Adventure Guide to

Provence
& the Côte d'Azur

HUNTER

Hunter Publishing, Inc.
130 Campus Drive
Edison, NJ 08818-7816
☎ 732-225-1900/800-255-0343/fax 732-417-1744
Web site: www.hunterpublishing.com
E-mail: comments@hunterpublishing.com

IN CANADA
Ulysses Travel Publications
4176 Saint-Denis
Montreal, Québec H2W 2M5 Canada
☎ 514-843-9882, Ext. 2232/fax 514-843-9448

IN THE UK
Windsor Books International
The Boundary, Wheatley Road
Garsington, Oxford OX44 9EJ England
☎ 01865-361122/fax 01865-361133

ISBN 1-58843-505-9
© 2005 Hunter Publishing, Inc.
Manufactured in the United States of America

All rights reserved. No part of this publication may be reproduced, stored in a retrieval system, or transmitted in any form, or by any means, electronic, mechanical, photocopying, recording, or otherwise, without the written permission of the publisher.

This guide focuses on recreational activities. As all such activities contain elements of risk, the publisher, author, affiliated individuals and companies disclaim any responsibility for any injury, harm, or illness that may occur to anyone through, or by use of, the information in this book. Every effort was made to insure the accuracy of information in this book, but the publisher and author do not assume, and hereby disclaim, any liability or any loss or damage caused by errors, omissions, misleading information or potential travel problems caused by this guide, even if such errors or omissions result from negligence, accident or any other cause.

Front cover: Villefranche-sur-Mer, © Steve Vidler/SuperStock
Maps by Toni Carbone,
© 2005 Hunter Publishing, Inc.

About the Author

London-based writer and journalist, Ferne Arfin has been traveling back and forth to France over more than two decades. She likes hiking and cycling and is especially fond of finishing off a hard day's activity with a French dinner and a bottle of wine.

Her travel articles and photography have been published in magazines and newspapers in the USA and the United Kingdom, appearing most recently in the *Los Angeles Times*, *The London Sunday Telegraph*, the *Christian Science Monitor*, and the *Travelers' Tales Anthology: A Woman's Europe*.

A graduate of Syracuse University and the University of East Anglia, Ferne also writes fiction. Her short stories have appeared in the *Literary Review*, the *Arkansas Review* and *Wild Cards*, an anthology of short fiction published by Virago.

She is currently traveling and working on a second novel — set all over the world.

Contents

Introduction	**1**
The Land: A Microcosm	1
History & Pre-History	4
500,000 BC	4
The Greeks & Romans	5
Medieval Provence	6
The Avignon Popes	8
The House of Savoy	9
The Revolution & the Age of Napoleon	10
The 20th Century	11
The Climate	12
The Economy	13
Agriculture	13
Industry	14
Flora	14
Fauna	15
A Bird Watchers' Paradise	15
Other Wildlife	15
Language & People	16
Art & Architecture	16
Modern Art	17
Performing Arts	18
Food & Drink	18
Boulangeries, Patisseries & Tea Shops	19
Fast Food	20
Bistros & Cafés	20
Fine Dining	20
Shopping	20
Eco-Travel	22
Adventures	22
Hiking	23
Cycling	23
Practical Advice for Cyclists	24
Specially Recommended Routes	25
Sources of Information	25
Getting Here	26
By Air	26
Contacts	26
By Rail	27
Contacts	27
Getting Around	27
Where to Stay	29
Travel Essentials	30

Entry Requirements	30
Customs	31
Tax Free Shopping	31
Money Matters	31
Currency	31
Traveler's Checks & Credit Cards	32
Where to Get Cash	32
Cost of Living	33
Tipping	33
Public Holidays	33
Health Services & Insurance	34
Mail	34
Telephones	34
Emergency Consular Services	35

The Alpilles & The Garrigues   37

Getting Here	38
Getting Around	39
Principle Destinations	39
Avignon	39
Sightseeing	42
Nîmes	42
Sightseeing	45
St. Rémy de Provence	46
Sightseeing	48
Worth a Side-Trip	49
Les Baux de Provence	49
Beaucaire	50
Eygalières	51
Maussane les Alpilles & Mouriès	51
The Pont du Gard	52
Uzès	53
Festivals & Fêtes	54
Shopping	54
Market Days	54
Department Stores	55
Sports & Cycling Shops	55
Where to Stay	56
Deluxe	56
Moderate	57
Budget	58
Camping	59
Gîtes	60
Where to Eat	60
Light Meals & Snacks	61
Adventures	62
On Foot	62
Rambling Near the Pont du Gard	63

Rock Climbing	63
On Wheels	64
Driving	64
Cycling	65
Where to Stay Along the Route	66
On Water	67
Canal Boating	67
On the Gardon River	68
In the Air	68
Hot Air Ballooning	68
Eco-Tourism	68
The Camargue	**71**
Getting Here & Getting Around	72
Four Habitats	72
La Grande Camargue	72
La Petite Camargue	73
Les Salins	74
The Crau	74
Principle Destinations	74
Arles	74
Getting Here	77
Sightseeing	77
Les Saintes Maries de la Mer	79
Getting Here	81
Sightseeing	81
The Great Outdoors	81
Aigues Mortes	81
Getting Here	83
Sightseeing	83
Camargue Beaches	85
Plage Est	85
Plage de Beauduc	85
Plage de L'Espiguette	86
Festivals & Fêtes	87
Arles	88
Les Saintes Maries de la Mer	88
Aigues Mortes	88
Shopping	89
In Arles	89
In Les Saintes Maries de la Mer	89
In Aigues Mortes	89
Where to Stay	90
Deluxe	90
Moderate	91
Budget	91
Camping	92
Gîtes	93

Where to Eat	94
Light Meals & Snacks	95
Adventures	96
On Foot	97
On Wheels	97
Cycling	97
Jeep Safaris	99
On Horseback	99
On Water	100
Windsurfing & Sailing	100
Canoeing & Kayaking	101
Power Boats & Jet Skis	101
Fishing Trips	102
Birdwatching	103

Vaucluse, the Lubéron & Mont Ventoux — 105

Getting Here & Getting Around	106
The Regions of Vaucluse	106
Haut Vaucluse	106
Mont Ventoux, Comtat Venaissin, Pays de Sault	108
Pays de Sorgues, Monts de Vaucluse	108
The Montagne du Lubéron	108
Principal Destinations	109
Apt	109
Sightseeing	111
Carpentras	111
Sightseeing	112
Gordes	113
Sightseeing	115
Orange	116
Sightseeing	117
Vaison la Romaine	118
Sightseeing	119
The Roman Ruins	119
The Medieval District	120
Worth a Side-Trip	121
Châteauneuf du Pape	121
Fontaine de Vaucluse	121
L'Isle Sur La Sorgue	123
Roussillon	124
Festivals & Fêtes	125
Music & Dance	126
Shopping	126
Markets	127
Carpentras	127
Apt	127
Châteauneuf du Pape	127
Gordes	127

L'Isle sur la Sorgue	128
Orange	128
Roussillon	128
Vaison la Romaine	128
Where to Stay	128
Deluxe	128
Moderate	130
Budget	130
Camping	131
Gîtes & Chambres d'Hôtes	132
Where to Eat	134
Deluxe	134
Light Meals & Snacks	135
Adventures	136
On Foot	136
Hiking in the Vaucluse	136
The Provençal Colorado	136
Rock Climbing	138
Accrobranching	138
Spelunking	139
On Wheels	139
Two Suggested Cycle Itineraries	140
Cycle Tours	142
The Luxury Tour	142
Ad Hoc Support	142
In the Air	143
On Horseback	144
Eco-Tourism	144

Marseille & Aix en Provence — 147

Principal Destinations	148
Aix en Provence	148
Getting Here	149
Getting Around	151
Sightseeing	151
Marseille	153
History	154
Getting Here	156
Getting Around	157
Sightseeing	157
Museums	161
Les Calanques	162
The Calanques of Marseille	162
Les Calanques of Cassis	165
Cassis	165
Getting Here	165
Sightseeing	165
Worth a Side-Trip	167

La Ciotat	167
Martigues	167
Salon de Provence	169
St Maximin La Ste Baume	169
Festivals & Fêtes	170
In Marseille	170
In Aix	171
Art & Architecture	172
Vasarely Foundation	173
Shopping	173
Department Stores & Shops	173
Markets	175
In Marseille	175
In Aix en Provence	176
In Cassis	176
Where to Stay	177
Deluxe	177
Moderate	178
Budget	179
Camping	180
Gîtes	181
Where to Eat	182
Light Meals & Snacks	183
Adventures	184
On Foot	184
Hiking & Climbing in the Calanques	184
Escalade	185
Mont Sainte Victoire	185
On Wheels	186
Cycling La Sainte Baume	186
A Scenic Drive Above the Coast	190
On Water	190
Diving	191
Windsurfing & Sailing	192
Beaches	192
Haute Provence	**193**
Getting Here	193
Getting Around	196
The Gorges du Verdon	196
Principal Destinations	196
Les Gorges du Verdon	196
Adventures on Foot	197
Trekking, Climbing & Escalade	197
Abseiling	197
A Three-Day Hike	197
Adventures on Wheels	204
Driving Tour	204

Adventures on Water	206
Whitewater	206
Extreme Fly Fishing	207
Family Watersports	207
Where to Stay	207
In or Near Castellane	207
Rougon	208
In or Near La Maline	209
In Moustiers Saint Marie	209
Refuges & Hostels	210
Where to Eat	210
Useful Contacts	211
Tourist Information Offices	211
Taxi Services	211
Worth a Side-Trip	212
Digne les Bains	212
Puget Theniers	213
Via Ferrata for Would-Be Mountaineers	213
The Route Napoléon	214
The Western Côte d'Azur	**215**
The Massif des Maures	215
Getting Here	218
Collobrières	218
La Garde Freinet	220
Climb to the Saracen Fortress	221
Pierrefeu du Var	221
Adventures on Foot	221
Rambles	221
Ecology Walks	222
Long Distance Paths	223
Adventures on Wheels	223
Cycling	223
The Wild Maures	223
The Corniche des Maures	225
Where to Stay	226
Camping	228
Where to Eat	228
The Mauresque Coast	229
St. Tropez	230
Sightseeing in St. Tropez	232
Shopping	234
Getting Here	234
A Day at the Beach – Plage Pamplonne	236
Le Lavandou	237
Getting Here	237
Grimaud & Port Grimaud	238
Getting Here	238

Ste Maxime	239
Getting Here	239
Where to Stay on the Mauresque Coast	239
Deluxe	239
Moderate	243
Budget	246
Camping	248
Where to Eat on the Mauresque Coast	248
Massif de l'Estérel	251
Getting Here	253
Getting Around	253
Fréjus	253
Sightseeing	255
The Roman Ruins	255
The Medieval Quarter	257
The Diocesan Group	257
The Chapelle Cocteau	258
Saint Raphaël	258
Sightseeing	260
The Center & Vieux Port	262
Santa Lucia Port	263
Boulouris	*263*
Le Cap Dramont	264
Agay	266
Anthéor & Le Trayas	267
Les Adrets de L'Estérel	268
Adventures on Foot	269
Mont Vinaigre	269
Guided Walks	270
Planning Your Route	270
Consulting the Experts	270
ONF Guided Walks	271
Green Walks	271
Group Walks	271
Adventures on Wheels	271
4X4 Tours	271
Mountain Biking	272
Adventures on Horseback	272
Ecotourism	273
Les Étangs de Villepey	273
Adventures on Water	274
Canoeing & Kayaking	*274*
Sailing & Windsurfing	*275*
Yacht Rentals	276
Powerboating	276
Boat Excursions	277
Diving	278

Dive Contacts on the Estérel Coast	279
Other Watersports	279
Where to Stay	280
Deluxe	280
Moderate	281
Budget	283
Chambre d'Hôtes	284
Gîtes	285
Camping	286
Where to Eat	286
The Massif du Tanneron	288
Cycling Around the Tanneron	289
Mimosa Circuit	289
Worth a Side-Trip: Le Pays de Fayence	290
Adventures in the Pays de Fayence	291
In the Air	291
Where to Stay in the Pays de Fayence	292
Where to Eat	293
Shopping in the Esterel	293
The Artists Circuit in Fréjus	293
Hypermarket Shopping in Saint Raphaël	294
Markets	294
Festivals & Fêtes in the Esterel	295
Mimosa Celebrations on the Mimosa Road	295
The International Air Festival	295
Fireworks in Fréjus	295
Fréjus Street Theatre Festival	296
Les Bravades	296
Chestnut Festivals	296
The Giant Omelet Feast	296
The French Riviera & the Maritime Alps	**299**
Principal Destinations	302
Cannes	302
History	302
The Capital of Cinema	303
Sightseeing in Cannes	304
La Croisette	304
Le Suquet	305
A Bit Farther Out	306
The Îles de Lérins	306
Getting Here	307
Antibes-Juan les Pins	308
The Birthplace of the Jazz Age	310
Antibes Today	311
Getting Here	312
The Beaches	314
Sightseeing in Antibes-Juan les Pins	315

Musée Picasso	315
The Archaeology Museum	315
Fort Carré	315
The Vieille Ville	316
Nice & the Haut Pays Niçois - The Flower of the South	316
A Unique History & Culture	318
Nice at Table	320
The Arrière & Haut Pays Niçois	321
Getting Here	322
Getting Around	322
Sightseeing in Nice	323
The Promenade des Anglais	323
Place Masséna	324
Cours Saleya	324
Opéra de Nice	324
Cathedrale Sainte Réparate	324
The War Memorial	324
The Russian Orthodox Church	324
Museums	325
Menton - A Town as Work of Art	326
The Grimaldi Connection	327
History - The Belle Époque & After	328
Getting Here	329
Getting Around	329
Sightseeing in Menton	330
The Palais Carnolès	330
The Bastion & the Musée Jean Cocteau	330
Basilique Saint Michel Archange	330
The Mentonese Faiences	330
The Gardens	331
Worth a Side-Trip	333
Biot	333
Grasse	334
Èze	335
Mandelieu -La Napoule	336
Mougins	337
La Turbie	338
Festivals & Fêtes	339
Antibes-Juan Les Pins	339
Nice	340
Menton	341
Shopping	341
Cannes	341
Market Days	341
In Antibes	342
Market Days	342
In Nice	342
The Markets	343

In Menton	343
Where to Stay	344
Deluxe	344
Moderate	350
Budget	352
Camping	354
Where to Eat	354
Light Meals & Snacks	358
Adventures	359
On Foot	359
Hiking in the Haut Pays Niçois	359
Three Days in the High Mountains	360
Where to Stay & Eat on this Itinerary	366
Mountain Guides	368
A Two-Day Trek in the Mercantour	
Accompanied Visits to La Vallée des Merveilles	371
In the Snow	372
Ski Resorts	372
Auron	372
Isola 2000	373
Valberg	373
Pra Loup	373
Adventures on Water	374
Le Ski Nautique & Water-Tow Sports	374
Deep-Sea Fishing	375
Diving	375
Adventures on Wheels	376
Mountain Biking	376
A Mountain Bike Circuit in the Black Forest	376
Driving the Corniches de la Riviera	377
In the Air	379
Paragliding	379
Eco-Travel	380
Mercantour National Park	380

Appendix — **383**

Tourist Information Offices	383
Regional Tourist Boards	387
Useful Contacts	389
Information	389
Accommodations	389
Activities	390
Cycling	390
Fishing	390
Riding	390
Walking & Hiking	390
Paragliding	390
Transportation	390

Air	390
Rail	391
Car	391
Local Bus Services	391
Emergencies	391
Consular Services	391
Maps & Guidebooks	391
IGN Maps	391
Glossary	393

Maps

Provence	2
Avignon	40
Nîmes	43
Arles	75
Camargue Beaches	84
Vaucluse	107
Bouches du Rhône, Aix & Marseille	145
Aix-en-Provence	146
Marseille	150
Vieux Marseille	155
Haute Provence	194
Massif des Maures	216
Collobrières	219
St Tropez - Western Côte d'Azur	231
Massif d'Esterel	252
Fréjus	254
St Raphaël Region	259
St Raphaël Center	261
Cannes	301
Cap d'Antibes	309
Vieille Antibes	312
Pays Niçois	317
Old Town Nice	320
Menton Region	328

Introduction

■ The Land: A Microcosm

All of Provence could be tucked into an area one-fifth the size of New England. From the Rhône on its western edge, to the Italian border on the east, it is barely 150 miles wide. North-to-south, the region stretches a mere 100 miles, from Lac de Serre-Ponçon, Europe's largest artificial lake, to a scattering of Mediterranean islets off Hyères. Yet, the variety of the landscapes and ecosystems crammed into this relatively compact region rivals that of many countries.

IN THIS CHAPTER	
■ History	4
■ Climate	12
■ Economy	13
■ Flora & Fauna	14
■ Language & People	16
■ Art & Architecture	16
■ Food & Drink	18
■ Shopping	20
■ Adventures	22
■ Getting Here	26
■ Getting Around	27
■ Where to Stay	29
■ Travel Essentials	30

Alpine peaks, hidden valleys and gorges, arid plateaus, even a stony desert, The Crau, are all part of the Provençal experience. In the southwest, the Rhône Delta spreads and floods, forming a vast and mysterious salt marsh, The Camargue. Here, sea and sky merge across flat vistas, punctuated by plantations of salt pans and mountains of drying salt. The Camargue is a naturalist's paradise, home to feral white ponies, herds of black bulls and thousands of migratory birds, including flocks of African flamingos.

Inland, much of Provence is dry and stony. Some areas are virtually paved with pale, calcareous pebbles that give the land a characteristic sun-baked look. Yet the region also supports vineyards, olive and almond groves and acres of nodding sunflowers. It is the fruit basket of France and its floriculture provides a large percentage of the raw materials for the world's perfume industry. Provence boasts mountain lakes, vast caves, thick Mediterranean forests of umbrella pine and cork oak, soft hills fragrant with wild herbs and cultivated lavender and, arguably, the most naturally glamorous coastline in the world.

This is a land that supports an exceptional range of outdoor activities – from spelunking to hang-gliding, whitewater rafting to skiing (on water or snow), cycling to rock climbing to bird watching. The French occasionally boast that they have no need to travel abroad for their vacations because they have everything they need – plus exquisite food and wine – right at home. After even a short visit to Provence, it is hard to argue.

Geology has been almost artful in Provence. Caught between the Pyrénnéan and Alpine folds, the land mounts toward the Alps from the broad alluvial plain of the Rhône. Most of Provence east of the river is criss-crossed by a complex system of small, east-to-west mountain ranges,

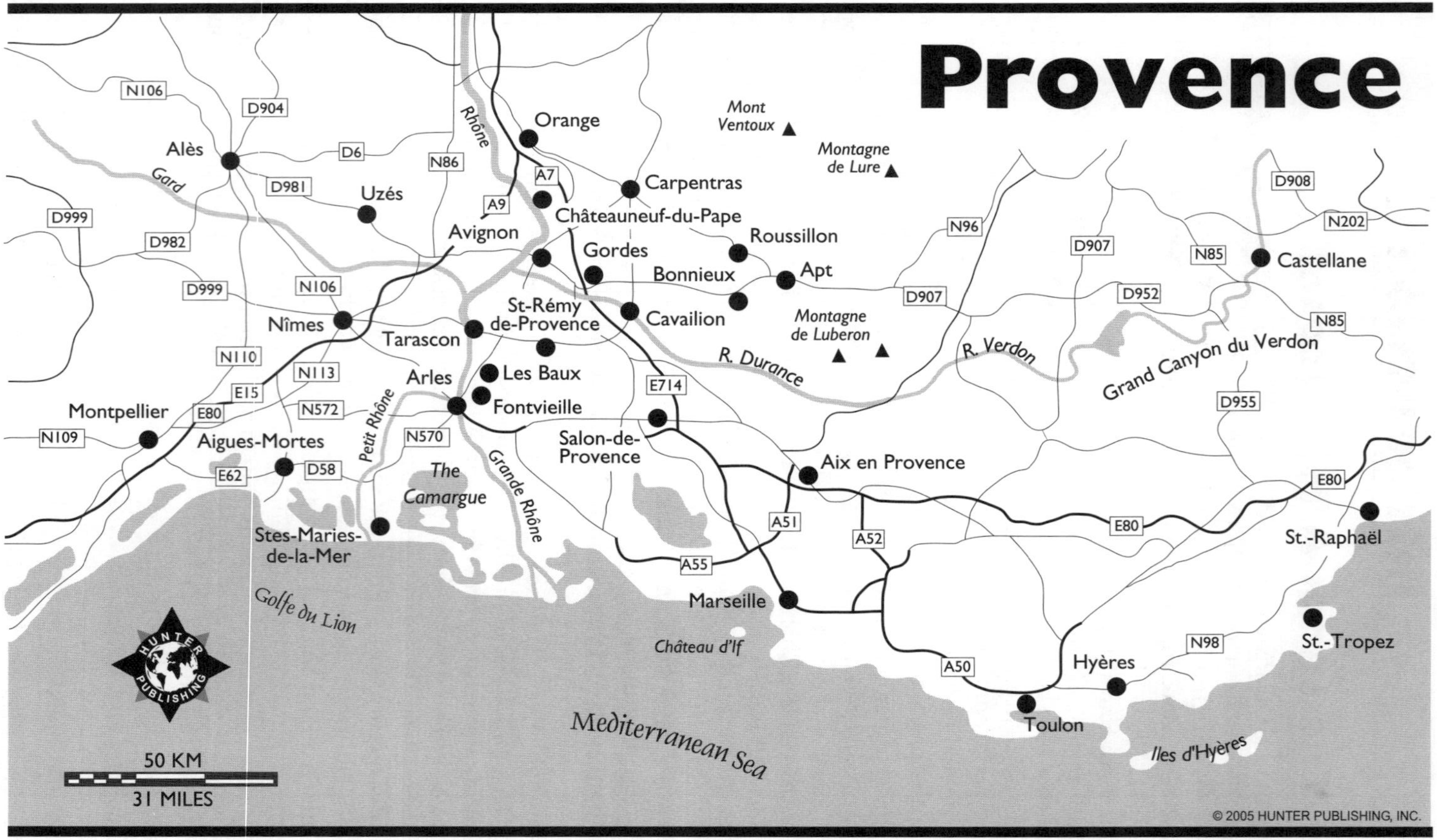
Provence
Mont Ventoux
Montagne de Lure
Orange
Carpentras
Châteauneuf-du-Pape
Roussillon
Apt
Gordes
Bonnieux
Cavailion
Alès
Gard
Uzés
Avignon
St-Rémy de-Provence
Nîmes
Tarascon
Les Baux
Fontvieille
Arles
Montpellier
Aigues-Mortes
Petit Rhône
Rhône
Grande Rhône
The Camargue
Stes-Maries-de-la-Mer
Salon-de-Provence
Aix en Provence
Marseille
Château d'If
Montagne de Luberon
R. Durance
R. Verdon
Grand Canyon du Verdon
Castellane
St.-Raphaël
St.-Tropez
Hyères
Toulon
Iles d'Hyères
Golfe du Lion
Mediterranean Sea
N106
D904
D6
N86
A7
A9
D981
D999
D982
N106
N110
E15
E80
N113
N572
N109
E62
D58
N570
E714
A51
A52
A55
A50
N98
E80
D955
N96
D907
D952
D907
N85
D908
N202
N85
HUNTER PUBLISHING
50 KM
31 MILES
© 2005 HUNTER PUBLISHING, INC.

high or enclosed plateaus and dense mountain clusters, called *massifs*. Glaciation, rushing rivers and Mediterranean downpours have shaped the underlying structure of soft, sedimentary rock, limestone and bauxite. Today, millennia of erosion show in the precipitous slopes and deep ravines that give an awesome appearance to mountains barely 3,000 feet high. Snow-capped **Mt. Ventoux** is one eccentric exception. Although, at 6,263 feet, it is surpassed by a number of Provence's Alpine and Pre-Alpine peaks, its splendid isolation on the plains above Carpentras gives it a particular grandeur.

Mt. Ventoux (© D. Basse, Collection CDT Vaucluse)

The **River Durance** and its tributaries, including the green **Verdon**, were tamed by a series of dams about 30 years ago. Today, they are nothing more than sluggish waterways as they snake through the region. But they were once wild seasonal torrents flooding their valleys with Alpine melt. Depending upon the time of year (even the time of day) and the operation of the hydroelectric dams, they can still be counted on for whitewater adventure. The evidence of their past is visible in several kinds of geological formations.

Most mysterious are the **cluses** (*clues* in Provençal), deep, transverse valleys. These are often so narrow that they are virtually hidden beneath arid, highland plains. Thousands of years of rushing water have undercut their vertical walls so that, at the bottoms, they often widen into cool, moist secret worlds. Deep pools, waterfalls and shaded microclimates that harbor lush ecosystems are not uncommon.

Water has also riddled the Provençal hills with networks of **caves**. Some of the best show caves in Europe are here, and many are open to the public. Some feature prehistoric cave paintings. Others can boast history of a more recent and daring kind. During World War II, local caves provided excellent cover for the French Resistance and Allied soldiers.

The **Grand Canyon of Verdon** is worth a trip all on its own. Thirteen miles long and between 1,000 and 2,000 feet deep, it is one of Europe's outstanding natural features. Access to the bottom has been possible only since the late 1970s when a series of dams reduced the flow of the Verdon 100 fold (from 28,000 cubic meters per second to 280 cubic feet per second). Even now, the canyon is an exciting place of rocky, whitewater straights and challenging hiking trails for fit travelers.

The **Mediterranean Alps** traverse the entire eastern border of Provence, separating France from Italy with a thick wall, 5,000 to 9,500 feet high. The Pre-Alps, along the coast between Nice and Menton, are nowhere near as high but their position, crowding the coast, makes them equally dramatic. Most Pre-Alpine peaks are about 3,000 feet high, and plunge abruptly to the sea. Looking up, snowy peaks dotted with perched villages form the backdrop for the chic yacht harbors of Villefranche, Beaulieu and Monte Carlo. Looking down, the prospect from the famously vertiginous Riviera road, **The Grande Corniche**, encompasses the golden beaches of Cap Ferrat and Èze-Bord-de-Mer beside the teal blue waters of the Mediterranean. It is impossible to say whether up or down is the better view.

■ History & Pre-History

500,000 BC

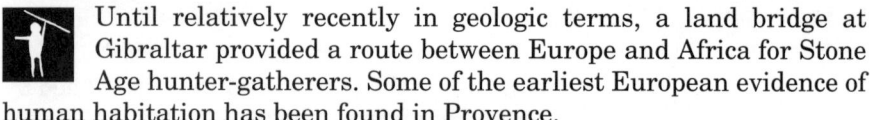

Until relatively recently in geologic terms, a land bridge at Gibraltar provided a route between Europe and Africa for Stone Age hunter-gatherers. Some of the earliest European evidence of human habitation has been found in Provence.

At the **Terra Amata** site near Nice, the remains of shallow huts, made of wooden poles supported by stones, have been found. Some of the huts, which date between 450,000 and 380,000 BC, had hearths which are believed to be the earliest evidence of humankind's controlled use of fire. A dwelling of animal skins draped over a wooden framework, found inside **Lazaret Cave**, may be even older; at between 500,000 and 400,000 BC, it predates Neanderthal man. These finds, which can be viewed nearby at the **Prehistoric Museum of Terra Amata** (page 319), include axes and stone tools as well as the bones of elephants, rhinos, red deer and giant oxen.

The first visitors were probably seasonal nomads. For many years, archeologists believed that poor local hunting precluded any long-term, early settlement in Provence. As proof, they cited the absence of early cave paintings of large game animals such as those found at Lascaux. But in 1991, a remarkable discovery by a local diver, **Henri Cosquer**, changed everything.

COSQUER'S CAVE

Diving in the **calanques**, deep narrow inlets in the rocky coastal cliffs between Cassis and Marseilles, Cosquer entered a cave about 120 feet below sea level and, after swimming upward into a vast, air-filled chamber, found himself surrounded by pictures of stenciled human hands, animals and, unusually for Paleolithic cave paintings, sea creatures. Scientists found enough charcoal and carbon in the primitive artwork for very accurate radio carbon dating. Tests showed that **Cosquer's Cave** was in continuous use over a period of almost 9,000 years, until the seas rose and concealed the entrance after the last Ice Age. The stenciled hands have been firmly dated to 27,000 years ago. Some of the animals, including aurochs, horses, chamoix and megaloceros, a giant Ice Age deer, are about 18,500 years old. Cosquer's Cave is considered one of the most important and well-dated Paleolithic caves in the world. The entrance is now blocked, but Henri Cosquer still takes divers on tours of the calanques.

Elsewhere in Provence, the **bories** (pages 114-15) provide more evidence of Prehistoric, probably Iron Age, habitation. Thousands of these beehive-shaped, mortarless stone dwellings are scattered across the Lubéron and the Vaucluse Plateau. Water-tight, thick-walled and relatively warm inside, Bories remained in use as animal pens, tool sheds and, occasionally, dwellings, through the 18th century.

The Greeks & Romans

Provence seems to have provided a meeting ground for the mingling Northern European and Southern Mediterranean cultures for as long as humans have had the urge to travel. From about 1000 BC, there is clear evidence that Ligurians from Northwest Italy were well-established along the coast. Germanic Celts, noted for their pottery, were settled inland, north of the Durance. It is likely that the two groups had social and trade connections even earlier. Some examples of etched Celtic pottery dating from the Bronze Age, around 6,000 BC, have been found in the area.

In any case, by the time the Phocean Greeks arrived in 600 BC, a local culture was already flourishing. According to legend, the Greeks acquired the harbor at **Massalia** (modern Marseille) as part of the marriage dowry for a Ligurian princess. (We'll never know, but there seems no evidence that they acquired it through warfare.)

Massalia was a perfect trading base. Located near the mouth of the Rhône, it provided easy communication for inland trade. Soon, the Greeks were exporting local livestock, pewter and pottery, as well as tin from Brittany and copper from Spain. Along the nearby coast, adventurous divers have located a range of sunken vessels still carrying evidence of these trade goods.

In their turn, the Greeks bartered their ancient Mediterranean crops – olives, figs, walnuts, cherries and grape vines – changing local agriculture forever. They prospered here for several centuries, establishing colonial outposts at **Hyères, St. Tropez, Antibes, Nice** and **Monaco**, and intermarrying with the local population.

Massalia earned itself the mixed blessing of Roman favor when, in the third century BC, it sided with Rome against the Carthaginians. At the time, many other Provençal towns supported Hannibal, who crossed Provence on his way to Rome via the Alps. A century later, the Greeks called upon Rome to defend them against pirates attacking Antibes and Nice, as well as Celtic tribes attacking from the North. Romans came to the rescue and, as was so often the case, decided to stay. Massalia became Massilia under the Romans.

Transalpine **Gaul**, established about 121 BC, was the first Roman province in France. Initially, the Romans looked to routes through Provence to protect their trade with Spain. By the time Julius Caesar officially conquered Gaul (58-51 BC), Roman garrisons reached from the Alps to the Pyrénées. The Romans built more than 13,000 miles of road, some of which can still be seen today. Vestiges of the **Domitian Way**, the route from the Italian Alps, are visible in Cavaillon, Bonnieux and Apt. **Pont Julien**, a three-arched bridge on the D149 between Bonnieux and Apt, is still in use. Also in use, the **Aurelian Way** took travelers from Rome to Arles. Its modern features included raised sidewalks and milestones marking each Roman mile along the way. A good section of it can be seen east of Tourtour, and the RN7 between **Aix en Provence** and **Nice** follows this route.

The Romans called the area **Provincia Romana**, from which modern Provence takes its name. Evidence of the Roman era, in the form of villas, temples, baths, theaters, arenas, aqueducts, triumphal arches, circuses and forums, can be visited all over Provence. It is, in fact, the rare village that lacks a Roman site. Altogether, the Romans prospered here for more than 600 years. A remarkable percentage of these antiquities are still being used for their original purposes.

Medieval Provence

The Middle Ages were marked by cycles of plague and almost ceaseless warfare. Following the fall of the Western Roman Empire, various warrior tribes – Vandals, Visigoths, Ostrogoths and Burgundians – coursed through Provence. The area was subdued in the sixth century by the Franks, who were constantly called upon to expel invaders. Between the eighth and the 10th century, Saracens (a name used interchangeably by contemporary historians for Arabs, Berbers, Moors and Turks) sacked the entire coast. From their stronghold on the Massif des Maures (Maures=Moors in French) they regularly descended to the inland villages to plunder and loot. They were finally expelled by Count William the Liberator, in 974. Today, from the ruins of the Saracen fortress at **La Garde-Freinet** (page 221), near St. Tropez, the nearly 360° panorama gives a clear indication of why they chose this easily defended spot as a base for their raids.

For centuries, between invasions by outsiders, the region was wracked by internal conflicts among the ruling Franks. Strife was partly encouraged by their Germanic inheritance rules. Under Frankish law, kingdoms were divided between all surviving sons, but land was inherited for *use* rather than *ownership*. As a result, disagreements were frequent and bloody.

Bonnieux (Village Perchée, © J.L. Seille)

The Kingdom of Provence passed from hand to hand until the 11th century, when it was incorporated into the Holy Roman Empire.

A key feature of this period was the development of the *village perchée* (perched village), defensive settlements where local inhabitants could retreat from the chaotic warfare and waves of disease that regularly raged below them. Provence is particularly noted for these small settlements, balanced like eagles' nests on steep slopes or isolated pinnacles. Perched villages are walled and clustered around an abbey or a feudal lord's watchtower. Their narrow, pedestrian streets twist and turn like the flights of stairs in an etching by Escher, unexpectedly becoming tile-roofed steps or passing through the lower halls of private dwellings. Some of these villages have been abandoned for centuries; some are restored for tourism, but a remarkable number are still inhabited. The Pre-Alpine area, inland from Nice to Menton, is particularly rich in picturesque examples.

In the 12th century, the **Compté de Provence** was re-established as an autonomous earldom, centered around Aix en Provence and ruled by the Counts of Provence. Known for the refinement of their court, the Counts ushered in a golden age of courtly love, poetry and music, including the tradition of the Provençal troubadour.

CELEBRATIONS & FESTIVALS

Music and dance still thrive in Aix. Home of the **Conservatory of Music of Aix en Provence**, the city hosts music festivals, concerts and open-air performances almost year-round. For the 50-year-old **International Festival of Lyric Art** in June and July, leading opera stars and soloists gather to perform Mozart, fully mounted operatic productions and Italian Bel Canto. The unusual *Tambourin* festival, held annually, in April, is sponsored by the **Academie du Tambourin Musique de Provence**. It features the ancient music of the tambourin, a long, cylindrical drum, accompanied by the *galoubet*, a three-holed flute. A highlight of the year is the *Roumavàgi* **of Sainte Victoire** when a procession of drummers winds its way up the crested peak so often painted by local artist Paul Cezanne. At the Chapel of the Priory on the summit, Provençal songs accompany a mass and traditional blessings of the mountain and of Aix.

The Avignon Popes

At the beginning of the 14th century, following a disagreement between Pope Boniface VIII and King Philip the Fair of France, a French pope, Clement V, was elected. Within four years, civil unrest in Rome and riots between rival factions drove him to take shelter with a Dominican order in **Avignon**.

The move was intended to be temporary, but a number of factors combined to make it a longer sojourn. Avignon adjoined church land and belonged to Charles II of Anjou, a faithful ally. Equally important, after the separation of the Roman and Byzantine churches, Avignon was closer than Rome to the center of Catholic Europe. Its primacy as a papal city eventually lasted nearly 100 years, through the reigns of seven popes, two of whom are usually referred to as the **anti-popes**. During that time, despite being twice decimated by plague, the city grew from a population of about 4,000 to more than 40,000, becoming one of the largest and most cosmopolitan centers in Europe.

Cloister of the Palais des Papes (© Ferne Arfin)

The **Palais des Papes**, which took about 17 years to build, looks more like a colossal fortress than a papal residence. But, rather than being an expression of temporal political power, the fortifications were made necessary by roving bands of mercenaries who formed during breaks in the Hundred Years War. These so called "Great Companies" menaced the countryside, sacking villages and slaughtering local populations to fill their own pockets. Avignon's wealth drew their attention and several popes were forced to pay ransoms so that the city, and the residences of its wealthy cardinals, would be spared.

THE GREAT SCHISM

The most remarkable episode in the story of the Avignon popes was the Great Schism and the period of the anti-popes. In 1378, the cardinals, meeting to elect a new pope, were besieged by rioting Romans. In fear for their lives, they elected an Italian. The French cardinals revolted. Feeling they had been coerced by the rioters, they declared the first election null and void and chose their own French pope, Clement VII. For 30 years, Rome and Avignon each supported its own pope, dividing the Church into warring factions.

Eventually, the political backers of a French papacy faded away. The people of Avignon, tired of being the focus of so much dissention, laid siege to the Papal Palace. For five years, Benoit XIII, the last Avignon pope, became a prisoner in his own palace. In 1405, he sought refuge from the King of Spain, his last ally, with whom he remained until his death in 1409.

Did you know? Visitors often assume that the spacious esplanade of the **Place du Palais,** outside the Palais des Papes in Avignon, was designed for displays of papal pageantry. After all, it makes a fine setting for outdoor music and theater during the annual Avignon Festival (page 54). In fact, this void was created by Rodrigo de Luna, nephew of the last Avignon pope, who defended the palace for 17 months after his uncle escaped to Spain. Rodrigo demolished every house near the palace so that he could see his enemies coming.

The House of Savoy

Eavesdrop on the conversations of old men along the French Riviera and you might think you are in Italy. There is a good reason for this. From the 14th to the mid-19th century, a large stretch of Mediterranean Provence was controlled by the **House of Savoy** which, in turn, ruled parts of Italy until just before World War I.

The Italian connection originated through the heirs of Queen Jeanne of Naples and Sicily, an adopted heir of Count Louis d'Anjou and his cousin the Prince of Naples. It is a tangled story. Parts of Provence passed back and forth so many times that even local historians have a hard time keeping track. Basically, except for a few brief interruptions, Nice and its surrounding area belonged to the Dukes of Savoy, who became the Princes of Piedmont and ultimately Kings of Sardinia from 1388 until 1860.

SAVOYISMS OF TODAY

The legacy of Savoy remains as a distinct Italianate lilt in the local culture. The Belle Époque hotels along **Nice's Promenade des Anglais** seem just a bit more Rococo than anywhere else in France. The local language, *le Nissart*, a Latin-influenced variant of Provençal spoken almost exclusively until the end of the 19th century, is now experiencing a revival. Classes are offered in local schools – *escola* in Nissart instead of *école* in French. Visitors should listen for le Nissart in the names of popular local snacks. ***Pan bagnat***, or "bathed bread" for example, is a kind of meat or tuna and salad hero sandwich made with olive oil and garlic. Everywhere, older local people speak French with a strong Italian accent. In the kitchen, specialties have direct Italian parallels – *fougasse*, an olive oil bread, and *pissaladière*, a flat anchovy and tomato tart, are the focaccia of Tuscany and the pizza of Naples. It is probably no coincidence that Niçoise **pizza *feu de bois*** (made in wood burning ovens) is the best this side of Queen Jeanne's Naples. Even the name of the Côte d'Azur between Nice and the Italian border changes to the Riviera, an Italian word.

The Revolution & the Age of Napoleon

The French Revolution caught hold quickly in Provence and along the Côte d'Azur. But it was not long before independent southerners were chafing under the iron rule of Paris. As in the rest of France, the period of revolutionary harmony was brief and the chaos of the reign of terror bloody. Monuments commemorating this difficult period in French history are rare, but damage to some of the older churches still recalls the period's anticlerical fervor.

Napoleon Bonaparte is the greatest hero of French history – just ask any Frenchman. But during his lifetime, and during his 16 years in (and briefly out of) power from 1799 to 1815, he was not universally esteemed by the Provençal. Perhaps that's because, although he passed through Provence at several key points in his career, he never seemed to stay long enough to appreciate the region's charms.

En route from victories in Egypt to the coup d'état that brought him to power in 1799, he landed his forces in the port of St. Raphaël (page 258), now a resort near the Roman town of Fréjus (page 253). Fifteen years later, in 1814, following defeats at the hands of the Austrian, English, Prussian and Swedish armies, he departed from the same port to exile in Elba. A year later, in 1815, landing with more than 1,000 troops at Golfe Juan, up the coast near Cannes, he began the "100 days" grab for power that was ended by the Duke of Wellington at the Battle of Waterloo. To avoid troops garrisoned at Marseille, as well as the hostile local population, Napoleon did not take the easy route north along the valley of the Rhône. Instead, he led his troops to Grenoble though Grasse and the pre-Alpine passes at Digne and Sisteron. The legacy of that march is preserved today in The Route Napoleon.

THE ROUTE NAPOLEON

The well-marked Route Napoleon is popular with history buffs and scenery junkies alike. As it winds up from the coast at **Golfe Juan**, it passes through dramatic cluses and under layered, vertical cliffs, offering sudden, sparkling vistas of the distant Mediterranean and the Massifs des Maures and L'Estérel. Visitors can spend a day climbing the 112-mile motor route, with plenty of stops. Ambitious, and very fit, cyclists should head southwards from Sisteron to the coast. The four- or five-day run, covering just under 200 miles, alternates between somnolent river valleys and screaming downhills, passing through lavender fields, Roman towns and typical villages along the way. (More about The Route Napoléon, page 214.)

The 20th Century

Although the countryside was largely untouched by World War I, Provence, like much of Europe, lost a generation of young men in the "Great War." With insufficient manpower to wrest a living from the land, much of the remaining population migrated to emerging urban industrial centers. Many small holdings merged into larger, commercial farms and vineyards – a process that, sadly, continues today. Nevertheless, the trend for processing and sales cooperatives has enabled enough family farms, orchards, olive groves and vineyards to survive for the area to retain its highly independent character.

All sorts of tribes have invaded Provence; Greeks, Ligurians, Romans, Moors and Celts have all, at one time or another, coveted and occupied the Côte d'Azur. But the Roaring Twenties brought an invasion of a completely different kind. Rich and carefree, artistic and bohemian, mostly American but a few Europeans as well, the new invaders heralded the Jazz Age, gambled at the Riviera's first casinos and created the glamorous ambience for which this corner of Provence is still justly famous. F. Scott Fitzgerald, Hemingway, Aldous Huxley, Thomas Mann, Douglas Fairbanks and Mary Pickford were among those who rode the deluxe *Train Bleu* from the Channel port of Calais, through Paris, to the Côte d'Azur at Nice. It was an era of hedonism and free spending that lasted until the Great Depression destroyed many of the fortunes that had made it possible.

World War II ushered in a very dark period in the region's history. Partly occupied by the Italians, who moved into Menton as early as 1940 and partly under the control of the Vichy government, as a kind of "free" zone, Provence remained outside of German occupation until the invasion of 1942. The German's fortified the coast, their pillbox bunkers commanding wide sea views. In August, 1944, the area was liberated by the Americans and the Free French after 14 days of fierce fighting, a week of it centered around Marseille. During the war, the maze of caves laced throughout the Alpilles, the Verdon, the Pre-Alpes and the Alpes Maritime provided perfect shelter for cells of French Resistance fighters who harried the Germans, rescued Allied soldiers and launched daring hit-and-run attacks. Jean Moulin, the great hero of the French Resistance, was active in Provence. Look for the **Route Jean Moulin**, a marked scenic route that follows the hero's travels, winding through the small towns here.

Tip: To appreciate the panoramic sweep of a World War II German lookout post, ask locals to direct you to the pillbox bunker in the hills above Vallauris). On a clear day, the coastal view extends from the Massif des Maures, in the west, to as far east as the Italian border and beyond. While in Vallauris, home of Picasso's pottery and today a major center for ceramics, visit Picasso's murals, *La Guerre et la Paix* (War and Peace), installed in the chapel of a ruined castle. Now a national museum, the murals can be viewed from 10 am to 12 noon and 2 to 6 pm (5 pm in winter), daily, except national holidays. Adults €3, youth ticket (18-25 years) i1.50, children and teenagers up to 18 years, free. Group tickets can be ordered in advance: ☎ 33 01 40 13 49 13, museecie@rmn.fr.

■ The Climate

Deceptively mild average temperatures conceal dramatic extremes. Hot, dry summers can be plagued with forest fires. If the **Sirocco** (a gusty wind off the Sahara) blows, it sometimes deposits a fine layer of red desert sand along coastal areas and turns dusk purple or yellow. Relief comes in the form of short, violent thunderstorms that can drop more than five inches in an hour.

Autumn and spring are the rainiest seasons and, in winter, the steady howl of the **Mistral** can make temperatures that rarely drop below 50°F seem much colder. Thanks to the moderating influence of the Mediterranean Sea, the Côte d'Azur enjoys the warmest winter temperatures.

AVERAGE TEMPERATURES (°F)	
January	54
February	53
March	58
April	65
May	70
June	80
July	83
August	83
September	77
October	71
November	62
December	57

Regardless of the season, dry days bring brilliant light and deep turquoise skies.

The Wind That Drives Men Mad

The legendary Mistral is the result of cold northern air, channeled southward by the void between the Pyrénnées and the Alps. Pressed by mountains on both sides, it barrels down the Rhône Valley at speeds of up to 60 mph, dropping temperatures and often lasting for days on end. According to local stories, the Mistral can drive men mad and some accounts suggest that Van Gogh cut off his ear after several days of severe Mistral weather.

■ The Economy

Ancient crops and modern technology co-exist amicably throughout Provence. The almost quilted landscape (small plateaus and valleys enclosed by mountain ridges and massifs) encourages a range of micro-climates and micro-cultures.

Agriculture

"Le Vendange," the grape harvest in Provence (© lefrance,CDT Vaucluse)

Every area has its agricultural speciality: cherries, and table grapes from the Vaucluse; citrus fruits and orange blossom products from the *arrière pays* behind the Côte d'Azur; rice and cattle in the Camargue; lavender along the higher slopes; flowers and flower seeds from Grasse; almonds apricots and grain in the dry climate of the Alpilles; truffles (called *rabasses*) in the Luberon; melons from Cavaillon.

But everywhere, the ancient Mediterranean cultivation of vineyards and olive groves gives Provence its special character.

A diversity of grapes – table grapes as well as those grown for red and white wines – thrive in the Mediterranean climate. There are six regional AOC (Appellation d'Origine Contrôlée) classifications, including Côtes du Rhône, Côtes du Rhône Villages, Côtes de Provence, Baux de Provence, Coteaux d'Aix and Coteaux Varois, as well as distinctive local wines – Cassis, Bandol, Châteauneuf de Pape, Gigondas, Vacqueyras, Lirac and Tavel.

> **Tip:** Locals save money buying their everyday wine *en vrac* at the supermarket or specialist wine merchant. Wine is decanted from big wooden barrels by the liter into whatever bottle you bring. While most people keep special containers for the purpose, nobody will bat an eyelid if you bring plastic cola bottles.

Olives were brought to Provence by the Greeks and have been a staple crop ever since. They too are occasionally awarded an AOC designation. Maussane, in the valley below Les Baux de Provence, produces AOC table olives as well as an olive oil that is used by chefs from the best restaurants in Paris and Lyon.

Olives at Les Halles covered market in Avignon (© Ferne Arfin)

At the end of the 19th century, the French government introduced lavender to Provence to make use of poor quality, under-used land. Today the crop, bursting into bloom in June, is among the area's most important – turning up in perfume, laundry detergent, soap and insect repellents. The best places to see the rows of lavender shrubs are in the Alpes de Haute-Provence, the Vaucluse, Drôme and the Rhône Valley.

Industry

Fishing, **aquaculture** and **shipping** are major industries. From the Port of Marseille, one of Europe's most important seaports, France and much of Europe send fruit and vegetables, oil and oil products and manufactured goods to Africa, the Middle East and the Far East.

A large **petrochemical** industry is clustered around Fos, an industrial zone extending from the Port of Marseille. **Microelectronics** (a third of the total French industry), **robotics** and **aeronautics** are also major industries.

In recent years, Arles has become a center for **multimedia**, particularly digital and 3-D animation. And, since the 1960s, a sort of parallel universe of high technology, commercial and academic research has quietly grown up in Sophia Antipolis, between Antibes and Cannes. More than a science park, Sophia Antipolis is home to some of the world's biggest names in **computers** and **biotechnology**, along with about 3,500 residents.

Tourism is, of course, a major industry. Most Europeans – including the French themselves – consider Provence a top vacation destination. As a result, there are plenty of accommodations, restaurants and activities, and English is widely spoken. That so much of Provence remains relatively laid-back and apparently unspoiled is a remarkable achievement given the area's popularity.

■ Flora

Green oak and **kermes oak**, deciduous in other parts of the world, hang onto their leaves and are virtually evergreen here. Other common sights are the tall, slim **cypress trees** that line roads or form windbreaks on the hills. **Pine woods**, prone to forest fires in the high summer, include typically Mediterranean Aleppo and Maritime pines. **Parasol pines** (easy to spot because they look like their name) are distinctive in the headlands above the coast. The shade of *micocouliers* (nettle trees) and **plane trees** give Provençal village squares their typical character.

Since their introduction at least 2,500 years ago, **olive trees** have so taken to local conditions that they are often found naturalized, mingled with wild fig and almond trees. In the wild, they can reach as much as 60 feet in height, with trunks of 12 feet or more in circumference.

As with agriculture, other plant life tends to be typical of local microclimates: bamboo along water courses; fragrant herbs such as rosemary, thyme, savory and mint in the garrigues (the arid limestone areas), and sturdy alpines on the higher slopes.

Fauna

A Bird Watchers' Paradise

Hawks, **buzzards** and **falcons** – several different varieties of each – cruise the thermals in the Alpes Maritimes and the Alpes of Haute Provence. One of the great sights of the Camargue are crowds of **pink flamingos** that nest there between April and May – some years as many as 20,000 pairs. Elsewhere, bird life runs the gamut of **woodland species** (cuckoo, hoopoe, nightjar, magpie, jay, woodpecker), shore, wetlands and **wading birds** (godwits, sandpipers, black-winged stilts, herons, egrets, gulls, terns, coots, diving ducks), and **birds of the garrigue** (grouse, partridge, ptarmigan, thrush, pheasant). Those with good night vision should watch for several different varieties of **owl** – tawny, long-eared and eagle.

Other Wildlife

Wild boar are legendary throughout France, including Provence. They are, fortunately, very shy. You are more likely to meet up with one at table than in the wild. **Ponies** and **bulls** run wild in the Camargue. For the most part these are not really wild, but simply reared in freedom among the salt plains. **Beaver**, **ferret**, **deer** and several varieties of **mountain goat** populate Alpine areas. The symbol of Provence is the large, loud **cicada**, which can be heard throughout the summer. The image of this insect decorates soaps, fabrics and all kinds of handicrafts. The climate tends to encourage generally larger insects – some of the biggest **dragonflies** we've ever seen were in Provence – but they are, for the most part, harmless. And there are no poisonous snakes.

■ Language & People

The French are generally cosmopolitan and English is widely spoken in Provence. Even in the smallest villages, someone with a working knowledge of English can usually be found. If you have a little school French, do try it out. The local people here can be remarkable generous if you make an effort in their language.

One gift of this region's complex history is the variety of colorful local dialects, some of which constitute languages of their own. **Provençal** (often paired with the slightly different **Langue d'Oc** spoken to the west) is the medieval language of the troubadours and rarely spoken in its pure form. But its words, syntax and expressions crop up in conversations and in writing throughout the region.

As a visitor, you will be considered an *estranger*, although the word is *étranger* everywhere else in France. Look out for *pan bagnat* (pronounced *pan banYAH*), a popular sandwich of cold meats or tuna, onions, peppers and olive oil. In proper French its name (translated as "bathed bread") would be pain baigné. *Panisse* is the local name for a flour made of chick peas. And a barren salt plain in the Camargue is *la sansouire*.

Like any great city, Marseille has an idiom and argot of its own that is continually changing. You know you are in its sphere of influence when you begin to hear the distinctive Marseillaise accent. A key marker is the word *vingt*, French for 20. Elsewhere in France it is pronounced a bit like *vaah*. Around Marseille, that changes to *vang*.

As you near Italy on the Côte d'Azur and in the Alpes Maritimes, the language you hear sounds almost Italian.

■ Art & Architecture

Provençal Mas

Domestic architecture throughout the region is unmistakably Provençal. One- and two-story houses of pale local sandstone or limestone dot the rural landscape. Window shutters are painted pale aqua or periwinkle blue and roofs are almost invariably covered with terra cotta tile from Marseille. They pose against rows of cypress trees as if waiting to inspire a passing artist – which they often do. The classic, rustic *mas* is a building that once housed animals in a lower story with humans living above. Today *mas* often have large, vaulted lower rooms. A *mas* has no windows on its northern side, the direction from which the Mistral comes. Village houses follow the same boxy shape, although they often have a third story. Stonework is frequently concealed with rendering and then lime-washed or painted with pastels. Substantial village or rural houses are called *bastides*.

Civic architecture ranges from Roman and Gallo-Roman through Gothic to Baroque. Provence has some of the finest examples of classic Roman architecture outside of Italy. In fact, Roman buildings and monuments are so common in Provence that it is easier to list the towns and villages that don't have any than those that do. The arena in Arles

The Roman Theater at Orange
(© J.L. Seille, Collection CDT)

and theaters in Orange (pages 116 ff) and Vaison la Romaine (pages 118 ff) are still in use for open-air summer performances. Nîmes boasts a fine Roman temple, La Maison Carré. Several excavated Roman villas can be visited – most notably in Vaison la Romaine – and the Roman aqueduct, the Pont du Gard (page 52), stands nearly intact after more than 2,000 years.

Examples of medieval and Gothic architecture remain in fortified churches and abbeys and in the region's many perched villages. The Palais des Papes in Avignon is probably the best-preserved example of the Gothic style in the region.

The elegance of the 17th and 18th centuries, what the French call the Classical period, characterizes some of the larger towns. In Aix en Provence, large urban mansions called *hôtels* parade down beautifully proportioned, tree-lined avenues or cluster around fountains in small squares.

Did you know? Aix is often called the city of fountains.

Baroque architecture, in all its wedding cake frippery, along with its more modern relative, Belle Époque, is much in evidence on the Côte d'Azur, especially along The Promenade des Anglais in Nice.

Modern Art

From the mid-19th century, when the Impressionists focussed the art world's attention on the quality of light, Provence has been the place to paint. The list of artists who have made their homes here, or who have stayed long enough to paint significant works, reflects every major art movement of the modern age. Most large towns have art museums or connections with giants of 19th and 20th century art. Cezanne, Chagall,

Dufy, Léger, Matisse, Picasso, Renoir, Vasarely, Vlaminck and of course, Van Gogh all lived and worked here. Museums devoted to their lives and work are scattered all over Provence.

■ Performing Arts

Music, dance and theater abound with world-renowned summer festivals held in Avignon, Aix en Provence and centered around the Roman theaters of Orange, Vaison la Romaine, Arles and Nîmes. Aix en Provence, with it is troubadour heritage, is known for music – hosting opera, lyric singing and jazz festivals every summer. During the **Avignon Festival** (page 54) in July and August, these take over the whole town. For **Les Choralies** (page 126; held every three years – the next is in 2007) thousands of choral societies from all over Europe descend on Vaison la Romaine, for performances, competitions and impromptu street performances.

■ Food & Drink

Wild mushrooms in Avignon market (© Ferne Arfin)

The Provençal table is blessed with a rich variety of fresh, local ingredients. The cuisine is informal, colorful and strongly flavored. Olives, olive oil, tomatoes, chick peas and fresh herbs – basil, thyme, rosemary, savory, marjoram, mint – play important roles. So does garlic, ranging from mild and sweet to hot and pungent.

Although the region doesn't produce any of France's most distinguished wines, its microclimates foster a large variety of wines – more than any other comparable part of France.

Here are some typical Provençal specialties:

- **Aïoli** – a garlicky mayonnaise used for dipping cooked vegetables and fish. A Grande Aïoli, sometimes served as a celebration meal for a whole town, can include boiled potatoes and carrots, tomatoes, salt cod, shellfish, shrimp, langoustines, artichokes, cauliflower, boiled eggs, dry sausages, green beans, grilled sardines, all served with huge bowls of glistening aïoli.
- **Pistou** – a basil, garlic and parmesan paste (similar to pesto but without the pine nuts) served with vegetable soup.

- **Soupe de poisson** – a pungent soup made from several kinds of fish, including the Mediterranean rascasse, and served with rouille (pronounced roo-EEE), a fiery, saffron-colored mayonnaise.
- **Fougasse** – a dense braided or twisted bread made with olive oil.
- **Brandade de Morue** – a thick, paste of salt cod, mashed potato, garlic and, sometimes, ground olives. Eaten on bread or toast as an hors d'oeuvre.
- **Tourte aux blettes** – a specialty of Nice, this is a sweet pastry filled with Swiss chard! Delicious, believe it or not.
- **Socca** – crisp pancake made with chick pea flour, most often seen along the Côte d'Azur.
- **Bouillabaisse** – a stew of fish, tomatoes and garlic which must include the rascasse or scorpion fish to be a real bouillabaisse. Try it along the seafront in Marseille, Nice, Antibes or Juan les Pins.
- **Grilled sardines** – nothing like our teensy canned sardines, these are fat little fish, five or six inches long, eaten with the fingers. Ask a local to show you how to remove all the bones with one deft twist.
- **Pizza feu de bois** – a Riviera specialty, this pizza is cooked on hot stones in wood-burning ovens. It is a real surprise and worth stopping for.
- **Muscat de Beaumes de Venise** – a very rich dessert wine similar in fragrance and syrupy texture to the finest Sauternes.
- **Vin Cuit de Provence** – a local wine specialty made from cooked grapes that is usually made for Christmas.
- **Tapenade** – a salty blend of ground olives, used as a spread on bread.

Boulangeries, Patisseries & Tea Shops

There are several different kinds of bakeries; some with seating or counters for light breakfasts or quick snacks. Even if they don't have seating, no one minds if you buy something and take it to a café or bar tabac (see below) as a nicer, sometimes cheaper, alternative to the continental breakfast served in your hotel.

Boulangeries sell breads, croissants and sweet breakfast pastries. *Patisseries* specialize in fancy cakes, tarts, pastries, and other sweet-tooth fantasies such as *confiserie* (handmade candy), *chocolat* and *glace* (ice cream). If the sign also says *Salon de Thé*, you can sit down for beverages and light meals – grilled sandwiches or quiche, for example.

Fast Food

A *bar tabac*, as the name implies, sells drinks (both alcoholic and non-alcoholic) and cigarettes. At lunchtime, they sometimes sell baguettes filled with ham, *saucisson sec* (salami) or cheese. You have to ask. Just say "Casse Croûte?" – which literally means breaking crust. *Pan bagnat*, a more interesting choice, is a kind of Mediterranean sub sandwich often sold by sidewalk vendors or from shop fronts.

Bistros & Cafés

Sidewalk cafés and moderately priced bistros are everywhere. You'll almost always find a few casual places to dine in the town center. Quality varies, but the standard is generally quite high. Menus posted outside will give you an idea of what to expect. Prix fixe menus, which are customarily two courses with dessert or cheese, are usually good value. They often include a half-liter or *pichet* of house wine. During the popular spring and summer months, you may have to make reservations for dinner, even at the most informal places.

> **Author's Tip:** The red and blue sign of *Les Routiers*, posted outside a restaurant, is a good indication of decent meals at fair prices. The sign means the restaurant is recommended by *Guide Des Relais Routiers* (Routiers are long distance truck drivers) which has as its slogan "Good, moderately priced restaurants for all." They have an interactive website – www.relais-routiers.com – to help find restaurants along your route.

Fine Dining

The French are serious about their cuisine and the finest restaurants may be destinations in their own right. As a rule, the most celebrated restaurants are expensive – you can easily spend €75 or more per person for a two-course meal with wine. Sometimes lunch (*déjeuner*) is a lower-cost way to experience two- or three-starred culinary artistry. If you can afford it, it is worthwhile to fit in at least one – but don't plan too much rigorous activity the next day! "Destination restaurants" are pointed out in the regional chapters.

DINING PRICE CHART	
Prices are for a typical prix fixe menu of two courses and a glass of house wine for one.	
	€14-€19
€	€21-€34
€€	€35-€49
€€€	€50-€69
€€€€	€70-€140
€€€€€	The sky's the limit

■ Shopping

Provence is full of temptation. Most of the larger towns have a good selection of stores. Although you will find chain stores (and even department stores in the biggest towns), the French are particularly fond of **bou-**

tiques and **specialty stores**. It is worth exploring the narrow lanes of the larger towns for local designers and galleries.

Every town has at least one **market** day. Try to schedule your visit to take in one of the markets recommended in later chapters. Some of them are truly spectacular – in **St. Rémy**, the market takes over the entire town once a week, drawing vendors from throughout the region. Along the **Côte d'Azur**, antique markets and flea markets are especially popular.

If you are planning to stay in one place for a while and cook for yourself, make sure you stock up at the local *hypermarché*. The selection of meats, fish, cheeses, fruit, vegetables, baked goods and interesting groceries is stunning; you can buy wine *en vrac*, and prices are very competitive.

Clothing & shoes – French fashion companies compete with local designers and craftspeople, especially in the bigger towns – Aix en Provence, Avignon, Arles and Nîmes – and just about everywhere along the Côte d'Azur. You may find prices on the high side, but quality is impeccable. Look, especially, for unusual clothing for children, infants and toddlers.

Antiques – Watch for the word *brocantes* on shop fronts if you enjoy poking around in bric-a-brac. Weekly flea markets are popular and some towns are particularly good hunting grounds. **Isle sur la Sorgue** (page 123) has about 300 permanent dealers and Easter and August fairs that attract hundreds more.

Sporting goods – The French are particularly keen cyclists so a good selection of European cycling clothing and gear is easy to find in most of the larger towns and even many smaller ones.

Local specialties – In shops and markets look for local honey, handmade sweets, including *calissons d'Aix*, (page 174) olive oil, olive oil-based or *vegetale* soaps, including *Le Vrais Savon de Marseille,* lavender- and *neroli-* (orange blossom-) scented products, hand-blown glass from Biot, carved *santons*, bright printed fabrics, fruits in eau de vie (strong and unsugared, a really grown-up treat).

Specialty nougat in a Provence confiserie (© Ferne Arfin)

Did you know? Santon means "little saint" in Provençal and are an essential part of Provençal Christmas celebrations. These painted figures were originally based on bib'lical characters of the nativity. Later, local peasants were added, representing the characters of a Provençal village who bring their gifts to the Christ child, along with their farm animals and produce.

Eco-Travel

Provence has three "regional nature reserves": **The Camargue** (pages 71 ff), **The Lubéron** (pages 108 ff) and **Haute Provence** (pages 193 ff). **Le Mercantour** (page 380), a national park in the Alpes Maritime, is also in Provence. "Regional nature parks" are chartered to protect areas of natural and cultural importance where the balance of nature is seen as threatened. Unlike nature reserves which you may be accustomed to elsewhere, towns and villages can be included in these parks. The boundaries of the parks are negotiated by the townships that ratify their charters. These charters usually include commitments about conservation, management of nature and landscapes, land use planning and education. French "national parks" are run along similar lines but are administered nationally as part of a European initiative. Their aim is to foster conservation, protect biodiversity and promote environmental protection.

Well-marked hiking and cycling trails are a feature of these parks, as are information and education centers. Other low-impact activities, such as climbing, ballooning, riding, canoeing and sailing, may also be permitted. Look for more information about the nature reserves and the national parks in the regional chapters that follow.

L'evasion verte (green escape) is the French way of suggesting an eco-friendly vacation in a rural or parkland *gîte*. *Gîtes* are self-contained houses where you do your own cooking and cleaning – what Europeans call "self-catering." A gîte may be a bungalow built specifically for family vacations or it may be a fully equipped, luxury home, rented out for part of the year. They range from rustic simplicity – the French version of a log cabin – to Riviera elegance. In some areas, trailers or RVs may be offered as *gîtes*. Local suppliers of this kind of accommodation are listed in the regional chapters.

> **Note:** The national organization, **Gîtes de France**, sets standards and has a comprehensive directory of *gîtes* on its website, www.gites-de-france.fr/eng.

Adventures

The wide variety of landscapes and microclimates, bordered by the sea and the Alps, offer a varied choice of adventure activities. Hiking, cycling and watersports are the most popular and the most widely available, but just about every outdoor pastime you can think of can be enjoyed here – horseback riding, rock and cliff climbing, spelunking, diving, sky diving, hot air ballooning, hang-gliding, fishing, boating, kayaking and, in season, whitewater rafting and Alpine skiing, to name a few.

Hiking

Hundreds of thousands of miles of marked and maintained trails range from national long-distance paths, crossing vast tracts of the country, to local paths that provide a few hours of interesting walking. French hiking trails tend to connect rural villages where food, lodging and basic supplies are available so that it is usually possible to trek for several days without needing to camp and carrying a light pack. Paths are classified as follows:

- **GR** *(Sentiers de grandes randonnées)*: GRs are long paths that criss-cross the entire country. They are numbered, well-mapped and marked with white over red blazes. Many of the itineraries suggested in this book pick up portions of GR trails. For an overview of all 38,000 miles, check out **IGN map 903 France**, Grande Randonnée (a huge, 1:1,000,000 scale map produced by The Institut Géographic National). See *Sources of Information* below for places where the map may be available.

- **GRP** *(Grandes Randonnées Pédestres)*: Regional trails, indicated by a yellow mark over a red blaze, explore regions, usually in a circuit. There are about 25,000 miles of them, some more than 100 miles long.

- **PR** *(Randonnées Pédestres)*: These are local paths, close to or heading out of towns and villages and covering short hikes of a day or less. They are marked with a yellow blaze or, if there are many local paths, any single color. The best sources of information on PRs are local tourist offices, or the Fédération Française de la Randonnée Pédestre (the French Ramblers' Association, info@ffrandonnee.fr, www.ffrandonnee.fr). About 50,000 miles of these paths are listed officially, but in fact, that is probably just the tip of the iceberg.

Cycling

Road cycling in Provence is easy and relatively safe because so many French people do it themselves. There are plenty of quiet backroads and many of the busier, numbered national routes have bicycle lanes or paved cycle paths running alongside. Drivers coming up behind you will tap their horns just to let you know they are there or to give you a bit of encouragement and it is not at all unusual for passing truckers to call out "Courage!"

The network of dedicated cycling routes is not as extensive as the ramblers network, but it is growing. **Green** *(Véloroutes Voies Vertes)* designates easy routes and urban cycleways, while **Blue** *(Véloroutes Voies Bleus)* signifies moderate to difficult routes. **IGN map 906** covers all mountain biking sites and the main tourist cycling routes. The IGN 1:250,000 scale series even features suggested tourist sites along the way.

Practical Advice for Cyclists

Judging distances: All the itineraries in this book give distances in both kilometers and miles (1 km=.62 miles). Itineraries and maps available from tourist offices in France provide distances and times based on km only.

Sometimes an average time for the route is suggested. This is based on an average speed of 20 km per hour

Cycling break (courtesy of Trek Travel)

(three minutes per km), which is what French cycling organizations expect that a trained cyclist who is reasonably fit and cycles regularly can cover. For uphill routes, add one hour per 1,000 m (3,280 feet) of climbing (six minutes per 100 m/328 feet). Adjust this rate to suit your own fitness and the weight of your backpack or panniers.

Rules of the road: When using public roads, cyclists are subject to the same rules as motorists. During daylight hours, cyclists can ride in pairs but must go back to single file when a motor vehicle approaches to pass. During darkness, cyclists must ride single file. When passing a cyclist, motorists must give the cyclist one meter (about three feet) of clearance in built-up areas and 1½ m (about five feet) of clearance elsewhere.

Road signs for cyclists: Signs follow international agreements and most are easy to understand. These road signs are particularly important for cyclists:

Start of cycle path   End   Cycle crossing

No cycles permitted   No vehicles   No motor vehicles

Compulsory equipment: Your cycle must have certain equipment. Most cycles available to rent will have everything required by law, but it's wise to double-check for the following:

- Two working brakes
- A bell or horn that can be heard at a distance of 50 m (165 feet)
- Several red reflectors visible from the rear
- Several red reflectors visible from the sides
- One white reflector, visible from the rear

Specially Recommended Routes

The French seem to love to hand out certificates and diplomas testifying to the guaranteed quality of this or that. The whole Appellation d'Origine Contrôlée (AOC) system – for wines, olives, olive oil and various other products – is a case in point.

In a country with so many avid cyclists, it is only natural that a national system of rating cycle routes and handing out certificates would apply. There are two such systems, called *Brevets de Cyclotourisme* (Certificates of Tourist Cycle Routes). They are intended to call attention to routes and will give you better understanding of the character and aspects of a region.

Routes marked **BPF** *(Brevet de province française)* must have at least six points of special regional interest. If, in addition, the route has a point of special national interest, it will be marked **BCN** *(Brevet de cyclotourisme nationale)*. It is worth following up these indicators if you come across them on road signs or in itineraries offered by local tourist authorities.

■ Sources of Information

i **Institut Géographique National** (IGN, www.ign.fr), the French government mapping organization, produces a wide range of detailed topographic maps with ramblers' and cycling routes superimposed on them. Maps can be purchased online from their French-language site or from:

- In the US – **Map Link Inc**., Map Distributors, has a large selection of maps, but very few from IGN. They are at 30 S. La Patera Lane, Unit 5, Santa Barbara, CA 93117, ☎ 805 692 6777, billhunt@maplinkinc.com.
- In the UK – **Navigator Maps Ltd.**, 4 Devonshire Street, Ambergate, PO Box 6242, DE56 2GJ, Derby, ☎ 01773 857 996, www.navimaps.co.uk. **Stanfords**, in London, usually has a good selection of IGN maps with facilities to purchase online or by telephone. Stanfords, 12-14 Long Acre, London, WC2E 9LP, ☎ 0207 8361321, fax 0207 8360189, customer.services@stanfords.co.uk, www.stanfords.co.uk.

- **Fédération Française de la Randonée Pédestre** offers information, Topo-Guides, and maps of GRP and PR routes. Contact FFRP, 14 Rue Riquet, 75019 Paris, ☎ 33 01 44 89 93 90, www.ffrp.asso.fr.
- **Fédération Française de Cyclisme** provides information about regional and departmental cyling committees and addresses of local cycling clubs. Contact Fédération Française de Cyclisme, Bat. Jean Monnet, 5, Rue de Rome, 93561 Rosny Sous Bois, ☎ 33 01 49 35 69 00, www.ffc.fr.

How to Dial French Telephone Numbers

You will find the numbers in this book look a bit different from telephone numbers you may have seen before. Here is a typical format: 33 04 12 23 34 45.

In the sample above, the first pair of numbers (33) is the country code for France. If you are phoning France from overseas, you must dial 33 after your own country's international access code.

The second pair of numbers includes 0 and a number – which, in this book, is usually 4, but may be another number. This is the regional or local code. If you are dialing from outside of France, do not dial the zero. Use the zero, in combination with the number next to it, if dialing from within France.

These numbers are followed by four pairs of numbers. In France, these telephone numbers are almost universally given in pairs.

Getting Here

By Air

Two international airports serve this region: **Marseille** and **Nice Côte d'Azur**. You can fly non-stop to Nice from New York JFK or with one connecting flight to Marseille from most major US airports. Both airports are only short hops from either Paris or London, with plenty of direct flights run by most European airlines.

Contacts

Marseille-Provence Airport: contact@marseille-provence.aeroport.fr, 24-hour information desk, ☎ 33 04 42 14 21 14. Convenient for western Provence, this is one hour and 25 minutes from Paris, two hours from London. Delta Airlines connect to Marseille through Charles De Gaulle Airport, Paris, from several US cities. British Airways serves Marseille from London Gatwick.

Delta Airlines: www.delta.com; in the US, ☎ 800 221 1212; in the UK, ☎ 0800 414767.

British Airways: www.britishairways.com; from the US, ☎ 800 403 0882; in the UK, ☎ 0845 7733377.

Nice Côte d'Azur Airport: www.nice.aeroport.fr, ☎ (from within France only) 08 36 69 55 55. This is useful for eastern Provence, the Riviera and the Maritime Alpes. It's one hour and 35 minutes from Paris, two hours from London, and about 8½ hours from New York. Air France flies non-stop from New York JFK once a day, while Delta Airlines connects from the US through Paris-Charles de Gaulle. British Airways flies from London Gatwick. In addition, British Midlands flies from London Heathrow and EasyJet flies from London Stansted or London Luton.

Air France: www.airfrance.us, US Reservations ☎ 800 237 2747.

British Midlands: www.flybmi.com, from the US, ☎ 44 01332 854854; from the UK, ☎ 0870 6070555.

EasyJet: www.easyjet.com, ☎ 44 0870 6000000.

By Rail

TGV Méditerranée, www.tgv.com, tgv@voyages-sncf.com, the Southern branch of the French high-speed rail network, offers direct links from Paris to Marseille, Avignon and Nîmes. TGV stands for Trains à Grande Vitesse (high speed trains) and the trains reach more than 186 miles per hour in some stretches. The journey from Paris to Avignon, a distance of about 440 miles, takes only 3½ hours. Fares vary seasonally and by duration of stay. Promotional fares are usually available and Eurail Pass holders can travel on TGV Méditerranée routes on payment of a reservation fee. Local trains connect the TGV hubs with most larger towns and also run along the coast. If you are traveling with your own car from the UK, you can also book French Motorail journey to Avignon, which takes about 11 hours.

Contacts

Rail Pass: www.railpass.com, from the US, ☎ 877 RAILPASS.

Rail Europe: www.raileurope.com, from the US, ☎ 877 257 2887; from Canada, ☎ 800 361 RAIL. From the UK, contact www.raileurope.co.uk, reservations@raileurope.co.uk, ☎ 08705 848 848.

Getting Around

By Train: Local trains run by **Trains Express Regionaux (TER)** connect most of the larger towns. Fares vary but are generally fairly low. Service may be direct (Avignon to Nîmes, for example, in 35 minutes) or may involve changing trains, depending on the time of day. Fare and schedule information can be obtained from SNCF train stations all over France.

> **Did You Know?** Romantics or the just plain curious may be interested to know that the name of the French national rail company, SNCF, is short for Société Nationale du Chemin de Fer.

By Bus: Services tend to be local, based in the major towns and serving their surrounding area or *banlieue*. Scheduling fast journeys between destinations can be a problem. But for the independent traveler, who isn't in a hurry and wants to do some local exploring, they can be a useful alternative to the car or bicycle.

> **Tip:** If you are planning to use local buses a lot, pick up a free copy of the very useful *Guide Régional des Transport, Trains Express Régionaux (TER)*. This great mouthful of a guidebook covers local trains and bus services and is available at any SNCF train station.

By Car: Car touring is an excellent way to see this area and most destinations are connected by "RN" roads or *Routes Nationales*. These were France's biggest roads before the Autoroutes, or "A" roads were built. They are wide and well-maintained, but a little more scenic than "A" roads. Off the main highways, "D" roads vary in size but are safe and clearly marked with good surfaces. With the exception of a few breath-catching routes in the Alps of Haute Provence and the Maritime Alps, the roads aren't particularly challenging, allowing you to cruise along and enjoy the scenery. It is a good idea to buy a French road atlas or the Michelin Green map that covers this area to a scale of 1/100,000 (1 cm=1 km) to discover the many out-of-the-way routes and twisting country lanes.

> **Caution:** Be wary of other drivers. The French drive much faster than you may expect, and they are impatient daredevils when it comes to passing.

Cars are easy to rent, with most major companies represented at airports and TGV stations. Try to choose a compact or even sub-compact car – roads can be narrow and European gasoline prices can be shocking – $6 a gallon or more. **Rail Europe** (☎ 1 888 382 7245) offers below advertised rates for **Hertz** and **Avis** cars. **France Car Rental** (US ☎ 786 866 2865, info@francecarrental.net) acts as an agent for **National Car Rental** and offers good value deals on a range of models.

Tip: France uses the metric system of measurement and road signs are in kilometers. A km is .62 miles so a sign that says, for example, "Marseille 100" means Marseille is 62 miles away.

By Bicycle: This area is particularly popular with cyclists, it is relatively safe. Motorists expect cyclists to appear, singly or in packs, around every bend and tend to be on the lookout for them. Still, it is wise to avoid RN roads and to wear bright clothing. If you're planning a bicycle tour, make sure you allow plenty of time between scheduled stops. Parts of Provence are flatter than others but those long, apparently gentle, ascents can be real killers if you're in a hurry.

The French call bicycles *vélos*. Mountain bikes (called V.T.T. for *vélo tout terrain*) are catching on as well and are widely available for rent. Local tourist offices always have information and maps about nearby bicycle routes.

A familiar sight in Provence (courtesy of Trek Travel)

Tip: Avoid renting the cycles available at SNCF stations. They can be expensive and are often poor quality. Even the tiniest village is accustomed to catering to cyclists' needs so decent cycle shops are just about everywhere.

■ Where to Stay

There are several different kinds of accommodation. Unless meals are included, prices are almost always quoted per room rather than per person. **Auberges** are country inns, sometimes the equivalent of staying in rooms over a British pub, but usually a bit more *charmante*. An auberge usually has a restaurant.

Hotels in France carry a government star rating, ranging from one star for a simple inn up to four stars for deluxe accommodation. Star ratings – which are based on room size, facilities, elevators, plumbing – are only loosely connected to price. A very

HOTEL PRICE CHART	
Rates are per room based on double occupancy.	
	Under €55
€	€56-€96
€€	€97-€135
€€€	€136-€195
€€€€	Over €195

charming three-star hotel may be more comfortable (and more expensive) than a nearby four-star.

> **Logis de France** – *Fédération Nationale des Logis de France, 83 Avenue d'Italie, 75013 Paris,* ☎ *33 01 45 84 83 84, fax 33 01 45 83 59 66, www.logis-de-france.fr.* This organization rates some 3,000 independently owned restaurant-hotels, which must meet strict standards of quality and service. Their ratings of one to three "chimneys" are reliable indicators. **One chimney** means simple but comfortable furnishings, good cuisine, excellent value; **two chimneys** indicates a high level of comfort and tasty cuisine for the price; **three chimneys** is for an extremely comfortable hotel, elaborate cuisine, and attentive service.

A *ferme* or a *chambre d'hôte* is an informal, often family-style accommodation. *Chambre d'hôtes* include meals – either full or half-board (breakfast and dinner). A *ferme*, which means farm, may often be a *chambre d'hôte* as well. *Gîtes* (see *Eco-Travel*, page 22) are for the do-it-yourselfer and can be an economical solution for families or larger groups planning to stay in one location.

Slightly up the scale are **villas**. Not as grand as the word might suggest, villas are privately owned homes and cottages rented out through brokers. Usually very well-equipped (kitchens may even have food processors and balloon whisks!), often with swimming pools, they can be a reasonably priced base for three couples sharing.

Because much of this region is dry for three-quarters of the year and vulnerable to forest and brush fires, **camping** is permitted only in designated areas, some of which may be municipal but are usually privately owned. Campgrounds are subject to a governmental star system, depending on the level of comfort and facilities such as showers, platform tents and utility link-ups for caravans (the European term for small trailers and RVs). Camping areas will be suggested in each chapter. For more information and a fuller list of campsites, try the website of the **Fédération Française de Camping et de Caravaning**, www.ffcc.fr (French-language site with links to English-language campsites).

■ Travel Essentials

Entry Requirements

Citizens of the **United States** and **Canada** do not need visas for tourist visits of up to 90 days. You'll need to have a passport, valid for three months longer than you intend to stay, tickets and documents for your return or onward travel. Occasionally, you may be required to prove you have the means to support yourself during your stay so it is wise to have your credit cards or traveler's checks within reach. As members of the European Union, subjects of the **United Kingdom** should carry their passports but are otherwise free to travel in France without restriction.

Customs

Non-Europeans who live outside the EU can bring 400 duty-free cigarettes, 200 cigarillos, 100 cigars or 500 grams of smoking tobacco into France. Customs also allow two liters of wine (coals to Newcastle?) and one liter of alcohol over 22 proof as well as two liters of wine under 22 proof. You can bring €175 of general merchandise if you are over 15 or €90 worth if you are 14 or under. No limitations apply to EU citizens as long as the goods are intended for personal use.

Tax Free Shopping

Value Added Tax (VAT or TVA in France) is a sales tax charged across Europe. If you are a non-European and stay in France less than six months, you can get a tax refund on purchases of €183 or more. It is a bit complicated but can be worth it on larger purchases (the standard French VAT rate is 19.6% but it can be as high as 33%!). First, get a completed VAT refund form from the store where you make your purchase. When you leave France, have Customs stamp the form. Then mail it back to the store. Refunds are credited to your credit card account or mailed to you and can take as long as six months to arrive.

Money Matters

Currency

The euro (€) is now the only currency in use in France. There are seven denominations of bills – €5, €10, €20, €50, €100, €200 and €500 – used by participating European Union countries (the "Euro zone" does not include the United Kingdom, which has not yet adopted it). There are €1 and €2 coins along with six denominations of euro cents – 50, 20, 10, 5, 2 and 1. Each coin denomination has a common face on one side but the issuing countries decorate the opposite face in their own ways. All can be freely used throughout the zone. The European Central Bank website, at www.euro.ecb.int/en/section.html, has pictures of all the notes and coins.

> **Tip:** The value of the euro fluctuates. Where specific prices are quoted in this book, they are given in euros, up-to-date at the time of going to press. Exchange rates are usually carried in the financial pages of most daily newspapers. A universal currency converter is available on the Internet at www.xe.com/ucc/. At press time, the euro was worth US$1.30, Can$1.58 and £.69.

Traveler's Checks & Credit Cards

It is wise to carry a minimum amount of currency. Traveler's checks are useful but in smaller towns you may have to cash them at a bank. Credit or debit cards are by far the most convenient way to pay or to get local currency. They are accepted everywhere. When you use plastic to get local currency from a cash machine, you don't pay a commission and the amount is converted to your own currency at the best interbank rate available on the day. Visa and MasterCard are the most widely accepted cards. American Express and Diners Club cards are also usually accepted, although some merchants may charge extra for their use.

To Report a Lost or Stolen Credit Card in France

American Express . . . . ☎ 01 47 77 72 00
Diners Club. . . . . ☎ 08 10 31 41 59
MasterCard . . . . ☎ 08 00 90 13 87
VISA global assistance . . . . ☎ 08 00 90 11 79
or call US collect 001 410 581 9994 or 001 410 581 3836

Where to Get Cash

- **Banks**: To cash traveler's checks and for cash advances on credit cards (if you forget your pin number!). Banks are usually open between 9 am and 4 pm, closing from noon to 2 pm for lunch. Some are closed on Mondays and some close at noon the day before a legal holiday.
- **Post Offices**: Most post offices have ATMs (called DABs, for *distributeurs automatiques de billet*s, in France) with round-the-clock service. During office hours (8 am to 5 pm) bureau de change and travelers' check cashing facilities are available. Look for yellow signs with the word La Poste, in blue. In smaller towns, they may close for lunch between noon and 2 pm.
- **Bureaux de Change**: These are small, money changing offices available all over Europe. They offer a range of services including local check cashing, travelers' check cashing and cash advances on credit or debit cards. Some will also make funds-by-wire transactions. Because they are open late and on weekends, they charge a premium for their services.
- **ATMs**: Cash machines are everywhere and are the most convenient, and usually cheapest, way to obtain local currency. You'll need a four-digit pin number. Check with your card issuer about any hidden transfer charges.

Above: Vines and Lavender (© N&F Michel, CDT Vaucluse)

Below: This very olive grove, outside St. Paul de Mausole asylum, was a frequent inspiration for Van Gogh (© Ferne Arfin)

Above: Les Antiques, St. Remy de Provence (© Ferne Arfin)

Below: The 2,000-year-old Pont du Gard, one of the world's finest examples of Roman arch construction (© Ferne Arfin)

Above: Camargue horses grazing *(© Ferne Arfin)*

Below: Graceful Arlesian houses beside the Rhone in Arles *(© Ferne Arfin)*

Above: *Les Belles Vieux Quais* – evening festivities during Beaucaire's Fête de la Madeleine (© OT Beaucaire)

Below: *Gardians de Taureaux* – Camarguaise "cowboys" escort their bulls through town during the Fête de la Madeleine in Beaucaire (© Ferne Arfin)

Cost of Living

There's no getting around the fact that France is not cheap. While Provence is not as expensive as Paris (where you can spend €5 on a capuccino) many things will cost more than they do in the US and Canada (though less than in the UK). Gasoline, which is sold by the liter (1.05 quarts) can cost €5 per gallon or more. Personal electronics, CDs and clothing in retail shops all cost more than they do in the US. If you are very frugal, picnic on bread, cheese and local *vin du table* and stay in tent campsites, you might get away with spending about €50 per day, per person. A budget of €125 to €175 per day, per person is more realistic. If you have a student or senior citizen's card, don't be embarrassed to use it – discounts are common (for movies, transportation, museum entries) and a big help.

> **Tip:** During festivals, avoid cafés on the streets most popular with tourists. Prices can double or even triple. I once paid the equivalent of $9 for a Coke in Avignon during the summer festival. A week later, the same drink was less than $3.

Tipping

A 12-15% tip is often included in the bill at restaurants and cafés. If it is, the menu will say *service compris* and the same words will be printed or written on your bill. If you are unsure, simply ask. Try the French *Est-ce que le service compris?* (pronounced Es-kuh luh sairvis compri?) if you are adventurous. Unless service was really terrible, it is customary to leave some extra small change. Where service isn't included, leave 12 to 15%, more in stylish restaurants. Taxi drivers will expect about 10% of the amount on the meter. Small tips for other services – room service, maid service, porters (about €1.50 per bag) – are common but not required or demanded.

Public Holidays

Avoid starting your vacation in France on a public holiday as car or cycle rental shops and other services may be closed. Legal holidays include:

January 1 . . . . New Year's Day
March/April . . . . Easter Sunday & Monday
May 1 . . . . May Day
May 8. . . . . Victory in Europe Day
40th day after Easter (May or June) . . . . . . Ascension Thursday
7th Sunday & Monday after Easter (mid-May or June)
. . . . Pentecost/Whit Sunday & Whit Monday
July 14 . . . . Bastille Day/National Day

August 15 . . . . Assumption Day
November 1 . . . . All Saints' Day
November 11 . . . . Remembrance Day
December 25 . . . . Christmas

Religious holidays, such as Ascension and Pentecost, usually mean long holiday weekends and the start of school vacations. If you can, avoid traveling across France by car or bus then because all the motorways going south turn into parking lots.

Health Services & Insurance

US and Canadian citizens should carry up-to-date travel health insurance. The French Health Service is first class – hospitals, clinics and medical specialists are well distributed throughout Provence – but it is not free to non-Europeans. For UK subjects, health care is free at the point of delivery but you must present a form **E111**, which you can pick up at any UK Post Office. Alternative practitioners, such as osteopaths, homeopaths and chiropractors, are popular and easy to locate in the bigger towns.

Pharmacies able to dispense prescription drugs are always indicated by a green cross sign (usually in neon). They are open between 9 am and 7 pm (closed noon to 2 pm). For emergencies, the details of a local, after-hours pharmacy (*pharmacie de garde*), and doctor (*médecin*) are posted on pharmacy windows.

Mail

Blue and yellow French mail boxes are easy to spot in town centers or in the outer walls of post offices (indicated by the words *La Poste* in blue and yellow). Stamps can be purchased from machines or from bar tabacs. The mail service is comparable to North American and UK services, with letters taking from one to five days to reach overseas addresses.

Telephones

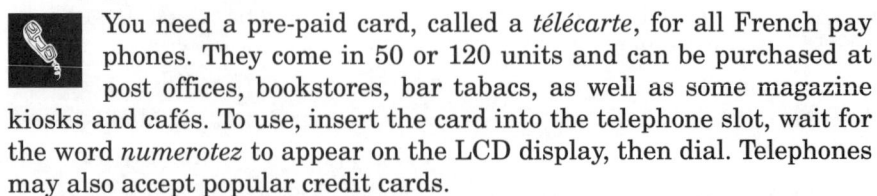

You need a pre-paid card, called a *télécarte*, for all French pay phones. They come in 50 or 120 units and can be purchased at post offices, bookstores, bar tabacs, as well as some magazine kiosks and cafés. To use, insert the card into the telephone slot, wait for the word *numerotez* to appear on the LCD display, then dial. Telephones may also accept popular credit cards.

Most US and Canadian long-distance calling card services can be used in France. If your service provider has an 0800 number, you can dial that free from a public pay phone. Otherwise, you'll need to use a French *télécarte* or a credit card to access your long-distance service.

EMERGENCY PHONE NUMBERS

(Free from public pay phones)

Ambulance 15
Police 17
Fire.................................... 18

Emergency Consular Services

The US, Canada and the United Kingdom all maintain emergency services for their citizens. While most embassies are in Paris, local consular services are available in Provence. Your own country's consul can help with a variety of crises, from replacing a lost or stolen passport to repatriating a deceased relative. Most will not, however, advance funds except under the most urgent and unusual circumstances.

USA: US Consul General Marseille, Place Varian Fry, 13286 Marseille Cedex 6, ☎ 04 91 54 92 00, amcongenmars@fr.inter.net.

Canada: 24/7 Emergency assistance for Canadian citizens in distress. Dial the Canadian Embassy switchboard at ☎ 01 44 43 29 00 or paris-consulaire@dfait-maeci.gc.ca.

United Kingdom: British Consular Services, 24 avenue du Prado, 13006 Marseille, ☎ 04 91 15 72 10, consulare-mailpavis.consulare-mailpavis2@fco.gov.uk.

Going Metric

To make your travels in this region easier, we have provided the following chart that shows metric equivalents for the measurements you are familiar with.

GENERAL MEASUREMENTS

1 kilometer = .6124 miles

1 mile = 1.6093 kilometers

1 foot = .304 meters

1 inch = 2.54 centimeters

1 square mile = 2.59 square kilometers

1 pound = .4536 kilograms

1 ounce = 28.35 grams

1 imperial gallon = 4.5459 liters

1 US gallon = 3.7854 liters

1 quart = .94635 liters

TEMPERATURES

For Fahrenheit: Multiply Centigrade figure by 1.8 and add 32.

For Centigrade: Subtract 32 from Fahrenheit figure and divide by 1.8.

Centigrade	Fahrenheit
40°	104°
35°	95°
30°	86°
25°	77°
20°	64°
15°	59°
10°	50°

The Alpilles & The Garrigues

Van Gogh's Provence

If you have ever dreamed of Provence, it probably looked like Vincent Van Gogh's wheat fields and cypress trees, stony white hills and starry nights, tumbling clouds in brilliant blue skies. These images have made this part of Provence so familiar that it has become a kind of collective fantasy. Van Gogh spent his last and most prolific years painting the fields, farmhouses (*mas* in Provençal) and people of this corner of Provence. He produced so many images of the area that stretches from **Avignon**, west to **Nîmes** and south to **Arles** (the gateway to the Camargue) that visiting it, you might feel as if you're walking around a living art gallery.

IN THIS CHAPTER	
■ Avignon	39
■ Nîmes	42
■ St-Rémy de Provence	46
■ Les Baux de Provence	49
■ Beaucaire	50
■ Eygalières	51
■ Maussane les Alpilles & Mouriès	51
■ Pont du Gard	52
■ Uzès	53
■ Festivals & Fêtes	54
■ Market Days/Shopping	54
■ Where to Stay	56
■ Where to Eat	60
■ Adventures	62

There is, of course, much more to enjoy here besides the buzz of *déjà vu*. Rustic villages of great charm and individuality punctuate a varied, distinctive and lightly populated landscape. From the walled city of Avignon, above a wide and fertile reach of the Rhône Valley, the 14th- and 15th-century Papal vineyards of **Châteauneuf-du-Pape** are just visible in the distance. The **Pont du Gard** rises out of the mists of the River Gardon. This, the world's most complete example of a three-tiered Roman aqueduct, can still be crossed. And local history, from outstanding Greco-Roman and Medieval ruins to the caves of the French Resistance, is within easy reach of all of the region's key destinations.

The Alpilles are a range of abrupt and jagged limestone hills forming a geological extension of the Lubéron between Avignon and Arles. Though only 1,000 to 1,500 feet high, they have bare summits and strangely eroded shapes, which create the illusion of high mountains. In fact, they are almost intimate in scale. The landscape is arid but not barren. Olive and almond trees soften the lower slopes and dry valleys of the Alpilles, while scattered oak, pine and brush weave patterns on the outcrops of pale, exposed limestone.

The Garrigues region takes its name from its stony landscape. The term *garrigue*, used in both France and Spain, refers to stretches of dry, pebbly soil and stone table land that cannot hold rainwater and, therefore, is able to support only rough, scrubby plants. The Garrigues of Provence are of a particularly vast extent, reaching from just north of Nîmes to the edge of the Massif Central, France's central mountain region. Composed of gentle, rounded hills (which the French evocatively call *mamelons*), covered with rockrose, thistle, thorn and broom, the Garrigues are characteristically harsh and dry. But this is Provence, where even hard and austere landscapes have soft pleasures. Wild lavender, thyme and rosemary flourish here and other aromatic plants (basil, sage, marjoram and savory) are cultivated, keeping the air scented year-round. The Gorges du Gardon divides The Garrigues almost in half and marks the border between Provence and the Cévennes Region.

GORGES DU GARDON

The languid Gardon, flowing between broad, sandy banks and widely spaced cliffs, is peaceful for swimming, kayaking and hiking in good weather. But watch the clouds and beware of *gardonnades,* sudden flash floods that can be sparked by a storm in the Cévennes Mountains.

■ Getting Here

Avignon is the most convenient gateway for touring this region, with easy air and rail links to Paris as well as good local rail services for cyclists and hikers. Well-maintained and well-marked roads between Avignon and other regional destinations make the town a useful and cosmopolitan base for visitors touring by car as well.

By Air: Air France schedules four or five flights per day, from Paris Orly to **Avignon Airport**, about five miles from the town center. There are no bus or shuttle services from the ai;rport but local taxi service is reasonably priced. For airline fares and schedules, in the US call **Air France** at ☎ 800 AF PARIS. **Marseille Airport** has direct flights from Paris and the UK, and connecting flights from the US. It is about a 40-minute drive from town. There are also bus and train connections from Marseille to Avignon.

By Rail: The sleek and amazing TGV (Trains à Grand Vitesse) trains whiz passengers between Paris and Avignon at speeds approaching 200 miles per hour. The trains, which are comfortable and equipped for handicapped travelers, leave Paris Gare de Lyon at approximately three-hour intervals throughout the day. The new **Avignon Gare TGV**, located on the southern edge of the city, near the ring road, is almost two miles from the center. A shuttle bus, or *navette,* runs between the station and the bus terminal (*gare routière*), just outside the city walls, every 15 minutes. A variety of RailPass packages for French rail travel can be obtained through **Rail Europe,** ☎ 877 257 2887 in the US; ☎ 800 361 RAIL in Canada.

By Car: Avignon is directly linked to Paris via the **A7**, or *Route du* but driving from Paris or elsewhere in Northern France is not mended. During the off-seasons (which aren't often), Europeans u French motorways as if there are no speed limits (which, in essence, there aren't), with speeds of more than 100 mph not uncommon. Then, throughout the summer vacation season, as Northern Europeans make a beeline for the Mediterranean, everything slows to a crawl. And in August, when it can seem like all of France is heading for the Med, the road can become a parking lot 550 miles long. Renting a car locally is a better bet.

■ Getting Around

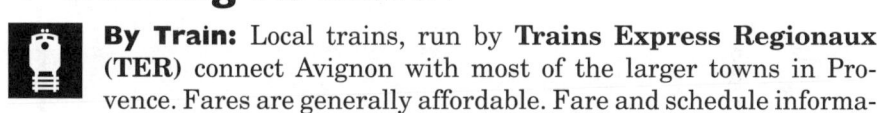

By Train: Local trains, run by **Trains Express Regionaux (TER)** connect Avignon with most of the larger towns in Provence. Fares are generally affordable. Fare and schedule information can be obtained from the **SNCF Train Station**, Boulevard St. Roch, 84000 Avignon, ☎ 33 08 36 35 35 35. The station is located along the medieval wall, between **Porte St. Charles** and **Porte St. Michel**, on the south side. It has its own gate, or *porte,* through the wall, connecting to **Rue de la Républic**, which leads directly to the center of town.

By Bus: Bus schedules can be obtained from the Gare Routière (the bus station), next to the SNCF Train Station at 5 Avenue Montclar, 84000, Avignon, ☎ 33 04 90 82 07 35.

■ Principle Destinations

Avignon

In the year 2000, UNESCO listed **The Historic Center of Avignon** as a **World Heritage Site**. The award recognizes the 13th- and 14th-century papal palaces and cathedrals massed inside Avignon's remarkably intact 14th-century walls. But visitors have always loved Avignon. In fact, this small city, set above a lazy bend in the Rhône, has attracted appreciation since the Stone Age. Maybe the first Neolithic settlers chose the heights of **The Rocher des Doms** to be safely above the Rhône's fertile flood plain; we're romantic enough to hope they also liked the view. Today, the Rocher des Doms is a scented formal garden overlooking the **Pont St. Bénézet**, with extensive vistas of the surrounding country, reaching as far as the Alpilles, **Mt. Ventoux** (pages 108 ff) and the **Dentelles de Montmirail** (page 106).

Before the Romans arrived in the first century BC, Avignon was a Celtic-Ligurian river port called Cavares. The Romans named the town *Avenio* (town of the river), from which Avignon is derived, and stayed about 600 years.

Avignon

1. Espace Jeanne Laurent
2. Rocher des Doms; Musée du Petit Palais
3. Palais des Papes
4. Musée du Mont de Piété
5. Maison Jean Vilar; Bureau du Festival
6. Opéra
7. Hôtel de Ville
8. Palais du Roure
9. Musée Vouland
10. Musée Calvet
11. Musée Requien
12. Bibliotheque Ceccano
13. Musée Lapidaire
14. Musée Angladon Dubrujeaud
15. Musée Vouland
16. Gare SNCF
17. Gare Routiere
18. Office de Tourisme
19. Les Halles
20. Université

© 2005 HUNTER PUBLISHING, INC.

Avignon Festival dancers, outside le Palais des Papes
(© J.L. Seille, CDT Vaucluse)

It was, however, the Middle Ages, and in particular the 13th- and 14th-century era of the French popes and anti-popes that gave Avignon the character for which it is still renowned.

Modern Avignon is a city of about 90,000 people and capital of the Vaucluse département of France. A major commercial center, its principle activities are food processing, civil engineering and high technology. Within the seven gates of the walled city, however, tourism and the arts reign supreme. Palaces, cathedrals and museums, theaters, cinemas, music clubs and restaurants, terrific shopping – in chic boutiques or traditional markets – shade-dappled squares lined with sidewalk cafés, sunny plazas ringing with song; there is so much to do and see here that visitors should plan on spending at least a few days. During the **Avignon Festival of Theatre and Dance**, which now rivals Edinburgh as Europe's pre-eminent arts festival, it is possible to see a different performance every night for a month. *Jongleurs*, mime artists and musicians turn the festival city into a continual open-air performance for most of July.

This is a genuinely seductive place. And since many of its narrow, winding streets are for pedestrians only, it manages to be peaceful yet lively and entertaining at the same time. Before you leave, be sure to cross the river to **Villeneuve-les-Avignon** for an unforgettable view of Avignon glowing golden in the sunset.

SUR LE PONT D'AVIGNON...

The curious **Pont St. Bénézet**, famed as the Pont d'Avignon of the children's song, didn't always end abruptly in the middle of the river. The bridge, an extension of the city walls near the Palais des Papes, was once the only Rhône crossing between Lyons and the Mediterranean. Built as a penance by St. Bénézet in 1185, legend has it that a dream vision led him to the spot. According to the story, the bishops of the day scoffed at Bénézet, refusing to help him, so the people of Avignon pitched in to build it. The bridge was regularly damaged by seasonal tides. In fact, St. Bénézet himself was forced to rebuild it several times. Finally, in the early 18th century, the Avignon authorities became fed up with the cost of regular repairs and left the bridge to its picturesque fate.

By the way, did you know that the words of the traditional song, as sung today, are wrong? The familiar verse, *Sur le pont d'Avignon, on y danse, on y danse...* (On the bridge of Avignon, people dance, etc...) was originally *Sous le pont* ...or under the bridge. Apparently, at one time people danced at a tavern on the shore, under the arches. A tiny set of steps tucked away beside the bridge will take you to the spot. They danced *under* the bridge – the bridge itself being too narrow to dance in a circle anyway.

Sightseeing

Tourist information: Office de tourisme, 41 cours Jean Jaurès, ☎ 04 32 74 32 74, information@ot-avignon.fr.

The Palais des Papes: The 14th-century palace of the French popes, with its 150-foot towers, parapets and crenelated battlements, dominates Avignon as well as the countryside for miles around. The chronicler Froissart once called it Europe's most beautiful and powerful château. Today, it is an enormous maze of deserted rooms, corridors and chapels, with only a few surviving murals, tapestries and paintings suggesting its sumptuous past. Exhibitions are held throughout the summer and fall, and guided tours (in French) are available every half-hour during the summer.

Follow Rue de la République north from the SNCF station and across the Place de l'Horloge. If you can resist the many shops and shady cafés along the way, a narrow passage at the northern end of the square will lead you into the Place du Palais and the Palais des Papes.

Open from 9:30 am to 5:45 pm, November 2 to March 31; 9 am to 7 pm, April 1 to August 2; 9 am to 8 pm, August 3 to September 30. Late opening to 9 pm during Avignon Festival.

Admission of €7 includes the Palais des Papes and exhibitions as well as the Pont St. Bénézet.

Tip: Pick up a free **Avignon Passeport** for discounts of between 20% and 50% on admission to more than 16 museums and historic monuments, including the **Palais des Papes** and the **Petit Palais**, as well as reduced fares on local tour buses. Just ask for the pass after paying the full admission at any of the participating sites. Then enjoy the discount on admission to all the museums you visit that day.

Nîmes

In a region saturated with Roman monuments and the echoes of Roman culture, Nîmes is the most Roman of cities. The well maintained state of its ancient monuments and public buildings is due to the fact that several

Nîmes

1. Jardins de la Fontaine
2. Place Picasso
3. Square de la Bouquerie
4. Opéra
5. Coupole des Halles
6. Les Halles Covered Marketplace
7. Église St.-Charles, Place St.-Charles
8. Place du Château
9. Université des Carmes
10. École des Beaux Arts
11. Place des Arènes
12. Palais de Justice
13. Esplanade
14. Gare SNCF
15. Temple; Place de l'Oratoire

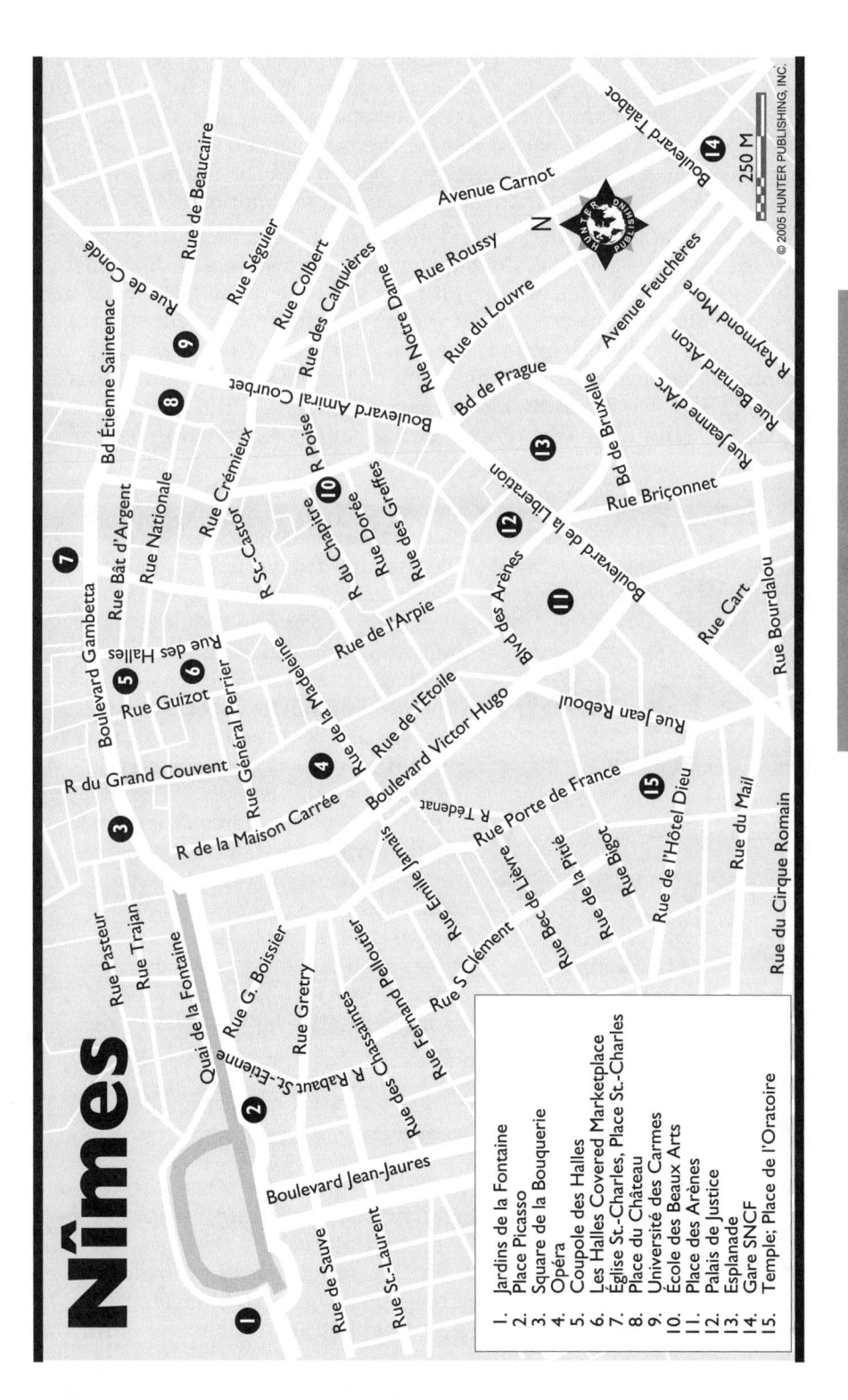

The Alpilles & the Garrigues

of them have been in virtually continual use since they were built. The **Amphitheater**, built by the Romans in about 40 or 50 BC, is still the main venue for all kinds of festivals and spectacles. The classical, colonnaded **Maison Carré**, once a Roman temple, has been the town hall, a private home, a stable, a monastery, a church and the regional archives before its current incarnation as a museum of antiquities.

Nomadic Celts had settled around an abundant spring in the sixth century BC, calling the place *Nemausus* (a name eventually shortened to Nîmes) in honor of their water spirit. By the time the Romans colonized the area, about 500 years later, it was already a thriving center of trade. Located on the Via Domitian, the main route road between Italy and Spain, Nîmes eventually became one of the most important cities in Roman Gaul. The **Pont du Gard** (page 52) is part of the 50-km/31-mile aqueduct, built in the first century BC, to supplement the original spring that was Nîmes' main water supply.

PUBLIC SPECTACLES

The Romans also brought their love of spectacle. Their gladiatorial contests evolved into less violent and dangerous entertainments but the local population's taste for games involving wild animals lasted well into the 18th and 19th centuries. In the mid-19th century, Spanish-style bullfighting, the *corrida*, was imported to Nîmes, where it remains popular with a substantial minority. More popular still – and perhaps more acceptable to a wider audience – is the *Course Camarguaise*. In this game, athletic young men, dressed completely in white, compete to grab various tokens from the horns of small native bulls. Both the human and taurine competitors can become local stars and a lively, intelligent bull can have a high-earning career lasting several years.

Bulls are the real stars of the Course Camarguaise (© Ferne Arfin)

The history of Nîmes is one of religious ferment. From the fifth century onward, various heresies including Aryanism and Albigensianism struggled with the power of the church. In the 13th century, the Jews, who had enjoyed the freedom of Nîmes from the seventh century onward, were expelled. And in the 16th century, the city became a Huguenot stronghold and a focus of religious warfare and persecution that lasted until the French Revolution.

In the Middle Ages, the quality and quantity of the Nîmes water supply led to the growth of textile manufacturing, tanning and dyeing – industries that have continued to the present day. At one time, during the 18th century, at least two-thirds of the town's working population were engaged in silk-making for stockings. Modern Nîmes remains a center for the manufacture colorful Provençal fabrics, table linens and clothing.

With a population of about 135,000, Nîmes is an intriguing mixture of classical, medieval, Baroque and cutting-edge modern architecture (Norman Foster, Jean-Michel Wilmotte, Jean Nouvel and others have designed its public buildings). It offers several first-rate museums, some of the best Roman sites in the world and the relaxed street life of a typically southern city.

> **Did you know?** That blue jeans have their origin with the textile makers of Nîmes? It all began with a tough cotton fabric, made here for sails, sheeting and other heavy-duty uses. It was known as *serge de Nîmes* – say that fast and you've got "denim." The fabric was especially popular with sailors from Genoa (some people think that the sails on Christopher Columbus' ships were made of *serge de Nîmes),* who liked the material dyed blue. Eventually indigo-dyed denim came to be called *Gènes*, after the Genovese sailors. And there you have it – blue jeans!

THE CROCODILE & THE PALM

Nîmes' coat of arms, the crocodile and the palm, is visible all over the town – on signs, in the gates of public buildings, even in bronze studs in the sidewalks of the old town. In 31 BC, Octavius defeated Anthony and Cleopatra and became Emperor Caesar Augustus. Veterans of the victorious campaign were rewarded with lands in the new colony of Nemausus (Nîmes), where a special commemorative coin was struck. It featured the crocodile chained to the palm tree under a wreath of laurel leaves, symbolizing the conquest of Egypt.

Getting Here: Nîmes is about half an hour drive southwest of Avignon on the A9. It is well connected to Avignon and Arles, as well as other local communities by train and bus.

Useful Contacts: SNCF train station Boulevard Talabot, ☎ 33 08 36 35 35 35. Bus Station Gare Routière, Boulevard Natoire, ☎ 33 04 66 29 52 00.

Sightseeing

Tourist information: Office de Tourisme, 6 Rue August, ☎ 33 04 66 67 29 11, info@ot-nimes.fr. www.ot-nimes.fr.

The Amphitheater: Built in the first century BC, Nîmes' oval arena was once the scene of gladiatorial battles and lion hunts. During the Dark Ages, the people of Nîmes took shelter from marauding barbarians within its walls. At one time it contained a church and a small village! Today it is used for festivals, sports and cultural events year-round – in winter, a lentil-shaped roof is pulled over. Constructed in 34 tiers to seat more than 20,000 spectators, the games held here led to the codification of modern bullfighting.

Place des Arènes. Open daily 9 am to 6:30 pm, April through October, daily 9 am to 5:30 pm November through March. Admission: adults €4.45, students and children €3.20.

The Maison Carré: A Greek-style temple surrounded by Corinthian columns, it was built to honor the young sons of the Emperor Augustus Caesar. It has been in continual use and today houses a museum of antiquities.

Place de la Comédie. Open daily 9:30 am to 6:30 pm, April through October, 9 am to 5 pm, November through March. Admission free.

The Carré d'Art: Opposite the Maison Carré, this modern art museum was designed by renowned British architect Sir Norman Foster and echoes the shapes of the classical building in a modern idiom.

Open daily, except Monday and holidays, from 11 am to 6 pm and, from 10 am between April 1 and September 30. Admission €4.45, students and children €3.20.

Les Jardins de la Fontaine: Beautifully landscaped gardens, popular with the Nîmoise themselves, surround the original spring, dedicated to Nemausus, around which Nîmes was founded. Within the gardens is the mysterious **Temple of Diana**, which may, in fact, have been dedicated to Nemausus (the Celtic god of the spring) and the **Tour Magna**, a 100-foot defensive watchtower built by the Romans.

St. Rémy de Provence

Once in a great while, you may come upon a place that is so completely inhabited by the spirit of an area that you need go no farther to experience and understand the entire region. St. Rémy de Provence is such a place. If can visit only one town in the Alpilles, make it this one.

With a population of about 9,500, St. Rémy is a small gem of a town. It offers some of the oldest evidence of settlement in France (the ruins of Glanum, page 48); a town center of winding lanes and tree shaded avenues; several grand 14th- and 15th-century town houses and historic connections to musicians, artists, poets and philosophers. It has plenty of restaurants for every budget, ranging from casual sidewalk cafés and pizza joints to Michelin-starred eateries; a good selection of hotels, dozens and dozens of lovely shops and, arguably, one of the best markets in Provence (see *Market Days*, page 54) when the entire town fills up with stalls and vendors.

St. Rémy is surrounded by several wonderful villages (Maussane, Eygalières, Les Baux de Provence – see *Worth a Side-Trip*, page 49) and is in the center of an area rich in opportunities for such outdoor adventures as hiking, cycling, climbing, caving, riding, hang-gliding and parasailing.

You may find that some of the countryside around St. Rémy looks very familiar. That's because you have probably seen it before. Vincent Van Gogh spent most of the last year of his life, from 1889 to 1890, painting frantically in St. Rémy. While voluntarily committed to an asylum there (St. Paul de Mausole, see below), he produced 150 canvases. Some of these – including *Starry Night* and *Irises in a Vase* – are among his most famous paintings. Parts of the asylum can still be visited. From the olive groves to the cypress trees to the views of the rocks and mountains, Vincent's views are all around.

For Van Gogh Enthusiasts

Marie-Charlotte Bouton, journalist, translator and author of *Van Gogh, L'homme qui Aimait les Fleurs et la Lumière* (*Van Gogh, the Man Who Loved the Flowers and the Light*) offers excellent and informative personalized tours of Van Gogh's St-Rémy and its environs for individuals and groups of up to 25. Two-hour tours, including St. Paul de Mausole and Glanum, cost €60 for two people, €90 for groups of five people. She also offers full-day tours that take in Les Baux de Provence, St. Rémy de Provence, Arles or Avignon. Contact her at boutoncharlotte@club-internet.fr or fax 33 04 90 92 40 85.

NOSTRADAMUS, THE PROPHET OF ST. RÉMY

The lasting fame of Nostradamus (born Michel de Nostredame at St. Rémy in 1566) owes as much to good medieval public relations as it does to the accuracy of his obscure and much debated predictions. Catherine de Medici consulted him about the fate of her husband, King Henry II, and her three sons. Impressed with his predictions, she gave him her protection and enabled him to publish his prophesies. Nostradamus also successfully treated victims of the bubonic plague by boosting their immune system with tablets made from an extract of roses, inadvertently inventing the first vitamin C supplement.

Getting Here: St. Rémy is about half an hour's drive south of Avignon. Take the A7 18 km/11 miles south to the Cavaillon exit, then west on the D99, 15 km/9.3 miles to the center of St. Rémy. The D99 can be a busy road but sections of it are lined with trees that arch over the road. Very scenic and typically Provençal.

Sightseeing

Tourist Information: Office du Tourisme, Place Jean Jaurès, 13210 Saint Rémy de Provence, ☎ 33 04 90 92 05 22. Free brochures and other information is available by fax at 33 04 90 92 38 52. The St. Rémy tourist authority also has a very good website: www.saintremy-de-provence.com.

The Ruins of Glanum: A 15-minute walk south of the center of town, Glanum is one of France's major classical sites. The Roman town occupies an even more ancient site. Recent excavations have uncovered an Iron Age settlement. Celto-Ligurians, in the first millenium BC, were followed by Phocean Greeks, who established a religious and commercial center. Roman occupation in the first century BC followed the usual pattern of their towns – thermal baths, villas, religious sites and fortifications. Much of this can now be visited. From May to December, you can sample typical Roman dishes at the **Taberna Romana**, ☎ 33 04 90 92 23 79.

The ruins are on Avenue Van Gogh. Open 9 am to 7 pm, May 1 to August 31; 10:30 am to 5 pm September 1 to April 30. Admission: €6.10, reduced price €4.10 (18 to 25-year-olds and teachers), children under 18 free.

Detail of L'arche de triomphe, Les Antiques (© Ferne Arfin)

Les Antiques: These two first-century BC Roman monuments probably marked the entrance to Glanum on the Via Domitia, the Roman road between Italy and Spain. The Mausolée des Jules is not, as you might think, a memorial to Julius Caesar, but is an unusual funerary monument built for a family known as the Julii about 30 BC. The Arc de Triomphe, built about 10 years later, commemorates and illustrates the Roman conquest of Gaul. On Avenue Van Gogh, South of St. Rèmy. Admission free.

Monastery of St. Paul de Mausole: Across the road from Les Antiques and Van Gogh's sanctuary until about three months before his death, the monastery is today a private sanitorium for women. A church has existed on this site since the 10th century; some say since the beginning of Christianity in Provence. Parts of the site, including the church, cloister, gardens and olive groves, as well as Van Gogh's room, are open for

discrete visits. Interestingly, art is used as therapy here and it is fascinating to look at the patients' paintings, which are for sale in the gift shop.
Open November to March, 10:15 am to 4:45 pm; April to October, 9:15 am to 7 pm. Admission: €3.20, children 12 to 16 €2.40, children under 12 free. Closed Christmas, New Years and November 1. ☎ *33 04 90 92 77 00, maison.sante.st.paul@wanadoo.fr.*

■ Worth a Side-Trip
Les Baux de Provence

According to some legends, the ancient Lords of Les Baux de Provence threw enemies from the ramparts of their 11th-century castle, overlooking the Val d'Enfer (the Valley of Hell). The Lords were an argumentative bunch and in 1633 Louis XIII had the castle destroyed to quash their rebellious tendencies. The remains of the castle and the medieval ghost town (the *Ville Morte*), perched on a plateau at the highest point in the Alpilles, still lord it over the countryside. The rest of Les Baux is a pretty – if slightly touristique – village of winding streets and ancient stone houses, designated one of the *Plus Beaux Villages de France* (Most Beautiful Villages) by the French Tourist Authority. It's full of shops, restaurants and narrow, walled *ruelles* – tiny streets that open to amazing vistas at every turn. If you're not worried about heights, climb up to the Saracen Tower on the southern edge of the plateau and you may be able to see all the way to the Mediterranean at **Aigues-Mortes**. For the most dramatic views, follow one of the many footpaths leading down the western slope from the **Rue Porte Eyguières** to the **Vallon de la Fontaine**.

The Château and Ancient Village:
Château des Baux de Provence, 13520 Les Baux de Provence, ☎ 33 04 90 54 55 56, fax 33 04 90 54 55 00, www.chateau-baux-provence.com. Open every day from 9 am, spring to 7:30 pm, summer to 8:30 pm, autumn to 6:30 pm, winter to 5 pm. Admission: Adults €7, concessions €5.50, children up to 18 years €3.50, children under seven free.

Getting Here: 4.8 miles south of St. Rèmy on the D27; watch for a left turn onto the D27A which winds up the short distance to Les Baux. Automobiles are prohibited and the streets are too steep and cobbled for cyclists. Park in the Pay and Display areas at the bottom of the town. July and August are the most crowded. If you have no other choice, aim to arrive very early or after 5 pm.

i **More Information:** Municipal Office of Tourism des Baux de Provence, Maison du Roy, Rue Porte Mage, 13520 Les Baux de Provence. ☎ 33 04 90 54 34 39, fax 33 04 90 54 51 15, tourisme@lesbauxdeprovence.com, www.lesbauxdeprovence.com.

Author's Tip: The area around Les Baux and the Val d'Enfer is rich in short, rugged and rewarding footpaths Check out IGN's French **TOP 25/Série Bleue Topographic Survey Map 30420T** (see *Introduction* page 25 for suppliers).

LA CATHÉDRAL DES IMAGES

Many years ago, a good friend took me to see La Cathédral des Images, just below Les Baux, and I was, as the British say, gob smacked. Enormous underground rooms (about 40 feet high) in a former limestone mine form the backdrop for a unique photographic artform. Slides, choreographed to music, voice and sound effects, are projected onto columns of stone left when mining ended. The columns become natural screens, 15 to 30 feet wide by as much as 30 feet high, for a dizzying array of images that completely envelopes the viewer. They even wrap across the ceiling and creep along the floor. Founded in the 1970s by photographer and writer Albert Plécy, La Cathédral des Images is still run by his family, who organize a new show annually. Like nothing else you've ever seen! And bring a sweater or jacket. It's very cold almost 200 feet underground.

Located just before Les Baux on the D27 south of St. Rèmy. *☎ 33 04 90 54 38 65, fax 33 04 90 54 42 65, contact@cathedrale-images.com, www.cathedrale-images.com.*

Beaucaire

Until the early 19th century, this pretty little pleasure port at the intersection of the Rhône and the Canal du Rhône à Sète hosted the richest commercial fair in Europe. For 400 years, the week-long fair attracted up to 50,000 visitors a day. Fortunes were made and the evidence is all around in the form of grand 16th-, 17th- and 18th-century mansions.

Today, Beaucaire is an excellent place to begin – or end – a canal trip into the Camargue. It has a summer full of festivals, one after the other, and is a center for the popular **Course Camarguaise** (Nîmes, page 44), making it a lot of fun for a family vacation.

Because this stretch of the Rhône is quiet, the town has very good facilities for watersports, including canoeing, kayaking, rowing, surf-boarding, jet skiing and dinghy sailing (*Adventures on Water*, page 67).

Getting Here: About 15 km/9.3 miles west of St. Rémy de Provence on the Nîmes Road (D99/D999), across the Rhône from Tarascon.

More Information: Beaucaire Office of Tourism, 24 Cours Gambetta, BP 61, 30301 Beaucaire, ☎ 33 04 66 59 26 57, fax 33 04 66 59 68 51, info@ot-beaucaire.fr, www.ot-beaucaire.fr.

Eygalières

In 1660, when the nobleman who owned it went broke, he sold all the land in Eygalières to its peasants. They thus became emancipated landowners more than 130 years before the French Revolution. Today, it is hard to believe that this tiny village of stone houses, fountains and Gallo-Roman remains has such an illustrious past.

Eygalières, wrapped around a small hill about 12 km/7.45 miles from St. Rémy, is itself wrapped in the small, rock-strewn peaks of the Alpilles and the footpaths redolent of wild rosemary. Just east of the village center on the D24B, the **Chapelle de St. Sixte** is a 12th-century saint's chapel and hermitage. It is open only on the saint's day and Easter but, if you visit on a Saturday, you may be lucky enough to see a local wedding party posing for photographs. With several outstanding restaurants, comfortable small hotels and a bar-tabac that is basic but très typique, Eygalières makes an excellent stop on a cycling circuit in the area.

Getting Here: From St. Rémy, take the D99 about 10 km/6.2 miles east. Turn right (south) onto the D24, which leads to the center of the village.

Maussane les Alpilles & Mouriès

Most people know that the best French wines have pedigrees that not only identify regions, but also vineyards and sometimes even particular slopes. But did you know that olives and olive oils can have pedigrees too. Olive oil from la Vallée des Baux de Provence is one of three AOC (Appelation d'Origine Contrôlée) "pedigrees" granted to the olive growers in the area south of Les Baux. Together, the villages of Maussane and Mouriès, about four km/2½ miles apart, form one of France's most important olive oil producing areas. Between them, they have more than

100,000 trees. If you're cycling through, stop at a local café to taste the oil that Parisian chefs travel south to buy. Locals dip it in bread and drizzle it on goat cheese or ripe tomatoes. Both towns have oil-producing mills, where you can taste and buy. The tourist office in Mouriès can also steer you to short hikes through the olive groves.

Getting Here: Reach Maussane on the D27 just four km/2½ miles south of Les Baux or take the D24 from Eygalières to Mouriès. Maussane and Mouriès are connected by the D17.

More Information: Maussane Tourist Office, Place Laugier de Monblan, 13520 Maussane les Alpilles, ☎ 33 04 90 54 52 04, contact@maussane.com, www.maussane.com. The office is closed between noon and 2 pm. **Mouriès Tourist Office**, 2 Rue du Temple, BP 37, 13890 Mouriès, ☎ 33 04 90 47 56 58, office@mouries.com, www.mouries.com. The office is closed between noon and 3 pm.

The Pont du Gard

The Pont du Gard is iconic; truly one of the "must see" monuments of any trip to Provence. A 2,000-year-old Roman span near Remoulins, it was built to carry the aqueduct of Nîmes across the Gardon. Three tiers of arches – the topmost being the aqueduct itself – stand about 165 feet above the river bed. In 1985, it was named a **UNESCO World Heritage Site**, recognizing it as a technical and artistic masterpiece. More than a million visitors a year make this one of France's most popular historic sites.

Up until recently, visitors could cross the upper level of tiers, walking through the aqueduct, but to preserve the bridge for another millennium, that option is no longer available. It is, however, quite safe

Pedestrians crossing the Pont du Gard as their Roman predecessors did

to walk across the roadway on the first tier of arches (cyclists must dismount). There, 18th-century graffitti testify to earlier waves of visitors.

On the left bank, a national park includes picnic areas, a visitors' center, a café and shop. Steep stone steps lead to a spectacular view from above. A few hundred yards downriver, the broad and dazzling pebble river bank provides easy access to the Gardon itself. It is a dream of a river – clean, cold and safe – for swimming, fishing, rowing, canoeing and kayaking

(*Adventures on Water*, page 67). Popular for walking, cycling and horseback riding as well, the area is laced with trails. Maps and brochures are available in the visitors' center or from the tourist office in Remoulins.

Getting Here: Leave Remoulins in the direction of Uzès and follow signs to the Pont du Gard, rive gauche (left bank). For the rive droit (right bank), leave Remoulins in the direction of Nîmes. After the bridge over the Gardon, take the D981 on the right. Parking €5. An annual parking pass for €8 allows unlimited visits – a good buy for anyone interested in easy access to watersports on the Gardon.

More Information: Tourist Office of the Pont du Gard, Place des Grands Jours, 30210 Remoulins, ☎ 33 04 66 37 22 34, ot.remoulins@free.fr, www.ot-pontdugard.com./ang/index.htm.

Uzès

Le Duché d' Uzès: The De Crussol d'Uzès family own the **castle** (Le Duché d'Uzès) in the town center and have been living there, on and off, for more than 1,000 years. That may be why this *village perché*, on a high plateau overlooking the Vallon de l'Alzon, preserves so much of its past in such good condition. The castle, although a private home, can be visited. In addition, there are a 12th-century clock tower, a mostly 18th-century church (St. Etienne) with a 13th-century square tower and several 16th- and 17th-century mansions. The curious **Tour Fenestrelle** (roughly, tower of windows) is the only circular Romanesque tower in France.

Le Duché, Place du Duché, 30700 Uzès, ☎ 33 04 66 22 18 96, www.duche-uzes.fr. Open daily, except Christmas; from July 1 to mid-September, 10 am to 1 pm and 2 to 6:30 pm. Earlier closing from mid-September to the end of June. Admission includes the tower and a guided tour. Adults €11, children 12 to 16 years €8, seven to 11 years €4, children under seven free.

Musée du Bonbon: At one time, Uzès was a center for licorice-making. Candy-makers Haribo-Riqclès-Zan (a popular mass-market brand in Europe), are still active in the town and if you are on a family holiday – or have a sweet tooth – you might want to visit their museum, Le Musée du Bonbon, at Pont des Charrettes.

Haribo, Pont des Charettes 30700 Uzès, ☎ 33 04 66 22 74 39, www.haribo.com. Open daily throughout the summer from 10 am to 7 pm and from October 1 to June 30 until 6 pm.

Getting Here: 18 km/11 miles north of Nîmes on the D979. Cyclists coming from the direction of the Pont du Gard face a mostly uphill 11-km/6.8-mile ride that can be tough in places but very scenic.

More Information: Office de Tourisme d'Uzès et de l'Uzège, Chapelle des Capuçins, Place Albert 1er, BP 129, 30703 Uzès, ☎ 33 04 66 22 68 88, otuzes@wanadoo.fr.

Festivals & Fêtes

This area boasts dozens of celebrations, almost year-round, so it is worth checking tourist authority websites to find out what is going on where you want to go. Meanwhile, here are just a few of the best:

Avignon Theater Festival: Usually held in July and August, this rivals Edinburgh as one of Europe's largest and most important theater, music and dance festivals. It includes a huge Fringe component, with as many as 350 companies performing all over town. Even if you don't speak a word of French, the atmosphere is loads of fun.

Beaucaire, Fête de la Madeleine: Every year, from about July 21-31. Bull-centered festivities commemorate the historic St. Magdalen's Fair which was once this town's raison d'être. You'll see non-lethal bull games in the arena, bull running through the streets, free live music and performances most nights.

Nîmes, Pentecost Feria: The biggest of Nîmes' many *ferias* (fiestas) is held in June. It attracts nearly two million visitors for a riot of music and dancing in the streets, flamenco, gypsy music, Spanish-style bull fighting most afternoons and partying all night.

Shopping

Market Days

Many places have different kinds of markets on different days. This is just a selection:

St. Rémy: Wednesday mornings, the center of St. Rémy de Provence fills up with market stalls selling everything imaginable – from clothing and household goods to locally made perfumes and olive oil soaps, 50 different kinds of olives, wines, cheeses, pets, hardware, jewelry, printed Provençal fabrics, shoes, dozens of kinds of honey, locally made candy, dried herbs and spices. Though some of the goods are clearly targeted at visitors, this is a working village market and most of the town turns out. The market spills from the town square down dozens of little, winding streets, some of which open into hidden, shady squares. This is one of the best markets in Provence.

Avignon: Bric-a-brac, Brocante des Halles, Place St. Jean le Vieux, Sunday, 7 am to 2 pm.

Nîmes: Art market, Boulevard Gambetta, around the cupola of Les Halles, first Sunday of every month, 8 am to 1 pm, sculpture, ceramics, painting and photography. Nîmes has many markets every day. Ask at the tourist office.

Eygalières: Small traditional market, Friday mornings.

Maussane des Alpilles: Small traditional market, Thursday mornings.

Uzes: Traditional local market, Wednesday and Saturday mornings.

LOOK OUT FOR...

- **Olive oil** from Maussane, said to be the best in France. You can watch it being made, taste and buy at **Moulin à huile**, Mas des Barres, 13520 Maussane les Alpilles, ☎ 33 04 90 54 44 32.
- **Provençal fabrics** from Nîmes, where the tradition of colorful local prints began. Table linens, bed linens and clothing from **Les Indiennes de Nîmes Mistral**, Boulevard des Arenes, 3000 Nimes, and **Les Olivades**, 4 Place Maison Carrée, 3000 Nîmes, with branches in Avignon, St. Rémy and Uzès.

Department Stores

Galeries Lafayette: High fashion and expensive designer clothing and household goods. Cap Sud shopping area, just south of Avignon on the N7. Buses from Avignon bus and train stations.

Monoprix: Moderate to bargain-priced clothing, household goods, and sometimes groceries. Branches are everywhere. **Avignon**: Rue de la Républic, open 9 am to 7 pm. **Nîmes**, 3 Boulevard Admiral Courbet, open 8:30 am to 8 pm.

Sports & Cycling Shops

All the larger towns have cycle shops for accessories and repairs to mountain (VTT) and road (Vélo) bikes. For rentals, try **Holiday Bikes**, a company well represented in the south of France. Their range includes kids' bikes (€6 per day, €25 per week), three-gear town cycles (€10 per day, €50 per week), 21- to 24-gear mountain, as well as road and racing bikes (starting at €14 per day, €65 per week). Helmets (required by French law) and child seats are free on request. If you are over 18 and can present a valid driver's licence, the company also rents motorcycles. *In **Avignon**, 20 Boulevard St. Roch (near the SNCF Station),* ☎ *33 04 90 27 92-61, motovelo@provencebike.com. For other locations, contact@holiday-bikes.com, or check www.holiday-bikes.com.*

SPORT 2000 is a large sporting and outdoor equipment department store. Branches in ***Nîmes**, 421 C. Monnet-Ville Active, and **Uzès**, 13 Boulevard Gambetta.*

Where to Stay

Note: *Hotels in France carry a government star rating, ranging from one star for a simple inn up to four stars for deluxe accommodation.*

Deluxe

☆☆☆☆ **Hôtel Cloître Saint Louis** *(20 Rue du Portail Boquier, 84000 Avignon, ☎ 33 04 90 27 55 55, fax 33 04 90 82 24 01, hotel@cloitre-saint-louis.com, www.cloitre-saint-louis.com, 80 rooms and suites, three with handicapped access, direct dial phone, mini-bar, cable TV with BBC World Service, room safe, hair dryer, air conditioning, pool and roof-top sun terrace, shaded cloister courtyard, bar, lounge and restaurant, elevators. Private parking, buffet or continental breakfast and room tax extra, €€€€).* Once the cloister of a 16th-century Jesuit school, the hotel was renovated in 1990, with a new wing added by the trendy French architect Jean Nouvel. Rooms are well-appointed and tranquil – some with exposed stone walls – although the standard rooms can seem a bit bare if Minimalism is not your style. Most rooms overlook the splendid cloistered courtyard, all pale stone and empty but for a half-dozen majestic plane trees. Well-located, on a quiet back street inside the city walls, not far from the SNCF Station.

☆☆☆☆ **L'Hôtel Les Ateliers de l'Image** *(36 Boulevard Victor Hugo, 13210 Saint Rémy de Provence, ☎ 33 04 90 92 51 50, fax 33 04 90 92 43 52, info@hotelphoto.com, www.hotelphoto.com, 24 rooms, seven suites, three with handicapped access, two pools, cinema bar, restaurant, direct dial phone, modem socket, satellite TV, hair dryer, air conditioning, parking, buffet and cooked breakfast, photo exhibition gallery, black and white darkrooms, photoshop, billiards, airport transfers. Local room tax extra, €€€€).* How can you even begin to describe a place that lists one of its rooms as giving "access to a cabin perched by a drawbridge"? One featuring Bang & Olufson Hi-Fi/CD/DVD systems that swivel to face you when you turn them on? And that, in addition to being a hotel, provides photographic darkroom facilities? Luxury here is modern and the design is very high-concept –

even the key rings and door knobs match! A sense of fun keeps it all from becoming too precious – indie movies play over your head in the spacious bar that was once a movie theater; we received a packet of tomato seeds as a comment on the accent color in our room. Located on the ring road, immediately outside the center of St. Rémy.

HOTEL PRICE CHART	
Rates are per room based on double occupancy.	
	Under €55
€	€56-€96
€€	€97-€135
€€€	€136-€195
€€€€	Over €195

☆☆☆☆ **Mas de la Brune** *(13810 Eygalières, ☎ 33 04 90 90 67 67, fax 33 04 90 95 99 21, contact@masdelabrune.com, www.masdelabrune.com, 10 rooms and suites, one with handicapped access, telephone, mini-bar, television, air conditioning, pool, extensive gardens, enclosed parking. Breakfast and room tax extra, €€€€).* This 16th-century mansion is a romantic fantasy overlooked by the Alpilles and the town of Eygalières. Rooms are individually decorated with simple elegance – in the Pierre Isnard suite, an airy, muslin-draped wrought iron bed and a vaulted ceiling. There's an old olive press in the dining room and a huge, original fireplace in the living room. Pierre Isnard, who built the house in 1562, may have been an alchemist, which inspired current owners, Marie and Alain de Larouzière, to create an extensive and unusual Alchemist's Garden. Culinary and horticultural visits are held throughout the year. There is no restaurant but a chef can be arranged for parties of 10 or more.

Moderate

☆☆☆ **Hotel Robinson** *(Route de Remoulins, 30300 Beaucaire, ☎ 33 04 66 59 21 32, fax 33 04 66 59 00 03, contact@hotel-robinson.fr, www.hotel-robinson.fr, 30 terraced rooms with bath or shower, several with handicapped access, direct dial phone, hair dryer, automatic wake up, satellite TV, pool, tennis, boules, woodland paths, bar, sitting room and restaurant. Parking lot and garage. Breakfast and local room tax extra, €-€€).* A big, rambling white house set in acres of pine woods beside a wide stream. The Blanc family have run the hotel for four generations, which may explain the relaxed and unpretentious atmosphere. Guest rooms are large, comfortable and immaculate. The sprawling public rooms have a lived-in feeling that, depending on your age, could remind you of family vacations in the "country" when you were a child. The indoor/outdoor restaurant is an endless sea of tables that is very popular with locals for *cuisine du terroir* (regional cooking). The local Rotarians meet here every Thursday night – honest.

☆☆☆ **Hotel Mercure Cité des Papes** *(1 Rue Jean Vilar, 84000 Avignon,* ☎ *33 04 90 80 93 00, fax 33 04 90 80 93 01, H1952@accor-hotels.com, www.mercure.com. 85 rooms, level ramp handicapped access, phone, satellite and cable TV, pay-per-view channels, mini-bar, room safe, hair dryer, air conditioning, voice mail, USB and ethernet sockets, bar and restaurant, elevators, parking. Breakfast and room tax extra, €€-€€€).* Mercure is a French chain of reliable, comfortable, mostly mid-priced hotels. Every room in this one looks out on the Palais des Papes, so what it lacks in excitement it makes up for in location. If you are in Avignon, you can't get more central. Rooms are decorated in warm, Provençal colors and breakfast is served on a terrace with panoramic views.

☆☆☆ **L'Orangerie** *(755 Rue Tour de l'Evèque, 30000 Nîmes,* ☎ *33 04 66 84 50 57, fax 33 04 66 29 44 55, hr-orang@wanadoo.fr, www.hotel-lorangerie.com, 31 rooms, two with handicapped access, three with Jacuzzis, phone, satellite TV, pool, sauna, gym, air conditioning, parking. Breakfast and room tax extra, €-€€).* A lot of charm for the money. This is a relatively new building decorated to resemble a traditional Provençal *mas*. Rooms are individually decorated in warm colors and the public rooms are pretty enough to photograph. Located less than a mile from the historic center of Nîmes.

Budget

☆☆ **Hotel Central** *(2 Place du Château, 3000 Nîmes,* ☎ *33 04 66 67 27 75, fax 33 04 66 21 77 79, www.hotel-central.org. 15 double rooms with bath or shower, phone, TV, fan, room tax included. Breakfast and parking extra. Prices during Feria festival on request. Other times € or less).* Family-run and idiosyncratic – room doors have been decorated by a local artist. This hotel is close to the Augustus Arch, the rail station and many of Nîmes' major monuments. Good views can be had from the top floors. Special rates for stays longer than five days.

☆☆ **Villa Glanum** *(46 Avenue Van Gogh, St. Rémy de Provence,* ☎ *33 04 90 92 03 59, fax 33 04 90 92 00 08, villa.glanum@wanadoo.fr. 28 rooms, pool, television, handicapped access, locked parking, no restaurant but breakfast and snacks for guests, closed from the end of October to mid-March, €)* Next to Les Antiques, this hotel has large, looked-after rooms, a lush garden and a colorful history. Vincent van Gogh painted it in *Le mas dans les oliviers*, while staying at the mental hospital across the road, St. Paul de Mausole. French writer Alphonse Daudet lived here for a while as well.

Domaine des Clos *(Route de Bellegarde, 30300 Beaucaire, ☎ 33 04 66 01 14 61, fax 33 04 66 01 00 47, contact@domaine-des-clos.com, www.domaine-des-clos.com. Bed and Breakfast, Gîte de France, six rooms with private W.C. and showers, small shared kitchen, washing machine, pool, barbecue. Four apartments, rented weekly, are also available, €-€€).* Hosts David and Sandrine Ausset gave up Parisian life to return to their roots and restore this ancient Provençal *mas* and wine estate. It is all pale stone, exposed beams and rooms decorated with eccentric charm.

Camping

Camping costs vary and some campgrounds charge separately for parking, electricity link-ups, and use of showers. Some also charge a small reservation fee (during the busy summer months, it is probably a good idea to reserve a place). Because of the danger of forest fires, most do not allow barbecues or open cooking, except in designated areas.

☆☆☆☆ **Le Mas de Nicolas** *(Avenue Plaisance du Touch, St. Rémy de Provence, ☎ 33 04 90 92 27 05, fax 33 04 90 92 36 83. Open mid-March to mid-October).* St. Rémy's municipal campsite has 140 places. The basic price of about €14 includes two adults, car, trailer, and use of showers and swimming pool. Electricity, local tax, pets and use of washer and dryer are extra. There is also a €17 deposit.

☆☆☆ **Camping Municipale de la Laune** *(Chemin St. Honoré, 30400 Villeneuve Lez Avignon, ☎ 33 04 90 25 76 06, fax 33 04 90 25 91 55).* Close to Avignon. Everything is separately priced but two adults with a tent, a car and an electrical hook-up should cost less than €15.

☆ **Camping Les Oliviers** *(Avenue Jean Jaurès, 13810 Eygalières, ☎ 33 04 90 95 91 86, reservation@camping-les-oliviers.com. Open end of March to end of October).* One place for two people with electricity should cost €10-12. Local tax is extra. Caravans (trailers) for two or four people and a small studio can be rented. This is a large campsite, well located for the Alpilles.

☆☆☆☆ **Camping Municipal les Romarins** *(St Rémy Road, Maussane, ☎ 33 04 90 54 33 60, fax 33 04 90 54 41 22, camping-municipal-maussane@wanadoo.fr, open mid-March to mid-October).* 145 places in the heart of the Alpilles, close to les Baux, a daily package for under 15 includes two adults, one child, car and warm water shower. Electricity, power, pets and local tax are extra. There is a reservation fee and various redeemable deposits (for electric link-up, entry badge, etc).

Gîtes

Below is just a sampling of what's available in this area. It is usually wise to contact the local tourist authority or Gîtes de France (www.gites-de-france.fr/eng) for an up-to-date list. Most *gîtes* are rented by the week, but some may be available for a weekend.

Gîte "Le mas de la Pierre Blanche" *(Mme. Tessier, Chemin du Tourdre, 13810 Eygalières, ☎/fax 33 04 90 95 91 90)*. About a mile from the center of the village, this 19th-century house has period details. The gîte is on the second floor of the *mas*, reached by an external staircase. Suitable for four or five people, it includes a large room with a sofa-bed, kitchenette and dining area, and a large bedroom overlooking the garden. Linen is provided and pets are welcome.

Les Gîtes "Mistral" *(Joëlle Mistral, 39 Rue Jean Jaurès, 13890 Mouriès, ☎ 33 04 90 47 57 93, jomistral@yahoo.fr)*. A small house in the village with a fully equipped kitchenette, available year-round.

Gîtes "La Galinette" *(M. and Mme. Jacques Vidal, Chemin Jean Piquet, 13210 St Rémy de Provence, ☎/fax 33 04 90 92 29 39, contact@la-galinette.com)*. This group of apartmen*t gîtes*, a little over a mile from the center of town, boasts "American kitchens" with ovens and refrigerators.

Gîtes "La Balancelle" *(Beth and Stephane, Voie Aurelia, 13210 St. Rémy de Provence, ☎ 33 06 22 05 02 05, info@laBalancelle.com, €-€€)*. These are three really pretty apartments on the Aurelian Way – the Roman Road on the edge of town. They're arranged around a swimming pool and they are fully equipped – even microwaves and hair dryers, room safes, linens, barbecues, or, as the British say, "all mod cons" (modern conveniences).

■ Where to Eat

Le Petit Bru in Eygalières *(18 Avenue Jean Jaurès, 13810 Eygalières, ☎ 33 04 90 95 98 89, closed Thursdays, Friday lunch and from November 12 to December 12, €€)*. We ate here under the stars before a sudden summer storm. The menu, prepared by Irish chef Helen O'Neill (poached by the owners from a resort in Rosslare, Co. Wexford), was simple – a *mille feuille* of grilled feta, a filet of salmon, guinea fowl in a cheese sauce – but perfect. The ambiance, on a terrace hugged by the bare stone walls of

DINING PRICE CHART

Prices are for a typical prix fixe menu of two courses and a glass of house wine for one.

	€14-€19
€	€21-€34
€€	€35-€49
€€€	€50-€69
€€€€	€70-€140
€€€€€	The sky's the limit

adjoining village houses, was laid back and welcoming. When the storm surprised us, a cream protective canvas was unrolled in seconds.

Well-heeled gourmets head for Le Petit Bru's Michelin-starred big brother, the **Bistro d'Eygalières "Chez Bru"** *(Rue de la République, Eygalieres,* ☎ *33 04 90 90 60 34, sbru@club-internet.fr, €€€€)*, under the same ownership and right around the corner. Le Petit Bru is still little known. It won't remain so for long. At €30 per person for a prix fixe menu that includes three courses, cheese and a bottle of wine for two (lunch or dinner) and a simpler pasta menu at €11 in the winter, this is top value for cooking of a very high standard.

Also good value for excellent cooking is **L'Ail... Heure** in Beaucaire *(48 Rue du Château, Beaucaire,* ☎ *33 04 66 59 67 75, lunch €, dinner, €€)*. It occupies a vaulted stone "cave" and a terrace under the town's castle. The chef, Luc Andreu, is just beginning to build a national reputation in France for his unusual dishes (sea bass with truffles, bull steak, wheat risotto) – so much so that the French magazine *Le Point* said the €15 prix fixe lunch was "like a gift." If you visit Beaucaire, try to have one meal here.

Oustau de Baumanière *(Val d'Enfer, 13520 Les Baux,* ☎ *33 04 90 54 33 07, fax 33 04 90 54 40 46, contact@oustaudebaumaniere.com, www.oustaudebaumaniere.com, €€€€€)*. If you are thinking about pulling out all the stops, and I do mean all of them, this is the place. Founded by a legendary chef, the late Raymond Thuilier, in 1946, Oustau de Baumanière was once considered the best restaurant in France. It still holds two Michelin stars and the wine list is amazing – 1964 Petrus, 1870 Château Lafite Rothschild Paulliac. I fondly remember enjoying ravioli of leeks and truffles while sitting on a plane tree-shaded terrace beside a swimming pool. A small wedding lunch was underway at the next table. That was years ago but the dish is still on the menu and the pool at the base of a cliff looks just as inviting today. The restaurant is a sort of foodie pilgrimage place. And, as you might expect, the prices are high. You can easily spend more than €250 per couple here.

Light Meals & Snacks

It is almost pointless to single out one budget place over another when there is so much decent, simple food around. The truth of the matter is that you can find good, inexpensive meals and snacks just about anywhere in this part of France. Bistros, sidewalk cafés, even street vendors on market days can offer carefully made salads, soups, omelets, seafood dishes, sandwiches, drinks and sweets. And don't pass up the pizza places, especially those that promise *pizza feu de bois* (cooked in wood burning ovens), which are usually quite good.

Because of its setting, **La Grotte** in Beaucaire *(Avenue des Anciens Combattants d'Afrique du Nord, 30300 Beaucaire,* ☎ *33 06 21 87 87 01)* stands out for a drink, a snack or an inexpensive meal. The restaurant, in a cave at the base of a cliff in the middle of town (actually, it is one huge piece of rock the size of a 10-story building, heavily draped in vines) has to be the most dramatic place I've ever lifted a Stella. Open for lunch and dinner every day, the restaurant's four-course meal of salad, grilled meat, cheese and dessert is only about €12. It specializes in such local specialties aïoli, boeuf à la mode de Beaucaire and rouille.

■ Adventures

The varied landscape of this region, with the small but rugged Alpilles overlooking wide plains and river valleys, makes it an ideal vacation destination for couples or families with mixed abilities. Walking varies from easy to moderately challenging; beginner and intermediate cyclists will find plenty of trails, while the hills around Les Baux de Provence give the more experienced cyclist and mountain bike enthusiast a bit of a workout. Some of the rock climbing in the cliffs around Mouriès has been graded at 7 or 8 on the French scale (equivalent to 5.11d to 5.14b on the US scale, 6a to 7b on the UK scale).

> **Nota Bene:** Spring and fall are the best times to visit. Because of the risk of fires, foot and cycle paths in the Alpilles are closed between June 30 and September 15 (the dry season); camping is only allowed in designated areas.

Visitors to this area are rewarded with the chance to see a wide variety of birds. All kinds of Mediterranean species are common – warblers, crag martins, eagle owls blue rock thrush, swifts. If you are lucky you may spot a Bonelli's eagle or snake eagle, a kestrel or peregrin falcon. Other than birds, wildlife is relatively thin on the ground, although domestic goats sometimes take to the hills and forage in small, semi-wild groups.

Flora is the typical garrigue combination of spiky plants – thistles and teasels, tough-leaved evergreens and conifers. Hardy herbs such as rosemary and thyme can bloom two or three times a year. In spring look for rock lilies and *cystes or* wild Provençal roses. The most common variety of cyste has crumpled-looking purply pink petals around yellow centers.

On Foot

Eygalierès Loop – The GR6 Long Distance Path (marked with white over red blazes) forms an eight-km/five-mile loop that passes right through the town. It is suitable for hiking or mountain biking. It crosses between a series of steep foothills on the north side of the Alpilles, gradually climbing to a height of about 220 m/722 feet. Cliff views on the south side of le Calan de Rousset, le Petit Calan and le Gros Calan (together, Les Calans) are worth the relatively modest effort.

Eygalières to St. Rémy – A somewhat more challenging walk of about 15 km/9½ miles leaves the Eygalierès loop and continues west along the main branch of the GR6. This path takes you to the edge of the Calan cliffs and climbs steadily along the cliff edges to 390 m/1,300 feet at the Plateau de la Caume, before a gradual descent into St. Rémy. Heading south on the GR6 from Eygalierès, cross the D24 (leaving the loop path) and continue in a northwesterly direction along the GR6. Turn left at the edge of the Aerodrome for a short, steep hike (two km/1.25 miles) over the crest of Les Calans into the Col de Vallongue (alt. 250 m/820 feet). The path continues westward, steadily climbing the escarpment for about six km/3¾ miles. Bring plenty of water and trail mix. This is a long, satisfying and occasionally challenging hill walk. A taxi back to Eygalierès is relatively inexpensive. Or book in advance to stay over in St. Rémy.

Town & Themed Walks – Tourist authorities in most villages can provide maps and itineraries for short, local walks. Mouriès, for example, has several signposted walks:

- Route de l'olivier – through olive groves and past oil mills, oil production.
- Sweet shops and museums.
- Route des vins – visits the local vineyards and estates.
- Route des maisons nobles de la vallée des Baux – a historic house trail in the Baux Valley, taking in 16th-, 17th- and 18th-century houses.

Rambling Near the Pont du Gard

The GR6 and GR63 long-distance paths wander this area, passing through Remoulins, Vers Pont du Gard, Sanilhac, Collias, St. Bonnet du Gard, Sernhac and other small towns. Hiking and rambling here offers the opportunity to walk the ruins of the aqueduct that crosses the Gardon at the Pont du Gard and to see a variety of religious and secular ruins, ranging across the region's 2,000-plus years of history.

Shorter local trails (PR paths) range from two km/1.2 miles up to about 20 km/12 miles and lead to ancient churches, scenic viewpoints and prehistoric sites in the vicinity. The Topo Guide, *Le Gard à Pied* (Walking in the Gard) is offered for sale at tourist information offices in Remoulins and Uzès.

Rock Climbing

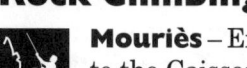

Mouriès – Experienced climbers and mountaineers are attracted to the Caisses de Jean-Jean, level 7 and 8 cliffs near Mouriès. In France, rock climbing goes by the romantic name of *escalade* and the Mouriès tourist office will arrange rock climbing lessons and outings for less experienced visitors. Monday to Friday outings in the Baux Valley last from 9 am to 7 pm and cost €54, including equipment and lunch. Groups of up to eight people, as young as nine years of age, can be accommodated. Book through the Mouriès tourist office *(Office de Tourisme, BP 37, 2 Rue du Temple, 13890 Mouriès,* ☎ *33 04 90 47 56 58, fax 33 04 90 47 67 33, office@mouries.com, www.mouries.com.)*

Collias – Several rock climbing routes are easily reached from this riverside village, a few miles west of the Pont du Gard on the D112.

Les Escollettes – Follow the GR6 along the Gardon River for two km/1.2 miles toward La Baume.

Les Falaises and Grottes de Pâques – High cliffs, an equipped site. Follow the river seven km/4.3 miles toward La Baume.

La Rouquette – An equipped training site. Along the Gardon, follow the direction of the current (toward Pont du Gard) for one km/.6 miles.

HIRE A GUIDE

The Pont du Gard area is rich in historical monuments that include Roman ruins, the aqueduct, medieval churches, ancient wash houses, and prehistoric stone dwellings. One way to understand the region and make the most of your walk or rock climbing experience is to hire a local guide. The Pont du Gard tourist office recommends:

- **Alain Paul** – mountain guide, available year-round for footpath hikes and climbing. *Rue du Gardon, 30190 Dions,* ☎ *33 04 66 63 18 94 or 33 06 03 05 15 17.*

- **Daniel Tort** – accompanied rambles, *30210 Remoulins,* ☎ *33 04 66 37 27 97.*

- **François Tournois** – guided climbing on all the Pont du Gard and Uzege sites, via ferrata, abseiling. Year-round. *Le Murellet, 30210 Pouzilhac,* ☎ *33 04 66 03 00 94 or 33 06 09 85 57 34, francoistournois@hotmail.com.*

On Wheels

Driving

To make a circuit of the region, take the N7 south from **Avignon** to **Plan d'Orgon**, then turn right (west) onto the D99, passing through **St. Rémy** and **Tarascon** before crossing the Rhône to **Beaucaire**. At Beaucaire follow signs to the D999 toward **Nîmes**, about 14 miles away. Take the N86 north from Nîmes to **Remoulins**, turning left on the D981 for the left bank of the **Pont du Gard**. Return to Remoulins to join the N100 East for the short run back to Avignon. This route can be driven in a morning (with no stops!) but, ideally, forms the basis of a two- or three-day itinerary.

Author's Choice: For a slightly more adventurous journey, leave **Nîmes** by the D979 north toward **Uzès**. Just before Uzès, take a right turn onto the D981 towards the Pont du Gard, which will be a well-signed turnoff. Take a right turn marked D981 bis (*bis* means an alternate route). If you are on foot or cycling, this little road can actually take you over the Pont du Gard itself and onward to the road to Remoulins.

Cycling

As you move west and south from Avignon, the cycling becomes easier. Much of the **Bouches du Rhône** is relatively flat. The area around the **Alpilles** is good for couples or families with mixed abilities as it offers a good variety of satisfying rides on the level or in gentle hills, as well as more challenging mountain bike routes on the **Alpilles Massif** and road bike climbs up to Les Baux. Farther north, near the Pont du Gard, trails suitable for mountain and road bikes are bit more challenging but still of only moderate difficulty. **Holiday Bikes** in Avignon *(contact@holiday-bikes.com, or check www.holiday-bikes.com)* rents motorcycles – ranging in price, per day, from about €53 to about €240 – and can organize guided or independent motorcycle tours.

Suggested Cycling Route:
The Roman Aqueduct & the Pont du Gard

Because cycling is so popular in France, tourist information offices in every town can supply maps and local route advice. This itinerary covers a particularly scenic and historic area:

Thirty miles, rolling terrain, moderate difficulty. Mountain or road bikes. A fit cyclist can easily do this circuit in a day, but there is more than enough to stop, see and admire for a two- or three-day itinerary, with overnight stops in Uzès, Collias or Vers Pont du Gard. This is a departmental Balisage cycle trail. Watch for white and green arrow-shaped signs that mark the trail. You can find them in all the village centers.

Start at Vers Pont-du-Gard. Before you go, visit the 12th-century village walls, the three ancient dry stone *lavoires* or wash houses and the Château St. Privat.

- Leave town on the **D227** towards Remoulins and the Pont du Gard. Turn left on the **D981** (it is a busy road, so take care!).
- After about one km/.6 mile, take the first right onto the **D981 bis** (watch for a sign for Pont du Gard parking). Visit the **Pont-du-Gard** (page 52) and swim in the river below it.
- Take the **GR6** west, toward Collias. If you have a road bike rather than a mountain bike, you may want to walk for part

- of this stretch. Follow the footpath to the scenic viewpoint overlooking the **Gorges du Gardon**. The Gorges du Gardon Highlands will be over your left shoulder.
- At **Collias**, which rests at the foot of the Gorges, stop for a swim, rent a canoe for the afternoon or do a bit of rock climbing. (Collias has campsites, *gîtes*, chambres d'hôtes and hotels.)
- Leave Collias on the **D112** and climb through holly and *arbousiers* (strawberry trees) to **Sanilhac**.
- From the center of Sanihac, pick up the **D212** to **Sagriès**. The two villages are three km/1.8 miles apart. About halfway between them, stop to admire a great view of Uzès.
- Continue on the D212 toward **Uzès**. Cross the **D981** and look for green and white circuit signs to Uzès, about 2.2 km/1.4 miles ahead. The cycle route follows a stream called the Alzon. Stop to visit Uzès. The town has more than 50 restaurants and cafés, seven hotels, *gîtes*, chambres d'hôtes, camping and a group hostel.
- Leaving Uzès, return to the intersection of the **D981** and turn left onto it.
- After about 250 m/820 feet, look for a left turn onto the cycle circuit. Along this stretch of the circuit, sharp eyed cyclists should spot ruins of the Roman aqueduct. The trail winds along toward Saint Maximin, under Mt. Bouquet.
- At **Saint Maximin**, visit Jean Racine's house and tower, and wander the narrow alleys and lanes, punctuated by tiny squares called *placettes*.
- Follow trail markers east toward Argilliers. About halfway there, the trail joins the **D3bis**. Near **Argilliers**, look for Roman chariot tracks in the ancient quarry used to build the Pont du Gard.
- Continue east along the D3bis to return to **Vers Pont du Gard**, where you'll find the most extensive remains of the aqueduct.

Where to Stay Along the Route

Collias: ☆☆☆ **Le Castellas**, very charming 17th-century village house with individually decorated rooms and gastronomic restaurant, €€-€€€. Contact: *Chantal et Raymond Aparis, Grand'Rue, 30210 Collias,* ☎ *33 04 66 22 88 88, fax 33 04 66 22 84 28, info@lecastellas.com.* Camping at ☆☆☆ **Le Barralet**, *30210 Collias,* ☎ *33 04 66 22 84 52, fax 33 04 66 22 89 17, www.barralet.fr.*

Uzès: ☆☆☆ **Hotel Mercure**, popular and reliable French hotel chain, €. *Contact: Mercure Uzès, Pont du Gard, Route de Nîmes, 30700 Uzès,* ☎ *33 04 66 03 32 22, fax 33 04 66 03 32 10, mercure.relaisuzes@wanadoo.fr.* Camping at ☆☆☆ **La Paillotte**, *Quartier le Grezac, 30700 Uzès,* ☎ *33 04 66 22 38 55, fax 33 04 66 22 26 66.*

Vers Pont du Gard: La Begude Saint Pierre, 17th-century *mas* recently restored to a restaurant-hotel (meals €€-€€€), close to the Pont du Gard and named for a nearby 11th-century Gallo-Roman church, €-€€. *Contact: La Begude Saint Pierre, D 981, 30210 Vers Pont du Gard,* ☎ *33 04 66 63 63 63, fax 33 04 66 22 73 73, begudesaintpierre@hotel-saintpierre.fr, www.hotel-saintpierre.fr.*

Remoulins: Camping at **III La Sousta**, *Avenue du Pont du Gard, 30210 Remoulins,* ☎ *33 04 66 37 12 80, fax 33 04 66 37 23 69, info@lasousta.fr, www.lasousta.com.*

On Water

Canal Boating

Boating on the **Canal du Rhône à Sète** is a gentle way to experience the changing landscape between Provence and the Camargue Provençal. From its beginning at **Beaucaire**, the canal winds through sun-bleached villages toward the sea. It crosses the Camargue salt marshes and, for its last stretch, rides over the edge of the Mediterranean itself. Canal boats, or *pénichettes*, for two to 12 persons can be rented without any special license or permit from: **Connoisseur Cruisers**, *14 Quai de la Paix, Beaucaire 30300,* ☎ *33 04 66 59 46 08, www.connoisseur.fr* or, in the USA, contact: *Connoisseur USA, 980 Awald Road, Suite 302, Annapolis MD 21403,* ☎ *888-355-9491, fax 410-280-2406, usa@connoisseurafloat.com.*

PICK YOUR ADVENTURE

La Lolotte, an adventure sport center in Nîmes, organizes training and outings for a variety of locally popular adventure sports, including canyoning, climbing, spelunking (potholing), canoeing, hiking and mountain biking. *Contact: La Lolotte, 145 Rue Louis Proust, ZI St Césaire, 30900 Nîmes,* ☎ *33 04 66 64 12 43, fax 33 04 66 23 30 75, contact@lalolotte.com, www.lalolotte.com.*

On the Gardon River

Canyoning, combining climbing and hiking with whitewater in the **Gorges du Gardon**, is permitted between April and October, when the river, squeezed between the narrow walls of the gorge, forms cascades. The Gardon can change very suddenly and it is wise to go canyoning in groups, accompanied by experienced guides.

Canoeing, fishing and swimming is available nearer the Pont du Gard where the Gardon widens into beautiful stretches of calm, crystalline turquoise waters.

Anglers will need a licence, available from local tourist offices, to fish for trout, pike and other game fish on the Gardon. More information from **Gard Fishing and Environment Association**, *34 Rue Gustave Eiffel, 3000 Nîmes,* ☎ *33 04 66 02 91 61.*

Canoes can be rented on the river bank in Collias from:

Canoë Collias, *4 Champs Ronde Fabré, 30210 Collias,* ☎ *33 04 66 22 87 20, fax 33 04 66 03 63 45, April 1 to September 30*; **Canoë le Tourbillon**, *Le Pont, 30210 Collias,* ☎ *33 04 66 22 85 54, fax 33 04 66 22 84 87, location@canoe-le-tourbillon.com, www.canoe-le-tourbillon.com.* Rental by the hour, half- or whole day, April to September; **Kayak Vert**, *Berges du Gardon, 30210 Collias,* ☎ *33 04 66 22 80 76, fax 33 04 66 22 88 78, kayak.vert@wanadoo.fr, www.canoe-france.com/gardon, March to October, rental and instruction.*

In the Air

Hot Air Ballooning

Follow in the footsteps of the Montgolfière brothers with a hot air balloon trip over the Pont du Gard and the Uzès countryside. Contact: **Les Montgolfières du Sud**, *64 Rue Sigalon, 30700 Uzès,* ☎*/fax 33 04 66 37 38 02, lms@sudmontgolfiere.com, www.sudmontgolfiere.com.* Every day, year-round.

Eco-Tourism

The **Gorges du Gordon** and the rocky massif that surrounds it support more than 4,500 varieties of plant life and numerous protected species of wildlife. There are groves of holm oaks, elms and white poplar. Silver-studded, blue butterflies and dragonflies visit the bee orchids, asphodel lilies and strawberry trees. Birds include bee-eaters, kingfishers, orioles and musical, ringed plovers. Bonelli's eagle soars overhead and, if you are lucky, you might spot a family of beavers.

Because of this variety, local and national authorities have designated this a protected area for conservation and environmental management (in the French terminology, a *site classé*). Several discrete areas alongside the river are Special Protection Zones for wildlife as well.

The GR6 and GR63 paths wind through the territory. In addition, regional tourist authorities maintain a number of PR (*Petit Randonée*) trails that allow careful exploration. The PR circuit known locally as **La Torte**, leading to the **Collias Hermitage**, is particularly worthwhile.

Suggested Itinerary:
La Torte, from Collias to the Hermitage

Start and finish in the **Collias village parking lot**. The path, marked with yellow blazes, is 11½ km/seven miles, climbing to 210 m/700 feet and should take average walkers three to four hours.

Cross the **Collias bridge** over the Gard in the direction of **Cabrières-Nîmes**. Turn left into the first street, which heads downward. The road follows the river. Look for a sign pointing out the direction to l'Ermitage. This is a large and sandy path in a deep narrow valley called the Combe de l'Ermitage. Looking up, you will see prehistoric caves. Most of these are closed or inaccessible. The **Hermitage**, at the base of the little valley, next to a spring, consists of a huge, open-air cross and cave that was inhabited from prehistoric times, before becoming a chapel. Stop and admire the fresco next to the entrance, a stone arch, before moving on. Pass through the arch and go up to the chapel. Facing the altar, take the little path on the left. It leads to limestone steps, with the stone cross on the right. The steps lead up into the garrigue. At the top of the steps, turn left and continue, straight, to the *mas de Laval*. Take the road on the right of the *mas*, through cultivated fields. Cross the D3 and take the path on the right, walking alongside some railings. At the end of the railings, on the right, take the road to the *mas de Saint Privat*. A meandering, stony path is indicated by boundary markers designated **DFCI B54**. This path leads you back to the village. At the place called **La Torte**, take the road to the left, which leads you back to your starting point.

The Camargue

Where Land & Sea Merge

Broad, flat and sunburnt, the Camargue is an almost surreal web of shallow, lakes (*étangs*), meandering rivers, canals, marshes and dunes. Part-desert, part-irrigated plain, part-grassland, part-nature reserve, it is an area of France truly unlike any other.

A rough triangle, bounded on the north by **Arles,** the west by **Aigues Mortes** and the east by the desert-like **Crau** and the industrial suburbs of **Marseille**, the Camargue has an elemental, almost primitive ambiance.

IN THIS CHAPTER	
■ Arles	74
■ Les Saintes Maries de la Mer	79
■ Aigues Mortes	81
■ The Beaches	85
■ Festivals & Fêtes	87
■ Shopping	89
■ Where to Stay	90
■ Where to Eat	94
■ Adventures	96

And, despite the lively resort towns of **Les Saintes Maries de la Mer** and **Aigues Mortes**, it is a virtually empty area, dotted with traditional stucco and thatch cottages (called *cabanes*). Fewer than 7,500 people occupy its 330 square miles – much of it protected wetlands. A map of the region resembles nothing so much as a piece of lace, the land area a mere web.

Several different layers of environmental protection cover the region, considered to be Europe's most important wetland. Any visit to the Camargue is, by its very nature, eco-tourism. Almost all of it, including its towns and hamlets, is protected or managed habitat. At the heart, the **Réserve Nationale**, created in 1927, covers 32,412 acres – about 50 square miles – around the shallow, salt lake, the **Étang du Vaccarès**. The area has been designated a UNESCO "Biosphere Reserve," one of only 300 in the world.

For birdwatchers, this is genuinely paradise. There are more than 350 resident and migratory species. The Camargue is the only place outside of Africa where you can see pink flamingos nesting in their tens of thousands. The habitat also supports about 1,000 species of flowering plants.

Most tourists in this small corner of France are French themselves. That's because even they find the ancient traditions, pastimes and occupations exotic and fascinating.

A salty atmosphere and shifting wetlands make agriculture challenging. There is some farming – rice, fruit trees and, remarkably, vineyards – but for many inhabitants life revolves around the semi-wild, cream- and dust-colored Camargue horse and the small, clever native bulls. The animals forage and breed in the wild, grazing on the glasswort-covered *sansouires,* dried and cracked salt plains.

Elsewhere on the *sansouires*, the Camargue supports a major salt harvesting industry and has done so since the Roman era. More than 34,000 acres, on both the eastern and western edges of the Camargue, are devoted to salt production. Mountains of drying salt can be seen for miles.

In May, the area hosts one of Europe's most colorful festivals, when more than 8,000 gypsies from all over Europe converge on Les Saintes Maries de la Mer to celebrate their patron saint, Sarah (see pages 79, 80, 88).

■ Getting Here & Getting Around

Arles is the gateway to all the destinations in this chapter. It is within easy reach of two major Provence termini – Marseille (served by international air and TGV rail from Paris) and Avignon (served by air from the UK and TGV rail from Paris). For information about using the TGV system as well as local rail and bus services, see pages 26-27.

By Car: From Marseille Airport in Marignane, take the N113 north toward Salon de Provence. Just before Salon, join the A54 (a toll road) at junction 14, going west toward Saint Martin de Crau. After the toll road ends, at junction 12, continue west on the N113 to Arles. The journey is about 95 km/59 miles and should take 1½ hours.

From Avignon, take the N570 directly south to Arles. The journey covers 37 km/23 miles and should take about half an hour.

■ Four Habitats

La Grande Camargue

The Grande Camargue, at the mouth of the Rhône, covers the entire Rhône Delta. Located between two arms of the river – the Grand Rhône to the east and the Petit Rhône to the west – and bounded on the south by the Mediterranean, the Grande Camargue is, in effect, an island and is sometimes referred to as L'Ile de la Camargue. Over millenia, the land was created from sedimentation deposited by the Rhône. Until the 19th century it was known to "drift." Even today as much as 26 million cubic yards of sand and gravel per year are carried downstream and deposited along the eastern edge of the Camargue. Most of the Grande Camargue consists of a fragile network of lakes and marshes, with almost no human habitation. The southernmost reach of la Grande Camargue includes the **Plage de Beauduc**, a 28-mile-long stretch of undeveloped "wild sand," the longest beach of its kind on the Mediterranean.

NATIVE HORSES

Camargue horses are legendary. White or grey and cream, short-legged and sturdy, with bushy tails and thick, glamorous manes, they are really a kind of pony. The origin of the horses, unique in the world, is something of a mystery. At one time, they were thought to be descendents of Arabian horses left behind by Saracen invaders. But they bear little resemblance to the tall, elegant Arabian breed. In all likelihood, they are the product of crosses between native, paleolithic horses and other breeds.

At one time, they were completely wild, but today they are semi-feral. They graze freely in the areas known as *sansouires* – salty, dry plains covered with grasses and glasswort – coexisting with herds, or *manades,* of native bulls. They form their own herds and breed in the wild. Once a year they are rounded up to inspect and brand the foals.

Gardians (Camargue cowboys) and *manadier*s (ranchers), use Camargue horses for working with cattle. Once broken to the saddle, they are considered reliable and sure-footed.

A number of stables rent horses out for guided rides. Confident riders, with a good knowledge of French, can live the fantasy of galloping through the surf on the back of a native pony. (See *Adventures on Horseback*, page 99).

La Petite Camargue

La Plaine d'Aigues Mortes, also known as La Petite Camargue or La Camargue Gardoise, extends west of the Petit Rhône to the Canal du Rhône à Sète. The canal, a natural waterway enhanced by man, carries pleasure boats from the Rhône to the Mediterranean. Though the Petite Camargue is made up of a fine balance of agricultural and ranch land, salt and freshwater marshes, lagoons, channels, ponds and pine forests, most of it, unlike the Grande Camargue, lies outside of the regional nature reserves and conservation areas. It has more paved roads, for exploring by bicycle or car. Several châteaux and the walled town of Aigues Mortes testify to crusader connections. Port Camargue, at it is southernmost tip, offers sailors the biggest pleasure sailing port in Europe.

Les Salins

Salins are saltworks. There are two major sea saltworks in the Camargue, one south of Aigues Mortes (25,000 acres) and one south of Salin de Giraud (27,000 acres). Together, the two areas export more than half a million metric tons of salt annually. Such industrial works may seem an odd inclusion in a travel guidebook. But, if you are in the region, the acres of salt pans and the long snakes of salt mountains, each as high as a seven-story building, are remarkable sights. Salt is extracted from evaporating seawater in much the same way as was done in ancient times. The Romans exported salt from this region throughout their empire. The existing industry was founded by monks in the 13th century and expanded in the 19th century.

The Crau

The Plain of the Crau (pronounced "crow") extends from just south of Arles to the Mediterranean along the eastern edge of the Camargue. It is is the closest thing to a real desert on continental Europe and, despite some recent agricultural development, has a brooding, desolate ambiance.

Formed from rocks and pebbles washed down from the Alps during the last two Ice Ages, the Crau's development was shaped by changing river patterns that prevented deposits of finer sediments and left, instead, a wide area of boulders and gravel. Just below the surface, a layer of calcium carbonate as hard as concrete cuts the surface off from the underlying ground water. For centuries, this was a barren, arid area – particularly during the hot summer months. In more recent times, irrigation has opened the northern Crau (about half its total area) to agriculture – in particular the cultivation of feed hay and fruit trees.

■ Principle Destinations

Arles

Sometimes referred to as the Gateway to the Camargue, technically, Arles is the Camargue. The township includes most of the land within the two branches of the Rhône – about two-thirds of the Camargue – making it, at 170,000 acres, physically the biggest town in France. Of course, since most of the population of 52,000 is concentrated in a relatively small area, just below the branching of the Rhône, Arles gives the impression of a compact, Gallo-Roman city.

Founded by the seagoing Phocéans in about 700 BC, it was originally called Theline, a name perhaps reflected in *tellines*, the prized local clams. The city was part of the trade route between Massalia (today's Marseille) and inland settlements. Three hundred years later, as a

Arles

1. Amphithéâtre
2. Place Notre Dame, Eglise Notre Dame de la Major
3. Cemetery
4. Jardin d'Ete
5. Théâtre Antique
6. Cloister & Cathedral Saint-Trophime
7. Arlaten Museum, Cryptoportico of the Forum, Hotel de Ville, Chapel of Saint Anne
8. Espace Van Gogh
9. Théâtre Municipal
10. Eglise St.-Césaire
11. Pavillon du Canal
12. Tower of the Ecorchoir
13. Eglise les Frères Prêcheurs
14. Place du Forum
15. Baths of Constantine
16. Réattu Museum
17. Eglise St.-Julien
18. Place Voltaire
19. Collège Saint-Charles
20. Anciennes Eglises St.-Blaise & St.-Jean de Moustiers; Tower of the Mourgues
21. Passenger boat pier
22. Roman bridge ruins
23. To Musée de l'Arles Antique (via Avenue Jean Monet)

100 METERS
© 2005 HUNTER PUBLISHING

The Camargue

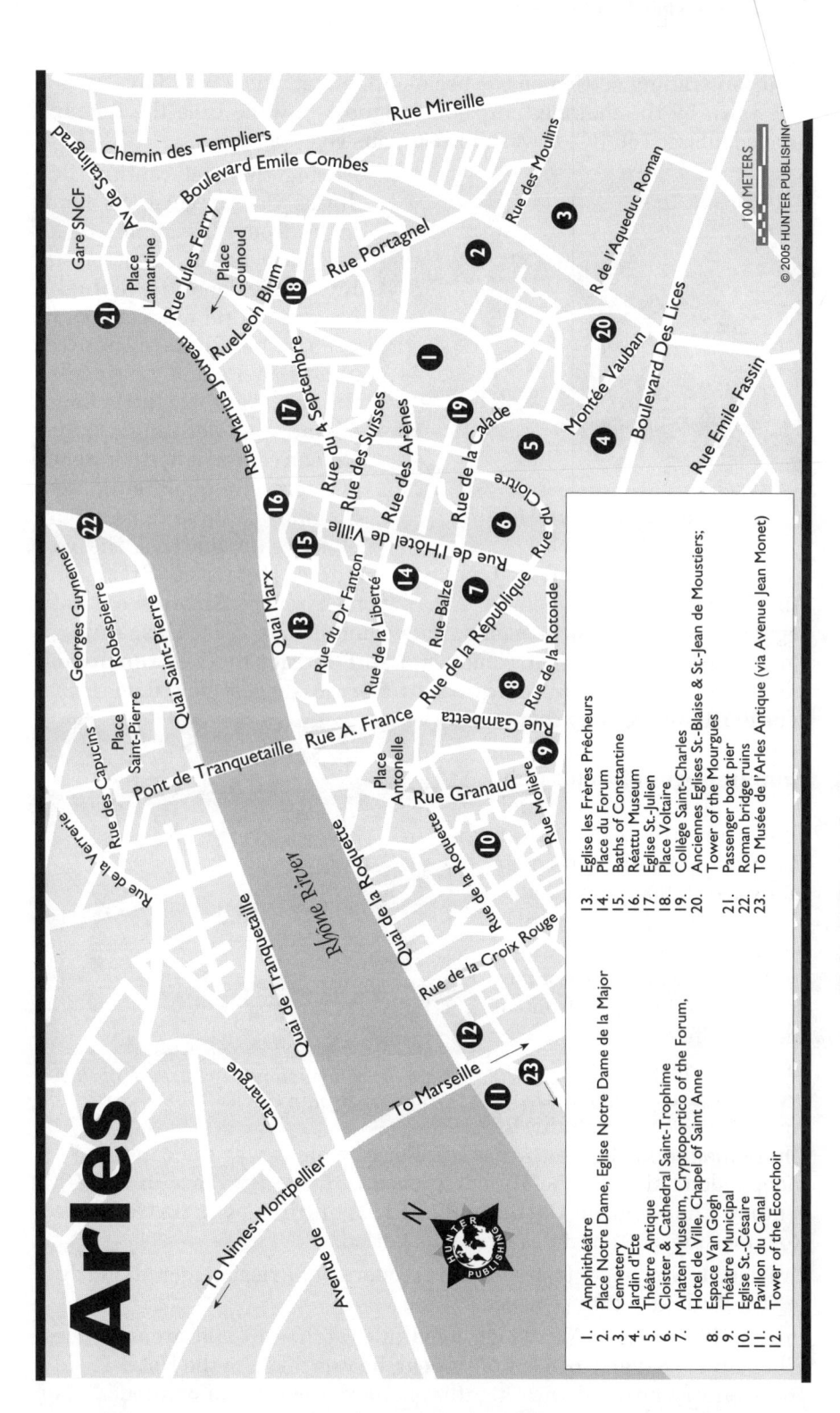

Ligurian trading settlement, it became Arelate, which may have meant "the town by the marshes" in their language. By the time the Romans arrived, about 150 BC, it was a prosperous river port.

During the first century BC, Julius Caesar gave the land, taken from Massalian Greeks and local tribes, to victorious Roman Legions. It eventually became a kind of second capital of the Roman Empire, known in Roman writings of the period as "The Little Rome of Gaul." As befitting a major Roman center, it had a number of impressive public buildings. So many of these remain part of Arlesian life that the city has been designated a UNESCO World Heritage Site. The **Amphithéâtre**, built about 90 AD, and the **Théâtre Antique** are both regularly used for sports events, music and drama. The **Alyscamps**, a Roman and early Christian cemetery, **Les Thermes de Constantin** and the mysterious **Cryptoportiques du Forum** suggest how Roman citizens lived. An archway that is one of the few remains of the **Roman Forum** is built right into the façade of a local hotel. The remains of a huge **Roman Circus** where as many as 20,000 could watch chariot races, is currently being excavated. An obelisque from the site graces the Place de la République, in front of the town hall.

Roman Amphitheatre in Arles (© Ferne Arfin)

Place de la République, Arles, with obelisk from the Roman Circus (© Ferne Arfin)

Virtually destroyed by barbarians during the Dark Ages, Arles was rebuilt by Charlemagne in the ninth century. For a while it was the capital of an independent kingdom before being absorbed into Provence in the 16th century. The beautiful **Cathedral of St. Trophime**, with its Gothic and Romanesque cloister, dates from this period.

Gracious town houses testify to the prosperity of Arlesian merchants during the 17th and 18th centuries.

In the 19th century, Van Gogh lived and worked in and around Arles. When, in 1888, Van Gogh cut off his ear, he was taken to the Hotel-Dieu, a 16th-century hospital with a galleried garden which he painted. Today, known as the **Espace Van Gogh**, the building is a cultural and educational center. The garden can be visited.

DID YOU KNOW...?

Vincent Van Gogh's stay in Arles was a period of feverish activity. Between his arrival in 1888 and his departure 15 months later to the asylum in St. Rémy, he completed 300 paintings. Fans will find a number of his works come to life here. Throughout Arles, historic markers – including a picture of the relevant painting – are placed at the exact spot where Van Gogh is likely to have set up his easel. The trail includes *Night Café, Starry Night, The Old Mill in the Rue Mireille*, the *Trinquetaille Bridge from Roquette Quay, The Langlois Bridge, The Yellow House, The Arena, The Sanitorium Garden, Les Alyscamps* (also painted by Gauguin) and many others. Guided tours (in French), following in the artist's footsteps, leave from the Tourist Office on Boulevard des Lices every Tuesday at 5 pm. The price is €4, children under 12 go free.

Getting Here

Arles is about half an hour by **car** from either Nîmes or Avignon and well signposted. From Nîmes, take the N113, southeast; from Avignon, take the N570 southwest. **Buses**, costing €6.90, leave from Avignon TGV Station every 15 minutes. From Avignon Center, TER (local commuter) **trains** leave regularly. The 20-minute journey costs €5.70. Regular train service is also available from Marseille and Nîmes.

Sightseeing

Tourist Information: Office de Tourisme, Boulevard des Lices, 13200 Arles, ☎ 33 04 90 18 41 20, ot-arles@visitprovence.com, www.ville-arles.fr.

MONUMENT PASS

If you plan on visiting a number of monuments and museums in Arles, a Monument Pass, available at the ticket windows of any of the museums and ancient monuments for €12 could save you money. But, before you buy one, consider that tickets for each attraction cost between €3 and €4, so you'd have to visit three or four attractions to make it worth your while.

Even if ancient monuments and museums are not your cup of tea, take some time to walk around Arles and down to the banks of the Rhône. It is one of the South's prettiest small cities.

The Amphithéâter: Built around 90 BC, this round arena was the site of gladiatorial contests and animal hunts until the sixth century. It was capable of seating 20,000 spectators. During the barbarian invasions of the Dark Ages and the warring period of the Middle Ages, Arlesians sheltered within its walls. At one time it held two chapels and more than 200 houses. Today it is used for

Arlesian café life, beside the Roman Amphitheatre (© Ferne Arfin)

concerts and drama, sports events and, during the season, Course Camarguaise (see page 44) and bull fights. In-between events, it can be visited. Rond Point des Arènes (just follow your nose to the top of the old town), ☎ 33 04 90 96 03 70, open year-round, 9 am to 6:30 pm, May to the end of September. Shorter hours in winter. A guided tour (in French), at 10:30 am every day, is included in the €4 price of admission.

Théâtre Antique: Completed a few decades before the birth of Christ, this semicircular theater was largely hidden by chapels and houses until the mid-19th century. When they were demolished, a marble-paved orchestra section, the area that housed theater machinery and some of the seats were revealed. The Théâtre Antique seats 10,000 in 33 tiers. Open year-round, it is a romantic setting for festival performances in the summer. Rue Porte de Laure, ☎ 33 04 90 96 93 30, open year-round, 9 am to 6:30 pm, May to the end of September. Closed for lunch between 11:30 am and 2 pm the rest of the year. Admission €3.

Place de la République in the center of the city is almost a catalog of Arles' historic periods and architectural styles. The Roman period is represented by an obelisque rescued from the Roman Circus; **St. Trophime's Cathedral**, built between the 12th and 15th centuries, features a magnificent

Detail, Romanesque Portal, St. Trophime's Cathedral, Arles (© Ferne Arfin)

Romanesque portal; **City Hall** and **St. Anne's Church** both date from the Baroque period of the 17th century; the 18th-century **Archbishop's Palace** runs along one side of the square and the former post office, built by noted 19th-century architect Auguste Véran, runs along another.

Buy an ice cream from one of the vendors and sit near the square's central fountain to enjoy it.

The Langlois Bridge: The little wooden drawbridge that Van Gogh named after the bridge guard was said to have reminded him of Holland. If you like Van Gogh, you will recognize it in an instant. Head south from the center of Arles on the D35 toward Port Saint Louis du Rhône. After about four km/2½ miles, look for very small signs for the Pont Van Gogh, which will be to the east.

The Langlois Bridge (© Ferne Arfin)

Les Saintes Maries de la Mer

For most of the year, this is a small but busy seaside town with a boardwalk, souvenir shops, an arena and cafés. Located on the Mediterranean, near the mouth of the Petit Rhône, it is the jumping-off point for some wonderful nature trails and deserted beaches. Despite calling itself the "Capital of the Camargue," if not for the towering presence of the 12th-century fortress church, there would be little evidence that Les Saintes Maries de la Mer is more than a beach resort. In fact, it has been a pilgrimage site for nearly 2,000 years and is, today, the scene of Europe's most remarkable pilgrimage festivals.

Easy-going Les Saintes Maries de la Mer (© Ferne Arfin)

Twice a year, in May and in October, the town is transformed as tens of thousands of gypsies from all over the world pour into the area for the **Pilgrimage Festivals of Les Saintes Maries de la Mer**. They come, many in their traditional caravans, to venerate the two Saint Marys and Sara, the gypsies' patron saint, whose relics are kept in the town's fortress church. During the festivals, the saints' relics, in elaborate reliquaries, are brought down from their chapels into the center of the church. Frag-

The Gypsy Pilgrimage re-enacts the landing of the saints (Gilles Martin-Raget, OT-Les Saintes Maries de la Mer)

ile, ancient statues of the saints are carried to the sea in processions led by women in traditional Arlesienne and gypsy costumes and accompanied by *gardians*, Camargue horsemen in traditional dress. In addition to the religious observances, there are parties, parades of gypsy caravans, music and bull games.

THE LEGEND OF THE SAINTS

According to Provençal tradition, a group of early Christians, including Mary Jacobe, sister of the Virgin Mary; Mary Salome, mother of the apostles James and John; Sara, a black woman who may have been their servant; Lazarus, and his sisters Martha and Mary Magdalen, were set adrift from Jerusalem in a boat without sails or oars. The vessel came ashore at Les Saintes Maries de la Mer in about 40 AD.

Though not uncontested, there is some evidence to support the stories. The area, then part of the Roman Empire, had been a trading outpost for the Egyptians and Greeks for many centuries and would have been well-known to anyone fleeing the Holy Land by sea. Martha is traditionally credited with converting Tarascon and in the Provençal town of St. Maximin la Ste Baume, a cave is associated with Mary Magdalen.

The identity of Sara, who is said to be the inspiration for many of the Black Madonnas in this part of France, is a mystery. In one charming story, she was the housemaid of the two Marys. Left behind on shore, she cried out to be taken. Mary Salome threw her a cloak which spread over the water so that Sara could join the others in the boat. Others believe she may have been an Egyptian living in the area who rescued the Christians from the sea or an indigenous Celto-Ligurian pagan who was an early convert.

An oratory, containing the relics of Marie Jacobe, Mary Salome and Sara was attracting pilgrims to Les Saintes Maries de la Mer as early as the second century AD.

Above: Elegant simplicity, the doors of St. Trophime's Cathedral, Arles
(© Ferne Arfin)

Below: The Langlois Bridge, just outside of Arles, as painted by Van Gogh
(© Ferne Arfin)

Relics of the two Saint Marys, in their fragile, boat-shaped casket, are carried to the sea during the Gypsy Pilgrimage in Les Saintes Maries de la Mer
(Gilles Martin-Raget, courtesy of OT-Les Saintes Maries de la Mer)

At Manade des Baumelles, near Les Saintes Maries de la Mer, clever bulls are chosen (© Ferne Arfin)

Above: The waterworld of the Camargue (Photo courtesy of Mas de la Fouque)

Below: Abandoned ochre diggings make for a fascinating hike in the Provençal Colorado near Rustrel (© N&F Michel, Collection CDT Vaucluse)

Getting Here

The town is 38 km/24 miles south of Arles on the D570. **Bus** service is available from Arles Station (see page 28 for information on local bus services).

Sightseeing

Tourist Information: Office de Tourisme et des Congrès, 5 Avenue Van Gogh, BP73, 13732 Les Saintes Maries de la Mer, Camargue, ☎ 33 04 90 97 82 55, info@saintesmaries.com, www.saintesmaries.com.

The Church of Notre Dame de la Mer: Built between the ninth and 12th centuries near the mouth of the Petit Rhône, the church served a dual purpose as a fortress where the local population could shelter from Saracens and raiding pirates. In addition to the saints reliquaries, a fourth-century pagan altar is preserved within it.

The Great Outdoors

Outside of the brief, colorful Pilgrimage periods, Les Saintes Maries de la Mer is primarily a family beach resort with little to see in the village besides the church. But the community extends well out into the Camargue, taking in bird sanctuaries and nature parks, Le Bac du Sauvage – a free ferry across the Petit Rhône, outstanding walks, cycle tracks and access to the extended Mediterranean beaches.

STAYING IN A CABANE

Cabanes de gardian or herdsmens' huts are the oldest form of dwelling in the Camargue. Built of all natural materials, with thick whitewashed walls and high, thatched roofs, they are spacious and well-adapted to the climate. In their time, they have provided shelter for shepherds, cowboys, farmers and fishermen. Today, they are offered as gîtes, ideal for vacationers who want to stay in traditional accommodation, close to nature. Information about renting a cabane is available from the tourist office in Les Saintes Maries de la Mer (see above).

Aigues Mortes

This walled town in the Petite Camargue owes its existence to the whim of a king. In the early 13th century, King Louis IX (Saint Louis) wanted a

Mediterranean port of his own so that he could launch his Crusades without going through the ports of his vassals, the Counts of Provence. Before it received this royal attention, Aigues Mortes was little more than an occasional settlement for salt workers, amid the salt marshes and malarial swamps ("Aigues Mortes" means dead waters).

The town, built in a strict grid pattern, was finished in less than 50 years and prospered briefly as a port of departure for North Africa and the Holy Land. It was also the main port for the large salt-producing area, **Les Salins du Midi**. Eventually, its access to the Mediterranean silted up and its role as a port was surpassed by other coastal towns.

The ramparts of Aigues Mortes

Despite Crusades, the Hundred Years War and various wars of religion, most of Aigues Mortes' impressive fortifications, and much of the atmosphere of the Middle Ages, remain intact. In a part of France that is characterized by Roman antiquities, Romanesque, Renaissance and Baroque architecture, Aigues Mortes is distinctively medieval. The town's thick ramparts are dotted with 20 towers. The **Constance Tower**, a massive medieval keep and dungeon, was used as a prison by the Knights Templar and later, during the persecution of the Huguenots, as a prison for Protestant women. The **Carbonnière Tower**, north of the town, guarded the approach to the main gates and offers outstanding views.

Modern Aigues Mortes is unashamedly geared to vacationers. It offers a colorful alternative for visitors to the Camargue nature parks, for campers and boating people who want an excuse to dress up and have a night (or day) on the town. Shops along the **Rue Jean Jaurès** and **Rue de la République** stay open late and offer a very good choice of traditional Provençal and Camarguaise goods – printed fabrics, *santons* (little painted statuettes of Nativity figures) sweets, leather goods, ceramics. **Place St. Louis**, which features a 19th-century statue of the crusader king, is lined with outdoor cafés and restaurants. On summer nights, live music and an animated international ambiance prevail.

Confits de fruits in a sweetshop in Aigues Mortes (© Ferne Arfin)

Getting Here

By **car**, from Arles, take the N572 west, turn south on the D979. Regular commuter **rail** service takes 41 minutes from Nîmes and costs €6.20. From Avignon, commuter rail runs from Avignon Center to St. Césaire, then coach from St. Césaire to Aigues Mortes. The journey takes an hour and 49 minutes and costs €11.80.

Sightseeing

Tourist Information: Office de Tourisme, Porte de la Gardette, BP 32, 30220 Aigues Mortes, ☎ 33 04 66 53 73 00, ot.aiguesmortes@wanadoo.fr, www.ot-aiguesmortes.fr.

The Ramparts and the Constance Tower: Exhibits in the tower, a 13th-century castle keep, document its role in the Crusades and as a prison over the centuries. Panoramic views of the Camargue, the salt mountains of les Salins du Midi and the modern, pyramid-shaped apartment buildings of La Grande Motte, a new town to the West. Hours: May 2 to August 31, 10 am to 6 pm; September 1 to April 30, 10 am to 4:40 pm. Admission: adults, €6.10, youth ticket (18-25) €4.10, under 18 admitted free. Closed January 1, May 1, November 1 and 11, December 25.

La Tour Carbonnière

La Tour Carbonnière: An ancient watchtower, about three km/two miles northwest of town, that defended the only approach. It offers an exceptional view of Aigues Mortes. Always open, no admission. Take the D979 north to the D58, turn left on the D46.

Les Salins du Midi: The oldest cultivated salt marsh on the Mediterranean. Tours of 1½ or 2½ hours, in either little trains or open-topped buses, take in salt production areas, including *les camelles* (massive salt pyramids), and visit marshes and wild beaches. Bring binoculars and a bird book – there are hundreds of varieties of birds (about 270 species are resident or migratory) – including pink flamingos. The longer tours are guided and include a visit to a salt museum. Take the D979 south towards le Grau du Roi and turn right at the sign for Jarras Listel vineyard. Entrance is through the Jarras Listel caves. Hours: every day, from March to October, 9:30 am to 6:45 pm. Children under four are free. The short tour, which costs €6.80, departs frequently throughout the day. The longer tour with guide costs €9.90 and departs at 10:30 am, 2:30 and 4:45 pm. *Salins Patrimoine, BP 84, 30220 Aigues Mortes,* ☎ *33 04 66 73 40 24, fax 33 04 66 73 40 21, salins@salins.com, www.salins.com.*

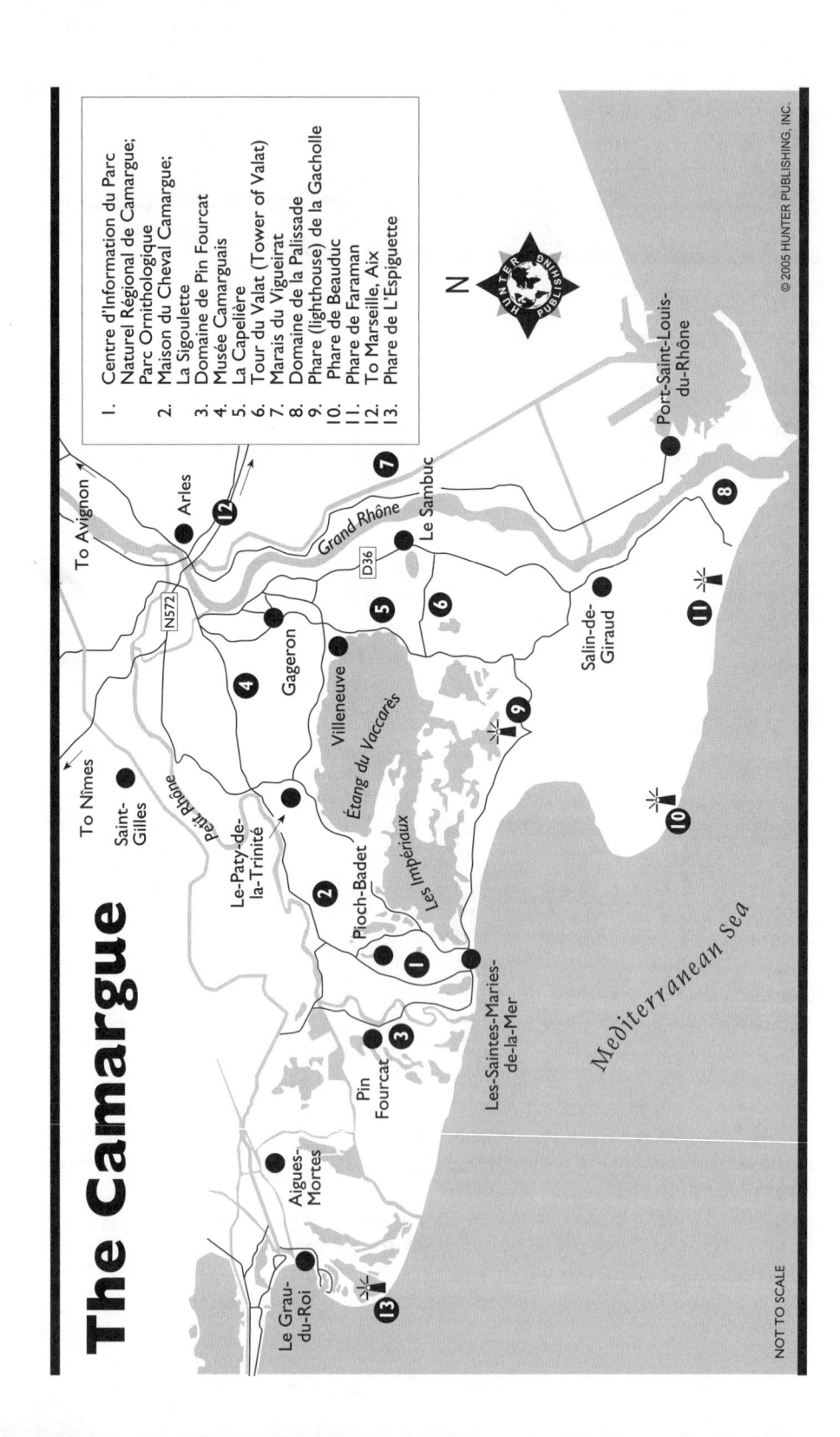

The Camargue

1. Centre d'Information du Parc Naturel Régional de Camargue; Parc Ornithologique
2. Maison du Cheval Camargue; La Sigoulette
3. Domaine de Pin Fourcat
4. Musée Camarguais
5. La Capelière
6. Tour du Valat (Tower of Valat)
7. Marais du Vigueirat
8. Domaine de la Palissade
9. Phare (lighthouse) de la Gacholle
10. Phare de Beauduc
11. Phare de Faraman
12. To Marseille, Aix
13. Phare de L'Espiguette

NOT TO SCALE

© 2005 HUNTER PUBLISHING, INC.

■ Camargue Beaches

Sad to say, no matter where you go on the Mediterranean coast these days, the RVs and tent campers have gotten there before you. Nevertheless, the beaches of the Camargue are probably about as unspoiled as is possible in modern Europe. Miles of white sand, grass-covered dunes and white ponies galloping in the surf are not just fantasies here. Several beaches are worth visiting.

Plage Est

If you continue eastward along the The East Beach at the end of Les Saintes Maries de la Mer, you may see signs announcing *Zone Naturiste* – that's the **nude beach**. It is about five km/three miles outside the village. To get there, follow the beach road east. After about three km/1.9 miles the road becomes a dirt track. Leave it here and walk along the beach. The Mediterranean will be on your right, dunes, ponds and marshes on your left and you will only be able to proceed on foot or mountain bike. Bring your own water, refreshments and shade because all you'll find are sand dunes, sea and loads of sea birds.

Plage de Beauduc

Beauduc Beach is the hardest to find and the best – 28 km/17.4 miles of natural, wild white sand beach. A shambling assortment of (illegal) fishermen's shacks, caravans and trailers at the end of a track includes two remarkably popular restaurants on the sand, **Marc et Mireille** and **Chez Juju** (see page 95). Otherwise the wide, empty beach feels like the end of the world. To get there from Arles, take the D570 South (or the D570 North from Les Saintes Maries de la Mer) to the D36 South (signposted Le Sambuc, Salin de Giraud and Plage de Piémançon). Turn right onto the D36b (follow signs for La Capelière). You will be skirting the Camargue Nature Reserve so watch for birds and wildlife. Continue past Salin de Badon (a large house near a big pine tree) for about eight km/4.8 miles. Watch for a small sign directing you to Restaurant Marc et Mireille. This will be a right turn onto an even smaller, unpaved road. If you arrive in the small town of Salin de Giraud, you have gone too far. When the road widens out to white sand, you are there. One word of warning – the tracks wind through marshland and lagoons so leave plenty of daylight for your return journey. Also, be careful not to park facing the wind. This beach has sufficient wind for kite surfing 300 days per year and it will drive sand into your engine.

> ### LA CAPELIÈRE 
>
> On the way to Beauduc, it is worth stopping at La Capelière on the D36b. It is prime birding territory. A log book for visitors lists some of the birds you can expect to see, such as tufted ducks (left), scaups, red-crested pochards (below), tits, spotted eagles, marsh harriers, flamingos and great white egrets, among others. A marked, 1½-km/.9-mile trail has conveniently placed hides. The center is open every day, from April 1 to September 30, 9 am to 1 pm and 2 to 6 pm. Between October 1 and March 31, it closes an hour earlier and is completely closed on Tuesdays.

Plage de L'Espiguette

Ten km/six miles of wide, sandy beach backed by pine woods and sand dunes, the beach extends from the marine resort of Port Camargue to the lagoons and canals of the Petite Camargue. It's near the Espiguette lighthouse, and dress is optional. Snacks, umbrella and beach chair rentals are available near Les Baronnets parking. Parking is by the hour and can be expensive. The best time to appreciate this beach is early or late in the day and out of season. To get there from Aigues Mortes, take the D979 South toward the small fishing village of Le Grau du Roi. Just before the village, turn left onto a new road, the D62b, towards Port Camargue. After about one km/.6 mile, turn left onto a narrow paved road marked Phare de L'Espiguette. At the lighthouse, look for parking signs.

> ### A Visit to a Manade
>
> Like Camargue horses, Camargue bulls (*biòu* in Provençal) are an ancient, local breed with origins in prehistory. Some think they may be the westernmost descendents of cattle from Asia Minor. Small and wily, the bulls roam free, grazing the *sansouires* in small herds called *manades*. The ranches where they are raised are also called *manades* and the ranchers are known as *manadiers*.
>
> *Camargue bull in the Course Camarguaise (© Ferne Arfin)*

Too independent for work and of limited use for meat (although you will find *taureau* on Provençal menus), the bulls are kept almost exclusively for the Course Camarguaise, the modern game in which players compete to snatch paper rosettes, bits of string and other tokens (called *attributs*) from their lyre-shaped horns (see Nîmes, page 44). Popular in just a tiny corner of Provence and southwestern France, the games are played at 600 to 700 events each year. Successful bulls can make a fortune for their *manades*.

There are only about 30 *manades* in the Camargue. Some allow visitors to come and watch, or even participate in, *le triage du bétail*, when the cleverest bulls are selected and prepared for the games and for *abrivados* – bull running in the streets. **Manade des Baumelles** offers a variety of taurine demonstrations, equestrian activities, and traditional meals *(Domaine des Baumelles, Cabanes de Cambon, Route d'Aigues Mortes, 13460,* ☎ *33 04 90 97 84 37, mas-des-baumelles@camargue.fr or sylvie.linsolas@free.fr, www.manade-des-baumelles.camargue.fr)*. A *journée Camarguaise* (a Camarguaise day out) including various demonstrations and a traditional meal, costs €30 per person; half-price for children under 10. Boat trips on the Petit Rhône, from Les Sainte Maries de La Mer to the *manade's* own dock, can also be arranged.

Manades may also offer Camargue "safaris" on horseback or in four-wheel-drive vehicles, *journées champêtre* (basically rural days out), and a *Course Camarguaise*. Some have overnight, *chambre d'hôte* accommodations with full- or half-board as well. The best way to find a *manade* that suits your interest is to contact the very helpful English-speaking tourist office staff at *Porte de la Gardette, BP 32, 30220 Aigues Mortes,* ☎ *33 04 66 53 73 00, ot.aiguesmortes@wanadoo.fr, www.ot-aiguesmortes.fr*.

Manades are working ranches and agricultural estates so what's on offer when you visit will depend on their routine. Few *manadiers* cater for English speakers, but they are popular with French families and if you are game, you can usually connect with friendly English speakers among the French vacationers.

■ Festivals & Fêtes

History and tradition are celebrated throughout this region. Festivals often feature women in Arlesian costume and many include bull games. Mounted *gardians* wearing brightly printed shirts, brimmed leather or felt hats and carrying *tridents* – long lances with very small, three pointed forks at the end – usually participate in traditional events. Nowadays it is not uncommon to see *gardiennes* (cowgirls).

Arles

Feria de Pâques: Arles seems to have one festival after another. There's a costume festival in July, a rice festival in September and an epic film festival the last week in August during which movie spectacles like *Gladiator* and *Spartacus* are projected in the Roman Theater. The *Feria de Pâques*, or Easter Festival, has all the key elements – musical performances, markets, parades, *Course Camarguaise* and bull running. The dates depend on Easter so it is best to check with the tourist office (page 383) for specific dates and events.

Pegoulado: On the last Friday in June Arlesians – men, women and children – come out in costume for the *Pegoulado*, a long lamplight parade along the Boulevard des Lices. If you are in the area, it is worth seeing. Arlesian traditional dress is lovely.

Les Saintes Maries de la Mer

Thousands turn out to venerate the Gypsy Patron Saint Sara, said to be the inspiration for the region's tradition of the Black Madonna (Gilles Martin-Raget, courtesy of OT-Les Saintes Maries de la Mer)

The Gypsy Pilgrimage: On May 24 and 25, thousands of gypsies from all over the world gather here to pay homage to their patron, Sara, and the two Saint Marys (see box page 80). The town and the countryside all around are packed with colorful gypsy caravans. Processions, accompanied by mounted *gardians* and Arlesian-costumed women, re-enact the saints' arrival from the sea. This is a remarkable and unique event.

Tip: If you plan to attend, you need to reserve accommodation well in advance because hotels throughout the region, as far away as Nîmes and Arles, fill up for this event.

Aigues Mortes

Fêtes de la Saint Louis: In honor of its 13th-century origins, the town goes completely medieval on the third Saturday and Sunday in August. A pageant features local people in traditional costumes and events include knightly chivalry, tournaments, horsemanship, a medieval market, strolling troubadours and bonfires.

If you are nearby around Bastille Day (July 14), Aigues Mortes is a good place to watch the traditional fireworks. They start at 11 pm near the

South Ramparts. Bastille Day celebrations actually start a day earlier with a torchlight procession from Place St. Louis, at 9 pm on July 13.

■ Shopping

Key items to look for in this area are *santons* (see page 161), traditional clothing – including Arlesian costumes, ceramics and colorful Provençal printed fabrics.

In Arles

Arles is the best town for serious shop hounds, with outstanding craftsmen who work with leather, wood, metal and ceramics. The town also has several good art galleries and antique dealers. Most shops are liberally salted in the streets and lanes between Boulevard des Lices and the Rhône quays, particularly in the pedestrian areas off Rue de la République.

Custom-made *gardians'* boots are sold at **La Botte Camarguaise**, 22 Rue Jean Granaud.

Hand-made *santons* are at **Le Cloître**, 1 Rue Jean Jaurès, which has a huge selection of sizes and styles.

Arlesian costumes are sold at **L'Arlésienne**, 12 Rue du Président Wilson.

Traditional printed fabrics can be found at **Soleiado**, 4 Boulevard des Lices, including yard goods, bed linens and ready-to-wear clothing.

Market Days: Saturday sees a **Provençal Market**, along Boulevard des Lices and Boulevard Clémenceau, and a **Farmers' Market**, along Esplanade Charles de Gaulle.

On Wednesday a **traditional local market** opens along Boulevard Emile Combes.

In Les Saintes Maries de la Mer

This is not really a shopping town, but look for *gardian* gear – boots, clothing, hats, even tridents – at **Boutique le Gardian**, 9 Rue Victor Hugo. Gypsy-inspired fashions for women are sold at **Boutique Maria Maria**, 7 Place des Remparts. The selection includes fashion from Christian Lacroix, an Arlesian.

Market Days: Monday and Friday in the summer.

In Aigues Mortes

More than 100 art galleries and almost as many antique shops are tucked away in the little streets within the city walls. Expect tourist prices. Shops along the **Grand Rue Jean Jaurès** are mostly tourist tat but stay open late and are fun to browse for surprises. Bypass the snazzier looking sweet shops and head for **Poitavin**, 8 Grand Rue Jean Jaurès, for handmade chocolates and great slabs of soft nougat with nuts and fruits kneaded in.

Market Days: A market is held on Wednesday and Sunday mornings at Avenue Frédéric Mistral.

■ Where to Stay

Deluxe

☆☆☆☆ **Grand Hotel Nord-Pinus** *(14 Place du Forum, 13200 Arles,* ☎ *33 04 90 93 44 44, info@nord-pinus.com, www.nord-pinus.com. 24 rooms and suites. Breakfast and room tax extra. €€-€€€€).* Idiosyncratic and independently run, this is an Arlesian mansion in a pretty square just across from Van Gogh's Café de Nuit. Hemingway, Churchill, Jean Cocteau, legendary bull fighter Luis Miguel Dominguin and Picasso have all been guests. Restored about a decade ago to reflect its raffish, Bohemian past, the hotel was once owned by a cabaret dancer and her husband, a tight-rope walking clown! Photos by Karen Blixen are displayed in public rooms.

☆☆☆☆ **Jules César** *(9 Blvd. des Lices, 13631 Arles,* ☎ *33 04 90 52 52 52, julescesar@wanadoo.fr or julescesar@relaischateaux.com, www.hotel-julescesar.fr. 55 rooms, breakfast and room tax extra, €€€-€€€€).* A 17th-century Carmelite convent hidden behind a mock-Roman façade. Spacious rooms with pastel or pale stone walls, furnished with antiques. The *chapelle*, complete with Baroque altarpiece, is used for meetings and seminars and you can lunch in the cloister. Ask to stay in the Mother Superior's room.

☆☆☆☆ **Mas de la Fouque** *(D38, Rte. du Bac Sauvage, 13460 Les Saintes Maries de la Mer,* ☎ *33 04 90 97 81 02, info@masdelafouque.com, www.masdelafouque.com. 17 rooms and suites, €€€-€€€€).* On the edge of the Camargue, near the mouth of the Petit Rhône and about half a mile from a deserted Mediterranean beach, this is an isolated and romantic farmhouse with individually decorated suites, built on piles over a lagoon. Watch the bulls and horses from the window; take the hotel's boat waterskiing or for a picnic on a private beach; or arrange to visit a *manade*. This place is popular with French movie stars. Maybe that's why it has its own heliport for the short flight from Marseille Airport.

HOTEL PRICE CHART	
Rates are per room based on double occupancy.	
	Under €55
€	€56-€96
€€	€97-€135
€€€	€136-€195
€€€€	Over €195

Moderate

☆☆☆ **Hotel Mireille** *(Rive Droite, Trinquetaille, 13200 Arles,* ☎ *33 04 90 93 70 74, contact@hotel-mireille.com, www.hotel-mireille.com. 34 rooms, satellite TV with CNN and BBC, pool. Bed and breakfast, €€).* Across the road from the town center. The small rooms are brightly painted and evocatively named – Romarin, Lavande, Basilic, Pomme d'Amour.

☆☆☆ **Le Boumian** *(Route d'Arles, 13460 Les Saintes Maries de la Mer,* ☎ *33 04 90 97 81 15, leboumian@camargue.fr, www.leboumian.camargue.fr. 28 rooms, bed and breakfast, €€)* Hotel-restaurant just outside of town with its own stable of horses for guided promenades into the Camargue. All rooms face a very pretty pool.

☆☆☆ **Les Cabanettes** *(RN 572, 13200 Arles,* ☎ *33 04 66 87 31 53, BW.hotel.lescabanettes@wanadoo.fr, 29 rooms, handicapped access, €-€€, breakfast and local taxes extra).* A simple but comfortable hotel 16 km/10 miles outside of Arles along the St. Gilles road. The hotel is well-located for explorations of the entire region. Rooms are arranged on one level along a spiral, giving each room a sheltered, private patio. Part of the Best Western Group.

Budget

☆☆ **Hotel de L'Amphithéâtre** *(5 to 7 Rue Diderot, 13200 Arles,* ☎ *33 04 90 96 10 30, contact@hotelamphitheatre.fr, www.hotelamphitheatre.fr. 28 rooms, €, breakfast and local taxes extra).* Wildly decorated in the Provençal manner – painted wood, wrought iron, printed fabrics. In the heart of the old district and convenient for visiting the Amphitheater and Roman Theatre.

☆☆ **Hotel de La Muette** *(15 Rue des Suisses, 13200 Arles,* ☎ *33 04 90 96 15 39, hotel.muette@wanadoo.fr, http://perso.wanadoo.fr/hotel-muette. 18 rooms, breakfast and local taxes extra, €).* In the historic district, this is an ancient "maison" dating from the 12th to 15th centuries. Many of the rooms incorporate the original stone walls and beams. Part of the rated, Logis de France group.

☆☆ **Mas des Salicornes** *(Route d'Arles, 13260 Les Saintes Maries de la Mer,* ☎ *33 04 90 97 83 41, info@hotel-salicornes.com, www.hotel-salicornes.com. 16 rooms, breakfast and room tax extra).* A *mas* or farmhouse in the local tradition and a genuine bargain. Rooms, small but complete, are arranged around the pool. A tiny restaurant serves traditional food and offers flamenco evenings and cooking classes. The *mas* has its own horses and offers guided rides ranging from two hours in the marshes or seashore to sunrise excursions along the Étang de Vaccarès.

Camping

Almost all of the Camargue is included in the Regional Naturel Park and the most interesting wildlife area, the National Nature Reserve, is off-limits except for specified viewing areas. So, unless you plan to unroll a sleeping bag on one of the wild beaches (frowned upon but not unheard of), camping is quite organized, with facilities, entertainments and often bungalows or camper vans rather than tents.

☆☆ **Camping City** *(67 Rte. de la Crau, 13200 Arles,* ☎ *33 04 90 93 08 86, fax 33 04 90 93 91 07, informations@camping-city.com or service-reservations@camping-city.com, www.camping-city.com).* Tents, RVs or camper vans. This is a big, busy, family camping facility near Arles, with pool, laundry, recreation facilities, restaurant. Set price for two adults with a car and caravan, camper or tent is €16. Tourist tax and electricity hook-up are extra.

☆☆☆☆ **Le Clos du Rhône** *(Route d'Aigues Mortes, 13460 Les Saintes Maries de la Mer,* ☎ *33 04 90 97 85 99, fax 33 04 90 97 78 85, leclos@saintesmaries.com, www.saintesmariesdelamer.com).* A family-style, seashore campsite near the mouth of the Petit Rhône, about a mile from the center of Les Saintes Maries de la Mer. It has a full range of the typical facilities and a heated pool, laundry, shop, snack bar. About €15 to €22 for two adults. Electricity and water are extra. The site is closed between December 12 and February 28.

☆☆☆ **Fleur de Camargue** *(D46, Ancient Rte. d'Aigues Mortes, 30220 St. Laurent d'Aigouze,* ☎ *33 04 66 88 15 42, fax 33 04 66 88 10 21, sarlaccv@aol.com, www.fleur-de-camargue.com).* Convenient for visiting Aigues Mortes. Tent camping as well as campers. Pool open from mid-May to September. Provençal entertainments, including *pétanque* (the popular outdoor bowling game), accordion music, gastronomic evenings. €15 to €23 for two adults, car, electric hook-up and use of facilities. There is a non-refundable reservation fee of €16.

> **Author's Tip:** Les Campings de France has a useful Internet portal with access to thousands of campsites all over France at www.lescampingsdefrance.com. For this region, enter the site and select 13 on the interactive map or 13-Bouches du Rhône on the dropdown menu.

Gîtes

Because of associations with the Crusades and the ancient pilgrim route to Santiago de Compostela in Spain, *gîtes* in this region can sometimes be medieval crusaders' guardhouses, old monastic dwellings and pilgrimage inns. They are usually rented by the week, though some may also have chambre d'hôte (bed and breakfast) rooms that are available by the night. The local tourist authorities or **Gîtes de France** (www.gites-de-france.fr/eng) are the best sources of up-to-date lists. In Aigues Mortes and Les Saintes Maries de la Mer, ask about the availability of *cabanes* (see box, page 81). This small selection is typical:

Mas de la Grande Rougnouse *(Rte. de Salin de Giraud, D36, 13200 Arles, ☎ 33 04 90 96 45 98, fax 33 04 90 96 45 98, rougnouse@wanadoo.fr, www.rougnouse.com, €-€€)*. About five km/three miles from Arles, these Mediterranean-styled accommodations (white walls, blue and ochre decor, wrought iron furniture) cluster around a 15th-century fortified tower built to protect the approach to Arles and as a pilgrim shelter. Four of the *gîtes* are suitable for four people, one larger gîte will house up to six. French or Oriental dinners, served in 15th-century rooms, can be arranged. The owners offer three-hour Camargue tours in four-wheel-drive vehicles.

Mas du Petit Prince *(Patrick and Anne-Marie Castan, Mas du Petit Prince et de Beynes, Gageron, 13200 Arles, ☎ 33 04 90 97 07 29, contact@maspetitprince.com, www.maspetitprince.com, €€)*. Only two *gîtes* and three chambre d'hôtes (bed and breakfast rooms) in a luxuriously decorated, 15th-century *mas* about 11 km/seven miles from Arles. Many of the rooms feature original bare stone walls and beamed ceilings (what the French call *pierres et poutres*). Bathrobes are supplied in the chambre d'hôtes and the property has a pool.

Mas du Grand Antonelle *(Mme. Dominique Plan, Mas Antonelle, Villeneuve-Camargue, 13200 Arles, ☎ 33 04 90 97 00 32, fax 33 04 90 97 0129, antonelle@wanadoo.fr, http://perso.wanadoo.fr/antonelle.net/indexus.htm, €)*. On a spur off the D36b just north of the crossroads at Villeneuve, this is a long 17th-century farmhouse divided into several units and furnished in a rustic style. Rooms feature sunny colors and Provençal antiques. Most boast an "American" kitchen, including stove, refrigerator/freezer, microwave and electric coffeemaker. About 13 km/eight miles from Arles, the *gîtes* are within the Camargue Regional Nature Park on the edge of the National Reserve and convenient for the information center and nature trails at La Capelière.

Domaine de Paulon *(Madame Brigitte Blanc, Le Sambuc, 13200 Arles, ☎ 33 04 90 97 27 73, fax 33 04 90 97 21 61, domaine-de-paulon@camargue.fr, www.domaine-de-paulon.camargue.fr. Weekly rental, €)*. *Gîtes* for three to 10 people on a working *manade* with a chance to watch the rearing of Camarguaise bulls used for the local games. Neat and well-equipped units share the grounds of a *mas* that was once the headquarters of the crusading Knights of Malta.

Le Mas des Sables *(D 979 – Route de Nîmes, 30220 Aigues Mortes,* ☎ *33 04 66 53 79 73, fax 33 04 66 53 77 12, masdessables@camargue.fr, www.lemasdessables.com. Weekly rentals, €).* Fully equipped apartments for five to eight people on the grounds of a country inn. Simply furnished in a rustic style, with terra cotta floors and beamed ceilings in some rooms.

■ Where to Eat

We picked the **Café du Commerce** *(11 Place Sainte-Louis, 30220 Aigues Mortes,* ☎*/fax 33 04 66 53 71 71, €€)* from the various restaurants and cafés that line two sides of **Aigues Mortes**' central plaza because I wanted oysters and the restaurant's display of shellfish on ice looked tempting. It was a lucky choice – we were not disappointed. The *plateau* of oysters was generous and absolutely fresh. A wide selection of seafood and grilled meats was unadventurous but nicely prepared.

DINING PRICE CHART

Prices are for a typical prix fixe menu of two courses and a glass of house wine for one.

	€14-€19
€	€21-€34
€€	€35-€49
€€€	€50-€69
€€€€	€70-€140
€€€€€	The sky's the limit

Like all the other restaurants in the Place Saint Louis, the Café du Commerce benefits from the festive and friendly holiday atmosphere in the plaza. In the summer, there's live music and the shops and galleries stay open late for strolling and browsing. We had to wait about half an hour for a table, so reserving ahead is probably a good idea.

Elsewhere in Aigues Mortes, **Restaurant La Camargue** *(19 Rue de la République, 30220 Aigues Mortes,* ☎ *33 04 66 53 86 88, fax 33 04 66 53 72 69, brahic.web@wanadoo.fr, www.restaurantlacamargue.fr, closed Mondays in winter, €€€)* offers gypsy music and occasional flamenco in an 18th-century building (they claim it is the oldest restaurant in town). A big inglenook fireplace dominates the main room and the patio is shaded with vine leaves. It is probably a bit *touristique*, but gastronomy isn't this area's strong point so you might as well have fun soaking up atmosphere. Alongside various grilled foods, local specialties include *gardianne de taureau* (a long-simmered stew of marinated bull, olives and vegetables) and *rouille de poulpes* (octopus in a strong, garlicky sauce).

The **Brasserie Nord-Pinus** *(Place du Forum, 13200 Arles,* ☎ *33 04 90 93 44 44, info@nord-pinus.com, www.nord-pinus.com, closed February and Wednesdays in winter, €-€€€)*, attached to the hotel of the same name (see *Where to Stay*, page 90), is the place for celebrity spotting and posing in Arles. Décor is retro and Bohemian and food reflects the lighter side of the Provençal style. You can have anything from a snack to a full three-course meal. The terrace faces Van Gogh's model for *Café de Nuit*.

Le Cloître *(Hotel Jules César, Boulevard des Lices, 13633 Arles,* ☎ *33 04 90 52 52 52, julescesar@wanadoo.fr or julescesar@relaischateaux.com, www.hotel-julescesar.fr, closed mid-November through December, €-€€)*, offers a less expensive, and less formal, version of the cooking available in the hotel's main restaurant **Lou Marquès** (€€€-€€€€). Le Cloître, open only for lunch, spreads out in the cloister and cloister garden of an 18th-century Carmelite convent. Cooking mixes classical French and Provençal styles. Save up some calories for the terrific rice pudding with honey.

For a really special experience, make your way over the trails to the beach at **Beauduc** and then hike over the sand to lunch al fresco at either **Chez JuJu** *(Beauduc Beach,* ☎ *33 04 42 86 83 86, €€)* or **Chez Marc et Mireille** *(Beauduc Beach,* ☎ *33 04 42 48 80 08, €€)*. Both are little more than shacks in the sand – you eat at picnic-type tables – where freshly caught sea bass, prawns and bream are grilled or simply prepared in wood-burning ovens with garlicky sauces. The tiny local clams, called *tellines*, are so good that Marc et Mireille supply them to some of the region's top restaurants, like le Bistro d'Eygalières (page 61). Both places are tiny and wildly popular with local people and beach aficionados, so make reservations well in advance. And, since getting to Beauduc is something of an adventure, don't try to cram too much else in on the day you go.

HOTEL BREAKFASTS

Unlike other parts of France, cute cafés and *boulangeries* that serve coffee are thin on the ground here. While searching out a cosy little place for breakfast can be fun and economical in Paris, it is just a time-waster in the Camargue. Unless it costs more than €10, you're better off sticking with whatever your hotel provides.

Light Meals & Snacks

Real gastronomy is hard to find in the Camargue, but carefully prepared snacks and salads are everywhere. Look for *pizza feu de bois* (cooked in wood-burning ovens often fueled with vine wood) crêperies, omelettes and salads with *frites* (French fries) in most sidewalk cafés for about €10 or less. At this level, it is really hard to go wrong.

The Spanish influence on Arles is evident at **L'Affenage** *(4 Rue Molière, 13200 Arles,* ☎ *33 04 90 96 07 67, €)*, where a buffet of Provençal hors d'oeuvres is reminiscent of a Madrid tapas bar – fried vegetables, tapenade and marinated olives, seafood, slices of ham.

Locally popular, **L'Affenage** is off the tourist radar and the owners take the traditional French vacation, closing for most of August. **Vitamine** *(16 Rue du Docteur Fanton, 13220 Arles, ☎ 33 04 90 93 77 36, closed on Sunday and Saturday for dinner in winter)* is a friendly, casual (and cheap!) place to give your digestive system a break. Their menu features loads of different salads and a few pasta dishes.

■ Adventures

Primarily wetland, the Camargue is a flat world of salty plains, shallow lagoons and seasonal marshes encircled by sand dunes and centered on the Étang de Vaccarès. Vaccarès is a vast (15,000 acres), shallow (about 6½ feet deep) body of water that provides nesting and feeding areas for hundreds of resident and migratory birds. As a UNESCO World Heritage protected area, the Camargue's many fragile eco-systems are monitored and protected. Vehicle access – and often human access as well – is strictly limited. For the adventurer on foot, cycle or horseback, this is a peaceful, undisturbed landscape with much to see and enjoy. The Mediterranean beaches and the canals provide opportunities for watersports and boating.

Besides flamingos, the ponds and marshes are habitat for egrets, herons, bitterns, mallards, diving ducks, and all kinds of fishing birds. Sterns and avocets are a common site along the sea dike, on the southern edge of Vaccarès. (See *Birdwatching*, page 103.) Small mammals, including foxes and otters hide among the reeds and the Camargue is a habitat for rare European beavers.

WEATHER WATCH

The Camargue is worth visiting year-round, but each season has its own advantages. The spring and fall are mild and provide the best opportunities for seeing the famous flamingos as well as enjoying some of the major festivals. During the hot summer months, the salt marshes turn into hard, cracked plains (*sansouires*) where small groups of bulls and Camargue horses graze. For wind- or kite-surfers, ocean breezes, while steady, may be lighter. During the winter months, the salt marshes flood beneath eight to 10 inches of water and Mistral winds can make the ambient temperature seem much colder. Nevertheless, many birdwatchers enjoy the opportunity of spotting southern birds at the point of their northernmost migrations, in relative privacy.

On Foot

None of France's long-distance paths cross the Camargue but several short walks will give a good idea of the variety of wildlife and environment. (For a longer challenge, try one of the cycle itineraries listed in *Adventures on Wheels*, page 97.)

La Maison du Cheval Camargue *(Mas de la Curé, Rte. d'Arles, 13460 Les Saintes Maries de la Mer, ☎ 33 04 90 97 58 47, fax 33 04 90 97 58 48. Monday through Friday, 1:30 pm to 2 pm, Sunday at 10 am, admission €5 for adults, €3 children, reservations required).* Guided walks along a two-km/1.2-mile pedestrian path to discover the breeding of Camargue horses in their natural environment.

Domaine de la Palissade *(BP5, D36, Salin de Giraud, ☎ 33 04 42 86 81 28, fax 33 04 42 48 82 18, palissade@free.fr. Daily except holidays from 9 am to 5 pm. Small entrance fee).* A protected freshwater environment along the banks of the Rhône. Trails include information boards and hides.

La Capelière (see *Making Sense of the Park System*, page 103). A network of trails, with hides and observation platforms, allows limited access to the Camargue National Reserve. A log book at the visitors' center details visitors' bird sightings. The paths are relatively short but this is the closest you will get, on foot, to the National Reserve.

> **Mosquito warning!** The Camargue is mostly marshland, prime breeding territory for mosquitoes. Be warned. If you leave your insect repellent at home, you have no one to blame but yourself.

On Wheels

Cycling

Les Saintes Maries de la Mer is a good base for cycle touring of the Camargue and the tourist information office there can provide useful trail information and maps. Although there are few conventional trail markers, there are very few paths and trails. Those that exist are usually signposted with the direction of the next hamlet or *mas*. Routes may be either unpaved, dirt lanes or partially paved and partially unpaved roads so mountain bikes are recommended. Some trails flood during the winter months; before setting out, check that your route is open.

Le Vélo Saintois *(19 Avenue de la République, 13460 Les Saintes Maries de la Mer, ☎ 33 04 90 97 74 56, fax 33 04 90 97 60 81, velosaintois@aol.com or loc@levelosaintois.com, www.levelosaintois.com)* rents all types of cycles – even tandems – and can provide maps and advice. In Aigues Mortes, **The Bike Rental Agency** *(14 Rue Théaulon, ☎ 33 04 66 51 56 03 or 33 06 15 37 88 45)* rents bicycles by the day, half-day or week.

SUGGESTED CYCLING ITINERARIES

Digue à la Mer (The Sea Dyke): 24 km/15 miles over dirt tracks and sandy paths, moderate difficulty, for mountain bikes. A three-hour circuit with some of the best views into the nature reserve and opportunities to spot sea birds and marsh wading birds. The trail is passable year-round and can be done as a five-hour hike. Carry water, refreshments and sun protection as there are no restaurants, snack bars or sources of water and the route is very exposed.

Leave Les Saintes Maries de la Mer on the beach road, heading east past the thalassa therapy center. There is only one road, which turns into a dirt track. About three km/1.9 miles outside the town, you reach the dyke, running between the Mediterranean and the marshland of Étang de Vaccarès. Follow the dyke to the Gacholle Lighthouse. Return the same way.

Méjanes: 30 km/18.6 miles, a third paved roads, two-thirds sand trails, moderate difficulty, for mountain bikes. The trail skirts the western edge of the Étang de Vaccarès through the nature reserve. It is passable only from June to October and should be avoided after heavy rain. The round-trip will take about six hours. It can also be done as an eight-hour hike. There is a restaurant for refreshments in Méjanes, but it is probably wise to carry water and sun protection.

Just east of Les Saintes Maries de la Mer, pick up the D85A – "The Route de Cacharel" north. After four km/2½ miles on the paved road, just before the Mas de Cacharel, turn right onto the sandy track signposted for Méjanes, which is 17.7 km/11 miles farther along. Return the same way.

Bac du Sauvage-Cacharel: 30 km/18.6 miles over paved roads and sandy trails, moderate difficulty, for any bicycle. This five- to six-hour circuit takes in some of the Petite Camargue, with views of varied landscapes – the Petit Rhône, marshes and ponds. It includes the Bac du Sauvage – a free ferry across the Petit Rhône. (Before setting out, ask about the ferry schedule in the tourist information office in Les Saintes Maries de la Mer.) The trail is passable year-round. Bring water, refreshments and sun protection.

West of Les Saintes Maries de la Mer take the D38 for six km/3.7 miles, then cross the Petit Rhône on the Bac du Sauvage, the free ferry boat. Continue on the D85 toward Aigues Mortes, passing the Mas du Juge. Re-cross the Petit Rhône at the Sylvéréal Bridge. Immediately after the bridge, take the small trail on the right, marked Mas d'Astouin. After the sign for the Petit Astouin, turn right onto the D38, then take the left fork (D38b) towards Pioch Badet. Turn left onto the D570 – a busy road. After about 350 m (a fifth of a mile), take the right fork to Pioch Badet. At Pioch Badet, turn right, and return following the sign for "Les Saintes Maries de la Mer par Cacharel."

Jeep Safaris

Touring with a guide in a 4x4 vehicle is a popular way of getting close to *manades* of bulls and herds of horses, as well as visiting private beaches.

Several companies offer day and half-day safaris. **Camargue Safari 4x4 Gallon** offers 4x4 tours by the hour, half-day and full day. Day-long safaris, including lunch, go for €92, children under 10 half-price. *(Gallon Organisation Loisirs en Camargue, 22 Ave. Van Gogh, 13460 Saintes Maries de la Mer,* ☎ *33 04 90 97 86 93 or 33 04 90 97 84 12, fax 33 04 90 96 31 55, camargue-safari.gallon@camargue.fr, www.safari-4x4-gallon.camargue.fr).*

Le Gitan Safari Nature Camargue claims to be the only safaris organized by professional *manadiers*. They offer half-day and shorter tours of the Petite Camargue (leaving from Aigues Mortes) or the Grande Camargue (leaving from Les Saintes Maries de la Mer) year-round. *(M. Trazic, 17 Ave. de la République, 13460 Saintes Maries de la Mer,* ☎ *33 04 90 97 89 33 or 33 04 66 53 04 99, fax 33 04 66 70 22 47, leGitansafari@libertysurf.fr, www.manade-safari.com).*

Several of the *mas* and *manades* listed in the accommodation section of this chapter will also arrange 4x4 safaris.

On Horseback

Covering the countryside on the back of a gentle, intelligent Camargue horse is fantasy riding. You've probably seen it in the movies – galloping along a beach, manes flying, hooves slapping the surf, or splashing through the marshes. This is one dream that doesn't have to be debunked.

Riding here is well-organized for both experts and novices. It is the best way to take in the wildlife – not just birds and beasts but also butterflies, dragonflies, iridescent frogs, otters, foxes and other small mammals that wink in and out of the tall, rustling reeds. And, because it is an important part of the local way of life, it is a good way to get to know the Camarguaise. There is even an "equestrian gîte" organized by an English expatriate, Brenda Gatti, where you can learn to ride without taxing your high-school French.

Mas des Salicornes and **Le Boumian** (see *Where to Stay*, pages 91-92) both offer riding, ranging from days out to several-day treks. In addition to stables, the facilities at **Cabanes de Cacharel** include traditional herdsmens' huts that have been featured in French films. Horses can be hired by the hour or you can join a two- to five-day trek, including meals and overnight stays in rustic equestrian *gîtes*. *(M. Terroux Olivier, Mas de Cacharel, Route de Cacharel-D85A, 13460 Les Saintes Maries de la Mer, ☎ 33 04 90 97 84 10, fax 33 04 90 97 87 97, info@camargueacheval.com, www.camargueacheval.com).*

Monsieur Gallo, at **Promenade des Rieges**, runs week-long pony treks for beginners to advanced riders in the Petite Camargue and the Grande Camargue. *(Route de Cacharel, 13460 Les Saintes Maries de la Mer, ☎/fax 33 04 90 97 91 38, info@promenadedesrieges.com, www.promenadedesrieges).*

At **Brenda - Centre Tourisme Equestre**, English-born Madame Brenda Gatti offers five-day programs that include lessons (what the French call *formations*) and Camargue treks. *(Mas Saint Georges, Astouin, 13460 Les Saintes Maries de la Mer, ☎ 33 04 90 97 52 08, fax 33 04 90 97 50 19, BrendaCTE@aol.com, www.brendatourismeequestre.com).*

Most Camargue stables belong to the Association Camarguaise de Tourisme Equestre (ACTE), which has set a range of registered prices with the Les Saintes Maries de la Mer tourist office. An hour's horse rental should cost between €14 and €16. A full day out will cost between €55 and €80 and starts at 9:30 am. A.C.T.E. suggests a standard day out that includes a ride across the interior of the Camargue, taking in étangs, rice paddies, and so forth; a crossing of the Petit Rhône on the Bac du Sauvage, and then a ride along a pine-bordered beach. A supplement is charged for a picnic or barbecue on the beach. Multiple-day treks with A.C.T.E. members cost from €80 to €115 per day depending on the standard of accommodation and meals. A list of members of A.C.T.E. can be obtained from *Association Camarguaise de Tourisme Equestre, Service Élevage du P.N.R.C., Rte. d'Arles, Centre Joseph d'Arbaud,* ☎ *33 04 90 97 58 45, fax 33 04 90 97 58 48, elevage.parc@wanadoo.fr.*

On Water

Windsurfing & Sailing

Les Saintes Maries de la Mer has become a windsurfing destination because of its specially built speed canal, next to the yacht harbor, where professional windsurfers regularly break world records. Amateur speed freaks prefer conditions off the East Beach, but the steady breezes channeled down the Rhône Valley make conditions for sail-based sports good off-shore from most beaches. The local sailing school, **École Française de Voile**, offers lessons in windsurfing – which the French call *planche à voile* – sailing and catamaran sailing. They also rent canoes and sea kayaks. *(École Française de Voile, S.E.M.I.S. Capitainerie Port Gardian, Avenue Théodore Aubanel, BP74, 13460 Les Saintes Maries de la Mer,* ☎ *33 04 90 97 85 87 or 33 04 90 97 77 40, fax 33 04 90 97 97 82, e-mail through the tourist authority at info@saintesmaries.com or at portgardian@saintesmaries.com).*

The new extreme sports of **kite-surfing** and **fly-surfing** are popular at Beauduc Beach, where good wind conditions prevail for a reputed 300 days a year. The stretches of hard, empty sand see the occasional sand yacht as well.

> **Tip:** The **Camargue Wind Club** is a group of 10 enthusiasts who take part in windsurfing, fly- and, kite-surfing and sand yachting. They don't offer any services, but if you too are an experienced windsport enthusiast you might find some kindred spirits willing to share local information. *(Espace Paul Ricard, 13460 Les Sainte Maries de la Mer, ☎ 33 04 90 97 98 28 or 33 06 61 82 49 74).*

Cool-Kite, a Swiss-based school *(info@coolkite.ch, www.coolkite.ch/men122.htm,* ☎ *41 78 628 44 78)* offers kite and fly surfing courses at Beauduc. A description of the course is available on their French-language website.

Canoeing & Kayaking

The tranquil Petit Rhône meanders from Arles to the Mediterranean beach at Grand Radeau. It passes between banks covered in white poplar, ash and elm, brambles and hawthorn, occasionally opening on views of ancient *mas*, rice paddies, reed beds, sand dunes and herdsmens' huts. Paddling down, you might see rare birds of prey in the trees – a great spotted or a rare short-toed eagle among the dozens of species – or drift past shores covered with narcissi, yellow flags and tamarisk. A canoe trip serves up yet another – and completely different – Camarguaise habitat. **Kayak Vert Camargue**, based at the Mas Sylvéréal, rents unsinkable canoes by the hour or day and organizes two- and three-day river trips with overnight accommodations, meals and mini-bus shuttles. They also run combination canoe and cycle trips. *(Kayak Vert Camargue, M. and Mme. René Amar, Mas Sylvéréal, Route d'Aigues Mortes, 30600 Vauvert,* ☎ *33 04 66 73 57 17 or 33 06 09 56 06 47, fax 33 04 90 97 80 32, seminaires@camargue.fr, www.kayak.camargue.fr or www.canoe-france.com/petit-rhone/indexa.html).*

Power Boats & Jet Skis

Generally, permits are not required for river and canal boating or to captain boats with engines of 6CV capacity or less. Because some of the more powerful Jet Skis have engines of larger capacity, they are classed as boats and may require a permit. (For permit requirements, see page 102.)

These companies rent river, canal and small sea-going boats, with and without permits:

- **Rivage**: Motorboats without permits include inflatable Zodiacs or rigid 16-foot power boats. Water ski and wake board equipment can also be rented by the hour, day or week. *(Port Gardian, 13460 Les Saintes Maries de la Mer, ☎ 33 06 11 04 05 00, fax 33 04 66 53 33 57, info@rivage.fr, www.rivage.fr).* Rivage also rents Jet Skis, with and without permits, from its Port Camargue location. *(La Base Nautique de Port Camargue, ☎ 33 06 23 84 13 08).*

- **Nautic Camargue**: River and canal cruisers, by the day, hour or week, for two to 12 people, without permits. *(27 Quai des Croisades, 30220 Aigues Mortes, ☎ 33 04 66 51 56 73 or 33 04 67 94 78 93, fax 33 04 66 51 56 32 or 33 04 67 94 05 41, www.nautic.fr/uk/index.html, e-mail via the English-language website).*
- **Artimon**: Sail and motorboats from Port Camargue. Zodiac inflatables and 16-foot motorboats available without permits. *(Central Reservations, Zone Technique number 2, 30240 Port Camargue, ☎ 33 04 66 53 40 18, info@artimon.com, www.artimon.com).*

Fishing Trips

Ocean fishing is not a major activity in this area but a few boats do go out. The best way to find out about fishing trips is to visit the town harbor master's office (called the *Capitainerie*) and ask. You can also write to the local tourist information office, but be sure to ask for up-to-date information.

> **Tip:** Whatever you do, avoid the tourist excursion boats that ply the Petit Rhône and the canals. There is even a paddle wheeler! They are overpriced, overcrowded and so noisy they scare away all the wildlife.

Do I Need a Permit to Rent a Boat?

Inland waters: Although boating in rivers and canals is highly regulated, most charterers can issue a **temporary pleasure boat card** which is good for a limited time on certain waters where conditions are known to be safe – i.e., the Petit Rhône below Arles and the Canal du Rhône à Sète, but not the Grand Rhône, which is a major, commercial waterway.

Coastal waters: The French don't require permits for sailboats or for slow boats with motors of less than 6CV capacity. For anything larger, there are three levels of permits:

- La Carte Mer – for motors from 6CV to 50CV, daytime sailing within nine km (5.4 miles) of the coast.
- Le Permis Mer Côtier – for motors 50CV and higher, night sailing within a limited distance of the coast.
- Le Permis Mer Hauturier – awarded after a full boating course, for all types of boating.

If you have a registered US qualification it may be sufficient but you may need an International Certificate of Competence (ICC) to charter the larger boats. In the UK, this can be obtained from any RYA accredited school. In the US, you should check with authorities who issue your qualification.

Birdwatching

In 2002, The European Union's Convention on the Conservation of European Wildlife and Natural Habitats declared the **purple gallinule** rare in Europe. Of the estimated 6,000 breeding pairs around the Mediterranean, only six to 16 have ever been seen in France. At least one of those pairs, maybe more, enjoys the rice paddies of the Camargue.

Marsh harriers, penduline tits, Cetti's warbler, nightingales, all kinds of herons, egrets, ducks, geese, warblers, larks, shrikes, avocets, buzzards, hawks, falcons, terns and eagles, plovers, storks, cranes, not to mention greater flamingos – more than 200 bird species, many of them rare in Europe, have been reported in the Camargue wetlands.

Spring and fall are the best times of year for birding. Bring a bird book and a set of binoculars to just about any quiet spot around the marshes, the dunes and the seashore, and especially along the edge of the Étang de Vaccarès, for world-class birding.

In addition to the paths around **La Capelière** (page 97), the **Ornithological Park of Pont de Gau** (page 104) and the **sea dyke** (page 98), several other spots offer good birding opportunities. The stretch of the **D37** along the northern edge of the Étang de Vaccarès is prime territory. Look for a viewing platform at a converted pumping station on the side of the road.

Eagles are often reported in the grazing meadows, between Le Sambuc and the Gacholle Lighthouse. There are posted guides, foot and cycle paths and observation points around the **Gacholle Lighthouse** as well.

Making Sense of the Park System

The Camargue is protected by several layers of national and regional parks and nature reserves. It helps to understand these layers when enjoying the various walks, rides and visitors' centers.

- **The Camargue National Reserve**: Established 1927, the Réserve Nationale de Camargue, covers more than 32,000 acres around and including the Étang du Vaccarès. It is a UNESCO "Biosphere Reserve," one of 300 such sites in the world. The National Reserve can only be visited from the designated center at La Capelière. It can also be viewed from the sea wall and various paths along its edges. *(Camargue National Reserve, 13200 Arles, on the D36, 20 km / 12 miles from Arles.* ☎ *33 04 90 97 00 97, fax 33 04 90 97 01 44. Open 9 am to 1 pm and 2 to 6 pm, April through September. Closes one hour earlier and on Tuesdays, October through March; small entrance fee.)*

- **The Regional Natural Park**: Created in 1970, the Parc Naturel Regional de Camargue is intended to balance the ecology and human activities of the area and to preserve much of the traditional lifestyle of the *mas* and *manade*. It covers all of the Île de la Camargue, the Rhône Delta area between the arms of the Petit and Grand Rhône. It includes freshwater marshes, temporary marshes and periodically flooded saltwater marshes. *(Musée Camarguais, Mas du Pont de Rousty, 13200 Arles, on the D570, 12 km / 7½ miles from Arles,* ☎ *33 04 90 97 10 40 or 33 04 90 97 86 32, fax 33 04 90 97 12 07, info@parc-camargue.fr, www.parcs-naturels-regionaux.tm.fr/lesparcs/camaa_en.html).*

- **The Ornithological Park of Pont de Gau**: Four km/2½ miles from Les Saintes Maries de la Mer, an information center gives way to acres of marshland, laced with paths and dotted with blinds from which to watch hundreds of species of birds as well as herds of bulls and horses. The center of the park is devoted to birds of prey. Some larger birds are caged. A visit to the Parc Ornithologique du Pont de Gau is a useful introduction to the Camargue for both experienced and inexperienced bird watchers. *(RD570, Quartier Pont de Gau, 13460 Les Saintes Maries de la Mer,* ☎ *33 04 90 97 82 62, fax 33 04 90 97 74 77, open every day, 9 am to sunset, April through September. 10 am to sunset, October through March. Small entrance fee.)*

Vaucluse, the Lubéron & Mont Ventoux

The Scented Hills

Head north and east of Avignon and the landscape of Provence changes dramatically. The fertile plains of western Vaucluse, known as the Comtat Venaissin, give way to rising, forested hills and mountains. It is here that the South of France begins to lift itself into the first intimations of the Pre-Alpes.

Vineyards, olive groves and orchards spread across valley floors. Three wine growing areas contribute to the region's prosperity. Both the Côtes du Ventoux and the Côtes du Lubéron produce delicate young wines, while several world-class Côte de Rhône vineyards are located within Vaucluse. The valleys and plains are also known for cherries, apricots, figs and melons, including the small, rich Cavaillon melons grown around their namesake town.

IN THIS CHAPTER	
■ Apt	109
■ Carpentras	111
■ Gordes	113
■ Orange	116
■ Vaison la Romaine	118
■ Châteauneuf du Pape	121
■ Fontaine de Vauclude	121
■ L'Isle Sur La Sorgue	123
■ Rouissillon	124
■ Festivals & Fêtes	125
■ Music & Dance	126
■ Shopping	126
■ Where to Stay	128
■ Where to Eat	134
■ Adventures	136

Wild boars prowl the oak and chestnut forests of the uplands where farmers gather prized black truffles. Locals who, like mushroom gatherers, keep their fields secret, call these *rabasses*. At least 75% of all the truffles sold in France come from the Vaucluse and more than 50% exchange hands in the Carpentras truffle market (page 127).

There are dense pine woods where cicadas, the symbol of Provence, sing, deep limestone canyons and foothills covered with fragrant herbs. The colorful, ochre-rich area is known as the *Provençal Colorado* because of the flaming colors of its soils. Ochre mining was once a traditional activity in

Above the lavender, snow-capped Mont Ventoux (© N&F Michel, Collection CDT Vaucluse)

this part of the Apt region. For many generations, it moulded both the landscape and the men who lived there.

Vaucluse is considered the center of Provence and provides some of the region's most iconic images – from the rows of blooming lavender to the isolated summit of Mont Ventoux, scourge of cyclists and famous "killer" climb of many a Tour de France.

And while there are opportunities for hiking, climbing, canoeing, swimming, fishing, spelunking, hang-gliding, ballooning, skiing and snow-shoeing, it is cycling for which Vaucluse is best loved by adventure travelers. Its rolling hills present cyclists at every level of experience with moderate to challenging ascents. The scenery – golden hamlets, proud perched villages, sweeping vistas – make for some of the best cycling in France.

There are also nearly 2,500 miles of well-marked hiking paths and three important climbing areas – **Buoux, Bédoin** and **les Dentelles de Montmirail**.

> **Did you know?** *The word Vaucluse comes from Vallis Clausa, Latin for "closed valley" – the location of the Fontaine de Vaucluse (page 121), the source of the Sorgue River and one of the area's most mysterious and remarkable natural features. In fact, Vaucluse is divided into several distinctive areas, each with a slightly different micro-climate.*

■ Getting Here & Getting Around

Avignon is the most convenient gateway to this region. **Orange**, which is also on the TGV rail line from Paris, is an alternative. Local train service is poor to non-existant in the Lubéron and the Vaucluse, but regular bus services link most villages to hubs in Avignon, Carpentras, Apt, L'Isle Sur La Sorgue, Cavaillon, Orange. (See pages 26-27, and specific destination pages for bus services).

■ The Regions of Vaucluse

Haut Vaucluse

Also known as Provence des Papes or The Papal Enclaves, Haut Vaucluse covers the region of vineyards and estates once controlled by the Avignon popes. The northernmost section of Vaucluse, it includes some of the best Côte de Rhône vineyards – Châteauneuf du Pape, Gigondas and Vacqueyras, large areas in lavender cultivation and the wonderful Roman towns of Orange and Vaison la Romaine. Hiking or rock climbing on Les Dentelles de Montmirail – so named because of the lacy limestone formations at the summit – offers great views of Mont Ventoux and the surrounding countryside.

Vaucluse

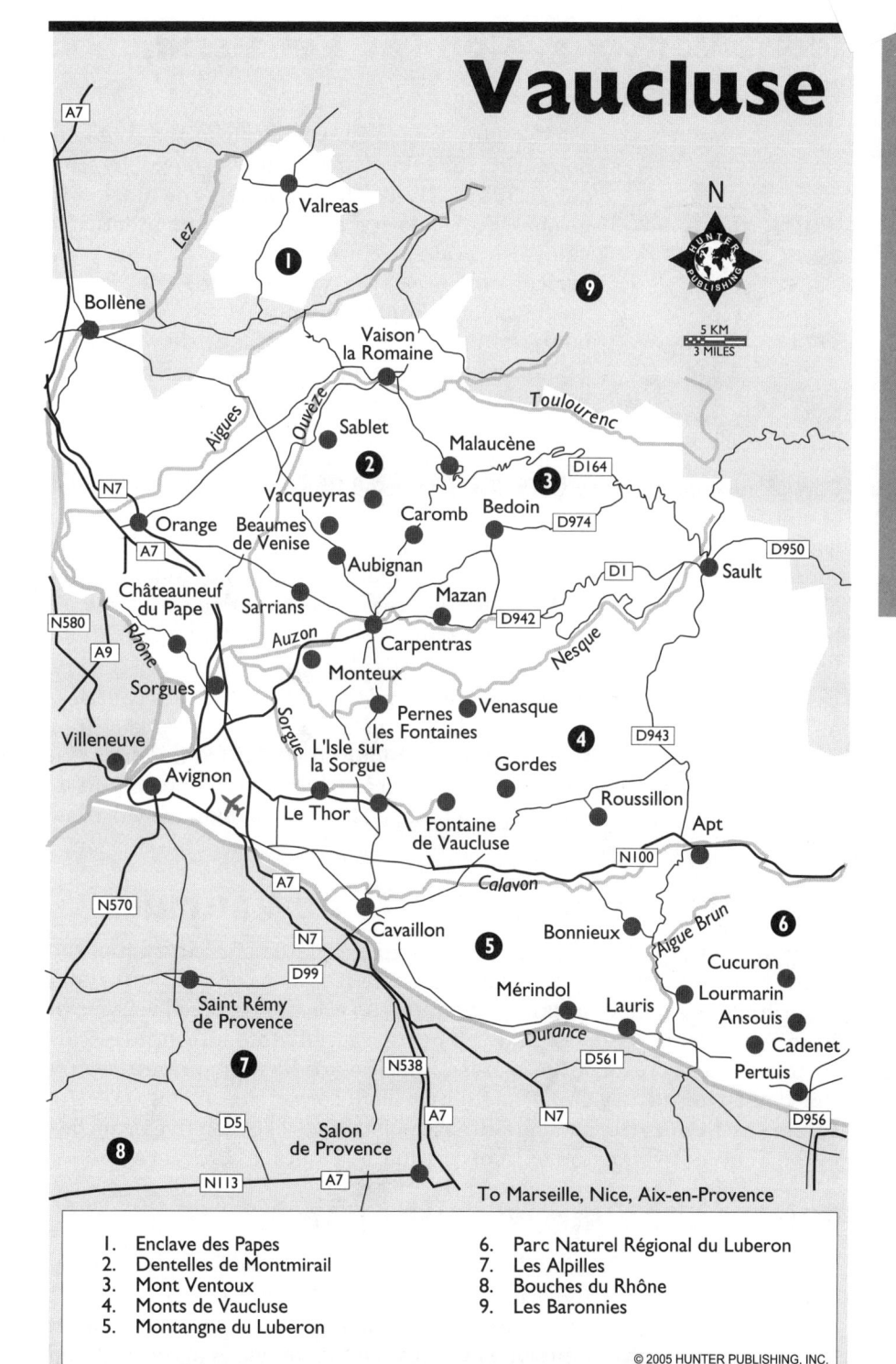

1. Enclave des Papes
2. Dentelles de Montmirail
3. Mont Ventoux
4. Monts de Vaucluse
5. Montangne du Luberon
6. Parc Naturel Régional du Luberon
7. Les Alpilles
8. Bouches du Rhône
9. Les Baronnies

© 2005 HUNTER PUBLISHING, INC.

Mont Ventoux, Comtat Venaissin, Pays de Sault

The Comtat Venaissin was given to the Avignon popes in 1274 by King Philip (known by the delightfully silly epithet of Philip the Rash). It formed the majority of their income-producing vineyards and agricultural estates. Primarily an agricultural area, the villages here are rich in medieval and Roman history. Mont Ventoux, at more than 6,200 feet, is sometimes snow-capped. The name is a Provençal variation of the French word for windy – *venteux* – and from late autumn to early spring, a windplume of snow from the summit can be seen from most vantage points. Part of the mountain is a UNESCO Protected Biosphere. At the changing of the seasons, Mont Ventoux slices through the climate; it is always warmer and sunnier on the southern slope. Villages with picturesque squares and evocative names like St. Pierre de Vassols, Modène and Mazan – often little more than a few houses, a church with a wrought iron bell tower, and a café or bar tabac – hug its lower slopes and hide in its folds, offering lots of possibilities for exploration.

Below it, the Côte de Ventoux vineyards and the fruit orchards of cherries, apricots and figs turn red and golden in the autumn. The area is rich in cycling and hiking paths – including mountain bike trails *down* the mountain (for the brave) and the Mont Ventoux circuit (for the very fit or slightly mad!). Lavender covers the hills in the Pays de Sault at the eastern reach of this area.

Pays de Sorgues, Monts de Vaucluse

Despite the use of "mountain," or sometimes "plateau," in its name, the range that gives this *département* its name is a mass of small hills and bluffs hugging tight little valleys. Some of the prettiest perched villages in France, including **Gordes** and the ochre-colored **Roussillon**, are scattered along the crests of these steep hills. So are Roman antiquities and the dome-shaped dry-stone shelters called *bories* (see pages 114-15). **L'Isle sur la Sorgue**, a village situated on islands between five branches of the Sorgue River, is the unlikely antiquing capital of Provence.

The Montagne du Lubéron

Separated from the Vaucluse by the broad expanse of the **Calavon Valley** and the **Imergue,** the Lubéron spreads across the landscape like a giant slab of bread dough. The mountain is divided in two by the **Lourmarin Valley** and the **Aigue Brun River**, with the higher peaks to the east and

The mass of the Lubéron, seen from Gordes on the edge of the Vaucluse. Tiny villages, just visible, shelter in the folds of its base. © Ferne Arfin

the **Petit Luberon** to the west. The entire area is included in a regional nature park, criss-crossed with well-marked hiking and cycling trails, including an outstanding, 100-km/62-mile cycle circuit (See *Adventures on Wheels*, pages 139 ff). It also has some outstanding rock climbing, notably at **Buoux**. Near **Rustrel**, the **Provençal Colorado**, a man-made "canyon" created by several hundred years of ochre mining, is a fascinating and colorful hike. The climate here is more Mediterranean than the rest of Vaucluse. Drier and warmer, it is protected by massed hills from the Rhône Valley's Mistral winds. Côte de Lubéron villages on the north slope, following the path of the narrow, bamboo-lined Calavon River, can be quiet and magically strange to cycle through. Once again, part of the Luberon is a UNESCO Protected Biosphere.

■ Principal Destinations

Apt

The mysteriously silence of Maubec, a village in the shadow of the Lubéron. © Ferne Arfin

The market in Apt. ©BisetValerie, Collection CDT Vaucluse

With a population of more than 11,000, Apt is a relatively big town by local standards. It is surrounded by industrial suburbs and apartment houses. Most remnants of its days as an important Roman city are hidden in private cellars, unexcavated, or locked inside its currently closed museum. So it may seem, at first glance, an unlikely choice of destination.

But Apt, in the Cavalon Valley between the Vaucluse Plateau and the Lubéron, is at the very center of the **Lubéron Regional Nature Park** and sits at the mid-point of the 100-km/62-mile Lubéron cycle route (page 140) between **Cavaillon** and **Forcalquier**. It is in the middle of very good hiking country, at the convergence of several Grandes Randonées, the French long-distance paths (the GR4, GR6 and

GR92 are nearby and the GR9 goes right through the center of town). It is also within easy reach of the **Provençal Colorado** and the wide, equipped climbing cliffs at **Buoux** (page 138). Add to this the fact that it is surrounded by some of the Lubéron's most picturesque perched villages and, all in all, it is an ideal base for exploring the entire region.

The old town, surrounded by walls, dates mainly from the Middle Ages. It is a warren of narrow streets, vaulted passages and small fountain-centered squares built around the 11th- and 12th-century **Cathedral of Ste Anne**. The church, at left, which contains the saint's relics, was the first sanctuary in France dedicated to her and was an important pilgrimage center. A traditional pilgrim procession still takes place on the last Sunday of July.

A few remains of Roman monuments can be seen below the church (a second-century chapel and fourth-century sarcophagus), in the town center and in the Place Jean-Jaurès, which may have been the Forum.

It was probably pilgrims who originally turned Apt into a bustling market town. A market has taken place there since the 12th century. The French love to classify and rate things – in 1996, the Grand Marché d'Apt was classified as one of France's 100 Exceptional French Markets because of its atmosphere, originality and permanence. It has been trading on Saturday mornings, in the same location, for at least 500 years, as ordered by the Sénéchal de Provence in 1504.

The ochre industry, which once contributed to the town's economy, died out in the 1930s when natural ochre, a pigment made of sand, clay and iron oxide, was replaced with synthetics. Today Apt is noted for its glacé fruit – the glistening melons, whole pineapples, peaches must be seen to be believed – lavender essence and faience pottery. From late November, black truffles, a regional treasure, can be found (for a price!) at the Saturday market.

Getting Here: 53 km/33 miles west of Avignon on the N100. Leave Avignon on the N7 South, signposted for Cavaillon. After about 11 km/seven miles stay on the right when the road divides; you will leave the N7 and pick up the D973 west for 4½ km/2.8 miles. Then continue on the right to join the D22. Just before Coustellet, this road becomes the N100. Apt is about 25 km/15 miles farther on this road. Local bus service is available from Avignon. (See pages 26-27 for local bus information.)

Sightseeing

Tourist Information: Office de Tourisme, 20 Avenue Philippe de Girard, 84400 Apt, ☎ 33 04 90 74 03 18, fax 33 04 90 04 64 30, ot@apt.fr, www.ot-apt.fr.

Cathedral of Ste Anne: This Baroque basilica was built in the 17th century after a pilgrimage visit by Anne of Austria. Parts of the crypt date from the Roman period. The Treasury in the sacristy includes rare religious objects, reliquaries, ancient manuscripts and incunabula (books printed before 1501). A flag, known as the veil of Ste Anne and used to cover the saint's relics during processions, is actually an Arab standard woven in the 11th century for a Kalif and carried back from the Crusades. The Treasury and Crypt, 8 Rue Ste Delphine. Open July, August and September, Tuesday to Saturday, from 3 to 5 pm, except during holy offices.

Carpentras

On the plains below Mont Ventoux and capital of the Comtat Venaissin area, Carpentras was an important market town and agricultural trading center for the local Celtic-Ligurian tribes long before the Romans arrived. A Roman colony under Julius Caesar, it was caught up in the warfare and turbulence that tore across much of Provence in the Dark and Early Middle Ages. Given to the Papal States in the 13th century, it offered refuge to Jews being expelled at that time from the rest of France and from as far afield as England. It did not become part of France until after the French Revolution.

Carpentras is famous for its **truffle market** (see page 127) and is also a center for cherries. During the summer months, the fruit selection at the Friday morning market is irresistable. With its surrounding villages, it has supported vineyards for 2,000 years. The locally invented hard candies, called *berlingots*, are a popular souvenir.

Today, this small, provincial market town retains several fine examples of 18th-century Italianate Baroque architecture. It is well-located for hikers or cyclists on Mont Ventoux and Les Dentelles de Montmirail who want a base with a reasonable selection of restaurants and shops as well as a big market.

Getting Here: 15 km/9.3 miles west of the Avignon TGV Station, 25 km/15½ miles from Avignon center. Leave Avignon on the N7 north, exit onto the D942 to Carpentras. Trans Vaucluse provides regular bus service from Avignon. Schedule information from their

French-language www.ville-carpentras.fr/transports/horairestransport.htm or inquire at Avignon TGV station.

Sightseeing

Tourist Information: Office de Tourisme, Hotel-Dieu, Place Aristide-Briand, Carpentras, ☎ 33 04 90 63 00 78, fax 33 04 90 60 41 02 tourist.carpentras@axit.fr, www.ville-carpentras.fr/english/index.html or www.tourisme.fr/carpentras/e-index.htm.

Cathedral of St Siffrein: Built over a period of more than 100 years in the 14th and 16th centuries, primarily in a style known as Southern Gothic. The façade was restored in 2004. Of particular interest, the Porte Juive is an example of the Gothic Flamboyant style and leads to a mysterious baptistry where converts first entered. You reach the pedestrian town center from the Rue de la République. The Cathedral is at the heart of the old town. Always open, free entry.

The Synagogue: The oldest synagogue in France and one of the oldest in Europe, this one dates from 1367. The basement, which is now a small museum, contains a bakery for unleavened bread and a mikvah, a bath for ritual cleansing, fed by a natural spring. Behind a plain façade, the sanctuary itself is an elegant example of 18th-century decoration. *(Place Juiverie off Rue de la Sous-Prefecture. Visits by arrangement.* ☎ *33 04 90 63 39 97.)*

The Hôtel-Dieu: Once the town's hospital, this 18th-century Baroque building on Place Aristide-Briand became a cultural center in time for the millennium and houses the tourist information center. It includes an Italian Baroque chapel decorated with colored marble and an 18th-century pharmacy, preserved with its original faience pots and jars as well as cabinets painted by Duplessis, Louis XVI's court painter. The pharmacy is open Mondays, Wednesdays and Thursdays from 9 to 11:30 am. There is a small entry fee.

Porte d'Orange: A 14th-century fortified gateway is all that remains visible of the town center fortifications and ramparts – now, as in many Provençal towns, hidden by houses built up against them. The Porte d'Orange guards the northern entrance to the town center off Boulevard Leclerc.

Place du 8 Mai: This terrace overlooking the Auzon River in the northern corner of the old town offers an excellent vantage point for viewing Les Dentelles de Montmirail.

The Pope's Jews

In Carpentras, the oldest synagogue in France, originally built in 1367, bears witness to a remarkable and little-known story of religious belief, interfaith tolerance and, probably, mutual convenience.

Jews arrived in Roman Gaul – i.e., the South of France – as early as the destruction of Masada, in the year 73. By the Middle Ages, small Jewish communities had become important minorities in most urban centers of the region. They lived in ghettos, called *carrières*, usually in the center of town, which were locked at night. Laws required both men and women to wear identifying items of clothing. But, otherwise, Jews participated in the society of the time – especially in medicine, philosophy, science and business, but also as bakers, stone cutters, masons and weavers. Nostradamas was said to have come from a family of Jewish doctors in St. Rémy.

After the Black Plague, in the 14th century, when Jews were expelled from most of France, they were welcomed and protected by the Avignon Popes who believed, in the words of St. Bernard de Clairvaux, "He who harms a Jew is as guilty as if he had set to the eye of Jesus himself, for the Jews are his flesh and bones."

They became known as The Pope's Jews and in the Papal lands around Avignon and the Comtat Venaissin, they enjoyed freedom of worship and residence. Communities flourished in Avignon, Cavaillon, Carpentras, Pernes les Fontaines and L'Isle sur Sorgue.

The Vaucluse Tourist Board has created a suggested itinerary of key Jewish sites in the region: **The Road to Jewish Heritage in the South of France**. Guided visits can be arranged in several towns along the route. For more information, and a copy of the itinerary booklet, contact: *The Comité Départemental du Tourisme de Vaucluse, 12 Rue Collège de la Croix, BP 147, 84008 Avignon Cedex,* ☎ *33 04 90 86 43 42.*

Gordes

Pedalling uphill along the D15, I thought I had used up my last reserve of strength and was about to dismount and push my bicycle the rest of the way when I saw Gordes. Is it possible to be energized by a view? If so, Gordes, as seen from this approach, is the one to do it. You round a hairpin turn and, without warning, you're facing one of the most famous views in Provence. In fact the Bélvèdere, a rocky vantage point along the way, is known locally as monkey rock because of all the tourists who stop there to gape and take photographs. Seen from this angle, the 12th-century perched village with its ramparts, spirals around a bluff at the edge of the Vaucluse. It has been the subject of thousands of paintings, possibly millions of postcards and no matter how familiar it may be, it is still breathtaking. The artists Marc Chagall, who summered here, and Vasereley, who lived in Gordes year-round, must have thought so too. Today it is as popular as ever with artists and celebrities – making for a lively art gallery and craft scene.

Tall, austere houses, built of the local, yellow sandstone, march up steep lanes. Though the buildings – including a castle and a church – date from the Middle Ages or later, the streets, paved with stepped river stones and called *calades*, are much older. Gordes was already an important fortified town before the Roman era.

Photogenic and well-located for both the Vaucluse and the Lubéron, Gordes has several good restaurants, guest houses and hotels and is understandably popular. Avoid the summer crowds and enjoy it in spring and autumn when the village is at its most mellow.

Getting Here: 35 km/22 miles west of Avignon on the N100. Leave Avignon on the N7 South, signposted for Cavaillon. After about 11 km/seven miles, the road divides; stay on the right. You will leave the N7 and pick up the D973 west for about 4½ km/2.8 miles. Then continue on the right to join the D22. Just before Coustellet, this road becomes the N100. Take a left turn onto the D2, then take the left fork onto the D15 into Gordes. There is twice-a-day bus service from Cavaillon. (See pages 26-27 for local bus information).

LES BORIES

Beehive-shaped stone shelters and dwellings are scattered all over the Lubéron. Some are of recent vintage, some appear to be ageless. In the 18th century, these shelters were often used as herdsmen's huts, but no one really knows how long ago the craft of building them, or the impulse to do so, originated. Evidence of bories has been found going back 3,000 years. Recent theories suggest they were simply a way to use up all the stones cleared from the fields. As many as 200,000 to 300,000 individually positioned stones are used in the construction of one borie. Given such utilitarian beginnings, their design is remarkable. Constructed of dry stone, without the use of mortar or cement, they are nevertheless watertight and symmetrical. The most important group of bories in Provence is just outside Gordes (page 115).

Sightseeing

Tourist Information: Office de Tourisme, Le Château, 84220 Gordes, ☎ 33 04 90 72 02 75, fax 33 04 90 72 02 26, office.gordes@wanadoo.fr, www.gordes-village.com.

The Village of Bories: Sheep-pens, stone bread ovens, wine vats, threshing areas, narrow alleys and "city walls," all built of dry stone. Classified by the French Government as a Historical Monument in 1977, the village is a rare example of "spontaneous architecture" and demonstrates a rural lifestyle with traditional objects and tools. A museum on the site documents their history and construction. Located on the D15, about a mile from the village. *Village des Bories, Les Savournins, 84200 Gordes, open every day from 9 am to sunset. ☎ 33 04 90 72 03 48, fax 33 04 90 72 04 39.*

The Castle: At the very top of Gordes, the castle dates from 1031, with additions made in 1525. It demonstrates both medieval and Renaissance styles.

In more recent times, the castle was touched with piquant scandal. It was owned and restored by the artist Vasarely, who created a foundation and museum to display his works. After he died in 1997, the foundation was accused of financial improprieties and alleged tax fraud, lost its tax-exempt status and saw one of its executives jailed.

Today, a museum devoted to a local artist, Pol Mara, occupies the castle, providing the opportunity to see the building, its Renaissance spiral staircase and monumental fireplace. Reach the castle by spiraling up to the very top of the town. There is a tourist office at the castle. *Open every day, except Christmas and New Year's Day, 10 am to noon and 2 to 6 pm. Information at the tourist office.*

Sénanque Abbey: Just outside Gordes, in a closed valley, this is a Cistercian Abbey in continual use since 1148. Although a community of monks still live and work here, all the original buildings can be visited. *Abbaye Notre Dame de Sénanque, 84220 Gordes. Leave Gordes on the D15 and take the D177 to the right. ☎ 33 04 90 72 05 72, fax 33 04 90 72 15 70, visites@senanque.fr, www.senanque.fr. Adult admission €6, children and students reduced rate, priests and members of religious orders, free. Open 10 am to noon and 2 to 5:30 pm.*

Le Moulin de Bouillons: This claims to be the oldest working olive oil press, still in working order, in the world. The axle of the press is made of a seven-ton oak trunk. The oil press itself is Gallo-Roman. A small museum presents the history of Le Vrai Savon de Marseille, the popular olive oil soap of the region. Located about six miles from Gordes in Saint Pantaléon. Ask at the tourist information office in the Castle for directions. *Musée du Moulin des Bouillons, Route de Saint Pantaléon, 84480 Gordes,* ☎ *33 04 90 72 22 11, fax 33 04 90 72 20 48. Open February 1 to October 30, 10 am to noon and 2 to 5 pm in winter. One hour later closing in summer. Closed Tuesdays.*

Orange

The main reason for coming to Orange is the city's Roman heritage. But don't dismiss the monuments here as yet more piles of ruins (let's face it, the Romans left behind so much in Provence, it is easy to become jaded). The UNESCO-listed **Triumphal Arch** and **Théâtre Antique** are really spectacular. In fact, the theater is

Les Choragies, France's oldest music festival, at the Roman Theater in Orange. © D.Lefranc, Collection CDTVaucluse

considered to be the most complete surviving example in the world. King Louis XIV called its gigantic exterior, "The finest wall in my kingdom."

The structure of the wall, which is pierced and chambered, creates outstanding acoustics, a fact discovered in the mid-19th century when, after 1,500 years of neglect, the restored theater became a performance venue again. Since 1869, it has hosted **Les Choragies** – an opera festival that is the oldest music festival in France. Other festivals and dramas of all kinds take place here from late spring to mid-fall.

Orange is a big town, with a population of about 30,000, ringed with industrial suburbs and apartment buildings. But the old town is comfortable and easy to explore, with café-lined boulevards, shops selling Provençal specialties and 2,000 years of history visible around every corner. In addition to Roman history, Orange was briefly a principality of Holland and was caught up in the religious and dynastic wars that wracked this region in the Middle Ages and early Renaissance. There is a good selection of hotels and restaurants and good access to Avignon, as well as hiking and cycling on *Les Dentelles de Montmirail.*

Tip: By one of those mysterious conjunctions of climate and geography, Orange regularly records the highest temperatures in France. What better excuse for frequent café stops to drink citron pressé!

Getting Here: Two TGV trains per day from Paris Gare de Lyon to Orange, three hours and 13 minutes. (See pages 26-27 for information on booking rail services.) By car, Orange is 29 km/18 miles from Avignon at the junction of the A9 and the A7 – the Autoroute du Soleil. Bus and taxi services are available from Avignon. Information about local buses from the bus station – Gare Routière d'Orange, ☎ 33 04 90 34 15 59.

Sightseeing

Tourist Information: Office de Tourisme, 5 cours Aristide Briand, 84100 Orange, ☎ 33 04 90 34 70 88, fax 33 04 90 34 99 62, officetourismeorange@wannadoo.fr, www.provence-orange.com/indexuk.htm. There is also a walk-in office, open from April to September, across from the Roman Theater in the Place des Frères Mounet. For information about performance schedules and booking Les Choragies, ☎ 33 04 90 34 24 24, fax 33 04 90 11 04 04, info@choregoes.asso.fr, ww.choregies.asso.fr/angl/bienvenue.htm.

The Théâtre Antique and Museum: The best-preserved Roman theater in the world. Its back wall, nearly 350 feet long and 118 feet high, supports a magnificent and nearly complete scena – the backdrop of a classic theater. Abandoned when Christian kings prohibited pagan entertainments in about 300 AD, it had filled up with houses – only the back wall suggesting what lay beneath. Restoration in the 19th century took nearly 40 years. Today, it seats 7,000 in a semi-circle of tiers built against a hill. The acoustics are superb and, if you have even a slight interest in theater, walking the stage area is magic. There is access to the ruins of a Roman Gymnasium and Capitol, next to the theater. A museum across the street details the town's colorful history and the restoration of the theater. Place des Frères Mounet. *Open every day of the year, 9 am to 5 pm, November through February; to 6 pm, October and March; to 7 pm April, May and September; and to 8 pm, June through August. There is a small admission fee.*

The Triumphal Arch: The Romans suffered one of their worst defeats here in 105 BC at the hands of Teutonic tribes. Three years later, they saw the "barbarians" off, but it was not until 70 years later that they founded a colony. Later, to mark a separation between the world of the dead (some 100,000 Roman legionnaires are said to have fallen) and the world of the living – and to put their Imperial stamp on the landscape – they built the great triumphal arch that still stands. The friezes on the northern side are nearly intact and tell the story of the battles and the founding of the Roman colony. The location is just north of the old town on the Roman Via Agrippa, now known as Avenue de l'Arc de Triomphe. It's about a 10-minute walk from town.

Colline St Eutrope: The hill overlooking the town is the site of the first settlements and the devastating battle of 105 BC. Now a park, it has a small temple at the site of the town's original spring, as well as traces of three other temples. It offers a splendid panorama of Orange.

Vaison la Romaine

The first time I saw Vaison la Romaine, people were singing in the streets. I had wandered out of lavender country and down through the wooded hills that encircle the town, not knowing what to expect. Small groups sang harmony around the fountains, à cappella quartets hummed in the parks and along a boulevard of cafés different choruses rehearsed, led by conductors in halter tops, shorts and straw hats.

I had, inadvertently arrived in time for *Les Choralies*, 10 days in August when choristers from all over the world descend on Vaison la Romaine (see *Festivals and Fêtes*, page 125).

Needless to say, I was enchanted. Yet *Les Choralies* is a mere sideshow to the real reasons for visiting – the Roman residential districts and the medieval *haute ville*.

Excavations of the Roman town began before World War I. Almost 40 acres (of an estimated 150 to 175) of streets, shops, large residential villas (some of the most spacious in Roman Gaul), thermal baths and working people's quarters have been unearthed. Compared to the monumental or triumphal Roman structures found elsewhere, these streets are distinctly domestic and exploring them is evocative and uncanny. Decorative details and objects, including a silver bust and a complex mosaic floor, can be seen in the adjoining museum.

Across the Ouvèze River, linked to the (mainly) 18th-century town and the Roman districts by an unusual, single-arch Roman bridge, is the medieval town. Built on a hill for defensive reasons in the 14th century, it was virtually abandoned in more peaceful periods as residents moved down to the fertile valley floor. It has been restored in recent times, primarily through residential development, without losing its distinctive medieval character.

In 1992, the Ouvèze flooded, destroying or damaging more than 300 modern homes along the river and washing out the modern bridge. Older buildings and the Roman bridge were undamaged.

Getting Here: 47 km/29 miles northeast of Avignon, 27 km/16.8 miles northeast of Orange. Take the A9 north to the Orange-Centre Ville exit, then the D975 northeast to Vaison la Romaine. There is bus service from Orange or Carpentras. The Office de Tourisme can provide details of bus and taxi companies.

Sightseeing

Tourist Information: Office de Tourisme, BP 53 Place du Chanoine Sautel, ☎ 33 04 90 36 02 11, fax 33 04 90 28 76 04, tourisme@Vaison la Romaine.com or ot-vaison@axit.fr, www.vaison-la-romaine.com.

ALL-IN-ONE TICKET

Admission tickets are a good value in Vaison la Romaine. One ticket lasts the duration of your stay and is valid for all sites in the town – the Roman Ruins, the Museum, the Théâtre Antique, the Cathedral and Cloister and the guided tours of the medieval town. The ticket is also good for up to five guided tours in a four-day period. Price for adults is €7, students, €3.50, children, €3, under 12, free. See the tourist office.

The Roman Ruins

There are two distinct districts of Roman ruins, on either side of Avenue Charles de Gaulle in the center of the lower town and north of the Ouvèze River. *Both are open from 10 am to noon and 2 to 4 pm from November to January; from 10 am to 12:30 pm and 2 to 6 pm, October and March through May. From June to September, the two archaeological sites, the Quartier de Puymin and the Quartier de la Villasse, have different hours. The Archaeological Museum stays open about a half-hour longer.*

The Quartier de Puymin: Includes the remains of a substantial mansion of a rich family, La Maison des Messii; an enclosed promenade, Le Portique de Pompée; terraced, working-class quarters, Les Maisons de Rapport; and a public bath house, called a nymphée. The Museum, where you can see decorative details excavated from the houses, along with a silver bust and elaborate mosaics, is part of this site. The Théâtre Antique, smaller than those at Orange or Arles but restored and in regular use, adjoins the Puymin site. *Summer hours are 9:30 am to 6 pm, June and September; to 6:30 pm in July and August.*

The Quartier de la Villasse: Includes two mansions, La Maison Dauphin and La Maison Buste D'Argent (where the silver bust was found), a street of shops, a street lined with columns and a central square with a basilica. *Summer hours are 9:30 am to 12:30 pm and 2 to 6 pm, June and September; to 6:30 pm in July and August.* Night-time visits, called **Les Nocturiales**, to the la Villasse district, accompanied by illuminations and readings, are held several nights a week, from 10 to 11 pm, June through September. Check with the tourist information office for dates.

The Roman Meal: On Friday nights, during July and August, the tourist authority organizes a Roman meal, based on ancient recipes and prepared by a local restaurant. Information and tickets at the tourist information office.

The Medieval District

The *Haute Ville,* on the hill south of the river, is mostly residential but its small restored stone houses, narrow cobbled lanes and small squares, decorated with fountains, are very atmospheric and make for an interesting afternoon stroll. There is a Bishop's palace, a 14th-century fortified gateway, a bell tower and a 14th-century church. Guided walks are available through the tourist office for holders of all-in-one tickets.

The Château: Climb the steep path above the *Haute Ville* to the ruins of the 12th-century castle of Count Raymond of Toulouse for good views over the town, the Ouvèze Valley and Mont Ventoux.

The Cathedral of Notre Dame and Cloister: North of the river, adjoining the Quartier Puymin and open the same hours, the Cathedral was started during the sixth or seventh century, in the Merovingian period, and, along with the Cloister, was rebuilt in the 11th and 12th century. It is considered one of the best examples of an early Romanesque cathedral in Provence.

La Ferme des Arts: An ancient farmhouse on the Puymin hill, adjoining the Théâtre Antique, is the venue for a changing series of contemporary art exhibitions.

> **Did you know?** The Italian poet Petrarch climbed Mont Ventoux early in the 14th century and wrote about it in a classic of Renaissance humanism, *The Ascent of Mont Ventoux*. From the top, he described views of Lyons, the Italian Alps, the Bay of Marseille. "I stood in a daze, to see the clouds beneath our feet," he wrote. Petrarch began his climb from Malaucène, a village not far from Vaison la Romaine, on the northern slope. Today, the tourist office there organizes night climbs along Petrarch's route. For more information contact *Malaucène Tourist Office,* ☎ *33 04 90 65 22 59, ot-malaucene@axit.fr.*

■ Worth a Side-Trip

Châteauneuf du Pape

The 14th-century summer residence of the Avignon Popes (the name literally means the "Pope's new castle"), Châteauneuf du Pape now exists primarily as a place to taste and buy its famous Côtes de Rhône wine – with an opportunity to do both seemingly every 50 feet. Dominated by the towering ruins of the Papal summer palace (destroyed in WWII), the town's narrow streets of golden medieval houses, with their red tile roofs and pastel shutters, wind down into the vineyards. There are pleasant and relatively undemanding opportunities for hiking and cycling through the vineyards and along the Rhône. A local circuit for walkers loops through the vineyards and along the river, passing several lovely wine estates. Information on local paths is available from the Tourist Information Office.

Getting Here: 18 km/11 miles north of Avignon. From Avignon, take the N7 north to the D66. Turn left (west) on the D66 and follow signposts. Nearest local rail service: Sorgues (4½ miles) or Orange (eight miles).

More Information: Tourist Office, Place du Portail, 84230, Châteauneuf du Pape, ☎ 33 04 90 83 71 08, fax 33 04 90 83 50 34, tourisme-chato9-pape@wanadoo.fr, http://perso.wanadoo.fr/ot-chato9-pape.

Fontaine de Vaucluse

A scenic, museum-filled village on the site of one of the most powerful natural springs in the world. It is located in a dramatic closed valley, *vallis clausa* in Latin (the origin of the name Vaucluse), surrounded by towering limestone bluffs and steep, stony hills. The Italian poet Petrarch, who lived here in the 14th century pining for his muse, made the *"Fontaine"* world famous. One of the town's more interesting museums (and there are seven rather good ones here) is **The Petrarch Museum and Library**, which commemorates him. There is also a glass-blowing museum, the **Cristallerie des Papes**, and the **Moulin à Papier Vallis Clausa**, a paper mill that demonstrates how water power has been used here for papermaking since the 15th century. Shops in the **Vallis Clausa Covered Arcade** are geared to souvenir hunters but offer a good selection of gifts.

Water has powered fine paper making in Fontaine de Vaucluse since the 1400s.
© *Ferne Arfin*

Tip: Try to avoid visiting in July and August, when the village is bursting with vacationers. Also, be prepared to pay for parking. There is absolutely none that is free.

Getting Here: About 35 km/22 miles west of Avignon. From Avignon, take the N100 to L'Isle sur la Sorgue. In the center of L'Isle sur la Sorgue, join the D938 north. After just under a mile, turn right onto the D25 and follow it to Fontaine de Vaucluse. Daily bus service from Cavaillon, Apt, Fontaine de Vaucluse, Avignon, Marseille, Aix en Provence and Carpentras, through **Voyages Arnaud**, ☎ 33 04 90 38 15 58.

More Information: Maison de Tourisme, Avenue Robert Garcin, ☎ 33 04 90 20 31 44, office-tourisme.vaucluse@wanadoo.fr or fontaine-devaucluse@oti-delasorgue.fr, www.oti-delasorgue.fr/fontaine.php.

Outside the village of Fontaine de Vaucluse, at the base of high limestone cliffs, the River Sorgue rises mysteriously from the ground. The *Fontaine*, which gives its name to this entire region, is one of the

The bottom of the Fontaine de Vaucluse, at untold depths, has never been discovered.
© *D.Basse.Collection CDT Vaucluse.*

most powerful natural springs in the world. From May to early September, thousands throng the riverbanks to witness the phenomenon. Souvenir tents spring up like mushrooms after rain. By late October, the circus has moved on, giving those wise enough to visit in the autumn the time and space to really appreciate one of the genuine wonders of France.

The Fontaine de Vaucluse, a clear, green, apparently motionless pool, is fed by rainwater that filters down from as far as 20 miles away on the Plateau de Vaucluse. The stillness is an illusion caused by the pool's depth. In the 1980s, a robot submarine plunged more than 1,000 feet and failed to find the bottom. Churning rapids just downstream of the pool reveal the powerful flow, which can reach as much as 7,000 cubic feet per second. Within about a mile, by the time it passes the waterwheel and scenic bridge in the center of town, the spring has widened and formed the broad, clear Sorgue River.

L'Isle Sur La Sorgue

A large but compact medieval town, seven km/4.3 miles down the Sorgue from its source at the Fontaine de Vaucluse, this was originally a fishing village built on stilts. The river divides here and is further branched by canals so that today the town is actually spread out on islands between five branches of the river. It is sometimes known as the Comtadine Venice. Several waterwheels, some of which still turn, line the tree-shaded canals. As pretty as it is, the town's main claim to fame is as the antique capital of the region. At least 30 antique shops are open year-round along the Quai de la Gare, across from the railway station, and there's a flea market with 50 traders every Sunday, all day. At Easter and Assumption (August 15), as many as 900 dealers gather for massive antique fairs. The town has a good selection of shops and restaurants, as well as several pleasant hotels.

Antiques fair in L'Isle Sur La Sorgue. ©BisetValerie Collection CDT Vaucluse

Getting Here: 25 km/15½ miles southeast of Avignon on the N100. There is local rail and bus service from Avignon.

More Information: Office de Tourisme, Place de la Liberté, 84800 Isle sur la Sorgue, ☎ 33 04 90 38 04 78, fax 33 04 90 38 35 43, contact@ot-islesurlasorgue.fr, www.ot-islesurlasorgue.fr.

Roussillon

Roussillon glows with dozens of shades of natural ochre, mined nearby. The town's ruddy glow is visible for miles. © J.L.Seille Collection CDT Vaucluse

This perched village is remarkable, first and foremost, for its colors. Built in the middle of what is claimed to be the world's largest and richest deposit of natural ochre, it was once the center of the region's trade in these iron oxide pigments. The startling colors of the local houses remain as evidence. There are 15 or 16 different shades, ranging from white, through yellows to reds and purples. A lane from the middle of the village leads directly to the ochre cliffs in the Val des Fées or Fairy Valley. A marked path, **Le Sentier des Aiguilles**, is a half-day hiking itinerary, set out by the Lubéron Natural Regional Park (contact@parcduluberon.fr, www.parcduluberon.com), featuring informational signs about the formation and uses of ochre.

Though largely replaced by synthetics, natural ochre is still highly prized. The local factory just outside the village produces about 2,000 metric tons annually and can be visited. *The **Mathieu Factory**, Conservatory of Applied Pigments and Ochres, Association OKHRA, 84220 Roussillon, contact Mathieu Barrois,* ☎/fax 33 04 90 05 66 69, info@okhra.com, www.okhra.com.

Author's Advice: Roussillon is picturesque, with steep, narrow streets, some of which (such as the Rue de l'Arcade) are undercover. But cars are not allowed into the village and there is a bit of a climb from the parking lot, so access may be an issue for some visitors. Be aware, also, that this is a popular town. If visiting during the summer months, try to arrive very early (or very late) to avoid the crowds.

Getting Here: 46 km/28.6 miles southeast of Avignon. Take the N100 toward Apt. At the Pont Julien (a three-arched Roman bridge that will be well signposted) look for a left turn onto the D108 and follow signs to Roussillon. Local buses stop at this intersection, five km/three miles from the town.

More Information: Office de Tourisme, Place de la Poste, 84220 Roussillon, ☎ 33 04 90 05 60 25, fax 33 04 90 05 63 31, ot-roussillon@axit.fr, www.roussillon-provence.com.

■ Festivals & Fêtes

Villages and towns seem to celebrate their traditions, harvests, and products practically every weekend, all year. There are literally hundreds of festivals, fairs and fêtes. The best way to find out what's going on is to consult the local tourist office. Here are just a few that are fun.

Foire à la Brocante de l'Isle sur la Sorgue: A huge flea market held over the Easter weekend. As many as 900 dealers fill just about every street of the town, selling anything from antique counterpanes and furniture to pottery, paintings, games, curios. Serious collectors and browsers are equally welcome.

Arts Marathon, L'Isle sur la Sorgue: A wild 24 hours, the first Friday in July, during which visual artists of all kinds take over the center of town. A huge workshop on the river bank becomes the scene of non-stop creativity for painters, sculptors, graphic designers, creators of recycled art and photographers. Onlookers can see the work take shape – and sometimes join in the creative process. Time is up late Saturday afternoon, when the tired artists and contributors drink a toast and exhibit their work. *Organized by Association 7ART,* ☎ *33 04 90 38 67 31, isabelleetthierrysavini@club-internet.fr or inquire at the tourist office.*

La Véraison, Châteaunef du Pape: Three days in August, the village celebrates La Véraison – the Grape Ripening – with a medieval festival. Costumed knights, lords and ladies take part in pageants, parades, public entertainments, medieval shows and feasts, under the authority of a costumed, medieval Pope. Contact the tourist information office (page 123) for exact dates.

The Village Soups Festival, Vaison la Romaine area: In late October, 14 villages all around Vaison la Romaine compete to create prize-winning soups. Over 14 nights, villagers – ranging from grannies to teenagers to Cordon Bleu chefs – prepare soups for everyone in town. Competitions for the best soup in each village are held every night. At the end of the 14 evenings, the champion soup maker of each village competes in the finals at Les Journée Gourmandes (yet another food festival, held in November in Vaison la Romaine). Soups are judged by The Venerable Brotherhood of Voconces Louchiers (literally, "ladlers of Voconces"), but anyone can have a bowl in one of the many soup dining rooms – usually set up in village halls. Information about dates and locations from the Vaison la Romaine tourist office (page 386).

Music & Dance

July and August mean culture, music and dance festivals in Provence.
© D.LefrancCollCDTVaucluse

Les Choragies, Orange: This annual festival of opera and lyric singing in the Roman Theater is the oldest music festival in France, www.choregies.asso.fr/angl/bienvenue.htm. For more details, see Orange, page 116.

Les Choralies, Vaison la Romaine: For an eight-day period in August, every three years, more than 4,000 choristers and musicians from all over the world come to Vaison la Romaine for master classes, performances and a giant 3,000-voice sing-along in the Roman Theater. The next Choralies will be held in August 2007.

Festival of Choir Prizewinners, Vaison la Romaine: Choirs that have won competitions throughout Europe perform in the town's Romanesque Cathedral from the end of July to the beginning of August. Details from the tourist office (page 386).

The Vaison Dance Festival: Major festival of dance companies from throughout Europe, performing every night in the Roman Theatre. Held the last two weeks in July. Program and reservation information at www.vaison-festival.com.

Les Estivales de Carpentras: All kinds of performance – music, dance, theater and variety acts – enliven Carpentras, the capital of the Comtat Venaissin, for the last two weeks of July. Information from the tourist office (page 383).

Shopping

L'Isle sur la Sorgue has a good range of interesting shops. Otherwise, wherever you go, the best shopping will be in the local markets (some of which have existed in the same location for five or six hundred years), as well as the shops that line their edges. Visit the *caves du vin* and *négociantes* in key Côte de Rhône towns to taste wines before you buy.

LOOK FOR...

- **Côte de Rhône** wines such as Châteauneuf du Pape, Vacqueras, Gigondas.
- **Truffles** (in tins or small glass jars to take home) and truffle oil.

- **Glacé fruits** from Apt – a surprisingly wide range, often beautifully packaged. These are not cheap.
- **Scented products** made with local lavender. French lavender has a fresher, younger scent than English lavender.
- **Muscat de Beaume de Venise**, a honey-scented dessert wine that is almost like drinking the very best Sauternes.
- **Rasteau**, another sweet wine that often accompanies fois gras in the best restaurants.

Markets

Carpentras

Wander into Place Aristide Briand in the center of Carpentras, any Friday morning between November and March and you will see small sacks of wrinkled black funghi being exchanged for astronomical prices. If you're up on celebrity chefs, you might spot a few of them as well.

The **Truffle Market**, in Carpentras, has been held for hundreds of years. It's small and discreet – just a tiny section of the Friday market, which takes over most of the town center – but a magnet for connoisseurs. Brokers, négociants and sellers from at least eight French départements come to the Carpentras market to trade. About 50% of all the truffles sold in France are traded here. Even if you're not buying, it is fun to watch the cagey traders and their customers – and to enjoy the aroma. Place Aristide Briand, 8 to 10 am, Fridays from the end of November through March.

Known locally as *le Marché Bio*, the "organic market" market offers all natural products, including bread, fruit and vegetables, cheeses, juice, honey, fabrics and paper goods. Tuesday mornings, from 8 am to noon on the Rue Raspail.

Apt

Named one of France's 100 most exceptional markets, the **Apt market** has been held in the center of the town's *quartier antique* since 1504. Buy fresh fruit and local produce but, for the glacé fruits that are the town's specialty, choose the smart shops along the market route.

Châteauneuf du Pape

Every Friday morning, there's plenty of opportunity to taste and buy one of the jewels in the crown of the Côte de Rhône at the **wine market**. Forget how early it is (or do as the professionals do and spit it out) and have a go. Place de la Renaissance.

Gordes

Tuesday mornings before noon, at the top of the town, the square outside the church fills up with dealers selling everything from local produce, wines and soaps to amateur paintings, sunglasses and leashes for Fido. It is a small but typical **town market** with enough tempting items to weigh down your backpack.

L'Isle sur la Sorgue

People come to this market town to shop so there are plenty of opportunities. Thursday and Sunday mornings in the town center look for fruits, vegetables, cheeses, fabrics, ceramics, soaps and scents. A **flea market** spreads out along the Quais on Sunday. Once a year, on the first Sunday in August, a **floating market**, in old-fashioned river boats, lines the canals. If you are nearby, plan to visit this with your camera and some spending money.

Orange

On Thursday mornings at least 300 traders fill the old town for a **general market**. On Saturdays, from 6 am to noon, the specialty is *brocante* (a cross between junk and antiques) specializing in old **Provençal furniture** and **decorative objects**. Between August 15 and October 15, there is a market every day. During the rest of the year, a general **food market** is held on Mondays, Wednesdays and Thursdays.

Roussillon

A small **village market**, similar to the market in Gordes, is held every Wednesday mornings in the town center.

Vaison la Romaine

Since 1483, a general market has filled all the main squares and streets of the lower town every Tuesday morning. Today it is held from 8 am to 2 pm. There is a smaller, Provençal market on summer Sunday mornings in the medieval upper town. An **organic farmers' market** takes place Tuesdays and Saturdays, from 7:30 to 11:30 am, mid-October to mid-June, as well as Thursdays during the summer, at Place François Cévert. There is a **flea market** on the third Sunday of every month, from 7 am to 7 pm.

■ Where to Stay

See also Avignon, Where to Stay, pages 56-60, for hotels convenient to this region.

Deluxe

☆☆☆☆ **Hostellerie de Crillon le Brave** *(Place de l'Église, 84410 Crillon le Brave,* ☎ *33 04 90 65 61 61, fax 33 04 90 65 62 86, crillonbrave@relaischateaux.com, www.crillonlebrave.com. 32 rooms and suites with private bath and showers in seven different restored village houses. Direct-dial telephones and free access to AT&T, Sprint, MCI, etc. Heated pool. Breakfast and room tax extra, €€-€€€€).* Just

Above: Sénanque Abbey near Gordes has been in constant use by Cistercians for more than 850 years (© D.Basse.Collection CDT Vaucluse)

Below: One of several village houses at Hostellerie de Crillon le Brave (Photo courtesy of Hostellerie de Crillon le Brave)

The Panier District, the oldest "Old Town" in France
(© Alain Sauvan, OTCM Marseille)

Above: Spelt wheat and lavender are traditional and colorful companion crops
(© D.Basse.Collection CDT Vaucluse)

Below: The Belle Epoque Leonard Parli Calisson factory and shop is a landmark in Aix en Provence (©Ferne Arfin)

Glorious technicolor! Roussillon blazes in its cloak of ochre
(© PhotoX, CDTVaucluse)

outside of Carpentras and close to Mont Ventoux, this hotel is popular with Tour de France followers. It sprawls across seven luxuriously restored medieval stone houses – almost a third of the village – linked by a cobbled courtyard and a terraced Italian garden. This setting, on a steep hillside, makes for a lot of up and down but also stunning views. Little luxuries include Provençal toiletries in

HOTEL PRICE CHART	
Rates are per room based on double occupancy.	
	Under €55
€	€56-€96
€€	€97-€135
€€€	€136-€195
€€€€	Over €195

the sumptuous bathrooms, fluffy white bathrobes and English-language newspapers with breakfast. Fabulous food is served in the elegant restaurant (€€€€) or more casual **Bistro** (€€€) and, during the autumn and spring the chef holds cooking classes for guests. Packages also include visits to wineries and private estates. This place is a real knockout. If you plan to give yourself a brief treat, you can't go wrong with a night or two here. Ask about the town's Mechanical Music Museum before you leave.

☆☆☆☆ **Bastide de Gordes** *(Le Village, 84220 Gordes, ☎ 33 04 90 72 12 12, fax 33 04 90 72 05 20, mail@bastide-de-gordes.com, www.bastide-de-gordes.com. 37 rooms and suites with private bath and showers. Heated pool. Breakfast and room tax extra, €€-€€€€).* The 16th-century Bastide de Gordes clings to the cliffs and ramparts of the town; part of it was built into the restored fortifications, part carved from virgin rock. The

View from Bastide de Gordes. The hills of the Vaucluse disappear in the mist. ©Ferne Arfin

pool is on a terrace perched at the edge of the world, overlooking the Lubéron. Rooms are spacious and, with their vaulted ceilings, manage to be rustic and luxurious at the same time. After a long ride or hike, the deep bathtubs are heaven for aching muscles. It delivered just what we need after 34 miles on bicycles. The food is exceptional (€€€€) and the wines are supervised by a knowledgeable and passionate sommelier (who introduced us to a deep, nutty and local Vin Cuit de Provence – an unusual cooked wine). This spot offers a dramatic, moonlit view of the Lubéron.

☆☆☆ **Hotel du Poète** *(84000 Fontaine de Vaucluse, ☎ 33 04 90 20 34 05, fax 33 04 90 20 34 08, contact@hoteldupoete.com, www.hoteldupoete.com. 24 rooms and suites with private bath, direct-dial phones, air conditioning, satellite TV, mini-bar. Pool. Breakfast and room tax extra, €-€€€).* A

19th-century mill, complete with waterwheel, beside the Sorgue in the center of the village. Designed to resemble a private home, each room is individually, and recently, decorated in a modern interpretation of the Provençal style. Very comfortable. The sound of the river is soothing, making the place remarkably calm in a village that can become a bit hectic during July and August.

Moderate

☆☆☆ **Hostellerie Le Beffroi** *(Rue de l'Evêché, Cité Médiévale, BP 8584110 Vaison la Romaine, ☎ 33 04 90 36 04 71, fax 33 04 90 36 24 78, lebeffroi@wanadoo.fr, www.le-beffroi.com. 22 rooms with private bath, direct-dial phones, television, mini-bar, hair dryer. Pool and gardens. Breakfast, room tax and covered parking extra. Open March through January, €-€€).* Two private homes, one dating from 1554, have been linked and converted into an inn. The public rooms retain some period features – including a spiral staircase up a tower. Guestrooms are individually decorated, some featuring original beams. They are, nevertheless, relatively basic. The setting, in the upper village, is charming and the views are good.

☆☆ **Hotel Burrhus** *(1 Place Montfort, 84110 Vaison la Romaine, ☎ 33 04 90 36 00 11, fax 33 04 90 36 39 05, info@burrhus.com, www.burrhus.com. 38 rooms, six rooms with private bath or shower €€).* An emphasis on art makes this an interesting place to stay in a town devoted to the arts. Six rooms have been recently architect-designed in a French minimalist modern style, including high-tech bathrooms (the French are particularly good at these). Others have been decorated by various local artists. The oldest rooms retain a rustic, Provençal style. The hotel has regular art exhibitions in its public rooms.

☆☆ **Le Mas des Grès** *(RN 100 Route d'Apt, 84800 Lagnes, ☎ 33 04 90 20 32 85, fax 33 04 90 20 21 45, info@masdesgres.com, www.masdesgres.com. 14 rooms with private baths, telephones and CD radio alarm clocks. Terrace, pool, gardens and protected parking. Open March 15 to November 10, €€-€€€€ – half board for two people).* More than a hotel, this *mas*, about three miles from L'Isle sur la Sorgue, is like a rustic home and reflects the multicultural passions of its owner. Thierry Crovara, a Moroccan-born Swiss citizen with French and Italian ancestors, is an accomplished and trained cook as well as a passionate golfer. The *mas* offers cooking classes and golf packages. Room décor is basic but typically colorful. The public rooms are gorgeous, with lush decoration in the local style. The *mas* is good value when you consider that rates, starting at €129 per night, include breakfast and dinner for two.

Budget

☆☆ **Le Manoir Hôtel Restaurant** *(Quartier Salignan, RN 100, 84400 Apt, ☎ 33 04 90 74 08 00, fax 33 04 90 74 19 72, hotel.lemanoir@free.fr, www.hotel-lemanoir84.com. 20 rooms with French television, direct tele-*

phone. Pool. Breakfast and room tax extra, €). A pale stone *bastide* (a kind of grand farmhouse) with a noted chef, set in comfortably landscaped grounds about four km/2½ miles from the center of town. A good base if you are planning to visit the Apt market or tour "ochre country." *Logis de France* has rated this hotel two chimneys for value and comfort.

> **Author's Tip:** Ibis Hotels *(€)* operate several hotels in this area – in Avignon, Cavaillon, Orange and Manosque. Hotels in this international economy group provide basic but relatively up-to-date bed and breakfast accommodation. Rooms have phones and televisions. The hotels usually have a bar and some have pools. They have very little local character, but if you are just looking for a modern bath and a bed for the night, they are cheap and reliable. Reservations are easiest online. Their website (www.ibishotel.com/ibis) has a good interactive map.

☆☆ **Auberge du Lubéron** *(8 Place du Faubourg du Ballet, 84000 Apt, ☎ 33 04 90 74 12 50, fax 33 04 90 04 79 49, contact@auberge-luberon-peuzin.com, www.auberge-luberon-peuzin.com/index-gb.html. 14 rooms with television, covered parking, €)*. *Logis de France* gives this chef-owned hotel/restaurant three chimneys for good value meals and accommodation. Serge Peuzin is a Maître Cuisinier de France and his *cuisine du terroir* (i.e., based on local specialties and ingredients) menu at only €29 is not to be missed. He also makes his own glacé fruit (the Apt specialty), which is sold in the hotel shop. The rooms are comfortable and old fashioned in a 19th-century French *petit bourgeois* sort of way. You half-expect someone's maiden aunt, dressed in black silk, to show up offering her special cordial on a silver tray.

☆☆ **Hôtel du Fiacre** *(153 Rue Vigne, 84200 Carpentras, ☎ 33 04 90 63 03 15, fax 33 04 90 60 49 73, contact@hotel-du-fiacre.com, www.hotel-du-fiacre.com. 20 rooms, some with private terraces or patios. Private baths, direct telephones with modem connections, satellite TV in some rooms, enclosed parking. Open year-round. Breakfast and room tax extra, €)*. A genuine find, this place has a genteel, Belle Époque charm. Every room is different, with chandeliers, great antique sleigh beds, impressive Art Deco armoires and mirrors the order of the day. All have modern, colorfully tiled bath or shower rooms. Ask for Room Number 1 for a real treat.

Camping

Some campgrounds charge separately for parking, electricity hook-ups and use of showers. Some also charge a small reservation fee (during the busy summer months, it is probably a good idea to reserve a place). As in other parts of Provence, forest fires are a summertime danger so open-air cooking may be restricted.

Note: Prices are per night for one tent or trailer space, two adults, electricity and car parking. Local taxes may be charged in some areas.

☆☆☆ **Camping Le Jonquier** *(Monsieur Joel Denis, 1321 Rue Alexis Carrel, Orange, ☎ 33 04 90 34 49 48, fax 33 04 90 51 16 97, joel.denis@waika9.com. Open March 27 to September 30; €19.50 to €24.40).* Eighty places, less than 15 minutes from the Roman monuments of Orange. The site is spread over five acres and has a swimming pool, laundry facilities, running water hook-ups.

Did you know? Because the French are very fond of their bread, most campsites have it delivered fresh every morning!

☆☆☆☆ **Camping du Théâtre Romain** *(Monsieur Jean Pruvot, Quartier des Arts, Chemin du Brusquet, Vaison la Romaine, ☎ 33 04 90 28 78 66, fax 33 04 90 28 78 76, info@camping-theatre.com, www.camping-theatre.com. Open March 15 to November 15; €17.10 to €21.30).* Seventy-five places with electricity, drinking water and wastewater disposal. The campsite is well located, only 200 m/650 feet from the Roman ruins and 500 m/about a third of a mile from the town center and shops. Quiet and partly shaded, the campsite has special handicapped and baby units, washing machines and a swimming pool. Games include fussball and billiards.

☆☆☆ **Camping le Lubéron** *(Monsieur Jean Claude Marie, Route de Saignon, D48, Apt, ☎ 33 04 90 04 85 40, fax 33 04 90 74 12 19, luberon@wanadoo.fr, www.camping-le-luberon.com. Open April 1 to September 30; prices for camping, €11 to €16 per night; gîtes and chalets are rented by the week).* High above Apt, this is a wooded site with 110 camping places as well as *gîtes* and chalets. Full facilities, pool.

Tip: The **Vaucluse Departmental Tourist Board** publishes a free camping guide, updated annually. Write to Comité Départemental du Tourisme de Vaucluse, 12 Rue Collège de la Croix, BP147, 84008, Avignon, or e-mail info@provenceguide.com.

Gîtes & Chambres d'Hôtes

Below is just a sampling of what's available in this area. Most *gîtes* are rented by the week but some may be available for the weekend.

Gîtes le Pont des Aubes *(M. Patrice Aubert, 189 route d'Apt, le Pont des Aubes, 84800 Isle sur a Sorgue, ☎ 33 04 90 38 13 75, fax 33 04 90 38 13 75, patriceaubert@wanadoo.fr, perso.wanadoo.fr/lepontdesaubes, €).* Two apartments in a large house beside the river, not far from the village center. Behind a typically rustic Provençal exterior, interiors are modern and utilitarian. Kitchens include microwaves. Le Pont des Aubes also has two rooms on a B&B basis which are very good value at €60 per night for two.

Gîtes and Chambres d'Hôtes Chez Alice *(La Croix des Aires, 84830 Sérignan du Comtat,* ☎ *33 04 90 70 08 19 or 33 04 90 70 06 59. chezalice@netcourrier.com, www.serignanducomtat.com/chezalice.htm, €).* About seven km/four miles from Orange off the D976. A tile-roofed, walled compound of farmhouse and out buildings, with a garden and olive groves. The gîte also has a private courtyard. The B&B rooms are sunny and colorful, if a bit basic. They are fairly priced at €50 per night for two with *petit déjeuner* (breakfast).

Colline des Puits, Chambre d'Hôtes *(Monsieur André Pin, 84400 Apt,* ☎ *33 04 90 74 66 33, fax 33 04 90 74 66 33, call 33 06 70 64 54 42. Open year-round. B&B, €).* In the Parc Naturel Régional du Lubéron, this traditional house is well-located for hikes and cycle trips in the region. It's only 2½ km/1½ miles from Apt and within 10 minutes of the Provençal Colorado (page 136). Rooms have shady terraces, independent entrances and outdoor cooking facilities. The owners speak English and are proud of serving generous breakfasts that include their own homemade jams.

Chambres d'Hôtes la Bastide des Beaumes Rouges *(Madame Claudette Bauer, 84800 Fontaine de Vaucluse,* ☎ *33 04 90 20 34 18, fax 04 90 20 34 18. Open April or March to November. B&B, €).* A stone farm house, surrounded by olive trees about 100 m/330 feet from the village. The views are lovely and private parking is included – a very important plus in this busy little town where there is little parking and all of it costs a bundle. The owner speaks English and rooms are furnished with antiques. In good weather, you can enjoy breakfast in the shade of a 100-year-old vine arbor. Half- or full board can sometimes be arranged. The property also includes two independent *gîtes*.

Chambres d'Hôtes les Floralies *(Monsieur and Madame George and Théa Janssen, Avenue de Verdun, 84340 Malaucène,* ☎ *33 04 90 65 14 35, fax 33 04 90 65 14 35. Open mid-March to mid-November. B&B, €).* A substantial, early 19th-century house in a walled garden with views of Mont Ventoux. The hosts speak English and serve their generous breakfasts anywhere you like around their beautiful house – in the orangerie, the dining room or the garden. A larger studio is available and half- or full board can be arranged. Malaucène is a small, medieval village close to Vaison la Romaine.

For more information about *gîtes* in this region, contact local tourist authorities or www.gites-de-france.fr for an up-to-date list. Or **Gîtes de France Alpes de Haute Provence** *(Rond Point du 11 Novembre, 04000 Digne-le-Bains,* ☎ *33 04 92 31 52 39, fax 33 04 92 32 32 63)* and **Gîtes de France Vaucluse** *(Place Campana, BP 164, 84008 Avignon,* ☎ *33 04 90 85 45 00, fax 33 04 90 85 88 49).*

■ Where to Eat

Deluxe

At the top end, you cannot beat the restaurants at Hostellerie Crillon le Brave and Le Bastide de Gorde. But you will pay for the privilege, so save the experience for one of your big blowouts. I've found through experience that you can eat with such extravagance only once or twice in a week-long vacation – if you want to be fit to do anything else! At **Hostellerie Crillon le Brave** (Place de l'Église, 84410 Crillon le Brave, ☎ 33 04 90 65 61 61, fax 33 04 90 65 62 86, crillonbrave@relaischateaux.com, www.crillonlebrave.com, restaurant €€€€, bistro €€€) Chef Philippe Monti was born and raised in nearby Bédouin. His cuisine makes adventurous use of local specialties. In the restaurant – a series of stone-vaulted chambers under a 16th-century village house – we ate pink, pan-roasted foie gras in a sweet wine sauce, shoulder of wild boar (roasted and stewed) and cinnamon crème brûlée with roasted figs. If you think you can manage seven courses, try the chef's sampling menu at €64. **The Bistro** is slightly more casual – decorated in bright Provençal colors. Both are open for dinner only and offer dining under the stars in good weather.

DINING PRICE CHART

Prices are for a typical prix fixe menu of two courses and a glass of house wine for one.

	€14-€19
€	€21-€34
€€	€35-€49
€€€	€50-€69
€€€€	€70-€140
€€€€€	The sky's the limit

At the **Bastide de Gordes** (Le Village, 84220 Gordes, ☎ 33 04 90 72 12 12, fax 33 04 90 72 05 20, mail@bastide-de-gordes.com, www.bastide-de-gordes.com, €€€-€€€€€) we dined in a bright, elegant room decorated in pinks and creams, with flowers. Specialties included mushroom ravioli with Lubéron truffles and an amazing fruit soup with homemade honey ice cream. There are good value tasting menus of local specialties for €54 and, unusually for a restaurant of this class. If you aren't very hungry you can choose a single dish, starting at about €13. A "Grill," open for lunch, is reasonably priced. The manager is the sommelier and is passionate about his subject, so ask his advice in choosing a wine. If you are lucky, he may have some *vin cuit* – cooked wine – a local Christmas specialty, for dessert.

While we're on the subject of big blowouts – the **Moulin à Huile** in Vaison la Romaine (Route de Malaucène, 84110 Vaison la Romaine, ☎ 33 04 90 36 20 67, fax 33 04 90 36 20 20, info@moulin-huile.com, www.moulin-huile.com/uk, €€€-€€€€€), offers seasonal menus and internationally influenced cuisine. You might find lobster or a tandoori dish on the menu. Try fois gras, simply cooked and served with a Beaume de Venise jelly. Wines are distinctly local – specialiszing in Châteauneuf du Pape and Gigondas. The chef, Robert Bardot, has won loads of awards and is a bit of a character. His own watercolors decorate the menus. The restaurant is in a brightly painted, converted olive oil mill. Dining is on a colorful veranda overlooking the river, or in a vaulted chamber. The restaurant is also open for lunch at about half the price of dinner.

A bit more down to earth is **Chez Serge** in Carpentras *(90 Rue Cottier, 84200 Carpentras,* ☎ *33 04 90 63 21 24, fax 33 04 90 60 30 71, up to €€)*. It has fixed-price menus of €12 at lunchtime, €25 for dinner. The *pizza feu de bois* is worth the visit. Other specialties might include salmon braised in cider or beef in a Vacqueras sauce. The ambiance is rustic/designer trendy; the other diners are stylish. There's a good value children's menu too.

Épeautre – New Life for an Old Staple

Spelt, a form of wheat that was grown in the Middle Ages and eaten as a whole grain, has recently become popular on French gourmet tables. Grown alongside lavender on the Provençal uplands, it provides a lovely golden counterpoint to the rows of purply blue. On menus, it's called épeautre and is served as a risotto, instead of potatoes or rice. It tastes like a cross between barley and rice. Look for boxes of it in French supermarkets. A popular brand is called Eblé and it's sold near the rice, lentils and grains.

Light Meals & Snacks

As elsewhere in Provence, local cafés are easy to find and usually good value.

> **Warning:** This is a popular vacation area for French families as well as tourists from all over the world so, unfortunately, there are quite a few ripoffs. Beware of restaurants that seem to offer elaborate menus at prices too good to be true. They probably are. Elegant cooking is expensive.

Look instead for open-air cafés offering pizza *feu de bois*, composed salads, omelets, steak frites, and you won't go wrong. Aim for a few local specialties – for example, dishes with cherries, apricots and peaches. In Apt, look for tea shops (salons de thé) that serve sweets made with glacé fruits. And, of course, follow the French example and have a glass or two of a local Côte de Rhône wine with lunch – even if you're eating a tuna sandwich.

Adventures

On Foot

Hiking in the Vaucluse

It is almost impossible to single out one area of this region that is better for hikers than another. There are gentle hikes around vineyards, hearty hill walking on the slopes of Mont Ventoux – in the steps of Petrarch, perhaps or around the Dentelles de Montmirail – and dramatic walks in the area of the Provençal Colorado (see below). At least five of France's Grande Randonée (GR) paths criss-cross the region.

Whether or not you are a serious hiker, it's wise to take along an IGN 1/25000 TOP25 map of the area you want to explore. There are 18 for this region and each covers about 12 square miles. (See *Sources of Information*, page 25).

A TOURING NETWORK

The department, including 130 of the 150 towns in the Vaucluse, has mapped more than 5,000 km/3,000 miles of paths suitable for hiking, cycling and riding. Since the late 1990s, the regional government has been rolling out a program of maintaining and marking these paths so that today almost the entire region is covered. At intersections, trail markers have names and altitude markings as well as indications of the distance to the next trail marker. In the Mont Ventoux range, markers at intersections also point out the nearest village in case you get lost. Within the network, GR trails are marked with a white horizontal stripe over a red one. Short local (PR) paths are marked with yellow horizontal stripes and local long-distance paths are marked with a yellow stripe over a red one.

The Provençal Colorado

A nine-km/5.6-mile walk, with altitude changes of 227 m/745 feet, this route circles the abandoned ochre pits with views of wildly colored ravines and ochre sands. It will take about 3½ hours at a brisk pace. Start at Rustrel, a few km northeast of Apt.

- From the village, follow the GR 6/GR97 to the trail marker at Cornet. Turn left along the GR6, passing next to several small parking areas.
- After the parking, at the first left curve, take the path on the right, toward the Doa, a small branch of the Calavon River.
- Cross the stream and continue past a ruined cabin. The path climbs, overlooking a box canyon of ochre sands. At the *Barriés* marker, the G6 goes off to the left. Take the path that overlooks the Barriés ravine.

- At the top of the valley, take the path to the left. At the next crossroads, by the *Pradenques* marker, turn right. You will pass a small farm.
- At the *Ubac de Pradenques* marker, take the path on the right, along the edge of the plateau. To your right, the many colors of the ochre quarries come into view. There is a short downhill, then go uphill to the right along the top of the *Gourgues* ravine. Stay to the right.
- At the second fork, take the path left, going west, and climb toward La Croix de Christol.
- At the *Croix de Christol* marker, take the path on the right, downhill and north, towards the Doa and Istrane. Cross the Doa.
- At the crossroads at Istrane, turn right and follow the ochre factory path past Bouvène and back to the *Cornet* marker. Turn left and return to Rustrel along the GR6/GR97.

> **Did you know?** You can let a donkey do the donkey work. Hiking at a gentle pace (two or three miles per hour) with a donkey to carry your luggage and supplies is a fun way to explore mountain paths in the Lubéron and Mont Ventoux. For about €40 per day, several companies will provide donkeys equipped with pack saddles and lanyards, as well as detailed itineraries for a few hours or a few days in the protected biosphere areas. For information, contact **Les Ânes des Abeilles** *(le Col Abeilles, Les Isnards, 84390 Monieux,* ☎ *33 04 90 64 01 52, anesdesabeilles@wanadoo.fr, www.ane-et-rando.com / Site / AnesAbeilles / AnesDesAbeilles.html)* or **Eric Moreau** *(Domaine de Bélèzy, 84410 Bédoin,* ☎ *33 06 77 56 63 49).*

WINTER ON MONT VENTOUX

Although there are both Alpine and cross-country skiing on Mont Ventoux (at the Mont Serein snowpark), snow is really too unreliable to make a special trip for it. But if you are in the area after a snowfall on the mountain, you can go on a snowshoe hike. Half-day tours for five to 12 people explore the forest slopes of the mountain in the UNESCO protected biosphere reserve. The price – adults €22, children between €8 and €12; €15 includes a professional guide and snowshoe rental. (***Agarrus**, Maison des Dentelles, Place du Marché, 84190 Beaumes de Venise,* ☎ *33 04 90 65 06 41 or 33 06 80 43 12 12, fax 33 04 90 62 93 25, agarrus@wanadoo.fr).* Check out whether there is snow on the mountain via Mont Serein station's live webcam at www.stationdumontserein.com.

Rock Climbing

The long, south-facing gray limestone cliffs of **Buoux**, not far from Apt, are considered to be among the best and most difficult rock climbs in France – 100 m/328 feet high, they are classified 4 to 8c in the French system. They are also popular; most experts suggest going in spring or autumn to avoid crowds. Notable limestone climbing sites near Bédouin at **Combe Obscure** and the "**four seasons**" sites in Les Dentelles, near Gigondas, are well-equipped, with instruction and guides available. Information about climbs and guides can be obtained from *Comité Départemental Fédération Française de la Montagne et d'Escalade (FFME) du Vaucluse, 54 route de Morières, Les Aubépines A1, 84000 Avignon, fax 33 04 90 14 6 10.* Also contact *roger.maurel@wanadoo.fr or pierre.duret@wanadoo.fr.* If you are confident in French, the FFME's website may be useful – www.ffme.fr. Local guide **André Charmetant** offers instruction and guided climbs of the Dentelles de Montmirail, including seven-day programs for children. *(André Charmetant, 98 Avenue de Tarascon, 84000 Avignon, ☎ 33 04 90 82 20 72, fax 33 04 90 14 96 03, andre@charmetant.org, www.charmetant.org.)*

A REGION OF ADVENTURES

The Vaucluse is one of France's smaller *départements* but it packs in a great deal of outdoor activity. The departmental government supports 15 sports commissions (*Comité Départemental de...*), many of which are listed as sources of information in this section.

In addition, two **Vaucluse Leisure and Outdoor Activity Centers** (*Centres Départementaux de Plein Air et de Loisirs*), located in Fontaine de Vaucluse (Route de Cavaillon, 84800 Fontaine de Vaucluse) and Sault (Route des Cartouses, 84390 Sault en Provence), offer mountain biking, climbing, spelunking, canoe-kayaking, cycle touring, hiking and orienteering. For information about programs at either, ☎ *33 04 90 20 32 33, fax 33 04 90 20 22 13, cdpal@cg84.fr.*

Accrobranching

Did you ever want to swing from the trees like Tarzan or his simian pals? Accrobranching is a new French sport that tries to approach that sensation by walking in the trees. Essentially, you progress from one tree to another by using monkey bridges, catwalks, swings, suspended beams and various other equipment. The basic "equipment" is the forest itself and the sport is suitable for both children and adults. In the Vaucluse, you can take a one-day accrobranching course near **Buoux** *(Amethyst, La Baume, Quartier la Combe, 84489 Buoux, ☎ 33 04 90 04 71 29, fax 33 04 90 74 05 92)*, at **Lac Les Salettes** in Mormoiron *(Lionel Fonquiernie,*

Plan d'Eau des Salettes, 84570 Mormoiron, ☎ 33 04 90 65 76 84, llfonker@aol.com) or at **Lagnes** *(Passerelles des Cîmes, les Cadenieres à Lagnes, Bat. D, 24 Allée Jean Giono 84800, L'Isle sur la Sorgue,* ☎ *33 04 90 65 76 84, passerelles.cimes@caramail.com).* Prices range from €35 to €125, depending upon how many people are in your group. The more the merrier – and the cheaper.

Spelunking

If you are keen on caves, there are plenty of galleries, swallow-holes, pits and kettles to explore in the Vaucluse. Sites tend to be in the northern half of the region. There is no caving to speak of in the Lubéron. For information about sites and local clubs, contact:

- **Comité Départemental de Spéléologie de Vaucluse**, *President Didier Delabré, 6 Rue Julien de la Rovère, 84000 Avignon,* ☎ *33 04 90 87 67 96, didier.delabre@free.fr.*

- **Accueil Spéléologique du Plateau D'Albion** (ASPA), *Refuge Francis Belin, Rue de l'Église, 84390 Saint-Christol,* ☎ *33 04 90 75 08 33, contact@aspanet.net, www.aspanet.net.* The spelunking discovery and exploration center offers a two-day spelunking course in the area around Mont Ventoux and Sault for adults and children over 12. The fee of €116.63 per person covers instructor, accommodation, breakfast, equipment, clothing and membership in the ASPA Refuge.

On Wheels

Climate, geography and history make the Vaucluse/Lubéron one of the best cycling areas in all of France.

Spring and fall are warm and mild but usually cool enough for a comfortable ride. Sunshine is relatively reliable and, while it may rain now and then, the drenching thunderstorms of the summer months have mostly passed.

The choice of cycle routes varies from easy (on the plains of the Comtat Venaissin or the Calavon Valley between the Monts de Vaucluse and the Lubéron) through to extremely challenging (the Mont Ventoux circuit) with plenty of moderate hills for in-betweeners. The views – orchards and vineyards, rolling hills, ravines and limestone cliffs, ochre canyons, snow-covered peaks – are constantly changing and surprising. Add to this a large number of tiny villages, at Roman springs, at the crossroads of Roman roads or along the pilgrimage routes of the Middle Ages. Usually no more than five or six miles from each other, they are just far enough apart for either a short ride or a long cycle trek with plenty of diverting stops.

The Lubéron Natural Regional Park, together with several government departments and tourist authorities, has put together the **Lubéron Cycling Circuit**, covering routes for all abilities. The circuit stretches from Cavaillon, on the plains, via Apt, to the steep, hilly terrain around Forcalquier on the north.

Its southern reach also goes from Cavaillon to Forcalquier, this time passing through Lourmarin and Manosque. In all, there are 230 km/143 miles of trail, all of it marked, maintained and easy to follow. Most of the route travels over dedicated off-road cycle paths or quiet roads. Between Cavaillon and Apt, a disused railway line has been turned into the cycle path. Signs at every village on the route provide information about accommodation, services, sites and local itineraries.

Lubéron Cycling Circuit – Essential Information

Map: IGN 1/60,000 tourist map, *Parc naturel régional du Lubéron*.

Brochure: *Le Lubéron en vélo, Tour du Lubéron* – practical information about the circuit and facilities. Available from the Parc du Lubéron and from regional tourist offices.

Contact for information and brochures: *Parc Naturel Régional du Lubéron, Maison du Parc, 60 Place Jean Jaurès, 84404 Apt,* ☎ 33 04 90 04 42 00, info@parcduluberon.fr, www.parcduluberon.fr. The website is entirely in French, but, as with most French contacts, you can correspond via e-mail in English.

Two Suggested Cycle Itineraries

Caromb to Fontaine de Vaucluse, return by bus, via L'Isle sur la Sorgue

This itinerary takes you across the plains and up on the Vaucluse, then down into the cool, mysterious closed valley of the Fontaine. You will encounter several short but tough climbs on roads carved through the native limestone. This is 40 km/25 miles of moderate to hard cycling. Bus service is available from L'Isle sur la Sorgue to Carpentras. If you leave Carpentras by 8:30 am you should arrive in Fontaine de Vaucluse in time for lunch.

- Leave Carpentras, going east on the D942 to Mazan.
- At Mazan, go right on the ring road, then right onto the D1 toward Pernes les Fontaines. At the next traffic circle (about .5 km/.33 mile) go half-way around and exit onto the D1 toward Pernes les Fontaines.
- After 4.4 km/2¾ miles, you will come to another traffic circle. Exit onto the D4A toward St. Didier.
- Three-quarters of a mile further (1.2 km), you will come to a T-junction. Turn left onto the D39 into St. Didier. If you are bushed, St. Didier is a good place to stop for a bit of refreshment because the short, sharp

climb starts here. The town has a pleasant bar/tabac with sidewalk tables and a Monday morning market in the center of the village.

- If you go into the town center, you will have to backtrack. Look for a sign toward Pernes. This will be a right turn coming into St. Didier or a left turn if you have visited the village center. It's a small sign and easy to miss, so look sharp. Almost immediately, turn left toward Saumanes and, again immediately, turn right, uphill onto the D210 toward La Roque sur Pernes.
- Climb La Roque sur Pernes (2.4 km/1½ miles). After four miles (6.4 km), veer right onto the D57 toward Isle sur la Sorgue – watch your signs here, because this one is easy to miss.
- After a mile (1.62 km), turn left onto the D57 toward Fontaine de Vaucluse.
- Two-thirds of a mile later (one km), turn left at the stop sign onto the D25 to Fontaine de Vaucluse. Continue to the center of the village, park your bike and look around. Ask a local for directions to the Fontaine itself.
- To return, retrace your route out of the village along the D25 and continue west (past the D57) to L'Isle sur la Sorgue. In town, ask someone for directions to the Gare Routière (bus station) and take a local bus back to Carpentras.

The Mont Ventoux Circuit

A difficult, 56-km/34.8-mile circuit, with a steep 20-km/12½-mile climb, followed by an equally steep, and slightly longer, descent. This legendary mountain circuit is not for the faint-hearted. It is a notorious dasher of athletes' hopes when it forms part of the Tour de France. Don't attempt Mont Ventoux unless you are very fit and a speed freak. Carry a fleece and waterproofs – it may be snowing at the top. The average time for the circuit is six to seven hours.

Mont Ventoux is shaped something like a child's drawing of a mountain: straight up and straight down! Start climbing to the east at Malaucène and pray the wind isn't against you. You'll be on the D974 most of the way. The circuit is a wide, paved road that you share with a few cars and lots of other would be iron men and iron women. You'll climb 1,600 m/5,250 feet in 20 km/12½ miles. If you can look around, particularly on the hairpin turns and switchbacks, the views are sensational.

Stop at the Mont Ventoux observatory, at the summit (you will probably have to!) and enjoy the scenery. You can see all the way across the Vaucluse and south to the Mediterranean. The descent, beginning at the Col des Tempêtes (Tempest Pass), is slightly longer than the ascent but equally steep. It features a chain of about 15 dizzying switchbacks. Be careful to take the hard right on the hairpin turn at le Chalet Reynard or you may end up on the wrong road.

Stay with the D974, now heading west. Once you reach Bédouin, at about the 40-km/25-mile mark, the route levels out. At Bédouin, look for the limestone bluffs, popular for climbing, on your right. From the center of Bédouin, join the D19, a winding but level road, back to Malaucène.

Cycle Tours

Cycle touring packages make good sense if you are a first-time visitor to Provence, are uncertain of facilities, concerned about safety, unsure of the language, feel more comfortable in a group or just want to be pampered.

The Luxury Tour

There are dozens of cycle tour packages, available online or through travel agents. The first time we cycled in Provence, we joined **Trek Travel** for a luxury tour *(801 W. Madison, Waterloo WI 53594, ☎ 866 GO4 TREK or 920 478 4672, www.trektravel.com)*. We stayed at deluxe hotels, ate gourmet meals, attended wine tastings, visited markets, picnicked on choice morsels beside a rushing stream under limestone cliffs. Our tour guides were knowledgeable, experienced and fluent in French; one accompanied us on a bicycle while the other cruised the route in a van, collecting stragglers, repairing cycles and offering snacks and drinks. Our bags disappeared every morning, only to turn up in our rooms at the next hotel. We cycled with detailed route guides on state-of-the-art bicycles. The company, an offshoot of Trek Bicycles, sponsors the US Postal Service cycling team. For around $3,000, all-inclusive from Avignon, the company offers five-night leisure trips for cyclists of moderate abilities; challenging performance trips, and specialty trips accompanied by US Postal Service cycling team members (Lance Armstrong has ridden along in the past).

If we had one little quibble with this fabulous trip it was that sometimes it seemed to be more about cycling than about touring. We would have liked to spend more time exploring but we felt a certain pressure to keep up.

Still, independence comes at a price and organizing all the details on our own – or carrying heavy packs while cycling – was too daunting to contemplate. Recently, a new kind of mix-and-match service has become available in the Lubéron, offering cyclists a middle ground.

Ad Hoc Support

An association of 25 cycling-related business along the Lubéron Cycling Circuit are offering cyclists the ability to combine some of the more reassuring features of a package tour with the freedom of independent cycling.

The businesses provide cycle and equipment rental and repair, transportation, accommodation, meals, guide services, itineraries and maps. Through **Vélo Loisir en Lubéron**, cyclists can arrange their own tours, covering as many or as few miles as they choose – self-guided or accompanied – and cherry-pick the services they need: transportation at the beginning and end of tours, transport of luggage between stops, accommodations, meals, snacks, cycle rental, repair and on-the-road support. The upside is freedom to plan a tour that suits individual strengths and interests. If you only want to cycle 10 miles a day, so be it. On the downside, accommodation may be at a more utilitarian level and member hotels may not be in the towns you'd visit if you were completely independent. *(Vélo Loisir en Lubéron, BP14, 04280 Cereste, ☎ 33 04 92 79 05 82, info@veloloisirluberon.com, www.veloloisirluberon.com.)*

THE LAVENDER ROADS

From July to the end of August, lavender blooms and is harvested in the **Pays de Sault** on the eastern slopes of Mont Ventoux. The delicate scent is everywhere and all kinds of events, workshops, demonstrations and sales are organized for visitors. Tourist authorities throughout the lavender-growing areas have jointly published *The Lavender Roads*, a brochure full of useful information including suggested itineraries for motorists, cyclists and walkers; accommodation, restaurants, a lengthy schedule of special events and a list of lavender "stays" for independent travelers or groups.

For a copy of the brochure contact **Les Routes de la Lavande**, *2 Avenue de Venterol, BP 36, 26111 Nyons,* ☎ *33 04 75 26 65 91, fax 33 04 75 26 32 67, info@routes-lavande.com, www.routes-lavande.com.*

In the Air

Pre-Alpine terrain – rugged and rising but not precipitous – wide valleys and open plains, make much of the Vaucluse and the Lubéron ideal for **ballooning** and **wing sailing**. There are three popular launching sites for **hang-gliders** and **parasailers** – Rustrel, Cabrières d'Aigues and Mont Ventoux – as well as several aero clubs in the region. Information is available from:

- **Comité Départemental de Vol à Voile**, *President Gilles Laurent, Valla d'Hubert, 84360 Mérindôl,* ☎ *33 04 90 60 08 17 or 33 04 90 72 87 97.*
- **Association Vaucluse Parapente**, *Maison IV de Chiffre, 26 Rue des Teinturiers, 84000 Avignon, 33 04 90 85 67 82.*
- **Rustr'aile** (*roost-RYE*) **Colorado**, *Stade Brieugne, 84400, Rustrel,* ☎ *33 06 80 40 23 42 and 33 06 86 00 19 73, fax 33 04 90 04 96 53, rustraile@libertysurf.fr.*

For beginners, the Vaucluse Tourist Board recommends a five-day paragliding vacation available through Rustr'aile Colorado (above). It includes five four- to six-hour sessions, instructors' fees and use of equipment for around €400. Compulsory insurance is extra.

If you'd rather let someone else do all the hard work, you could cruise in a **hot air balloon** over the rolling lavendar hills, orchards, vineyards and golden fields of spelt wheat. Balloon trips can be arranged through:

- **BRIO Provence**, *BP432, Avignon 04,* ☎ *33 04 90 86 27 65, fax 33 04 90 86 27 68, jeromebillo@wanadoo.fr.* A half-day flight for three costs €262 per person, including lunch, champagne and a certificate.
- **Montgolfière Provence**, *Le Mas Fourniquière, 84220 Joucas, Gordes,* ☎ *33 04 90 05 76 77 or 33 04 90 05 79 21, fax 33 04 90 05 74 39, mongolfiere@free.fr or montgolfiere@infonie.fr, http://avignon-et-provence.com/ballooning/uk/index.html.* A standard flight of one to 1½ hours, followed by a champagne picnic and a certificate, costs €230 per person. Mongolfière also organizes adventure ballooning trips at sunrise and sunset, winter Alpine ballooning and "château-ballooning" departing from an 18th-century château.

On Horseback

A network of marked trails suitable for experienced riders criss-crosses the region. Itineraries, available through the **Association Départementale de Tourisme Equestre en Vaucluse (ADTEV)**, include suggested lodgings for both riders and horses. The ADTEV can also supply a list of riding centers for beginners, offering classes, half-day and all-day accompanied trail rides. *Contact: ADTEV, Comité Départemental D'Equitation, President René Francois, Chemin de Saint Julien, 30133 Les Angles,* ☎*/fax 33 04 90 25 38 91.*

Eco-Tourism

Departmental Nature Discovery Centers at Mérindôl, Apt and Sault en Provence combine outdoor activities with information about this region's natural resources.

- **The Lubéron Birdwatching Observatory** *(Observatoire ornithologique, Maison du Parc du Lubéron, 84360 Mérindôl)*, on the banks of the Durance just outside Mérindôl, is one of many good birdwatching points in the region. Look for Bonelli's eagles, Egyptian vultures, kites, all kinds of warblers, golden orioles, Alpine swifts, crag martins and penduline tits. White egrets and cormorants winter here. Information is available at the center about flora and fauna to watch for and other good sites to visit.
- **The Lubéron Regional Natural Park Center** *(60 Place Jean Jaurès, BP 122, 84404 Apt,* ☎ *33 04 90 04 42 00, fax 33 04 90 04 81 15, PNR.Luberon@wanadoo.fr, www.parcduluberon.org)*. Exhibitions and documentation about environmental issues at the park and the Lubéron UNESCO Protected Biosphere. "Discovery" stays with an environmental focus are offered at the park's group lodging center near the Buoux Fort.
- **Environmental and Hunting House and Nature Discovery Center** *(Avenue de l'Oratoire, 84390 Sault en Provence,* ☎ *33 04 90 64 13 96, fax 33 04 90 64 15 64)*. Exhibitions about the flora and fauna of Mont Ventoux and theme-based, guided outings.

Bouches du Rhône, Aix & Marseille

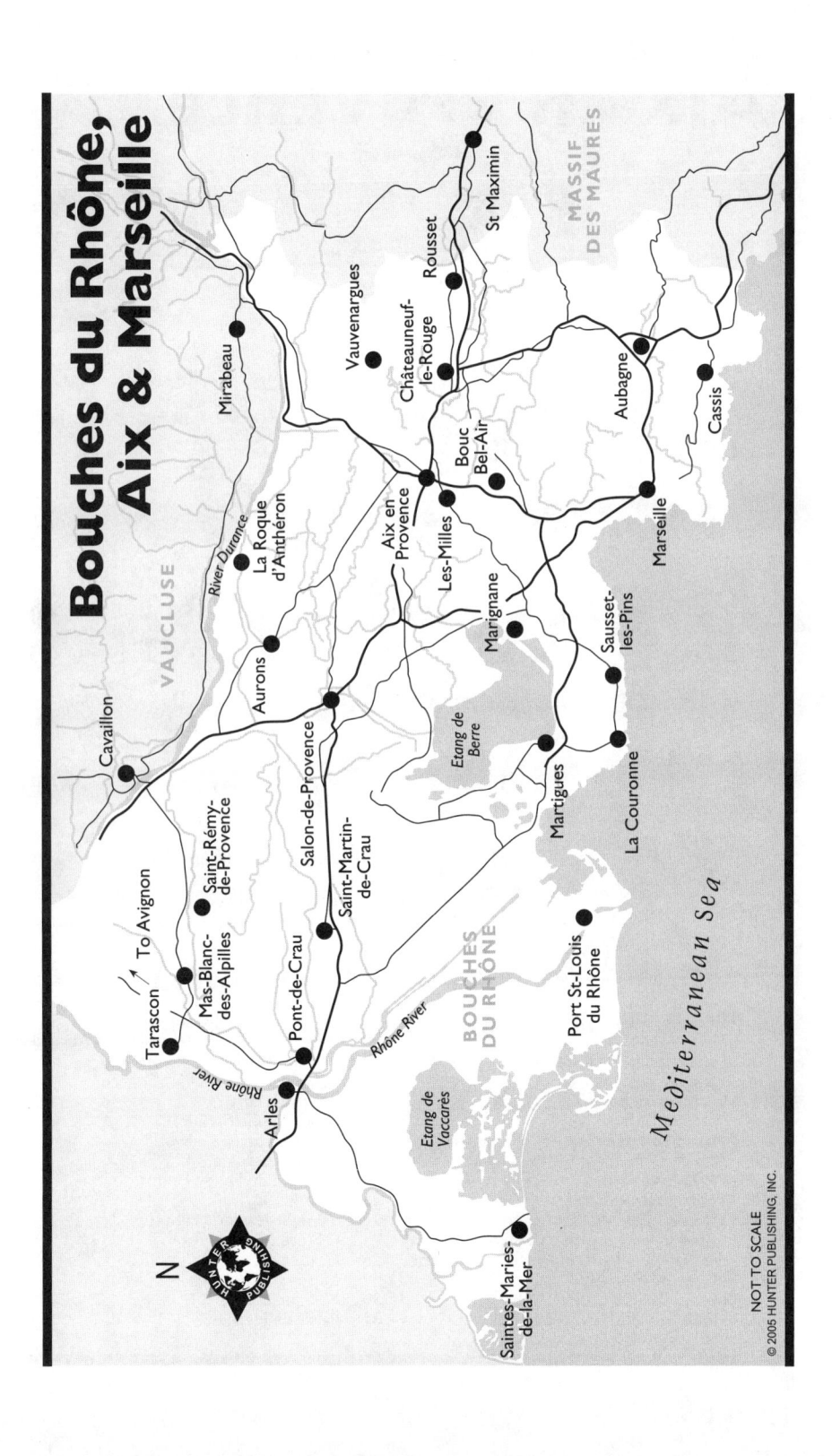

Aix en Provence

1. Place de Gaulle
2. Place Jeanne d'Arc
3. Fontaine des Neuf Canons
4. Fontaine d'Eau Chaud
5. Fontaine du Roi René
6. Passage d'Agard
7. Mausolée Joseph Sec
8. Atelier Cézanne
9. Pavilion Vendôme
10. Thermes Sextius
11. Medieval City Walls
12. Cathédrale St-Sauveur Cloître
13. Festival d'Art Lyric; Musée des Tapisseries
14. Musée du Vieil Aix
15. Forum des Cardeurs
16. Hotel de Ville; l'Ancienne Halle aux Grains
17. Église St-Jean Baptiste
18. Église du St-Esprit; Clocher des Augustins
19. Muséum d'Histoire Naturelle
20. Église de la Madeleine; Collège des Prêcheurs
21. École Ste-Catherine
22. Lycée du Sacré Coeur
23. Théâtre des Ateliers
24. Fontaine du Jeu de Paume
25. Petit Palais
26. Église St-Jean de Malte
27. Collège Mignet
28. Conservatoire
29. Musée Arbaud
30. Pôle Judiciaire
31. Palais de Justice

Marseille & Aix en Provence

A Story of Contrasts

From the industrial edge of the Camargue, barely above sea level, to the small but rugged massifs – *Chaine de l'Estaque, Chaine de L'Etoile* – that surround Marseille, this is a region of dramatic contrasts.

Gigantic ocean liners and massive cargo ships crowd the modern docks that are virtually around the corner from a 2,600-year-old harbor and golden beaches. Modern apartment blocks (including Le Corbusier's landmark Radiant City) jostle for space beside some of the oldest religious and military buildings in France, all of them tumbling in a cosmopolitan chaos to the edge of sea.

IN THIS CHAPTER	
■ Aix en Provence	148
■ Marseille	153
■ Les Calanques	162
■ Cassis	165
■ La Ciotat	167
■ Martigues	167
■ Salon de Provence	169
■ St Maximin La Ste Baume	169
■ Festivals & Fêtes	170
■ Art & Architecture	172
■ Shopping	173
■ Where to Stay	177
■ Where to Eat	182
■ Adventures	184

Basilica of Notre Dame de la Garde watches over Marseille Vieux Port from the city's highest point. ©Alain Sauvan, OTCM Marseille

Even the region's two main cities, **Aix en Provence** and **Marseille**, couldn't be more different. Marseille, an industrial, trade and transport capital, is a genuine crossroads of the world – and has been for thousands of years. Aix is a small, conservative, art- and music-oriented city, noted for its fountains and springs. Roman in origin, the look of modern Aix owes much more to the 17th and 18th centuries. It is often compared to a prim, good-mannered woman of a certain age. If that's the case, then the cultural melting pot of Marseille, France's oldest and second-largest city, could be her big, brawling, rough companion.

Between them, **Mont Sainte Victoire** rises in a familiar silhouette. Olive groves and *almandiers* begin to outnumber vineyards. It is just possible that some of these ancient trees may spring from the earliest groves in France, carried here by the first Greek traders.

In less than the 20 miles between Aix and Marseille, Provence wakes up – making the transition from a soft, dreamlike ambiance to the hurly-burly of the coast.

Candy-colored Mediterranean resorts like **Martigues**, **Cassis** and **La Ciotat** jostle for coastal space with the major industrial and technology center at **Fos**, the refineries and petrochemical plants around **L'Etang Berre**, and the pristine, vertical landscape of **Les Calanques**. L'Etang Berre, a huge (38,375 acres), almost landlocked body of calm water between Marseille and the Rhône, makes for dramatic views while driving west of Marseille but is surrounded by heavy industry and is of little interest to visitors.

Wine tasting at a Sunday Market on the Cours Mirabeau in Aix en Provence. © Ferne Arfin

With direct flights from the UK and Paris and regular high-speed rail service from London or Paris, Marseille is a convenient gateway for Western Provence and the Western Côte d'Azur (see pages 26-27).

■ Principal Destinations

Aix en Provence

Small, prim and proper, Aix en Provence bills itself as a town of water and a town of art. About 20 miles north of Marseille, it is a million miles away in terms of its spirit and style. Aix is quiet, provincial, tame and, frankly, a bit frosty. Despite this, the town of about 140,000, offers history, culture and charm in the middle of some very pleasant hiking country.

Like much of this region, the area around Aix was already part of a loose trading federation of Celto-Ligurian tribes when the Romans arrived. Their fortified settlement and capital, the Oppidum of Entremont, lies just under two miles from the center of Aix old town.

In 122 BC, the Romans were secure enough in their control of the area to move down from the defensive plateau of Entremont and establish a spa town at the crossroads of their major European routes and about halfway between their colonies in Italy and Spain. They founded what is now Aix en Provence under the bare limestone peak of Mont Sainte Victoire – the familiar peak so often painted by Paul Cézanne.

Very quickly, the town became noted for the purity of its springs, some of which are thermal. They named the town *Aquae Sextiae* – the waters of

Sextius – after the Roman consul Sextius Calvinus. Over a period of nearly 2,000 years, that name migrated through various Gallic and Provençal dialects to become the present-day Aix en Provence.

Near the end of the 12th century, Aix became the court of the **Counts of Provence**, who kept the region virtually independent of the Kings of France and Savoy for about 300 years.

The origin of the troubadour tradition and the roots of French literature in courtly romances and Provençal poetry arose within their palaces. The **University**, which is still a center of learning, was founded in 1409 by Louis II, Count of Anjou and Provence. Its Faculty of Law, now The Institute of Political Studies, had far-reaching influence. Written law, which (in France) originated in Aix, spread from there, eventually replacing the common law practiced throughout the rest of Northern Gaul. Louis' son, the legendary **Roi René**, with his queen, **La Reine Jeanne**, fostered art and music and presided over a period that is generally regarded as the town's golden age. Music and dance – traditional, classical and contemporary – remain important in Aix, with several major festivals taking place throughout the year (see *Fêtes & Festivals*, below).

Following his reign, Provence was incorporated into the Kingdom of France but Aix remained rebellious for several hundred years. This is probably why a small section of ramparts, near the northern edge of the old town, is virtually all that is left of the medieval city.

It was not until the reign of **Louis XIV**, the Sun King, in the 17th century, that Aix returned to prosperity as a courtly center of judicial and ecclesiastical power. Today's town is a feast of 17th- and 18th-century, Baroque urban mansions. Most of the fountains, for which Aix is well-known and which give some areas the constant sound of splashing water, date from the Baroque era as well.

Getting Here

By Air: Aix is about 31 km/20 miles from Marseille. It is served by Marseille-Marignane Airport – direct from Paris or the UK, connecting flights from the US. Buses travel between Marseille-Marignane Airport and the Aix en Provence bus station (Gare Routière) about every half-hour, every day, from 5 am to 11:30 pm (last bus to the airport leaves Aix at 10:45 pm). The same bus stops at the Aix en Provence TGV station and will make request stops at Les Milles. The one-way fare is €7.50 and the ticket office is near the front of Terminal 1. The Aix bus station is near the town center and has a taxi stand.

By Train: Links to Paris or Lyon take about three hours and service is frequent throughout the day. The **TGV** station is eight km/five miles from town with bus links into the town center. Frequent, regular train service (**SNCF**) is available from Marseille's Saint Charles Station. The station is near the town center.

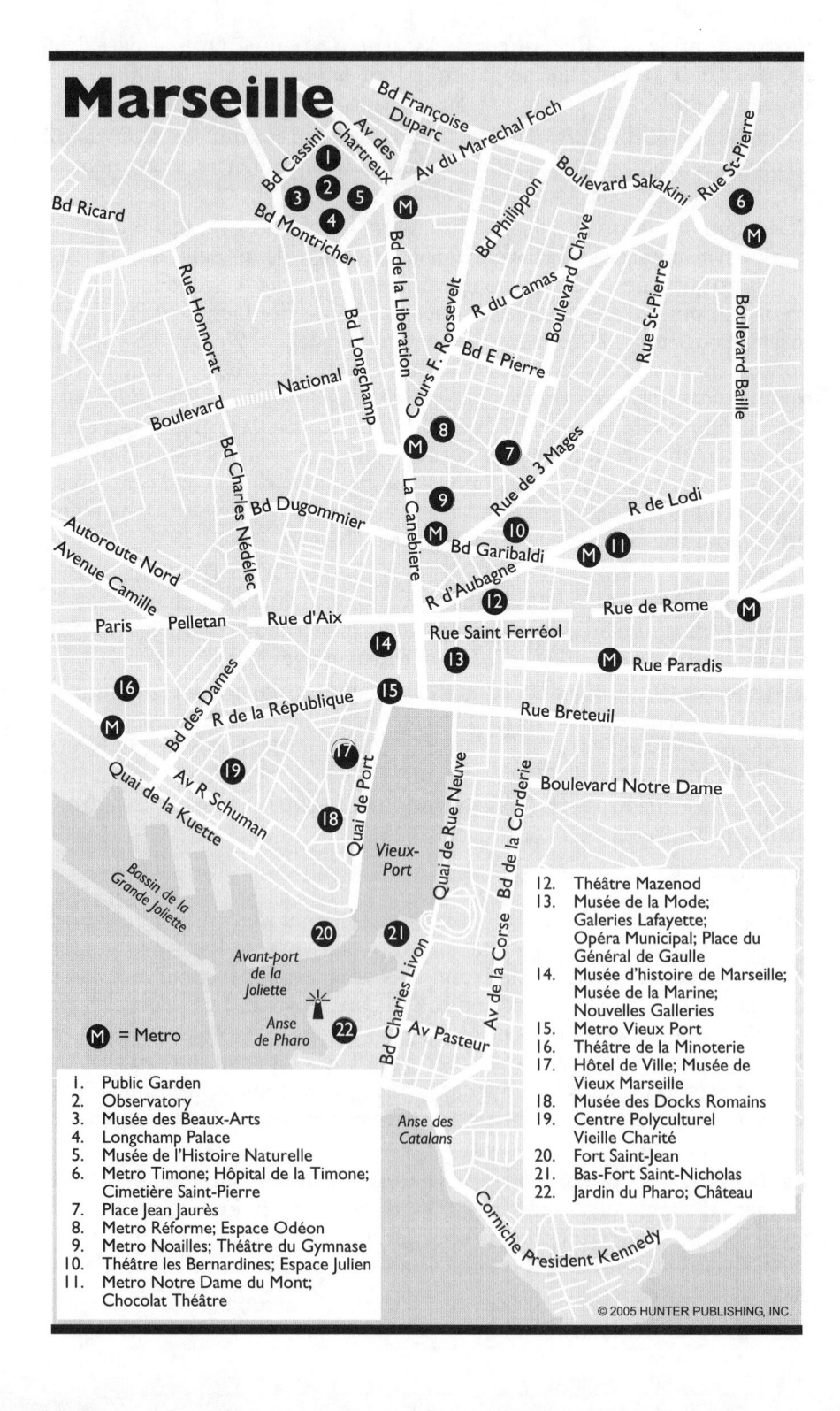

Marseille

M = Metro

1. Public Garden
2. Observatory
3. Musée des Beaux-Arts
4. Longchamp Palace
5. Musée de l'Histoire Naturelle
6. Metro Timone; Hôpital de la Timone; Cimetière Saint-Pierre
7. Place Jean Jaurès
8. Metro Réforme; Espace Odéon
9. Metro Noailles; Théâtre du Gymnase
10. Théâtre les Bernardines; Espace Julien
11. Metro Notre Dame du Mont; Chocolat Théâtre
12. Théâtre Mazenod
13. Musée de la Mode; Galeries Lafayette; Opéra Municipal; Place du Général de Gaulle
14. Musée d'histoire de Marseille; Musée de la Marine; Nouvelles Galleries
15. Metro Vieux Port
16. Théâtre de la Minoterie
17. Hôtel de Ville; Musée de Vieux Marseille
18. Musée des Docks Romains
19. Centre Polyculturel Vieille Charité
20. Fort Saint-Jean
21. Bas-Fort Saint-Nicholas
22. Jardin du Pharo; Château

© 2005 HUNTER PUBLISHING, INC.

Getting Around

Aix is a relatively compact walking town, but some of the sites (Atelier Cézanne, Entremont, Les Milles) are far enough outside of town to require bus or taxi. Most buses leave frequently from La Rotunde. The tourist information office, near La Rotunde, has bus routes and schedules posted. All stations (bus, train, TGV) have taxi stands and the town has several taxi companies. Try **Taxi Radio Aixois**, ☎ 04 42 27 71 11, **Taxi Cézanne**, ☎ 33 04 42 15 30 30, or **Taxi Mirabeau**, ☎ 33 04 42 21 61 61.

Sightseeing

Note: We fondly remembered Aix en Provence as a tree-shaded, typically bourgeois town full of Baroque mansions, lovely fountains, back streets echoing with the sounds of music students rehearsing. It is famous for its year-round calendar of music and heritage festivals. When we visited recently, a great deal of construction in the new *Sextius-Mirabeau* quarter made coming and going from the center difficult. We also found graffitti and trash defacing some of the prettiest fountains and squares. And, sad to report, the welcome, compared to other Provençal towns, was a little cool. Maybe this was just an aberration brought on by that summer's long and extremely unpleasant heat wave. We hope so.

Tourist Information: Office de Tourisme, 2 Place du Général de Gaulle, BP 160, 13605 Aix en Provence, ☎ 33 04 42 161 161, fax 33 04 42 161 162, info@aixenprovencetourism.com, www.aixenprovencetourism.com.

The Fountains: About 40 public fountains dot the old town and Mazarin Quartier so that wherever you go, in the older part of Aix, you are never far from the sound of splashing water. The fountains range from tiny wall-mounted basins to the massive fountain at the base of the tree-lined Cours Mirabeau, La Rotonde. Some others worth seeing include:

- **The Four Dolphins** (Place des Quatre Dauphins, Mazarin Quartier). Dolphins with flippers raised, on a bed of waves. Installed in 1667, the fountain centers a square of Baroque mansions.
- **The Town Hall Fountain** (Place Hôtel de Ville, Old Town). 18th-century fountain with a Roman column.
- **Le Moussue** (Cours Mirabeau). One of the three beautiful fountains on the Cours Mirabeau, this one is really unusual in that it is covered with moss – thus its name. It flows from a hot spring and is also known as The Fountain of Hot Water.

Paul Cézanne

If the distinctive limestone peaks of Mont Sainte Victoire look familiar, you have probably seen one of the more than a dozen versions of it painted by Paul Cézanne. One of the founders of Impressionism, the artist was born into a bourgeois Aix family in 1839 and studied law at the university there before going on to art school. Although he occasionally lived and worked in Paris and elsewhere, he spent most of his life in Aix and there he built his reputation. Although he painted landscapes, still lifes and portraits, he was obsessed with the shape and bulk of the mountain and painted it again and again.

In the Footsteps of Cézanne (available from the tourist office) is a detailed self-guided pedestrian tour of the key sites associated with Cezanne. **Cézanne's Atelier**, where he painted during the last years of his life, is open to the public and provides an insight into his methods as well as the objects and landscapes that inspired him. The Atelier is a few miles north of the Avignon Center, but is easily reached via a Number 1 Bus. The bus leaves every 20 minutes throughout the day from La Rotonde fountain, in front of the St Christophe Hotel, Avenue Victor Hugo. *(Atelier Cézanne, 9 Avenue Paul Cézanne, 13090 Aix en Provence, ☎ 33 04 42 21 06 53, fax 33 04 42 21 90 34, infos@atelier-cezanne.com, www.atelier-cezanne.com. Open Oct. 1 to March 31, everyday from 10 am to 12 noon and from 2 to 5 pm; an hour later from April 1 to June 30 and from September 1 to September 30. During July and August, the Atelier is open through the lunch hour and until 6 pm. Closed Christmas Day, New Years Day and May Day. Admission: adults, i5.5, children under 16, free.)*

Cathedral of Saint Sauveur: Considered by many to be a virtual catalogue of Provençal architecture, the Cathedral, on the site of a temple to Apollo, was built, changed and expanded between the fifth and the 18th centuries. Its façade has a bit of Roman wall, a 12th-century Romanesque gate, a 15th- to 16th-century carved Gothic gate and a 14th-century steeple. Inside, there are Romanesque, Gothic and Baroque naves and the baptismal font is supported by a fifth-century octagonal base. Lovers of Renaissance sacred art will want to see the 15th-century *Burning Bush* tryptich by

Nicholas Froment, inside. (Place de l'Université, opposite the old Faculty of Law, now the Institute of Political Studies.)

Architectural Walks: Much of the Old Town (north of the Cours Mirabeau) and the adjoining Mazarin Quartier (south of the Cours Mirabeau) will be of interest to lovers of Renaissance and Italian Baroque domestic and public architecture. Aix is crammed full of urban mansions, academic and administrative buildings of distinction. The tourist office can suggest a variety of walking tours, including tours with guides.

Entremont Oppidum: About two miles north of the old town, excavations, have uncovered the pre-Roman remains of the original Celto-Ligurian tribal capital. The site includes shops, warehouses and workshops as well as a large shrine. Finds from the site are kept in the Granet Museum in the Mazarin Quartier, which, unfortunately, is closed for renovation until at least 2006.

The Milles Memorial: Milles Tile Factory (*Tuileries des Milles*) was used for internment, transit and deportation of Jews from France during World War II. Thousands of Jews passed through Les Milles to Auschwitz. Today, the external appearance of the factory, a large, red-brick structure, stands unchanged. Murals in the guards' refectory were painted by interned artists. The Memorial includes a commemorative pillar along the deportees path and a train carriage of the period. An exhibition inside the carriage can be viewed by appointment. *(3¾ miles south of Aix on the Marseille Road. Open for unaccompanied visits, Monday to Friday 9 am to noon and 12:45 to 5 pm, ☎ 33 04 42 24 33 02. Guided tours of the site and the train carriage exhibition, from the Souvenir Carriage Association, by appointment, ☎ 33 04 42 24 34 68.)*

Marseille

Marseille was already an established trading post in 600 BC between the Ligurian and the Celtic tribes of the hinterlands when Phocaen Greeks sailed up the creek that is now its Old Port. In fact, cave paintings found in **Cosquer's cave** (see pages 4-5) in the nearby calanques (narrow coves cut by water out of the rock), show signs of some kind of social organization in this area going back as much as 27,000 years – during the last Ice Age!

But it was the **Phocaens** (not to be confused with that other seagoing people, the Phonecians) who really put Marseille – they called it *Massalia* – on the map. The Phocaens, who came from an island near the Turkish coast, were the earliest Greeks to make long-distance voyages. They must have liked what they discovered because, in addition to founding France's oldest city, they planted their key crops – vines, almonds, olives, apricots and cherries – establishing most of what is, today, considered Mediterranean agriculture.

They established other cities as well. By the time the Romans arrived (at the invitation of the Greeks in the second century AD), their empire included Arles, Nice, Antibes, Agde, La Ciotat and the Iles d'Hyères.

Roman domination (they changed the name to *Massilia*) was short lived, but long enough to bring the first monastic communities, leading to the spread of Christianity in Provence. By the third century, barbarians and plagues had turned the city into a backwater, but the crusades ushered in a new seagoing era. The shipbuilding and navigational skills of the Marseillaise brought the city to prominance once again, and its merchants competed with the Genoese to outfit and supply the Crusaders.

How the French National Anthem Got Its Name

The people of Marseille have always been independent – so much so that the city was, briefly, an independent republic in the Middle Ages. They've been royalist when everyone else was republican and vice versa. In 1792, however, the workers took up the Revolutionary spirit and Marseille became the first community to demand the abolition of the French Monarchy.

At about the same time, a young French officer named Rouget de Lisle, serving in Strasbourg, composed a rousing anthem – *The Hymn of the Army of the Rhine*. The song was published and circulated among a 500-strong volunteer force about to leave Marseille for Paris to join the revolution.

They marched on Paris, singing the song all the way. By the time they arrived they had perfected a chorus of such harmony and fervor that they inspired the mobs wherever they went. Hearing them approach, people would exclaim : *It's the regiment from Marseille!...C'est la Marseillaise!* Soon, the song they sang took on their name. And that, truly, is how the French national anthem got its name – *La Marseillaise*.

History

The resilient spirit of Marseille and its powers of recovery are almost legendary. Twice the city provided the entry point for Plague into Europe and was devastated by it – most recently in 1720 when it opened the door to the last major outbreak of Plague in Europe and lost 50,000 people as a result.

In the 19th century, before the French conquered Algeria, its shipping trade was regularly ravaged by Barbary pirates from the North African coast.

During World War II it suffered bombardment by the Germans, Italians and Allies. In 1943, in the guise of a civic cleanup (but more likely to destroy the hiding places of the Resistance), the Nazis evacuated 40,000 people from the city's oldest and most picturesque quarters and then

Vieux Marseille

Marseille & Aix en Provence

NOT TO SCALE

1. Musée de la Mode
2. Musée de la Marine
3. Tourism Office (two locations)
4. Square Belsunce
5. Jardin des Vestiges
6. Hotel de Ville
7. Théâtre du Lacydon
8. Musée du Vieux Marseille
9. Cathédrale
10. Square Protis
11. Place de Lenche
12. Place aux Huiles
13. Fort-St-Jean
14. Bas-Fort-St-Nicolas
15. Abbaye St-Victor
16. Tunnel du Vieux Port

© 2005 HUNTER PUBLISHING, INC.

razed the neighborhoods, leaving only a single row of older buildings around the harbor. Nearly 2,000 buildings north of the Old Port were destroyed. A large proportion of the inhabitants were sent to the death camps.

After the war, Marseille saw the rise and fall of its steel industry, the decline of its ship-building trade and the creation of an industrial super-port at Fos, west of the city, that produced fewer jobs than expected. Nevertheless, despite high levels of unemployment and poverty, today it remains one of the most important ports in Continental Europe, a center for the French film and animation, petro-chemical, high tech and logistics industries and a premier port of call for the major Mediterranean cruise companies.

MARSEILLE IS NOT FOR EVERYONE

It must be said that Marseille is not a very tourist-friendly place. This city of one million has only recently begun to promote itself as a Mediterranean resort and the local tourist authority is working hard to make it easier to visit.

It isn't a typical vacation destination. With its international airport in Marignane and its TGV link to Paris, it *is* a Provençal gateway. But, as a place in which to stay or spend time, it may not be ideal for the first-time visitor to France or for anyone easily intimidated by cities.

Nevertheless, for the urban connoisseur, Marseille has a lot to offer. Its setting, between the sea and the mountains – with amazing, long vistas across the Bay of Marseille – is almost aggressively dramatic. Along its edges, it offers some of the best diving in the European Mediterranean (in the calanques) and is surrounded by good beaches, interesting hiking and climbing areas.

It has a lively, cosmopolitan arts scene that mingles both classical French culture with North African and Middle Eastern influences; chic department stores; some excellent museums; a Second Empire palace, and the infamous Château d'If – the prison setting for both the *Man in the Iron Mask* and *The Count of Monte Cristo*.

And, of course, if you want to eat bouillabaise where it was invented, this is the place.

Getting Here

By Air: Marseille is served by Marseille-Marignane Airport (direct flights from the UK and Paris, connecting flights from the US) and by TGV from Paris. There is frequent bus service from the airport to Saint Charles Station in the center of Marseille. Buses travel every 20 minutes between the airport and the Gare Saint Charles in the center of Marseille. The fare is €8.50. The last bus leaves the airport at 10:50 pm but service is guaranteed for flights scheduled to arrive later. The bus ticket office is near the front of Terminal 1.

By Train: Marseille is served by **TGV** from Paris and by local **SNCF** and **TER** services to Gare St. Charles, ☎ 33 08 36 35 35 35.

By Bus: Buses to many surrounding communities, leave from the Gare routière, ☎ 33 04 91 08 16 40.

Getting Around

As a large, urban center, Marseille has a good range of public transportation that is easy to use and not too expensive. The same tickets and fare structures apply to buses, Metro and trams. If you are driving, it really makes sense to leave your car in a municipal garage – there's a big one near the Hotel de Ville close to the Vieux Port – and use public transportation:

The Metro: A single Metro journey costs €1.50, a day pass with unlimited journeys costs €4, or you can buy a CityPass for unlimited access to the public transportation system as well as museum admissions and tours (see box, page 158). There are two Metro lines and a short tram line that cover most of the tourist sites. It is even possible to combine Metro, bus and boat services to reach the beaches, the calanques and the harbor islands, including the Château d'If.

Buses: If you are staying close to the Vieux Port, local buses are a good bet. The Number 83 bus – La Joliette to Métro Rond Point du Prado – goes all around the Vieux Port and connects with most other bus lines. The Number 60 bus – Ballard to ND de la Garde – stops at both Abbaye St Victor and Notre Dame de la Garde. Ask at the tourist information office for other bus routes.

Ferry: A five-minute ferry trip takes you across the Vieux Port (which is bigger than it looks on most maps!) all day long, between the Quai de Rive Neuve and l'Hotel de Ville.

Power Launches: GACM *(1 Quai des Belges, 13001 Marseille, ☎ 33 04 91 55 50 09, fax 33 04 91 55 60 23, gacm@wanadoo.fr, www.answeb.net/gacm/if.html)* operates water taxis ranging from 20-minute journeys to Château d'If and the beaches of Frioul to four-hour calanque cruises to Cassis. There are also voyages to the calanques and beaches to the east of Marseille as well as a "Histoboat" tour of the entire port area. For fares, stop in at the office, located at the head of the Vieux Port, not far from the tourist information office.

Sightseeing

Tourist Information: Office de Tourisme et des Congrès, 4 La Canebière, 13001 Marseille, ☎ 33 04 91 13 89 00, fax 33 04 91 13 89 20, info@marseille-tourisme.com, www.marseille-tourisme.com. Also Bouches du Rhône, Comité Departmental du Tourisme, Le Montesquieu, 13 Rue Roux de Brignoles, 13006 Marseille, ☎ 33 04 91 13 84 13, fax 33 04 91 33 01 82, www.visitprovence.com.

Le Vieux Port: Marseille's Old Harbor is the inlet around which Marseille was first settled in 600 BC. Today, it is a scenic pleasure port and marina, surrounded by a promenade with cafés clustered around its eastern end. The west-facing entrance to the Vieux Port is protected by two forts. On the north, **Fort Saint Jean** was begun in the 15th century as a headquarters for the Hospitallers of St. John of Jerusalem. Additions were made by Louis XIV in the 17th century. **Fort Saint Nicholas**, a star-shaped fort guarding the southern side of the harbor, also dates from the 17th century. The forts were not built to protect the harbor but to keep an eye on the notably rebellious Marseillaise! Because it overlooks the city and represented the power of the monarch, Fort Saint Nicholas was partially destroyed during the French Revolution. Both forts have pedestrian access and offer good views of the Vieux Port as well as the 19th-century Joliette docks. (Both forts are on Bus Route 83, which makes frequent stops around the Vieux Port.)

The Panier District: Just north of the Vieux Port, this area of pastel-painted houses and architectural artifacts is where the original Phocaens settled 2,600 years ago. This makes it the oldest "old town" in France. You won't find any trace of the Phocaens – above-ground anyway. Or much that is genuinely old either, because this was one of the areas virtually destroyed by the Nazis and largely restored or reconstructed. The tourist authority has planned a two-hour walk through the district, marked by plaques and a red path on the pavement. A booklet for this and several other city walks is available from the tourist office.

La Canebière: Marseille's most famous street heads uphill from the Vieux Port. It is lined with luxury shops, mansions, sidewalk cafés, museums and banks.

MARSEILLE CITYPASS

If you plan to spend a few days sightseeing, including visits to the Château d'If and one or more museums, consider buying a one- or two-day CityPass. The pass, available at the Marseille Office de Tourisme, is good for all forms of public transportation, including the Marseille Metro, buses, trams, sightseeing trains and the GACM launch to the Château d'If. The CityPass includes free or half-price admission to 14 of the city's most important museums and monuments as well as discount tickets to performances, guided tours and discount shopping offers. The CityPass costs €16 for one day or €23 for two days.

Basilica of Notre Dame de la Garde (courtesy of www.tgveurofrance.com)

The Abbaye Saint Victor: This 12th- and 13th-century fortified church and monastery were built over a Greek quarry and Hellenic crypts that date to the second century BC and earlier. It is said to be the site of the first monastic order in Provence and the place from which Christianity spread throughout the region and contains third- and fourth-century sarcophagi and carvings of great archaeological interest. Despite a period as a fodder store, prison and barracks during the French Revolution (which probably saved it from destruction), the church is now a consecrated place of worship. Sacred music concerts are regularly held there. (Rue d'Endoume, behind the Bassin de Carenage on the east side of the Vieux Port. Take Bus Number 60 from the Vieux Port Metro Station, near the tourist office. Open every day from 8:30 am to 6:30 pm.)

Basilica of Notre Dame de la Garde: Whether or not you are interested in this church, built on an ancient fortified site, climb up anyway to enjoy the panoramic view of virtually all of Marseille. Garde Hill, the highest point in the city, has been a defensive lookout and communications beacon site since Roman times and possibly even earlier. The current church is built in a Romano-Byzantine style that was fashionable in the mid-19th century. It stands on foundations that were part of a 13th-century fortified church. The bell tower is crowned with an enormous gilded statue of the Virgin which can be seen from everywhere in Marseille and is known by one and all as *La Belle Mère*, the Beautiful Mother. (Bus Route 60.)

The Château d'If: Legends, fiction and fact mingle on this grim and evocative prison island just off Marseille. Edmond Dantès, Alexandre Dumas' the Count of Monte Cristo, was a fictional character – but guides will point out the hole he dug in the castle walls to escape. Similarly, the Man in the Iron Mask, title character of another Dumas novel, did exist but was never imprisoned here – yet his "cell" is still being shown. Built as a fortress in 1531 by King Francis I, the dungeon served as a prison from the late 16th century up until the 1880s. With its castle keep and three squat towers, set on a rock in the Bay of Marseille, this is a dungeon in the truest sense. The voyage across to the island via GACM launch takes about 25 minutes. There is a bar-restaurant, **Le Donjon**, on the island. *(Open Tuesday through Sunday, October 1 to April 30 from 9:30 am to 5:30 pm and closed Mondays and holidays. From May 1 to September 30, open every day from 9:30 am to 6:30 pm. Admission of €4.60 is not included in the price of the launch and is sold at the site. GACM launch, €10, from Quai des Belges, near Vieux Port Metro 1 Station. GACM, 1 Quai des Belges, 13001 Marseille, ☎ 33 04 91 55 50 09, fax 33 04 91 55 60 23, gacm@wanadoo.fr, www.answeb.net/gacm/if.html.)*

Museums

Marseille has 22 museums, most of which are open Tuesday through Sunday from 10 am to 5 pm in winter and from 11 am to 6 pm in summer. Here are a few that we found interesting:

- **Palais Longchamp** *(Metro line 1, 5 Avenues Longchamps)* – an extravagant 19th-century water tower complex houses the **Musée des Beaux Arts** *(☎ 33 04 91 14 59 30)*, a collection of French, Italian and Flemish paintings as well as the Provençal School for the 17th to 19th centuries; **Musée Grobet-Labadié** *(☎ 33 04 91 62 21 82)*, sculpture, paintings, drawings, furniture, tapestries and earthenware from the 13th to 18th century in the atmosphere of a 19th-century private mansion; **Musée d'Histoire Naturelle** *(☎ 33 04 91 14 59 50)*, with zoology and 400 million years of Provençal history.
- **Musée des Docks Romains** *(Place Vivaux, ☎ 33 04 91 91 24 62, Metro line 1, Vieux Port)* – in-situ remains of a Roman warehouse and archaeological finds illustrating Marseille's trading history from 600 BC.
- **Musée d'Archeologie Mediterranéenne** *(Centre de la Vieille Charité, 2 Rue de la Charité off Avenue de L' Évèche, ☎ 33 04 91 14 58 80, Metro line 2, Joliette)* – pre-historic collections of Celtic-Ligurian and Egyptian civilizations. Paintings and sculpture from the third century BC. Ancient history of Near East, Cyprus, Greece and Etruria.
- **Musée Cantini** *(19 Rue Grignan, ☎ 33 04 91 54 77 75, Metro line 1, Estrangin-Préfecture)* – a collection of Fauvist and Surrealist paintings, considered to be the best in France, including works by Bacon, Dufy, Ernst, Le Corbusier, Léger, Matisse, Miro, Picasso, Giacometti, Dubuffet and others, housed in a 17th-century mansion.
- **Musée de la Mode** *(11 la Canebière, ☎ 33 04 91 56 59 57, Metro line 1, Vieux Port)* – hundreds of items demonstrating the history of fashion, Mediterranean fashion in particular. Think bikinis. This is the place to get inspired before moving on to retail therapy at the chic Galeries Lafayette department store nearby.

SANTONS

Shops all over Provence display small clay figurines of rustic or biblical characters. Don't pass them by – they are not mass-produced tourist souvenirs. *Santons* (*Santouns* in Provençal – the word means saint), are a genuine and historic craft dating back to the French Revolution. During the Revolution, churches were closed. Local people made the little figures to replace church crêches during Christmas, the celebration of which was briefly banned. Aubagne, near Marseille, is now a renowned center of Santon making.

Les Calanques

Les Calanques are submerged valleys formed before the last Ice Age and then flooded when the ice melted and the oceans rose. Today, they are deep, narrow inlets, lined with jagged limestone cliffs, that stretch between Marseille, Cassis and La Ciotat along the Mediterranean coast. These "fjords" of the south were carved into the limestone massifs by rivers flowing to the sea, forming the dramatic coastline.

For thousands of years, sailors have used the inlets as safe havens during storms. In fact, that may be how the adventurous Phocaens found Marseille in the first place.

Every calanque is different. Some have small beaches at the ends – there are at least 70 sand or fine pebble beaches scattered among Les Calanques. Others have tiny harbors. Some can be reached over footpaths, others by boat from Cassis or another nearby town. There are even one or two that are accessible via public transportation from Marseille. Some are walled by an especially hard, fine-grained limestone known as **Cassis stone**. This stone has been quarried since ancient times and was used to build the quays of Alexandria and the Suez Canal, even the base of the Statue of Liberty. Others are made of softer stone and riddled with caves – many of them underwater. In a few places, most of the surrounding landscape has eroded away leaving needles and masses of isolated limestone that seem to grow from the sea.

Lovers of adventures and active vacations will find plenty to do here. Adventures include challenging cliff climbs and spelunking, boating and sailing, as well as moderate hikes suitable for families or groups of mixed abilities.

> **Tip:** Most of all, the Calanques are noted for astonishing dives in crystal-blue waters and underwater cave diving. It was in this area, not far from Marseille, where, in 1991, diver Henri Cosquer discovered the caves now named for him, with evidence of the earliest human society in Europe (see pages 4-5). Although Cosquer's Cave is now closed to the public, you can still dive with Monsieur Cosquer (see *Adventures in Water*, page 191).

Because of very high summer temperatures and lack of fresh water, most local footpaths in the Calanques are closed during the summer months. But access from the sea is possible year-round.

The Calanques of Marseille

From Marseille, you can take public transportation to the Calanques of the massifs de Marseilleveyre and Puget. One of the pleasures of Marseille is that you can combine an urban vacation with hiking and swimming around some of the wildest coast in Europe. The following routes will take you to points from which you can hike through the Calanques and down to the sheltered beaches. Hiking access is forbidden between June 10 and September 15 because of the heat and lack of drinking water.

- **Les Goudes or Callelongue**: Metro Line 1 to Castellane, then Bus 19 followed by Bus 20. Follow footpath signs to the Calanque de Callelongue.
- **La Cayolle**: Metro Line 2 to Rond Point du Prado, then Bus 23 to Beauvallon, followed by one hour on foot to the Calanque de Sormiou. (Cosquer's Cave is in a mystery location, somewhere near this calanque).
- **Luminy**: Metro Line 1 to Castellane, then Bus 21. Follow footpaths to the Calanque de Morgiou and the Calanque de Sugiton.

You can also drive to some of the Calanques (except from July 1 to September 3, when land access to the massif is closed). Callelongue, Sormiou and Morgiou all have automobile access during the cooler months.

Excursion boats from the Vieux Port will take you to one or more the Calanques near Marseille. Boats leave from the GACM dock on Quai des Belges for a four-hour cruise in the Calanques to Cassis (2 pm departure, daily in the high season, Wednesday, Saturday, Sunday and public holidays the rest of the year, €25). You can walk around the Vieux Port to find other boats that will drop you off at a calanque, but this is easier to do from Cassis (below).

Allow at least half a day for boat excursions and a full day for a hike.

THE CALANQUE DE CALLELONGUE

On its eastern edge, Marseille comes to an abrupt end at the Marseilleveyre, a massif of vertical limestone peaks and needles that rise up around the Calanque de Callelongue. We could see it from the roof of our hotel, but from a distance it merged with other hills and peaks. When our innkeeper described it as being "another world, like being on the moon" we thought he was exaggerating.

He wasn't.

What really recommends this beautiful, rugged landscape, is that it is less than half an hour from the center of Marseille and it has a charming restaurant where you can break up a day's gentle hiking and hill walking.

Buy a day travel pass (€4.50) and take the Number 19 bus to Goude at the end of the line. Try to time the 20-minute bus ride to arrive a little before the hour. The Number 20 bus, which takes you the 10 minutes further to **Callelongue**, leaves hourly and if you miss it, there's not much to do or see in Goude.

The Calanque of Callelongue is a miniscule working harbor, crammed with *pointus*, traditional fishing boats. A few pastel summer houses, known locally as *cabanons,* and a deceptively casual looking restaurant, called the **Bar Restaurant Pizzeria de la Grotte**, make up the entire hamlet. The two cave-riddled peaks of the Marseilleveyre, **Rochers de St. Michel** and the **Rochers des Goudes**, wrap themselves around it like a fortress. They rise nearly vertically, for about 1,000 feet.

In the hills below them, several well-marked and -maintained trails, including the famous **GR51** (pages 223, 237, 270) the **Balcon du Côte d'Azur** (blazed in red and white), and local paths (blazed in black and yellow) criss-cross. Paths and trails begin just beyond the end of Callelongue's one short street. A trail map is posted about 50 feet up and to the right of the head of the little harbor. Consult the map, reserve a table for lunch and head out.

The trails are easy here but paved with rough, loose limestone, so good walking shoes are essential. The views are spectacular amid pines, rock roses and rosemary. Bring a camera.

Lunch at **La Grotte** *(Calanque de Callelongue, 13008 Marseille,* ☎ *33 04 91 73 17 79, fax 33 04 91 73 20 54, €-€€)* was a another surprise. Inside, once past the sun-filled, enclosed terrace (from under the glass canopy, the mountains seem to hang over your head), the place is an extravagant celebration of Louis XVI and pre-Revolutionary France. Considering that Marseille was one of the first cities outside Paris to join the French Revolution, the theme seems ironic. There are massive fireplaces, enormous flower arrangements, gilt mirrors and portraits of royals. A painting of Marie Antoinette dominates a pink and furbelowed powder room where swan-shaped faucets emerge from a huge and astonishingly ornate, pink and grey marble, mirrored vanity. Out back, a pretty walled garden completes the picture.

Given the elegant décor, the well-prepared food is reasonably priced and ranges from small but very good pizzas to *soupe de poisson* with croutons and *rouille* (*rouille* is a fiery-flavored, rust-colored sauce of hot chiles, garlic, fresh bread crumbs and olive oil pounded into a paste and often mixed with fish stock). We had the daily special, *Pot au Feu* – a classic dish of boiled beef and vegetables in a fragrant broth – followed by *crème brûlée* in a wide, shallow dish. The place is definitely a local secret. We were surrounded by Marseillaises.

Afterward, we continued exploring the trails for another few hours before catching the bus back to the center of Marseille in time for a night on the town.

Les Calanques of Cassis

Three of the most beautiful Calanques are within easy reach of Cassis:

- **Calanque de Port Miou**: The closest to Cassis, it's about one km/.62 miles long and ends in a small, sheltered port.
- **Calanque de Port Pin**: Pine trees cling to the steep, rocky walls of this calanque, giving it the name. At the base is a small, shaded beach.
- **Calanque d'En Vau**: This is one of the most famous Calanques. Its cliffs and limestone needles rise straight out of the calm sea. It has a sandy beach at its base.

Cassis boats to the Calanques leave from the little town center harbor as soon as they fill up. Walk around the harbor until you find a boat heading for one or more of the Calanques, get on board and wait. Generally, excursion boats will visit several Calanques. Plan half a day for the outing.

Alternatively, you can walk to all three from an access point near Port Miou. The vista from the viewpoint above Calanque en Vau, which takes in Cap Canaille to the east, is really spectacular. (More details about these challenging hikes, as well as climbing and diving in the Calanques in *Adventures*, pages 184, 191.)

Cassis

Getting Here

Cassis is about 20 miles east of Marseille on the D559, Marseille-to-Toulon road. There is frequent **bus** service from the Marseille Bus Station (Gare routière – see page 157).

Sightseeing

Tourist Information: Office de Tourisme, Oustau Calendal, Quai des Moulins (on the port), 13260 Cassis, ☎ 33 04 42 01 71 17, fax 33 04 42 01 28 31, omt@cassis.fr, www.cassis.fr.

This lively and colorful fishing port is set like a jewel between the Massif de Puget and its Calanques, on the west, and the spectacular cliffs of Cap Canaille on the east. Cassis may seem, at first, an odd choice for a "Principle Destination." Its tile-roofed houses, prinked out in Provençal pastels, are typical of many villages along this coast. Its architectural highlights are minimal. It has no distinguished museum. The shops are charming but average.

But stretch out on one of its small beaches under the mist-shrouded **Grande Tête du Cap Canaille** – at nearly 1,400 feet, the highest sea cliff in Europe – and you will begin to see what some of the most important artists of the 20th century (Vlaminck, Matisse, Dufy) came here to capture.

Or taste the fresh fish, crustaceans and *fruits de mer* accompanied by a crisp, cold glass of the local white wine.

> **Did you know?** Cassis, which produces red, white and rosé wine, became an appellation contrôlée in the 1930s but it is actually the oldest wine-making region in France. In 600 BC, when the Phocaen Greeks arrived to establish nearby Marseille, Cassis wine making was already well established.

The harbor is a real sweetheart, where tourist boats for the Calanques and gorgeous private yachts share moorage with local fishing boats of very ancient origin. Cassis is one of the few fishing harbors left on the Mediterranean where fisherman still use a small, double-ended boat called a *pointu*. The high bow posts probably originated as phallic symbols and have been a feature of the boats for at least 2,000 years.

TAKE A TRIP IN A POINTU

The traditional, double-bowed fishing boat, the *pointu*, so evident in Cassis, is also seen in the small Marseille harbors away from the center – Vallon des Auffes (left) and l'Estaque, Malmousque. The tourist office organizes day trips in *pointus* that sail around Château d'If and harbor islands and explore the small coves and havens. Trips cost €42 and can be booked at the Tourist Information Office on the Quais des Belges (page 165).

On either side of the port, Cassis **beaches** are small but clean and sandy. **Plage de la Grand Mère**, just outside the port, is an especially nice sand beach. West of the port between **Plage du Bestouan** and **Plage Bleue**, a wide stone shelf is, by common consent, enjoyed by nude bathers.

Cassis is mellow, lacking much of the hype and glamour of the Côte d'Azur, farther east. It is an ideal base for divers, hikers, cliff climbers or anyone who enjoys spectacular scenery beside the sea. (Henri Cosquer is based here; see pages 4-5, 162-63.)

Worth a Side-Trip
La Ciotat

Although at least as old as Marseille, La Ciotat is basically a modern industrial city. It is at one end of the Corniche des Crêtes, a hair-raising 15-km/9.3-mile road that goes over the top of Cap Canaille from Cassis (*Adventures*, page 190). If you manage the drive, you will probably want to stop in the old center of La Ciotat for refreshment and retail therapy.

> **THE FIRST HORROR FILM?**
>
> Movie buffs may have another, much more compelling reason for making a quick side-trip to La Ciotat. Billing the town as *La Ville des Lumières*, the local tourist authority is not referring to the fine Provençal sunlight but to the home of the Lumière Brothers – early movie pioneers, who lived and worked here in the 19th century. Their film, *The Entrance of the Train into La Ciotat Station*, drove terrified spectators into the streets in 1895 – becoming not only the first film given a public showing, but possibly the first horror film as well! You can see an exhibition about the Lumières at Espace Simon-Lumière. (*Association Berceau du Cinema, 20 Rue Maréchal Foch, ☎/fax 33 04 42 08 94 56.*)

The game of *pétanque*, a variation of *boules*, was invented here in 1910, by Jules Lenoir. The association that organizes tournaments is located in town and you can contact them about forthcoming events. (*Association Jules Lenoir, Berceau de la Pétanque, Traverse de la Pétanque, ☎ 33 04 42 08 08 88. juleslenoir@wanadoo.fr, www.berceaupetanque.fr.st.*)

Getting Here: About 19 km/12 miles from Cassis on the D559 or 9.3 km/15 vertiginous miles along the Corniche des Crêtes.

More Information: Office Municipal du Tourisme, Boulevard Anatole France, 13600 La Ciotat, ☎ 33 04 42 08 61 32 and 33 04 42 08 43 80, fax 33 04 42 08 17 88, tourismeciotat@wanadoo.fr, www.laciotatourisme.com/accueil.swf.

Martigues

Four hundred years ago, three villages, l'Isle, Jonquière and Ferrières, united to form Martigues. Today, this apparently small town, divided by canals and laced together with bridges, is actually one of the largest in the Bouches du Rhône region, with a population of about 45,000. Luckily, the explosion of growth, fostered by the development of major oil refineries in the suburbs, has left the center relatively untouched and totally charming.

Known as the "Venice of Provence" (not be be confused with l'Isle sur la Sorgue, the "Venice of the Vaucluse"), it straddles one end of the Canal de

Caronte, which links the Etang de Berre with the Mediterrandean about 38 km/23.6 miles from Marseille.

Fishermen used to occupy the narrow streets around the Canal St. Sebastian, still known as the fisherman's quarter. Their pastel-colored, 17th-century houses now provide weekend homes for film stars and wealthy Marseille residents.

Sunset casts a painterly light over the canals of Martigues, near Marseille.
© *Ferne Arfin*

There are several cramped and atmospheric old districts, their lanes filled with shops and cafés. Each of the three original villages has an ancient church – the most impressive being the **Cathedral de la Madeleine**, in the center, with its wrought iron, Provençal bell tower.

Today, the center of Martigues (the island that was once the village of l'Isle) is a popular pleasure boat harbor. Its pedestrian quays are good places to look for lively of cafés and restaurants.

Throughout the summer, Martigues hosts performances and music festivals in its multi-stage, festival center, and on a temporary stage floated in the Canal St. Sebastian. **Ferrières**, the section north of the l'Isle, also has some pretty beaches on the Etang Berre. The island is probably the most picturesque part of Martigues but the best shops are scattered in the old district of **Jonquières**, the southern section.

A floating stage is set up in the Canal St. Sebastian for the Festival of Martigues.
© *Ferne Arfin*

Getting Here: 38 km/23.6 miles west of Marseille on the A55. Bus and local train service is available from Marseille.

More Information: Tourist Office, Rond Point de l'Hôtel de Ville, Avenue Louis Sammut, 13500 Martigues, ☎ 33 04 42 42 31 10, fax 33 04 42 42 31 11, ot.martigues@visitprovence.com, www.visitprovence.com (choose Martigues from the drop-down menu).

Salon de Provence

Driving around between the Bouches du Rhône and Vaucluse regions of Provence, it seems as though every road leads to Salon and every journey takes you around its many, many rotaries.

A sprawling modern town, with industrial parks and big retail outlets, Salon de Provence has a small Vieux Ville (old town) on a hill in the center, topped by a 13th-century château built by the Archbishops of Arles. **Nostradamas** grew up in Salon in the 16th century and lived here most of his life. His home, with a small exhibit about his prophesies, is open to the public. The town has also been a center for the manufacture of "le Veritable Savon de Marseille" since the 15th century. This is a dense, olive oil-based soap that is among the "must have" purchases of Provence. Two small soap-making companies still operate.

But the most important reason to visit Salon is to do some real, everyday shopping. When the charming boutiques and colorful markets pale, you still might want some ordinary shops and a few medium-sized department stores to buy batteries, underwear, disposable diapers and six-packs of diet soda. Salon is central, handy and full of modern stores.

Getting Here: At the crossroads of the A7, A54, N113, D15 and N538, about halfway between Avignon and Marseille.

More Information: Office de Tourisme Salon de Provence, 56 Cours Gimon, 13300 Salon de Provence, ☎ 33 04 90 56 27 60, fax 33 04 90 56 77 09, ot.salon@wanadoo.frwww.visitprovence.com (choose Salon de Provence from the drop-down menu).

St Maximin La Ste Baume

If you are planning to cycle in St. Baume (see *Adventures*, page 186), it is worth making some time to see this village of 12,000 at the base of the Ste Baume mountain. According to legend, Mary Magdalene lived the last years of her life and died nearby. Her relics were discovered in the late 13th century, in a fourth-century crypt, and are preserved in a sarcophagus in the town's huge royal **Basilica de Ste Marie Madeleine**, considered one of the most important tombs in Christendom.

The story is not as far-fetched as it might seem. This area was an important part of the Roman empire during the early Christian period and many towns in Provence are associated with the first saints and evangelists.

St Maximin La Ste Baume also had a thriving Jewish community in the Middle Ages. The old **synagogue** and the **Rabbi's house** can still be visited.

Getting Here: On the A8 and the N7, 36 km/22.3 miles south of Aix en Provence.

More Information: Office de Tourisme, Hotel de Ville, 83470 Saint Maximin la Sainte Baume, ☎ 33 04 94 78 00 09, fax 33 04 94 78 09 40, sce.communications.culture.st.maximin@wanadoo.fr.

■ Festivals & Fêtes

Celebrations of heritage (what the French call *patrimoine*), harvest and just high spirits take place year-round, all over the region. Local and regional tourist offices usually can provide descriptions and schedules of events.

All over the Mediterranean coast, port villages bless their fleets during the **St Pierre Fête**, a sea and fishermen's festival. There are sea parades of small decorated boats, sea-front parades, Provençal boat jousting events *(joutes)*, and singing. Often, a *grand aïoli* is served. In Cassis, they have been celebrating this fête, on June 29 and 30, since 1717. The event in this lovely little port is picturesque and worth seeing.

In Marseille

Marseille Carnival is a mad, one-day event in March, when floats from the city's different neighborhoods pour onto the Canebière and the Vieux Port for a themed parade. The parade starts after lunch on Avenue Prado, not far from the Vieux Port Metro Station, and finishes at Parc Borely.

Float themes can be quite modern, but probably not as wild and modern as the **Marseille Gay and Lesbian Pride parade**, which launches itself from the Parc du 26th Millénaire on the first Saturday in July. That parade ends with a dance party that runs from about 11 am to early next morning at Docks du Suds (pronounced soood, it means "southlands" or "southerners"). *GBLT Marseille, Lesbian & Gay Pride de Marseille, 8 Boulevard de la Libération, 13001 Marseille,* ☎ *33 04 91 50 50 12 or 33 06 14 01 32 39.*

A much gentler sort of celebration, the **Festival of the Wind**, scatters colorful kite-flying events over the Plage du Prado, an artificial beach in East Marseille. Teams from France, Italy, Switzerland and Spain compete for prizes. There are children's workshops and a variety of day and evening festivities. To get there, take Bus 19 or 83 from the Vieux Port. The four-day festival usually takes place near the beginning of September – check with the tourist office for exact dates.

During July and August, when the French take their vacations and head south, music and dance festivals bloom all over Provence. Both Marseille and Aix have cultural festivals worth scheduling your vacations around. Their styles are as different as the cities that stage them.

The **Marseille Festival**, over four weeks in July and August, is a big, brash mix of contemporary dance, theater, music and classic silent films accompanied by music. All kinds of venues, indoor and out, are used. The idea behind the festival is to involve everyone, from all walks of life and every social group. Every year is different. Details from *Festival de Marseille, 6 Place Sadi Carnot (one floor up), Marseille 13002, info@festivaldemarseille.com, www.festivaldemarseille.com.*

In Aix

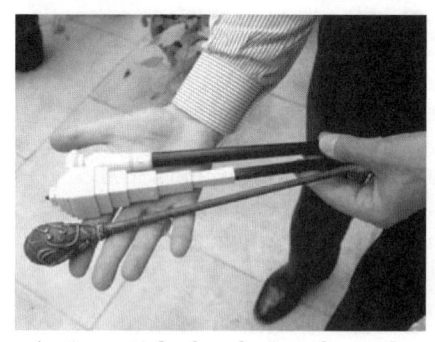

Antique sticks for playing the traditional tambourin, from the collection of André Gabriel, tambourinaire, professor, musicologist and performer.
© Ferne Arfin

The **Tambourin Festival** is held in Aix en Provence every year near the end of March/beginning of April. A *tambourin* is a traditional Provençal drum – about 3½ feet high – played alongside the *galoubet*, a traditional flute. One person plays both instruments at the same time. Events, which kick off with a blessing of the *tambourins* in Place Forbin, highlight traditional music and costumes, local life and customs.

The **Roumavàgi** is an ancient event. It is a pilgrimage procession, accompanied by medieval Provençal music, to the Priory at the top of Mont Sainte Victoire. Costumed participants, some singing and some playing *tambourins* and *galoubets*, walk up the mountain for a mass at 11 am on the last Sunday in April. The mass is accompanied by traditional songs and is conducted in the Provençal language. Folk dancing, refreshments and, oddly, a life-saving demonstration by the Vauvenargues fire department follow. This is an easy one to miss so call ☎ 33 04 17 97 00 and ask for details of the "Pèlerinage de Ste Victoire."

Most of July is devoted to the **Aix en Provence Lyric Festival and European Music Academy**. International opera performers and orchestras fill four historic buildings with operas and concerts. The European Music Academy highlights young musical talent from all over the world. Tickets are not cheap (€25 to €185), but the quality of the performances and staging is world-class. More information from *Festival Lyrique Aix en Provence, Palais de l'Ancien Archeveche, 13100 Aix,* ☎ *33 04 42 17 34 34, fax 33 04 42 63 13 74, secretariat.general@festival-aix.com, www.festival-aix.com/index.asp?lng=en.*

No sooner does opera finish than dance begins. The **Dance in Aix Festival** takes place over three weeks, from the middle of July to the beginning of August. Again, this is a major international festival with dance companies from all over the world participating. Some of the events take place in theaters but there are outdoor performances in Parc Jourdan, in the city center and in villages and castles nearby. Tickets range from €6 to €26. More information from *Danse à Aix, 1 Place John Rewald, Espace Forum, 13100 Aix en Provence,* ☎ *33 04 96 05 01, fax 33 04 96 65 30,* *danseaix@ten.fr, www.AixenProvence.com / danse-a-aix / festival / festival.htm.*

With its music schools and traditions, Aix has many more music festivals – including jazz, sacred music, Baroque music – throughout the year. Check the Tourist Authority website (www.aixenprovencetourism.com) to find out what's going on.

HAVE A PLAN B

Some of the music, dance and theater festivals described in this book are important enough to plan your vacation around. In July and August of 2003, a combination of a brutal heat wave throughout France, coupled with poor tourism numbers and a strike, led to the cancellation of almost all of the major music festivals in Provence. This was an extremely rare situation, but it is a good idea to think about what else you'll do while there, just in case.

■ Art & Architecture

Le Corbusier's **Cité Radieuse** (The Radiant City) is on Boulevard Michelet in Marseille's 8th arrondissement. It is a seminal building of modern, brutalist architecture and one of the few complete examples of the architect's theories and philosophies. If you are interested in 20th-century urban architecture, this is one of the most important residential structures in the world. Le Corbusier called it a machine for living and saw it as a vertical community, with apartments, a hotel and restaurant, an internal shopping street (half-way up), recreation areas, a children's nursery on the roof and about eight acres of parkland. It was completed in 1952 and today 1,600 people live and work in it. You can still dine in the restaurant and stay in the hotel (see page 179), which both preserve the original 1952 décor.

The **Mazarin Quartier** of Aix en Provence is crammed with Italianate Baroque architecture of the 17th and 18th centuries. The district – designed in a grid pattern – was laid out by Archbishop Mazarin in the late 17th century to provide a sort of luxury housing development for members of the Provençal Parliament and the bourgeoisie. Most of the "hotels" (urban mansions) are private, but the tourist authority organizes visits to the **Hôtel de Caumont** on Rue Cabassol. Built between 1715 and 1742 for the president of the National Audit Office, it is now the Darius Milhaud Conservatory of Music and Dance. The **Arbaud Museum**, nearby at 2 Rue du 4 Septembre, is a collection of Provençal earthenware and paintings, housed in a late 18th-century mansion. It is open to the public every day except Sunday and holidays, from 2 to 5 pm. The quarter was originally laid out along the Rue Cardinale and the Rue du 4 Septembre, where the bulk of the Baroque domestic buildings can be found. There are also several distinguished buildings along the Cours Mirabeau, which marks the northern border of the Mazarin Quartier. Among these are **Hôtel de Villars** (number 4), **Hôtel Isoard de Vauvenargues** (number 10), **Hôtel Forbin** (left, at number 20, one of the largest and oldest), and **Hôtel Maurel de Pontevès** (at number 38), the oldest house in the Mazarin Quartier.

Vasarely Foundation

Modern French artist Victor Vasarely lived and worked in Gordes and, in the mid-1970s, established a foundation there to promote his ideas about integrating art and architecture. He even restored Gordes castle to house his work. Unfortunately for Gordes, after his death, his family became embroiled in financial disagreements over the foundation, there were court suits and some scandal. The Aix area benefitted as a result. The ultimate home of Vasarely's monumental work became an equally monumental museum in **Jas de Bouffan**, a village on the western edge of Aix en Provence where Cézanne's mother had a farm. *Open every day except Monday, from 10 am to 1 pm and from 2 to 6 pm, Fondation Vasarely, 1 Avenue Marcel Pagnol, Jas de Bouffan,* ☎ *33 04 42 20 01 09, fax 33 04 42 59 14 65, fondation.vasarely@wanadoo.fr. Exit Aix-West from the A8 or A51 highways.*

■ Shopping

Department Stores & Shops

For France's second-largest city, Marseille has fewer of the big, glamorous department stores than you might expect. Nevertheless, if you are determined to visit one of the country's *grand magasins*, you will find branches of a few good ones. **Les Galeries Lafayette** *(40-48 Rue Saint-Ferréol,* ☎ *33 04 96 11 35 00, Metro Line 1, Estrangin Prefecture)*, not far from La Canebière, is a center for French and European designer fashion. Its sister store, **Les Nouvelles Galeries** *(Centre Bourse, 28 Rue Bir Hakeim,* ☎ *33 04 91 56 82 12, Metro Line 1, Vieux Port)* is nearby in a big, in-town, multi-story mall. It has similar merchandise from newer designers and more housewares. **Printemps** *(Centre Commercial La Valentine, Chemin de la Sablière,* ☎ *33 04 91 45 65 00, fax 33 04 91 45 65 01)* is farther out, both in terms of its ambiance and its location. Located in a big, edge-of-town shopping center, it carries trendy young designer fashion and housewares.

The in-town multi-story mall, **Centre Bourse**, has branches of most of the key national and regional chain stores, including **FNAC**, which carries books, CDs and small electrical equipment. Trendier shops and cafés can be found around the **Cours Julien** (Metro 2, Notre Dame du Mont) The neighborhood is full of used bookstores and record stores that specialize in the latest alternative and indie sounds, boutiques and second-hand stores.

Monoprix, in Aix, is a big town-center, budget-priced shop with clothing, toys, electronics, household goods and groceries. It is impossible to miss as it is right in the middle of the Cours Mirabeau, between the cafés and bars. Elsewhere in Aix, the small lanes in the triangle between the Cours Mirabeau, Rue Fabrot and Rue Marius Reynard are cheek-by-jowl designer boutiques – in fact, many more designer shops are here than in Marseille. And, with so many designer outlets in this rich little town, it is a fair bet that there are also a number of good second-hand shops – or dress agencies, as Europeans call them – where you can get very lightly worn, top label apparel. Try **Trifouille Boutique** (1 Rue Laurent Fauchier) near the Hôtel de Ville, for immaculate pre-worn clothes. Standards are high – only top designer labels are accepted and they must be from collections no more than two years old. **Trouvailles** (26 Place des Martyrs de la Résistance) in the old town, is another good one. It is slightly less pricey, but clothing is still in very good shape and service is better than usual in France. Both shops close for lunch between noon and 2 pm and stay open until 7 pm.

CALISSONS D'AIX

When it comes to tradition, no special event in Aix would be complete without a box or two of Calissons d'Aix to sweeten the occasion. Christmas, New Year's, weddings, birthdays, christenings, feast days – these pretty, iced sweetmeats are *de rigueur*. There are a handful of different stories about their origin, but most people agree that *calissons* have been made here since the 15th century, possibly created for the wedding of Roi René and Reine Jeanne, who was known to be fond of sweets.

Renée Maucort in her jewelbox of a shop.
© Ferne Arfin

A confection of almonds and candied melon, blended and slowly cooked to a supple paste, the ingredients are layered onto communion wafers before being cut and iced. Their precise ingredients are secrets, jealously guarded by the handful of businesses that make them. Whatever their origin, their manufacture is unique to Aix.

At **Confiserie Léonard-Parli**, housed in a large, yellow, Belle Époque house, fronted by a small, exquisitely decorated display window, the same family has been making *calissons* since 1874. Founded by a Swiss candy maker who emigrated to France, the company then passed down through the women in his family. According to the current matriarch, Madame Renée Maucourt, the company established the first *calisson* factory when Léonard Parli invented the machine that mechanized cutting of the bite-sized pieces and also created their distinctive lentil shape.

Madame Maucourt, granddaughter-in-law of the founder, enjoys the fact that a business established by a man has been run by strong women ever since. She is keeping up the tradition by training her daughter. In a remark that only a French woman could carry off so matter-of-factly, she said, "Myself, I like to hire strong, smart women and sweet men."

Mme. Maucourt explained that *calisson* making probably originated here because Aix was the center of both melon and almond growing in France. She suggested that the quality of the local water, for which Aix is famed, might have also contributed. "In Aix, the water is very light and hot. It is spa water. When they make bread it is crusty and light. Whatever is cooked with this water is very light."

The 22 employees of Léonard Parli make their own glacé fruit for the secret recipe. They also make chocolate-covered *calissons* – called *cabossons* – and the "13 desserts" that are a Christmas tradition in Provence. Even if you don't have a sweet tooth, visit the chic little shop at the front of the factory just to feel as though you're surrounded by edible jewels.

Confiserie Léonard Parli, 35 Avenue Victor Hugo, ☎ 33 04 42 26 05 71, fax 33 04 42 26 42 76, leonard-parli@wanadoo.fr, www.leonard-parli.com.

Markets

In Marseille

The **Annual Santon Market Marseille** is one of the more important centers of handmade *santons* (small painted Nativity figures), which are absolutely essential to a Provençal Christmas. The annual market takes place from the last Sunday in November, every day from 10 am to 7 pm, until the end of December in the Allées de Meilhan off la Canebière (Metro Line 1, Réformée).

There are loads of daily and weekly markets all over Marseille. Here are a few good ones:

- **Quai des Belges**, along the Vieux Port. Daily fish market, including Sundays, 8 am to 1 pm (Metro 1 Vieux Port).
- **Cours Julien**. Fruits, vegetables and food products every day, plus... stamps – Sunday, 8 am to 1 pm; second-hand – alternate Sundays, 8 am to 7 pm; old books – alternate Saturdays (Metro 2, Notre Dame du Mont or Place Paul Cezanne).
- **Place Carli**. Books and records, every day (Metro 2, Noailles).
- **Allée de Meilhan**. Flowers, Tuesdays and Saturdays, 8 am to 1 pm (off la Canebière, Metro 1 Réformée).
- **Marché aux Puces** (flea market). Antiques, Friday to Sunday 10 am to 7 pm; flea market, every Sunday 9 am to 7 pm (Avenue du Cap Pinède, Eastern edge of town, Bus 35 or 70).

In Aix en Provence

Market day in Aix en Provence.
© Ferne Arfin

Zola was born and raised here – he went to school with Cézanne – so it's kind of cool to buy an old book on one of the streets he walked. The **used-book market** takes place on the first Sunday of the month in front of the Hôtel de Ville, from 9 am to 6 pm. Rare old books do occasionally turn up but don't count on it. Go instead for the atmosphere and the buzz of French intellectuals and serious book lovers.

Important French Provincial **antiques** change hands on Tuesdays, Thursdays and Saturdays near the Fontaine Pascal. You can drool, but remember, if you buy it, you also have to get it home.

Other Aix markets include:

- **Place des Prêcheurs**. Fruits, vegetables and food products, Tuesday, Thursday and Saturday.
- **Place Richelme**. Fish, Tuesday to Saturday.
- **Place de la Mairie Flower Market**. If the Aix flower market feels familiar, that's because artists and photographers are continually drawn to the scene, under the belfry clock. The market is held every Tuesday, Thursday and Saturday.

Above: The Chateau d'If, legendary prison, off the coast near Marseille, where fact and fiction mingle (© Alain Sauvan, OTCM Marseille)

Below: Les Calanques of Marseille (© Alain Sauvan, OTCM Marseille)

Above: Pastel houses that once sheltered fishermen are now weekend retreats Martigues (© Ferne Arfin)

Below: Martigues' best shopping is hidden away along the lanes of Jonquière (© Ferne Arfin)

Along the Corniche in Marseille (© Alain Sauvan, OTCM Marseille)

The mysterious grotto and legendary burial place of Mary Magdelene is hidden behind the House of the Parisians, a convent at the base of La Sainte Baume (© CDT VAR / www.wallis.fr)

In Cassis

Market days are Wednesdays and Fridays in the **Place Baragnon**, from 8 am to 1 pm. A free shuttle bus, called a *navette* by locals, circulates around the town taking passengers to the center on market days.

■ Where to Stay

Deluxe

Hôtel le Petit Nice – Passédat *(Anse de Maldormé, Corniche John Fitzgerald Kennedy, 13007 Marseille,* ☎ *33 04 91 59 25 92, fax 33 04 91 59 28 08, hotel@petitnice-passedat.com, www.petitnice-passedat.com, €€€€).* Two Belle Époque Greek-style villas with a pool between them overlook the Mediterranean at one of Marseille's more distinctive hotels. Every room has a terrace with a sea view that looks like a postcard and is equipped with just about the best of everything. Chef Gérald Passédat, who serves unusual seafood (sea anemone fritters, oyster *nem*) in his two-star restaurant, is the major draw to this family-owned hotel. It is expensive and exclusive. Expect to spot movie stars, captains of industry, maybe even a few heads of state.

☆☆☆☆ **Le Pigonnet** *(5 Avenue Pigonnet, 13090 Aix en Provence, 33 04 42 59 02 90, fax 33 04 42 59 47 77, reservations@hotelpigonnet.com, www.hotelpigonnet.com, breakfast buffet and room tax extra, €€€-€€€€).* A gracious stately home on the outskirts of Aix, this hotel is surrounded by a shady garden with views of Mont Sainte Victoire. According to legend – which the hotel keepers are happy to encourage – Cézanne often painted the mountain from here. Rooms are luxuriously appointed in a 19th-century bourgeois style. Even in some of the nicest hotels, French beds and pillows can seem a bit skimpy. Not here.

HOTEL PRICE CHART	
Rates are per room based on double occupancy.	
	Under €55
€	€56-€96
€€	€97-€135
€€€	€136-€195
€€€€	Over €195

GETTING CLOSER TO HISTORY

If you've ever wondered what it might be like to stay in a medieval castle or an ancient priory, a group called **La Société Hôtelière France Patrimoine** (The French Heritage Hotelier

Society, www.hotels-francepatrimoine.com) has come up with just the thing.

Since 1987, the group has worked with owners of historic properties – usually the state or local organizations – to restore them for use as two- or three-star accommodation (sometimes higher) and as venues for cultural activities. The list of 20 establishments includes ancient châteaux, stately homes and several convents and monasteries.

One such place, offering a standard of luxury well beyond its price, is the ☆☆☆☆ **Hôtellerie le Couvent Royal de Saint Maximin la Sainte Baume** *(Place Jean Salusse, 83470 Saint Maximin La Sainte Baume, ☎ 33 04 94 86 55 66, fax 33 04 94 59 82 82, contact@hotelfp-saintmaximin.com, www.hotelfp-saintmaximin.com, €-€€).* The convent was built in 1290, by Charles Duke of Anjou, adjoining the Basilica said to hold the relics of Mary Magdalene. As a hotel, it is an unforgettable experience. (You won't find the local tourist office giving guided tours of most hotels). The accommodation itself is built around the convent cloister and includes the refectory, chapel and a tower that is a remnant of the town's ancient ramparts. The 67 rooms, with bare stone walls and terracotta floors, were once monks' cells. They are spacious and stylish, decorated with traditional Provençal furniture. Renovations were completed in 2003 so bathrooms and other features are modern and luxurious.

The **Hotel Cloître St Louis**, in Avignon, is also a member of this group.

☆☆☆☆ **Les Roches Blanches** *(Route des Calanques, 13714 Cassis, ☎ 33 04 42 01 09 30, fax 33 04 42 01 94 23, hotel@roches-blanches-cassis.com, www.roches-blanches-cassis.com, open March through mid-November, breakfast and room tax extra, €€€)* is a family-owned luxury hotel on a headland that overlooks the Calanques to the east of Cassis. Most of the 24 rooms have balconies or terraces with views of Cap Canaille. The hotel features an "infinite edge" swimming pool and gardens cascading to the sea. Charming and very Côte d'Azur.

Moderate

☆☆ **The Europe Hotel** *(12 Rue Beauvau, 13001 Marseille, ☎ 33 04 91 33 65 64, fax 33 04 91 33 80 30, air conditioning, satellite TV, breakfast and room tax extra, €).* This is a recently renovated, family-run establishment near the Vieux Port and convenient to St Charles train station. Some rooms have good views over the harbor.

☆☆ **Hôtel Mercure Paul Cézanne** *(40 Avenue Victor Hugo, 13100 Aix en Provence, ☎ 33 04 42 91 11 11, fax 33 04 42 91 11 10, mercure.paulcezanne@free.fr, www.hotelaix.com/english_v/hpcezane.html, breakfast and room tax extra,*

€-€€). Close to the SNCF train station and the center of town, every room is individually decorated in Provençal colors and prints. They have armoires, four-poster beds and charming tiled bathrooms. There is a breakfast room and a small honor bar, but no restaurant. We thought the rooms were terrific but the welcome could have been warmer. Pay parking on the street was a problem when we unloaded our luggage as well.

☆☆☆ **Les Jardins de Cassis** *(Rue Auguste Favier, 13260 Cassis,* ☎ *33 04 42 01 84 85, fax 33 04 42 01 32 38. contact@hotel-lesjardinsde-cassis.com, www.hotel-lesjardinsde-cassis.com, open April to November, breakfast and tax extra,* €-€€). A Provençal *mas*, decorated simply but traditionally. Most rooms have patios or terraces.

☆☆☆ **Mahogany – Hotel de la Plage** *(Plage du Bestouan, 13260 Cassis,* ☎ *33 04 42 01 05 70, fax 33 04 42 01 34 82, info@hotelmahogany.com, www.hotelmahogany.com, air conditioning, satellite TV with English-language channels, bed and breakfast,* €-€€). Overlooking the small, sandy Bestouan beach, a few hundred yards from the village and its fishing port. Rooms are well-equipped and smallish – you pay for the view here. But what a view it is – including the Mediterranean and the dramatic cliffs of Cap Canaille.

Budget

Like everything else in this an area, contrasts apply in the realm of hotels and accommodation as well. Because Marseille is a major city, hotels tend to be more expensive and, in the middle and budget ranges, seem to offer less value. If you are visiting Marseille and want charming, typically Provençal accommodation on a tight budget, consider staying in the **Camargue**, which is within easy reach: try the Budget hotel recommendations starting on page 91. But Marseille has lots of business visitors and, if a standard business class hotel with good, modern facilities will suit you, there's a good choice of French chain hotels.

A BUDGET STAY IN A LANDMARK

Stay in a landmark for the price of a budget hotel. **Hôtel Le Corbusier** occupies several floors of Le Corbusier's landmark building, Le Cité Radieuse (see *Art and Architecture*, page 172). The building is listed for historic conservation and hasn't changed since 1952, when it was completed. Short-term rental rooms for visitors were part of the original concept and these, with their original period décor preserved in pristine condition, constitute the hotel. The style is minimalist; the smallest rooms were based on monastic cells. Larger rooms, which can accommodate four, have the view of Marseille harbor as their only decoration and oak floors that, the hotel literature declares, "… give a lot of charm without any useless luxury." The small number of "studio" rooms include 1952 designer kitchens (which can't be used but are kept for their historic interest), and artist-designed staircases. *(Hôtel Le Corbusier, 280 Boulevard le Michelet, 13008 Marseille, ☎ 33 04 91 16 78 00, fax 33 04 91 16 78 28, contact@hotellecorbusier.com, www.hotellecorbusier.com, restaurant, breakfast extra, €.)*

The **Ibis Hotel Group** *(www.ibishotel.com, €, see box, page 131 for full details)* offers clean modern rooms with basic but adequate facilities and has six two-star hotels in Marseille, three of which are convenient for the Vieux Port, most sightseeing and shopping: ☆☆ **Marseille Prado**, ☆☆ **Marseille Gare Saint Charles**, and ☆☆ **Marseille Centre Bourse**.

Etap Hotels *(www.etaphotel.com, €)* is another chain, affiliated with the same group. They are a bit cheaper and more family-oriented in that the price of the room stays the same for up to three people and breakfast buffet is included. Two are convenient for vacation visitors to Marseille: **Etap Hotel Marseille Vieux Port** *(46 Rue Sainte, Vieux Port, 13001 Marseille, ☎ 33 08 92 68 05 82, fax 33 04 91 54 95 75)* and **Etap Hotel Marseille Prado Parc Des Expositions** *(35 Boulevard Rabatau, Rond Point du Prado, Rabatau, 13008 Marseille, ☎ 33 08 92 68 31 86, fax 33 04 91 25 49 88, E2136@accor-hotels.com)*. Another is close to Aix en Provence and is a good, low-cost option for a relatively expensive town: **Etap Hotel Aix en Provence East Meyreuil** *(Lieu dit le Canet, 13590 Meyreuil, ☎ 33 08 92 68 31 74, fax 33 04 42 58 64 95)*.

Some other, less expensive hotels in the region worth considering include several interesting small hotels in Aix en Provence:

☆☆ **Hotel Artea** *(4 Boulevard de la République, 13100 Aix en Provence, ☎ 33 04 42 27 36 00, fax 33 04 42 27 28 76, contact@hotel-artea-AixenProvence.com, www.hotel-artea-AixenProvence.com, breakfast and tax extra, €)*. This was the home of French composter Darius Milhaud and its central location a block away from La Rotunde make this basic hotel worth considering. Rooms are of a decent size but, with their tile floors and simple furnishings, slightly monastic.

☆☆ **Hotel des Quatre Dauphins** *(54 Rue Roux-Alphéran, ☎ 33 04 42 38 16 39, fax 33 04 42 38 60 19, breakfast extra, 12 rooms, €)*. Close to the Four Dolphins Fountain, this tiny place is a five-storey, 18th-century townhouse. Rooms are decorated with tiles, toiles and Provençal fabrics and the owners have a reputation for being attentive. Reservations are by telephone or fax; no e-mail as yet but the hotel occasionally pops up as bookable through Internet travel sites. Best bet, telephone or write to them by snail mail.

Camping

Camping tends to be family-oriented with entertainment and facilities such as refrigerators and microwaves available to rent. Private, open-air cooking is almost always prohibited.

Note: Prices are per night for one tent or trailer space, two adults, electricity and car parking. Local taxes may be charged in some areas.

☆☆☆☆ **Silvacane en Provence** *(BP 47, 1340 La Roque d'Antheron,* ☎ *33 04 42 50 40 54, fax 33 04 42 50 43 75, www.campoclub.com / campoclub / silvac_phot01_fr.htm).* The village of La Roque d'Antheron, just north of Aix en Provence, is the only place in France where Lipizzaner horses are raised. It has a 12th-century abbey and is connected with the history of the Waldensians, an early Hugenot sect. The campgrounds are large and organized, with entertainment and sports. There are 140 spaces as well as a few bungalows and trailers. The campsite makes a point of highlighting its handicapped facilities. The basic package ranges from €10.50 to €22 in the high season, tourist tax extra.

☆☆☆ **Camping Saint Jean** *(30 Avenue de Saint Jean, 13600 La Ciotat,* ☎ *33 04 42 83 13 01, fax 33 04 42 71 46 41, stjean@easyconnect.fr, www.asther.com / stjean. Open end of March to beginning of October).* Right on the beach, this is a tent campground with facilities on the grounds of a seaside hotel. It is convenient for both Cassis and Marseille, but is less family-oriented than some others in the area and more geared to the surfing and windsailing crowd; surfing, sailing and scuba diving centers are all within a mile. There are no reservations – first-come, first-served. At about €26 per night for a sea view campsite, rates are at the high end, but smaller tent sites, with parking for one motorcycle, can be had for about a third less.

Gîtes

There is a large selection of rural *gîtes* around Aix en Provence, Salon de Provence, and La Ciotat. They change all the time so your best bet is to go to the regional information website, www.visitprovence.com. On the left of the screen, click Holiday Rentals, then Gîtes de France. A tiny Union Jack, on the upper right side of the page, translates the text to English. You can also go to the main Gîtes de France site, www.gites-de-france.fr. Expect to pay in the range of €56-€96 per night for seven nights, with a security deposit of about half the high-season rate.

If you are a fan of Marcel Pagnol and the film *Jean de Florette*, you might want to look for **Les Jujubiers**. Find it at number 294 – Aubagne, in the listings on the Visit Provence website above. *(Site booking service:* ☎ *33 04 90 59 49 40, fax 33 04 90 59 16 75, resa13.gitesdefrance@ visitprovence.com.)* Monsieur Félix Richeda and Mme. Clémentine Richeda's five-person *gîte*, in an 18th-century farmhouse, is right in the middle of the countryside where the movie was set and filmed.

■ Where to Eat

If you are going to go for broke in Aix, everyone recommends **Le Clos de la Violette** *(10 Avenue de la Violette, 13100 Aix en Provence, ☎ 33 04 42 23 30 71, fax 33 04 42 21 93 03, www.si-web.net/closdelaviolette/english.asp, €€€€)*, which has two Michelin stars and "crossed forks" all over the place. Spread across several rooms, it might offer parsnip ravioli, wild asparagus with poached eggs and morels, sea bass, pear soufflé or savory tarts dressed with balsamic vinegar. Also in the stratospheric class is the **Hotel Passédat-Petit Nice** in Marseille (see *Where to Stay*, page 177 for full details), another two-star establishment where Gérard Passédat, one of France's world-renowned chefs, cooks innovative seafood.

DINING PRICE CHART	
Prices are for a typical prix fixe menu of two courses and a glass of house wine for one.	
	€14-€19
€	€21-€34
€€	€35-€49
€€€	€50-€69
€€€€	€70-€140
€€€€€	The sky's the limit

BOUILLABAISSE

In Marseille, a meal of bouillabaisse is a must. The stew (a mixture of seven or eight different Mediterranean fish and shellfish, with garlic, herbs, tomatoes, onions and olive oil) was created here by local fishermen. Some fish considered absolutely necessary for the dish – rascasse, galinette – can be found only in local waters. Restaurants jealously guard their secret recipes. Several claim to be keepers of the flame, so to speak.

Here's a rundown of a few places that could have come right off the pages of Marcel Pagnol's Marseille novels:

- ☆ **Le Miramar** *(12 Quai du Port, 13002, Marseille, ☎ 33 04 91 91 10 40, contact@bouillabaisse.com, www.bouillabaisse.com, €€€€)*. Michelin, which rates this family-run restaurant with three crossed forks and one star, says it is *the* reference for bouillabaisse. Expect to wait 20 minutes for the preparation and to pay €48 per person for the dish. Don't worry, you won't be hungry for anything else.

- ☆ **Chez Michel** *(6 Rue Catalans, La Corniche, 13007 Marseille, ☎ 33 04 91 52 30 63, fax 33 04 91 59 23 05, €€€€)*. Slightly scruffier and retro, but with a star from Michelin nonetheless, Chez Michel is considered another *conservatoire* of bouillabaisse. The same family has been dishing up seafood here since 1946.

- ☆ **Chez Fonfon** *(140 Vallon des Auffes, 13007, Marseille,* ☎ *33 04 91 52 14 38, fax 33 04 91 52 14 16, chezfonfon@aol.com, www.chez-fonfon.com, €€€€).* Don't let the basic décor and raffish ambiance fool you. Bouillabaisse takes lots of time and bags of ingredients to make, so expect to pay for it. The tiny port of Vallon des Auffes, south of the Vieux Port under the Corniche John F. Kennedy, is a real working fishing port. Chez Fonfon has served locals here for for more than 50 years.

Of course, its possible to dine well for considerably less. Look for restaurants specializing in regional Provençal cooking and, particularly along the Mediterranean, seafood and you can hardly go wrong. In Aix, **Café Bastide du Cours** *(43-47 Cours Mirabeau, 13100 Aix en Provence,* ☎ *33 04 42 26 55 41, fax 33 04 42 93 07 65, info@cafebastideducours.com, €€€)* offers seafood, duck and lamb and an extravagant dessert menu that includes baked red fruit in batter with mousse and a terrific chocolate cake.

Cassis is full of charming, small restaurants and bistros overlooking its various beaches and the fishing port. **Fleurs de Thym** *(5 Rue Lamartine, 13260 Cassis,* ☎ *33 04 42 01 23 03. Open for dinner only, between October 1 and March 1, €€-€€€),* serves traditional Provençal dishes and seafood in the colorful local décor of tiles and printed fabrics. **Restaurant Romano** *(Port de Cassis,* ☎ *33 04 42 01 08 16, €€)* is a marine bistro with a terrace overlooking the tiny fishing port, specialising in bouillabaisse or fisherman's casserole. **Nino** *(1 Quai Jean Jacques Barthélemy, Port de Cassis,* ☎ *33 04 42 01 74 32, €€€)* is yet another restaurant where you can enjoy bouillabaisse overlooking the old port – this time in front of a house built in 1432.

Light Meals & Snacks

Pizza, as always, is good in this part of France and, along the coast, you'll start seeing *pan bagnat*, the specialty sandwich of the Côte d'Azur and the Riviera. All the towns featured in this chapter have dozens of casual sidewalk cafés where you can find an omelet, a salad or a stuffed baguette.

When we first rolled into Aix en Provence, we were too exhausted from a long drive in the heat to look for a restaurant. Just across the street from the Hôtel Mercure Paul Cézanne, we found a sort of hole-in-the-wall snack bar so basic that buying food there was probably the equivalent of buying a *Sabrett's* hot dog on the street in New York. The care they took in putting together our take-out *salades composées* was just amazing.

The Cours Mirabeau, near the fountains in Aix, is lined with bistros and bars. We tried **Café le Grillon** *(31-49 Cours Mirabeau, 13100 Aix en Pro-*

vence, ☎ *33 04 42 27 58 81)*, which serves sandwiches, salads, pasta, snacks and full meals all day. The food, as always, was well prepared and presented though, as elsewhere in Aix, the reception was frosty.

In Marseille, at the head of the Vieux Port, in an atmosphere that is at once urbane and earthy, try **Le Suffren** *(31 Quai des Belges,* ☎ *33 04 91 33 36 66, fax 33 04 91 33 38 88, info@lesuffren.com, www.lesuffren.com, €)*, a traditional *brasserie*. On Thursdays, you can have your fortune told over tea when their resident astrologer is on call – a consultation, plus a drink and dessert costs about €15. At any other time, they offer salads, pasta, pizza, desserts and drinks, à la carte or from very reasonable (€) prix fixe menus.

■ Adventures

On Foot

Hiking & Climbing in the Calanques

Vertical limestone peaks and needles rising above the clear, teal blue Mediterranean, steep, narrow paths lined with wind-sculpted pines, winding down to tiny, almost private beaches – the Calanques offer breathtaking scenery, well-marked hiking trails and well-equipped and maintained *escalade* (climbing) sites.

Hiking paths vary from moderate to very challenging. The **GR98** connects Marseille to Cassis along 28 km/17.4 miles of crests and coastline, a difficult, 11-hour hike.

> **Note:** There is no natural fresh water in the Calanques so you must bring your own. Because of the lack of water and danger of fire, local paths across the Calanque Massif, are closed from July to mid-September.

If you are a confident and very experienced hiker, you can go it alone, using Map: IGN "Plein Air" Collection, 1/15,000 scale – "Les Calanques de Marseille à Cassis." The Marseille Office de Tourisme (page 157) can provide a list of local climbing and hiking clubs, many of which will arrange guides. Both the Marseille and Cassis tourist offices can furnish maps of local cycling and hiking routes.

It is possible to enjoy the Calanques even if you have less experience. About 80% of the Calanque Massif is within the municipality of Marseille and the city itself owns about 20% of it. The local tourist authority has made the most of providing access to this striking natural area. Group tours accessible to anyone, in the company of professional guides, leave regularly from the tourist information office on the Quai des Belges. The cost is €15; children 12 and under go free. The guide provides knowledgeable commentary on the flora and fauna in this fragile ecosystem. Paths in the Calanque Massif can turn suddenly treacherous, so this is a good idea for first-timers to the area.

A more challenging hike, the **Adventure Trail in the Calanques**, which can also be booked at the tourist office, lasts three hours and includes **zip lines** and **abseiling** as well as hiking. The cost of the tour, which leaves from Calanque gateways at Callelongue and Sormiou, is €35.

Escalade

Sparkling white limestone cliffs above a sea that in good weather is really the color of sapphires, have drawn cliff-climbers to the Calanques for decades. Claiming to be the cradle of modern escalade, the area boasts cliffs that range in difficulty from 3 to 8, according to the French system. The main equipped climbing sites are located in the Calanques of Les Goudes, Marseilleveyre, Sormiou, Morgiou, Luminy and La Gardiole. Although the tourist office can advise you on how to find these, a local guide makes more sense. **Les Guides des Calanques**, an association of outdoor sports professionals, can suggest individual guides and group leaders for the Calanques as well as the cliffs between Cassis and La Ciotat. *(Les Guides des Calanques, Rue Lorraine, Plan de Cuques, 13013 Marseille, ☎/fax 33 04 91 07 46 96, cell 33 06 80 00 49 41, info@lesguides.net, www.les-guides.net/agences.htm.)*

Mont Sainte Victoire

A challenging four-hour round-trip itinerary takes you up the north slope of Mont Sainte Victoire, past an unusual prehistoric burial site and on to outstanding viewpoints of the Alps and the surrounding countryside.

The hike begins at the Domaine Départementale parking de La Sinne-Puits d'Auzon, just past Col des Portes on the D10 (east of Vauvenargues). Follow yellow path markers until Col des Portes then red path markers to the summit.

- Leave the parking area, and continue along the D10 for about 200 m/650 feet, then take the Puits d'Auzon path (northeast, and then north) toward la Sinne. La Sinne is a farm and astronomical observatory, located in the midst of a large forest. On reaching a deep hollow you will see la Sinne, on the heights opposite. (estimated time for this lap of the hike is about 20 minutes).

- Leave the observatory on the path to the left, and follow it as it climbs gently through junipers. You will pass a cable across the road to prevent vehicular access. The path crosses a plateau used as pasture for sheep. Enjoy the scent of thyme, juniper and wild roses.

- About 300 m/985 feet after the cable, leave the marked trail – which climbs to the right – and, instead, take the path on the left, toward la Citadelle. This leads from one cairn to another, up to the crest. There is an ancient tumulus on the right. The rock piles you will see are most likely Bronze Age markers of a burial site.

- Continue left, toward the south, for a short distance until you rejoin the yellow-marked trail. From here, in good weather, you can see the summits of the Alps.
- As you continue toward the crest of la Citadelle, the path crosses an important fortification. Look for a painted stone marker on the ground, which indicates the directions to Col des Portes, la Citadelle and la Sinne (estimated time from la Sinne to the Citadelle, 25 minutes).
- From the painted stone, take the trail toward le Col des Portes, following a sheep path and keeping to the left, across a garrigue with juniper and herbs. Look for *santoline*, with small greyish leaves and white flowers, also called *pebre d'aille*. This is a uniquely Provençal herb with no English equivalent. It is sometimes used to season chèvre (goat cheese).
- Cross a trail and climb toward a smaller path. Near the crest, head south, toward a little stand of pines and green oaks. Cross the little wood.
- Leave the path (which now descends steeply toward the right) and continue straight, walking beside a stone wall for an gentle descent towards le Col des Portes (estimated time, 20 minutes).
- At the Col, take the path opposite (red trail markers), which climbs toward the southwest through mixed vegetation of junipers, lavender, thyme, cypress and boxwood. The climb is steady and pleasant, despite several steep passages. There are excellent Alpine views.
- Briefly, the path follows along a false summit, bare of vegetation and parallel to the crest of Sainte Victoire, which it quickly rejoins at the Col de Cagoloup (this is the GR9 trail, marked with red and white blazes). Just north of the Col de Cagoloup, you will see the Gouffre de Garagai, a chasm, 15 m/50 feet across.
- Continue along the GR9, toward the west to Pic des Mouches (the summit), where there is an orientation table and fabulous views (estimated time, one hour).
- Return along the path you came on as far as Col des Portes, then take the path that follows the D10 to your departure point (estimated time, one hour 15 minutes)

On Wheels

Cycling La Sainte Baume

This ride along the crest of the Chaine de la Sainte Baume offers stunning views of the wide, cultivated plain of Saint Maximin and the historically and spiritually important village of Saint Maximin la Sainte Baume, which is held by many to be the last resting place of Mary Magdalen. This is a well signposted, 55-km/34.2-mile circuit on paved roads and cycle trails, suitable for riders of intermediate ability. The estimated time is three hours and 25 minutes. There is one steepish, off-road climb, rising steadily through about 500 m/1,640 feet over a distance of nine km/5.6 miles. After that it's level or downhill most of the way. Watch for green and white, arrow-shaped Départemental Cycle route signs, marked "3." Until you clear Saint Maximin la Sainte Baume, you'll be following a cycle lane along the busy RN7 so you're likely to encounter traffic for the first few miles. After that, most roads are very quiet.

- Leave Saint Maximin la Sainte Baume from Place Malherbe, going south along **Boulevard Jean Jaurès (RN7)**. Follow the RN7 left onto Boulevard Victor Hugo. At the traffic lights, turn right onto Avenue du XVe Corps and Avenue d'Estienne d'Orves. (Streets in French towns sometimes have two names, but don't worry, you're still on the RN7.)
- Go straight across the rotary onto the **RN560** toward **Saint Zacharie**. Continue along the RN560. You will cross a railroad bridge. About 1½ km/one mile south of the town, look for the **Oratory of Saint Pilon**. This small 15th-century chapel marks the spot where, according to local legend, the dying Mary Magdalen was carried by angels to receive her last communion from Saint Maximin.
- At the traffic lights, turn left toward **Mazaugues**, along the **RD64**. Cross the Cauron River at the Mazaugues Bridge and, a bit farther along, cross the Canal de Provence.
- At the next intersection, take a right onto the **RD1**.
- Then, at the next intersection, take a left toward Rougiers and head for the center of the village. **Rougiers**, at the 11-km/6.8-mile mark, sits at the base of the Massif de la Sainte Baume. It is overlooked by the ruins of the medieval village of **Saint Jean**, which was inhabited between the 12th and 15th centuries. If you need to take a break, this is a good spot because the steepest, off-road part of the route starts here.
- At the intersection on Avenue de Brignoles, turn left onto **Rue Ste Anne**. Continue straight until you join the **Route des Glacières**, a forestry road that climbs the first foothills of la Sainte Baume. Above you, on the right, look for the **Chapel of Saint Jean de Solférino**.

   Note: Before leaving Rougiers, check the information board near the Mairie (the village hall) to make sure the Route des Glacières is open. It is sometimes closed when there is a risk of forest fires. Whatever you do, don't cross the safety barriers.

- The climb continues to the domain of **Font-Frège** at the 20-km/12.4-mile mark. You can turn right here, onto the RD 95, or you can take a left for a short detour to explore several 13th- to 19th-century ice houses, the **Glacières**, of this area.

Glacières Detour

The Massif de la Sainte Baume has the largest collection of ancient ice houses in the Mediterranean basin. The first of these small stone structures was built around 1650.

At the intersection of the RD 95, turn left towards Mazaugues. After about 250 m/820 feet, in the domaine of Font-Frège, you'll see a series of ancient ice houses. Continue toward Mazaugues for 2.2 km/1.4 miles. Near the sign for the **Glacière de Pivaut**, take a right onto a dirt track. The track climbs 80 m/260 feet, over a distance of 200 m/650 feet. The Glacière, which is owned by the departmental council, can be visited free, whenever the trail is open.

Retrace your path to return to the intersection of the RD95.

- At the intersection of the RD95, follow signs toward **Plan d'Aups la Sainte Baume**. The road winds through the protected St. Baume Forest and past the *maison forestière* (forest ranger station) at **Les Béguines**.
- Turn left onto the **RD80**. Leave this intersection to the left on the **Chemin des Rois** and, after passing several small chapels, arrive at the **Grotto of Mary Magdalen**. Whatever your religious inclination, it is hard not to find the grotto and forest that surrounds it magical. The grotto is at the bottom of a natural dome, carved from the native rock, several hundred feet high. Stop to appreciate the setting and it becomes easy to understand why early Christians in the region found it awe-inspiring. After your visit, backtrack the short distance to the RD80.

THE MYTHICAL FOREST & GROTTO

In Provençal, the word for grotto is *baumo* – the Sainte Baume of this area is not a person but the *Holy Grotto,* which is believed to have sheltered Mary Magdalen during the last years of her life and which gave its name to the mountain and region. The grotto, which became a recognized shrine in the Middle Ages, is one of the West's most frequently visited pilgrimage sites and also one of its oldest. During the Middle Ages, eight popes and 18 kings made their way into this forest to visit it.

The forest itself is extremely ancient, filled with the kind of moisture-dependent flora and fauna that is relatively rare in Provence. It harbors very old trees – some yew trees are nearly a thousand years old. The forest has been protected since the early Middle Ages, through papal bulls and royal decrees. In modern times, it came under the protection of the French National Forestry Office (ONF) and remains an environmentally protected site.

- The **Hôtellerie de la Sainte Baume**, on the RD80 at the 26-km/16.2-mile mark, is an international cultural center and the Écomusée de La Sainte Baume. Stop to see the permanent and temporary exhibits before continuing on to La Magdala at the 28½-km/17.7-mile mark.
- Turn right onto the **RD480** or continue straight ahead for another 1.2 km/.74 mile for a break in **Plan'd'Aups La Sainte Baume**.

A Break Along the Way

Try **Lou Pebre d'Ai**, a two-star hotel and restaurant. Recommended (with three chimneys) by *Logis de France*, the hotel is surrounded by the cool forests of La Baume. Lunch on the terrace, under a striped awning beside the pool, is very affordably priced with three-course menus starting as low as €20. If you decide to stay, the rooms are simply, but comfortably furnished in colors that echo the shady grounds. *(Quartier Sainte Madeleine, 83640 Plan d'Aups, ☎ 33 04 42 33 04 50 42. lou.pebre.dai@wanadoo.fr, www.loupebredai.com, meals €-€€, rooms €)*

- If you have gone into Plan d'Aups, return to the La Magdala intersection and descend, to the left, on the RD480 to the **Pas de Peyruis**, a beautiful, wild valley. This is another road that is sometimes closed in the forest fire season. Check for signs announcing closures outside the Mairies of the villages you pass through along the way. The road descends along ledges to the bottom of a deep ravine where you can visit the **Chapel of Notre Dame d'Orgnon**, a private chapel built in 1609 in the ruins of a Roman building.
- Continue, crossing over the Huveaune Bridge to **Saint Zacharie**, at the 38-km/24-mile mark. This is a big town with large, shady squares. The narrow lanes hide picturesque old portals and 16 lovely fountains.
- From the Place du 4 Septembre, turn right onto the **Rue Jean Jaurès** (the **N560**). Take care, this is a busy road.
- Staying on the N560, turn right onto **Avenue Frédéric Mistral** and climb the valley of the Huveaune toward Saint Maximin la Sainte Baume (another busy stretch of road).
- Continue across the plain, taking the left fork at the Châteauneuf intersection (46 km/29 miles) with the D280 and staying on the N560.
- When the D280 rejoins the road, at an intersection that also includes the D1, stay to the left on the N560.
- A few miles southwest of St. Maximin, on the N560, after a crossing to avoid the highway access route, look for the Roman columns of **Saint**

Pilon, which mark the passage of the **Aurelian Way**. Continue straight on the N560 to return to the starting point.

A Scenic Drive Above the Coast – the Corniche des Crêtes

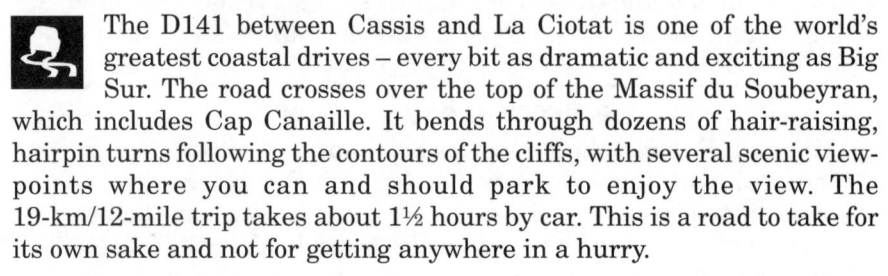

The D141 between Cassis and La Ciotat is one of the world's greatest coastal drives – every bit as dramatic and exciting as Big Sur. The road crosses over the top of the Massif du Soubeyran, which includes Cap Canaille. It bends through dozens of hair-raising, hairpin turns following the contours of the cliffs, with several scenic viewpoints where you can and should park to enjoy the view. The 19-km/12-mile trip takes about 1½ hours by car. This is a road to take for its own sake and not for getting anywhere in a hurry.

- Leave the town center of Cassis, going east toward Toulon on the **D559**, signposted for the **A50** to **Toulon**. As you climb away from Cassis, look for the **D141**, a right turn signposted Cap Canaille.
- At the sign for Pas de la Colle, turn left (off the D141, which turns sharply right here) and climb **Mont de la Saoupe**. Stop at the summit, park and enjoy the view, looking west over Cassis.
- Return to **Pas de la Colle** and rejoin the **D141**, which is now straight ahead, across the intersection. This road winds back and forth over the top of the massif. The views from **Cap Canaille**, and **Semaphore** (right turn and a short way off the D141) are outstanding and vertiginous but there are scenic vistas all along this route. Watch for them and stop wherever you can park.
- Continue southwest along the D141, which will eventually lead to La Ciotat.

On Water

The French call diving *la plongée* and the Mediterranean between Marseille and Cassis is recognized as one of the best diving areas in France – so much so, in fact, that the two main French organizations regulating the sport (The French Federation for Underwater Sports and Studies and The National Professional Divers Institute) have their headquarters there. It all began, of course, with diving pioneer Jacques Cousteau, who tested his early equipment here.

Diving

Off Marseille, the main draw is a remarkable collection of diveable wrecks. **D'If** and the **Friol Islands** that dot the harbor, have been collecting unfortunate ships for thousands of years. The index includes everything from Phoenician and Roman galleys to World War II remains. There are even remnants of the *Grand Saint Antoine*, the ship that brought the last plague epidemic to Europe in 1720.

Red coral, until quite recently processed for jewelry, and yellow coral, along with a wide variety of fish and crustaceans, also draw divers to the clear, blue waters. Several areas are recommended for their wildlife, including:

- **The Coral Cave**: South of Maïre Island, noted for red coral beds in less than 15 m of water. It is popular for night dives.
- **Les Moyades**: A small islet near the harbor island of Riou. At 20 to 40 m/66 to 130 feet, rock lobsters, conger eels and sea urchins hide among the blue gorgonias (a variety of sea polyp).
- **Impérial de Terre**: The smallest area, and the easiest to reach, off the east side of Riou, where all kinds of colorful wildlife contrast with the white limestone of the island.

The **Marseille Tourist Office** (☎ 33 04 91 13 89 00) will provide a list of diving clubs and instructors, as well as information about specific dive sites. Experienced divers who want to spend a bit more time can arrange local diving cruises. **Croisières Plongée Mediterranée** operates two- to seven-day diving cruises on their boat *La Revatua*, for experienced, qualified divers, between Marseille and the islands of Hyères. They'll also organize group day-cruises (for a minimum of 18) costing €90 per person for two dives and lunch. Equipment rental is €80 per week. *(Croisières Plongée Mediterranée, 10 Traverse de la Gaye, Soleil 4, 13009 Marseille, ☎/fax 33 04 91 74 75 23, boat, 33 06 84 49 01 49, info@revatua.com, www.revatua.com/english/accueil.htm.)*

If you want to dive with France's most famous diver since Monsieur Cousteau, you have to go to Cassis, where Henri Cosquer, discoverer of the 27,000-year-old painted caves of the Calanques, maintains a dive center for beginner to experienced divers. **Cassis Services Plongée** is located in the center of Cassis harbor. Prices range from €55 for a first dive (including one-on-one instruction, equipment rental, insurance plus first dive certificate) to several hundred euros for lessons to various certificate standards. Experienced divers may also join the team at Cosquer's dive center for night dives and exploration of the Calanques. Sadly for divers, the famous underwater cave is now protected and closed to the public, but there are still wonderful discoveries waiting to be made. *(Henri Cosquer, 3 Rue Michel Arnaud, BP 65, 13714 Cassis Cedex, ☎ 33 04 42 01 89 16, fax 33 04 42 01 23 76, henri.cosquer@cassis-services-plongee.fr, www.cassis-services-plongee.fr/anglais/default.asp.)*

Windsurfing & Sailing

There are so many places to rent boats, to learn to sail and to windsurf in Cassis, Marseille and La Ciotat that your best bet is to contact the local tourist offices. The area is undergoing a yachting and sailing boom and you can find anything from a one-man Laser or Mercury up to a fully crewed yacht. It is even possible, in Marseille, to rent out an old schooner.

Windsurfers are attracted to surfing areas at **Pointe Rouge** and **Prado**, where international competitive windsurfers train.

Beaches

If lying about in the sun, combined with a bit of snorkeling, sounds like just about enough activity, you're never far from a good beach. Marseille is lined with beaches, but, except for Prado, they are not wide and, as a major city, Marseille has a big working population who take to the beaches on hot days.

If you want a quiet, uncrowded beach, try a boat trip to the Calanques (see page 165) or take a GACM water taxi from the Vieux Port to the magical beaches of the **Frioul Islands** in Marseille harbor. These include sand beaches at **Maison des Pilotes** and **Saint Estève Calanque**, and pebble beaches at **Havre de Morgiret** and **Debarcardére**. Boats cost €10 and leave the Quai des Belges every hour during the summer and every hour and a half the rest of the year. The trip takes about 25 minutes. This is really worth doing. Once you arrive at a beach on le Frioul, you won't believe you are within shouting distance of France's second-largest city.

Haute Provence

Canyons, Gorges & Hidden Valleys

Along the Côte d'Azur and the Riviera, this region is usually referred to as *l'arrière pays* – the back country. And, like "the sticks" the world over, it isn't known for its cosmopolitan centers, historic treasures or sophisticated resorts.

The Pre-Alps that stretch across the top of Provence from the edge of Vaucluse to the Italian border are scattered with tiny villages, some pretty, others rugged and workaday, one (Dignes) big enough

IN THIS CHAPTER	
■ Getting Here	193
■ Getting Around	196
■ Les Gorges du Verdon	196
■ Where to Stay	207
■ Where to Eat	210
■ Useful Contacts	211
■ Worth a Side-Trip	
Digne les Bains	212
Puget Theners	213
The Route Napoléon	214

to be called a town. None of these places, of themselves, could be considered a "destination," principal or otherwise.

But if you love dramatic landscapes, nearly vertical gorges, calm mountain lakes and valleys so deep and tight they have their own climates, you can't help finding Haute Provence thrillingly beautiful.

This is where the mellow- , vine- , olive- and lavender-covered hills give way to abrupt and challenging Alpine landscapes. There is no clear line of demarcation. Instead, the landscape folds back and forth upon itself, seeming to suggest the giant tectonic forces that created the Alps. One moment, you will be staring up at arid, deeply eroded limestone peaks – hot and almost lifeless, some of the least populated areas in France. Turn a corner for a rapid descent to the floor of a gorge only six m (20 feet) wide, so damp and cool that water seems to seep out of its moss-covered walls.

This is kayaking, rafting and canyoning territory, an area for real, open-air or lodge camping, for *gîtes* and hostels. There are splendid hikes, lake-based watersports, heart-stopping drives, mountaineering and the uniquely European climbing sport of *via ferrata* (see page 197). In this chapter, the principal destinations are the gorges and mountains themselves, rather than the villages and towns that provide stopping places in a landscape so wild that much of it was undiscovered before the beginning of the 20th century.

■ Getting Here

By Air: Nice and Marseille are the most convenient gateway airports to this region, with Nice being the closest. From Nice Airport take the shuttle bus, which leaves every 20 minutes, to Nice Bus Station (Gare Routière) in Nice Center. The Chemin de Fer de Pro-

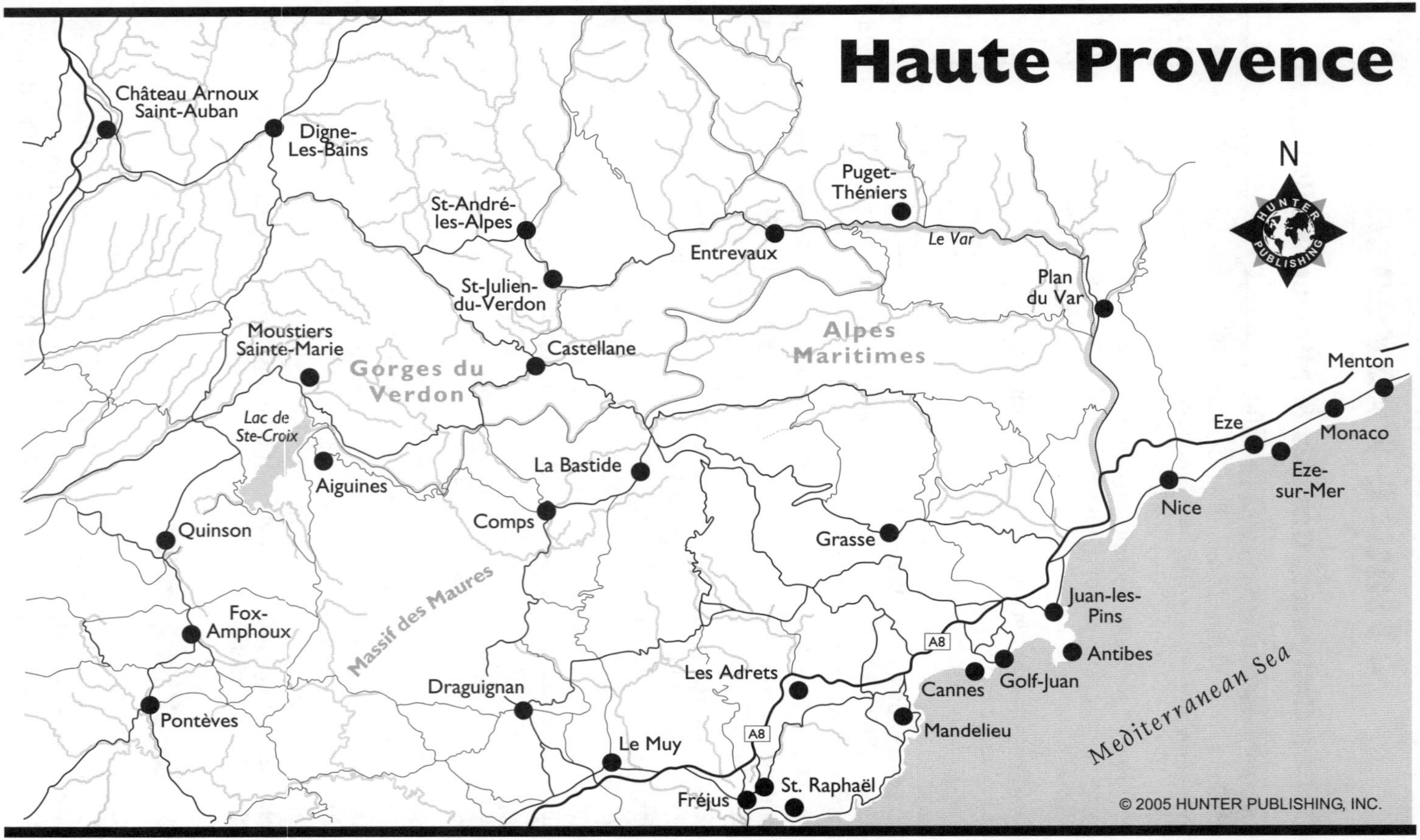
Haute Provence
N
HUNTER PUBLISHING
Château Arnoux
Saint-Auban
Digne-
Les-Bains
St-André-
les-Alpes
St-Julien-
du-Verdon
Puget-
Théniers
Entrevaux
Le Var
Plan
du Var
Moustiers
Sainte-Marie
Gorges du
Verdon
Castellane
Alpes
Maritimes
Menton
Lac de
Ste-Croix
Aiguines
La Bastide
Eze
Monaco
Eze-
sur-Mer
Nice
Comps
Quinson
Grasse
Massif des Maures
Fox-
Amphoux
Juan-les-
Pins
A8
Antibes
Les Adrets
Draguignan
Cannes
Golf-Juan
Pontèves
Mandelieu
Mediterranean Sea
Le Muy
St. Raphaël
Fréjus
© 2005 HUNTER PUBLISHING, INC.

vence (see *Le Train de Pignes*, below) leaves from Nice Gare du Sud, at 9 am daily for Saint André. From Saint André, take a taxi to Castellane or Moustiers. If you are lucky enough to be staying at the Bastide de Moustiers, you could, of course, charter a helicopter and land on the hotel's own helipad.

From Marseille Airport, take a shuttle into Marseille Center. From the SNCF train station, catch the bus service run by **Autocars Sumian** (☎ *33 04 42 67 60 34*) to the Gorges du Verdon. The service leaves Marseille at 8:30 am, reaching Moustiers at 10:50 and continuing on to La Palud sur Verdon, Rougon and Castellane (arrives at noon). The cost to the end of the line is €19.90. The service runs three times a week (Monday, Wednesday and Saturday, except holidays) from July 1 to September 15 and Saturdays only from September 16 to June 30.

LE TRAIN DES PIGNES

The Chemin de Fer de Provence between Nice and Digne Les Bains is more than just transportation between the coast and the high country. The narrow gauge train that makes the 151-km/90-mile, three-hour journey four times a day is an institution, a fun way to travel and a tremendous scenic outing in its own right.

The route, takes in 50 tunnels, bridges and viaducts, rising to an altitude of 1,000 m/3,280 feet as it connects a string of small mountain villages with tiny, picturesque stations. The narrow, metric gauge enables the train to take very tight curves and steep climbs, opening up wild landscapes, many of which cannot be seen any other way. Between Annot and Entrevaux stations, watch for a deep V-shaped cleft in the mountains. This is the **Gorge de Daluis**.

Despite its recently adopted official name, people still call it the Train de Pignes, which means Pine Cone Train. No one is quite sure where the name comes from. One story has it that the train travels so slowly you can get out and collect pine cones. Another suggests that pine cones were once used as tinder to fire up the engines. Either way, the name is unrelated to the countryside through which the train travels.

Using the same ticket, you can get out anywhere along the route for a picnic, a hike or a restaurant meal, then return on another train later in the day.

You can take the Train des Pignes to Saint André Les Alpes (€13.20) for **The Gorges du Verdon**, to Puget Theniers (€8.20) for **Via Ferrata** or all the way to **Dignes** (€17.64) to connect up with main SNCF rail for onward journeys.

During the summer, the line runs an old-fashioned **steam train** between Puget Theniers and Annot, with open benches for seats,

In addition to the daily steam train, Chemin de Fer de Provence operates four daily runs between Nice and Digne. Between Christmas and Easter, the line also runs snow trains into the ski areas of the Southern Alps.

For more information about the Train des Pignes, visit www.trainprovence.com/index_provence.asp. Or you can contact the Chemins de Fer de Provence station at Nice, 4 bis Rue Alfred Binet, 06000 Nice, ☎ 33 04 97 03 80 80, fax 33 04 97 03 80 81, or the station at Digne les Bains, 1 Avenue Pierre Sémard, 04000 Digne les Bains, ☎/fax 33 04 92 31 01 58.

Getting Around

The Gorges du Verdon

By Bus: A free shuttle bus service operates twice per day in each direction between the key stopping places along the Gorges hiking paths. It runs every day between July 1 and August 31, weekends and holidays between April to the end of June and during the month of September. If your timing is right, it is an alternative to taxi pick-ups.

Principal Destinations

Les Gorges du Verdon

The Gorges du Verdon, which mark the border between the French Départements of Var and Alpes de Haute Provence, were carved into the limestone by the Verdon, plunging down from its source, about 2,500 m/8,200 feet higher up in the Alps.

Without a doubt, the most spectacular gorge is the 21-km/13-mile stretch known as the **Grand Canyon of Verdon**. Though much smaller than the Grand Canyon in Colorado, its scale makes its vital statistics all the more dramatic up-close. The colorful walls of the gorge rise up to 700 m/2,300 feet above the opaque green river.

> **Did you know?** The emerald green color, by the way, is not the result of pollution. The river has always been thus and, in fact, its name comes from the French for green – *vert*. The color and opacity may be the result of dissolved limestone mixing with microscopic plant life.

At its base, the canyon measures between six and 100 m (20-328 feet) wide, while at the rim it spreads to between and 200 and 1,500 m (650 to 5,000 feet).

The gorge, a protected Regional Nature Park, is Europe's deepest. As such, it has its own, colder climate – parts of it barely see the sun. While you will find typical Provençal flora and fauna, including the common plants of the garrigue along the hot, arid rim, the deep, cool reaches of the gorge are scattered with Alpine plants, boxwood and, in spring, pomponium lilies, small Alpine mammals. Chamois are a common sight. Vultures, which were nearly extinct in this area, have been successfully reintroduced. The colony of about 60, including a dozen nesting pairs, populate the cliffs near Rougon and La Palud.

GORGE DU VERDON SHUTTLE BUS SCHEDULE		
Castellane to La Maline		
	am	pm
Castellane	8:05	4
Chasteuil	8:25	4:15
Ponts de Soleils	8:33	4:23
Carajuan	8:35	4:25
Point Sublime	8:45	4:40
La Palud	9	5
La Maline	9:20	5:20
La Maline to Castellane		
La Maline	9:30	5:30
La Palud	9:45	5:45
Point Sublime	10	6
Carajuan	10:10	6:10
Ponts de Soleil	10:12	6:12
Chasteuil	10:20	6:20

Adventures on Foot

Trekking, Climbing & Escalade

See Les guides du Verdon, above. Also:

- **Bureau des Guides du Verdon**, *La Palud sur Verdon*, ☎ *33 04 92 77 30 50*.
- **Mountain Guide Gabriel Maurel**, *Quartier de l'hôpital, 04120, La Palud sur Verdon,* ☎ *33 04 92 77 32 73, gabrielmaurel@yahoo.fr*.
- **Mountain Guide Les Allaves**, *04120 La Palud sur Verdon,* ☎ *33 04 92 77 31 24, fax 33 04 92 77 37 30, beachyludo@hotmail.com*.
- **Les Pionniers du Verdon**, *04129 La Palud sur Verdon,* ☎ *33 04 92 77 38 80.* Pony trekking and riding.
- **Verdon Passion**, *Avenue Frédéric Mistral, 04360 Moustiers Sainte Marie,* ☎ *33 04 92 74 69 77, cell 33 06 08 63 97 16, info@verdon-passion.com, www.verdon-passion.com/Defaulthtm.htm*a. A professional school of paragliding, canyoning and escalade.

Abseiling

To arrange abseiling from cliffs near **Castellane** as well as other sites throughout the region, contact **Abseil Canyon**, ☎ 33 06 79 75 32 85, contact@abseilcanyon.com, www.abseilcanyon.com.

A Three-Day Hike

In 1905, French explorer and speleologist E.A. Martel became the first person to pass through the Grand Canyon of Verdon. It took him three days. His route, known as the **Sentier Martel** or Martel Path, is today an offshoot of the GR4 long-distance path. It's a little bit easier now that it is marked and some of the route is carved into the stone walls of the canyon. But this is still a very difficult hike that will take you at least three days. It should be attempted only by experienced hikers and canyoners. Even they should consider hiring a guide or joining a guided group for the trek between **Castellane** and **Moustiers Sainte Marie**.

Essentials

Maps: IGN TOP25, 1:25,000 – 3442OT, Gorges du Verdon; IGN TOP25, 1:25,000 – 3542OT, Castellane.

Guidebook: *Topo-Guide GR4, La Haute Provence par les Gorges du Verdon*, published by the Fédération Francaise de la Randonnée Pédestre. Unfortunately, the only detailed guidebook currently available for this hike is in French. If you aren't confident in French, consider employing a guide, for about €60 to €100 per day, or joining a guide-led group.

- **Day 1 - Castellane to Point Sublime**

The Town: A compact 16th-century town, Castellane is hidden between the hills of the Gorges du Verdon – a sort of *village perchée* in reverse – only the Chapelle Notre Dame du Roc visible from the distance. The "roc" in question is an astonishing block of limestone that rises straight up behind the village to an altitude of 903 m/2,962 feet. Maybe even more astonishing is that the path up to the 18th-century chapel, which starts from behind the parish church in the village and is punctuated by stations of the cross, is fairly wide and not too difficult.

As one of the gateways to the Gorges du Verdon, the town is well equipped with shops, restaurants, guide services, hotels and campgrounds. It is also well served by public transportation (see *Useful Contacts* at the end of this section, page 214).

Three Quick Tours Around Castellane

Before heading out on your hike, you might explore the lakes and dams northeast of town.

1. Take the **D955** north out of Castellane. About five km/three miles from the town, at the Col de la Blanche, turn left onto the **D402**. This is a narrow, climbing road with several hairpin turns. After seven km/four miles, just before the hamlet of **Blaron**, stop at the scenic viewpoint for views of **Lac de Castillon**, one of the the lakes formed by the series of dams on the Verdon.

2. Follow directions to the Col de la Blanche, above, but remain on the **D955**. After about three km/two miles, you will arrive at

the **Castillon dam**. Stop at the viewpoint to see the dam in action (there is information). The route then crosses the top of the dam. Continue on the D955. One km/.6 miles after the dam, turn right on the **Route de Demandolx** which climbs the side of a mountain, for more views of the lake and dams.

3. Alternatively, after crossing the dam, turn left onto the **N207** toward Saint Julien de Verdon, for access to **Lac de Castillon**, a long, calm artificial lake, where a wide range of watersports are available.

The Hike: Day 1 of the hike takes about five hours. Join the GR 4 (the trail is blazed white above, red below) behind the Hôtel du Verdon on the Boulevard de la République.

- Cross the **Plaine des Listes**, a flat area of washed stones on the north bank of the river, and then turn right toward the **D952** (the **Route des Gorges**), which is a left turn after about 200 m/660 feet. The route climbs to the hamlet of **La Colle**, which you should reach after about 30 minutes from the start of the hike.
- At La Colle, cross a stream at the bridge and continue along the access route to the hamlet of **Villars-Brandis**. To the north, you will see the dramatic vertical promontories of the **Cadières de Brandis** (a popular, ecologically delicate climbing site).
- Where the route branches uphill (to the right), toward Villars-Brandis, leave it and instead take the path on the left, which follows a Roman mountain road to the **Col de la Chapelle Saint Jean** (1½ hours).
- At this point, you can take a 10-minute detour, on a path to the left, to see the **Chapelle**. Otherwise, continue along the Roman road (**GR4**) on the mountainside for another 45 minutes to **Chasteuil**. This charming village has been restored by potters and artisans working in stone, leather and wood. There is a very nice gîte/chambre d'hôte here (**Le Gîte de Chasteuil**, page 208), whose owners make and sell handmade soaps.
- Another hour of uphill walking will take you to a high pass (1,200 m/3,937 feet) between two rounded massifs. Stop and enjoy the view – to the east, the village of **Talloire**, to the north and west **Robion** mountain and another spectacular view of Les Cadières de Brandis.
- After the pass, the path plunges down a grassy sinkhole or *doline*. Pass under two electric lines and continue down to **Rougon** (one hour farther at an altitude of about 930 m/3,050 feet).
- After 20 minutes more, you come to **Chalet du Point Sublime**, which, at 787 m/2,580 feet, marks the start of the **Sentier Martel**. Leave the

path for a few minutes to enjoy the view from the **Belvedere du Point Sublime**. The first day of the hike ends here.

There is a hotel at Point Sublime, the **Auberge de Point Sublime** *(04120 Rougon, ☎ 33 04 92 83 60 35, 33 04 92 83 74 31, point.sublime@wanadoo.fr)*, but it fills up early and, at the height of the season, you may have to spend the night in the nearby villages of **Rougon**, **La Palud** or **Chasteuil**. There is also **Municipal Camping** in Rougon (☎ *33 04 92 83 70 94, fax 33 04 92 83 66 32)*. It is easy to get taxis from this point to various accommodations and there is a minibus service during the summer months.

● **Day 2 - Point Sublime to La Maline**

The Sentier Martel: This is a difficult hike for fit and experienced hiker/climbers. Horizontal stretches of the path cross moss-covered rockfalls at 45° angles and there are ladders bolted into the rocks in several places that have you climbing straight up over nothing.

RULES OF THE WAY

Since the mid-1990s, the nearby municipality of **La Palud sur Verdon**, into whose jurisdiction the Martel Path section of the GR4 falls, has issued strict regulations for hikers:

- The Martel Path is restricted to well-equipped, experienced hikers, wearing mountain boots.
- Access is prohibited to children under six and dogs – neither of whom could deal with the ladders and steps.
- Hikers must follow the marked path and carry flashlights to cope with several lengthy tunnels.
- Because of the unpredictable operation of the Verdon dams, hikers are forbidden to cross the Verdon except at specified places. And don't sunbathe on the sandy beaches either. You can never tell when the dams upstream will suddenly send down a tidal bore.

More Tips: Experienced guides suggest that you attempt this path only in good weather. Allow at least seven hours and bring adequate supplies of food and water. Beware of rock falls and avoid metal ladders and railings during storms. Use only marked tunnels and avoid those partly filled with scree and rockfall. Don't attempt direct descents of rock falls where there is a clearly marked path across them.

It can be very cold at the bottom of the gorge and very hot near the top. You should plan on approaching La Maline, in particular, in the latter part of the day to avoid the midday sun while crossing a very exposed area.

The Hike: Day 2 of the hike takes six to seven hours. From the Chalet du Point Sublime, the **GR4** follows the **D952** and backtracks toward Castellane.

- After 200 m/660 feet, it leaves the road for a path that descends on the right to the D234 which you take, to the right, to the entrance to the Gorges du Verdon and the beginning of the Martel Path.

  Once you enter the Martel Path, there is no way halfway point at which to quit.

- The GR4 descends across bolders and rockfalls to a footbridge over a stream.
- A bit farther along, climb stairs to the entrance of the first tunnel. This is an S-shaped tunnel, 670 m/2,200 feet long. Two windows in the tunnel overlook the narrow channel called the Couloir Samson.
- Shortly after you leave the first tunnel, you'll enter the second, the **Trescaire Tunnel**, about 45 minutes into the walk. This tunnel is 100 m/330 feet long. After leaving this tunnel, follow the horizontal path across a rock fall.
- After the third tunnel, known as **la Baume**, you will see the **Encastel towers** that mark the end of a stretch known as the **Chaos de Trescaire**. The path goes up and down along the **Rue de l'Eau du Verdon**.
- Skip the third, fourth, fifth and sixth tunnels, which are all considered dangerous.
- After an hour and a half, you'll arrive at the seventh tunnel, called both the **Tunnel des Guegues** and the **Tunnel de l'Artuby**. It sits about 50 m/165 feet above the path. In bad weather or if it is getting dark, use this tunnel to avoid the ladders of the Imbert Breach.

  Note: Less experienced hikers should use the tunnel rather than the Imbert Breach as well. If you take the tunnel, rejoin the GR4 at ++ below.

- After you pass the entrance to the tunnel, the GR4 trail descends to a path which makes a further gentle descent to the right, to a point above a sand beach.
- Follow a stretch on the path above the river. Then climb to the right along a winding path. You will pass several caves cut into the cliffs, eventually arriving at the foot of six metal ladders which can be climbed to reach the top of the **Imbert Breach** (40 minutes). The breach takes you over the rocky spur of **La Mescla**. There are outstanding views from the top. Only qualified hikers should attempt the ladders – all others should take the Artuby Tunnel (above).
- Descend to the intersection with the **Mescla Path**, on the southwestern side of the Mescla spur. The path, which turns off the GR4 to the

left and is a few meters above the river, takes you to the site of **La Mescla** (15 minutes) at the confluence of the Verdon and the Artuby. This site is considered to be one of the most dramatic of the canyon.
- Return to the GR4 and follow the foot of the rock face to **Baume aux Boeufs** (25 minutes), a vast cave where you can bivouac, though tent camping and fires are prohibited. The GR4 then climbs, in three loops, to the ++ **Éboulis (Rockfield) des Guegues** (15 minutes). This is also the exit from the seventh tunnel. Cross the rockfield, following the cable handrail and the steps.
- The path descends gently to the **Cavaliers Straits** (L' Étroit des Cavaliers) which opens out, after about 40 minutes, into the **Issane Meadow**. The meadow is an unusual oasis of greenery in the Canyon.
- Continue on the path, which runs about 30 m (100 feet) above the river, to the **Carrefour de l'Estellié**. There is a footbridge over the river at this point.
- The GR4 turns right and climbs through an oak wood to the foot of stairs that take you across the rocky ridge of the **Pas d'Issane**. The path climbs toward the north, across the Charençon ravine and then toward the west arriving, after about an hour, at the **Chalet de la Maline**. This is the end of the second day.

There is a refuge for overnight lodging at **La Maline** or you can take a taxi to **La Palud** for other accommodation.

● **Day 3 – Chalet de La Maline to Moustiers-Sainte-Marie**

The Towns: La Palud sur Verdon (950 m/3,117 feet) is a tourist center for the region, offering shops, restaurants, hotels, *gîtes*, campsites, a tourist information office and bus connections. It has a church with a 13th-century bell tower and an 18th-century castle. Located on a high, wide plateau, surrounded by views of even higher mountains, it is a good place to relax and recover from the Sentier Martel before taking up the last leg of the three-day hike.

> **Author's Choice:** The two-hour route from Chalet de la Maline to La Palud is over a paved road, the D23, also called the **Route des Crêtes**. Even if you arrange a taxi pickup and spend the night in La Palud, it's worth going back to **La Maline** to start the next day's hike just so you can enjoy the scenic road. It hugs the rim of the gorge pretty tightly here and the views from the top put where you've just been into a new perspective.

Moustiers Sainte Marie, where the hike ends, has been known since the 16th century for its blue and white faïence ware. Still a town of potters, it has 19 pottery studios to visit. The town's setting, in a natural amphitheater of limestone cliffs, makes it one of the most dramatically beautiful in the region. The two rocky towers above the town's church are linked with a 750-foot forged chain from which a golden star has shone for hundreds of years. It was placed there by a local nobleman, thankful for his return from the crusades. There are some very good restaurants (at least one of which, Alan Ducasse's **Bastide** (see page 209) is a destination on its own), shops, hotels and camping, as well as public transportation links. Moustiers is a popular town, so if you are planning to end your hike there, make reservations for a place to stay.

The headquarters of the **Parc Naturel Régional du Verdon** (Regional Nature Park of Verdon), which includes 43 towns and spreads over almost half a million acres, is here. Information about a variety of local paths for hikers and mountain bikers of different abilities is available at the park center in Moustiers Saint Marie (see *Useful Contacts*, page 211).

The Hike: Day 3 of the hike takes about eight hours (or six, if you start from La Palud).

- From Chalet de la Maline, the **GR4** follows the **D23** road to **La Palud sur Verdon** (two hours).
- Leave the town center in the direction of **Châteauneuf les Moustiers**, leading to a small wayside chapel.
- Join the path to the left which climbs along the thalweg (a geological term for the point at which two opposing slopes meet). The path winds back and forth along a forestry path and follows a stone wall before climbing steeply to the right toward Mont Barbin, which rises over the gorges.
- Climb for about an hour and a half to the **Source de Barbin**, a high pass at 1,330 m/4,400 feet.
- Follow the flank of the mountain and take the forestry path that descends to the left, through a stand of pines. The route joins a wider forestry road.
- Descend to the **Jas de Barbin**, a small Provençal farm in a clearing (about half an hour). Pass it on the left side. Then, 300 m/980 feet further, take the lane to the right.
- A bit further along, you will cross another path before rejoining the **GR4**, slightly lower down.
- Follow the GR4 to the right. After crossing a second small valley, reach the **Barbin Plain**. Continue to the first intersection of paths and turn onto the path to the right.
- A little farther, take the forestry road that goes off toward the right, into the pine woods. You will pass some ruined huts and, just after, reach **Col de Plein Voir** (Clear View Pass) at an altitude of 1,200 m/3,900 feet (about an hour). There is a scenic viewpoint here, overlooking Lac de Sainte Croix. You should also be able to see the

Lure, Mont Ventoux, Mont Sainte Victoire and the Lubéron in the distance.
- Follow the crest, reaching **Col de L'Ane** (Donkey Pass) after half an hour. After another half-hour, reach the **Ourbès** signal tower. After the signal tower the path descends down a rocky ridge past **Beylière Farm**, reaching the **D952**, the Route des Gorges, in about 1½ hours.
- At the crossroads, take the road to **Moustiers Sainte Marie** and follow it to **Chapelle Saint Pierre**. About 200 m/660 feet beyond the chapel, take the road to the left (going southwest).
- After another 200 m/660 feet, turn right. 500 m/1,600 feet farther, you will come to an intersection (about an hour). Continue straight through to the **Moustiers Sainte Marie** shelter.
- Ford a small stream, going north, and join a small road that leads to the town, about 15 minutes away.

EASIER HIKES

The **Sentier Martel** through the Gorges du Verdon is, for hikers, a little bit like K2 is for mountain climbers. It is considered one of Europe's great hiking challenges. But this area is crisscrossed with dozens of easier local paths for hikes that range from an hour or two to a day. The best sources of information about local and regional (PR) trails are the tourist information offices or the local hiking outfitters shops – of which there are many. Tourist offices usually have walking itineraries of special interest, such as the **Sentier Botanique** (Botanical Path) available from the tourist office in Moustiers Saint Marie.

Adventures on Wheels

Driving Tour

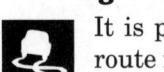

It is possible to make an automobile circuit of the Gorges. The route is dramatic, hugging the crest, with many belvederes – scenic viewpoints – along the way. Allow at least two days for the journey, stopping overnight in Moustiers Saint Marie or Castellane.

Day 1: From Castellane to Moustiers Saint Marie along the Corniche Sublime (81 km/48 miles, half-day drive).
- Leave Castellane driving southwest on the **D952**, following the contours of the river. This is a beautiful drive, between cliffs.
- After **Porte de Saint Jean**, the road begins a long turn and, to the north, you will see the **Cadière de Brandis** rising up like something out of a Spaghetti Western.
- At the **Pont de Soleils**, turn left onto the **D955**. The road leaves the Verdon River. Stay with the D955 through the Jabron Valley.

- At **Comps sur Artuby**, do some sightseeing before leaving the village, going west on the **D71**. There are several marked belvederes on this road. Try to stop at all of them – but don't miss the one called the **Balcons de la Mescla**. This overlooks the most dramatic part of the gorge from a height of 500 m/1,640 feet. Here the river makes a virtual hairpin turn as it is joined by the waters of the Artuby – *Mescla* means mingling of the waters.

  > **Tip:** After this point, the route can be blocked by snow in winter, so don't try this drive between December and March.

- Shortly after the Balcons de la Mescla, you will cross the **Pont de l'Artuby**, a stunning mountain bridge. The D71 winds through several switchbacks, going through a pair of tunnels before emerging atop the **Falaise des Cavaliers**.
- You are now on the **Corniche Sublime**, a road that will take your breath away as it leads through narrow turns and switchbacks on the side of a mountain opposite the vertical cliffs of the Verdon.
- After the **Col d'Illoire**, go through the tunnel and begin to descend toward **Aiguines** – another village to stop for a breather and a look around. Leave Aiguines on the **D19**, which winds down toward **Lac de Sainte Croix**.
- At the lakeside, turn right onto the **D957**, which skirts the lake, before crossing the Verdon.
- After another 9½ km/six miles, the road rejoins the **D952** to **Moustiers Saint Marie**.

Day 2: Moustiers Saint Marie to Castellane along the Route des Crêtes (73 km, a half-day drive). Directions may be easier but this is an equally white-knuckle drive.

- Leave Moustiers Saint Marie on the D952 going east toward **La Palud sur Verdon**. As before, stop at every belvedere you see. Between Belvedere Galetas and Belvedere de Mayreste, the road is cut into the face of the cliffs, which show the colors of many different ochres.
- Continue to La Palud. As soon as you enter the town, turn right onto the **D23**, the Route des Crêtes. The last time I drove this road, there was no sign to indicate the D23 and I got lost. That was a long time ago and the road is probably marked now, but be alert, just in case.
- The drive continues along the rim of the gorge, eventually turning away from it and back toward La Palud after the **Belvedere de Trescaire**. The route crosses through woods before rejoining the D952.
- Turn right onto the **D952** and continue on toward **Castellane**.

- After **Point Sublime**, the road dives into the gorge for several miles.
- At the **Pont de Soleils**, stay to the left and return to Castellane.

> **Author's Tip:** Tunnels along this route are narrow and dark. They go around corners in the dark. The protocol is to turn on headlights as you enter. Drive slowly, flashing lights and occasionally sounding your horn. If there's the slightest chance that you might be affected by vertigo, let someone else drive. These roads are perched on the flanks and edges of very high and sometimes nearly vertical mountains. If you meet an oncoming car in a tunnel, one of you may have to reverse out.

Adventures on Water
Whitewater

White water experience in the Gorges du Verdon. © CDT VAR / WWW.WALLIS.FR

The French rate their white-water challenges from Classe I to Classe VI according to level of difficulty and excitement. The reach of the Verdon between Castellane and Point Sublime is rated Classe II (small rapids, simple waves) and Classe III (sport rapids, large waves), suitable for novices, younger children and anyone nervous about the sport.

Farther along, in the Grand Canyon stretch, the rapids range from Classe III to Classe V (sequences of very big rapids, close together, S-bends and significant drops). They're suitable for rafters and kayakers who like a fair bit of bouncing around.

Guides and tours for rafting, kayaking, canyoning and hot canoeing (inflatable craft, a cross between a canoe and a raft) operate out of Castellane, La Palud and Moustier Saint Marie. Costs vary but are about €60 for a full day. Generally, the same guide companies offer most of the boat- or craft-related sports and one or two of the other activities (canyoning, hiking, aqua trekking, which is like canyoning but without cliff climbs and usually includes some swimming). Some will even teach you white-water swimming (known in French as *nage en eau vive*) and hydrospeed, which involves putting on a helmet, life vest, protective suit and flippers, then riding the rapids on a craft that's an unsinkable cross between a sled and a hydrofoil. It is a bit like water luge.

The best sources for guides and outfitters are the local tourist offices. Here are a few to start with:

- **Les Guides du Verdon**, *Le Galetas 83630 Aiguines,* ☎/*fax 33 04 94 84 22 55, info@les-guides.net, www.les-guides.net.* Rafting, kayaking, canyoning, escalade, hiking guides. They will also recommend local accommodation close to adventure sites.
- **Action Adventure Rafting**, *Philippe Rufin, 12 Rue Nationale, Castellane,* ☎/*fax 33 04 92 83 79 39, accueil@action-aventure.com, www.action-aventure.com.* Canyoning, rafting, hot canoe.
- **Acti-Raft**, *Relais de l'Eau Vive, Route des Gorges du Verdon, Castellane,* ☎ *33 04 92 83 76 64, fax 33 04 92 83 76 74, accueil@actiraft.com, www.actiraft.com.* Rafting, canyoning, kayaking, hot canoeing and white-water swimming.
- **Buena Vista Rafting**, *31 Rue Nationale, 04120 Castellane,* ☎/*fax 33 04 92 83 77 98, info@buenavistarafting.com, www.buenavistarafting.com.* Rafting, canyoning, hydrospeed, aqua trekking, hiking, mountain bike and climbing. They will also help you find local accommodation.

Extreme Fly Fishing

Have you ever considered being lowered on a rope to trout fish in rapids? Professional guide **Christophe Pironnie** leads groups on fishing expeditions that range from half-days to full weeks. A full guided day costs about €150.

A full season's trout season licence (the season runs from mid-March to mid-September) costs €60. You can also buy a vacation licence, good from June 1 to September 30, for €25. Have a look at all Monsieur Pironnie's press clippings at the Verdon Pêche website, www.verdonpeche.free.fr. Contact: *Christophe Pironnie, 82 Impasse de la Pastourelle, La Vieille Bergerie, 83600 Fréjus,* ☎/*fax 33 04 94 19 16 24 or 33 06 07 14 51 14, ch.pironnie@free.fr.* Or e-mail Nick@gourmetfly.com to arrange a complete fishing vacation, including accommodations.

Family Watersports

Sailing, pedal boats, windsurfing and swimming are popular in the calm waters of the **Lac de Sainte Croix** and **Lac du Castillon**.

Where to Stay

In or Near Castellane

The **Nouvel Hotel du Commerce** *(Place de l'église, 04120 Castellane,* ☎ *33 04 92 83 61 00, and 33 04 92 83 72 82, accueil@hotel-fradet.com, www.hotel-fradet.com/1024/index_gb.html, open March through October, €)* is dramatically located at the base of the huge rock topped by Notre Dame du Roc, that overlooks the town. Rooms are simple but clean and reasonably equipped and the hotel has a large restaurant serving traditional food. This is a comfortable base for exploring the Gorges du Verdon. Groups are offered bed and breakfast at reduced rates with one person going free for every €20.

Just a few miles outside of Castellane, in the 16th-century hamlet of Chasteuil, **Le Gîte de Chasteuil** *(Hameau de Chasteuil, 04120 Castellane, ☎/fax 33 04 92 83 72 45, info@gitedechasteuil.com, www.gitedechasteuil.com/english.htm, € or less depending upon the season)* is a charming and quiet alternative base. Nancy Herfeld, who, with her partner Pascal Beguin, owns and operates this tiny bed and breakfast, is originally from California and at least one of the rooms is decorated with images of California wild flowers. Nancy makes essential oil soaps that are available for sale. Simple evening meals are served during the summer. Book early because the inn has only four guest rooms – one equipped with a kitchenette – and it fills up quickly during the season.

Rougon

Dining "almost" al fresco in the fresh mountain air at the Gîte de Chasteuil, a convenient stop for hikers in the Gorges du Verdon. Photo courtesy of Gîte de Chasteuil

The **Auberge du Point Sublime** *(D952, 04120 Rougon, ☎ 33 04 92 83 60 35, fax 33 04 92 83 74 31, point.sublime@wanadoo.fr, 15 rooms, open mid-April to October 19)* is located precisely on Point Sublime, at the starting point for the Sentier Martel. During the summer it's busy, so book early. The hotel is a member of *Logis de France*, which rates and maintains standards across France. It offers reasonably priced traditional meals and comfortable rooms. It doesn't really have to try very hard because of its amazing location.

Alternatively, Rougon, itself a village of only about 85 people who are accustomed to catering for the needs of hikers and and climbers, runs a 10-acre muncipal campsite on the banks of the Verdon. **Camping municipal de Carajuan** *(Route des Gorges du Verdon, 04120 Rougon, ☎ 33 04 92 83 70 94, camping@rougon.fr, open April 1 to September 30)* has 100 shaded spaces, a sandy, riverside beach, sanitary facilities, a *buvette* (snack bar) and shop.

The tourist office in Rougon also has a listing of *chambre d'hôtes* and *gîte d'etapes* (lodges for one-night stays, used by hikers and cyclists). Typical is **Le Mur d'Abeilles** *(04120 Rougon, Gorges du Verdon, ☎ 33 04 92 83 76 44, murabeille@wanadoo.fr)*. It has five rooms, two of which sleep four and all of which share common sanitary facilities. It has a shared portable gas stove, a small refrigerator and what the owner, Monsieur Jacqueson, describes as "petit material de cuisine" – ie, pots and pans. The cost is €16 per night with breakfast extra. The owner runs a small local crêperie so half-board of a simple meal of crêpes can also be arranged. Unlike some *gîtes d'étape*, this one provides sheets and blankets. Often, you are expected to carry your own.

In or Near La Maline

Le Refuge De La Maline *(Route de la Maline, ☎ 33 04 92 77 38-05)*. This is a very basic park refuge and gîte d'étape or hikers' lodge. It has sanitary facilities, drinking water, 82 spaces and a basic restaurant. By the time most people finish the Sentier Martel, all they want to do is crash anyway, so, if you are carrying a sleeping bag, it is adequate. You can catch the Castellane-to-La-Palud bus to the nearby village of La Palud sur Verdon or arrange for a local taxi to take you from here to other *gîtes* and inns in the area.

Accommodation in this one plays second fiddle to the glorious scenery and outdoor activities. Hotels have all the facilities but not much charm. Among them, the most expensive is **Les Gorges Du Verdon** *(Route de la Maline, 04120 La Palud sur Verdon, ☎ 33 04 92 77 38 26, fax 33 04 92 77 35 00, bog@worldonline.fr; www.hotel-des-gorges-du-verdon.fr/index-gb.htm, €€)*. Another, **L'Auberge des Crêtes** *(04120 La Palud sur Verdon, ☎ 33 04 92 77 38 47, fax 33 04 92 77 30 40, aubergedescretes@wanadoo.fr)* is a less expensive, but even more basic mountain lodge.

La Palud has six campsites, an equal number of *gîtes* and refuges, and dozens of casual rooms to rent. Because these come on and off the market so often, your best bet is to contact the Syndicat d'Initiative (see *Useful Contacts*, below) or Gîtes de France (www.gites-de-france.fr/eng).

In Moustiers Saint Marie

If you want to treat yourself well for all the hard work of the three-day hike in the gorges (or the taut nerves of the half-day drive!) then **La Bastide de Moustiers** *(Chemin de Quinson, 04360 Moustiers Sainte Marie, ☎ 33 04 92 70 47 47, fax 33 04 92 70 47 48. contact@bastide-moustiers.com, www.bastide-moustiers.com, €€€-€€€€)* is definitely the place to aim for. This elegant house on the edge of town once belonged to a master faïencier. Today it is owned by world-renowned chef, Alain Ducasse, who says he developed it as his own home away from home. The 12 rooms are individually decorated, in styles that range from romantic to rustic, with antiques and samples of Moustiers' signature blue and white faïence. One room has a freestanding Empire-style bathtub, another a bath and shower suite designed by Philippe Starck.

All the chefs in the Michelin-starred restaurant have been trained by Ducasse. If you plan on dining here (more details in *Where to Eat*, below) carry your *tenue de soirée* (that's French for smart duds) in your backpack.

You could, of course, save up for a meal here by staying at more moderately priced accommodations like **La Bastide du Paradou** *(04360 Moustiers Sainte Marie, ☎ 33 04 92 74 13 60 and 33 04 92 74 67 97, fax 33 04 92 74 13 61, noaille@aol.com, http://bastide.paradou.free.fr/gb/index.htm, €-€€)*. This bastide is a restored 17th-century house featuring bare stone walls, whitewashed beams and gorgeous views.

Le Relais *(04360 Moustiers Sainte Marie, ☎ 33 04 92 74 66 10, fax 33 04 92 74 60 47, Le.Relais@wanadoo.fr, www.provenceweb.com/04/ukrelais.htm, €-€€)* has a tablecloth signed by Picasso testifying to the quality of the cooking. Rooms are comfortable, decorated like a cared for Provençal home and the hotel's location, right in the center of town, near a scenic bridges over an abyss, can't be beat. You won't be able to peel yourself away from the terrace views.

La Ferme des Felines *(Route de la Palud sur Verdon, 04360 Moustiers Sainte Marie, ☎ 33 04 92 74 64 19, contact@ferme-de-felines.com, www.ferme-de-felines.com)* is not only a very good value, but it offers winter and early spring visitors the unusual opportunity of participating in a truffle hunt. A stylish and modern chambre d'hôte, with huge windows overlooking Lac Sainte Croix as well as a private path down to the lake, it's located in the middle of a rich truffling territory. The owners, Francis and Rita Ravez, run truffle-hunting stays between December and March.

Refuges & Hostels

Gîte L'Oustaou – *Chemin des Listes, Castellane, open year-round, 34 places, ☎ 33 04 92 83 77 27.*

Gîte d'Etape Au Soleil Levant – *Castellane, open year-round, 27 places, ☎ 33 04 92 83 70 82.*

Auberge de Jeunesse (Youth Hostel) – *La Palud sur Verdon, closed in winter, 65 places, ☎ 33 04 92 77 37 40.*

Gîte d'Etape Les Cavaliers du Verdon – *Moustiers Saint Marie, open year-round, 22 places, ☎ 33 04 92 74 60 10.*

■ Where to Eat

Hundreds of sports- and adventure-hungry vacationers lose themselves in these mountains all day during the high season, only to emerge at dinner time looking for one of the few tables around. If you want to dine well, you need to make reservations.

In Moustiers, restaurant standards were already high even before Alain Ducasse established the Bastide de Moustiers with its Michelin-starred *restaurant gastronomique*. But with the arrival of a team trained by the world-famous chef, competition has really heated up and there are several excellent restaurants in the town.

The **Bastide de Moustiers** *(04360 Moustiers Sainte Marie, ☎ 33 04 92 74 13 60 and 33 04 92 74 67 97, fax 33 04 92 74 13 61)* is not cheap (€€€ +) but, compared to other restaurants in the region of similar reputation, not badly priced. The cooking is adventurous modern French.

Les Santons *(Place de l'Eglise,04360 Moustiers Sainte Marie,* ☎ *33 04 92 74.66 48, fax 33 04 92 74 63 67, €€-€€€)* is a well-established restaurant spread over several village houses. Decorated in ravishing Provençal style, it's situated against a cliff. Food is contemporary and imaginative – lavender ice cream, spiced chicken in lavender honey.

With menus in the € to €€ range, **Le Relais** *(04360 Moustiers Sainte Marie,* ☎ *33 04 92 74 66 10, fax 33 04 92 74 60 47),* offers good value for cooking that received Picasso's seal of approval – the tablecloth with his sketch and comment "Here you eat well" is on display. The menu offers lamb so local that they will happily tell you where it grazed.

Near Castellane, the **Auberge de Teillon** *(Route Napoleon, La Garde, 04120 Castellane,* ☎ *33 04 92 83 60 88, €-€€€)* serves good-quality, rustic cooking and a variety of traditional, local dishes.

You'll find crêperies, pizza places and bistros in Castellane, La Palud and Moustiers. Most villages that cater to hikers have *boulangeries* (bread bakers), snack bars or shops selling bottled water and high-energy snacks. All the campgrounds have snack bars as well.

■ Useful Contacts

Tourist Information Offices

i **Alpes de Haute Provence:** Alpes de Haute Provence Regional Tourist Board, Maison des Alpes de Haute Provence, 19 Rue Docteur Honnorat, BP 170, 04005 Dignes les Bains, ☎ 33 04 92 31 57 29, fax 33 04 92 32 24 94, info@alpes-haute-provence.com, www.alpes-haute-provence.com.

Regional Nature Park of Verdon: Parc Naturel Régional du Verdon, BP 14, Domaine de Valx, 04360 Moustiers Sainte Marie, ☎ 33 04 92 74 68 00, fax 33 04 92 74 68 01, info@parcduverdon.fr, www.parcduverdon.com/eau/infeau.html.

Castellane: Office de Tourisme, Rue Nationale, 04120 Castellane, ☎ 33 04 92 83 61 14, fax 33 04 92 83 76 89, www.castellane.org/index_gb.html.

Rougon: The Mayor, Jean-Pierre Clair, 04129 Rougon, ☎ 33 04 92 83 66 32, fax 33 04 92 83 66 49, infos_rougon@rougon.fr, www.rougon.fr.

La Palud sur Verdon: Syndicat d'Initiative, 04120 La Palud sur Verdon, ☎ 33 04 92 77 32 02, syndicat-initiative.x@wanadoo.fr, www.lapaludsurverdon.com/p1006001.htm.

Moustiers Sainte Marie: Office de Tourisme, Rue de la Bourgad, 04360 Moustiers Sainte Marie, ☎ 33 04 92 74 67 84, fax 33 04 92 74 60 65, moustiers@wanadoo.fr, www.ville-moustiers-sainte-marie.fr/indexot.htm.

Taxi Services

If you call a taxi from somewhere on your hike, you will pay from the time the driver leaves his base, so try to call one from the closest village:

- **Vincent Frères**, Castellane, ☎ 33 04 92 83 61 62.
- **Transports Guichard**, Route de Digne, Castellane, ☎ 04 92 83 63 27.
- **Gerard Susini**, Rougon, ☎ 33 06 08 05 67 78.
- **Taxis de Grand Canyon**, La Palud, ☎ 33 04 92 77 38 20.
- **Taxi de l'Etoile**, Moustiers, ☎ 33 04 92 74 66 87, 33 06 07 37 33 78, taxi.etoile@wanadoo.fr.

Worth a Side-Trip

Digne les Bains

A large spa and market town on the edge of the Alps, Digne is the capital of the **lavender** country of Haute Provence. It sits beside the fast-flowing Bléone river and is surrounded by heavily forested, steep and mountainous hiking country. The town has a compact center and a pretty main street lined with plane trees.

Digne's geological position, at the transition between the high plains of Provence and the Alps, puts it at the center of an area remarkably rich in **fossils**. The petrified remains of animals and plants, demonstrating more than 300 million years of evolutionary history, are protected in the **Haute Provence Geological Reserve**. The reserve, which covers 47 communities, is headquarted in Digne *(Geological Museum, Centre de Géologie Saint Benoît, 04000 Dignes les Bains, ☎ 33 04 92 36 70 70, fax 33 04 92 36 70 71, contact@resgeol04.org, www.resgeol04.org)*. Arrange for a guide through **Empreinte** *(c/o Joël Marteau, le Village, 04390 Beaujeu. ☎/fax 33 04 92 34 91 20, inforesa@empreinte-geol.com, www.empreinte-geol.com)* to find the fossil skeleton of a marine reptile, an ichtyosaurus, or the *Dalle aux Ammonites*, a huge slab of rock covered with more than 1,000 fossils.

> **Author's Tip:** Look for **Saint Vincent Stars** in Digne's jewelry and craft shops. Often mounted in gold or silver, these black limestone stars are the fossil remains of a plant that grew here 185 million years ago.

If chasing **butterflies** is more your bag than hunting fossils, you may be interested in the fact that Digne is also at the center of Europe's richest butterfly fields. A total of 115 species have been identified in the town's **Jardin des Papillons (Butterfly Garden)**. The most recent, identified here for the first time in 2004, is the Moiré Provençal *(Erebia epystigne)*.

The Butterfly Garden, an open-air center unique in France, can be visited only on guided tours, which are given at idiosyncratic hours. In April, May and September, tours are given Monday, Tuesday, Thursday and Friday, at 11 am and 2 pm. In June, tours at 11 am, 2 and 4 pm are available by appointment on Monday and Friday. In July, it's 11 am, 2 and 4 pm, and in August, 10 am, 11:30 and 2 pm tours are given every day. Tickets cost €4.60 for adults and €2.75 for children.

Getting Here: Dignes is served by the Train des Pignes (see page 195) as well as conventional (SNCF) rail service from Nice. Nice Côte d'Azur International Airport is the nearest airport.

By car, leave the A51 at exit 21, south of Sisteron and join the N85, also known as the Route Napoléan southbound. The N85 crosses the Durance and then turns towards the east, following the river Bléone to Digne les Bains.

More Information: For more about the Jardin des Papillions and other sites in Dignes, contact **Office de Tourisme**, Place du Tampinet, BP 201, 04001 Digne-les-Bains, ☎ 33 04 92 36 62 62, fax 33 04 92 32 27 24, info@ot-dignelesbains.fr, www.ot-dignelesbains.fr.

Puget Theniers
Via Ferrata for Would-Be Mountaineers

This mountain village is where the steam trains of the Train des Pignes are garaged. It is small and only moderately interesting as a town – though it is big enough to have some winding streets worth exploring.

The real reason for stopping in Puget Theniers is that it is the starting point for the **Via Ferrata des Demoiselles du Castagnet**.

Via Ferrata means "iron path" in Italian. It is a way of climbing using a series of metal climbing aids, ranging from hand and foot holds to long ladders enclosed in cages. The devices are bolted to cliffs, sheer walls and steep passes. The Via was first developed in World War I to allow untrained climbers to make their way through the Alps quickly and easily.

Over the years, Via Ferratas were maintained and new ones were added as the pastime became a popular European sport. There are Via Ferrata climbing sites throughout Italy, France and Switzerland.

The Via Ferrata des Demoiselles du Castagnet is rated D+ (for experienced climbers only). It has a wall 80 m/262 feet high for openers and the return journey involves a spidery suspension bridge of ropes and timbers (called a monkey bridge) and a zip line, although there are so-called "loopholes" to avoid both of these. If you've always wanted to try mountain climbing and lack the technical skills (but have the fitness and head for heights) this may just be the adventure for you. The Via, which rises 257 m/843 feet (to an altitude of 777 m/2,549 feet) over a distance of 750 m/2,460 feet, takes an estimated three hours to complete. Entrance is through the Maison de Pays located in the Train des Pignes train station. (Admission €3.05, equipment rental €11. Open every day, all year-round between 9 am and noon and between 2 and 6 pm. Closed in rain, stormy weather and snowstorms.

More Information: Maison de Pays, Gare de Chemin de Fer de Provence, R.N. 202, 06260 Puget Theniers, ☎ 33 04 93 05 05 05, fax 33 04 93 05 17 22, info@provence-val-dazur.com, www.provence-val-dazur.com. The Maison de Pays can also provide information about local hiking guides and whitewater sites.

The Route Napoléon

Most of the hiking and rafting through this area is challenging to difficult. If you'd rather not work so hard, but are are keen to see the many "cluses" – the steep-sided, transverse valleys that crisscross the area – to drive along the crests and ridges of the gorges and to enjoy the sweeping views of the Alps, the Mediterranean and the many perched villages, consider driving the Route Napoléon (www.route-napoleon.com/gb/index).

This is the route taken by Napoleon upon his return from Elba. Coming ashore with 1,000 troops at Golfe Juan in March 1815, he traveled through Haute Provence to Grenoble over the next six days, going from one sympathetic village to another, stopping here and there for meals or to await news of his supporters.

Besides being a tremendously scenic (and in some places a hair-raising drive for anyone with a fear of heights), the route is a sort of French pilgrimage, with historic markers along the way noting the houses, inns and châteaux that harbored the returning emperor – their version of "George Washington slept here."

The traditional way to drive is to follow Napoleon's route up from the coast to Sisteron, but you can just as easily reverse the journey. Either way, it's a 180-km/112-mile drive and should take most of the day.

From Sisteron, take the D4 South, passing through Volonne and Malijai, where Napoleon spent the night of March 4 in an 18th-century château beside the Bléone River. Leave Malijai, on the N85 in the direction of Digne. The road follows the river.

From Digne, abandon the historic route – which follows the D20 South – and remain on the **N85**, which will take you through the **Clue de Chabrières**. The N85 rejoins the historic route at Chaudon Norante. Remain on the N85, passing through **Barrème** (noted for its geology and for which a geological age has been named), and **Senez**. Between Senez and Castellane you will pass through the **Clue de Taulanne** before climbing to the scenic vista at **Col des Leques**. Farther south, the route passes through another "clue" near Seranon. After **Seranon**, the route rises in a series of what the French call *lacets* (and we refer to as hairpin turns or switchbacks). There are scenic vistas and lookouts all along the way. About one km/.6 mile before Seranon, watch for signs for the **Belvedere de Baou Mourine**, a right turn off the N85 up a steep and winding road (about one km/.6 mile plus a half-hour more on foot). From here you will see the **Golfe de la Napoule**, and the **Massifs de L'Estérel and des Maures**.

Rejoin the N85 and continue south to **Grasse** (see page 334). Exceptional views of the coast, of the Iles de Lerins, of Grasse and of countless perched villages, continue to open up. Leave Grasse for Cannes on the **N567**, passing through **Mouans-Sartoux** and stopping at the lovely village of **Mougins**. Leave Cannes on the N7, following the shore route to **Golfe Juan**.

The Western Côte d'Azur

The Mediterranean Meets the Massifs

Starting just east of la Ciotat, the great sweep of Mediterranean coast, all the way to the Italian border, is referred to as the Côte d'Azur or the Riviera. It is a large area with dozens of beaches and, despite the coast's reputation for toney glamor alternating with brash vulgarity, it's a great location for watersports, boating, parascending, climbing, hiking and gliding.

IN THIS CHAPTER	
■ The Massif des Maures	215
Collobrières	218
La Garde Freinet	220
Pierrefeu du Var	221
■ The Mauresque Coast	229
St Tropez	230
Le Lavandou	237
Grimaud	238
Ste Maxime	239
■ The Massif de l'Estérel	251
Fréjus	253
Saint Raphaël	258
Les Adrets de l' Estérel	268
■ The Massif du Tanneron	288
■ The Pays de Fayence	290

The Western Côte d'Azur, the section covered in this chapter, is a deeply indented coast, characterized by many small towns, miles of sandy beaches, and three great mountainous headlands, called massifs. The **Massif des Maures**, **Massif de l'Estérel** and **Massif de Tanneron** foreshadow the march of the Alps to the sea farther east along the Riviera. They offer stunning long-distance views and provide miles of good walking.

For years, French vacationers kept the region their secret, staying in their holiday homes or with friends and family. As a result, the massifs remain largely undiscovered territory for foreign visitors, who usually race around and between them on roads heading for the coast. If you stop to enjoy this region, you'll find it has its own personality and surprises.

■ The Massif des Maures

Between Hyères to the west and Fréjus-Saint Raphaël on the east, bounded by the valleys of the Gapeau and Argens rivers, the Massif des Maures is a succession of heavily forested ridges and hills, arranged like waves of land breaking toward the sea. Together with the Massif de l'Estérel, it is considered geologically to be some of the oldest land in France.

Though reaching only about 800 m/2,600 feet at its highest point, the massif has a distinctly mountainous atmosphere with sudden drops, winding roads and steep valleys.

Uniquely for Provence, it is densely forested and, despite being ravaged by devastating forest fires from time to time, remains evergreen year-round. Cork oak (which supports a small cork-making industry),

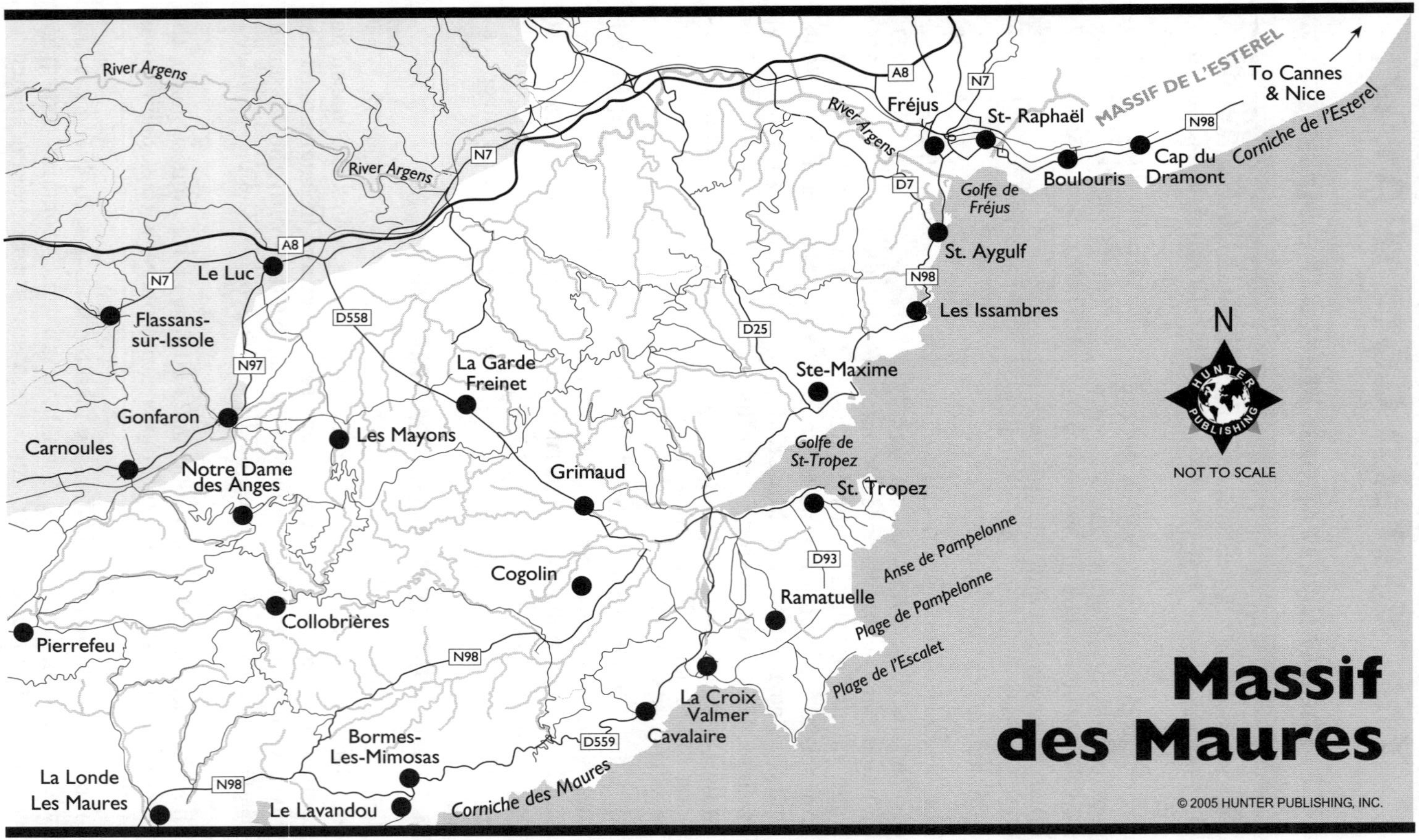
Massif
des Maures
NOT TO SCALE
N
HUNTER PUBLISHING
To Cannes
& Nice
MASSIF DE L'ESTEREL
Corniche de l'Esterel
Cap du
Dramont
Boulouris
St- Raphaël
Fréjus
Golfe de
Fréjus
St. Aygulf
Les Issambres
Ste-Maxime
Golfe de
St-Tropez
St. Tropez
Anse de Pampelonne
Plage de Pampelonne
Plage de l'Escalet
Ramatuelle
La Croix
Valmer
Cavalaire
Corniche des Maures
Bormes-
Les-Mimosas
Le Lavandou
La Londe
Les Maures
Pierrefeu
Collobrières
Cogolin
Grimaud
La Garde
Freinet
Les Mayons
Notre Dame
des Anges
Gonfaron
Carnoules
Flassans-
sur-Issole
Le Luc
River Argens
River Argens
River Argens
A8
A8
N7
N7
N7
N97
N98
N98
N98
N98
D7
D25
D93
D558
D559

holm oak, parasol and Aleppo pines, and holly flourish alongside fragrant sweet chestnut trees, lavender, rosemary, myrtle and heather. The forests of the Maures are among the last refuges of the rare Hermann's tortoise, a protected species than can live up to 100 years. Wild boars, attracted by acorns and chestnuts, populate the area and are hunted between mid-August and January. There are also hare, badger, fox and deer.

The **Corniche des Maures** is a spectacular drive along the coast. Inland, 26 villages are hidden away in the 386 square miles of the massif. It is a quiet, often isolated environment, intersected by wild and deeply shaded valleys. **Walking** is easy to moderate, so you can pay attention to the flora and fauna rather than the challenges of the climb. **Cycling** itineraries suggested by the departmental tourist board, on paved but very quiet roads, also suit beginner and intermediate cyclists.

Plan accommodations well ahead of time. This is not an area where you can wing it at any time of the year. Within the massif, accommodation is hard to find – there are only a few small and very basic hotels. Hotels in the nearby coastal towns and villages can be expensive. But you should be able to reserve a gîte or campsite. Or do as the French do and rent a vacation *immeuble* – a furnished apartment or family house – for a couple of weeks. See *Where to Stay in the Maures* (page 226).

HOW THE MOORS GOT THEIR NAME

From the eighth century right up to the 18th century, the Mediterranean coast of France was harrassed by an assortment of warriors and pirates from Spain, North Africa and the Levant. They included Barbary pirates, Saracens, Turks, and Muslims from Moorish Spain. Collectively, locals called them Les Maures (Moors). Between the eighth and 10th centuries, when they were expelled from most of the region, Arab invaders built and maintained a fortress at **La Garde Freinet** (page 220) in the Massif des Maures. The ruins can still be visited.

Most people believe the massif took its name from the Moorish invaders who had their citadel there. But there is some evidence to suggest that the place gave its name to the invaders rather than vice-versa.

A particular characteristic of the massif, unusual in this region, is its dark cover of evergreen forest. The word for dark forests in Provençal is *Maouro*, which became *Maure* in French and was applied to the densely wooded massif. Some people believe the massif actually gave its name to the people who held it and periodically came down to raid the surrounding country.

Getting Here

By Air: The towns of the Maures (as well as the nearby coast) are about halfway between Marseille and Nice airports (between 60 and 70 miles away).

By Train: Local trains stop at Toulon, Hyères, Saint Raphaël (bus service to La Garde Freinet) and Les Arcs-Draguinan (taxi to nearby towns). The **TGV** from Paris/Orly will deliver you to Toulon, which has regular bus service to Collobrières and Pierrefeu du Var (Transvar, ☎ 33 04 94 28 93 28, or ask at the tourist offices for bus times). Distances are small so if you arrive in one of the larger towns, your hotel or innkeeper will either arrange to collect you or advise you about local taxis.

Collobrières

Considered the capital of the Maures, Collobrières is hidden away at the center of more than 2,200 acres of sweet chestnut and cork oak forest. It is hard to imagine now, but in the 19th century this quiet village of 1,600 was a regional center of industry.

A local man, named Aumeran, brought the secret of turning cork oak into bottle corks. By 1850, the town had 17 cork factories, numerous sawmills plus lead, copper and iron mines. That industry is gone, leaving signs of 19th-century prosperity among the medieval, Roman (and possibly pre-Roman) ruins scattered around the town. Nearby, on the Plateau Lambert, menhirs or standing stones (the largest in France) testify to very ancient settlement. The Réal Collobrières River flows right through the center of town.

Today, Collobrières has turned to exploiting its natural resources – great forest walks and the noble chestnut. You'll find chestnuts made into ice creams and jams, bottled in syrup or brandy, combined with fruits in jellies and made into creams, liqueurs and candies. If you have a chance to taste chestnut honey, don't pass it up – it has a strong, dark taste unlike any other honey you are likely to find. The town also produces a respectable red wine.

Sitting on the crossroads of several long-distance paths, Collobrières is also surrounded by many short local paths. With several other towns, it participates in a program of guided nature walks (see page 223).

INFORMATION ABOUT LOCAL PATHS

Ask at the tourist office for the *Topoguide de 5 Randoneés Autour de Collobrières* (Five Walks Around Collobrières), which you can buy for €2. If you are planning to hike or cycle in the Maures during the summer, also ask there about forest closures, which may be issued from time to time because of fire risks. Information about forest path closures is also available on ☎ 33 04 98 10 55 41.

La Chartreuse de la Verne, a 12th-century convent 12 km/7½ miles from the village on the Route de Grimaud, is an imposing and curious compound that makes a worthwhile destination for a hiking or cycling circuit from Collobrières. Founded in 1170, it was sacked and abandoned after the French Revolution. It is currently being restored by the small community of Sisters of Bethlehem who live there. Look for arches and portals in serpentine, a distinctive local stone flashed with blue-green crystals. *(Open from 11 am to 6 pm in summer and until 5 pm in winter; http://la.verne.free.fr; admission €5, closed Tuesdays and religious holidays.)* **For more information:** *Office de Tourisme de Collobrières,* ☎ *33 04 94 48 08 00, fax 33 04 94 48 04 10, ot@collotour.com, www.collotour.com/index.php3.*

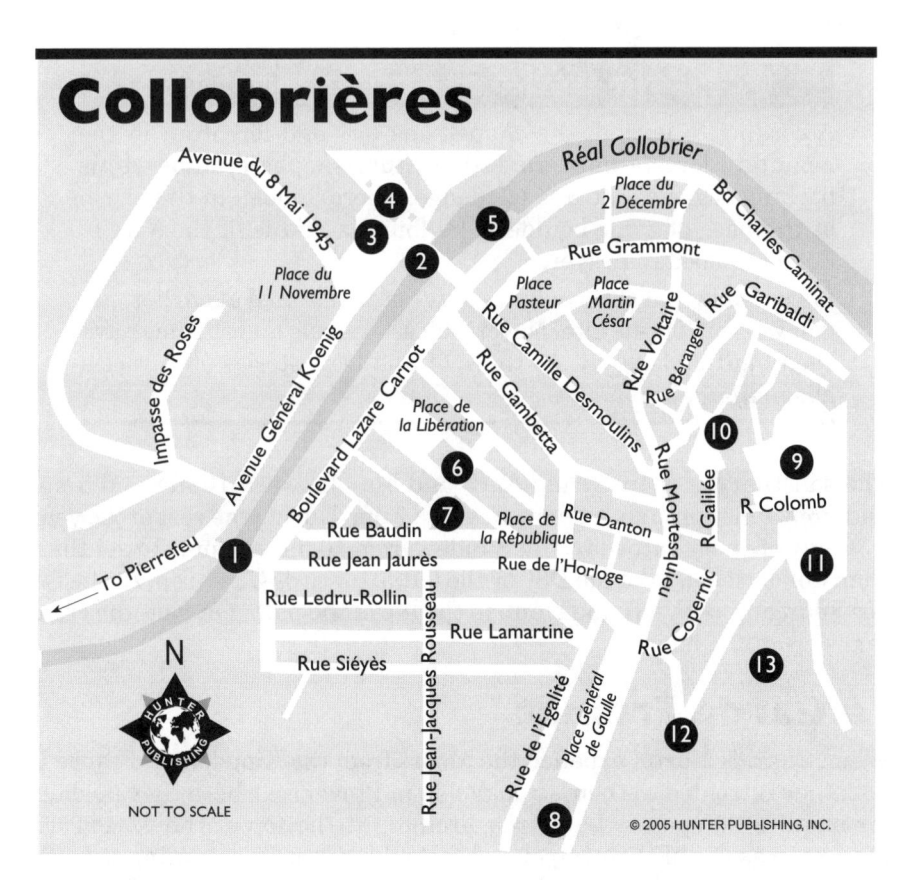

1. Pont Neuf
2. Pont Vieux
3. Chapelle Notre Dame de Pitié
4. Confiserie Azuréenne et Musée
5. Office du Tourisme
6. Mairie
7. La Poste
8. Église Notre-Dame-des-Victoires
9. Église Saint-Pons
10. Place Rouget de l'Isle
11. Point de Vue sur le Village; Départ Sentier Botanique
12. Camping Welcome Center
13. Campground

Notre Dame des Anges: The location of this shrine, about 17 km/10½ miles above Collobrières, makes it ideal for a hearty hike or cycle ride. At 771 m (2,530 feet), it is close enough to the summit of the Massif des Maures to offer good views along the coast as far west as Toulon and, on clear days, across the Mediterranean to Corsica. Whether you walk up along the **GR90** (which you can join near the tourist office in Collobrières), ride or drive up the **D39** (alongside and sometimes merging with the footpath), the journey winds back and forth through deep, cool forests, with newer and fresher views appearing around every hairpin turn.

The current chapel was built in the mid-19th century around ruins that go back to 517, when the cult of Notre Dame first began to appear in the region.

THE LEGEND OF NOTRE DAME

According to legend, the chapel was lost and forgotten in the mountain forests until an 11th-century shepherd followed his barking dog out onto a lonely ledge. There, hidden in the brush at the base of some boulders, he found a statue of the Virgin, hands clasped in prayer.

It's possible that the existence of the statue hinted at earlier, pagan worship on the site. Nevertheless, chapels and shrines have been built and rebuilt on the spot and local stories of miracles abound.

The sanctuary is open during April and May between 10 am and 5 pm, and from June through August, 10 am to 7 pm. During the rest of the year, it is only open on Saturday and Sunday, from 10 am to 5 pm. To get there from Collobrières, take the D39 or the GR90 towards Gonfaron. At the Col des Fourches, turn left and climb to the top of the path. On foot, the climb takes about 5½ hours.

La Garde Freinet

When Charles Martel expelled the Moors from the Kingdom of France in 732, they retreated to their strongholds in Provence, where they held out for another 200 years. La Garde Freinet, at the top of the Massif des Maures, was one of their important forts. From there, according to tradition, the Saracens surveyed the coast and surrounding countryside, descending from time to time for a bit of medieval pillage. The original name of the village, *Fraxinet*, is a Saracen word.

The ruins of the fortress are not much more than an archaeological site on a hill overlooking today's village. But the amazing views, of the coast as well as inland across the Maures and the Plaine de Luc, are worth the hike. The remains of a 12th-century fortified village are currently being excavated as well.

Below it, La Garde Freinet fills a narrow mountain pass on the GR9. Like other villages in the Maures, its economy includes cork manufacture and chestnut products as well as Côte de Provence wines and, of course, tourism.

Climb to the Saracen Fortress

Leave the village from the South side and join the **GR9** going west (right). It follows a paved road for about one km/.6 mile. From the parking area beside the road, a path leads to a cross. Climb a steep, stony path to the ruins. From the parking area, the walk should take about 45 minutes. **For more information:** *Maison du Tourisme, Chapelle Saint Jean, Place de la Mairie, 83680 La Garde Freinet,* ☎ *33 04 94 43 67 41, fax 33 04 94 43 08 69, ot_lgf@club-internet.fr, www.lagardefreinet-tourisme.com.*

Getting there: Only 20 km/12½ miles from Saint Tropez and the coastal beaches, La Garde Freinet has a bigger selection of hotels, restaurants and shops than most other towns on the Maures.

Pierrefeu du Var

At the edge of the Maures and surrounded by outstanding Côte de Provence vineyards (most of which can be visited for tastings), Pierrefeu du Var is ideally situated for a low-key rambling vacation. The most strenuous walk is about 15 km/9.3 miles to the sea at La Londe, along the GR51. The town itself is small and typical of the region, but if you like fountain squares, narrow lanes lined with ancient stones and tile-roofed houses, it is full of charm. At its highest point, near the Sainte Croix Chapel, it offers panoramic views of the Golfe de Saint Tropez.

Adventures on Foot

Rambles

Six marked hiking circuits, ranging in duration from about 1½ hours to seven hours (the 25-km/15½-mile Roudaïre circuit), start from different points in the village. Information, as well as a schedule of accompanied walks, is available from the tourist office. The nearby **La Marchande** recreation area, featuring nature trails and an arboretum with more than 300 tree species, is suitable for gentle rambles. Leave the village on the **D14** heading toward Collobrières. After about four km/2½ miles, look for a sign for the André Lugia Recreation Area, La Marchande, shaded in a grove of Aleppo pines. Along the trails birdwatchers may spot European rollers, red backed shrikes, golden orioles, ortolans and wood larks, which are beautifully named *alouette lulu* in French. Among the Mauresque flora, look for

Serapias, a rare Mediterranean orchid. The white flowers of *Gratiole officinale*, also known as "poor man's herb" and only found in the Maures and the Estérel, peek out along stream banks during July and August.

For more information: *Office de Tourisme, 20 Boulevard Henri Guérin, 83 390 Pierrefeu du Var,* ☎ *33 04 94 28 27 30, fax 33 04 94 28 21 78, contact@ot-pierrefeu.com, www.ot-pierrefeu.com.*

Plan an Adventure the Lazy Way

The Central Tourist Office of the Golfe Saint Tropez-Pays des Maures (http://www.golfe-infos.com/maison_du_tourisme_du_golfe_de_saint_tropez/default.php3), which represents 14 villages on the Massif des Maures and the Mauresque coast, can suggest various itineraries, including hotels and restaurants, and e-mail the itineraries to you. If you like their plan, they'll book it for you.

The free service is called the Pleasure Weekend, but you can actually plan a trip of any length this way. There is no obligation to take up any of the suggestions. The villages covered include: Saint Tropez, Sainte Maxime, Roquebrune sur Argens, Ramatuelle, Le Plan de la Tour, Le Rayol Canadel, La Garde Freinet, Gassin, La Mole, La Croix Valmer, Grimaud, Collobrières, Cogolin and Cavalaire.

Ecology Walks

Ten villages (including Collobrières, La Garde Freinet and Pierrefeu du Var) have joined forces with the Office of National Forests, the Departmental Tourist Board of the Var and the Provence-Alpes-Côte d'Azur Region to organize a year-round schedule of guided walks with local naturalists and experts.

The walks, which range in length from short local rambles to hikes of several hours, focus on key natural features, the flora and fauna and local history for each of the villages. Typical walks might include:

- **A walk along the Réal Martin** – following the river from Pierrefeu du Var with a forestry worker who explains the local riverside biosphere, called the *ripisylve,* and the importance of the vineyards in protecting the hills.
- **Plants and beliefs** – highlighting medicinal plants, plants used in witchcraft, magic places and the way that plants shape beliefs.
- **The Botanical Path** – a four-hour walk from Collobrières with a naturalist who explains local flora, birds and insects.
- **Mankind and the forests** – from La Garde Freinet, an easy 90-minute walk with a forestry technician who explains his work and the life of the forest

The accompanied walks cost between €6 and €8, with children under 10 free. They are conducted in French but you can enjoy them even if your French is limited to a few guidebook phrases. I've found that if you can master a little bit of the language, people will try to meet you halfway in English. **For more information:** www.webvds.com/sorties/index.php3, or ask about accompanied nature walks in the local tourist offices.

Long Distance Paths

Three **Grandes Randonées** traverse the Massif des Maures. The North-South **GR90** starts between Le Lavandou, on the coast, and Bormes les Mimosas and passes through Collobrières on the way to the east-west **GR9**. The **GR51**, also known as the Balcony of the Côte d'Azur, parallels the coast along the cliffs and ridges of the massif. The paths in this area range from gentle to hard walking but are recommended for hikers of average ability. **IGN Top25 maps 3445OT** and **3545OT** provide good coverage of this area.

GUIDED WALKS ON THE MAURESQUE COAST

Some of the coastal paths along the edge of the Maure offer spectacular views and wind through lovely villages and fishing ports. But here and there, the coastal walk can be surprisingly precipitous. If you like softer adventures, going with a guide is a good idea. There are a number of local and international companies that will show you the Cote d'Azur from this different perspective. One I've come across, **Headwater**, tours the coast from a base at the Hotel des Alcyons in Le Lavendou and offers quite a good variety of experiences – from a hike up into the Massif des Maures, to a boat ride to the botanical conservation area on the Ile de Porquerolles. The walks are circular during the course of the vacation, so you can stay behind for a lazy day or two at the beach if you prefer. If you are traveling from the UK with a dog under the Pet Passport Scheme, the company can also organize dog-friendly walking tours. *(Headwater, The Old School House, Cheshire CW8 1LE, UK,* ☎ *44 0 1606 72019, fax 44 0 1606 720098, info@headwater.com, www.headwater.com.)*

Adventures on Wheels

Cycling

• **The Wild Maures**

The route is 89 km/55 miles, for road or hybrid bikes, moderate difficulty, about six hours of steady cycling. Map Ref: IGN1/100,000 No. 68 (Toulon-Nice). This circuit takes you through the forests and some of the hidden villages of the Maures. Carry water and snacks because refreshments along the way are scarce.

- Leave Collobrières going east on the **D14**. At **Pra de Castel**, turn left onto the **D39** and climb above a small valley to **Col des Forches**. The trail climbs about 535 m/1,755 feet to this 12-km/7½-mile point. Descend in the direction of Gonfaron.
- Just before the A57 Autoroute, near Gonfaron (20 km/12.4 miles), take a little lane to the right to join the **D75**, going east toward **Les Mayons** (25 km/15½ miles). Stop in Les Mayons to admire the **Grandfather Chestnut** tree, planted in the Middle Ages.
- From Les Mayons, continue east on the **D75** to the **D588**. Take the road to the right and climb to **La Garde Freinet** (40 km/24.8 miles). This town has several restaurants, chambres d'hôtes and hotels as well as two large campsites (pages 226-28). So, depending upon how hard you choose to cycle, you could stop for lunch or spend the night here. If you decide to stay over, make sure to book ahead (even if you are camping). Accommodation is limited and in demand on the massif.
- Leave the village going left onto the D75. At the **Col de Vignon**, descend to the right, via the D74 to **Plan de la Tour** (51 km/31.7 miles). This pastel-colored village also has accommodations and restaurants, as an alternative stop on this circuit.
- Leave Plan de la Tour to the right via the **D44**, passing the tiny hamlets of **Préconil**, which has a Roman bridge, and **Courruero**.
- After climbing the pass at **Le Petit Col de Reverdi** (184 m/603 feet), take the D44 to the right past the hamlet of L'Avelan, before going right onto the **D14** towards **Grimaud** (64½ km/40 miles), a medieval village with a ruined château and a restored windmill. Grimaud, which is close to Saint Tropez, has restaurants, cafés and (often expensive) accommodations.
- Cross the village on the **D558**, then go left on the **D14**, descending into the **La Giscle** (ZHEE kluh) Valley. Keep to the right, staying on the D14, past the hamlet of **L'Amirauté** at the start of a panoramic climb to the **Perier Pass** (350 m/1,148 feet). From the pass you will be able to see **La Chartreuse de la Verne**.
- Continue on through the pass at the **Col de Taillude** (81 km/50 miles) at 41 m/1,348 feet elevation.
- Stay on the D14, returning to Collobrières through Pra de Castel.

Bicycle Rentals

Renting a bicycle is easiest along the coast and, despite the apparent majestic isolation of the Maures, the crowded coastal towns are never more than a few miles away. Most of them have at least one cycle shop and usually several. Whenever you go, it's wise to reserve a bike ahead of time. **Holiday Bikes**, the nationwide French company (contact@holiday-bikes.com, or www.hol-

The deep and mysterious Gorges du Verdon (© *CDT VAR/www.wallis.fr*)

Escalade or cliff climbing in the Var region of Provence
(© CDT VAR / www.wallis.fr)

Above: The mountain formation of Cadières de Brandis rises behind a village near the Gorges du Verdon (© CDT VAR/www.wallis.fr)
Below: The red volcanic peaks of the Estérel, along the Saint Raphaël coast (© J.F. Cholley, OT Saint Raphaël)

Vieux Port, Saint Raphaël (© *J.F. Cholley, OT Saint Raphaël*)

iday-bikes.com), is your best bet, with shops in Cavalaire sur Mer, La Croix Valmer, Hyères, Bandol, le Lavandou, Saint Tropez, Ramatuelle, Port Grimaud and Cogolin. You can book online at their informative English-language website, www.holiday-bikes.com/accueil/index_us.htm, which includes local maps and full descriptions of their cycles, accessories and rates.

● The Corniche des Maures

A relatively easy ride of 94½ km/59 miles, for road or hybrid bikes. There is one significant climb but it is short (you can always walk the bike for a while). It should take about 5½ hours if you cycle steadily. (Map Ref: IGN1/100,000 No. 68: Toulon-Nice.) This circuit follows the edge of the massif, overlooking the Mediterranean – a very scenic ride with fabulous sea views that passes through (or above) coastal towns and beach resorts. There are plenty of places to stop for drinks and meals, but it's always a good idea to carry water and snacks. Carry a swimsuit too; this route takes you along several beaches.

- Leave **Cogolin** going west on the **N98**, past the **Château de Tremouriès**. After the **Château de la Mole**, near the airport, take a left onto the **D27** and, at the 15-km/9.3-mile point, climb the **Col du Canadel**, 267 m/875 feet. From the top of the pass, enjoy a panoramic view of the mountains of Haut Var and Mercantour.
- Cross the **Col de Barral**, 372 m/1,220 feet, and continue along the ridge to the right. From here, you can see a panoramic view of the Mauresque coast and the Iles d'Hyères.
- From high above the tumbled rocks of **La Pierre d'Avenon**, begin the long descent along the **Col de Landon** and **Col de Caguo-Ven**. To the right of the Col de Caguo-Ven, come into **Bormes Les Mimosas** at the 36½-km/21¾-mile stage. This medieval perched village has a ruined 13th-century château. The hard part is now over and the rest of the route is nearly flat.
- Descend to **Pin de Bormes**. Just before the D559, take the coastal cycling path, east toward **Le Lavandou**. You've now gone 39½ km/24½ miles.
- Le Lavandou is a picturesque and popular fishing port and watersports center. Cross the village on the **D559**. In the summer, Le Lavandou is crowded, so watch the traffic. Although it can be expensive if you aren't careful, it's a good place to stop for some seafood.
- At the **Rond-Point de l'Europe**, take a left and rejoin the coastal cycle path. Pass through a series of hamlets that are basically beaches as you begin to climb the **Corniche des Maures**. Cross the beaches of Saint Clair, La Fossette, Cavaliere et Pramousquier.

- Rejoin the **D559** in the direction of **Rayol Canadel**, which culminates in a scenic lookout – **the Belvédère du Dattier** – overlooking the coast, before reaching **Cavalaire Sur Mer** at 59½ km/37 miles.
- Cavalaire Sur Mer is a bathing beach below the ruins of a castle destroyed in 1646. Continue along the beach, which was the World War II landing site for the Americans on August 15th, 1944. Take a left onto the **Chemin de Pardigon**.
- Follow the Chemin de Pardigon to **La Croix Valmer** at 65½ km/41 miles. La Croix Valmer has a wide sandy beach. In the village, take a right onto the **D93**, which rises gradually to the **Col de Collebasse**, above Cavalaire Bay, before arriving at Ramatuelle Plain.
- After the Co-Op wine merchant (*cave coopérative*), continue to the right via the D93, which parallels **Pampelonne Beach**. There are a number lanes leading down to the beach. Pampelonne Plage is a long and almost always crowded, sandy horseshoe divided into numerous private beaches. (As you ride past, try to imagine how lovely it might be if it were empty!)
- After the **Château de Sainte Anne**, turn right onto a local lane past the 13th-century **Chapelle de Sainte Anne** to enter **Saint Tropez** at 85 km/53 miles.
- Unless this is really your scene, ride on through Saint Tropez. It is crowded, expensive and full of people (and heavy traffic) looking to spot French movie stars, rappers and hip-hop stars.
- Leave Saint Tropez via the **D98A**. Cross the **Carrefour de la Foux** (a large intersection) to rejoin the N98 to **Cogolin** (94½ km/59 miles).

Where to Stay

☆ **Hôtel Restaurant Notre Dame** (*Logis de France, Collobrières, 15 avenue de la Libération, 83 610 Collobrières,* ☎ *33 04 94 48 07 13, fax 33 04 94 48 05 95, 14 rooms, with half-board,* €). Logis de France (see *Useful Contacts, page 389*) gives this hotel "one chimney" which, in their rating system, means "simple but comfortable furnishings, good cuisine, excellent value."

HOTEL PRICE CHART	
Rates are per room based on double occupancy.	
	Under €55
€	€56-€96
€€	€97-€135
€€€	€136-€195
€€€€	Over €195

☆☆☆ **Hotel La Sarrazine** (*La Garde Freinet, Route Nationale, 83680 La Garde Freinet,* ☎ *33 04 94 55 59 60, fax 33 04 94 55 58 18, reservations@lasarrazine.fr, www.lasarrazine.fr, four rooms and five suites, air conditioning, mini-bar, room service, private gardens and balconies,*

€-€€). A small charmer that offers terrific value for the standard. Rooms have beamed ceilings, stone walls, wrought-iron bedsteads and modern marble bathrooms. The hotel has an ambitious restaurant (€€-€€€).

L'Amandari *(Vallat d'Emponse, 83120 Le Plan de la Tour,* ☎ *33 04 94 43 79 20/33 06 03 45 37 39, fax 33 04 94 43 10 52, www.provence-holidays.com, B&B, six rooms, €-€€)*. Individually decorated, colorful accommodations in a friendly, family-run chambre d'hôte. Dinners can be arranged (€ without wine).

☆☆ **Mas de Brussaguières** *(Préconil near 83120 Plan de La Tour,* ☎ *33 04 94 55 50 55, fax 33 04 94 55 50 51, mas.brugassieres@free.fr, www.mas-des-brugassieres.com, €)*. A small, rustic hotel in a tile-roofed Provençal house. Rooms are decorated with considerable charm and flamboyance. If you have a funnybone, the English version of the hotel's website will tickle it. The restaurant serves breakfast and brunch.

La Broquière *(chambre d'hôte, Pierrefeu du Var, M. et Mme Schultz, 83390 Pierrefeu du Var,* ☎ *33 04 94 48 20 57, cell 33 06 15 25 60 60, la-broquiere@wanadoo.fr, www.guideweb.com/provence/bb/la-broquiere/loisirsa.html, €, half-board €€)*. Farm and family-run vineyard, producing AOC Côtes de Provence red and rosé wine. Bed and continental breakfast (fresh juices, warm croissants, homemade jams). Half- and full board are available and reasonably priced.

Gîte de la Portanière *(83390 Pierrefeu du Var,* ☎ *33 04 94 28 21 48 or 3 0 6 25 84 47 25, postmaster@gite-portaniere.com, www.gite-portaniere.com, B&B and rural gîte)*. This is very basic accommodation in a recently renovated 1930s schoolhouse. Painted in kindergarten colors, with bare floors and bunk beds, this is clean and modern but not someplace you'd stay very long. Still, its location on the GR51 makes it a convenient, budget stopover for long-distance hikers or riders at a price that is hard to beat – €15 for bed and breakfast. There is also an independent gîte for four, with its own kitchen and bath, available weekly. Stabling and mountain bike storage as well as linen rental can be arranged.

WHEN IN ROME…

Village houses and flats that rent by the week and sometimes the weekend are a good alternative in this region and certainly what most French visitors do. Homes are generally nicely furnished with well-equipped kitchens.

Because private rental accommodation tends to be less formal and more personal, the listings change from year to year. Local tourist offices and Gîtes de France (see *Useful Contacts*, page 389) are your best sources for finding what's available when you want to go. If you can handle French, *L'Annuaire Hébergement Rural en France* (HRFrance, www.hrfrance.com/index.php) is another good source for rural *gîtes* and online booking.

Here are descriptions of some typical properties:

Village house, sleeps six. Renovated house with reception, fully equipped kitchen, two rooms with double beds, one room with twin beds, two bathrooms with shower and WC. Washing machine, infant bed and chair, linens supplied. Weekly rental €350 to €540, depending upon the season.

Apartment for two. Village center above a restaurant. One double bedroom, living room, kitchen, bathroom, washing machine, television. €40 per night.

Three story village house for two. In the center of the old town, a restored character house. Fully equipped American kitchen opening onto a living room/dining room with chimney. One bedroom with bathroom and separate WC. One room with three single beds, bathroom and separate WC, terrace with panoramic views, barbecue, dishwasher, microwave, oven, wine cellar, fridge. Weekly rental €450.

Camping

Because of the danger of forest fires, campsites are close to the small villages.

Camping Saint Roch *(Office de Tourisme, Collobrières, ☎ 33 04 94 48 08 00, reservations ☎ 33 06 76 94 52 01)*. A municipal campsite above the village. 36 shaded spaces, sanitary facilities, electrical connections. Open from June 15 to September 15. Unsuitable for trailers and RVs because of the narrow access road.

Camping Saint Eloi *(Quartier Saint Eloi, D558, 83680 La Garde Freinet, ☎ 33 04 94 43 62 40)*. 100 spaces for tents and camper vans. RV rentals are also available.

Camping de Berard *(D558, direction Grimaud, 83680 La Garde Freinet, ☎ 33 04 94 43 21 23, fax 33 04 94 43 32 33)*. 160 spaces, tents, trailers and mobile homes to rent.

Farm Camping *(Camping à la ferme, 83120 Plan de la Tour, ☎ 33 04 94 43 77 59)*. Basic, open-air tent spaces with access to sanitary facilities and power.

Where to Eat

This is where the French take their family holidays so family-style restaurants abound. Very few will make the gourmet guidebooks but your average, run-of-the-mill restaurant around here offers good quality regional cooking at a fair price. This is also the area to start looking for North African influences. Couscous was recently named the most popular foreign food in France and Moroccan touches in presentation and spices have made it onto the menu of the most traditional restaurants.

Tip: *Plâteau de fruits de mer* (froo-EEE de mair) is a specialty of the cafés and bistros along the coast. Served on a dish with a pedestal, this is a selection of cold crustaceans and shellfish – oysters, clams, shrimp, langoustine, lobster – arranged on a bed of seaweed. It is a popular treat, often shared by two or more people as a first course. Wash it down with plenty of Provençal rosé or sauvignon blanc.

One note of caution – during the summer months, even the quiet backwaters of the Maures are full of French vacationers hiding away in their family vacation homes or summer rentals. So dinner (and sometimes lunch) reservations are necessary in restaurants. You can usually book a table earlier the same day though.

La Garde Freinet is one of the best towns for restaurants in the Maures. Check out the Place du Marché for the kind of summer vacation ambiance that manages to be lively and mellow at the same time. At **Le Lézard** *(7 Place du Marché, 83680 La Garde Freinet,* ☎ *33 04 94 43 62 73, www.aulezard.com/restaurant.htm, €-€€)*, which is a bar and art gallery as well as a restaurant, they devote one weekend a month to café theater. Try a *Gratin Fraxinois* – potatoes and cream flavored with local chestnuts.

Place Vieille is also good for restaurants – **La Colombe Joyeuse** specializes in pigeon dishes *(12 Place Vieille, 83680 La Garde Freinet,* ☎ *33 04 94 43 65 24, €€)*.

Relais Routier, which rates inexpensive, family-style restaurants, suggests **Auberge du Gisclet** in **Cogolin** *(Quartier Font Mourier, N98, 83310 Cogolin,* ☎ *33 04 94 56 40 39)* for pizza, pasta and a good-value menu. And we've had good reports about **La Grignotiere**, a gastronomic restaurant in **Pierrefeu du Var** *(19 Avenue des Poilus, 83390 Pierrefeu du Var,* ☎ *33 04 94 28 27 93, closed Monday night and Tuesday, €€€)*.

DINING PRICE CHART	
Prices are for a typical prix fixe menu of two courses and a glass of house wine for one.	
€	€14-€19
€€	€21-€34
€€€	€35-€49
€€€€	€50-€69
€€€€€	€70-€140
	The sky's the limit

■ The Mauresque Coast

A necklace of small villages, several with pretty ports, is strung out along the coastline of the Massif des Maures, culminating, in **St. Tropez**, one of the most famous (and arguably one of the most overrated) resorts of the Côte d'Azur. The mountains of the Massif des Maures march right to the edge of the sea, so, until you reach the fabulous beaches of Pampelonne Bay, the beaches tend to be long and narrow narrow. Nevertheless, several, including **St. Clair**, **Cavalière**, **Cavalaire-sur-Mer** and

Pramousquier, offer good stretches of fine, golden sand, several comfortable resorts (see *Where to Stay on the Mauresque Coast*, ppxx) and facilities for watersports and refreshments. **Le Lavandou**, with its good fishing off **Cap Bénat**, is noted for seafood (see *Where to Eat on the Mauresque Coast*, ppxx).

St. Tropez

Given its reputation for hedonism and excess, it is ironic that St. Tropez is named for a saint who defied the Roman Emperor Nero, a figure whose name is almost synonymous with excess.

According to the story, Torpes, Nero's highest steward, was converted to Christianity by Saint Paul himself. The infuriated Nero had Torpes beheaded and set afloat on the Arno. Legend has it that the Ligurian currents carried him ashore at St. Tropez, where the locals made him their patron saint.

The town, possibly founded by the Phocean Greeks of Marseille, shared this region's typically strife-riven history, with one group after another vying for its strategic bay. During the 19th century, it became an important naval and shipbuilding port.

If not for Roger Vadim and his young wife, Brigitte Bardot, St. Tropez might have remained just another sleepy seaside town. But after Vadim's film *And God Created Woman*, made on location here, and Bardot's decision to make the town her refuge for many years, movie stars, artists and jet-setters flooded in – followed by hordes of tourists.

Throughout the 1950s and 1960s, it really was possible to rub shoulders with the likes of Françoise Sagan, Alain Delon, Jean Seberg, French poet Jacques Prévert, or Picasso, while sipping pastis in a café or watching the boules players in the Place des Lices.

But the movie star parade moved on long ago. Even Bardot famously flounced out of St. Tropez in the mid-1990s, complaining of drugs and villains.

St. Tropez may still be popular with flash celebrities – supermodels, TV stars, DJs, rap stars and assorted Eurotrash, but today they stay well hidden on private estates, on the fabulous yachts in the marina, or locked away in the VIP rooms of the more expensive nightclubs.

During the summer months, St. Tropez is hectic and crowded. Traffic jams are notorious and you could spend the better part of a weekend just trying to drive into the town. Come in the spring or fall (or even mid-winter, when the town adorns itself for Christmas) and you'll have a better chance of seeing the charm that drew the beautiful people in the first place.

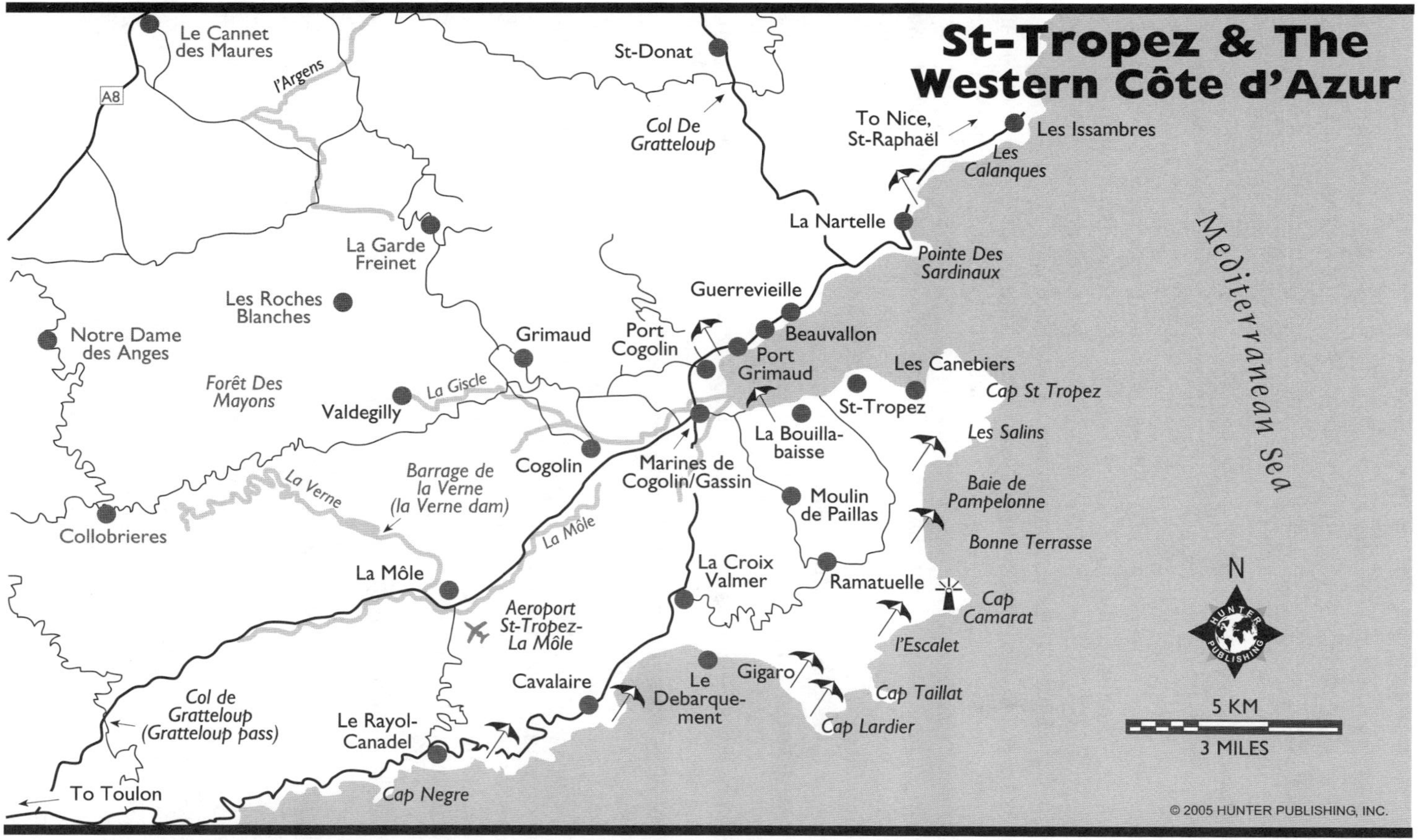
St-Tropez & The Western Côte d'Azur
Mediterranean Sea
Le Cannet des Maures
A8
l'Argens
St-Donat
Col De Gratteloup
To Nice, St-Raphaël
Les Issambres
Les Calanques
La Nartelle
Pointe Des Sardinaux
La Garde Freinet
Les Roches Blanches
Notre Dame des Anges
Forêt Des Mayons
Grimaud
Valdegilly
La Giscle
Port Cogolin
Guerrevieille
Beauvallon
Port Grimaud
Les Canebiers
Cap St Tropez
St-Tropez
La Bouilla-baisse
Les Salins
Cogolin
Marines de Cogolin/Gassin
Barrage de la Verne (la Verne dam)
La Verne
Collobrieres
Baie de Pampelonne
Moulin de Paillas
Bonne Terrasse
La Môle
La Croix Valmer
Ramatuelle
Cap Camarat
N
HUNTER PUBLISHING
Aeroport St-Tropez-La Môle
l'Escalet
Gigaro
Le Debarque-ment
Cavalaire
Cap Taillat
Col de Gratteloup (Gratteloup pass)
Le Rayol-Canadel
Cap Lardier
5 KM
3 MILES
To Toulon
Cap Negre
© 2005 HUNTER PUBLISHING, INC.

Sightseeing in St. Tropez

Tourist Information: Office de Tourisme de Saint Tropez, quai Jean Jaurès, BP 218, 83994 Saint Tropez, ☎ 33 04 94 97 45 21, fax 33 04 94 97 82 66, tourism@saint-tropez.st, www.ot-saint-tropez.com/en/accueil.htm .

Musée de l'Annonciade: Some consider this small art museum, in a deconsecrated chapel, one of the best modern collections on the Riviera. In addition to the usual suspects – Matisse, Dufy, Utrillo and Vlaminck – the museum houses works by Van Dongen, Bonnard, Braque, Rouralt, Signac, Seurat, Camoin and others. Place Grammont. Admission: adults €5.35, children €3.10. Open every day except Tuesdays. Summer, 10 am to 1 pm and 3 to 11 pm; winter, 10 am to noon and 2 to 6 pm.

Porte de la Poissonnerie: Next to the tourist office on Quai Jean Jaurès, this is both a gateway to the old town and a small market hall. Mosaic fish dance around the ceiling while a market, selling the real thing, spreads out everyday on the marble slabs below (closed winter Mondays). Walk through the Porte de la Poissonnerie to the adjoining **Place aux Herbes**, a sweet little square where a vegetable, fruit and flower market is a centuries-old tradition.

Rue Gambetta: Once known as Grande Rue, this street is lined with the great 17th- and 18th-century mansions of wealthy merchants and shipbuilders. The towering palm trees they planted still line the route. The 18th-century Miséricorde chapel on this street is one of the few landmark buildings in St. Tropez. Rue Gambetta opens up on the plane tree shaded Place des Lices.

Place des Lices: If it isn't a market day you might well wonder what all the fuss is about. The expansive plaza, with its even rows of shade trees and groups of old men playing pétanque (the Provence version of boules) can seem dusty and desolate. But come Tuesday and Saturday mornings, the atmosphere takes off with a huge and lively traditional market. Traders and shoppers come from miles around. In between forays among the stalls, grab a pew at one of the sidewalk cafés and watch the scene.

The Citadelle: The fortress overlooking St. Tropez was started in the 16th century, and expanded or rebuilt every century since. First created to protect the town from a Spanish or Savoyard invasion during religious wars between Catholics and Protestants, the Citadelle played a role in a list of conflicts and disputes that only the most avid local history buff could keep track of. A small museum explains some of it and there are good views of the town and the old port. During the summer, guided visits are conducted in English. From the tourist information office, follow Rue de la Citadelle to Montée de la Citadelle. Open every day, but closed on Tuesdays in November. April 1 to October 30, open 10 am to 12:30 pm and 1 to 6:30 pm; November 1 to March 31, closes at 5:30 pm. Guided visits in English, Mondays and Fridays during July and August at 4:30 pm. ☎ 33 04 94 97 06 53.

La Glaye and La Ponche: Side-by-side, these two areas reflect what is left of the original fishing village that first attracted artists, filmmakers and celebrities. Anse de la Glaye is a sheltered cove that extends between the Tour Portalet and the Tour Vieille, both remnants of the town's 15th-century defences. It's a lovely area for walking the Coastal Pathway, narrowly hemmed in by the sea on one side and the pastel houses, with their shuttered windows, on the other. La Glaye means "church" in a Genoese dialect and it is here, in one of the oldest areas of St. Tropez, that Genoese shipbuilders settled. The town hall now occupies the place where St. Tropez's first church once stood.

West of the Tour Vieille, La Ponche is a tiny fishing port which was the site of a small fish salting industry. Walk the narrow lanes of these districts to get a real feel for the town that still exists beneath the hurly burly.

Nightlife to Write Home About... If You Can Get In!

St. Tropez nightclubs are legendary. The party goes on all night in several self-consciously trendy and very expensive clubs. Among the many clubs and bars scattered about the town, these three are most likely to draw the beautiful people from their yachts and villas.

Les Caves du Roi, in the Hôtel Byblos, is probably the trendiest and the most select. Billing itself as "The Holy of Holies of frenetic glamour," the club boasts of being paparazzi-free and of cossetting celebs "who wish to remain anonymous." Beyoncé, Bruce Willis, George Clooney, Jack Nicholson, Ivana Trump and Naomi Campbell have all been recent patrons. If you aren't famous, you'd better be drop-dead gorgeous. The club is open from May through September, 11:30 pm to dawn. Admission is free but drinks start at about €20. *Hôtel Byblos, Avenue Paul Signac, 83990 St. Tropez.* ☎ *33 04 94 97 16 02, fax 33 04 94 56 68 01, saint-tropez@byblos.com, http://82.97.9.34/lcdr.*

The VIP Room draws much the same crowd for dining, in a 220-seat restaurant that specializes in Mediterranean and Italian food, as well as dancing, in a club that seats 300. Designed to resemble a white New York loft, the club promotes what it calls "art clubbing," with works by Jean-Michel Basquiat and Andy Warhol decorating the walls. Drinks are marginally cheaper than at the Caves du Roy. *Résidences du Nouveau Port, 83990 St. Tropez,* ☎ *33 04 94 97 14 70, fax 33 04 94 97 77 67, viprooom@viproom.fr, http://www.viproom.fr.*

Le Papagayo, virtually next door to the VIP Room, has a restaurant that's open 22 hours a day, and a huge nightclub decorated in wildly psychedelic neon colors. There's an admission fee of about €17, which includes the first drink. *Résidences du Nouveau port, 83990 St. Tropez,* ☎ *33 04 94 97 07 56, fax 33 04 94 97 10 22, contact@lepapagayo.com, www.lepapagayo.com.*

There are quieter bars, for late night drinking and talking, along the quais of the Vieux Port and around Place des Lices.

Shopping

St. Tropez has no particular shopping street or district. Instead, sophisticated boutiques, antique shops and most of the leading designer fashion stores are amply salted throughout the town. The streets of the old town, in the triangle between Place l'Ormeau, La Glaye and La Ponche are especially good hunting grounds.

If you like poking around in art galleries, this is a good place to do it. St. Tropez has dozens, representing all periods and media. **Le Mas des Palmiers**, the sunny yellow studio of artist Stefan Szczesny is particularly worth visiting for serious and spirited paintings, sculpture, glass and ceramics *(***Szczesny Factory Saint Tropez***, Espace des Lices, 7 Boulevard Louis Blanc, 83990 St Tropez,* ☎ *33 04 94 97 41 99, fax 33 04 94 54 83 35, sszczesny@aol.com, www.szczesny-online.com).* Or take home a well-above-average "souvenir" painting of the town by artist Henri Sie *(***Galerie Henri Sie***, 4 Rue du Clocher, 83990 St Tropez,* ☎ *33 04 94 97 09 64 or 33 04 94 97 58 59, fax 33 04 94 54 83 02, galerie.henrisie@wanadoo.fr, http://www.galeriehenrisie.com).*

Getting Here

By Car: From Marseille, take the A8 motorway to the "Cannet des Maures" exit, then follow the D558 for about 24 miles/38 km. From Nice, follow the A8 motorway to the " le Muy" exit, then take the D25 for about 25 miles/40 km.

> **Tip:** During July and August, roads in this area – particularly the D558, the D25 and the N98 shore route – are gigantic parking lots. Leave very early and allow plenty of time, even for relatively short journeys.

By Rail: Saint Raphaël, which has regular TGV service from Paris is the closest train station, about 24 miles/38 km away. From the station, regular buses serve St. Tropez between 6:30 am and 7:35 pm, Monday to Saturday. The journey takes about an hour and 20 minutes in the winter and up to 2½ hours in summer; cost is about €8.50. *Information from Société Départementale des Transports du Var (SODETRAV),* ☎ *33 04 94 95 24 82, www.sodetrav.fr).*

By Air: Of the major international airports, Nice is the closest. SODETRAV (see above) provides daily bus service through Saint Raphaël but, depending upon connections, the journey can take from an hour and

50 minutes up to four hours. Taxi fare is prohibitively expensive (€240 or more) so your best bet is car rental from the airport.

St. Tropez also has its own small airport, **St. Tropez-la Môle Aerodrome**, capable of handling private planes and small business planes with up to 40-seat capacity. The airport, 15 km/9.3 miles from the center of St. Tropez, with scheduled service from Geneva and helicopter flights from Nice during the summer and fall. (☎ *33 04 94 54 76 40, fax 33 04 94 49 58 08, sttropezairport@wanadoo.fr, www.st-tropez-airport.com*).

Helicopter services can also be chartered from **Heli Security** for transport from Nice, Cannes and other Riviera locations to nearby Grimaud. The cost for a private charter between St. Tropez and Nice is about €700, but includes VIP service for up to five passengers. So if you are traveling with a group, it could be a flashy – but not too expensive – way to arrive *(St Tropez Grimaud Helistation, Golfe de Saint Tropez, BP 39, 83316 Grimaud,* ☎ *33 04 94 55 59 99, fax 33 04 94 55 59 90, airhelico@aol.com, www.helicopter-saint-tropez.com).*

ST. TROPEZ BY BOAT

From late spring through early fall, traffic is a really concentrated nightmare along this section of the coast. So, whether you drive, take a bus or blow hundreds of euros on a taxi, the journey can take many stressful hours. Why not come by boat instead?

Regularly scheduled services from Nice, Cannes and Saint Raphaël don't take very long, are not too expensive and provide a really pleasant start to your visit. These services can sail you into the port of St. Tropez in style:

From Nice: Mid-June to mid-September, Tuesday, Thursday and Sunday at 9 am; July and August, departures every day. Round-trip fares, adult €43, child €26. ***Trans Côte d'Azur***, *Quai Lunel, Port de Nice, 06300 Nice,* ☎ *33 04 92 00 42 30, fax 33 04 92 00 42 31, carnal@trans-cote-azur.com, www.trans-cote-azur.com/ang/tca.html.*

From Cannes: June to end of September, Tuesday, Thursday, Saturday and Sunday at 10:15 am; July and August, departures every day. Round-trip fares, adult €31, child €16. ***Trans Côte d'Azur***, *Quai Laubeuf, 06400 Cannes,* ☎ *33 04 92 98 71 30, fax 33 04 93 38 69 02, carnal@trans-cote-azur.com, www.trans-cote-azur.com/ang/tca.html.*

From Saint Raphaël: Every day, year-round. The crossing takes about 50 minutes and there are two departures daily, at 9:30 am and at 2:30 pm. The fare is about €10. ***Bateau de Saint Raphaël****, Saint Raphaël Harbour Station,* ☎ *33 04 94 95 17 46, fax 33 04 94 83 88 55, bateauxsaintraphael@wanadoo.fr, www.tmr-saintraphael.com.*

A Day at the Beach – Plage Pamplonne

If you are after relatively empty, sandy beaches for active watersports and peaceful sun worshipping, go to the Camargue – or try your luck a bit farther along the coast in the Estérel. The beaches on this reach of the Côte d'Azur aren't about that. What they *are* about is posing, people-watching, celeb spotting, chic dining and drinking – some of them don't even have much sand between the chaise longues.

That said, they can be great fun in small doses and a jazzy tonic if you've been spending time in the peaceful forests of the massifs. The coastal area nearest to the Massif des Maures includes some of the most famous beaches in the world.

Even if you've never heard of Pampelonne Bay you've probably seen its beaches in magazine fashion layouts or movies. Located in **Ramatuelle**, which adjoins **Saint Tropez**, Plage Pampelonne is a huge stretch of white sand (about 67 acres) carved up into numerous private and public beaches.

One of them, the hot and glitzy **Plage Tahiti**, is where the bikini was first popularized and where topless sunbathing made its debut. Today, the beautiful people still enjoy topless (and very often bottomless) sunbathing there. All you have to do to join in is to pay an entry fee to rent a beach chair and umbrella for the day (from about €10 to €30) or have a drink or meal in an adjoining café. Or just bring a towel and sit on the beach for free. There are about 50 bistros and bars along the Plage Pampelonne, most of which are fairly chic (La Voile Rouge and the legendary Club 55 – see below – even have valet parking).

Have some fun and be faahbulous darling (for a few hours anyway) by booking a day or a lunch at one of the more famous beach clubs:

- **Le Club 55** is the granddaddy of them all. Founded in 1955, it began life as a sort of canteen for the cast and crew of *And God Created Woman*, the film that launched Brigitte Bardot. Nowadays it offers grilled seafood and Provençal specialties under a South Pacific-style thatch roof. Prices can be surprisingly reasonable for the location – if you select with care *(43 Boulevard Patch, Ramatuelle,* ☎ *33 04 94 55 55 55, €€-€€€).*
- Try **La Voile Rouge**, to soak up the scene while enjoying some nice seafood. It's a sort of open-air, daylight nightclub on the beach. There's music, champagne and a buzzy atmosphere. A beach mattress and space on the sand costs about €25 *(Boulevard Ratelli, Route des Tamaris, Ramatuelle,* ☎ *33 04 94 79 84 34, €€-€€€).*

- At **Chez Camille** they'll prepare your bouillabaise over a wood fire right before your eyes – if you can tear them away from the beach. *(Route de Bonne Terrasse, Ramatuelle, ☎ 33 04 98 12 68 98, €€€-€€€€).*
- At the newer **Millesim Beach Club**, where a beach mattress costs about €14, you could follow a lunch of salad and pasta or grilled fish with a Roméo y Julieta Churchill cigar or any one of a number of massages and spa treatments *(Plage de Tahiti, Ramatuelle, ☎ 33 04 94 97 20 99, beach@millesim.net, www.millesim.net/plage/, music on the beach from 3 pm, lunch from noon to 5 pm, dinner from 7:30 to 11 pm, à la carte menu, €€-€€€).*

Le Lavandou

About a half-hour west of St. Tropez, this busy little town was once a simple fishing port. Today, amid the usual Riviera trappings of luxury marina, restaurants, shops and nightclubs, a small fishing fleet remains active. Walk along the section of the marina closest to the quai to watch tradtional fishermen bringing in their catch. They sell their catch here every morning between 8 and 11 am.

Le Lavandou probably takes its name from an ancient wash house *(lavoir)* and its washerwomen *(lavandeuses)* rather than the more obvious Provençal lavender.

In addition to its 12 km/7½ miles of narrow, fine sand beaches (12 different beaches in all), the town is a good base from which to launch a walking tour into the Maures or along the coast. The **GR90 long-distance path** into the Maures begins on the road between Le Lavandou and its nearest neightbour, Bormes les Mimosas. The **GR51, The Balcony of the Côte d'Azur coastal path**, passes immediately north of the town. The tourist office will supply maps for dozens of local walking paths as well. The town website has live webcams aimed at several of the best beaches, so you can "look before you buy."

In the spring Le Lavandou becomes an active part of the Mimosa Trail (page 289). Its flower festival kicks off in mid-March with parades, floats, a Mimosa Queen and a *corso* or flower war (page 295).

Tourist Information: Central Welcome Point, Quai Gabriel Péri, 83980 Le Lavandou, ☎ 33 04 94 00 40 50, fax 33 04 94 00 40 59. **Cavalière Welcome Point** (June to October only), La Rotonde, Avenue du Golf, Cavalière, 83980 Le Lavandou, ☎ 33 04 94 05 80 50, fax 33 04 94 05 80 52, info@lelavandou.com, www.lelavandou.com.

Getting Here

By Car: About 38 km/24 miles west of St.Tropez via the N98 across the Massif des Maures, then east on the D559 via Bormes les Mimosas. From the north take the A8 motorway to the Hyeres exit, then the D98 east toward Bormes les Mimosas and the D559 into Le Lavandou.

By Bus: Service from Toulon and nearby towns is available from SODETRAV, ☎ 33 08 25 00 06 50 (toll free within France), www.sodetrav.fr.

Grimaud & Port Grimaud

Named for the Grimaldis, who once ruled it, the town dominated the Gulf of St. Tropez until the 17th century. The ruins of its castle can still be seen from the nearby coast. Grimaud's strategic coastal overview has meant that it has been continuously occupied since Roman times. It is a jewel of medieval and early medieval architecture with three separate and completely preserved chapels (one almost 1,000 years old), a recently restored windmill and an aqueduct known as the "fairy bridge."

Any place this pretty and this close to the Riviera is bound to be crowded in the summer. Try to get an early start to avoid the hordes and enjoy strolling along tiny lanes, between doll-sized houses to hidden squares awash with flowers. The hills leading up to the medieval village are criss-crossed with forest paths, many opening out onto terrific views over St. Tropez and the surrounding beaches.

You would not be far wrong if you thought that nearby **Port Grimaud**, laced with canals, looks a bit too perfect for the 16th-century village that it appears to be. It is, in fact, a Disneyesque fantasy – a marina and village built by developers since the 1960s. Mostly private and residential, it has a small number of public moorings available in each of its three marinas. The town also has several small but immaculate sand beaches along the route to Ste Maxime.

Tourist Information: Office de Tourisme de Grimaud, 1 Boulevard des Aliziers, 83310 Grimaud, ☎ 33 04 94 55 43 83, fax 33 04 94 55 72 20, bureau.du.tourisme.grimaud@wanadoo.fr, www.grimaud-provence.com/english/index.htm.

Getting Here

Grimaud and Port Grimaud adjoin St. Tropez and can be easily reached by taxi from there.

Mooring Information: Port Grimaud I, 287 public moorings, maximum length 55 m/180 feet; contact the harbor master at ☎ 33 04 94 56 29 88, capitainerie@port-grimaud.fr. **Port Grimaud II**, 66 public moorings, maximum length 18 m/59 feet; contact the harbor master at ☎ *33 04 94 56 73 65, aslpg2@wanadoo.fr.* **Marina**, 60 public moorings, maximum length 20 m/66 feet; contact the harbor master at ☎ *33 04 94 56 02 45, marinapg@infonie.fr.*

Ste Maxime

Halfway between Saint Tropez and Fréjus, the large town (population 11,000+) of Ste Maxime is relatively new by local standards. It was formed in the mid-17th century by linking two domains – the "Seigneurie" of Revest and the "Seigneurie" of the Bastides de Sainte Maxime and Saint-Pierre de Miramas. At the time, it is said, the only building between them was the 16th-century **Tour Carrée**, or square tower, which still stands – today housing the local history museum.

Ste Maxime, sheltered from the Mistral by the Massif des Maures, has several miles of warm, south-facing beaches. One of its most curious claims to fame, however, is that Jean de Brunhoff, creator of the *Babar the Elephant* stories, lived here. The first of the Babar series, *Voyage de Babar*, was written and illustrated in Ste Maxime. One of the town's beaches, now known as Elephant Beach, is pictured on pages four and five of the book. It's an apt association, since Ste Maxime is a bit more sedate and family-oriented than its near neighbors.

The town has a range of lively shops and modern shopping areas as well as a garden promenade and a pier overlooking the gulf. Beaches to the west of the town, particularly La Nartelle, are considered the best.

Tourist Information: Office de Tourisme, 1 Promenade Simon Lorière, BP 107, Ste Maxime, ☎ 33 04 94 55 75 55, fax 33 04 94 55 75 56, www.ste-maxime.com.

Getting Here

By Car: Leave the A8 motorway or the N7 highway at "le Muy" and follow the D25 for another 18 km/11 miles.

By Train: Saint Raphaël, 14 km/8.6miles away, is the closest station.

By Bus: There is regular local bus service between Ste Maxime and Saint Raphaël via Fréjus.

Where to Stay on the Mauresque Coast

Tip: Room taxes are set by the local community and almost never included in the price. At €2 per person/per day, St. Tropez adds one of the highest in the area. Breakfast is rarely included and can cost as much as €20 to €30 in the deluxe hotels.

Deluxe

If totally self-indulgent luxury is what you are after, this is the place to look for it. Deluxe hotels range from the extravagantly gaudy (where the parties go on till dawn) to the "discreet charm of the bourgeoisie" – establishments where luxe hides in quiet, shade-dappled gardens, behind vine-covered walls.

The **Hôtel Byblos**, with its famously expensive and exclusive nightclub, **Les Caves du Ro**y, is definitely the well-heeled party-goers choice. *(Avenue Paul Signac, 83990 Saint Tropez, ☎ 33 04 94 56 68 00, fax 33 04 94 56 68 01, saint-tropez@byblos.com, www.byblos.com; disco, bar, two restaurants, spa, €€€€)*. On a hillside, not far from the center of the town, the hotel was the brainchild of two billionaires – one Lebanese, one French. Built to resemble a Provence village street, the usual Provençal pastels have been replaced with the intense, Fauvist colors of a Moroccan souk. Rooms, 98 of them, all different, are wildly theatrical. Its patios, terraces and private courtyards are full of surprises. The party in the poolside courtyard goes on all night – probably why breakfast is served until 3 pm. Poolside is for recovering from the night before or strutting your stuff in a bikini, a teetering pair of Manolos and as much flashy jewelry as you dare. "Swim? Moi?"

Hôtel La Ponche *(3 Rue des Remparts, Port des Pêcheurs, 83990 St. Tropez, ☎ 33 04 94 97 02 53, fax 33 04 94 97 78 61, hotel@laponche.com, www.laponche.com, 18 rooms, €€€€)* could not be more different. Hidden away, it's a quiet secret behind the façades of several simple fishermen's cottages. Individually decorated rooms – only two or three per floor – have private terraces tucked into the corners under a jumble of red tiled roofs. Views are of the bay or of the evergreen slopes of the Citadelle. The pretty blue room, with its terrace between the Citadelle and the church, was apparently Romy Schneider's favorite. Staying here is a bit like staying in the private home of a very indulgent relative. The small adjoining beach has famous associations with the Brigitte Bardot/Vadim film, *And God Created Woman*.

Women of a certain age will probably remember St Tropez native, Alexandre de Paris. He was coiffing the rich and famous at about the time we were all discovering *Vogue*. His restored 1850 townhouse, **La Mistralée**, is one of St. Tropez's most eclectic and charming small hotels *(1 Avenue du Général Leclerc, 83990 St. Tropez, ☎ 33 04 98 12 91 12, fax 33 04 94 43 48 43, contact@hotel-mistralee.com, www.hotel-mistralee.com , eight rooms, two suites, €€€€)*. Décor in the individually decorated rooms runs from Classical through Renaissance to Baroque. Each is themed around a famous personality or region – Chanel, Hemingway, Chinoise, Maroc, Tarzan, Victor Hugo.

HOTEL PRICE CHART	
Rates are per room based on double occupancy.	
	Under €55
€	€56-€96
€€	€97-€135
€€€	€136-€195
€€€€	Over €195

There is even a 19th-century glass conservatory imported from England. Despite the multi-period decor, rooms are equipped with all modern conveniences – LCD satellite TV, WiFi, climate control. In the unusual private restaurant, chef Pascal Bouissie caters custom menus for guests in parties from two to 15.

You can't get more central than **La Maison Blanche**, a restored Belle Époque mansion *(Place des Lices, 83990 St Tropez, ☎ 33 04 94 97 52 66, fax 33 04 94 97 89 23, hotellamaisonblanche@wanadoo.fr, www.hotellamaisonblanche.com, €€€-€€€€)*. White inside and out, the house has been restored and decorated in a romantic, minimalist style. Details are chic and witty. Check out the very modern bathrooms – some with Jacuzzis and power showers – the billowing muslin curtains, the fluffy white robes. Ask for room number 7, in the loft, if you can get it.

Hôtel La Mandarine *(Route de Tahiti, 83990 St. Tropez, ☎ 33 04 94 79 06 66, fax 33 04 94 97 33 67, message@hotellamandarine.com, www.hotellamandarine.com; open May to October; some duplex suites, pool, private beach three km away, €€€€)*. This is like a tiny village set among vineyards yet less than a kilometer from Place des Lices. Part of the Alp Azur Group, which operates a number of nearby hotels, it offers the option of sharing the four private beaches and six restaurants of the other group members (see *Moderate*, below), with central billing for everything. The hotel's private beach, *Bora Bora*, is three km/1.8 miles away, but it's worth the trip to the very glamorous Pampelonne Bay.

The pink ochre-colored **Château de la Messardière** *(Route de Tahiti, 83990 St. Tropez, ☎ 33 04 94 56 76 00, fax 33 04 94 56 76 01, hotel@messardiere.com, website: www.messardiere.com, €€€€)* looks a bit like a children's book illustration of a fairy castle. The amber and yellow rooms are swathed in billowing nets. On a hill, in a 25-acre park, the hotel commands dramatic bay views. A 24/7 shuttle delivers guests to the harbor, the center of St. Tropez and the hotel's private, Tropeziana Beach.

Rumor has it that Winston Churchill was a fan of **Hotel Restaurant Les Roches**, a sort of beached cruise liner of a hotel near Le Lavandou *(1 Avenue des Trois Dauphins, Aiguebelle Plage, 83980 Le Lavandou, ☎ 33 04 94 71 05 07, fax 33 04 94 71 08 40, resa@hotellesroches.com, www.hotellesroches.com, €€€€)*. They've named a suite after him. Humphrey Bogart and Jean Cocteau were also regular guests. Right at the water's edge, the rooms are meant to resemble very high-class staterooms with huge sea views and terraces. The seagoing theme is continued at the hotel's beach restaurant,

Le Pirate, where diners gather under canvas sails for seafood cooked over a wood fire on the beach.

Also on one of Le Lavandou's many beaches, **Hotel le Club de Cavalière** *(83980 Le Lavandou, ☎ 33 04 98 04 34 34, fax 33 04 94 05 73 16, cavaliere@relaischateaux.com, www.clubdecavaliere.com, €€€€ includes half-board)* is a rambling, old-fashioned, family hotel. Thatch umbrellas give the private beach a slightly French West Indies feel. Rooms have beach or garden views and there are a few beachside bungalows.

Les Moulins de Ramatuelle, not far from St. Tropez, is the perfect setting for a wedding *(Route des Plages, 83350 Ramatuelle, ☎ 33 04 94 97 17 22, fax 33 04 94 97 11 46, info@christophe-leroy.com, www.christophe-leroy.com, five rooms, €€-€€€€)*. It's a small, vine-covered house, in the country, yet just a few hundred yards from the beaches of Pampelonne. Owned by a well known French chef (who runs dining rooms in Marrakesh, Avoriaz, and elsewhere along the Mauresque coast), it's basically a restaurant with rooms, set up to cater for private parties and receptions, inside and out. The well-shaded gardens, formal *potager*, or herb garden, and rooms decorated in soft Provençal colors are exceptionally romantic.

Halfway between Port Grimaud and Ste Maxime, **Hotel Le Beauvallon** is a Belle Époque grand hotel of the sort you might expect to find around Antibes, Cannes and Nice *(Boulevard des Collines, Beauvallon-Grimaud, 83120 Ste Maxime, ☎ 33 04 94 55 78 88, fax 33 04 94 55 78 78, info&reservation@lebeauvallon.com, www.hotel-lebeauvallon.com, €€€€)*. That's no accident. When it was built in 1914, the owners planned to emulate the grand palace hotels that were going up along the Riviera. It quickly had the stamp of approval from the Jazz Age celebrities who virtually invented the Riviera. According to legend, F. Scott Fitzgerald conceived *Tender is the Night* here. The hotel is a huge pink estate with 70 rooms, loads of salons, dining rooms and ballrooms, set on a hill, surrounded by acres of sweeping, manicured lawns. It promotes itself as a retreat for guests who want total privacy, within easy reach of the St. Tropez buzz. The private beach, reached through a tunnel under the road, is one of the largest along this part of the coast. The hotel's free launch ferries guests to St. Tropez and the beaches of Pampelonne throughout the day. There are private spa studios offering luxury treatment. And for golfers, the hotel adjoins two championship quality courses where guests have privileges. **Golf de Beauvallon** has a minimum handicap of 24 for men, 28 for women. There is no minimum handicap at the **Golf de Sainte Maxime**. During the off-season, the Beauvallon offers several golf packages.

The **Villa les Rosiers**, nearby, is also close to the Beauvallon Golf *(Chemin de Guerrevieille, Beauvallon-Grimaud, 83120 Ste Maxime, ☎ 33 04 94 55 55 20, fax 33 04 94 55 55 33, info@villa-les-rosiers.com, www.villa-les-rosiers.com, €€€€)*. A small hotel set amid rolling lawns and terraces, its 10 rooms and cooly modern public rooms have a Palm Beach feel. Elegant and perhaps a bit staid but probably a good place to retreat to after a few all-nighters clubbing in St. Trop.

If you've ever wondered how royalty live, you might like the **Hotel Villa Grimaldi** in the center of Ste Maxime *(44 Boulevard des Cistes, Montée du Sémaphore, 83120 Ste Maxime, ☎ 33 04 98 12 93 79, fax 33 04 98 12 93 89, info@villa-grimaldi.com, www.villa-grimaldi.com; open April 1 to mid-October; one room, four suites, €€€€)*. It was built in the 1920s as a second home for the ruling family of Monaco. The building itself is a beautiful example of Mediterranean Art Deco, made to resemble a yacht. Each of its four suites has a bathroom, living room and large south-facing terrace. The bathrooms carry on the shipboard theme and are finished in teak ship parquet. A fairly breathtaking array of original art and antiques is scattered about.

Moderate

> **Tip:** During the high season, between June and September, prices can double, taking even modestly priced rooms into the next price category. Quite a few of the less expensive hotels change to half-board only during the French school vacation periods. Dates for this vary from year to year so it's worth checking before you book.

St. Tropez's popularity makes it expensive. Hoteliers don't have to try very hard to fill their rooms, in or out of season. Because of this, moderate and budget rooms available in the town center are often spartan and of a generally lower standard than you might find elsewhere.

Just a couple of km out of town – along the beach roads or up into the hills – prices drop quickly and there's a reasonable selection of comfortable, moderately priced rooms. A bit farther afield, not more than seven or eight miles away in Le Lavandou, Grimaud and Ste Maxime, the selection of moderately priced accommodation is even better.

Hôtel le Baron Lodge is a pleasant surprise on the Citadelle hill, not far from the center of St. Tropez *(23 Rue de l'Aïoli, 83990 St. Tropez, ☎ 33 04 94 97 06 57, fax 33 04 94 97 58 72, hotel.le.baron@wanadoo.fr, www.hotel-le-baron.com, €€)*. More a guest house than a hotel, its simple rooms are decorated with flair and several have good garden views. There's a small, friendly bar where you are likely to meet French and European visitors.

Hôtel Brin D'Azur in the beach village of Gassin has a family atmosphere, a few hundred yards from the razzmatazz of St. Tropez *(Quartier Malleribes, RD 98 - Route de St.Tropez, 83580 Gassin, ☎ 33 04 94 97 46 06, fax 33 04 94*

97 19 01, hotelbrindazur@wanadoo.fr, www.hotelbrindazur.com, €-€€). All rooms have satellite TV, though why would you need it when they also have sea views? Marble baths, some with Jacuzzis.

La Bastide du Port *(Port du Pilon, 83990 St. Tropez, ☎ 33 04 94 97 87 95, fax 33 04 94 97 91 00, bastide-du-port@golfe-info, www.bastideduport.com, €€-€€€)* has simply furnished and decorated, adequate rooms, lifted by lovely views of the port. At the **Hôtel le Mouillage** in the same quarter on the edge of St.Tropez *(Port du Pilon, 83990 St. Tropez, ☎ 33 04 94 97 53 19, fax 33 04 94 97 50 31, contact@hotelmouillage.fr, www.hotelmouillage.fr, €€€)* all the rooms are different, comfortable and stylish, if basic. The pool is set in a pretty garden and a 100-year-old olive tree shades the terrace.

Ramatuelle is fringed by St. Tropez's sexiest beaches but immediately inland it's a green and quiet oasis with very comfortable hotels at competitive prices. **La Ferme d'Augustin**, a listed Relais de Silence surrounded by acres of parkland, is 100 m/330 feet from Tahiti Beach *(Tahiti, 83350 Ramatuelle, ☎ 33 04 94 55 97 00, fax 33 04 94 97 59 76, info@fermeaugustin.com, www.fermeaugustin.com, €€-€€€)*. Rooms are individually decorated with rustic antiques, while different local antique dealers decorate the public rooms. Behind the cosy charm, the hotel is geared to pamper St. Tropez party people. The gated grounds are attended 24/7, breakfast is served until 2 pm and there is 24-hour service on the terrace and in the garden, as well as in the rooms. The super-modern bathrooms have Jacuzzis, and there's a hammam, or Turkish bath, to detox. Light lunches and dinners are available for guests only.

Hôtel Saint Vincent *(Route de Tahiti, 83350 Ramatuelle, ☎ 33 04 94 97 42 48, fax 33 04 94 54 80 37, hotelsaintvincent@wanadoo.fr, www.hotelsaintvincent.com; open mid-March to mid-October, €€-€€€)* has spacious rooms, all with private terraces. It's set among quiet vineyards, less than a mile from one of the area's hottest beaches. Cool modern baths with colorful European tiles.

Nearby, is **La Vigne de Ramatuelle** *(Route des Plages, 83350 Ramatuelle, ☎ 33 04 94 79 12 50, fax 33 04 94 79 13 20, vigneramatuelle@aol.com, www.hotel-vignederamatuelle.com, €€-€€€€)*. It's small (10 rooms) but sophisticated. Rooms, with pool or garden views and long vistas, are decorated with a good deal of character. On weekends in the summer, star chef Laurent Tarridec of St. Tropez's celebrated Leï Mouscardins (page 249) provides special menus.

Les Moulins de Paillas and **l'Hôtel de Gigaro** are a pair of traditional *bastides* a few meters apart near the beach outside St.Tropez *(Plage de Gigaro 83420 La Croix Valmer, ☎ 33 04 94 79 71 11, fax 33 04 94 54 37 05, message@lesmoulinsdepaillas.com, www.lesmoulinsdepaillas.com; open May through September, €€)*. They are both decorated in the typical local style. Some rooms have beamed ceilings and bare stone walls, all have terraces or balconies. Features include 24-hour reception, pools, deck chairs, private car parks. Of the two, the Gigaro, which has a tennis court, is probably a bit more family-oriented. An added advantage to choosing one of these is that they are part of the Alp Azur Group, which operates a number of other local hotels. Guests can use facilities at all other nearby members of the group, which are then centrally billed. In the St. Tropez area, that includes several stylish restaurants and beaches as well as the deluxe Mandarine.

Le Rabelaise overlooks Le Lavandou's old fishing harbor *(2 Rue Rabelais, 83980 Le Lavandou, ☎ 33 04 94 71 00 56, fax 33 04 94 71 82 55, www.le-rabelais.fr, €-€€)*. Weekday mornings you can watch fishermen bring in their catch. The 20 simple and softly colored rooms have showers rather than baths and only some are air conditioned, but this little hotel is convenient to the town center and has excellent views from its terraces.

Le Lavandou is a long, narrow town with 12 different fine sand beaches pinched between the sea and the hills of the Maures. St. Clair and Aiguebelle are among the nicer ones and are good places to find pleasant, easy-going resorts. **Hôtel La Bastide** *(Plage de Saint Clair, 83980 Le Lavandou, ☎ 33 04 94 01 57 00, fax 33 04 94 01 57 13, contact@hotel-la-bastide.fr, www.lelavandou.com, €-€€)* is about one km/.6mile from the town center and 50 meters from the St. Clair beach. An unprepossessing exterior hides spacious and quite pleasant rooms with sea or garden views. Some sea-view doubles have balconies.

Unusual for this area, breakfast is included in the price at **Les Alcyons**, a laid-back, barefoot kind of place near Aiguebelle beach, about four km/2½ miles from the town center *(Avenue des Trois Dauphins, Aiguebelle, 83980 Le Lavandou, ☎ 33 04 94 05 84 18, fax 33 04 94 05 70 89, www.beausoleil-alcyon.com, €€-€€€)*. Rooms are simple but modern, most with blindingly clean white stucco terraces. The hotel's restaurant is known for local seafood.

One look at the **Hostellerie de la Croisette** in Ste Maxime and you just know that the breakfast chocolate will be served in a delicate, flowered china pot *(2 Boulevard des Romarins, 83120 Ste Maxime, ☎ 33 04 94 96 17 75, fax 33 04 94 96 52 40, contact@hotel-la-croisette.com, www.hotel-la-croisette.com, €€-€€€)*. A pink townhouse, with blue shuttered windows, though only recently opened, it is late 19th-century haut bourgeois style through and through. Rooms are daintily furnished. Windows swagged in chintz draperies frame views of the harbor and seafront. A new pool in the shady garden is lovely and private. Its sister establishment, **Les Santolines**, on the beach, outside of town, couldn't be more different *(La Croisette, 83120 Ste Maxime, ☎ 33 04 94 96 31 34, fax 33 04 94 49 22 12, hotel.les.santolines@wanadoo.fr or info@hotel-les-santolines.com, www.hotel.les.santolines.com, €€-€€€)*. The 12 rooms and the public spaces are relaxed and stylish. The there's an exotic garden, a large pool and comfortable, private terraces. Some of the rooms have very special tiled bathrooms. A visit feels a bit like a stay in a friends very smart beach house. Golf and tennis are nearby.

Hostellerie de la Nartelle *(48 Avenue du Général Touzet-du-Vigier, La Nartelle, 83120 Ste Maxime, ☎ 33 04 94 96 73 10, fax 33 04 94 96 64 79, hostel.nartelle@wanadoo.fr, www.hostellerie-nartelle.com, €-€€)* has everything you'd ask of a beach hotel at Nartelle. This is considered to be Ste Maxime's best beach. The rooms are cool and unfussy, with balconies over the beach and splendid Italian tile bathrooms to wash off all that sand.

Hostellerie La Belle Aurore on the beach outside of Ste Maxime is elegant yet comfortable *(5 Boulevard Jean Moulin, 83120 Ste Maxime, ☎ 33 04 94 96 02 45, fax 33 04 94 96 63 87, info@belleaurore.com, www.belleaurore.com; open mid-March to mid-October, €€€-€€€€)*. The location is magic – right on the beach, what the French call "Pieds dans l'eau," meaning feet in the water. Most rooms have private terraces overlooking the Med; the sitting rooms and salons are beautiful and the bathrooms are nicely done.

Budget

Inexpensive accommodations are hard to find here. The best way to stay for a while on a limited budget is to do what the French do and rent a small villa or holiday apartment (see box page 247).

Now and then you can come across a bargain surprise like the **Hôtel Mediterranée** *(21 Boulevard Louis Blanc, 83990 St. Tropez, ☎ 33 04 94 97 00 44, fax 33 04 94 97 47 83, contact@hotelmediterranee.org, www.hotelmediterranee.org; restaurant, half-board available, €)*. Well-located in the old center of town, rooms are small and tend toward old fashioned, but they are comfortable and overall the place is welcoming.

A bit farther from the center but still in St. Tropez, **Hôtel Lou Cagnard** *(18 Avenue Paul Roussel, 83990 St Tropez, ☎ 33 04 94 97 04 24, fax 33 04 94 97 09 44, €)* is a roadside spot that has its fans. Rooms over the road have double-glazed windows and rustic decor. Breakfast is in a pleasant garden. Nothing special but nice owners and good value.

Cheap digs with character are easier to find in Le Lavandou. **Hôtel de la Plage on Aiguebelle** *(14 Rue des Trois Dauphins, Aiguebelle, 83980 Le Lavandou, ☎ 33 04 94 05 80 74, fax 33 04 94 05 78 05, hotelbeachplage@free.fr, €)* is one of several beach hotels on the Rue des Trois Dauphins. It's a small, family hotel. Most rooms have balconies and sea views. This is a popular stretch of beach that can be quite crowded in the summer. The hotel is well-located for hikers, cyclists and nudists! Le Levant, this coast's popular nudist beach, is about a km/.6 mile away. The Coastal Cycle Path, that runs between Toulon and St. Raphaël, passes close to the hotel. Renovations in 2005 added air conditioning and satellite TV.

Rooms at the **Hôtel Raymond**, on the beach at Cavalaire sur Mer, have a kind of staying-at-Grandma's-house old fashioned charm *(Avenue des Alliés, 83240 Cavalaire sur Mer, ☎ 33 04 94 01 95 95, fax 33 04 94 01 95 96,* contact@hotelraymond.com, www.hotelraymond.com, €). But Grandma's probably doesn't have a large, pretty restaurant specializing in bouillabaisse and recommended, with two chimneys, by *Logis de France*.

Welcome to the **Hôtel California** *(Avenue de Provence, BP 2, 83980 Le Lavandou,* ☎ *33 04 94 01 59 99, fax 33 04 94 01 59 98, contact@hotelcalifornia.fr, www.hotelcalifornia.fr, € and under)*. A restored circa 1950s hotel near the harbor and five minutes from the town center. Rooms, with balconies, have either harbor or hillside views. Free parking is included in the bargain price.

Hôtel Belle-vue, on Le Lavandou's St. Clair beach *(Chemin du Four des Maures, St Clair, F-83980 Le Lavandou,* ☎ *33 04 94 00 45 00, fax 33 04 94 00 45 25, belle-vue@wanadoo.fr, www.lelavandou.com/bellevue, €€)* is rated by *Relais de Silence* and gets three chimneys from *Logis de France* for its rooms and dinner quality and value. Not far from Port Cros National Park, it is also within walking distance of the Levant nudist beach. Views are great, but you may want to consider that the hotel is across the road from the narrow beach and the steps down to the beach are steep.

Also on St Clair, **Les Flots Bleus** *(Plage de Saint Clair, F83980 Le Lavandou,* ☎ *33 04 94 71 00 9, fax 33 04 94 64 79 27, flots-bleus@wanadoo.fr, www.lelavandou.com/flotsbleus, €-€€)* is a typically French, relaxed beach resort. Light, airy rooms have beach or garden views and the hotel's restaurant, with bar and grill on the beach, is locally popular.

In Ste Maxime, up the coast from St. Tropez in the opposite direction, **La Villa et La Table** *(Le Val d'Esquières, FR-83120 Ste Maxime,* ☎ *33 04 94 49 40 90, fax 33 04 94 49 40 85, contact@lavillalatable.com, www.lavillalatable.com, €)* is exactly what its name suggests – a hotel and a restaurant in one. The public lounges are oddly old-fashioned and plain compared to the guest rooms, which are spacious, airy and well furnished. The restaurant holds the highest, three-chimney, rating from *Logis de France*. With dining indoors, on a covered terrace and in a garden, the restaurant is lively, decorated à la Provence and specializes in a changing seasonal menu based on the day's catch.

RENT A VILLA OR APARTMENT

Having a Riviera vacation without breaking the bank is easier if you look after yourself in a rented villa or apartment. The cost is usually a fraction of hotel costs for comparable accommodation and you almost always get well equipped kitchen facilities as well as access to beaches, pools or marinas. If you don't want to cook for yourself, use the savings to dine out well. The tourist information offices can provide up-to-date lists of local landlords, real estate agents and private individuals who have seasonal accommodation they rent by the week. Prices range from about €350 for a studio with a sea view in Le Lavandou, to thousands for villas around St. Tropez. Look for *locations saisonnières* (seasonal rentals) and *agences immobilières* (real estate agencies) in the tourist information listings.

Here are a few, just for guidance:

Maeva Orion *(1 Chemin du Préconil, 83120 Ste Maxime, ☎ 33 04 94 96 25 84, fax 33 04 94 49 73 77)*. Studio apartments for two to four people with balconies overlooking the Mediterranean, in a modern apartment building near the center of Ste Maxime. €721 per week in the high season.

Agence Michel *(2 Avenue General Leclerc, 83990 St Tropez, ☎ 33 04 94 97 82 71, fax 33 04 94 97 53 31, info@agence-michel.com, www.agence-michel.com)*. Studios, apartments, traditional fishermen's houses and villas in St. Tropez. From €720 per week in the high season.

La Cagnardette *(Mme Odile Laporte, Quartier du Pont de Bois, 83310 Grimaud, ☎ 33 04 94 43 25 25, mobile – English speaking, until 9 pm – ☎ 33 06 10 98 79 11, e-mail through website www.cagnardette.com)*. A studio for two or three in a detached cottage surrounded by vineyards about a mile from Grimaud. The furniture is homey and traditional; the owners are neighbors. Between €320 and €400 in the high season.

Camping

There is no camping in St. Tropez, but in nearby Grimaud, you can't see the forest for the tents. There are more than 3,500 *emplacements*, ranging from simple ope- air campsites and tent pitches to trailers, RV sites and small bungalows. "Prices range from about €14 to more than €20 for a space with electricity and waste water facilities for two people. *Camping à la ferme*, where you pitch your own tent in the open air (facilities are usually limited to a shared source of running water and a sanitary block) is also available near Grimaud. The best source of information on Grimaud's numerous campsites is the town's tourist information office (page 238), who provide details on dozens of sites.

Where to Eat on the Mauresque Coast

St. Tropez has the most adventurous and expensive food; the freshest seafood can be found in Le Lavandou – which still has a small, active fishing fleet. And, if you get hungry for a Big Mac or Ben&Jerry's, you can find them in St.Tropez. Several of the restaurants mentioned in this chapter offer serious cuisine. Check *A Day at the Beach* (page 236) for more bistros and restaurants on the water. One way or another, you won't go hungry on this coast.

Leï Mouscardins *(Tour du Portalet, BP 52, 83991 St Tropez, ☎ 33 04 94 97 29 00, fax 33 04 94 97 76 39, info@leimouscardins. com, www.leimouscardins.com, €€€€+)* comes garlanded with kudos from every quarter and is probably the most highly rated restaurant in St. Tropez. Breton chef, Laurent Tarridec prepares sophisticated Provençal cuisine with an outsider's iconoclasm. But the cuisine – sautéed monkfish, calamari with fennel, anchovy rissoles with celeriac and leaves, melon with spiced syrup, acacia and rosemary honey, pistachio oil and sorbet – is only part of the draw. The setting, opposite the 15th-century Tour du Portalet, straddling the end of the port and the opening of La Glaye, offers a 180-degree view of the sea and La Ponche. Book early.

DINING PRICE CHART

Prices are for a typical prix fixe menu of two courses and a glass of house wine for one.

	€14-€19
€	€21-€34
€€	€35-€49
€€€	€50-€69
€€€€	€70-€140
€€€€€	The sky's the limit

Spoon is a branch of star chef Alain Ducasse's high concept, multi-ethnic restaurant at Byblos *(Avenue Foch, 83990 St Tropez, ☎ 33 04 94 56 68 20, fax 33 04 94 56 68 01, spoonbyblos@byblos.com, www.byblos.com; evenings only, mid-April to mid-October, €€€€)*. The idea is that you taste the world's cuisine – a spoonful of this, a spoonful of that – and create your own menu. The carte suggests various themes. Dining is indoors and outdoors.

Michelin gives two crossed forks to **Le Girelier**, named after the woven straw trap used to catch Girelle fish used in the restaurant's *Soupe de Poisson. (Quai Jean Jaurès, 83990 St. Tropez, ☎ 33 04 94 97 03 87, fax 33 04 94 97 43 86, contact@legirelier.com, www.legirelier.com; lunch and dinner, mid-March to mid-October, €€€)*. Run by the same family since 1956, the restaurant serves seafood and grills, vegetable terrines, grand aioli, roasted crustaceans. The unassuming room, a typical seaside bistro, has art nouveau bentwood and wainscoting, blue striped wallpaper. The terrace overlooks the yacht haven. A thoughtful children's menu is about half-price and planned for fussy young palates.

Grand Joseph manages to be both chic and relaxed *(1 Place de l'Hôtel de Ville, 83990 St. Tropez, ☎ 33 04 94 97 01 66, chezjoseph@wanadoo.fr, www.joseph-saint-tropez.com; lunch and dinner, €€-€€€)*. Popular with fashionistas and gay celebrities – Elton John, George Michael. The food is theatrical and adventurous: barigoule of violet artichokes with tomato and fresh coriander, pressed duck fois gras with pistachio and dried figs, rare tuna steak with balsamic vinegar and curry cole slaw, pistachio crème brulée. Food is served until midnight but the party goes on all night.

Once a restaurant starts offering T-shirts and logo teapots, it's time to worry about the cuisine. But because of its prime location, opposite the best pétanque tournaments on the Place des Lices, **Le Café** can't help being popular with visitors *(Place des Lices, 83390 St. Tropez, ☎ 33 04 94 97 44 69, fax 33 04 94 55 84 95, raymond@lecafe.fr, www.lecafe.fr/st-tropez, €€)*. The unadventurous menu emphasizes well-prepared classics – boeuf en daub, moules marinières, Provençal monkfish soup with aioli, at reasonable prices.

Le Bistrot du Phare *(Chez Josie 1 Quai de l'Epi, 83990 St.Tropez, ☎ 33 04 94 97 46 00, fax 33 04 94 97 55 67, sirene83@tiscali.fr, www.bistrotduphare.com, €-€€)* serves up fisherman's stew, plank grilled fish, pasta, mussels for lunch and dinner with a view of the lighthouse.

Fuel to keep the all-night party going can be found in two famous brasseries at the port. **Le Gorille** *(1 Quai Suffren, 83990 St.Tropez, ☎ 33 04 94 97 03 93, €)* is open for drinking and light dining (poulet frites, croque monsieur) all year, round the clock. Not far away, **Sénéquier** *(Quai Jean-Jaurès, 83990 St. Tropez, ☎ 33 04 94 97 00 90, €)* is a place to drink late or breakfast early in the company of an arty, outré fashion crowd.

If French food begins to pale – and it can – **Banh-Hoi** is the place to go for top Vietnamese and Thai food *(12 Rue du Petit Saint Jean, 83990 St.Tropez, ☎ 33 04 94 97 36 29, fax 33 04 98 12 91 47; dinner only, late March to early October, €€€)*.

Asiatic food is also the specialty of stylish **Le Petit Joseph**, run by the owners of Grand Joseph *(6 Rue Sibile, 83990 St.Tropez, ☎ 33 04 94 97 03 90, fax 33 04 94 97 77 50, chezjoseph@wanadoo.fr, www.joseph-saint-tropez.com, €€€-€€€€)*. Cambodian and Vietnamese specialties at this smart, dinner-only restaurant.

Aux Fa.Da *(Avenue Général Bouvet, Le Lavandou, ☎ 33 04 94 23 34 07, €-€€)*. Couscous, Provençal seafood and fruit de mer in a lively room, on the seafront in Le Lavandou, with a covered terrace and small open terrace.

It's first-come, first-served at the popular **La Louisiane** *(Boulevard Front de Mer, Le Lavandou, ☎/fax 33 04 94 71 24 59, lalouisiane@lelavandou-resto.com, www.lelavandou-resto.com and www.lesbeauxpalmiers.com, €-€€)*. This huge place (the terrace seats 100) doesn't take reservations but its octopus stew, bourride, aioli and choucroute de la mer are always in demand. Don't plan on high season visits though – the casual restaurant accepts coach loads.

Chez Lulu *("Les Dauphins," Avenue Vincent Auriol, Le Lavandou, ☎ 33 04 94 64 95 23; open mid-March to mid-October, €€-€€€)* is a more intimate restaurant in which to sample regional food and the spicy, fish and tomato stew – *bourride*.

There's music and regional aperitifs like vin d'orange with the Provençal seafood dishes – *marmite du pêcheur*, aioli – at **La Favouille** in Le Lavandou's pedestrian area *(9 Rue Abbé Hélin, Le Lavandou, ☎ 04 94 71 34 29, €€)*.

For fish, fruit de mer and crustaceans straight out of the sea, try the restaurants of Le Lavandou Port, where the local fishermen land their catches: **Le Bosco** *(20 Quai des Pêcheurs, ☎ 33 04 94 71 09 88, fax 33 04 94 15 27 61, €€-€€€)*, **L'Algue Bleue** *(Auberge de la Calanque, 62, Avenue du Général de Gaulle, ☎ 33 04 94 71 05 96, fax 33 04 94 71 20 12, lacalanque@wanadoo.fr, €€-€€€).*

At **Les Santons** *(RD558, Grimaud, ☎ 33 04 94 43 21 02, fax 33 04 94 43 24 92, lessantons@wanadoo.fr, €€€-€€€€)* antiques, copper, flowers and santons establish a traditional atmosphere for a cuisine gastronomique menu that includes local truffles, lamb from the Sisteron and the best of the day's catch. Lunch, with wine included for €34, is a good value.

Auberge la Cousteline *(Quartier des Couzes, CD 14, Grimaud, ☎ 33 04 94 43 29 47, €€-€€)* serves rustic cooking in an isolated farmhouse in the woods. The terrace is lovely as is the market-inspired cuisine.

In Port Grimaud, **La Table du Mareyeur** will bring dinner to you if you'd rather stay in than dine at the restaurant's waterside terrace. *(10-11 Place des Artisans, 83315 Port Grimaud, ☎ 33(0)4 94 56 06 77, fax 33 04 94 56 40 75, info@mareyeur.com or equiries@mareyeur.com, www.mareyeur.com; open March to November, Christmas and New Years, €€-€€€€).* Fresh crustaceans, lobsters, crabs, langoustines, king prawns, fresh tuna tartare, can all be home delivered. The lunch menu at €25 is a bargain.

Nearby, try **Le Plaisancier** *(8 Place des Artisans. 83310 Port Grimaud, ☎ 33 04 94 56 07 04, sebboi@club-internet.fr; open March to November, Christmas and New Year, €-€€)* for grilled fish, gambas flamed in cognac, oysters, mussels, traditional dishes, on a canal-side terrace.

L'Amiral *(Le Port, 83120 Ste Maxime, ☎ 33 04 94 43 99 36, fax 33 04 94 43 99 36, € -€€)* serves reasonably priced grilled fish and regional cuisine on the jetty near the center of Ste Maxime.

La Gruppi *(Avenue Charles de Gaulle, 83120 Ste Maxime, ☎ 33 04 94 96 03 61, lagruppi@lagruppi.com, www.lagruppi.com, €€)* is an airy, traditional Provencal restaurant with a solid reputation for fresh, well-prepared seafood at moderate prices. Long-established and popular.

■ Massif de l'Estérel

North and east of the Massif des Maures, the Estérel stretches from Fréjus-Saint Raphaël in the west, to La Napoule, just south of Cannes. Much like the Maures in terms of its flora and fauna but about a quarter of its area, this is a densely forested, rugged terrain. Its volcanic origins show in a base of distinctive red porphyritic stone and in the profile of Mt. Vinaigre, at 614 m/2,000 feet, its highest point.

Once again, the contrast between the bustling coastal resorts and the quiet isolation of the interior is remarkable. It is possible to spend your

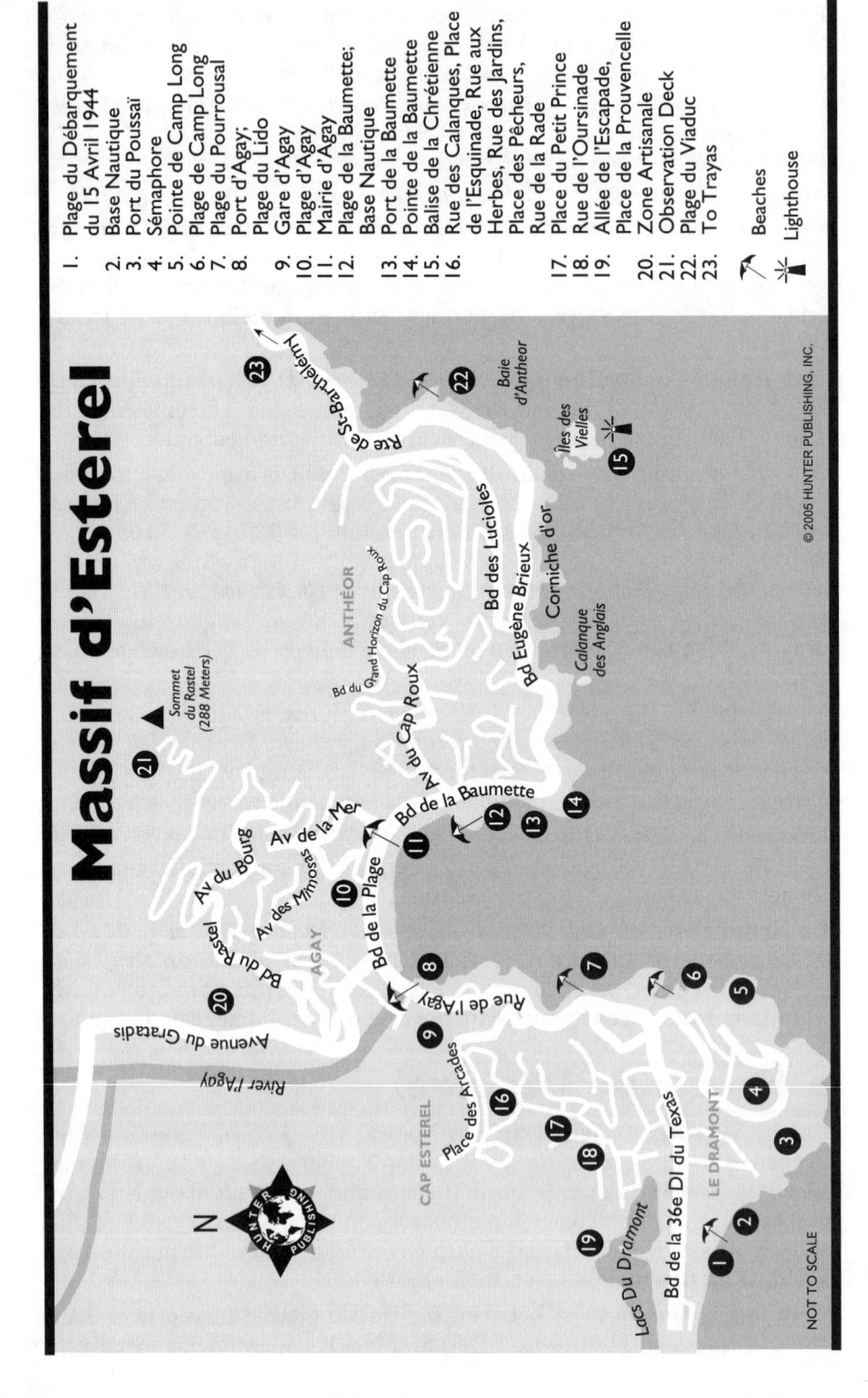

Massif d'Esterel

1. Plage du Débarquement du 15 Avril 1944
2. Base Nautique
3. Port du Poussaï
4. Sémaphore
5. Pointe de Camp Long
6. Plage de Camp Long
7. Plage du Pourrousal
8. Port d'Agay;
   Plage du Lido
9. Gare d'Agay
10. Place d'Agay
11. Mairie d'Agay
12. Plage de la Baumette;
    Base Nautique
13. Port de la Baumette
14. Pointe de la Baumette
15. Balise de la Chrétienne
16. Rue des Calanques, Place de l'Esquinade, Rue aux Herbes, Rue des Jardins, Place des Pêcheurs, Rue de la Rade
17. Place du Petit Prince
18. Rue de l'Oursinade
19. Allée de l'Escapade, Place de la Prouvencelle
20. Zone Artisanale
21. Observation Deck
22. Plage du Viaduc
23. To Trayas

⛱ Beaches
🗼 Lighthouse

days hiking or cycling along fragrant, silent trails, enjoying miles of coastal and mountain vistas, then dining and clubbing the night away along the coast

Of its 79,000 acres, 32,000 of the Estérel are managed and protected regional forest. The area, which has almost no towns and villages, is crossed by the Aurelian Way (the Roman road now running along the N7) and laced with about 45 km/28 miles of footpaths, 100 km/62 miles of signposted mountain bike trails and 100 km/62 miles of bridle paths. Following are the major destinations around the Massif de l'Estérel.

Getting Here

By Air: Nice is the nearest international airport, only 60 km/37 miles away. Regular bus service between Saint Raphaël and Nice Airport, via Le Trayas, Mandelieu and Cannes, is operated by **Beltrame** (☎ 33 04 98 11 97 60, sva.beltrame@wanadoo.fr, www.ste-varoise-des-autocars.fr).

By Rail: At least 20 TGVs per day stop at Saint Raphaël station (22 in the summer). The trip from Paris, Charles de Gaulle Airport takes almost five hours.

Getting Around

By Train: Local TER trains run along the coast, linking town centers and the beaches from Saint Raphaël TGV-SNCF station.

By Bus: Regular bus services link Fréjus and Saint Raphaël centers with each other and the surrounding countryside. **Fréjus buses** leave from the Kiosque Infobus on Place Paul Vernet (information, ☎ 33 04 94 53 78 46). Service is provided by **Estérel Car** (☎ 33 04 94 52 00 50). Services in Saint Raphaël leave from the Gare Routière in the town center, behind the train station. Regular urban services connect all the main districts as well as linking the town with Fréjus, Saint-Tropez, Draguignan, Fayence, Aix-Marseille, Cannes. **For more information:** www.ville-saintraphael.fr/services/transport_car.htm.

Fréjus

With a population of nearly 50,000 (that triples in the summer months), Fréjus is a very big town compared to the hamlets of the massifs. But the Mediterranean ambiance takes the edge off any sense of urban pressure. The Roman founders must have felt the call to what the locals term *la farniente* too (far-NYEN-tay, borrowed from Italian, means loafing around). Some of the many ruins scattered about suggest that, along with its sister town Saint Raphaël, right next door, Fréjus was a Roman vacation resort.

With origins in the first century AD as a stop along the Aurelian Way between Italy and Spain, the town was originally called Forum Julii.

Fréjus

Historic Town Center

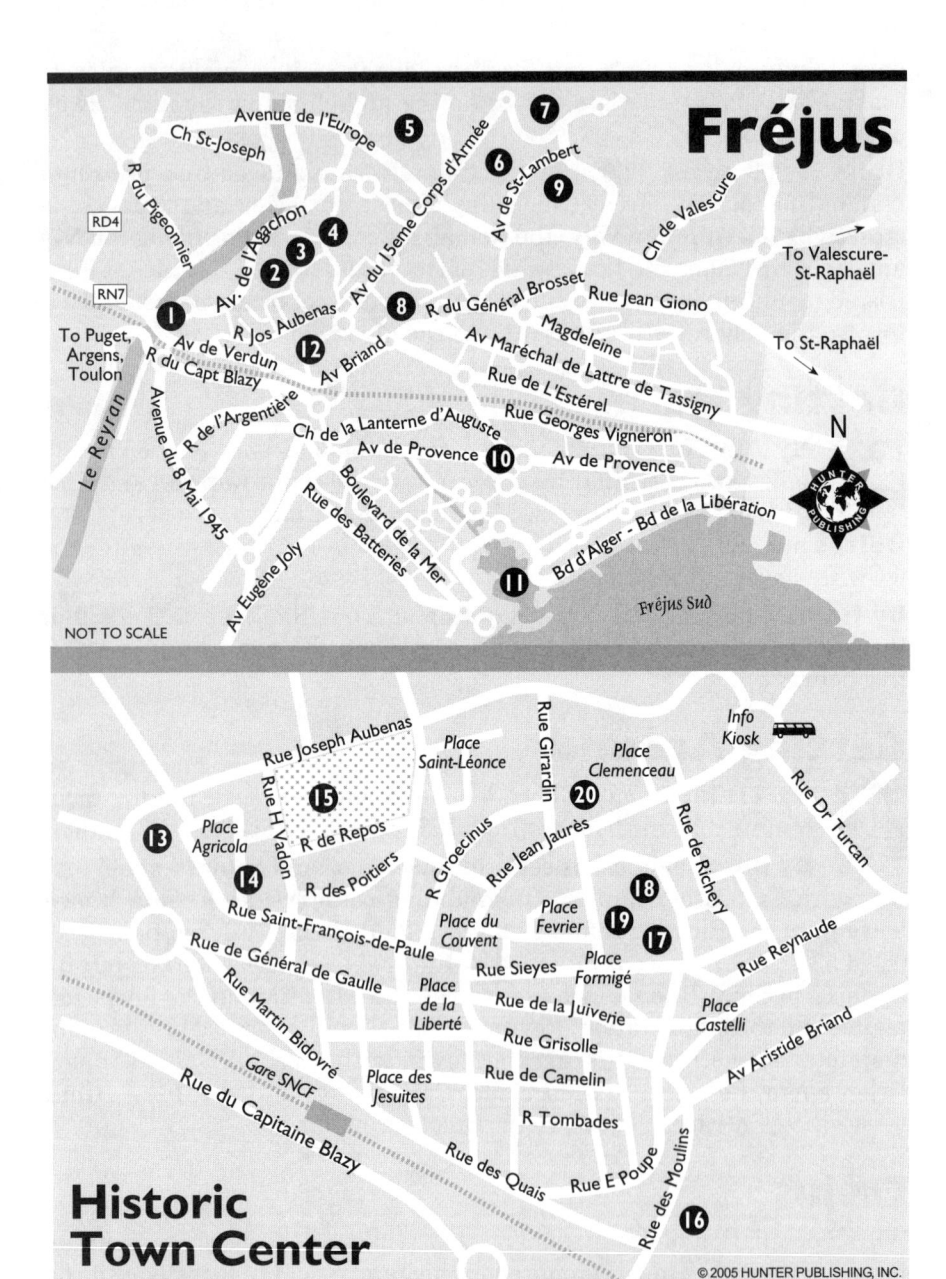

1. Amphithéâtre
2. Ramparts Romain
3. Théâtre Romain
4. Aqueduct
5. Villa & Parc Aurélien
6. Domaine Aurélien
7. Pagoda Hong Hien
8. Villa Marie
9. Le Parc de Valère
10. Lanterne d'Auguste
11. Port-Fréjus
12. Historic Town Center (see below)
13. Porte des Gaules
14. Église Saint-François
15. Cemetery
16. Porte d'Orée
17. Mairie
18. Musée Archéologique Municipal
19. Cathedral Close
20. Musée d'Histoire Locale et des Traditions "Les Amis du Pays de Fréjus"

Later it became a center of the early church and a fourth-century bishopric.

Today, it has 29 protected historic monuments from both the Roman and medieval periods, including the remains of a Roman arena, an aqueduct and a theater as well as a medieval baptistry that is one of the oldest in France.

Save them all for a rainy day and go to the beach! About a mile and a half outside the town center, the beach is a long expanse of soft white sand, 90 m/300 feet wide and more than a mile long. For the Med beyond the Camargue, this is very wide indeed.

There are plenty of places to arrange windsurfing, parascending and power boat rentals. Fréjus has a particularly good diving center and one of the only systems of wetland lagoons between the Camargue and the Italian border (see pages 268 ff).

The old town, a five-minute drive from the beach, is a complete change of pace from the flash of the coast. Its winding, cobbled streets and medieval stone houses are more like the rustic Provence of the interior. Even in the crowded summer months, the old town is relatively calm – and the shops are full of wonderful surprises.

Sightseeing

Tourist Information: Office du Tourisme de la Culture et de l'Animation de Fréjus, 325 Rue Jean Jaurès, 83600 Fréjus, ☎ 33 04 94 51 83 83, fax 33 04 94 51 00 26, tourisme@frejus.fr, www.frejus.fr.

The Roman Ruins

This group of monuments form part of the fabric of the town and can be freely visited at any time.

The Aqueduct: A few pillars and ruined arches are all that remain visible of what was once a marvel of Roman technology. Built in the first century, the aqueduct brought fresh water from a source 40 km/25 miles away to the highest point in the town, 30 m/100 feet above sea level. For security and to keep the water fresh, most of the aqueduct ran underground, surfacing only in arches to cross valleys. Today, much of that underground aqueduct remains under the pavement of the Old Town's ring road. The above-ground section is just north of the Old Town center on Avenue du 15ème Corps D'Armée.

La Porte des Gaules: The most important vestige of the town's first-century Roman ramparts. The tower beside the gate is one of two that would originally have flanked it. Located on Rue Henri Vadon. If you follow the topography of the land in the oldest part of the town, you will find other sections of both Roman and medieval walls marking the rocky butte on which Fréjus was originally built.

La Porte d'Orée: Located on the Rue des Moulins, beside the old port, this was the entrance to a monumental room that was probably part of the town's thermal baths. It dates from the third century.

The Roman Port: The vieux port of Fréjus is more "vieux" than many ports that carry the same title. The port is artificial, having been dredged out of the marshes near the rocky promontory that dominates it. It is at least 2,000 years old and may, in fact, be older. One of the most important maritime sites in the ancient world, it was the port that received the warships of Cleopatra after the battle of Actium in 31 BC.

La Butte Saint Antoine: For a long time this mysterious structure, sitting on a rocky outcrop above the Roman port, was thought to be the original Roman citadel. It is surrounded by Roman ramparts, which support it in several places and at least one of its semi-circular supports was thought to be a lighthouse. Recent archaeological excavations, however, tell a different story. It is now thought that the Butte Saint Antoine was the Iron Age dwelling of an important Celto-Ligurian leader, suggesting that Fréjus was already a fortified port when the Romans arrived.

The Lantern of Augustus: Follow the arrows from the Butte Saint Antoine to find a monument that is one of the most eloquent in the town. The tower, which signals the entrance channel between the sea and the port, is a remnant of the real working life of the Roman town. In the Middle Ages, when the tower itself was already a ruin, a signal light, then named the Lantern of Augustus, was erected. It is possible that the tower had been used for a signal light during the Roman era or earlier.

Amphitéâtre: The Roman arena here is somewhat smaller and less well preserved than the arenas in Arles and Nîmes. It was built of local stone in the first century AD and held about 10,000 spectators for gladiatorial contests, sports and water spectacles. The arena is unusual in that it was built outside of the town walls and against a hill. Entry is from Rue Henri Vadon, admission free. Open from 10 am to noon and 1:30 to 5:30 pm, November through March; 10 am to 1 pm and 2:30 to 6:30 pm, April through October. Closed Sundays.

Le Théâtre Romain: Built against a slope, the lowest level of seating and some of the supports of the upper tiers are still visible. The theater would have been built at about the same time as the arena. Some of the foundations of the *scena* (the Roman backdrop) and a channel through which the stage curtain may have been drawn give clues as to how the theater was used. *Rue du Théâtre Romain. Admission free.* ☎ *33 04 94 17 05 60.* Open from November through the end of March, 8 am to 5 pm every day but Tuesday. From April through the end of October, open 7 am and 7 pm. Closed Tuesdays, New Year's Day, May Day and Christmas Day.

Musée Archéologique: A worthwhile collection of Gallo-Roman relics. These include a marble head of Jupiter and a mosaic of a leopard above a two-headed Hermes, the town's symbol. The Archaeological Museum provides insight into the daily lives of people in the ancient town. It is free and a good way to take a break from the sun. *Salles du Vieux Fréjus, Place Calvini, ☎ 33 04 94 52 15 78. Admission free. Open November through March, Monday to Friday from 10 am to noon and from 1:30 to 5:30, Saturdays from 9:30 to 12:30 and from 1:30 to 5:30. From April through October, Monday to Saturday, 10 am to 1 pm and 2:30 to 6:30 pm. Closed Sundays and Tuesdays as well as New Year's Day, May Day and Christmas Day.*

The Medieval Quarter

• The Diocesan Group

From the fourth century, Fréjus was a seat of bishops and an important town in the early church. The compound of buildings, known as the Groupe Épiscopal, includes a 10th- to 13th-century cathedral, a 12th-century cloister and a baptistry that is one of the oldest buildings in France. The main entrance to all three buildings is through the Cloister, *48 Rue du Cardinal Fleury, 83600 Fréjus, ☎ 33 04 94 51 26 30, www.monum.fr.* The Cathedral is open mornings from 9 am to noon and from 4 to 6 pm, every day except May 1. Opening hours for the rest of the compound are 9 am to noon and 2 to 5 pm from October to through the end of March, 9 am to 7 pm from April through the end of September. Closed Mondays and New Year's Day, November 1, November 11 and Christmas Day. Admission €4.60.

The Baptistry: This unusual 5th-century building appears square on the outside and is octagonal on the inside. Columns used in the construction by the early Christian community who built it have white marble Corinthian capitals, taken from monuments in the Roman town. They are virtually the only decoration in the bare, blue-grey granite interior. An octagonal baptismal pool was discovered by archaeologists in the 1920s. It had been covered by later marble and decoration.

The Cathedral: As with the other buildings in this compound, the Cathedral was probably built on the foundations of Roman structures. It has two naves from distinctly different periods, separated by three large arcades. The Notre Dame nave, which has ribbed vaulting, is probably the earliest, while the Saint Etienne nave, which is barrel vaulted, dates from the 11th and 12th centuries. A 15th-century altarpiece by Pierre Durandi is notable in this simple and otherwise undecorated church.

The Cloister: On the north side of the Baptistry, a 12th-century Romanesque cloister maintains its peaceful, contemplative atmosphere around a small garden with a well. The ceilings of the galleries, on the other hand, are a riot of detail. They are covered with 1,200 painted wooden panels. The 400 of them still legible are decorated with men, animals and monsters. Local people entered the Cathedral through the cloister in the Middle Ages; the painted panels, which include military, secular and religious figures as well as a remarkably fantastic bestiary, was probably for their moral instruction.

The Diocesan Palace: Partially reconstructed in the 19th century, the ancient episcopal palace is a fortified residence with a crenelated tower that incorporates an ancient chapel. Much-restored, the side facing Rue du Beausset is the original 14th-century façade, built of red stone from the Massif de l'Estérel.

- **The Chapelle Cocteau**

In 1961, shortly before he died, France's latter-day Renaissance man, Jean Cocteau – who was playwright, filmmaker, poet and artist – designed La Chapelle Notre Dame de Jérusalem. The chapel, later completed by another artist, Edouard Dermit, retains Cocteau's unmistakable, childlike style. It is open to the public in the afternoons. *Avenue Nicolaï - La Tour de Mare, ☎ 33 04 94 53 27 06. Open from November through March, 2:30 to 5:30 pm, and from April through October, 2 to 6 pm. Closed Mondays.*

TOURS OF THE ROMAN & MEDIEVAL TOWNS

During the summer months, the tourist office organizes regular tours of The West Antique Quarter, The East Antique Quarter, The Roman Port and The Medieval and Modern City. The times and prices vary. Tours start at the tourist information office. They are conducted in French but, even if you speak only a little guidebook French, they are worth a try.

Saint Raphaël

Right next door to Fréjus – they even share a beachfront – Saint Raphaël was once a resort for the rich Romans of Fréjus, who came down from their villas in the hills to take in the fresh sea air at what was then called Epulias. Under its modern Casino, lie the ruins of thermal baths, a fishpond, terraces and buildings with mosaic floors.

It is not entirely clear why there are so many fewer Roman and medieval remains in Saint Raphaël. Perhaps the city was less important during those eras and fewer monumental buildings were created in the first place. But the fact that Saint Raphaël's outer harbor is deep and wide enough to shelter warships may provide a more likely hint.

During the late 19th century, it enjoyed a revival as a fashionable resort for the bourgeoisie of the Second Empire, who built themselves lavish and flamboyant villas. Much of the town's modern character can be attributed

St-Raphaël Region

The Western Côte d'Azur

1. Place Kennedy
2. Gare SNCF/TGV
3. Square Bir-Hakeim
4. Monument d'Afrique
5. Centre Nautique Municipal
6. Club Nautique
7. Place Amiral Ortoli
8. Palais des Congrès
9. Centre de Thalassothérapie
10. Gare, Poste, Mairie de Boulouris
11. Saint-Raphaël Town Center
12. Cimetière A. Karr
13. Notre Dame de la Paix
14. River *La Garonne*
15. To Cap Esterel
16. To Fréjus

NOT TO SCALE
© 2005 HUNTER PUBLISHING, INC.

Villa Mauresque, Saint Raphaël. Photo courtesy of Villa Mauresque

to its mix of 19th-century architectural styles – Palladian, Moorish, Anglo-Norman. Some of the grand houses of the past have been converted into hotels and chambres d'hôtes, but many are maintained as private homes.

Today Saint Raphaël is, first and foremost, a pleasure-boat haven and watersports center. One of only 27 resorts certified as a "France Station Nautique" by the French Sailing Federation, meaning that it offers the highest quality and widest range of watersports options. The quality rating symbol, shown at right, is displayed all over town.

Saint Raphaël's five separate ports, strung out along 42 km/26 miles of sheltered coastline, provide berths for 3,500 boats. They range in size from the new and bustling Santa Lucia Port, which can accommodate 1,800 yachts, to the sweet and tiny Port Toukan, with 60 berths in the middle of a necklace of sandy beaches.

Dozens of divable wrecks and underwater archaeology make Saint Raphaël a major diving center. Underwater finds in the town's archaeological museum testify to its antiquity as a thriving commercial port. The town's peaceful bays are virtually littered with history.

Unlike some Mediterranean towns that center around a harbor, Saint Raphaël snakes along the coast. The Massif de l'Estérel slides right down to the sea in several places along the town's seashore, dividing it into distinct districts, each with its own beaches and ambiance.

With the exception of Dramont, most beaches are relatively close to the Route de la Corniche (N98), the narrow but busy coastal road. This is a fact of life along the Côte d'Azur and Saint Raphaël's beaches are wider and more sheltered than many.

Sightseeing

This is a town completely devoted to the good life. Days are for boating, diving, sun worshipping, watersports or hiking in the Estérel – with a bit of shopping thrown in for good measure. Nights are spent dining, dancing, listing to music or gambling in the Casino.

Maybe because there are so few ancient and historic monuments on land, not much effort is made to point them out. If you dive, however, there is plenty to see – from wrecked Roman galleys to World War II landing craft. The tourist office, which has its main branch in the town center and a sat-

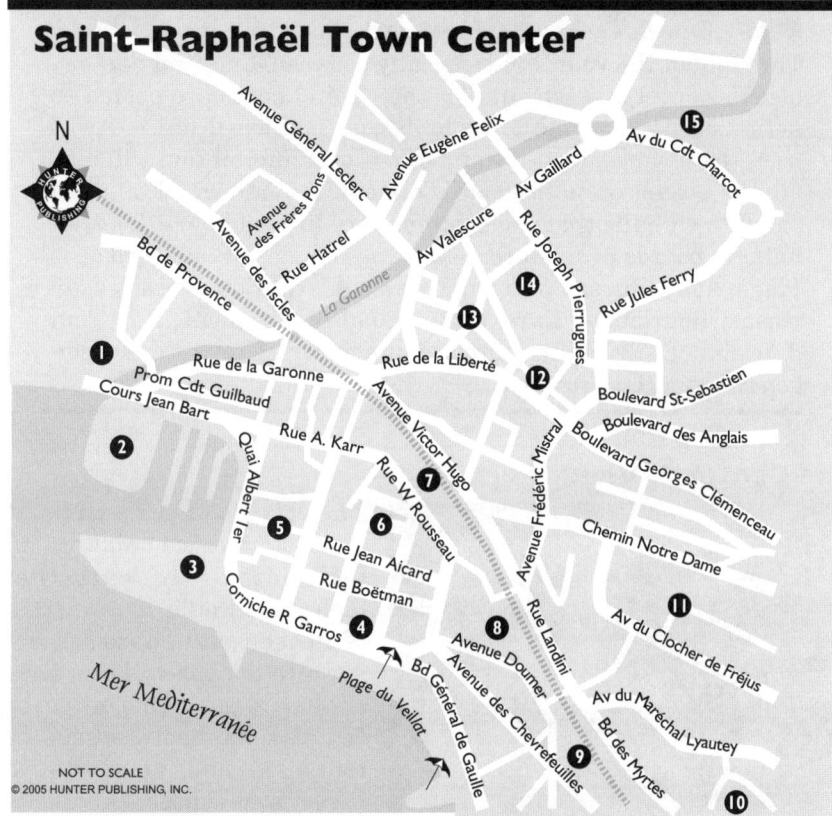

1. Square de Provence
2. Maison de la Mer; Place Kennedy
3. Gare Maritime; Quai Amiral Nomy
4. Promenade René Coty; Boulevard de la Libération; Promenade de Lattre de Tassigny
5. Rue Auble; Place du Parvis; Passage du Parvis
6. Place Coullet
7. Gare SNCF/TGV
8. Église Anglicaine
9. Église Orthodox; Maison de l'Hermitage; Square Berger
10. Parc St-Jacques
11. Allée Chapelle Notre Dame; Square St-Exupéry
12. Place Gabriel Peri
13. Rue des Lauriers, Rue de la Vieille Église, Place de la République
14. Place Châteaudun
15. Foyer des Acacias

ellite branch in Agay, can help you book accommodation, find restaurants or connect with a wide range of sports associations and clubs. They are also handy for providing directions to the many hidden trails, Calanques and sheltered beaches.

For More Information: Office Municipal de Tourisme et des Congrès, Rue Waldeck Rousseau, BP 210, 83702 Saint Raphaël, ☎ 33 04 94 19 52 52, fax 33 04 94 83 85 40, information@saint-raphael.com, www.saint-raphael.com. Except for July and August, when it is open non-stop from 9 am to 7 pm, the office normally closes for an hour and a half at lunchtime. Also *Office du Tourisme d'Agay, Boulevard de la Plage, next to the Gendarmerie*, ☎ 33 04 94 82 01 85, info@agay.fr or agay.tourisme@wanadoo.fr, www.agay.fr.

262 ■ Massif de l'Estérel

FIRE RISK

Throughout the year, but especially between June and September, risk level assessments for the Estérel paths are posted on noticeboards near the town halls and municipal office. Away from the town center, this and other local information will usually be posted on noticeboards outside the municipal offices – small town halls that are open for very limited hours. Look for bulletin boards near: Bureau Municipal d'Agay, Boulevard de la Plage, Agay; Bureau Municipal de Boulouris, Boulevard des Mimosas, Bourlouris; Bureau Municipal du Dramont, Rue Tour d'Armont, 83730 Agay; Bureau Municipal du Trayas, Rue Georges Hechter, Le Trayas.

The Center & Vieux Port

Café life near the town center. © J.F. Cholley, OT Saint Raphaël

The city center, with its multi-story office buildings and tall hotels (to call them high-rises would be something of an exaggeration) comes right down to the beach. Local boosters like to point this out as one of Saint Raphaël's assets, but that all depends upon what you expect from a beach.

The waterfront near the town center is quite urban. The **Promenade des Bains**, a wide esplanade, follows the route of the busy N98 coastal road and, just the other side of it, the shops, cafés and offices carry on their everyday life. You can rent a sun lounger and beach umbrella for the sandy beach, **Plage du Veillat**, which has a lifeguard in the summer, but you'll probably feel a bit odd in your beach attire when you cross the street.

Walk along the promenade for views of Saint Raphaël's wide bay and its two offshore volcanic rocks. The Vieux Port is a working fishing port with limited berths for passing boat traffic but with a great deal of character for the stroller on shore.

This area comes into its own at night. Saint Raphaël has a casino and a lively club scene.

Where else does garlic become an artists medium but the Cote d'Azur? © CDT VAR / WWW.WALLIS.FR

A moonlight promenade along the seafront near the Vieux Port is definitely part of a night out on the town.

Elsewhere in the town center, the market squares of **Place Coullet**, **Place Victor Hugo** and **Place de la République**, with their pastel-washed, tile-roofed buildings, remind you that you are still in Provence. Overlooking it all is the town's most striking monument, the **Eglise Saint Raphaël**, a 12th-century fortified church (also known as Eglise des Templiers). Lookouts in the 13th-century watchtower beside it gave early warning of Barbary pirate raids, summoning the townspeople to the protection of the church.

Santa Lucia Port

East of the town center, just beyond Plage du Veillat, Santa Lucia Port is a gigantic stretch of quays and floating quays with berths for 1,600 sail- and powerboats. Berths are available for rent by the day (as well as by the year), ensuring a regular turnover of yachts just passing through and giving the place a convivial and thoroughly relaxed, holiday atmosphere. To rent a berth, contact the *Capitainerie,* ☎ *33 04 94 95 34 30, fax 33 04 94 95 22 13, serpp-port-santa-lucia@wanadoo.fr, www.port-santa-lucia.com.*

The streets closest to the port are lined with shops selling the kinds of goods you might expect – swimsuits and resort fashions, diving gear, local products. There are plenty of cafés and bars, a couple of discos and a casual, laid-back style.

Santa Lucia Port has a sailing school (page 275). Nearby **Beaurivage**, west of the port itself, is a watersports center offering a range of activities, boat rentals and a half-mile-long shingle beach.

Boulouris

Next along, going east, Boulouris is a wide, quiet bay surrounded by rocky red spurs of the Estérel. In the inlets between them are eight separate, sandy beaches. These are among Saint Raphaël's best. Beach chairs and umbrellas can be rented on Plage de la Tortue.

Hotels, across the road from the beaches, are small and personal. This

A small corner of Port Santa Lucia.
© J.F. Cholley, OT Saint Raphaël

area is also popular for summer rentals and chambre d'hôtes. A thalassatherapy spa on the beach offers all kinds of European sea-water treatments, an aquagym in a heated seawater pool and a Turkish bath

(Thalasports, ☎ *33 04 94 19 87 94, info@thalasports.com, www.thalasports.com).* The tiny **Port du Toukan** is a complete change of pace from the huge ports of the center. It has space for only 60 boats. There is a good shopping area along the Esplanade Saint Jean. To rent a berth for your boat, contact the *Capitainerie,* ☎ *33 04 94 40 49 96.*

Le Cap Dramont

On August 15, 1944, during the liberation of France, the 36th Texan Division, about 20,000 GIs in all, came ashore on the east side of Cape Dramont at what is now referred to as the Plage du Débarquément. The event is commemorated with a memorial and landing boat on the shingle beach.

> **Did you know?** One of the few shingle beaches in this area, the grey stones were the leavings of ancient mines which now form a pair of large lakes, Lacs du Dramont, above the beach and across the N98.

Le Dramont is a wild coastal cape that shelters the deep bay of Agay and separates it from the rest of Saint Raphaël. It combines a variety of milieux – gentle beaches, forest paths for hiking and riding, a traditional fishing port, all in a relatively compact area served by a local rail connection to the town center. It is a fine place to fill a day with outdoor and marine activities and is close enough to the town to take advantage of the nightlife later on. Because of this, the paths and beaches of le Dramont are very popular during the summer months – especially during August when French vacationers hit the coast. May or September, when the weather is still very pleasant, are better months to appreciate this stretch of coast.

A jumble of mini-fjords and rugged red stones, Le Dramont forms part of the **Estérel National Forest**. Paths from the beaches that ring it lead up to a signal tower, **La Semaphore**, with panoramic views of the coast (see *Walking the Wild Coast,* below). In addition to the shingled beach, there are two sandy beaches –

Port Poussai in the Cap Dramont section of Saint Raphaël. The Semaphore signal tower, just visible at the top of the hill. © J.F. Cholley, OT Saint Raphaël

Plage du Camp Long and **Plage du Pourousset**, along its west side. A very good diving school for beginners and families, **L' Ecole de Plongée des Roches Rouges** (see pages 278-79) is based at the Camp Long beach. **Port du Poussai**, a traditional fishing port at the tip of Le Dramont, keeps a handful of its 90 berths available for short-term rental (*Capitainerie,* ☎ *33 04 94 82 71 31*). Offshore, there's good diving around **Ile d'Or**, which was once owned by a 19th-century eccentric who proclaimed himself king and built the sham castle still visible there.

WALKING THE WILD COAST

The **Sentier du Littoral**, or Coastal Path, was originally carved out to help French customs officers keep watch on approaching ships. It follows most of the French Mediterranean Coast, from Spain to the Italian border, shaping itself to the landscape – whether urban, beach, coastal plain or cliff top.

Wherever you are on the Côte d'Azur, it is easy to pick up the coastal path for a walk of a few hours or several days. Just ask the local tourist authority where the marked coastal trail begins and what the nearby terrain is like.

From **Port Santa Lucia**, east around **Le Dramont** to **Agay**, the path is particularly accessible. It begins in the town, east of Port Santa Lucia, passes through the manicured, palm-shaded lawns of **Beaurivage**, quickly crosses into rock-strewn headlands and climbs along the edge of the steep bluffs around Le Dramont. In a few places, where the path is particularly vertiginous, there are railings, handholds and steps chopped out of the rocks, making it within the reach of most walkers.

Along the way, the path gives glimpses of the volcanic geology that formed the Estérel. Just after Port Santa Lucia, there are a series red quartz-rich lava "pipes." Farther along, after **Aiguebonne beach**, black rocks formed of volcanic dust are more than 200 million years old. Among the maritime pines, coastal plants typical of the region include sea lavender and false laburnum.

There is regular bus service (Line 8, Autocars Raphaël) from Le Dramont, stopping all along the coastal road, to Port Santa Lucia, the Vieux Port and the Saint Raphaël Bus Station (Gare Routière).

The Semaphore: For a shorter, more dramatic walk, start at the free parking for the Plage du Debarquément. Take the steps down to the beach and pick up the coastal path. Follow it around the headland to **Port Poussai**. Then pick up any one of the narrow paths that snake their way up to the signal house at the top. The path is steep in places, but not difficult, and the walk should take about 90 minutes. On the way up – and from the Semaphore – enjoy dramatic views of Ile d'Or and the bay of Agay.

Agay

If a child drew it, the map of Agay could not be a more perfect, sheltered horseshoe of a bay. The deep turquoise water, fringed with sandy beaches, is wrapped in arms of the coast – Cap Dramont to the west and Pointe de la Baumette on the east – and overlooked by Rastel d'Agay, 309 m/1,000 feet of red volcanic stone.

Visitors come here to sail and windsurf, dive and canoe – the bay of Agay provides some of the best water for these pursuits along the coast of the massifs. The municipal Base Nautique offers lessons, rentals and excursions for all sorts of sailing and canoeing activities (page 275-76).

It is also a gateway to the Estérel, with lots of challenging day-long hikes, and the start of a particularly scenic stretch of the Corniche d'Or. East of Pointe de la Baumette, a series of calanques can be easily reached by canoe or kayak.

Agay is within reach of the center of Saint Raphaël by train, bus and taxi, but it has a good selection of camping and accommodations, plenty of restaurants, several markets and a lively life of its own.

Its natural harbor, Port d'Agay, has been a boat haven for more than 2,000 years. Before the Romans discovered and named it *l'Agathonis Portus*, it was a Celto-Ligurian fishing and trading port. The comings and goings of centuries of traders visiting the port have littered the sea floor with amphorae and fascinating evidence of ancient commerce – much to the delight of divers. From the bay, the port extends along the Agay River, making it a particularly scenic harbor for quiet walks. Evidence of the ancient port can still be seen on the left bank of the river, inland of the N98. During the summer months, traditional Provençal water jousting is organized on the river by the **Association Agay Nautique** (☎ *33 04 94 82 01 49).*

The modern port has 166 berths, with a limited number available for day rental. (Contact *Capitainerie,* ☎ *33 04 94 82 74 22).* Motorboat rentals are available from several companies (page 276).

At the bottom of the bay, east of the port, **Plage du Lido** and **Plage d'Agay** are long sandy beaches that stretch almost all the way around. Beach umbrellas and loungers can be rented on Plage du Lido. **Plage de la Baumette** is a bite-shaped scallop of quiet sandy beach near the Baumette Lighthouse (see Saint Exupery, below). There are cafés and bars scattered all around the bay and in the village of Agay, north of the N98.

Antoine de Saint Exupéry & Agay

Fans of Antoine de Saint Exupéry, France's pilot-poet, will find Agay particularly poignant because it was the last land he saw before his final flight. The author of *Night Flight, Wind, Sand and Stars* and the classic *The Little Prince* spent many childhood summers here and, through family, is closely associated with the Château d'Agay.

Saint Exupéry was a pioneering pilot as well as a philosopher and writer. Toward the end of World War II, on July 31, 1944, he took off on a reconnaissance mission from which he never returned. The lighthouse at Pointe de la Baumette, was the last monument he reported seeing before he crashed into the sea.

Today, a historic marker at the base of le Phare de la Baumette, tells Saint Exupery's story. The Fontaine Saint Exupéry à Agay, across the road from the Château, also commemorates this *monstre-sacré* of French literature and history.

Anthéor & Le Trayas

Beyond Agay, the coast becomes even more deeply indented with creeks and calanques. Between these two tiny communities, the Massif de l'Estérel rises up and plunges vertiginously into the sea. It dominates the narrow, sometimes nonexistant coastal plain. The stunning red stone mass of **Cap Roux** (452 m/1,500 feet) hangs above Anthéor, while **Pic de l'Ours** (496 m/1,630 feet) almost presses against Le Trayas. As mountains go, the coastal peaks of the Estérel are not very high. But there is no getting away from the fact that they are awesome. If you are able to rent a car, this stretch of coastal road (**N98**), known as the **Corniche d'Or**, is a terrific drive. The calanques between **Anthéor** and the **Maison Forestiere** (Ranger Station) on the N98 in Le Trayas are rugged and dramatic.

You could sample this bit of coast in a boat. About 10 km/6.2 miles of creeks, calanques and small sandy or shingle beaches are strung along the coast between Saint Raphaël's two most distant quartiers. The waters off Anthéor are popular with divers because of the large number of World War II barges and landing craft in the area. And despite the ruggedness of the coast, quite a few of these beaches are reachable if you park near the Corniche. Train and bus services will get you there as well.

Le Trayas, about halfway between Saint Raphaël center and Cannes, is also easily reached from Théoule sur Mer, farther east along the coast. The town is divided into two separate parts. One area, focussed around the beaches and calanques, is located below the coastal road, while the bulk of the village, including residential areas and a few shops, climbs the hill above the N98 and the railroad tracks. Of all of Saint Raphaël's seaside districts, Le Trayas is the least geared to passing tourism. It has a TER station, bus services and a post office but no harbor and very little else. This makes it one of the most peaceful, but also the most difficult, to visit.

CLIMBING PIC DU CAP ROUX

The path to the summit of Pic du Cap Roux is not too difficult. It is well signposted with arrows and orange blazes and when you arrive at the top you're rewarded with an orientation table to help you make sense of the coastal views. It is a two-hour hike from the parking lot.

By car, leave the N98 at the exit for **Agay** and follow the road signposted for **Valescure**. Turn right, toward **Pic de L'Ours** (there should be a directional sign). Pass the **Maison Forestière (Ranger Station) du Gratadis** and ford a stream. Leave the road for Pic de L'Ours, which goes off to the left and go around the north side of **Rastel d'Agay**. Continue toward the right in the direction of **Rocher de Saint Barthélemy** (signposted). Stop and take in the views from the picnic area on the **Plateau d'Anthéor**. Continue climbing. The road is narrow and the views drop away to the sea. If you don't like driving in high places, this might not be for you. When you have driven as far as you can up this road, there is a parking area. Leave your car for the two-hour hike to the summit.

Tip: The roads that climb Pic du Cap Roux are local and don't have national route numbers. The key landmarks are signposted but if you want to be certain, you can plot the route on IGN (1/25,000) MAP #3544 ET "Fréjus, Saint-Raphaël, Corniche Estérel." Or stop at the nearest tourist office – there is one in Agay (page 383) – for a local map.

Les Adrets de L'Estérel

Unlike the Massif des Maures with its handful of isolated villages, there are almost no villages in the interior of the Massif de l'Estérel. Les Adrets is an exception.

The village of about 2,000 is on the ancient Roman road, the Aurelian Way, equidistant from the coastal towns of Mandelieu and Fréjus. It probably owes its very existance to that fact. The distance – 17 km/10½ miles – was apparently as far as the post horses could travel over the dry, brutal terrain before needing rest and water.

At any rate, Les Adrets has been a resting place for travelers for more than a thousand years. There is a record of a meal taken in the Auberge by the Prior of Lérins in 824. And, until the early 1960s, when it was renamed, the town itself was called l'Auberge des Adrets.

On a clear day, the view from the top of Les Adrets extends along the coast from Nice to Saint Tropez. Deep in the forest, it is a convenient stopping place for hikes to the top of **Mont Vinaigre**, at 618 m/2,000 feet, the highest point in the Estérel. And it is within a short hike of the excellent fishing, rowing, windsurfing and lake swimming on **Lac Saint Cassien** (about six km/3¾ miles directly north; take the D237 north to the first intersection, bear left onto the D837, which becomes the D37 after it crosses under the A8 Autoroute, follow signs to lake-front facilities).

> ### IN THE FOOTSTEPS OF THE HIGHWAYMAN
>
> Les Adrets has a special place in French romantic history.
>
> In the late 18th century, the Estérel developed a fearsome reputation among travelers because of the bandits and brigands who regularly attacked the *diligences* (stagecoaches carrying the mail as well as passengers) that crossed its dark, mysterious forests. None was as celebrated as the **Highwayman Gaspard de Besse**, who became known as the French Robin Hood.
>
> According to the legend, Gaspard came to his life of crime by accident, after drunkenly enlisting in the civil constabulary, then deserting once he'd sobered up. He was known for his jokes and tricks, for his way with the ladies and, of course, for robbing the rich to give to the poor.
>
> His hideout was somewhere in the folds of Mont Vinaigre but he regularly came down from the hills to entertain his mistress and hold court at L'Auberge des Adrets – even then an ancient post house.
>
> Like all rebellious heroes who are the stuff of legends, Gaspard de Besse lived hard, drank hard, loved hard and died young. At the age of 24, after a short career, he was captured and executed.
>
> No one comes right out and tells you that **l'Auberge des Adrets**, the inn that still takes in guests, was Gaspard's love nest. But, since it is the original post house and is so old that it was "restored" in 1653, it probably was. It is also a luxurious, romantic place to spend a weekend (see *Where to Stay*, page 280).

Adventures on Foot

Mont Vinaigre

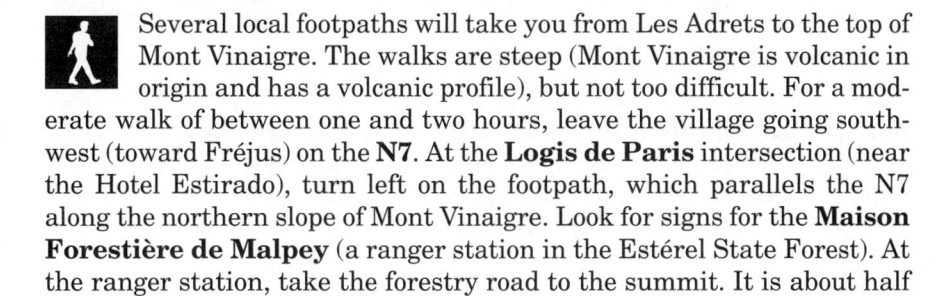

Several local footpaths will take you from Les Adrets to the top of Mont Vinaigre. The walks are steep (Mont Vinaigre is volcanic in origin and has a volcanic profile), but not too difficult. For a moderate walk of between one and two hours, leave the village going southwest (toward Fréjus) on the **N7**. At the **Logis de Paris** intersection (near the Hotel Estirado), turn left on the footpath, which parallels the N7 along the northern slope of Mont Vinaigre. Look for signs for the **Maison Forestière de Malpey** (a ranger station in the Estérel State Forest). At the ranger station, take the forestry road to the summit. It is about half an hour's walk from here. When I was last here, there was an old lookout tower you could climb for spectacular views. Even if you can't climb the tower, the panorama is terrific.

Guided Walks

Once a week, between June and September, volunteers from the Tourist Office lead walks into the Estérel. Groups meet at 8:30 am, Wednesday mornings, in front of the tourist office on the Place de la Mairie. **For more information: Office du Tourisme des Adrets de l'Estérel,** *Place de la Mairie, 83600 les Adrets de l'Estérel,* ☎ *33 04 94 40 93 57, fax 33 04 94 19 36 69, otsi@mairie-adrets-esterel.fr; www.mairie-adrets-esterel.fr / NewSite.*

Planning Your Route

Fire is a constant danger in the thick pine and cork oak forests that blanket the Estérel. Early spring and late autumn are the best times of year for hiking if you want to be sure your route will be open. During the summer, the massif is regularly swept by serious fires.

Damage caused by fires during the heat wave of 2003 forced local authorities to re-route some of the recommended cycling and hiking circuits on the Estérel. At the time of publication, the new trails were not fully complete. The GR51, the Balcony of the Côte d'Azur, was only partially open across the massif. Local tourist offices, along with the hiking and cycling clubs they recommend, are the best sources of information. Make a rough plan using IGN Blue Map (1:25,000) 3544 est "Fréjus, Saint Raphaël" or the Michelin Green Map #114 (1/100,000) – "French Riviera - Var." Then consult the following for local advice:

- **Office du Tourisme des Adrets de l'Estérel,** *Place de la Mairie, 83600 les Adrets de l'Estérel,* ☎ *33 04 94 40 93 57, fax 33 04 94 19 36 69, otsi@mairie-adrets-esterel.fr.*

- **Office Municipal de Tourisme et des Congrès Saint Raphaël,** *Rue Waldeck Rousseau, BP 210, 83 702 Saint Raphaël,* ☎ *33 04 94 19 52 52, fax 33 04 94 83 85 40, www.saint-raphael.com. E-mail through website.*

- **Office du Tourisme de la Culture et de l'Animation de Fréjus,** *325 Rue Jean Jaurès, 83600 Fréjus,* ☎ *33 04 94 51 83 83, fax 33 04 94 51 00 26, tourisme@frejus.fr, www.frejus.fr.*

Consulting the Experts

The scale of the Estérel and the number of signposted local walks makes this area tempting for hikers with little or no experience. There are even a large number of paths and forestry roads accessible to the physically handicapped. But don't underestimate the challenges of this volcanic landmass or the danger of fire risks (a couple of hikers died in the fires of 2003).

ONF Guided Walks

The **Office National des Forêts** (the French Forestry Commission) offers guided walks, year-round, which can be booked through the tourist offices in Fréjus, Saint Raphaël and Agay. They cost between €8 and €9 for adults, €5 for children under 12. The selection of themed walks includes the Estérel at dusk, "Stag calling in the Estérel," as well as spring and autumn flora and fauna tours.

Green Walks

Ecoloisirs Développement runs ecology-oriented walks for people of any ability, including children of elementary school age. It can also supply information about ecotourism around Saint Raphaël. Themes include flora and fauna, geology and land ecology. Contact *Ecoloisirs Développement,* ☎ *33 04 94 40 58 06 or 33 06 60 96 14 00, fax 33 04 94 40 58 12, ecoloisir@ wanadoo.fr.*

Group Walks

The Fréjus-Saint Raphaël Ramblers Club, **Randonneurs de l'Est Varois**, have a regular program of twice-weekly, day-long walks for their members and invite visitors to pack a picnic and join in. This being a French hiking club, the weekly walks are suspended during July and August, the inviolable French vacation period. Once a month, the group hires a bus to hike farther afield. The club takes mountain, forest and coastal walks.

If you have ever been a member of a rambler's association or hiking club, you know that this can be a sociable way to explore the countryside and get to know local people. They meet on Sundays and Wednesdays at Place de la République, near the Post Office annex, on Fréjus Plage (the beach). A schedule of walks is published on the group's website. Most hikes start at 7 or 7:30 am and last five or six hours. For more information and to see the schedule of hikes, contact Randonneurs de l'Est Varois R.E.V., *1098 Boulevard Jacques Baudino, 83700 Saint Raphaël,* ☎ *33 06 07 84 19 57 or 33 04 94 83 95 27, rev83@free.fr; http://rev83.free.fr.*

Adventures on Wheels

4X4 Tours

Tours in an open-topped Citroën Mehari are offered by **JDC Loisirs & Decouvertes** from the Cap Estérel parking lot. A Mehari is a funny little plastic car based on the design of the Citroën 2CV. A guide who goes only by the name of "Joseph" (and who is endorsed by the

French Forestry Commission) goes along, pointing out the highlights. This tour is a great way for softies to enjoy some of the best views from the top of the massif. It ends with a tasting of local products. Contact JDC Loisirs & Decouvertes, ☎ 33 06 09 09 73 90, *joseph@decouvertedelesterel.com*, *www.decouvertedelesterel.com*.

Mountain Biking

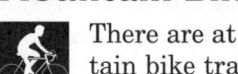

There are at least 100 km/62 miles of off-road, signposted mountain bike trails in the Estérel. At this writing, the long-distance itineraries laid out by the CDT Var were being re-routed because of the 2003 fires. Nevertheless, there are plenty of local tracks available for cyclists.

Estérel VTT-CDM Loisirs, based in the Cap Estérel car park in Agay, offers half- and full-day mountain bike rentals, including helmet and gloves. They provide trail maps or you can join a group for a guided bike tour into the massif. Contact ☎ 33 06 09 09 73 80, year-round. You can also find out about cycling conditions and services from the **Association Municipale des Sports et Loisirs de Fréjus** (AMSLF), which sponsors regular Sunday morning group rides, starting from the town tourist office. For times of the group rides and other cycling information, contact *Section AMSLF Cyclotourisme, Salle Sainte Croix, Avenue du XV Corps, Fréjus,* ☎ *33 04 94 51 55 39 or Monsieur Georges Flattet, Le Parc Adonis, 314 Rue du Suveret, Fréjus,* ☎ *33 04 94 83 24 39 or 33 06 87 00 44 20, gflattet@wanadoo.fr, www.amslfrejus.com*.

In **Les Adrets**, get in touch with **Estérel Cycliste Club des Adrets** *(André Hartz,* ☎ *33 04 94 40 96 06, andre.hartz@9online.fr)* for information about cycle trails, group outings and local cycling resources.

TO RENT A BICYCLE

Holiday Bikes, the national franchise chain, has a branch in **Fréjus** *(519 Avenue Corniche d'Azur, Saint Aygulf-Fréjus,* ☎ *33 04 94 81 35 94, fax 33 04 94 48 22 29, st-aygulf@holiday-bikes.com)*. There are a half a dozen cycle shops in **Saint Raphaël**. Try **Patrick Motos**, *280 Avenue du Général Leclerc,* ☎ *33 04 94 53 65 99*; **Atout Cycles**, *Boulevard Jean Moulin,* ☎ *33 04 94 95 56 91, contact@atoutcycles.com*; or **CyclesThierry**, *Rue Alphonse Karr,* ☎ *33 04 94 95 48 46/53*. In **Agay**, mountain bikes are available at **Camping de l'Ile d'Or** from **La Pecadille**, ☎ *33 04 94 19 48 54*.

Adventures on Horseback

Some of the best rides in this area are on the trails high above the coast. You can find horses to ride year-round, but spring and autumn are really the best seasons. The horses like the cool tem-

Fisherman seems to manage without the railings that are meant to help walkers cling to the coastal path (© J.F. Cholley, OT Saint Raphaël)

Easier than it looks, the Coast Path near Saint Raphaël
(© J.F. Cholley, OT Saint Raphaël)

From Agay, it's an easy kayak trip to tiny, sheltered beaches in the Saint Raphaël calanques (© J.F. Cholley, OT Saint Raphaël)

Hilltop village in the Pays de Fayence (© CDT VAR/www.wallis.fr)

peratures and the Mediterranean has an especially deep blue sparkle. **L'Estérel à Cheval** offers group and individual rides, ranging from a few hours to a full day, for beginners to experienced riders. At their "Pony Club," children from four years up can have day lessons or attend riding camps. They have just begun offering hour-long pony-riding lessons for children from two to four years old – *les bébés cavaliers!* Longer, multi-day trips, called *chevauchées*, journey into the massif from April to mid-June and from the end of September to the beginning of November. The *chevauchées* include meals and accommodation. The company operates from Le Domaine des Lacs du Dramont, near Agay. **For more information:** L'Estérel à Cheval, *Les 3 Fers, Centre Europe, BP 498, Boulevard du Cerceron, 83704 Saint Raphaël; adult tours,* ☎ *33 06 85 42 51 50, Pony Club for children,* ☎ *33 06 09 96 25 52, fax 33 04 94 82 72 03, info@les3fers.com, www.les3fers.com / index1.htm.*

Ecotourism

Les Étangs de Villepey

It is hard to believe, but the system of lakes and lagoons on the edge of Fréjus, reminiscent of the Camargue, is the positive result of interaction between man and nature. Initially formed as the delta of the Argens River, which separates the Massif des Maures from the Estérel, years of industrial sand dredging have produced an extensive wetland area stretching over 640 acres.

The French Coastal Conservation Agency (Conservatoire du Littoral) acquired the area with 24 separate purchases over a period of 15 years in the 1980s and 90s. Today, les Étangs de Villepey is the only major wetlands area between the Camargue and the Italian border.

The continuous tidal exchange of fresh and salt water fosters a diversity of plant and animal life. More than 250 species of birds have been spotted, including large migrating flocks of flamingos, once only seen in the Camargue, grey herons, ducks, grebes, a huge variety gulls, wading birds and birds of prey. The reserve also harbors tortoises, coypus (a beaver-like rodent) and other small mammals. It encompasses a variety of micro-habitats – lakes, lagoons, *sansouires* (salt plains on the edge of marshes in the Camargue and other littoral wetlands), dunes, prairies, salt marshes, riverbanks and pinewoods – encouraging enormous biodiversity. Plant life ranges from tough salt grasses, saladelle and salicorne, to sea lilies, maritime asters and rare serapia orchids. As a true estuarine habitat, fish in the étangs are as likely to be freshwater fish from the Argens as they are to be saltwater species.

An interpretation trail, an observation platform and footpaths, linked to the Massif des Maures and the Coastal Path, give visitors limited access to view the reserve. **For more information:** Les Étangs de Villepey, *RN98 Saint Aygulf,* ☎ *33 04 94 51 88 00, for the Environment and Forestry*

Service, *www.conservatoire-du-littoral.fr/front/process/Content.asp?rub=8&rubec=158.*

Adventures on Water

If you don't like being on, in, under – even over – the water, why on earth would you go to the Côte d'Azur? With its numerous ports, marinas, calanques, and dozens of sheltered harbors and bays, the Estérel Coast – particularly around Saint Raphaël – is watersports heaven.

This is the place to indulge in sailing, windsurfing, diving, parascending, power boating, sea canoeing, fishing, waterskiing. If you are qualified, you could rent a cabin cruiser for a week or two instead of staying in a hotel or villa. And, if you are interested in joining a crew for an extended cruise, the larger ports and marinas are prime job-hunting territory.

Canoeing & Kayaking

Canoe and kayak rentals, as well as lessons, are available from several of Saint Raphaël's smaller ports. **Agay** is chief among them because of its proximity to this coast's calanques and because its calm bay, carved so deeply into the coast, is the perfect place for canoeing enthusiasts of any skill level.

"Discovery" tickets for exploring the bay or the calanques are available from **Base de Plein Air d'Agay** located at the municipal Base Nautique d'Agay of l'Escale Beach. The center is open from 9 am to 5:30 pm every day, from mid-February to mid-December. Adults and children over eight who can swim can rent sea **kayaks** for use in the bay, for €4.50 per hour, per person. Tickets for kayaking in the calanques from Agay are available only on Saturdays between 10 am and 5 pm and only for groups of four or more. Half-day (four-hour) rentals cost €13.50 per person. Lessons and other group excursions can also be arranged. **For more information:** contact Base Nautique Municipale d'Agay, Plage de l'Escale, ☎/*fax 33 04 94 82 71 42, www.ville-saintraphael.fr/* (after you reach the site – which works only on Internet Explorer – choose "Sports et Loisirs" from the tool bar at the top and click on "stages" from the drop-down menu).

Canoeing is also popular along the sheltered beaches and creeks of Boulouris. **Terrescale**, based at Plage de la Tortue in Boulouris, has a selection of one- to four-person canoes, kayaks and inflatables (including 40 auto-emptying sea kayaks). The company offers supervised, in-shore outings in the Boulouris calanques and has a safety boat and changing rooms. Groups are accepted all year, individual rentals from mid-June to mid-September, 9 am to 6 pm. Prices range from €3.50 (for accompanied children from six to 12 in groups) up to €36 for three hours rental of an unsinkable Canadia canoe, suitable for two adults and two children. **For more information:** contact Terrescale, *Plage de la Tortue, Boulouris,*

Saint Raphaël, ☎ 33 04 94 19 19 79 or 0 6 19 26 26 69, fax 33 04 94 19 07 69, olivier.auneau@terrescale.com, www.terrescale.com. Or write to them at Port Santa Lucia, 83560 Saint Raphaël.

Sailing & Windsurfing

In both **Fréjus** and **Saint Raphaël** small sailboat rentals and sailing lessons are widely available, from both municipal and private sources. Windsurfing (*planche à voile*), including lessons and rental of equipment, is usually available at the same centers. Port Santa Lucia is the main sailing haven in Saint Raphaël but, once again, the quiet waters of Agay are great for windsurfers, as well as catamaran and dinghy sailing.

If you have bigger ambitions, or are thinking of buying a yacht yourself, it is possible to take a five-day sailing and navigation course on board a 13-m/42-foot single-masted yacht. One word of caution. If you are thinking of taking lessons, make contact and pin down arrangements before you arrive. Here's what's available on the Estérel coast:

- **Wind Club d'Agay** – Learn to windsurf on the bay of Agay. Plus catamaran and windsurf storage and rental. Catamaran courses, starting with eight-year-olds, and windsurfing lessons for 10-year-olds and up. Group and private lessons. Open year-round, except January. Located at the Complex Nautique on the N98 in Agay. Contact *Philippe Jard, 90 Rue des Pléiades, 83530 Agay,* ☎/*fax 33 04 94 82 08 08.*

- **Centre de Planche à Voile Freeride** – This is actually a surf shop in Fréjus where you can buy or rent pretty much whatever you need for surfing and windsurfing, including isothermic wetsuits. They offer lessons in windsurfing, fun boarding, canoeing, wake boarding and waterskiing. The website is so full of bells and whistles that it takes forever to load. But if you have patience, it has a terrific webcam aimed at Fréjus Plage. You can get a good idea of what the beach looks like and how busy it is. I watched a game of beach volleyball for a while! Contact Freeride, *Club Nautique, 769 Boulevard d'Alger, Fréjus,* ☎ *33 04 94 51 73 00 or 33 06 60 95 15 09, fax 33 04 94 51 73 01, contact@freeride-attitude.com, www.freeride-attitude.com.*

- **Club Nautique de Saint Raphaël** – Based in Port Santa Lucia, this is a sailing school offering beginner and "improvement" courses in windsurfing and catamaran and dinghy sailing. Open year-round, from 9 am to noon and 2 to 6 pm. Contact *Base Nautique de Santa Lucia, Boulevard. Du Générale de Gaulle, Saint Raphaël,* ☎ *33 04 94 95 11 66, fax 33 04 94 83 95 79, cnsr@free.fr.*

- **École Municipale de Voile** – At Fréjus Plage, with lessons in catamaran, sea kayak and dinghy sailing and windsurfing. Contact *École Municipale de Voile, Base de Voile, Boulevard d'Alger, Fréjus,* ☎ *33 04*

94 51 10 97, fax 33 04 94 51 97 43, macabou@club-internet.fr, www.ville-frejus.fr.

- **École de Croisière Sillages** – Ambitious sailors, including beginners, can learn yacht sailing and navigation or improve their skills on board a luxurious 13-m/42-foot, ocean-going yacht. This course is suitable for anyone thinking of buying a yacht or crewing on one. Week-long cruises depart from Saint Raphaël Vieux Port. The course is offered year-round and costs from €520 to about €600, depending upon the season. Guests under 17 years of age must be accompanied by an adult. For more information contact *École de Croisière Sillages, Capitainérie du Vieux Port, Saint Raphaël,* ☎ *33 04 94 40 83 80, fax 33 04 94 52 00 92, ecole@silages.fr, www.sillages.fr.*

Yacht Rentals

The harbour masters (*Capitainerie*) and tourist offices listed for each of the ports in this section can direct you to a range of skippered yachts to charter. If you are qualified to skipper a sailing yacht yourself and are up for spending between €1,000 to €5,000 per week for bareboat rental, contact:

- **Yachting Central**, *Immeuble "Le Consul," Avenue des Forces Françaises Libres, 83600 Port Fréjus,* ☎ *33 04 94 53 69 34, fax 33 04 94 52 21 78, info@centralyachting.com, www.centralyachting.com.*

- **Madraco Fréjus**, *Résidence Les Caryatides, Quai de la Foudre 83600 Port Fréjus,* ☎ *33 04 94 17 33 28,* ☎ *(Port) 33 06 20 93 33 98, fax 33 04 94 17 36 62, frejus@madraco.com, www.madraco.com.*

- **Sunsail**, *Port Santa Lucia, Saint Raphaël,* ☎ *33 04 94 95 63 73, www.sunsail.com.* This is an international bareboat charter company and, depending upon where you access their website from, you will get local contact information and prices in your own currency.

Powerboating

Small, open powerboats for fishing and waterskiing can be rented, with appropriate permits, for under €200 per day or about €1,000 per week. In Port Agay, **Plaisance Service S.A.S.** rents boats for a one-day minimum, with permit, for about about €170 and up. Some UK and US permits may qualify you for a temporary French permit (see below). You can contact Plaisance in advance to find out whether yours does. *Plaisance Service S.A.S., 1627 Avenue du Gratadis, Zone Artisanale, 83530 Agay, Saint Raphaël,* ☎ *33 04 94 82 04 76, fax 33 04 94 82 07 46, plaisance-service@wanadoo.fr or infos@plaisance-service.com, www.plaisance-service.com.*

France Yachting, in the Saint Aygulf section of Fréjus, brokers rentals for private owners and sometimes has small, older cabin cruisers (9.3 m/30 feet) available for under €1,000 per week. Their website has facilities to search your dates and requirements. *France Yachting, Chantier Naval de St Aygulf, 83370 Port de St Aygulf, Fréjus,* ☎ *33 04 94 81 43 86, fax 33 04 94 81 47 71. france.yachting2@wanadoo.fr, www.franceyachting.com.*

For larger yachts and skippered charters, contact the local tourist authorities or harbor masters (listed with each port).

EARN A FRENCH BOATING PERMIT

The *bateau-école* (boating school) in Saint Raphaël's Port Santa Lucia, runs short courses to gain French boating licences. Courses include inshore boating license, extension to ocean-going license, river license and VHF certificate. See page 102 for a full description of the French permit system. During vacation periods, teaching and exams take five days. The courses are taught over weekends other times of the year. The courses aren't cheap – from €80 for a VHF certificate up to €600 for an ocean-going extension, but if you think you might enjoy boating the French waterways, it's worth looking into. For more information, contact **Bateau-École**, *Port Santa Lucia,* ☎ *33 04 94 83 11 21 or 33 0 6 09 46 00 90, fax 33 04 94 95 53 50, www.bateau-ecole-var.com.*

Boat Excursions

If the urge for "messing about in boats," as the British say, is irresistable, but you have no desire to be at the helm yourself, there are all kinds of excursions available from most of the ports and marinas. Deep-sea fishing boats leave regularly from Saint Raphaël Vieux Port and Fréjus Vieux Port, and there are sightseeing excursions that range from a couple of hours exploring offshore islands to full- and half-day outings up and down the coast. **Les Bateaux de Saint Raphaël**, based in the Vieux Port, runs several trips to Saint Tropez daily. Round-trip fare for the hour-long voyage costs €20 for adults, €11 for children under nine years of age. On Tuesday and Saturday mornings, trips are scheduled in time for the Grand Marché Provençal à Saint Tropez – a particularly colorful market. The company runs a variety of cruises into the calanques and around the offshore islands in catamarans and motor launches (visit www.tmr-saintraphael.com/flotille.htm to see the fleet). From April to September, there are 45-minute glass-bottom boat cruises around Cap Dramont. A changing schedule, including fishing cruises, is published on their website and is available from their dock in the Vieux Port. For more information, contact *Les Bateaux de Saint Raphaël, Gare Maritime de Saint Raphaël,* ☎ *33 04 94 95 17 46, fax 33 04 94 83 88 55, bateauxsaintraphael@wanadoo.fr; www.tmr-saintraphael.com / index.htm.*

Diving

Between 35 and 50 shipwrecks, ranging from pre-Roman, Celto-Ligurian trading vessels in the Bay of Agay, to American mine sweepers from World War II, are within easy reach of divers off Saint-Raphaël's 42 km/26 miles of coast. Added to that, natural underwater arches and cliffs covered with yellow and red coral create an exceptional diving environment. A handful of diving clubs and schools, based in Saint Raphaël and Fréjus, regularly arrange dives to key sites of archaeological interest and natural beauty. Much of the area's underwater riches is between three and 50 m (10 to 150 feet) below the surface, accessible to beginners and intermediates as well as divers of mixed ability.

Key diving sites include:

- **L' Île du Lion de Mer** – The south face of this offshore islet is covered with young shoots of coral, down to about 40 m/131 feet. At only 10 m/30 feet, two sites, The Virgin and The Siren, are within reach of beginners. The site includes a natural arch.

- **Le Dramont** – The stepped bottom falls away in levels, from 3-50 m (10-150 feet), alternating rocks and boulders with stretches of sand. The underwater landscape encourages intense submarine life and great biodiversity.

- **La Balise de la Chrétienne** – At least a dozen ancient shipwrecks met their end along this rocky outcrop, now marked with buoys. Archeological finds stretch from earliest times through the medieval period. The amphoras and debris still scattered on the bottom reveal the nature of ancient trade to this area. The wrecks themselves are of interest in terms of the history of marine architecture.

- **Les Péniches d'Anthéor** – The *Jean Suzon* and the *Saint Antoine* were two river barges, commandeered by the Nazis to carry armaments from Italy along the French coast to Marseille. They were torpedoed by the British in July, 1944 and rest at 28 m/92 feet, with their lethal cargo.

- **The Mine Sweepers** – Two American mine sweepers, one of them a sister ship to Jacques Cousteau's *Calypso*, went down in St. Raphaël Bay, off Fréjus, in August 1944. The wreck lies between 41 and 46 m (135-150 feet) down.

Dive Contacts on the Estérel Coast

Individual and group dives are organized by several clubs and diving schools throughout this area. Some can also arrange accommodation close to the dive center or diving sites. Following are some of the best contacts for dives in this area.

Aventure Sous Marine (ASM), *56 Rue de la Garonne, 83700 Saint-Raphaël,* ☎ *33 04 94 19 33 70, didier-asm@wanadoo.fr, www.plongee83.com/plongee.htm.* Group and individual rates, specialists in training beginners. Dive sites are posted at the beginning of each week. ASM organizes accommodation at La Bonne Auberge or Les Pyramides (see *Where to Stay*, pages 283-84).

Club Sous l'Eau, *Port Santa Lucia, 83700 Saint Raphaël,* ☎ *33 04 94 95 90 33, fax 33 04 94 95 53 96, sousleau@wanadoo.fr, www.clubsouleau.com.* Open in good weather from March 15 to November 15, the club organizes dives for groups year-round. Teachers and monitors are experts in teaching beginners and children, but have plenty of activities and dives for experienced divers. Initiation and underwater orientation start at €35. This is a family-oriented club.

Roches Rouges Diving School, *Plage de Camp Long, Cap du Dramont,* ☎ *33 06 17 97 29 45 or 33 06 62 48 40 63, fax 33 04 94 81 63 34, www.rochesrouges.com.* This is a popular and highly regarded diving school. They specialize in dives for families and children, with early lessons given in the safety of Agay Bay. They are equipped and qualified to work with handicapped divers. Personalized and group dives as well as night dives all along the Estérel coast.

Euro-Plongée, *2170 Route de la Corniche, Port de Boulouris, Saint Raphaël,* ☎ *33 04 94 19 03 26 or 33 06 09 18 53 74, fax 33 04 94 95 50 76, europlongee83@aol.com, www.europlongee83.fr.st/.* Initiation and exploration dives and certificates. Open April to September but will operate group dives on demand year-round. They can recommend a good selection of budget digs near their base.

Terrescale, Port du Poussaï, Le Dramont, ☎ 33 04 94 19 19 79 or 33 06 19 26 26 69, fax 33 04 94 19 07 69, olivier.auneau@terrescale.com, www.terrescale.com. Night diving, wreck diving, explorations. From initiation dives to advanced explorations. The boat visits L'Ile d'Or and and Roches Rouges diving sites within minutes of the port. Like others, they're open from April to September and year-round for groups.

Centre International de Plongée, *Aire de Car énage, Port Fréjus Est,* ☎ *33 04 94 52 34 99, fax 33 04 94 53 44 39.*

Other Watersports

From May 15 to October 30, the **Fun Ski School**, based in Agay, offers waterskiing, wake boarding, and solo or double parascending for adults and children over eight years old. Private waterskiing and wake boarding lessons are available for adults and children over five years old. The center is normally open between 9 am and 7 pm, but extended hours, from 7 am to 8 pm, are in effect during July and August. *Fun Ski School, Epis du Gratadis, Plage d'Agay,* ☎ *33 06 07 08 17 17, fax 33 04 94 82 03 75.*

On the Lacs du Dramont, groups, families and individuals can try freshwater activities, such as speedboating and water carting, or oxoon (like surfing on a contraption that combines a bicycle-type seat, pedals and handlebars with an arrangement of pontoons). Contact **Sud Concept**, *Rue des Calanques, Cap Estérel, 83530 Agay,* ☎ *33 04 94 52 40 40, fax 33 04 94 82 87 29, Sud.concept@club-internet.fr, www.sudconcept.com.* The center is open year-round, from 9 am to 7 pm.

At Beaurivage, the neatly manicured park and beach west of Port Santa Lucia, wakeboarding and other water games are available from spring through fall. ☎ *33 06 09 84 23 41.*

Where to Stay

Sometimes it is hard to understand why the whims of fashion and celebrity land on one place and not another. Just a few miles to the west, around Saint Tropez, you can easily spend more than €700 a night on a hotel room and €15 or more just to put your feet on the sand.

Fréjus Plage and the many beaches and inlets of Saint Raphaël are just as glorious, and maybe a little less crowded, the Mediterranean is every bit as dazzling, the forests of the massif as deep and fragrant and, arguably, prettier against the red rocks of the Estérel. Yet you can stay along this coast for a fraction of the cost. About the only difference (aside from the potentially astronomical prices up the road) is that Fréjus/Saint Raphaël is slightly more family-oriented.

HOTEL PRICE CHART	
Rates are per room based on double occupancy.	
	Under €55
€	€56-€96
€€	€97-€135
€€€	€136-€195
€€€€	Over €195

Deluxe

There are fewer places at the deluxe end of the market (luxury-seekers can ask harbor masters about chartering a skippered yacht), but those that are around are particularly romantic.

☆☆☆☆ **L'Auberge des Adrets** *(Lieu-dit Auberge des Adrets, Route Nationale 7, 83600 Fréjus,* ☎ *33 04 94 82 11 82, fax 33 04 94 82 11 80, info@auberge-adrets.com, www.auberge-adrets.com,* €€€-€€€€*).* With its reputed connection to Gaspard de Besse, the French Robin Hood, this may be the most romantic of all. The Auberge is a 17th-century coaching inn with 10 recently renovated rooms, each named to reflect its ambiance – *Dolce Vita, Gala, Paloma, Bohème, Tosca* and so forth. One room has a huge bathtub reached by a flight of marble steps, another a piano. This is definitely the spot for a lovers' tryst; a private sitting room is available on request. If you aren't planning to spend time in your room (as opposed to the sitting room), pick someplace else. The hotel features a gastronomic restaurant and offers room discounts with some of its more expensive menus. Given the quality of the accommodation and setting, the prices are really remarkable. It is possible to stay here at the height of the summer season for well under €200 per night. For romantic adventurers, the hotel also offers a good value package that includes two nights, breakfast, one dinner, a half-day of canyoning and a mountain bike outing with trail maps and picnic.

La Villa Mauresque *(1792 Route de la Corniche d'Or, 83 700 Saint-Raphaël, ☎ 33 04 94 83 02 42, fax 33 04 94 83 02 02, contact@villa-mauresque.com, www.villa-mauresque.com. Open all year round, €€€-€€€€).* In Saint Raphaël, this is not actually a hotel but a pair of palatial villas, built in 1860 to resemble a Moorish castle.

Luxury villa on the Saint Raphaël coast. Photo courtesy Villa Mauresque

During the season, the villas are rented out to large groups – big families and their servants, rock stars and their entourages; use your imagination – both houses can accommodate between 26 and 30 people. But for the rest of the year, the Villa, in its huge park, operates like a hotel, renting out the rooms individually. Every très chic guest room has a marble bath and a spectacular sea view. Each house has jacuzzis, steambaths, a private dock and a heated swimming pool. There's a boat house and a multi-lingual caretaker.

Moderate

Hôtel l'Estirado des Adrets *(83600 Les Adrets de l'Estérel, ☎ 33 04 94 40 90 64, fax 33 04 94 40 98 52, estirado@estirado.com, www.estirado.com, 24 rooms, bed and breakfast, €).* This gets two chimneys from *Logis de France* for the value and ambiance of accommodation and dinner. Perched on a hill, most rooms, as well as the restaurant terrace, take advantage of expansive, panoramic views. The place has a slightly Spanish feel – stucco and dark wood trim. Rooms are simple but comfortable and menus in the restaurant (€€) are reasonable for the quality.

☆☆☆ **Hotel La Potinière** *(169 Av. de Boulouris, 83700 Saint Raphaël, ☎ 33 04 94 19 81 71, fax 33 04 94 19 81 72, hotel@la-potiniere.com, www.la-potiniere.com/, 29 rooms, €-€€).* In Boulouris, this is another *Logis de France*, with three chimneys. This rambling, family-run, house-hotel is not on the beach but overlooks the sea. Rooms are decorated in cool tones and quiet floral prints. Most have shaded terraces. Open year-round, the hotel has a heated indoor pool as well as an outdoor pool. The restaurant, which specializes in seafood, spreads across a pine-shaded terrace and has a wonderfully mellow, Provençal ambiance. They'll pack a picnic basket if asked.

Hotel Esterella *(197 Bord de Mer, 83530 Agay,* ☎ *33 04 94 82 00 58, fax 33 04 94 82 02 05, hotelesterella@aol.com, www.hotelesterella.com/indexUK.htm, €).* In Agay, this rates two *Logis de France* chimneys. A lot of hotels in this area have simple, almost spartan decor compared to the extravagantly colorful style of hotels elsewhere in Provence. That's probably because anything more would compete with the wonderful sea views. This place is no exception. It is an old-fashioned seaside hotel with basic, but comfortable, rooms and a restaurant with an unpretentious, relaxed atmosphere. The hotel also has a separate cottage available.

☆☆☆ **L'Arena Hôtel Restaurant** *(145 Rue Général de Gaulle, 83600 Fréjus,* ☎ *33 04 94 17 09 40, fax 33 04 94 52 01 52, info@arena-hotel.com, www.arena-hotel.com/larena.htm, €-€€).* In Fréjus, this place is a hard-to-miss 19th-century three-story building painted a bright Pompeian red. Inside, the rooms are comfortable – and less flamboyant. Some have terraces. The restaurant is good enough to have earned three *Logis de France* chimneys for value and quality.

The outside of the ☆☆☆ **Parc Hôtel Du Soleil** in Fréjus *(566 Via Aurélia, 83670 Fréjus,* ☎ *33 04 94 53 21 35, fax 33 04 94 53 28 21, 70 rooms, B&B, €-€€)* is a wild-looking yellow, blue and white trompe l'oeil, so it comes as a shock that the rooms are so mid-price-conventional. But then, as always, there is that million-dollar view, so why bother with decor?

You can't get much more *centre ville* than the ☆☆☆ **Hôtel Excelsior** in St. Raphaël *(193 Promenade du Président-René-Coty, Saint Raphaël,* ☎ *33 04 94 95 02 42, fax 33 04 94 95 33 82, www.excelsior-hotel.com, 40 recently refurbished rooms, B&B €€-€€€, town-view rooms are about 15% less).* It's right on the Promenade des Bains, across from the beach, near the Casino and the train station (SNCF and TGV). The rooms can be on the small side, but they're comfortable and reasonably equipped with air conditioning, phones and satellite TV. Here you are paying for location, views (most rooms have sea views), and the opportunity to have a beach vacation in the middle of the city. Public rooms and the restaurants are pretty. Sitting on the shady terrace in front of this wedding cake of a building, across from the beach, is a real "Riviera" experience. The hotel also boasts an English pub. Breakfast is included.

Also in the center of Saint Raphaël, the small (20 rooms) ☆☆ **Hôtel Ambassador** *(89 Rue Boetman, 83700 Saint Raphaël, contact through the Saint Raphaël Central Booking Service,* ☎ *33 04 94 19 10 60, reservation@saint-raphael.com, 20 rooms, €-€€)* is in the old quarter, not far from the Vieux Port and the train station. A pink-washed house, it has the curious distinction of being entirely furnished with wrought iron. Rooms are a good size and brightly painted.

☆☆ **Hotel Lido** *(Boulevard de la Plage, Agay,* ☎ *33 04 94 82 01 59, fax 33 04 94 82 09 75, €)* is on the beach in Agay, what the French charmingly call *les pieds dans l'eau* (feet in the water). This is a restaurant-hotel with one chimney from *Logis de France* and grilled fish a specialty. Rooms are compact but all have terraces on or overlooking the beach. How can you beat that for under €100?

Budget

☆☆ **Les Amandiers** is a big, bourgeois house with a good-sized swimming pool, about halfway between the thalassatherapy center in Boulouris and Port Santa Lucia *(874 Boulevard Alphonse Juin, 83700 Saint-Raphaël,* ☎ *33 04 94 19 85 30, fax 33 04 94 19 85 31, sarlj@aol.com, 11 rooms, €)*. The rooms are colorfully decorated, some with draped four-poster beds. It has two *Logis de France* chimneys for the value and quality of its table. And the location is only about 220 yards from some interesting calanques.

☆☆ **Le Thimothée** is another grand Victorian-era house in Boulouris, with a dozen rooms, a shady garden and a nice private pool *(375 Boulevard Christian Lafon, 83700 Saint Raphaël,* ☎ *33 04 94 40 49 49, fax 33 04 94 19 41 92, info@thimothee.com, www.hotel-thimothee-saint-raphael.cote.azur.fr, 12 rooms, €)*. The rooms are equipped with satellite TV, hair dryers and all the usual accoutrements. The hotel also has a few studio apartments, with kitchenettes, available on a weekly basis.

If you're not worried about sea views, ☆☆ **L'Oasis**, in Frejus-Plage, not far from the Vieux Port, is an inexpensive alternative *(Impasse Jean-Baptiste Charcot, 83600 Frejus-Plage,* ☎ *33 04 94 51 50 44, fax 33 04 94 53 01 04, 27 rooms, €)*. It's a big pink house, a bit overgrown with evergreens, on a quiet street. The rooms are homey but basic and, while most hotels in France now provide at least one handicapped-access room, L'Oasis has four.

CHEAP DIGS FOR DIVERS

Scuba diving is one of Saint Raphaël's biggest draws and a few hotels are set up to provide very low-cost accommodation, often with meals, specifically geared to the needs of divers. They are sometimes very basic but usually friendly and will often make special arrangements or offer deals to diving groups. Local diving clubs recommend these:

- **Les Pyramides**, *77 Avenue. P. Doumer, 83 700 Saint Raphaël,* ☎ *33 04 98 11 10 10, fax 33 0498 11 10 20, alayamard@wanadoo.fr.* Between the beach and the train station in the town center, this is one of the nicest, with pretty

rooms and terraces and a price that remains under €60 year-round.
- **La Bonne Auberge**, *54 Rue de la Garonne, 83700 Saint Raphaël,* ☎ *33 04 94 95 69 72.* A town-center restaurant-hotel with two dining rooms, a bar and terrace. Cooking is Provençal family-style and inexpensive full board is offered.
- **Hôtel Cap Boulouris**, *RN 98, Boulouris, 83700 Saint Raphaël,* ☎ *33 04 94 95 45 45, fax 33 04 94 95 71 49.* From March to June 15 and from September to November 3, divers can add inexpensive full board to the budget accommodation. Rooms have two, three or four beds and are equipped with linens, but you have to bring your own towels. They have private baths but no direct phones. The hotel has a pool. Discounts are available for groups.
- **Le Manoir**, *Chemin de l'Escale, Boulouris, 83700 Saint Raphaël,* ☎ *33 04 94 95 20 58, fax 33 04 94 83 85 06, manoir@cei4vents.com.* On a residential district about 400 feet from the beach, Le Manoir is a group hostel and is the most basic. It offers accommodation geared to the needs of each group. Its 26 rooms (with showers, sinks and private toilets) cost €19 per person per night. Breakfast is €4 extra. Le Manoir has the use of a private park next to the beaches and calanques.

Chambre d'Hôtes

Because this part of France is so geared up for vacations, it's not easy to meet the locals. You are more likely to strike up a passing friendship with a visiting Parisian – or a Dane for that matter – than to get to know any real Provençals. Chambre d'hôtes (guest houses and usually B&Bs) are almost always family-run; they're the best way to get close to the local culture on the Côte d'Azur.

Le Mas Blanc, in les Adrets, is a substantial, traditional farmhouse set in beautifully landscaped grounds, surrounded by forest *(Chemin de Beillesse, 83600 Les Adrets de L'Estérel,* ☎*/fax 33 04 94 40 92 05, or mobile 33 06 82 66 52 25, and 66 0 620 89 23 77, lemasblanc@laposte.net, three rooms, €).* It is only about 15 minutes to the beaches of Saint Raphaël, Fréjus or Cannes and about three km/1.8 miles from Lac St. Cassien, for fishing and lake sports. There are only two rooms and a suite that includes a child's room on the ground floor, so chances are, you'll to get to know your hosts, James and Michelle Beauchamp. Rooms are informal, with recently redone tiled baths, and the *mas* has a really lovely pool.

Staying at **La Pomme d'Ambre**, in Fréjus, is a like staying in a friend's very well-kept guest room *(Via Aurélia-Ancienne Route d'Italie, La Tour* de Mare, 83600 *Fréjus*, ☎ *33 04 94 53 25 47, fax 33 04 94 52 95 50, info@gardeninprovence.com or nicole.arboireau@wanadoo.fr, www.gardeninprovence.com, two rooms with shared bath, B&B, €)*. The two rooms can be booked separately or as a pair with a shared bathroom between them. Lest you're worried that this sounds a little shabby, I should point out that the bathroom has a chandelier – as does the little kitchen where your breakfast is served. An added bonus is that the owner, Nicole Arboireau, is a well-known gardener and gardening book author. You can sign up for her gardening classes or just come to enjoy her splendid cottage garden and her homemade jams. Because the garden is not at its best in the hottest weather, the house is closed to guests from July 15 to September 15.

Gîtes

Gîtes are usually rural houses and as this isn't really a rural area, there aren't many available. The best way to find a traditional gîte is to contact the départemental section of Gîtes de France, namely Gîtes de France du Var, on www.gites-de-france-var.fr. (The site was available only in French at the time of publication, but a small Union Jack waving in the corner suggested an English language version was on its way.)

Meanwhile, you can have a similar kind of experience here in a serviced apartment or a *résidence de vacances* – a camp of summer cabins very much like the 1950s bungalow colonies of the Northeastern USA.

If you want to opt for glamor and independence at the same time, the **Villa Franz Lehar** in the center of Saint Raphaël offers both at per-night prices that compete with moderately priced hotel accommodation *(96 Avenue Franz Léhar, 83700 Saint-Raphaël,* ☎ *33 04 94 44 34 60, fax 33 04 94 95 45 32, info@villafranzlehar.com, www.villafranzlehar.com, €€-€€€)*. This is a new development of seven furnished apartments, finished to a very high standard and equipped with everything you'd expect to find in a luxury apartment – dishwashers, microwaves, washing machines, DVD players, private parking. The apartments have deep, shaded terraces, bright white kitchens and to-die-for sea views. The building's wrap-around balconies suggest an ocean liner and give it a retro, 1930s look. If you're prepared to rent for a month in the off-season, the price drops away to almost nothing: €500-600 for 30 days from January to mid-May and from mid-September to the end of December.

There are several very big vacation apartment developments in Fréjus. **Pierre & Vacances** offers modern, fully equipped apartments in a large complex overlooking Port Fréjus West *(46 Quai Dei Caravello, Port Fréjus Ouest, 83600 Fréjus,* ☎ *33 04 94 82 69 00, fax 33 04 94 17 15 79, frejus@pierre-vacances.fr, www.pierreetvacances.com, weekly prices are € in spring and fall, up to €€€ in July and August)*. The two-room apartments are suitable for two couples, which can bring the price down significantly. They also offer studios equipped for handicapped vacationers.

Les Hippocampes, sitting right on the sand at Fréjus-Plage, was one of the best we saw *(881 Boulevard d'Alger, 83600 Fréjus, ☎ 33 04 94 51 32 63, fax 33 04 94 52 31 40, reservation@hippocampes.fr, www.hippocampes.fr, weekly rentals at € per night or less)*. It's a small block of one-bedroom apartments and studios with kitchenettes. The units are modern and don't have much character, but that's provided by the picture-window views of the sea on one side, the massif and the foothills of the Alps on the other. The weekly rental prices are very reasonable for such a good beach location.

☆☆ **Agathos**, on the beach at Agay, is an old-fashioned bungalow colony right on the water *(1510 Boulevard de la Baumette, 83530 Agay, ☎ 33 04 94 82 86 38, fax 33 04 94 82 86 80, resagathos@wanadoo.fr, www.residence-agathos.com, weekly rentals, €-€€)*. Nineteen bungalows, each equipped for four, are scattered around acres of grassy park which ends on a wide, private beach. These are very basic accommodations – the summer cabins of a lot of people's childhoods – but the setting is really beautiful for a family vacation and the bungalows are well-priced, with discounts for multiple weeks and a fourth week offered for free.

Camping

☆☆ **Camping Les Philippons**, on the edge of Les Adrets, is a small wooded campsite with tent and camper van spaces *(83600 Les Adrets de l'Estérel, ☎ 33 04 94 40 90 67, fax 33 04 94 19 35 92, info@philipponscamp.com, www.provence-campings.com/esterel/philippons/ukindex.htm, campsite for two adults is €17 high season, €11.75 off-season)*. Not far from Lac St. Cassien for watersports and Lac l'Avellan for fishing, it has a pool and during the summer months a mini-market and snackbar. Small cabins are available to rent on a weekly basis.

Les Rives de l'Agay is a level site near Agay's picturesque river harbor, about a quarter-mile from the beach *(Route de Gratadis, 83530 Agay, ☎ 33 04 94 82 02 74, fax 33 04 94 82 74 14, reception@lesrivesdelagay.fr, www.lesrivesdelagay.fr, 96 spaces and 42 RVs, open March to November. space for two adults, €28 high season, €14.60 off-season)*. Although higher than inland prices, the rates for the coast and private dock facilities at €4 per day are good value. The camp has handicapped facilities and, during the off-season, mobile homes can be rented by the night.

Where to Eat

Not that food around here isn't often very good. But sitting on a shaded terrace beside the sea, it is hard to argue over the gastronomic value of a simple meal of grilled fish or a a plateau of crustaceans, a clean-tasting salad and a glass of cool white wine. The fresh flavors of herbes de Provence are everywhere and even vegetarians – who can have a tough time in France – will find plenty to enjoy. But, the point is, unless your palate has led a very sheltered life, you won't find much that's original in this area.

Nevertheless, the general standard is quite high. The dining rooms of the hotels recommended in this section are all reliable, with beachside or shady garden terraces. Those rated by *Logis de France* are particularly recommended for value and quality. Expect to pay at least €18 to €24 for a three-course menu, going up to €35 to €55 for elaborate cooking. Watch for daily specials at €11 to €15.

DINING PRICE CHART	
Prices are for a typical prix fixe menu of two courses and a glass of house wine for one.	
	€14-€19
€	€21-€34
€€	€35-€49
€€€	€50-€69
€€€€	€70-€140
€€€€€	The sky's the limit

If you make a reservation for dinner for two from the "Menu à la Folie" (The Madness Menu) at **L'Auberge des Adrets,** you can stay overnight for half-price *(Lieu-dit Auberge des Adrets, Route Nationale 7, 83600 Fréjus,* ☎ *33 04 94 82 11 82, fax 33 04 94 82 11 80, info@auberge-adrets.com, www.auberge-adrets.com, €€-€€€€).* It isn't really that mad at €65 for five courses of adventurous gastronomy that might include a pumpkin cream soufflé with gnocchi and smoked bacon, crusty red mullet with chorizo oil, and a lemon and blackcurrant vacherin with fruit sauce and vanilla cream for dessert. The restaurant's three-course menus start a bit lower (€€€) and there's an à la carte menu, a relatively inexpensive children's menu (€), as well as lighter food served at lunchtime beside the pool. If you are looking for innovative, special occasion dining, there aren't many restaurants to choose from around the Estérel and L'Auberge des Adrets is one of the best.

L'Arbousier, in the center of Saint Raphaël, is regularly recommended by visitors *(6 Avenue de Valescure, Saint Raphaël,* ☎ *33 04 94 95 25 00, fax 33 04 94 83 81 04, open for lunch Tuesday-Sunday, dinner Tuesday-Saturday, €€-€€€).* Owned and operated by a couple – he's in the kitchen, she runs the dining room – it aims for the earthy, herby flavours of Provence in its seafood and game dishes. Rabbit and pigeon are specialties. Food is served in a colorful dining room or in a garden shaded by magnolias and arbousiers – a Provençal tree with round red fruit for which the restaurant is named. Try the mint and peppered strawberries for dessert.

Du Thym à l'Ail, next to the harbor master's offices in Port Santa Lucia, has a breezy, casual atmosphere and a good-value lunchtime special during the week – €12 for one course and dessert *(Port Santa Lucia, 83700 Saint Raphaël,* ☎ *33 04 94 83 93 99, open year-round, closed Tuesdays, €).* Three-course menus are budget- to medium-priced and feature such old standbys as moules marinères with French fries, salade niçoise, crême caramel and chocolate mousse. There's also a good selection of seafood and shellfish.

The wide terrace of the **Hotel Excelsior**, on the Promenade des Bains in Saint Raphaël, is the perfect place to indulge in that popular French café pastime, watching the world go by *(Promenade des Bains, Saint Raphaël, ☎ 33 04 94 95 02 42, fax 33 04 94 95 33 82, info@excelsior-hotel.com, www.excelsior-hotel.com, €-€€)*. The terrace serves morning coffee, afternoon tea, cocktails and *boissons* (cold soft drinks), all day long, every day, all year. Locals as well as visitors rate the hotel's pretty restaurant highly, where the *plat du jour* costs €11 and a traditional menu of two courses is available for €18.50. Taboulé Provençal, casseroled red mullet fisherman style and roti de porc Orloff are the kinds of dishes that show up on the menu, which changes daily.

Restaurant La Bouillabaisse is the kind of tiny place you wish you could claim to have discovered all by yourself *(50 Place Victor Hugo, ☎ 33 04 94 95 03 57, closed Mondays, €-€€€)*. This totally unpretentious bistro, in Saint Raphaël's Old Town, serves terrific bouillabaise on a Provençal terrace or in a dining room that looks like a sailors' joint.

Lastly, if the word "auberge" brings to mind a rustic coaching inn, all bare stones and exposed beams, think again. The **Restaurant Auberge de la Rade**, in Agay, couldn't be further from that image *(356 Boulevard de la Plage, RN98, 83530 Agay, ☎/fax 33 04 94 82 00 37, €-€€)*. This is a casual, beachside hangout – more like an old-fashioned American diner than a country inn. It's open from noon to midnight, every day, for just about anything you can think of – drinks, pasta, seafood, shellfish, pizza, omelets, salads – on an enormous menu. There's a daily special – paella, couscous, bourride (a spicy fish stew similar to bouillabaise) for between €8 and €13. Menus are reasonably priced, shellfish and crustaceans are specialties and you can sample a small serving of bouillabaise – *a marmite du pêcheur* – without selling your children. Forget about ambiance; this is the beach.

For **snacks and light meals**, you'll find pizza, salads and couscous all over the place. And every beach in Saint Raphaël and Fréjus has at least one – and usually several – beach cafés and snack shops serving inexpensive Provençal menus, salads, grilled fish and shrimp, pizzas and stuffed baguettes.

The Massif du Tanneron

The Massif du Tanneron is a small extension of the northeast corner of the Estérel, separated from it by a valley through which the A8 Autoroute now runs. Unlike both the Estérel and the Maures, the Tanneron is not a conservation area or nature reserve but is mostly cultivated land. What makes it unusual is its crop – mimosas.

Mimosa, a variety of acacia originally from Australia, was brought to the region by the English upper classes who "discovered" the Côte d'Azur as a winter resort in the late 19th century. The climate suited the plant and before long it had naturalized, spreading from the gardens of the grand houses to the whole of the Côte d'Azur.

The hills of the Tanneron suited it in particular. Eventually, early in the 20th century, local people realized the plant's commercial potential. Today, as a cut flower and for use in the perfume industry, mimosa from the Tanneron is sent all over the world.

From January through the beginning of March, the hillsides explode with fluffy, yellow blooms. At least eight towns and villages, including **Grasse**, **Saint Raphaël**, **Bormes les Mimosas** and **Tanneron** itself participate in festivals to celebrate (see *Festivals & Fêtes*, page 295).

Cycling Around the Tanneron

The village of Tanneron has nothing much to recommend it to visitors, but if you are visiting this region during the winter and early spring, a hike or cycling trip around the massif combines clear, panoramic vistas and brilliant yellow fields of fragrant mimosa. Winter temperatures are mild – between 40° and 60°F – and they seem even milder because of the steady sunlight.

Another benefit of a winter visit is the chance to meet local people. Between harvest and planting season, and without the crush of the summer tourists, January to March is a slow and mellow season when people are more willing to stop and chat in the cafés and markets.

Lastly, during this time of year there is less chance that your itinerary will have to be changed or interrupted because of fire risks.

Mimosa Circuit

Intermediate ride, road or hybrid bikes. 55½ km/34½ miles, on roads that are quiet in the off-season. Dedicated cycle trails run alongside the roads in some areas. The circuit presents two longish but moderate climbs. Between Mandelieu-La Napoule the route climbs from sea level to 463 m/1,519 feet over about six km/3.7 miles and there is another relatively long climb (just under 300 m/984 feet over about eight km/five miles) between Lac Saint Cassien and Montauroux. The circuit should take about three hours and 45 minutes of steady cycling.

- Leave the Planestel section of Les Adrets de l'Estérel on the **D237**, going south. At the **Logis de Paris** intersection, descend toward the left along the **N7**, passing in front of the Auberge des Adrets and heading for Mandelieu-la Napoule Plage, a seaside resort in the Département des Alpes Maritime at the 15-km/9.3-mile mark.

- About 250 m/820 feet after passing under the Autoroute A8, climb to the left along the panoramic **D92**. Enjoying the views from this road, along the coast from Nice to Saint Tropez, should slow you down quite a bit.

- Bypass the summit of the Grand Duc along its northern side. You will see signs indicating you are re-entering the Département du Var. Take a right onto the **D38**, another scenic road, toward **Tanneron** (27 km/16.7 miles). In Tanneron, look for the the medieval **Chapel of Notre Dame de Peygros** on the left.

- Continue through Tanneron on the D38, then turn right onto the **D94**, which descends into the valley of the River Siagne.
- In the hamlet of **Saint Cassien des Bois** (33 km/20½ miles), stop to have a look at a medieval chapel with an unusual square tower that has no doors or other apparent means of entry. In times of strife – wars and pirate raids – monks would enter their towers (usually with the church valuables) via a rope ladder, then pull the ladder up after them.
- Continue on the D94 above the River Siagne, along the northern end of **Lac Saint Cassien**. At the D562 – a bigger road – remain on the D94, taking first a left and then a right to cross the D562 near the 15th-century **Château de Tournon**.
- Climb to the *village perchée* of **Montauroux** (41 km/25½ miles). Montauroux has a ruined fortress and a 16th-century tower with an 18th-century campanile. It is one of a group of villages perchées, centered on Fayence, that are collectively referred to as le Pays de Fayence. This is about two-thirds of the way around the route and a good place to stop for lunch or to spend the night. (see *Where to Stay* and *Where to Eat* in the Pays de Fayence, pages 292-93).
- Leaving Montauroux, take the left fork onto the **D37** and descend toward the D562, which you cross at **La Font d'Aragon**.
- Cross **Lac Saint Cassien** on the Pont Pré Claou bridge (46 km/28½ miles) and turn right onto the **D37** to follow along the edge of the lake.
- Watch for a left onto the **D837** which takes you through a tunnel under the A8 Autoroute. Then climb toward the settlement of **La Baïsse** just before returning to **Planestel** (55½ km/34½ miles).

Worth a Side-Trip: Le Pays de Fayence

North of the Estérel, in Saint Raphaël's *arrière pays*, a group of villages perchées, known collectively as the Pays de Fayence, clings to the tops of the highest hills.

Fayence, Seillans, Mons, Callian, Tourrettes, Montauroux and Saint Paul en Forêt are all tiny medieval villages with tall, narrow houses hanging over lanes that are sometimes barely an arm span across. Streets are cobbled, many paved with river-smoothed stones set in flights of stairs, called calades. In the oldest and highest parts of the villages, ancient archways carry the higher lanes over those below. Houses form vaults over the ruelles that pass below.

For thousands of years, these naturally fortified places with their panoramic views of the distant coast and countryside, provided refuge and safety from invaders, plagues, pirates and warring factions. The so-called "Saracen Gate" in Fayence is evidence of just one of the perceived threats to the medieval population of the town. Here and there in the villages there are remains of prehistoric and Celto-Ligurian fortresses.

Elsewhere in Provence, villagers moved down into valleys when the ages of plague and warfare passed. **Vaison la Romaine** (page 118) and **Oppède** in the Luberon (with abandoned Oppède le Vieux above it) are examples.

Here, however, this cluster of villages is one of several you will come across in the Côte d'Azur where the upper village has always remained occupied. Maybe the inhabitants liked the great views.

It is possible that the Pays de Fayence has kept so much of its medieval character because, at one time, the region was among the poorest in France. But fortunes were made in mimosa growing on the Tanneron hills in the early 20th century, followed closely by the growth of tourism.

Mimosa remains an important crop but today these village trade mostly on their charm. Footpaths connect several of them. Local maps are available from tourist information centers in the towns (see *Tourist Information Offices*, page 383 ff). For adventure travelers, Fayence has further significance as the location of one of Europe's largest glider centers.

Try to visit in the early spring (in March the mimosas bloom on the nearby Tanneron), in the autumn or even winter. But, unless you really, really like crowds and traffic jams, avoid these villages during July and August. **For more information:** Office de Tourisme de Fayence, Place Léon Roux, 83440 Fayence, ☎ 33 04 94 76 20 08, ot.fayence@wanadoo.fr, www.mairiedefayence.com. The regional website, www.paysdefayence.com, also has loads of useful links.

Adventures in the Pays de Fayence

● In the Air

The **Fayence-Tourettes Aérodrome** is one of Europe's largest gliding (*vol à voile*) fields. High-altitude and long-distance flights into the Alps are launched here 365 days a year. The center has 27 gliders corresponding to different flying levels.

To rent one, you need a flightbook, a valid licence and, either membership and insurance in the French Aéroclub for the year, or a 10-day, temporary membership and insurance card. The 10-day cards cost €59 and can be obtained through the club secretary at the Aerodrome. Holders of British or North American licences must have them validated by the French civil aviation authorities – Direction Générale de l'Aviation Civile (DGAC), based at Nice airport.

If you've never flown a glider, you can experience it on an initiation flight, which lasts 20 to 30 minutes, with a resident instructor pilot. Initiation flights cost €65. Licenced glider pilots who have never flown from this aerodrome before must take the initiation flight as well, to familiarize themselves with the terrain and landing areas.

The aerodrome has a relaxed café and a limited number of basic, budget-priced rooms available.

For more information: Association Aéronautique Provence Côte d'Azur, Aérodrome Fayence – Tourrettes, 83440 Fayence, ☎ 33 04 94 76 00 68, fax 33 04 94 84 14 81, aapca@wanadoo.fr, www.aapca.net/.

To validate a licence: Direction Générale de l'Aviation Civile (DGAC), District Aéronautique Côte d'Azur, Aéroport Nice Côte d'Azur, BP 3153, 06203 Nice Cedex, ☎ 33 04 93 21 44 15 or 33 04 93 21 40 64, fax 33 04 93 21 38 50, lambertin_daniel@dac-se.dgac.fr.

Where to Stay in the Pays de Fayence

The Pays de Fayence is close to Fréjus-Saint Raphaël (*Where to Stay in the Estérel*, page 280 ff), so the hotel and restaurant recommendations for those areas should be convenient.

The following suggestions could be useful if you are hiking in the area, cycling the Tanneron or gliding from the Fayence-Tourettes Aérodrome.

☆☆☆ **Hôtel Les Oliviers**, in Fayence, is a practical base for visitors to the glider center *(Quartier de la Ferrage, 83440 Fayence, ☎ 33 04 94 76 13 12, fax 33 04 94 76 08 05, hotel.oliviers.fayen@free.fr; http://hotel.oliviers.fayen.free.fr; €)*. Located at the bottom of the village, the hotel has 22 air-conditioned and soundproofed rooms and the usual – but nonetheless charming – Provençal terrace for breakfast. Rooms are equipped with either a bath or shower. The hotel has no restaurant.

The ☆☆☆ **Moulin de la Camandoule**, just west of Fayence, has its own Roman aqueduct – once used to bring water to this ancient oil mill – and the almost complete oil mill machinery still in place in its restaurant, bar and public rooms *(Chemin de Notre Dame des Cyprès, 83440 Fayence, ☎ 33 04 94 76 00 84, fax 33 04 94 76 10 40, moulin.camandoule@wanadoo.fr; www.camandoule.com, three-night minimum €-€€)*. It was a working oil mill from at least the 15th century, perhaps earlier, until the 1920s. Currently, it's a lovely hotel restaurant with 11 rooms, individually furnished. Two have separate sitting rooms. Ask to see the room with the stunning yellow bathroom. The pool is gigantic – almost Olympic-sized, the owners claim. During the summer, there's a poolside barbecue.

Montauroux has two nice camping areas. **Camping Les Chaumettes**, is large (120 spaces for tents and camper vans) but quiet and handy for Lac Saint Cassien. *(Plan qua Chaumettes, 83440 Montauroux, ☎ 33 04 94 76 43 27).* ☆☆☆ **Camping Les Floralies** has 65 spaces and promises that 90% of them are in the shade *(Route de Gare, 83440 Montauroux, ☎ 33 04 94 76 44 03).* The site has a pool, snack bar and entertainment. Studios and canvas "bungalows" are available by the week.

Where to Eat

Le Castellaras is one of those "destination restaurants" that people make pilgrimages to *(Route de Seillans, 83440 Fayence, ☎ 33 04 94 76 13 80, fax 33 04 94 84 17 50, www.restaurant-castellaras.com, €€€-€€€€)*. Rod Stewart and Sharon Stone were among recent visitors. The setting is superb – an old stone house with a series of picturesque dining rooms and a huge, rose-covered terrace with views that go on forever. The chef earned his Michelin star with dishes like tomato and crayfish gaspacho; wild duck in spices and lavender honey; lamb in a tapenade, walnut and pine nut crust; and pan-fried foie gras served with rhubarb and strawberry compôte, spice bread and vanilla sauce. There's ewe's milk ice cream and a dessert menu to kill for. Of course, dining like this is a very special occasion – with prices to match. Menus start at €43 (for two courses, cheese and dessert, not including wine or coffee) and go up to about €75 for the chef's "surprise" menu.

At **Auberge les Fontaines d'Aragon** in Montauroux, dining is special but prices are slightly less celestial *(Quartier Narbonne, 83440 Montauroux, ☎ 33 04 94 47 71 65, fax 33 04 94 47 71 65, contact@fontaines-daragon.com, www.fontaines-daragon.com)*. Run by Eric and Carine Maio, the restaurant specializes in truffles and offers a truffle sampling menu for less than €40 at lunch time. The dining room is rustic and the new terrace simple, but the chef's passion is evident in the quality of the cooking.

For something completely different, try lunch or dinner on a farm. **Le Jas du Soupié** means the farm of the soup eater *(Quartier Chambarrot, D562, 83440 Montauroux, ☎/fax 33 04 94 76 42 77, jasdusoupie@wanadoo.fr, € without wine)*. It offers reasonably priced, rustic, Provençal cooking based on its own organic vegetables, red fruits, chickens and rabbits. The farm-auberge is open weekends, from Friday dinner to Sunday lunch, but will open for groups of at least eight during the week, by special arrangement. During July and August, it is open nightly, except for Sunday dinner and all day Monday.

Shopping in the Esterel

The Artists Circuit in Fréjus

If you can pull yourself away from the beach and watersports, there are wonderful things to buy in the back alleys and lanes of Fréjus' Old Town.

Since the 18th century, artists and artisans have set up their studios in the historic center. The tradition may go back even further, to ancient potters, who worked in the middle of the ancient town and around its walls.

More recently, the town has encouraged artists in the area to open their studios (*ateliers*) to the public. The result is the *Circuit des Métiers d'Art* (the route of the craftsmen) *du Coeur Historic*.

A free route map, available from the tourist office, presents details on dozens of artists and craftspeople whose shops and studios are seeded throughout the winding streets of the town center. Included are painters, potters, graphic designers, mosaic artists, lithograph studios, jewelers, frame shops, tapestry makers – there is even a tattoo artist on the list.

Hypermarket Shopping in Saint Raphaël

If you need to stock up on low-cost goods and want to pick up jars of French jams or inexpensive wines in a hurry, the **LeClerc Hypermarché** on the edge of Saint Raphaël is a handy stop *(Boulevard de l'Aspe, Compexe Sportif de l'Estérel, 83700 Saint Raphaël, ☎ 33 04 94 19 51 70, open Monday through Saturday, 8:30 am to 9 pm)*. Even if you don't need a thing, if you've never been to a hypermarché, you owe yourself an eye-opening visit. These are giant French stores that combine supermarkets with delis, liquor stores, wine shops, furniture stores, hardware stores, clothing shops, sometimes pet shops – I could go on. Basically, a hypermarket is like a big suburban shopping mall all contained in one shop. LeClerc in Saint Raphaël lists these departments – food, drink, butcher, baker, fashion and accessories, health and beauty, household goods, furniture, tableware, linens, luggage, paints and papers, hardware, electrical appliances, flowers and plants, games, stationery, sporting goods, music and video, camping and outdoor goods, tools, home decorating, automobile accessories and a pet shop.

Markets

From mid-June to mid-September, every night between 8 pm and midnight, **Fréjus Port** lights up with a *marché nocturne* (night-time market). Everything is for sale and everyone seems to be on vacation and out for a promenade. The market spreads over the Boulevards de la Libération and d'Alger at Fréjus plage.

Elsewhere in Fréjus, there's a market somewhere, selling food, Provençal products and miscellaneous goods, just about every day between Tuesday and Sunday:

- Old town, Wednesday and Saturday mornings.
- Les Arènes, Saturday morning.
- Fréjus Plage, Place de la République, Tuesday and Friday mornings.
- Fréjus Plage, Boulevard d'Alger on the seafront, Sunday morning.
- Saint-Aygulf, Place de la Poste, Tuesday and Friday morning.
- Port de Fréjus, Thursday morning.
- La Tour de Mare, Place des Pyracanthas, Thursday morning.

If you get bored with the night market in Fréjus, scoot across to **Saint Raphaël** where the Promenade des Bains and Vieux Port area host a big **arts & crafts market** every evening from mid-June to mid-September. There's also a food market, every day in Places Victor Hugo and République. Other markets include:

- **Bric-a-brac**, Place Coullet, Tuesdays,

- **Food**, Rue de la Thé, Sunday mornings
- **Manufactured goods & clothing**, Parking Cagnat, Avenue de Valescure, Thursday mornings.

Festivals & Fêtes in the Esterel

Every community has a full calendar of festivals available from the local tourist office. There is usually something festive happening almost every month of the year. Besides the usual round of harvest and heritage festivals, there are few that are unique to this region.

Mimosa Celebrations on the Mimosa Road

At the beginning of February, when the Mimosa plantations on the hills of the massifs burst into bloom, this area goes wild with flower celebrations. Festivities vary from town to town along the 130-km/80-mile Mimosa Road, but they usually include a grand parade or *corso* with flower bedecked floats and loads of pretty girls. In **Saint Raphaël**, **Mimosa Week** lasts eight days and includes the crowning of Miss Mimosa, exhibitions, nature walks, visits to greenhouses and "flower wars," which involve a lot of mimosa throwing.

In **Bormes les Mimosas**, where the Mimosa Road begins, a week-long Carnival in February ends with what locals claim is the prettiest *corso* on the Côte d'Azur. The Route du Mimosa winds along the coast, below the massifs and includes eight towns and villages – Bormes les Mimosas, Le Rayol-Canadel, Sainte Maxime, Saint Raphaël, Mandelieu-la Napoule, Tanneron, Pégomas and Grasse. It is possible to spend a few days following a wave of Mimosa activities and festivities along the route. **For more information:** Contact the Saint Raphaël tourist office (page 260) or visit www.tourismevar.com/carnetsderoute/mimosas.htm.

The International Air Festival

Kite makers and kite fliers from all over the world come to Fréjus at the end of October to compete with each other and enjoy each other's kites. The three-day event has been held at the Base Nature, an old air base between the Argens Delta and Port-Fréjus, since 1996. In addition to filling the skies with hundreds of colorful kites and balloons, the event usually includes kite-making and kite-flying workshops, aerial ballets and Japanese kite battles. Around the fringes of the festival, all kinds of wind-based activities, including paragliding initiation flights and demonstrations of kite-surfing, usually take place. For more information, contact the Fréjus tourist office (page 255).

Fireworks in Fréjus

If you like fireworks (*feux d'artifice*) find a comfortable viewing point along the quais of Port Fréjus in August. Spectacles designed by the best fireworks designers in France are staged on the first three Fridays in August at 10:30 pm.

Fréjus Street Theatre Festival

For two nights and days in early July (check with the tourist information office for dates) popular street comedy and improvisation groups from all over France perform along the Port Fréjus quais. Performances, which are free, take place all day long and into the evening.

Les Bravades

If you are around Fréjus in mid-January or Saint Tropez from May 16th to 18th, don't be surprised to see squadrons of "toy" soldiers, looking like they've just stepped out of an operetta, forming up to let off noisy musket volleys in the public squares. The *bravades*, a local tradition, recalls the region's earlier, warring history. Nowadays, musketeers honor the towns' patron saints by loudly demonstrating how they held off hordes of Saracens and Barbary pirates in the old days.

Chestnut Festivals

In October, **Collobrières** and **La Garde Freinet** celebrate their autumn chestnut harvest with Sunday Fairs. Collobrière's *Fête des Châtaignes* takes place on the last three Sundays in October and includes a chestnut market, artists in the street and special events. Not far away, in La Garde Freinet, the *Fête de la Châtaigne* is held on the last two Sundays in October and includes all-day Provençal markets, and the opportunity to taste and buy chestnuts, *marrons glacés* (candied chestnuts), chestnut liqueur and roasted chestnuts. If you are lucky, you may get to participate in a great public feast, a grand aïoli, at the chestnut festivals.

The Giant Omelet Feast

Actually, *La Fête de l'Omelette Géante*. The feast takes place early in September when chefs from several communities get together in the Saint Aygulf area of Fréjus, mix up several hundred dozen eggs and make a gigantic omelet, which they then cut up and distribute to the public. Why? Who knows, but it's fun to watch if you happen to be in the area.

At sunset, Menton glows before its protective amphitheater of mountains.
© Komenda, OT Menton

The French Riviera & the Maritime Alps

Even the Scenery Says Glamor

Like a lot of people, I got my first glimpse of the Riviera watching classic movies on television. Cary Grant and Grace Kelly trading barbs on a balcony overlooking a yacht-filled harbor, in *To Catch a Thief*; one of any number of James Bonds or Simon Templars stepping out of the Casino at Monte Carlo; *Pink Panther* movies, car chases on the Grande Corniche, David Niven in *Casino Royale*.

IN THIS CHAPTER	
■ Cannes	302
■ Antibes-Juan les Pins	308
■ Nice and the Haut Pays Niçois	316
■ Menton	326
■ Biot	333
■ Grasse	334
■ Èze	335
■ Mandelieu/La Napoule	336
■ Mougins	337
■ La Turbie	338
■ Festivals & Fêtes	339
■ Shopping	341
■ Where to Stay	344
■ Where to Eat	354
■ Adventures	359
■ Eco-Travel	380

They all created an indelible impression of a gorgeous, glamorous and expensive jetsetters' paradise. The term *jetsetter* is a little dusty these days, but substitute *Eurotrash,* and the idea is the same; celebrities, minor royals and fashionistas mingling with arms dealers, deposed dictators, media tycoons and shipping magnates while gossip columnists write about their lifestyles of apparently endless leisure.

Classic Riviera view, the old port, Antibes. © M Boisnard, OT Antibes

This is not an entirely imaginary picture. There's no denying that the Riviera is a playground for the rich and famous. Behind the walls and towering hedges of Cap Ferrat and other such places, most of what all the money in the world will buy can probably be found.

But don't be put off if you're traveling on a modest budget. It is the glamor of the landscape, and all the outdoor activities to which it lends itself, that was probably what attracted the beautiful people in the first place. And that is within reach of everyone.

Breathtaking drives along *Les Corniches de la Riviera* (page 377) and coastal walks that range from gentle strolls to challenging climbs are laced between the distinctive towns and villages – Antibes, Nice, Menton, Beaulieu sur Mer, Villefranche – scattered almost artfully along the coast. In the skies, paragliders float down like flower petals from a handful of exceptional launch sites.

Jardin Maria Serena in Menton, the most temperate spot in Provence. Photo Courtesy OT Menton

Starting around Antibes and heading east, the back country rises and the Alps crowd down to the water. Along the way, the *villages perchées* become ever more dramatic: **Èze**, at 427 m/1,400 feet, tops a narrow dome of rock; **La Turbie**, at 500 m/1,640 feet, is where the Emperor Augustus planted the Trophée des Alpes, a 165-foot monument to the power of Rome that still lords over the coast and looks down on Monte Carlo; the medieval village of **Sainte Agnès**, just inland of Menton, at 800 m/2,600 feet claiming to be the highest coastal village in Europe.

And perhaps most surprising of all, only a short train journey from a coast dotted with lush tropical vegetation – bananas, dates, carob trees, oranges and lemons, are the ski resorts. In the Alpes de Haute Provence and the Alpes Maritime you can ski throughout most of the winter into the early spring, snow shoe, even scuba dive under the ice at some ski resorts. Here, in warmer weather, you can hike and mountain bike on high trails and mountain passes between peaks that reach 8,000 to 10,000 feet or more.

The variety of environments and experiences you can have on (or near) the 50-mile stretch between Cannes and the Italian border is genuinely outstanding. The French have a word for it – *éblouissant* – which means ravishing, fantastic, extraordinary, overwhelming, all rolled into one. If you are a fan of adventure travel and outdoor activity, don't be put off by the Riviera's glitzy reputation. Here, you will find some of the best mountain and airborne adventure in all of Provence. The glamor is built into the landscape.

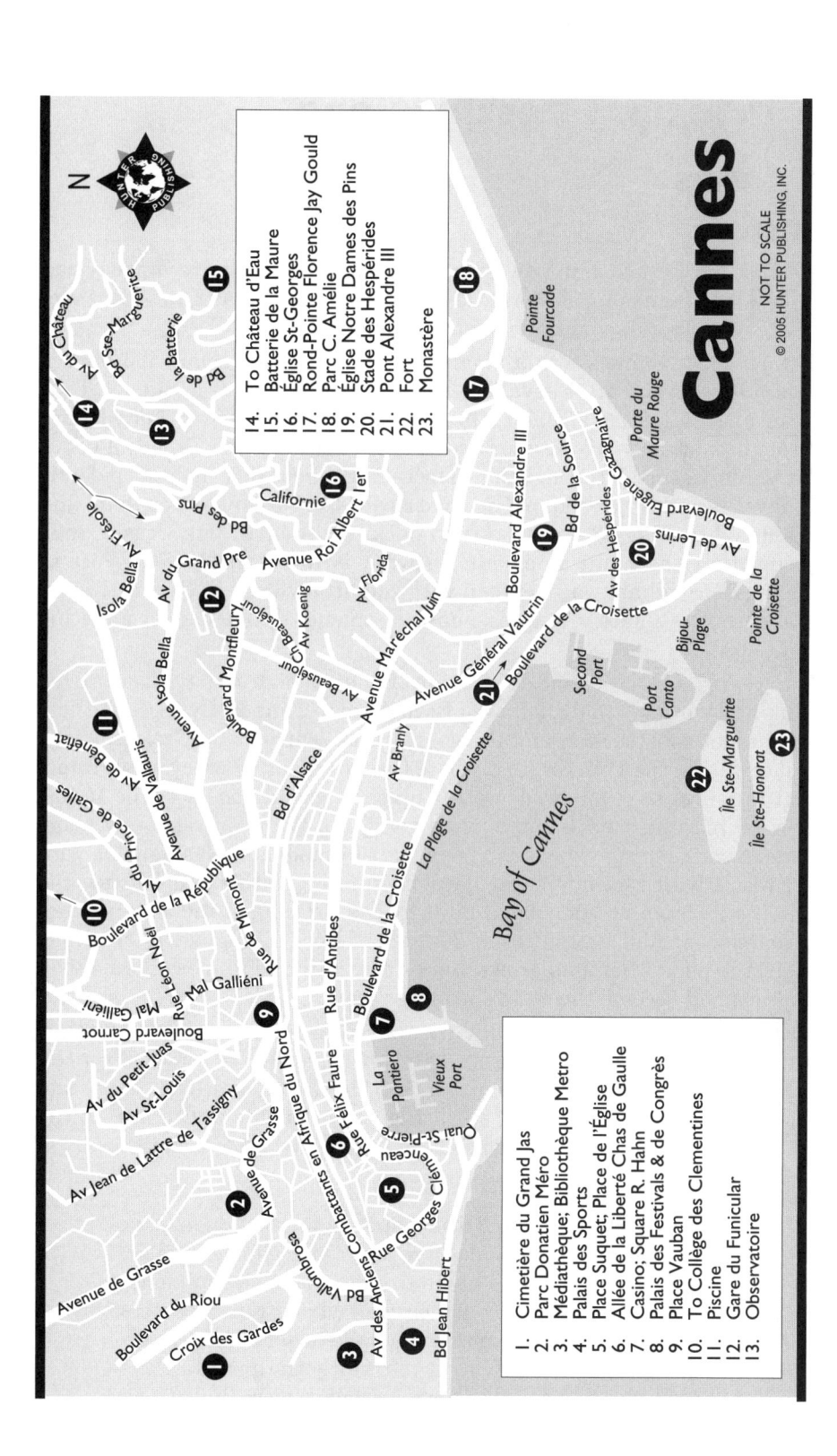

Cannes

1. Cimetière du Grand Jas
2. Parc Donatien Méro
3. Médiathèque; Bibliothèque Metro
4. Palais des Sports
5. Place Suquet; Place de l'Église
6. Allée de la Liberté Chas de Gaulle
7. Casino; Square R. Hahn
8. Palais des Festivals & de Congrès
9. Place Vauban
10. To Collège des Clementines
11. Piscine
12. Gare du Funicular
13. Observatoire
14. To Château d'Eau
15. Batterie de la Maure
16. Église St-Georges
17. Rond-Pointe Florence Jay Gould
18. Parc C. Amélie
19. Église Notre Dames des Pins
20. Stade des Hespérides
21. Pont Alexandre III
22. Fort
23. Monastère

NOT TO SCALE
© 2005 HUNTER PUBLISHING, INC.

The French Riviera & Maritime Alps

■ Principal Destinations

Cannes

History

The French didn't discover what a gem of a winter resort they had in Cannes until about 50 years after British and then Russian aristocrats virtually invented the place.

Before 1834, Cannes was a small fishing port, with about 500 houses around the base of Mt. Chevalier – the area now known as la Suquet. That year, as was his usual habit, the British Lord Chancellor, Lord Henry Brougham, was on his way to Nice, still part of Italy and already a popular winter resort with English aristocrats. Because of a cholera epidemic in Provence, the governor of Nice had closed the border so Brougham and his daughter Eleanore were turned back. On their way to Grasse, they stopped for the night at an inn on what is today the Rue du Port in Cannes. Brougham was so taken with the little village of *Canoïs* that he stayed on, ultimately commissioning a splendid villa named after his daughter.

Two years later, the crème de la crème of London high society, fleeing Britain's dull winter climate, followed Brougham to Cannes. By 1838, the port was under construction and the spectacular seafront, La Croisette, was underway. In the 19th century, where the British aristocracy went, Imperial Russians soon followed, setting up their grand houses in the 1840s. Ten years later, palace hotels were going up, Within a relatively short time, a poor fishing village had been transformed into a fashionable winter resort with vast mansions, gardens bursting with exotic blooms (the water was brought via a canal built by the British), grand avenues and promenades. And within three decades of Lord Brougham's fortuitous visit, the population had grown from a few hundred to more than 4,000. Cannes had become the coast's leading resort.

In the 1880s, French society finally arrived in numbers. Some say they were drawn there by the accounts of the town, painted by some of France's 19th century literary lions. Prosper Mérimée, who wrote the story and then the libretto for *Carmen*, spent the end of his life in Cannes. In the 1880s, Guy de Maupassant cruised the bay and wrote enthusiastically of the experience.

> **Did you know?** The British game of tennis, invented in 1873, was an adaptation of a royal French game called *jeu de paume*. It takes its name from the French command, *tenez!* (meaning *hold!*), which was what French players said just before they served the ball – a sort of early version of *get ready!* In 1879, six years after the game first appeared, the first tennis courts in France were built by an English property developer in Cannes.

The Belle Époque was well underway, at the turn of the 20th century, when some of Cannes' most famous landmarks were being built. The Hotel Carlton was commissioned in 1910. Legend says that its familiar domes were inspired by the breasts of *La Belle Otéro*, a famous courtesan of the era. It is probably true. Cannes in those days had the faintly naughty whiff of a rich man's playground about it. Several well-known courtesans entertained princes and captains of industry in its luxurious palace hotels and in the salons of its fine urban mansions.

During World War I many of the hotels were converted to hospitals and shelters for wounded soldiers and refugees. The Allies Peace Conference of 1921 was held at the Carlton.

Glamorous environments drew a glamorous crowd and it wasn't long after the war that the rich and famous returned. During the Roaring Twenties, the first generation of real mass media darlings populated the growing resort. The Aga Khan of the day married a local girl who had been elected Miss France. There were Rothschilds and Citroëns (people – not cars!), artists like van Dongen and Domergue, politicians – young Winston Churchill came often – and royalty. The Duke and Duchess of Windsor became part of the social scene following his abdication as Edward VIII.

The Capital of Cinema

If you know only one thing about the Riviera, you probably know that the Cannes Film Festival is held there. Every May, film stars and starlets, filmmakers, film buyers, film investors, producers, publicists and autograph seekers take over the whole town. If you can elbow your way into Cannes during the festival season, you'll find them parading along La Croisette, partying on the yachts that fill the harbor, wheeling and dealing in hotel rooms, restaurants and bars, and, oh yes, watching the films entered in the competition in the Festival Hall.

When this circus arrives, its impact spreads for miles. During the International Film Festival, there's not a hotel room to be had in Cannes or its coastal neighbors within an hour's drive.

Today the festival is so genuinely global in scope that it's surprising to learn it was political disagreements within Europe that started it all.

In the early days of the movie business, the festival that really mattered – for both international sales and artistic recognition – was the *Mostra di Venezia*, the Venice Film Festival. But in the mid-1930s Italian and German fascists were on the rise and their influence on the Venice festival was heavy. Filmmakers and festival participants from the Western democracies wanted no part of it and looked for somewhere else to showcase their films. The French Minister of Fine Arts suggested Cannes.

The first Cannes Film Festival was scheduled for September 1939. Louis Lumière, one of the inventors of motion pictures was to be the host. The festival opened on September 1, 1939 at the Municipal Casino. The next day, World War II broke out and the festival was immediately halted. The poster for that first, aborted event, by Jean Gabriel Domergue, is now a valuable collector's item.

The films shown when the festival was finally held, in 1946, are legends today – Jean Cocteau's *Beauty and the Beast*, Alfred Hitchcock's *Notorious*, and *Gilda* with Rita Hayworth's career-defining performance.

Building on the success of that first festival, Cannes has now made itself a kind of "festival central." Besides the film festival, it hosts bridge and chess championships, broadcast advertising festivals, antique festivals, an International Pyrotechnics competition, auto shows, boat shows and regattas and one trade show after another. In fact, after Paris, it is France's biggest trade show center.

Sightseeing in Cannes

Tourist Information: Palais des Festivals et des Congrès, La Croisette, 06400 Cannes, ☎ 33 04 93 39 24 53, fax 33 04 92 99 84 23, tourisme@semec.com, www.cannes.fr.

La Croisette

Cannes is probably the most urban of all the Riviera resorts. When not lounging on terraces overlooking the water (the quintessential Cannes accommodation is a rented apartment with a sea or pool view), experienced visitors spend a lot of time *en promenade*. Before lunch on La Croisette is the traditional time and place to stroll, window shop, see and be seen.

The Boulevard de la Croisette, as it is formally known, is lined on one side with magnificent hotels, nightclubs and exquisite shops offering every sort of luxury goods. Across the road, fine sand beaches, some public stretch, for miles.

AN EVENING STROLL

A four- or five-kilometer (2½- to three-mile) walk along the seafront at dusk, as the sun sets and the lights of the Riviera begin to sparkle, is a romantic way to build up an appetite for dinner. Walk the whole route, or stop in a bistro along the way, then call Cannes' 24/7 taxi company (**Cannes Allo Taxis**, ☎ 04 92 99 27 27).

Start at the Tourist Information office near the Casino and the Festival Hall. Walk east along the **Boulevard de la Croisette**, taking in great views across the bay of Cannes to the Esterel. At the eastern end of the **Plage de la Croisette**, pass the Second Port and Port Canto, both glamorous marinas. **Bijou-Plage** is just what the name suggests – small jewel of a beach just before **Pointe de la Croisette**, named for a small cross that used to mark the end of the bay, but which no longer exists. This is a lively area with several cafés and is a great place to watch the sunset while sipping an aperitif. Continue around the point, via **Place Franklin Roosevelt** and **Boulevard Eugene Gazagnaire**. There's an artificial beach, a Casino in the summer and the Palm Beach marina, center of high society social life in the 1920s. From Boulevard Gazagnaire, a completely new view opens up of Golfe Juan and Antibes set before the pre-Alps. Time it just right and you'll see the lights of the coast strung out like a diamond necklace.

Near **Port du Moure Rouge**, another marina, take a sharp left onto **Avenue des Hesperides**, which rejoins Boulevard la Croisette after about one km (.62 mile).

La Malmaison: Now the site of temporary fine arts and cinema exhibitions, this is all that remains of The Grand Hotel, Cannes' first palace hotel, built by architects Vianey and Blondel in 1863. In its heyday, this building served as the Grand's gaming room and tea room. *(47 La Croisette, 06400 Cannes, ☎ 33 04 97 06 44 90, fax 33 04 97 06 45 31, closed Mondays; open October to March, 10 am to 12:30 pm and 2:30 to 6 pm, April to September, 10 am to 1 p.m and 2:30 to 6:30 or 7 pm.)*

Espace Miramar: The work of young artists from throughout the region is showcased here. Cannes is a center for media trend setters so this is a coveted gallery space where you can expect to see some of the best up and comers. *(Corner of La Croisette and Rue Pasteur, 06400 Cannes, ☎ 33 04 9343 86 26, open winter from 1 to 6 pm, summer from 2 to 7 pm. Closed Mondays and some holidays. Free admission.)*

Tip: If you plan to dip in and out of the museums and gardens of this area during your stay, buy a *Carte Musées Côte d'Azur Museum Pass.* It allows access to 62 museums, monuments and gardens along the Riviera Côte d'Azur. Passes are available for one, three or seven days and start at 8, going up to 25 for the seven day pass.

Le Suquet

For aficionados of "old towns," the area known as Le Suquet around Cannes' oldest harbor is where what little remains of the city's pre-19th century history can be found.

Allées de la Liberté: Between Place Charles de Gaulle and Place Bernard Cornut Gentille, this shady avenue is a good place to watch the activities of the Vieux Port. In the morning, a photogenic flower market takes place here.

La Musée de Castre: A medieval castle atop the old city, the views over La Croisette, the Bay of Cannes and the Iles de Lérins (page 306) make it clear why the first defensive structures of ancient *Canoïs* were built here. The castle now standing was built at the end of the 11th century. The keep, the Romanesque **Chapel of Sainte Anne**, and the cisterns date from the original structure. Next to the remains of the ancient ramparts, the 17th-century **Notre Dame de l'Espérance** incorporates an earlier Romanesque bell tower. A square tower dating from the 12th century is an ancient guard house. Within the castle, an extensive and very eclectic art collection features works from the Far East and Pacific, North and South America and the Himalayas, as well as Orientalist and Provençal painting, ancient Mediterranean finds and musical instruments from all over the world. *(Le Suquet - 06400 Cannes, ☎ 33 04 93 38 55 26, fax 33 04 93 38 81 50; open October to March, 10am to 1 pm and 2 to 5 pm, April to September, open until 6 or 7 pm; closed Mondays and public holidays; free the first Sunday of each month.)*

Rothschild Villa & Gardens: A villa that is considered to be one of Cannes' finest 19th-century mansions. A grab-bag assortment of Classical, Palladian, Renaissance and Baroque features, it was built in 1881 on the foundations of Villa Marie-Thérèse, which had belonged to Lord Brougham, the founder of modern Cannes. The house and its large park, filled with specimen plants and trees, are both listed national monuments. Since the late 1940s, the house has served as a municipal library and "mediatheque." *(1 Avenue Jean de Noailles, ☎ 33 04 97 06 44 83, fax 33 04 97 06 44 86; open Tuesday to Saturday, 9:30 am to 6 pm.)*

A Bit Farther Out

Le Grand Jas: A large terraced cemetery in the Mediterranean style, first opened in 1866. It is the largest park in the city and includes an English cemetery where Lord Henry Brougham is buried. It is a treasure trove of Victorian-era funeral statuary. Among its permanent residents are Russian aristocrats, French Resistance heroes and such notables as Prosper Mérimée, Carl Peter Fabergé, Lily Pons and Olga Khoklova, a prima ballerina with Diaghilev and Picasso's first wife. *(205 Avenue de Grasse.)*

Villa Domergue & Gardens: Painter Jean-Gabriel Domergue wanted to build a house like the ones he had seen in Fiesole, near Florence. During the 1930s, he built and decorated the house, designing every detail. His wife, a sculptor, was responsible for the gardens, with their terraces and water features. Domergue, who designed the poster for the one-day 1939 film festival, was a popular portrait painter and the villa formed the backdrop for paintings of Brigitte Bardot and Gina Lollobrigida, among others. Domergue and his wife are buried in the gardens. *(Avenue Fiesole; open year-round by guided tour – inquire at the tourist office.)*

The Îles de Lérins

Just offshore, the Iles de Lérins are quiet, wooded, historically fascinating islets that are close enough for a pleasant half-day outing.

Île Sainte-Marguerite, the larger and closer of the two, is the site of **Fort Royal**, built by Cardinal Richelieu as both a military prison and a fortress. It was, for many years, the home of the mysterious *Man in the*

Iron Mask, whose cell can be visited along with the state prisons of Louis XIV.

The **Musée de la Mer,** housed in the Fort, also holds a significant collection of undersea archaeology found in the area, including amphorae, glass and ceramics. The building originally consisted of four first century Roman cisterns to which dungeons and other structures were added in the 17th to 19th centuries.

The island is covered with fragrant pine forests and botanical gardens, laced with footpaths. *(Fort de l'Île Sainte-Marguerite,* ☎ *33 04 93 38 55 26 or 33 04 93 43 18 17, fax 33 04 93 38 81 50; open October to March from 10:30 am to 1:15 pm and 2:15 to 4:45 pm, April to September, until 5:45 pm. Closed on Mondays and some holidays. Free the first Sunday of each month.)*

Île Saint-Honorat is a Cistercian monastery that has been continuously occupied since 410 AD. Although most of the structures in use today are modern, the island is scattered with ancient chapels and fortifications. The monks of today cultivate rosemary and lavender and operate a small, highly regarded vineyard. But, in its heyday, the Lérins Monastery was one of the most important economic and political powers in Provence, owning not only Cannes but also nearby Mougins and Vallauris. In the sixth century, it was apparently the most famous monastery in all of Christendom, holding out against regular Saracen and Spanish attacks. In addition to the numerous chapels on the island, two cannonball furnaces, one on each end, are listed historic monuments. The island is private and owned by the monks, but regular visits, with guided tours, are operated throughout the year.

Getting to the Islands: A number of companies provide regular excursions throughout the day for a standardized, round-trip fare of €10, half-price for children between five and 10 years old. Boats leave, throughout the day, for the 15-minute ride to Île Sainte-Marguerite from the Gare Maritime, Quai des Iles at the end of Quai Labeuf on the Vieux Port. **For more information**, cmcriviera@wanadoo.fr, www.ilesdeslerins.com, or call the following operators:

- **Compagnie Esterel-Chanteclair,** ☎ *33 04 93 39 11 82.*
- **Compagnie Maritime of Cannes,** ☎ *33 04 93 38 66 33.*
- **Horizon IV,** ☎ *33 04 92 98 71 36, sarlhorizon@aol.com.*

Only one service, operated by the monks, sails to Île Saint-Honorat. For information about visiting the monastery island, contact **Planaria,** ☎ *33 04 92 98 71 38, info@abbayedelerins.com, www.abbayedelerins.com.*

Getting Here

By Car: Cannes is located on the A8 motorway or the N7, about 27km (16.6 miles) from Nice Airport.

By Air: Nice Côte d'Azur is the closest commercial airport. Regular bus service leaves the airport every 20 minutes for Cannes, departing from Terminal 1 and 2. The fare is €9.9, with tickets for sale in the parking lot bus office. Taxi fare is between €60 and €80, depending upon traffic and time of day. Nearby Cannes-Mandelieu Business airport can handle private planes up to 22 tons in weight.

By Train: Cannes is on the main **TGV** line, with four or five departures from Paris per day.

Antibes-Juan les Pins

I discovered that I loved Antibes on my first trip to the South of France. Maybe that is why it has remained my favorite town on the Riviera ever since.

In the *ruelles* of the *Vieille Ville*, every house seemed bursting with flowers. Geraniums, oleanders, bougainvilla, grape vines, palms and yucca plants framed windows, tumbled out of pots and covered golden stone walls. Their blooms glowed in light filtered through the fluttering linens of dozens of clothes lines, strung high up, from the tops of the tall, narrow houses.

Rounding a bend we would be surprised by a sudden view of one of the ports, of the ramparts and fort. Or a market table loaded with oranges and lemons, their fragrance saturating the air. Or a shady square. Or the tiny shop where I bought needles in paper packets, embroidery silk, brightly printed Provençal fabrics and armloads of fresh flowers.

Vieux Port, from the old town, Antibes. © B.Giani, OT Antibes

Cap d'Antibes

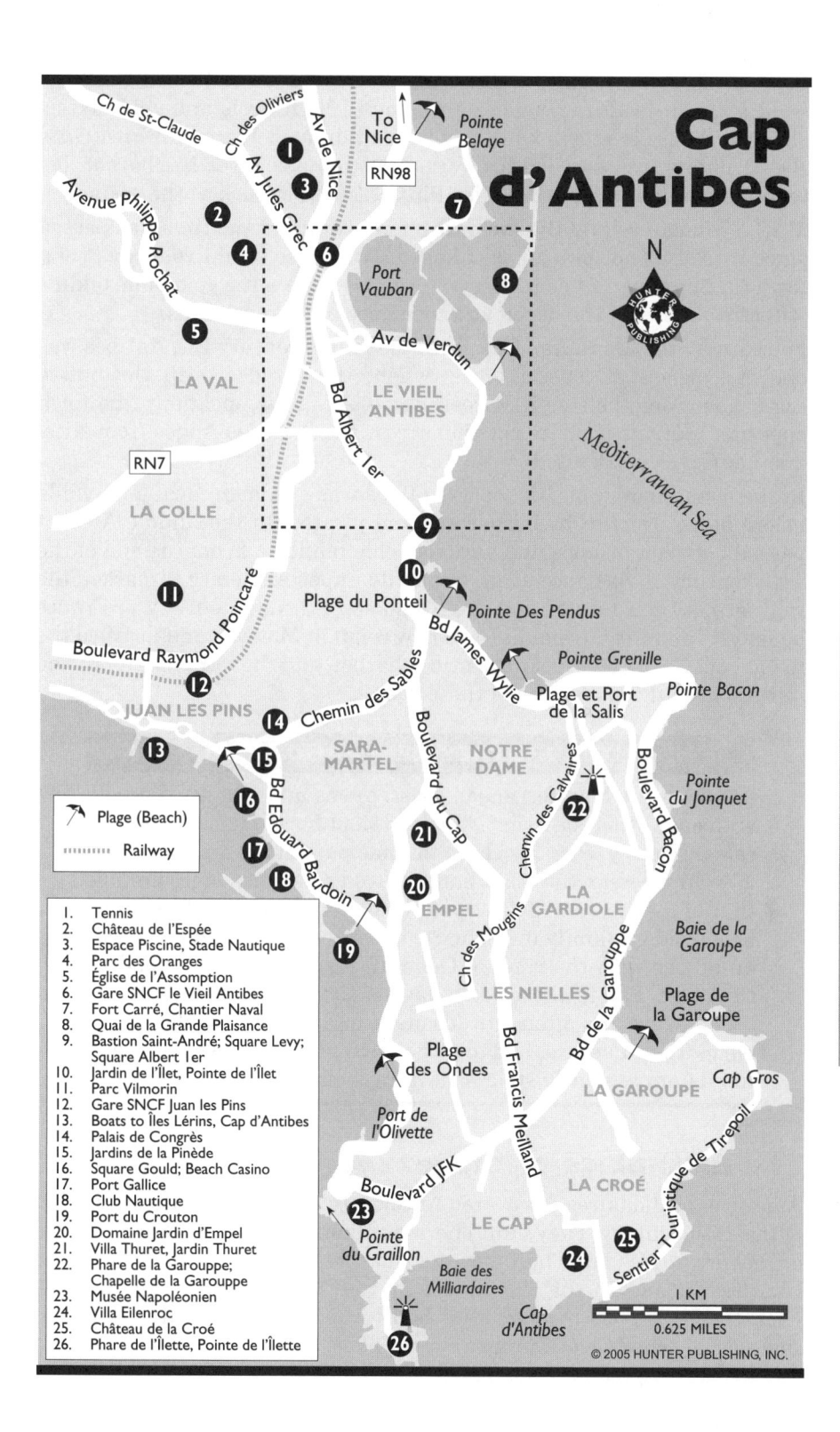

The French Riviera & Maritime Alps

1. Tennis
2. Château de l'Espée
3. Espace Piscine, Stade Nautique
4. Parc des Oranges
5. Église de l'Assomption
6. Gare SNCF le Vieil Antibes
7. Fort Carré, Chantier Naval
8. Quai de la Grande Plaisance
9. Bastion Saint-André; Square Levy; Square Albert 1er
10. Jardin de l'Îlet, Pointe de l'Îlet
11. Parc Vilmorin
12. Gare SNCF Juan les Pins
13. Boats to Îles Lérins, Cap d'Antibes
14. Palais de Congrès
15. Jardins de la Pinède
16. Square Gould; Beach Casino
17. Port Gallice
18. Club Nautique
19. Port du Crouton
20. Domaine Jardin d'Empel
21. Villa Thuret, Jardin Thuret
22. Phare de la Garouppe; Chapelle de la Garouppe
23. Musée Napoléonien
24. Villa Eilenroc
25. Château de la Croé
26. Phare de l'Îlette, Pointe de l'Îlette

© 2005 HUNTER PUBLISHING, INC.

Some afternoons we chilled, drinking *menthe et l'eau* or Ricard along the front at Juan les Pins, watching women in high heels and gold bikinis shop the designer stores while my friend hummed *Music to Watch Girls By*. At nights, we watched fireworks, set to music, over the harbor, listened to fabulous jazz in Juan les Pins or tried our luck at the casino.

Maybe you can tell by the musical reference that some time has passed since then. But not much has changed. What else would you expect of a town that has seen 24 centuries come and go? Even the gold lamé bikinis still stroll between the beach and the shops at Juan les Pins.

Founded by the Massalian Greeks in the fourth century BC, Antibes was one of a series of coastal towns where they traded with the native Ligurians. Some believe its Greek name, *Antipolis*, meaning "the town opposite," derives from its position across the Baie des Anges from Nice, another Greek settlement.

In the usual history of this coast, Antibes was a Roman town for a while before being overrun by barbarians and pirates. In the Middle Ages, it passed between bishops and various noble families. From the end of the 14th century, it was once again militarily important, since it marked the frontier between France and the Kingdom of Savoy. Henri IV of France bought it from the Grimaldis (who now reign in Monaco) and fortified the town. Fort Carré, overlooking Antibes harbor, and the ramparts along the seawall are all that remain of these works.

BEFORE THEY WERE FAMOUS...

All along the Mediterranean coast, towns and villages compete with each other for their "Napoleon slept here" moments and locales. Usually, they lay claim to some part in his "glorious" history. Antibes, on the other hand, played a part in a more humble time of his life. In 1794, the year he met and married Josephine, he moved his family into a house in Antibes. At the time, he was an officer with the rank of General, responsible for defending the coast. But in those early days of the French Republic, pay was meagre and often late. To make ends meet, Napoleon's noble mother, Laetitia, had to do her own laundry in a stream and his sisters regularly stole fruit from their landlord's garden.

The Birthplace of the Jazz Age

American millionaires discovered Antibes-Juan les Pins at the beginning of the 20th century. They built enormous mansions on the Cap d'Antibes or took over ones built half a century earlier, like Eilenroc, designed by Charles Garnier in the the 1860s. By the 1920s and 30s, the era the French call *l'age du pyjama,* they had turned it into a winter resort on their social schedule of Europe.

Among them, the legendary Murphys, immortalized by F. Scott Fitzgerald in his novel *Tender is the Night*, took up residence on Cap d'Antibes. Murphy was an early jazz afficionado. His collection included Louis Armstrong's first recording. Before long, his parties were drawing notable society beauties, flappers, musicans, artists and poets. F. Scott and Zelda Fitzgerald were regular visitors. So were Hemingway, John Dos Passos, Rudolph Valentino, Mistinguet and her lover Maurice Chevalier.

The Murphy's lifestyle inspired Fitzgerald's *Tales of the Jazz Age* and the term, which originated in the Casino at Juan, was taken up by all and sundry to describe the roaring twenties. The party went on right up until WWII and then continued again in the 1950s.

Picasso came to stay for a few years and so did Nikos Kazantzakis, author of *Zorba the Greek*. Grahame Greene moved to Antibes after the war. Jazz continued to be an established part of the of the scene, with Ray Charles, Ella Fitzgerald, Dizzy Gillespie and Fats Domino all performing at the Casino.

In the 1960s the jazz connection was formalized with launch of **Jazz à Juan**, one of Europe's oldest jazz festivals. Today, the festival, in a pine wood named after American millionaire Jay Gould, continues to attract top jazz musicans from throughout the world. Recent performers have included Marcus Miller, Wynton Marsalis, Salif Keita, Diana Krall, James Carter and Joshua Redman.

Antibes Today

Antibes is an important center of commercial flower growing. There are nearly 1,000 flower businesses, growing roses, carnations, anemones and tulips.

Just outside of the city, **Sophia Antipolis**, a vast and successful new town devoted to international development in science, technology, education and commerce, enables Antibes to remain vibrant and viable while protecting the serene ambiance of the town center.

Getting back to those cinema images of the Riviera, wasn't there always someone waterskiing in the background? It must have been Antibes because, according to the *Antibois*, waterskiing was practically invented here. Whether you've never done it before or water ski to championship standards, this is the place do it. Other watersports, including parascending, wake boarding and windsurfing, are available along the beaches. There are also a number of diving clubs and deep-sea fishing excursions.

The French, busy as always classifying everything in sight, have named Antibes "the second most athletic city in France." I have no idea what that really means, or which city is the *most* athletic. But I do know that whatever adventure activities you choose to pursue, leave some time for Antibes-Juan les Pins, to my mind one of the loveliest spots on the Riviera.

Vieille Antibes

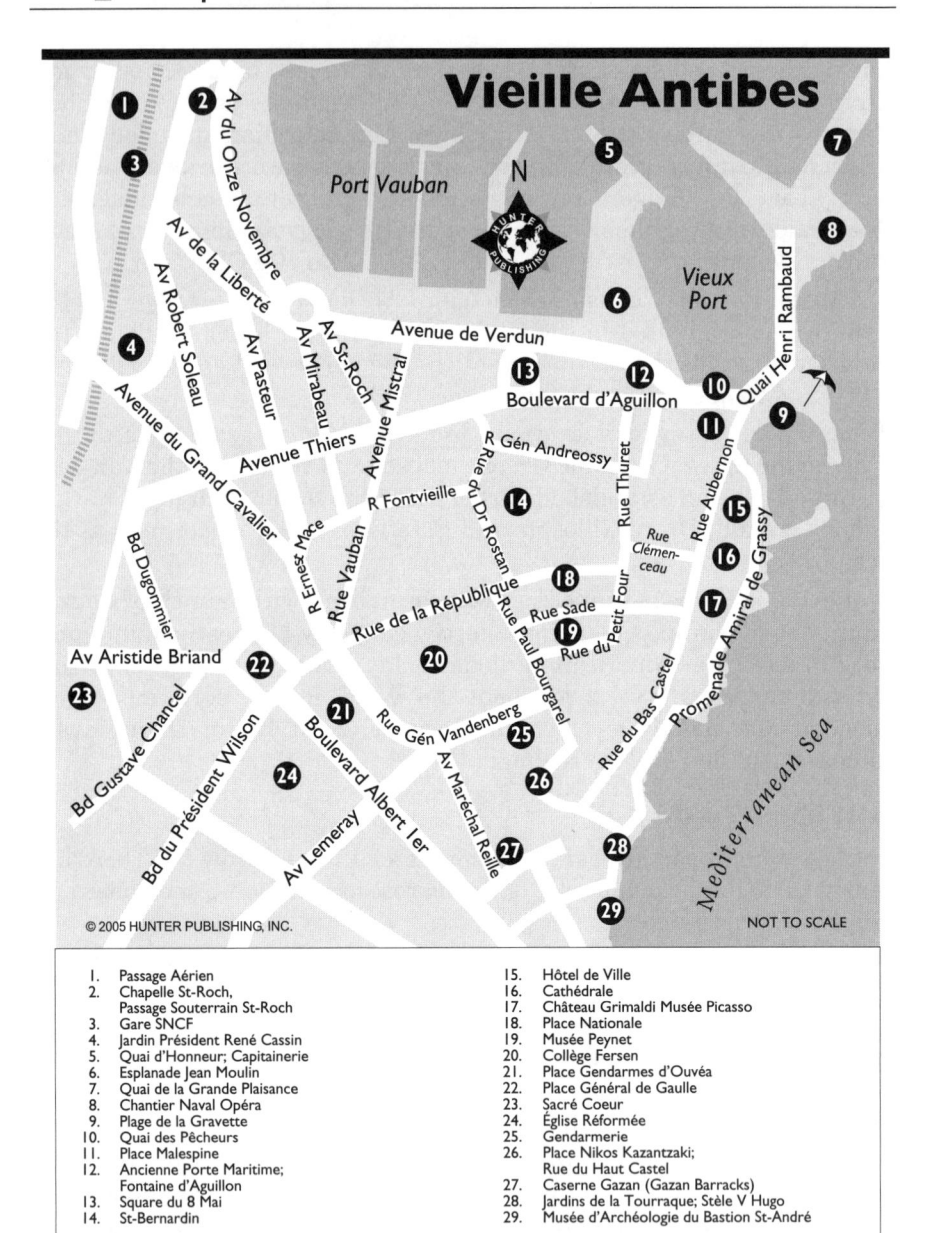

1. Passage Aérien
2. Chapelle St-Roch, Passage Souterrain St-Roch
3. Gare SNCF
4. Jardin Président René Cassin
5. Quai d'Honneur; Capitainerie
6. Esplanade Jean Moulin
7. Quai de la Grande Plaisance
8. Chantier Naval Opéra
9. Plage de la Gravette
10. Quai des Pêcheurs
11. Place Malespine
12. Ancienne Porte Maritime; Fontaine d'Aguillon
13. Square du 8 Mai
14. St-Bernardin
15. Hôtel de Ville
16. Cathédrale
17. Château Grimaldi Musée Picasso
18. Place Nationale
19. Musée Peynet
20. Collège Fersen
21. Place Gendarmes d'Ouvéa
22. Place Général de Gaulle
23. Sacré Coeur
24. Église Réformée
25. Gendarmerie
26. Place Nikos Kazantzaki; Rue du Haut Castel
27. Caserne Gazan (Gazan Barracks)
28. Jardins de la Tourraque; Stèle V Hugo
29. Musée d'Archéologie du Bastion St-André

Getting Here

Antibes is about halfway between Cannes and Nice.

By Car: Take the A8 motorway east from Cannes or west from Nice and exit to the D35 South.

By Train: Antibes is on the main coastal line and reachable by TGV from Paris or by local SNCF railway from most of the coastal stations from Marseille eastward (see page 27 for train information).

By Air: Nice Airport is only 20 km/12 miles away – about 20 minutes by car. **Taxi** fare is between €40 and €55. Daily **buses** to Antibes run regularly from Terminal 1 and cost €7.2 for a 40-minute trip (take Bus 200 Cannes RN7). The Nice Airport website (www.nice.aeroport.fr/include_en) has very good information in English about local transfers.

SAILING & THE PORTS

Antibes has five ports, ranging from the newest, Port Vauban – where some of the world's biggest yachts tie up – to the tiny, picturesque Port Olivette. Most sailing is at serious regatta level or connected with one of several residential or private club sailing schools. As a visitor, you may be able to rent a small sail- or powerboat if you have experience and appropriate qualifications. To find out, or to make marina arrangements for your own boat, contact the *Capitaineries* (harbor masters) of the individual ports. The harbor masters can also give you information on which captains are available for deep-sea fishing and whale-watch excursions:

Sailing in Antibes. © Monticelli, OT Antibes

- **Port Vauban** – in terms of tonnage, Europe's largest pleasure port. A total of 1,230 berths and 350 moorings. Capitainerie, ☎ *33 04 92 91 60 00*.
- **Port Gallice** – 525 berths for units no larger than 30 x seven m/98 x 23 feet. Capitainerie, ☎ *33 04 92 93 74 40*.
- **Port de la Salis** – 230 berths for small boats (5.99 x 2.3 m/19.6 x 7½ feet). Capitainerie, ☎ *33 04 93 67 12 70*.
- **Port du Croûton** – 390 berths for motor- or sailboats of less than 10 m/33 feet. Capitainerie, ☎ *33 04 93 67 32 31*.
- **Port Olivette** does not have berths available for visiting craft.

The Beaches

There are dozens and dozens of sandy beaches. Many are small and at least three times more are private than public. Don't be put off by that. With the exception of a small number of really private hotel beaches, most are available to the public for the payment of a fee. And since public beaches have no facilities, if you want to water ski or indulge in other beach sports – from volleyball to pedalos – you need to go to a private beach.

Admission prices may buy you a day's rental of a beach chair, air mattress or beach umbrella – or those may be extra. Some are connected with a restaurant and lunch or dinner guests will have free access to the beach. A few, geared to serious sun worshippers who haven't been paying much attention to modern medical advice, aren't really beaches in the true sense at all. They are simply rows of loungers lined up on piers – or "pontons" – in full sunlight all day long.

There is a good deal of variation in admission prices but most are reasonable. Since all the private beaches require advance reservations, the best way to find out the cost is to get a list of private beaches from the tourist office and call them.

Among the public beaches, those near the Garoupe Lighthouse on Cap d'Antibes are among the best. These include: **Plage de la Garoupe**, **Plage La Joliette**, **Plage de la Godille** and **Plage Le Rocher**, all along the Chemin de la Garoupe on Cap d'Antibes.

The shore walk at the end of Garoupe beach, Cap d'Antibes. © Monticelli, OT Antibes

There are quite a few private beaches with restaurants and facilities along this stretch, but if you think you might want to try one, make a reservation before you leave home for the beach.

> **Tip:** An interesting shore walk at the end of Garoupe beach takes you along the coastal path, around the headland at the base of the cliffs of Cap d'Antibes. Cover up and wear good walking shoes if you take this walk because a lot of it is over sharp and jagged boulders.

Sightseeing in Antibes-Juan les Pins

Tourist Information: Office de Tourisme et des Congrès, 11 Place de Gaulle, BP 37, 06601 Antibes, ☎ 33 04 92 90 53 00/05, fax 33 04 92 90 53 01, accueil@antibes-juanlespins.com, www.antibes-juanlespins.com.

Musée Picasso

In 1946, the curator of the Château Grimaldi, the 12th-century fortified house that the city had turned into a museum of history, offered Picasso some studio space in which to work. The post-war period was a time of hardship for everyone, including Europe's most celebrated living artist of the day. Out of gratitude, he gave the museum a large number of his works

Picasso Museum in the Chateau Grimaldi, at dusk in Antibes. © Monticelli. OT Antibes

– 28 paintings, 54 drawings, ceramics, prints and tapestries. Eventually, the Picasso Museum became the first one devoted to his work *(Château Grimaldi, 06600 Antibes, ☎ 33 04 92 90 54 20, fax 33 04 92 90 54 21, musee.picasso@ville-antibes.fr)*. The museum has grown substantially, with works by many of Picasso's contemporaries. It is said that if you want to see Picasso's Antibes paintings, you have to go to Antibes to see them. The Château Grimaldi is between the covered market at the Place Masséna and the ramparts. Open all year, except Mondays and public holidays. Winter hours from September 16 to June 14, 10 am to noon and 2 to 6 pm. Summer hours, from June 15 to September 15, 10 am to 6 pm. July and August, open Wednesdays and Thursdays until 8 pm. Admission €5 in winter, €6 in summer.

The Archaeology Museum

This houses an interesting collection of Greek and Roman artifacts – including ceramics, mosaics, coins, amphorae and objects of daily life, found in the city as well as underwater *(Musée d'Archéologie, Bastion Saint-André, 06600 Antibes, ☎ 33 04 93 34 00 39, fax 33 04 93 34 45 59, musee.archeologie@ville-antibes.fr, admission €3, same opening times as Picasso Museum above)*. The museum is housed in a fortification designed by the military architect, Vauban, at the end of the 17th century.

Fort Carré

The 16th- and 17th-century fortress that defends the Antibes coast stands on a site the Romans used as a temple to Mercury. The temple ruins make up part of a fifth-century chapel inside the fort. The most recent structures were designed by Vauban, which may be of interest to fans of military architecture. The view of Antibes from the fort makes it worth a visit for everyone else. The fort can be visited only on guided tours, which are run every half-hour, in both English and French. Until 1997, the Fort was the property of the French Army. It was opened to the public only after being acquired by the city. If you are a fan of Musketeer and Foreign Legion movies, the fort will probably seem familiar, as it has been filmed many times. *(Avenue du 11 Novembre, Route du Bord de Mer, 06600 Antibes, ☎ 33 06 14 89 17 45. Guided visits every half-hour from 10:15 am to 4 pm in winter and to 5:30 pm in summer. Free shuttle bus from parking at Port Vauban. Admission €3.)*

Inside Fort Carré, Antibes.
© M.Boisnard OT Antibes

The Vieille Ville

Tiny street in Antibes Old Town.
© Monticelli, OT Antibes

One of the best things to do in Antibes is to simply walk the streets of the old town, enjoying the ambiance, the squares, the shops and the lovely old houses. Climb the stairs to *le quartier le Safranier*, which is the most typically Provençal area of Antibes and a sort of town within the town – it even has its own mayor. Walking itinerary suggestions are available from the tourist office.

Nice & the Haut Pays Niçois - The Flower of the South

Nice is irresistably frivolous, like a dotty and unexpectedly girlish old lady. From the crisp meringue of the Belle Époque hotels on the Promenade des Anglais, to the candy-colored buildings along the Cours Saleya, it is a thoroughly delicious city.

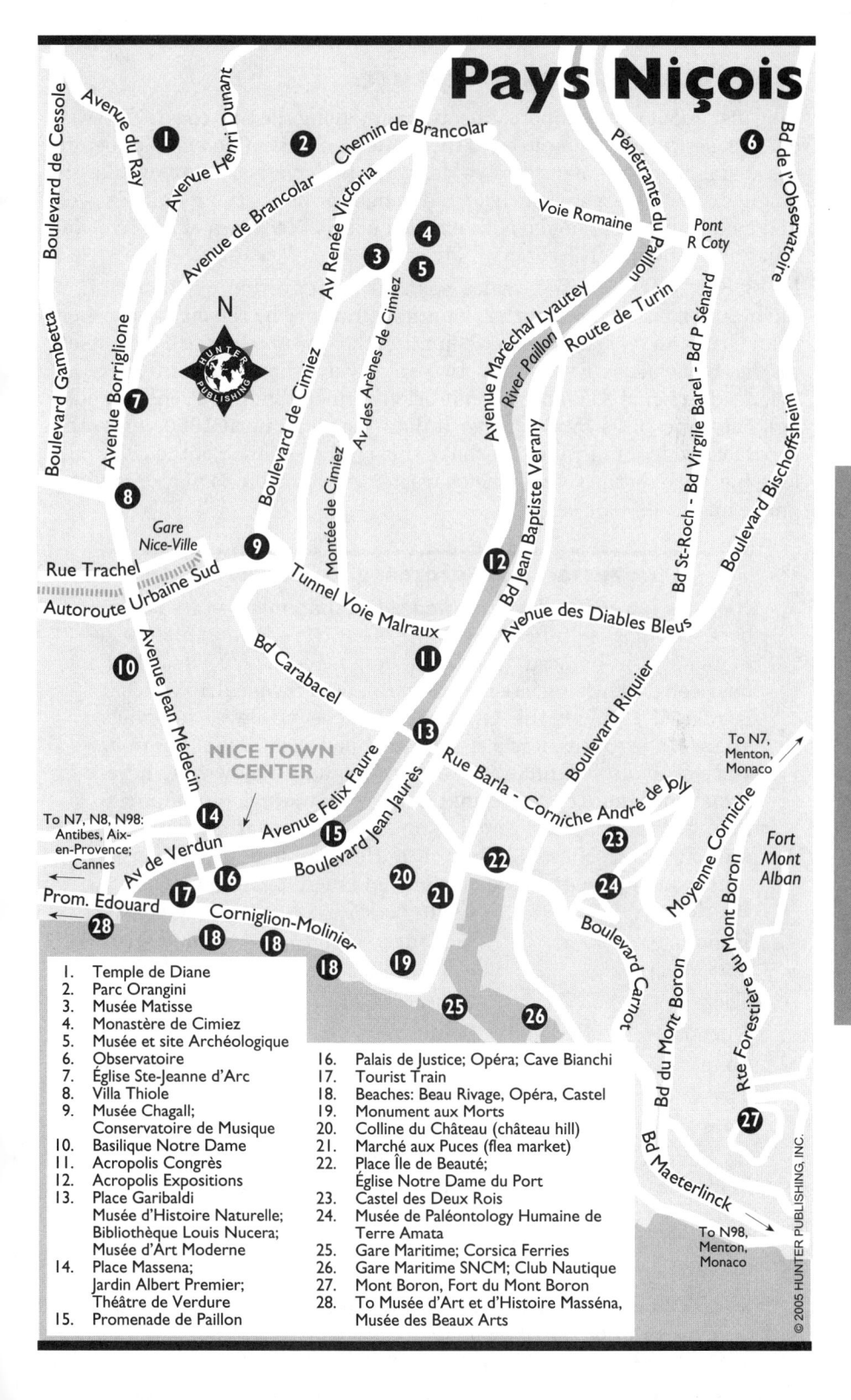

Pays Niçois

1. Temple de Diane
2. Parc Orangini
3. Musée Matisse
4. Monastère de Cimiez
5. Musée et site Archéologique
6. Observatoire
7. Église Ste-Jeanne d'Arc
8. Villa Thiole
9. Musée Chagall; Conservatoire de Musique
10. Basilique Notre Dame
11. Acropolis Congrès
12. Acropolis Expositions
13. Place Garibaldi
    Musée d'Histoire Naturelle;
    Bibliothèque Louis Nucera;
    Musée d'Art Moderne
14. Place Massena;
    Jardin Albert Premier;
    Théâtre de Verdure
15. Promenade de Paillon
16. Palais de Justice; Opéra; Cave Bianchi
17. Tourist Train
18. Beaches: Beau Rivage, Opéra, Castel
19. Monument aux Morts
20. Colline du Château (château hill)
21. Marché aux Puces (flea market)
22. Place Île de Beauté;
    Église Notre Dame du Port
23. Castel des Deux Rois
24. Musée de Paléontology Humaine de Terre Amata
25. Gare Maritime; Corsica Ferries
26. Gare Maritime SNCM; Club Nautique
27. Mont Boron, Fort du Mont Boron
28. To Musée d'Art et d'Histoire Masséna, Musée des Beaux Arts

The French Riviera & Maritime Alps

A Unique History & Culture

Like just about every important settlement along the this coast, Nice was a Greek settlement (*Nikaia*) and then a Roman town (*Cemenelum*) before the usual medieval period of raids, wars and plagues. But, unlike its neighbors, who were regularly forced to fight or flee to their walled towns and mountain strongholds, Nice enjoyed nearly 500 years of relative stability as part of the Kingdom of Savoy.

In 1388, after behind-the-scenes political maneuvering by the Count of Savoy and treason against the Counts of Provence by the city's governor, Jean Grimaldi (yes, that Monaco family), the city pretty much gave itself to the Savoyards. Except for two relatively short periods (when it belonged to Louis XIV and when it briefly joined the first French Republic), Nice was ruled by Savoy, an Italian kingdom, until 1860, when the people voted to join France. Perhaps this is why so much of the city's culture has such distinctive Niçois character, most visible to visitors in language and foods.

La Nissart – A Surprising Roman Relic

Nice has fewer Roman ruins and relics than many of its neighbors. The most significant evidence of the city's Roman history is in its Latin-influenced, traditional language – *La Nissart*, which has been undergoing a recent revival. Like Provençal, to which it is related through the Langue d'Oc, (the medieval language group of the south), it is a distinct tongue with its own grammar and vocabulary. Unlike its related languages, however, it retains much more of its original Latin vocabulary and pronunciation. In French, *Alors, ça va?* is an expression that means "How are you?" In La Nissart, it's *Alloùra*. Here are some other expressions you may hear or see on signs and menus around Nice:

English	French	Nissart
Hello	Bonjour	Bouangiou
Afternoon	Après-midi	Predina
Taste	Goûter	Tasta
Queen	Reine	Regina
Soap	Savon	Saboun
Tart	Tarte	Tourta
Eyes	Yeux	Uès

Le Nissart never really died out among the working people. More recently, theater companies and folk groups have been leading a revival. If you would like to see a performance of theater or songs in Nissart, look up these companies when you get to Nice:

- **Le Théâtre Niçois de Francis Gag**. Contact *Pierre Louis Gag,* ☎ *33 04 93 74 64 56.*

- **Lou Rodou Nissart**. Contact *J.C. Grasso*, ☎ *33 04 92 11 06 85*.
- **La Ciamada Nissarda**. Contact *Martine Salvatico*, ☎ *33 04 92 09 84 16, ciamadanissarda@wanadoo.fr*.

Everyone who visits Nice falls in love with the palm-shaded walks along the eight-km/five-mile sea front on the **Baie des Anges**, with Antibes in the distance. In the **Mont Boron Forestry Park** (created in 1866 with the planting of 142 acres of Aleppo pines) visitors climb miles of marked paths in search of rare flowers (wild orchids, lentiscus, miniature carnations) or to savor the views of Saint Jean Cap Ferrat. Or they are drawn to the exquisite daily flower market on the **Cours Saleya**. Nice flirts with tourists and knowing that it is a well-practiced flirtation doesn't diminish its charm in the least.

The Niçois have catered to a steady stream of visitors for nearly 150 years. Much of what is attractive and alluring about Nice today is a result of the waves of visitors who have come here and shaped their surroundings for their own pleasure.

From the Victorian period onward, Nice attracted wealthy foreign tourists. English aristocrats came first, building their gingerbread mansions in the **Cimiez quarter** and their sparkling Belle Époque hotels along the seafront named in their honor – **The Promenade des Anglais**.

American millionaires came later and then Czarist Russians. After the Russian Revolution, many came back to establish a Russian community and to build their elaborate mansions around the city's remarkable Russian Orthodox Church (page 324).

Countless important artists came here to work and some, like Marc Chagall and Henri Matisse, stayed – Matisse remaining for the rest of his life.

THE FIRST TOURISTS AT TERRA AMATA

Nice has been a destination for visitors longer than you might imagine. Some 400,000 years ago, when ice sheets covered most of Europe, elephant hunters, possibly chasing a herd across from Africa, set up temporary residence. They knew how to pick a good spot. Their camp was near the center of modern Nice on Boulevard Carnot, not far from the Port – still a good location. They left enough of their shelter and tools for paleontologists to identify the settlement. The **Terra Amata Human Paleontology Museum** is now located at the site. The museum includes a reconstruction of the prehistoric (Acheulean era) occupation from plaster casts and other findings. Contact: *Musée de Paléontology Humaine de Terra Amata, 25 Boulevard Carnot,* ☎ *33 04 93 55 59 93, closed Mondays.*

Old Town Nice

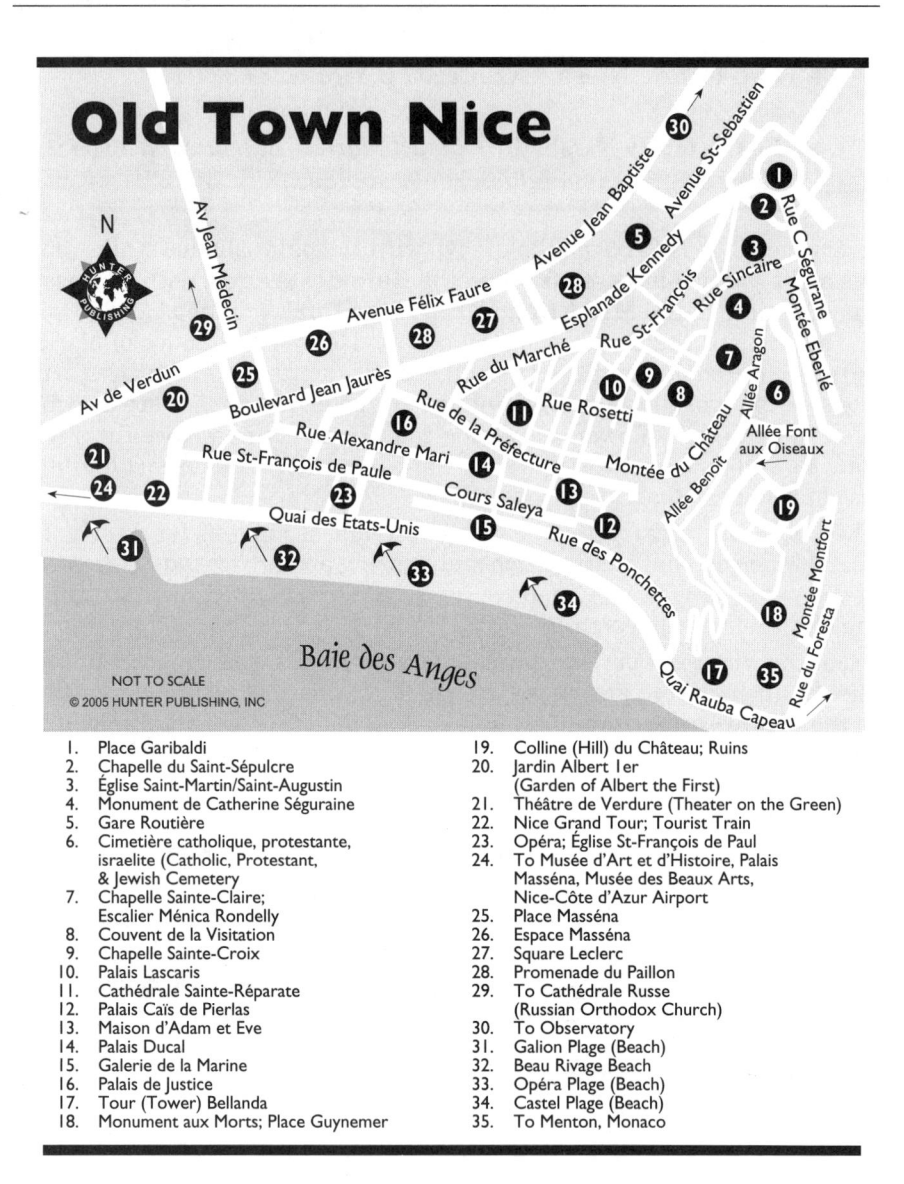

1. Place Garibaldi
2. Chapelle du Saint-Sépulcre
3. Église Saint-Martin/Saint-Augustin
4. Monument de Catherine Séguraine
5. Gare Routière
6. Cimetière catholique, protestante, israelite (Catholic, Protestant, & Jewish Cemetery
7. Chapelle Sainte-Claire; Escalier Ménica Rondelly
8. Couvent de la Visitation
9. Chapelle Sainte-Croix
10. Palais Lascaris
11. Cathédrale Sainte-Réparate
12. Palais Caïs de Pierlas
13. Maison d'Adam et Eve
14. Palais Ducal
15. Galerie de la Marine
16. Palais de Justice
17. Tour (Tower) Bellanda
18. Monument aux Morts; Place Guynemer
19. Colline (Hill) du Château; Ruins
20. Jardin Albert 1er (Garden of Albert the First)
21. Théâtre de Verdure (Theater on the Green)
22. Nice Grand Tour; Tourist Train
23. Opéra; Église St-François de Paul
24. To Musée d'Art et d'Histoire, Palais Masséna, Musée des Beaux Arts, Nice-Côte d'Azur Airport
25. Place Masséna
26. Espace Masséna
27. Square Leclerc
28. Promenade du Paillon
29. To Cathédrale Russe (Russian Orthodox Church)
30. To Observatory
31. Galion Plage (Beach)
32. Beau Rivage Beach
33. Opéra Plage (Beach)
34. Castel Plage (Beach)
35. To Menton, Monaco

Nice at Table

In addition to preserving their language and folk traditions, the Niçois give the preservation of their culinary traditions a good deal of attention. Restaurants bearing the trademark *Cuisine Nissarde* (which includes establishments in most price categories) have agreed to serve a selection of local specialties prepared in traditional ways. Salade niçoise is, of course, a basic. But don't be surprised if the real thing has only tuna, or egg – they're rarely used together. Cooked vegetables, including potatoes and green beans, are almost never used, though you may find small arti-

Along the rugged coast near le Trayas
(© CDT VAR / www.wallis.fr)

At Pra Loup in the Alpes de Haute Provence (© Manu Molle, OT Pra Loup)

In the old town, Antibes (© *Monticelli, OT Antibes*)

Above: Antibes port from inside Fort Carré (©Monticelli, OT Antibes)

Below: Port Vauban, Antibes (© Monticelli, OT Antibes)

chokes and broad beans in season. These are some other classics of Cuisine Nissard to look for:

- **Beignets** – Light, thin fritters, especially made with squash blossoms.
- **Farcis** – Small, stuffed vegetables. Every vegetable has a different, traditional stuffing.
- **Gnocchi** – Dumplings made with Italian semolina flour.
- **Mesclun** – A version of this is now available all over the US, but real mesclun is a wild salad of dandelion, rocket, chicory, purslane, chervil and bitter lettuce gathered in the hills of Nice.
- **Pissaladiere** – Flat onion tart with black olives and an anchovy condiment (*pissalat*) that may be Roman in origin.
- **Ravioli** – In Nice they're filled with swiss chard, pine nuts and cheese and they're used to garnish beef stew. Sometimes they are deep-fried and eaten as a snack.
- **Socca** – A large, thick crêpe made from chick pea flour. It is cut in squares, liberally peppered and eaten as a snack before lunch, with a glass of cold rosé.
- **Stockfish** – A very local fish stew made of dried haddock or cod with vegetables and tomatoes.
- **Tourta de bléa** – Also called *tourte de blettes*, this is a sweet or savory pie made with swiss chard and pine nuts.

The Arrière & Haut Pays Niçois

Nice has very good seafront and urban walks – there is even a mountain of sorts, Mont Boron, within the city limits. It is also noted for its underwater flora and fauna (see Adventures, page 359). For the serious adventurer, however, the real appeal of Nice is its proximity to the Alps.

In a way, Nice is like the frilly hem on a rough, peasant skirt. Its back country is the **Southern Alps** of the Alpes Maritimes and the Alpes de Haute Provence. Several mountains in this region are more than 2,700 m/9,000 feet high, with a number of big ski resorts higher than 1,500 m/4,920 feet. (see Adventures in the Snow, page 372).

The Alpine National Nature Park, the **Parc Mercantour**, is a wild and challenging high-mountain region where hikes will lead you to hidden and mysterious prehistoric carvings or to wildlife not seen anywhere else in this part of Europe – possibly even wolves. Just outside the park, there are more great hiking and mountain bike trails. They link small, medieval mountain villages, many with ramparts and castle ruins, where churches contain anonymous Renaissance masterpieces.

All of this is within two hours of Nice to the northeast by car or train. Or head northwest of Nice and you are into the gorges and clues of Verdon country. The famous **Train des Pignes** (see box, page 195), the scenic narrow gauge railway into the Alpes de Haute Provence and the Gorges du Verdon, departs from Nice several times a day.

The temperature in Nice rarely falls below about 51°F (11°C) – and that only in the coldest months – so it is possible to turn one trip into a virtual two-center vacation. In the spring and fall, you can combine a week in the snow-covered mountains with snorkeling, sunbathing, sailing, deep sea fishing and generally basking in the warm and giddy smile that is Nice.

Getting Here

By Air: Nice Côte d'Azur Airport (www.nice.aeroport.fr) is one of the major access gateways to Provence. It's 10 km/six miles from the center of Nice. **Taxis** to the city center cost about €25.

The most convenient and inexpensive way to get into the city from the airport is to take a **bus**. Direct buses, which take about 20 minutes, are run between the airport and the SNCF Railway Station. *(Route 99 SNCF Direct, ☎ 33 04 92 29 88 88, €3.50 per person, including luggage. Purchase ticket on bus. Departures every half-hour between 8 am and 9 pm from Terminal 2, Stand 4 and Terminal 1, Stand 1.)* Local buses, which cost a third of the price but take twice as long, are run by SUNBUS, Nice's mass transit company. *(Route 23, direction "St. Maurice," ☎ 33 04 93 13 53 13, www.sunbus.com, €1.30 per person. Buses leave every 10 minutes from Terminal 1, Stand 6 and take about 45 minutes to the SNCF Railway Station.)*

By Train: Nice is also on the main line SNCF national rail, TGV high speed rail and TER local train routes. (See pages 26-27 for more information about airports and train services).

Getting Around

By Taxi: You can't hail a taxi on the street, but you can order one by phone (**Central Taxi Riviera**, ☎ 4 93 13 78 78, 24-hour switchboard) or pick one up at an authorized taxi stand. The main taxi stands are at Esplanade Masséna, Promenade des Angais, Place Garibaldi, Hôtel des Postes, SNCF Railway Station, and Acropolis. Taxi rates go up between 7 pm and 7am.

By Bus: Bus routes, operated by **SUNBUS**, will take you all over the city and up into the surrounding hills. A single fare is €1.30, paid on the bus, but you can buy a one-, five- or seven-day Sun Pass for unlimited travel on all regular lines. The **Noctambus Service** operates four night bus lines from Place Masséna, between 9:10 pm and 1:10 am. A bus map and guide is available from the tourist office. To buy a Sun Pass, contact SUNBUS, Sun Boutique Grand Hotel, 10 Avenue Félix Faure, ☎ 33 04 93 13 53 13, fax 33 04 93 13 53 14, Monday to Friday 7:15 am to 7 pm, Saturday 8 am to 6 pm.

Sightseeing in Nice

Tourist Information: Nice Office du Tourisme et des Congres, 5 Promenade des Anglais, BP 4079, 06302 Nice. ☎ 33 08 92 70 74 07, fax 33 04 92 14 48 03, info@nicetourism.com, www.nicetourism.com. There are also branches of the Nice Tourist Office at Nice Airport, Terminals 1 and 2, and at the SNCF station on Avenue Thiers.

ADMISSION TO MUSEUMS & GALLERIES

Municipal art galleries are free and are open between 10 am and 6 pm, Tuesday to Sunday. Three galleries in the *Vieille Ville* specialize in the work of young artists:
- **Galerie Sainte Réparate**
- **Galerie du Château**
- **Galerie Renoir**

Most municipal museums are free for anyone younger than 18 and on the first and third Sunday of every month for everyone else. At other times, admission is €4. Hours are from 10 am to 6 pm. Check with individual museums for their annual closures. Museums covered by this plan are:
- **Museum of Art and History**
- **Museum of Modern and Contemporary Art**
- **Fine Arts Museum**
- **Anatole Jakovsky International Museum of Naive Art**
- **Matisse Museum**
- **Archaeology Museum of Nice-Cimiez**
- **Terra Amata Human Palaeontology Museum**

Three municipal museums are always free: **Museum of Natural History (Musée Barla)**, **Palais Lascaris** and **Prieuré du Vieux-Logis**.

This is one of the those places where you can't help saying "Oooh" and "Ahhh" every time you turn a corner. A walk around Nice repays your time. These are just a few of the highlights:

The Promenade des Anglais

Originally a footpath built by an English clergyman (at his own expense) in 1820, Nice's famous seafront boulevard follows the curve of the Baie des Anglais. The busy two-lane road of today is always flower-bedecked and adorned with exotic palm trees. Despite the traffic, this is an essential stroll, taking you past extravagant Belle Époque buildings like the **Hotel Negresco**, with its pink domes, and Art Deco masterpieces like the **Palais de la Méditerranée**.

Place Masséna

The heart of the city center pedestrian area, the square was built in an Italian style at the beginning of the 19th century. Many of the buildings surrounding it are coated in colorful ochres or painted the Pompeian red that you will see often in Nice. Adjoining the square, the vast **Jardin Albert I** is Nice's oldest public garden. Together with the **Esplanade du Paillon** and the **Promenade du Paillon** (with hanging gardens inspired by Babylon) this forms a two-km/1.2-mile green walk from the seafront toward the hills.

Cours Saleya

In addition to the daily flower market, this is a lively and entertaining area with sidewalk cafés, overlooked by the 17th-century **Préfecture** and 18th-century **Clock Tower**. The façade of the Préfecture is lined with alternating Corinthian and Doric columns.

Lively cafés on the Cours Saleya in Nice. Office du Tourisme et des Congrès de Nice

Chapelle de la Miséricorde: A lovely Baroque church on the Cours Saleya. Golden-colored, inside and out.

Maison d'Adam et d'Eve: At the corner of the Cours Saleya and Rue de la Poissonnerie, Adam and Eve's house is typical of the painted and decorated houses you'll find throughout the *Vieille Ville*. Its façade is covered with bas reliefs in cameo tones, created in 1584.

Opéra de Nice

Built in 1885, this is an outstanding example of Belle Époque architecture on the Rue Saint François de Paule.

Cathedrale Sainte Réparate

Built in the 17th century to honor Nice's patron saint, the colorful façade of the church fills one side of Place Rossetti (a great place for ice cream, with several ice cream parlors). Beside the church is a simpler, Neoclassical 18th-century bell tower.

The War Memorial

Near the Port, on Place Guynemer, this huge monument to the 4,000 Niçois lost in WWI is carved into the flank of Castle Hill. Worth seeing for the colossal high-relief carvings by Alfred Janniot.

The Russian Orthodox Church

Nice's émigré community built a monumental church on Boulevard Tzarevitch to remind themselves of the ones they'd left behind. Made of red brick, grey marble and painted ceramics, the church has six extravagantly decorated onion domes. Inside, there are serious icons, woodcarving and frescoes.

Museums

Archaeology Museum of Nice-Cimiez: This relatively new museum adjoins the ruins of *Cemenelum*, from the first to the fourth century the Roman capital of the Alpes Maritimes. The site includes an amphitheater, public baths, paved streets and a Paleochristian group of buildings dating from the fifth century. The museum houses collections from the Bronze Age through the dark ages, including sculptures, coins, jewelry, tools, ceramics and glass. *160 Avenue des Arènes, ☎ 33 04 93 81 59 57, closed Tuesdays.*

Matisse Museum: Matisse made Nice his home from 1917 until his death in 1954. This museum has a comprehensive collection of works from all periods of his life, including all the books he illustrated. In keeping with the Fauvist artist's colorful palette, the work is housed in a 17th-century, Genoan-style mansion painted a brilliant Pompeian red. *164 Avenue des Arènes de Cimiez, ☎ 33 04 93 53 40 53, closed Tuesdays.*

Fine Arts Museum: A very good (and very big) collection of paintings from the 17th to 19th centuries, including works by Fragonard, Dufy, Sisley, Boudin, as well as major works by Ziem and Van Dongen and sculpture by Rodin and Carpeaux. The building itself, once a private mansion, built in 1878 at the height of the Belle Époque, will knock your socks off. *33 Avenue des Baumettes, ☎ 33 04 92 15 28 28, closed Mondays.*

The Marc Chagall Museum: Based on a donation by the artist, this museum was built to house Chagall's work, *Message Biblique*, which includes 17 enormous paintings as well as mosaics, tapestries, and stained glass windows. The museum also includes more than 200 preparatory sketches, 39 gouaches, 105 engravings and 215 lithographs undertaken in the course of completing his great project – which took him 30 years. This museum, the largest collection of work by Chagall under one roof, is part of France's National Museum and therefore not included in Nice's municipal museum admission program. *Avenue Dr. Ménard, corner of Boulevard de Cimiez, ☎ 33 04 93 53 87 20. Admission €5.50, open July 1 to September 30, 10 am to 6 pm and October to June, 10 am to 5 pm. Closed Tuesdays.*

THE CIMIEZ DISTRICT

If you go up Cimiez Hill to visit the Matisse Museum or the Roman ruins, take some time to walk around the Cimiez gardens and the residential streets of the quarter. During the 18th and 19th centuries, this was the summer resort for most of the crowned heads of Europe and the streets are lined with their sumptuous villas.

Prieuré du Vieux-Logis: This small treasure features a late medieval interior in a 16th-century house. The collection includes 14th- to 16th-century everyday objects. Although one of Nice's municipal museums, it has its own, very limited, hours. *59 Avenue Saint Barthélémy, ☎ 33 04 93 84 44 74. Open 3 to 5 pm, Wednesday to Saturday and one Sunday a month.*

Menton - A Town as Work of Art

The last major town on the French Riviera before the Italian border is a Baroque masterpiece. It is hard to imagine an angle from which Menton could not be painted. Many artists did paint in Menton. Yet, given the profligate way important artists of the 19th and 20th century showered the Riviera with attention, only a few – Monet, Renoir, Dufy – actually painted it. Could it be because the town is a work of art itself?

Nature and man seem to have conspired in creating a perfect composition. Squeezed between a dramatic Alpine amphitheater and the mountain-shadowed sea (the Mediterranean is an undeniably darker blue here), Menton sparkles in endless sunshine.

From the old harbor, the old town – the heart of Menton – climbs steeply up the **Colla Rogna hill**, its ochre-colored houses arranged higgledy-piggledy around streets that near the top are little more than wide staircases. About halfway up, the **Basilique Saint Michel Archange** gives Menton its striking profile. The church, set before a plaza paved with the Grimaldi coat of arms, is considered one of the best examples of Baroque architecture on the Riviera. Not far from it, the more Rococo **Chapelle des Pénitents Blancs** sits behind an ornate façade of pinnacles, friezes and garlands. Higher up, the houses are medieval and several of the narrow streets are vaulted.

If the old town is a treasure trove of medieval and Baroque monuments, the "new town" is a bijou example of Belle Époque style and finesse. Like Nice and the surrounding area, it was "discovered" by wealthy English and Imperial Russian tourists from the mid-19th century onward. They filled the new town with their mansions and "follies" and gave the community fabulous

Along the pedestrian St. Michel in Menton, orange trees shade the walkers.
© Komenda, OT Menton

public gardens full of palms and exotic plants. Where else would you find Seville orange trees lining the avenues as shade trees? Visit Menton at the right time of year and breakfast drops right into your hand.

COCTEAU'S WEDDING ROOM

Separation of Church and State is so strong in France that, regardless of religious affiliation, only civil marriages are legal. In practice, French couples follow a quick legal ceremony at the town hall, with a more traditional religious ceremony afterwards. Every Mairie and Hôtel de Ville in France has a nicely decorated room for these civil unions. In Menton, the decoration of the wedding room is extraordinary. During 1957 and 1958, at the invitation of the mayor, who was apparently a pal, artist Jean Cocteau covered the walls and ceiling with romantic modern frescoes. The paintings depict eternal lovers, she wearing a traditional Mentonaise "capeline" and he in a Mediterranean fishing cap. Everyone who gets married in Menton uses the room – and that includes foreign visitors. Apparently, it is particularly popular with Japanese couples.

Cocteau's mural in the Menton Town Hall. © Ajuria, OT Menton

You can visit the Wedding Room to see the frescoes even when a wedding is taking place. *(Salle des Mariages, Mairie, Place Ardoïno, ☎ 33 04 92 10 50 00, open weekdays, 8:30 am to 12:30 pm and 1:30 to 5:30 pm. Admission €1.50).*

The Grimaldi Connection

In a history shared with other towns of the region, Menton was controlled in the Middle Ages by the Grimaldis, the ruling princes of Monaco (who bought it in the mid-14th century from the Ventimiglia, a Genoese family). The relationship endured here much later than elsewhere and the Princes of Monaco kept a summer palace in Menton well into the 19th century. In 1848, the town proclaimed itself a free city under the protection of Sardinia.

Then, in 1860, Menton joined other towns (including Nice) in a famous plebiscite and voted to join France under Emperor Napoléon III. It was only then that the Monegasque ruler, Charles III, finally relinquished all claim to the town and Menton joined the Alpes-Maritimes.

The connection with Monaco is still relatively strong. At night, the lights of the Principality blaze across the bay to the west. Monaco is only a 15-minute drive away and even less on the frequent local train service.

Menton

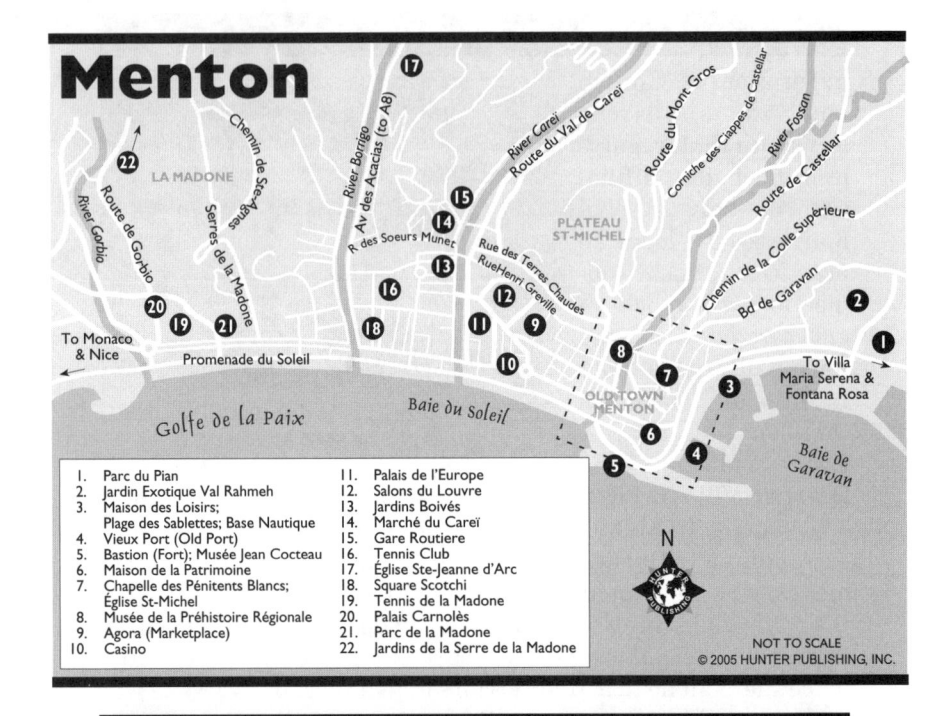

Map Legend:
1. Parc du Pian
2. Jardin Exotique Val Rahmeh
3. Maison des Loisirs; Plage des Sablettes; Base Nautique
4. Vieux Port (Old Port)
5. Bastion (Fort); Musée Jean Cocteau
6. Maison de la Patrimoine
7. Chapelle des Pénitents Blancs; Église St-Michel
8. Musée de la Préhistoire Régionale
9. Agora (Marketplace)
10. Casino
11. Palais de l'Europe
12. Salons du Louvre
13. Jardins Boivés
14. Marché du Careï
15. Gare Routière
16. Tennis Club
17. Église Ste-Jeanne d'Arc
18. Square Scotchi
19. Tennis de la Madone
20. Palais Carnolès
21. Parc de la Madone
22. Jardins de la Serre de la Madone

AUTHOR'S TIP

Monaco is an expensive and, in my view, stuffy place to stay. It's a bit like Geneva-on-Sea. But, if you think you might break the bank at Monte Carlo, why not stay in Menton and just pop over to try the Casino. It costs between €10 and €20 to get in, plus however much you throw away on chips. Built in 1878 by architect Charles Garnier, who also designed the original Paris Opera (now called the Opera Garnier), it is an extravaganza of Baroque/Rococo flash. The building, which also includes the Monte Carlo opera, has an atrium paved in marble and surrounded by 28 Ionic columns in onyx. The gaming rooms feature stained glass, bas reliefs, sculptures and brass lamps. Black tie is no longer required, though jacket and tie are required for men. The Casino is open daily, including Sunday, to anyone over 18 (ID/proof of age is required). Some of the rooms require an application and invitation.

For More Information: *Monte Carlo Casino, Place du Casino, MC 98000, Monaco, ☎ (377) 92 16 20 00, fax (377) 92 16 38 62, www.casino-monte-carlo.com.*

History - The Belle Époque & After

From 1880 to the First World War, Menton was a popular winter resort for the wealthy. They changed the face of the town, building ornate villas and hotels, taking advantage of the mild climate to create extravagant gardens (most of which are musts for visiting horticulturalists today). Because of the amphitheater of mountains that shields it from harsh northern weather – and particularly the Mistral – Menton has virtually no winter. It is possible to swim in the sea here all year-round.

Despite the damage of two world wars (the town was the only one in France occupied by the Italians) Menton managed to hold onto much of its original charm. The municipal market, the sunny, pedestrian Rue Saint Michel, the gardens and the lovely harbors and seafront all add to its considerable appeal. It is well located for watersports, for hiking (from easy rambles to strenuous hikes into the mountains), and for boating, and it has a good range of small but pretty public and private beaches.

The climate of Menton is perfect for citrus growing and in recent times, the local government has supported the restoration of citrus cultivation. Thousands of trees have been planted and the area produces more than 50 tons of fruit a year. Of those, about 17 tons of Menton lemons are supplied to France's top restaurants and, in a marketing success story, Menton lemons are close to receiving an AOC label from the French government. To celebrate, Menton's Lemon Festival is held for 15 days in February and March when the fruit ripens (see *Festivals and Fêtes*, page 341). During the festival, every open space is decorated with huge sculptures and works of art composed of lemons and oranges.

Getting Here

Menton is about 30 km/18½ miles from Nice on the A8 and the N7. A taxi from the airport costs between €80 and €90.

By Bus: Rapides Côte d'Azur Est *(RCA –* ☎ *33 04 97 00 07 00)* operates a bus service from Nice Airport, leaving hourly between 9 am and 9:15 pm, year-round. Buses (Route Number 110) leave from Terminal 1 and Terminal 2, Stand 2, and take an hour and 15 minutes to reach Menton, traveling through Monte Carlo along the way. The normal fare is €16.10 one-way, €26 round-trip.

By Train: The town is on the main coastal rail route to Italy. During the summer, there is **TGV** service directly to Menton. In the winter, take the TGV to Nice and change there for a local **SNCF** train to Gare de Menton.

Getting Around

Menton is small enough so you can reach most places on foot. A **bus** service, **Transports Urbains Mentonnaise** *(*☎ *33 04 93 35 93 60)* operates buses to outlying districts and nearby communities from the bus station on Avenue de Sospel. **Taxi** stands are located at the railroad station, the Mairie, the Casino, Port Garavan and the Hospital. **Bicycles** can be rented from **L'Escale Deux Roues**, *105 Avenue de Sospel,* ☎ *33 04 93 28 86 05.*

Sightseeing in Menton

Tourist Information: Office de Tourisme, 8 Avenue Boyer, BP239, 06506 Menton, ☎ 33 04 92 41 76 76, fax 33 04 92 41 76 78, tourisme@menton.fr, www.villedementon.com. Museums are open year-round, 10 am to noon and 2 to 6 pm; closed Tuesdays and holidays.

The Palais Carnolès

Built in 1717 as a summer palace for the Grimaldis of Monaco, the building's splendor gave it the title of Mini-Versailles. Today it houses Menton's **Musée des Beaux-Arts**, with a solid collection of contemporary art, as well as paintings going back to the 13th century. It is surrounded by one of Menton's classic gardens, full of palms and citrus trees. *3 Avenue de la Madone, ☎ 33 04 93 35 49 71, fax 33 04 92 10 05 40. Admission free.*

The Bastion & the Musée Jean Cocteau

A small fortress on the port, built in the early 17th century to defend the town, the Bastion was restored and redecorated in the 1950s to house works by Cocteau. The artist himself was involved in the restoration, in keeping with the Riviera's tradition of artists founding small, personal art museums. Work includes drawings, tapestries, watercolors, pastels, ceramics, faiences and mosaics made of pebbles. *Vieux Port, ☎ 33 04 93 57 72 30. Admission €3, free on the first Sunday of the month.*

Basilique Saint Michel Archange

The façade of the basilica that towers over the town was renovated in the 19th century, its simplicity concealing the explosion of Baroque decoration inside. Started in 1640, the church took several

The Bastion, Menton
© Ajuria, OT Menton

centuries to complete. More than 100,000 visitors a year come to see its exquisite interior. It is set on the Parvis, a public square paved with a pebble mosaic of the Grimaldi coat of arms. After visiting the church, continue uphill to the **Chapelle des Penitents Blancs**, which retains its more highly decorated Baroque exterior.

The Mentonese Faiences

If you are interested in Faience ware, this small museum may be of interest. 14 Promenade du Val de Menton. Open Monday to Friday.

Villages Perchées of the Mentonnaise Riviera

Menton is linked by dozens of footpaths to at least four nearby hilltop villages. Set on the crests of the mountains that encircle the town, they offer fascinating glimpses into the past – from Roman chapels to Baroque churches and from medieval seigneurial castles through to modern fortifications.

Trails range from leisurely walks to strenuous hikes, opening up to breathtaking views. The paths are well-worn and once you arrive you won't be alone. Most of these little hamlets are full of art galleries, artists' studios and restaurants.

The closest are **Gorbio**, **Castellar** and **Roquebrune**, all of which can be reached within an afternoon. Castellar, is about an hour from Menton over paths first blazed by English tourists in the 19th century. It is a meeting place for both the GR52 and the GR1. Its lovely yellow palace was the Baroque seat of the the Lascaris, a Genoese family who once ruled here.

The farthest village is also the highest. **Sainte Agnès**, about 10 km/6.2 miles away, is the highest hilltop village on the Riviera. It sits 800 m/2,625 feet above sea level, with visibility along vast stretches of the coast and deep into Italy. Sainte Agnès' panoramic views give it another, somewhat dubious distinction. It is one of the defensive points of the **Maginot Line**. The heavy fortifications of that 20th-century exercise in futility can be visited.

Information and walking maps for these villages are available from the Menton Tourist Office (page 330).

The Gardens

Almost anything will grow in Menton, a fact not lost on those keen gardeners, the English, when they "colonized" the Riviera in the 19th century. Besides several free public gardens, a number of specialist gardens of particular interest to amateur botanists can be visited. As a group, Menton's gardens are a considerable asset.

La serre de la Madone, Menton. OT Menton

Jardin de la Villa Maria Serena: The gardens surround a villa built in 1880 by Charles Garnier, architect of the Paris Opera. Famous for being the most temperate garden in France, it is full of exotic tropical and subtropical plants, including a rare dragon tree from the Canary Islands. The garden overlooks Menton and the *Vieille Ville*, with splendid views. *21 Promenade Reine Astrid, ☎ 33 04 92 10 33 66, fax 33 04 93 28 46 85. Guided visits only. Admission €5.*

Jardin Botanique Exotique du Val Rahmeh: Created in 1905 by Percy Radcliffe, a British plant collector, this is now the Mediterranean office of the French Museum of Natural History. The garden includes a large number of edible plants and more than 700 species of vegetables. It specializes in aromatic herbs and shrubs. One specimen, *Sophora toromiro*, is an almost mythical Easter Island tree and is believed to be the only live specimen of this plant in the world. *Avenue Saint-Jacques, ☎ 33 04 93 35 86 72, fax 33 04 93 28 89 75. Open 10 am to 12:30 pm and 3 to 6 pm from May 1 to September 30, closing one hour earlier from October through April. Admission €4.*

La Serre de la Madone: Designed between 1919 and 1939 by Lawrence Johnston, who also designed the English garden at Hidcote Manor. An exceptional botanical collection that includes many one-of-a-kind specimens. It was officially classified as a historic monument in the 1990s. *74 Route du Val de Gorbio, ☎/fax 33 04 93 57 73 90. Daily tours led by the gardeners at 2:30 in February and March, 2:30 and 4:30 in April and May, 10 am and 4 pm in June and September, 10 am and 5 pm in July and August. Admission €8.*

Fontana Rosa: Created in the 1920s by Spanish novelist Blasco Ibañez, this Spanish-style garden features ceramics dedicated to various important writers. Benches, pergolas, ponds and ceramic columns are scattered among the vividly colored plants. *Avenue Blasco Ibañez, ☎ 33 04 92 10 33 66, fax 33 04 93 28 46 85. Guided tours by reservation from Service du Patrimoine, €5.*

Parc du Pian: Seven acres of olive trees, 530 trees in all, some of which may be more than 1,000 years old, arranged on terraces overlooking the sea. This is a popular place for Sunday strolls. *Avenue Blasco Ibañez, open every day, free.*

Spanish ceramic follies at Fontana Rosa. OT Menton

Le Plateau Saint Michel: A fragrant forest of elderly olives, pines, eucalyptus, mimosas and heather on a plateau overlooking Menton. If you head uphill, virtually all roads lead here. From the Rue des Terres Chaudes, take the Escaliers des Rigaudis (steep, winding steps) or the Sentier du Plateau Saint Michel. Great for the viewpoints; bring your camera. *Open everyday, free.*

La Citronneraie: The lemon grove is a misnomer for this hillside grove created by farmers hundreds of years ago. It actually contains 200 olive trees at least 600 years old. Three hundred and fifty fruit trees were added in the 1950s. Now the grove contains kumquats, citrons, pink grapefruit, lemons, oranges, mandarins and clementines. Visitor information from the Tourist Office.

Private Gardens: In addition to this selection of public gardens, several important private gardens can be visited by arrangement with the owners. Information about visits to **Jardin des Colombieres**, **Le Clos du Peyronnet** and **Le Jardin de l'Esquinade** is available from the Tourist Office.

Worth a Side-Trip
Biot

Biot is yet another impossibly pretty medieval perched village, just back from the coast above Antibes-Juan les Pins. It's circled by forest paths that are accessible year-round.

Once the property of the Knights Templar and the Chevaliers of Malta, its vieille ville is a warren of steep, narrow lanes, tunnels and steps. The Rue du Templiers is particularly atmospheric.

Long before its involvement with crusading knights, Biot (founded about 165 BC) was an important source of glass and ceramics, an industry practiced from ancient times right into the modern day. Go for lunch in one of several excellent restaurants and spend the rest of the day wandering around the many glassworks or verreries. **La Verrerie de Biot**, founded in the 1950s, is a large complex at the base of the town where you can visit a gallery, see glass being blown, take lessons and, of course, shop. *(La Verrerie de Biot, 5 Chemin Combes, Biot, ☎ 33 04 93 65 03 00, verrerie@verreriebiot.com, www.verreriebiot.com.)*

You can tell when work has been bought in Biot by the rustic, slightly blue and bubbly glass characteristic of local makers. If you find La Verrierie de Biot a little too commercial, there are at least seven other master glassmakers, many glass galleries and several potteries in Biot. Some of the best include:

- **Verrerie du Val de Pome**, *Chemin du Val de Pome,* ☎ *33 04 93 65 03 78.*
- **Verrerie du Vieux Moulin**, Route de la Mer, ☎ 33 04 93 65 01 14.
- **Verrerie Silice Creation**, *173 Chemin des Combes,* ☎ *33 04 93 65 10 25.*
- **Verrerie Saba**, *407 Chemin des Près.* ☎ *33 04 93 65 52 99.*

- **Verrerie du Village**, *Rue saint Sébastien*, ☎ *33 04 93 65 06 50*.
- **Verrerie Farinelli**, *465 Route de la Mer (studio and shop)* ☎ *33 04 93 65 17 29 and 24 Rue St Sébastien (shop)*, ☎ *33 04 93 65 01 89*.
- **Verrerie Luzoro**, *1520 Route de la Mer*, ☎ *33 04 93 65 62 18*.

Southeast of the village, near the Verrerie de Biot, is the **Musée National Fernand Leger** *(Chemin du Val de Pome, 06410 Biot,* ☎ *33 04 92 91 50 30, fax 33 04 92 91 50 31, www.musee-fernandleger.fr; closed Tuesdays; admission €4, students 18-25, €2.60, under 18 free)*. This contains more than 300 works by the artist, left to the state by his widow, including paintings, drawings, tapestries and, of particular local interest, ceramics and mosaics, including a two-storey-tall mosaic celebrating sports motifs that was created for the stadium in Hanover.

Getting Here: Biot is about eight km (five miles) above Antibes-Juan les Pins. From Antibes take the RN7 east and turn left on the Route de la Mer, signposted for Biot, Valbonne and Grasse.

More Information: Office Municipal de Tourisme, Maison du Tourisme, 46, Rue St Sébastien, ☎ 33 04 93 65 78 00, fax 33 04 93 65 78 04, tourisme@biot.fr, www.biot.fr.

Grasse

Perched in the hills above Cannes, Grasse was a winter resort of royalty. Queen Victoria spent several winters here at the Grand Hotel or on the estates of the Rothschild family. The town, which has a compact *Vieille Ville* and a 12th-century cathedral (restored in the 17th century), is interesting on two counts.

Firstly, in the Middle Ages, it was a tiny republic, ruled by a council and entering into treaties with Italian city-states, including Pisa and Genoa. It had trade relations with Cannes, exchanging soap, oil and tanned leather for fresh hides and weapons.

Secondly, since the late 16th century and continuing into modern times, it has been the most important maker of floral essences for the French perfume industry. In spring and summer, Grasse is surrounded by flowers, all heading for distillation into concentrated essences. Fragonard and Molinard still make perfumes in the town, though most of the essences are sent to the perfumers of Paris.

You can learn about perfume making at the **Fragonard Museum** as well as the **Fragonard** and **Molinard perfumeries**.

Grasse is located near the GR51, and provides good access to the southern reaches of the Pre-Alps. It is at the heart of some very good hiking territory. There is also a launching site for paragliding and hang-gliding enthusiasts just outside of the town. (See *Adventures*, page 379.)

Getting Here: The town is directly north of Cannes on the **N85**. From either the Estérel to the west or towns to the east, take the **A8** to exit 42, direction Cannes-Grasse, and then the N85 to Grasse. Regular buses serve Grasse from both Nice and Cannes bus stations. From Nice center, take bus route number 500; from Cannes, route number 610.

More Information: Office de Tourisme, Place du Cours Honoré Cresp, 06130, Grasse, ☎ 33 04 93 36 03 56, info@grasse-riviera.com, www.grasse-riviera.com/en.

DID YOU KNOW?

Perfumerie, which is today Grasse's main industry, came to town by chance. For hundreds of years, the town had specialized in tanning leathers and in making fine gloves for the aristocracy. In the 16th century, perfumed gloves were suddenly all the rage. The tanners and glove makers learned to make the scents they needed to treat the gloves, making the perfumeries of Grasse among the most important in the world, almost by accident.

Èze

This Riviera village has its feet in the sand and its head in the clouds. Spread across all three of the Corniches de la Riviera, Èze Bord de Mer is a beach resort on the Corniche Inférieure between Nice and Monaco, with pine-shaded shingle beaches, wooded paths, villas and gardens. The music group U2 have a house here and, if you drop by La Cigale for a drink, you might run into a bandmember.

Higher up, south of (but towering over) the Moyenne Corniche, the 14th-century *village perchée* of Èze sits like an eagle's nest, strange and isolated on a peak 427 m/1,500 feet above the Mediterranean. Originally a Ligurian fortress, the village became a lookout for the Phocaens, the Romans and the Saracens before falling into the hands of the Counts of Provence. Much of its medieval character remains, inside the walls, along the tightly packed spiral of ancient houses. The town can only be entered through a double-fortified, machicolated gate. At the very top of the town, at the center of an exotic garden, the ruins of an ancient castle offer the best panoramic views – on clear days you can see Corsica. For more than a century, Èze has sheltered artists and writers. The **Frederick Nietzche footpath** is said to be where the philopher walked as he conceived the third section of his masterpiece, *Thus Spake Zarathustra*.

Èze continues upward to the heights of the Grande Corniche, through parks and paths that rise to the **Justice Plateau**, at 1,400 m/4,590 feet, a balcony over the sea. In all, the town maintains 30 paths and forest roads between its three levels. It's a hiker's paradise and a mountain-biking center along the Col d'Èze. You can learn escalade on one of several cliffs in the upper park (information, ☎ 33 4 93 41 17 20). And if you are an experienced paraglider or hang-glider, **Mont Bastide**, above the town is a recognized departure site (see *Adventures*, page 379).

Proximity to Nice, only a short bus or commuter rail ride away, makes Èze handy for a really nice "away day." A beach mattress and lunch on one of the private beaches is reasonably priced. The upper village is full of art galleries, a few diverting little boutiques and several places to have light meals or snacks while enjoying the sensational views.

Getting Here: The town is a 20-minute bus ride from Nice Bus Station. Take RCA bus, route number 100 – Nice-Menton (☎ 33 04 93 85 61 81). It's also easily reached by SNCF rail from Nice Station, just a few minutes away.

More Information: Office de Tourisme, Place du Général de Gaulle, 06360 Èze Village, ☎ 33 04 93 41 26 00, fax 33 04 93 41 04 80, www.eze-riviera.com.

Mandelieu - La Napoule

Mandelieu is a small town on the edge of the Massif du Tanneron, west of Cannes, and one of the stops on the Route de Mimosa (see page 289, *The Mimosa Circuit*). A leading resort of the Belle Époque, its popularity was later overtaken by the coastal towns of the Riviera. Today, it is known for several golf courses and extensive marina facilities, but it is primarily residential.

For casual visitors, one of the main attractions is the **Chateau de la Napoule**, a castle right at the water's edge that is not at all what it seems. *(Château de La Napoule, BP 940, 06210 Mandelieu-La Napoule, ☎ 33 04 93 49 95 05, fax 33 04 92 97 62 71, message@chateau-lanapoule.com, www.chateau-lanapoule.com.)* This massive 14th-century fortress had been a ruined glass factory when, in 1918, it was somewhat imaginatively restored and rebuilt by an American sculptor, Henry Clews, with the help of his wealthy architect wife. Two towers, Saracen and Romanesque, were added to the complex, as was a turreted gatehouse and various ramparts and terraces. The castle reflects the Clews' eclectic tastes rather than a truly historical restoration. Many of its turrets and walls are decorated with the artists' grotesquely imagined creatures.

Today, the castle operates as an arts foundation, offering residencies to talented young artists working in dance, design, film, literature, music, theater, visual and performance arts. The grounds and gardens, Clews studio and art collection are open to the public (with guided tours throughout the year) and there is a small tea room. Perhaps the most fun is the opportunity to swim at the foot of a castle – there is a small, beach between the château and La Napoule Port.

Getting Here: About six miles (10k) west of Cannes on the **RN98** (the scenic route) or the **A8** motorway. Buses between Cannes and St. Raphael stop at La Napoule Plage.

More Information: Office de Tourisme et d'Animation de Mandelieu-La Napoule, 340 Avenue Jean Monnet, 06210 Mandelieu-La Napoule, ☎ 33 04 92 97 99 27, fax 33 04 92 97 99 57, ota@ot-mandelieu.fr, www.ot-mandelieu.fr.

Mougins

It's not surprising that Catherine Deneuve, the cool and immaculate beauty, was a regular visitor to Mougins. This little medieval village, about four miles from Cannes, is lovely in a manner that can only be described as tasteful and immaculate. Ancient houses, winding around narrow, pedestrian lanes, have been carefully and precisely restored. Unlike the wild tumbles of blooms that pour out of cachepots and window boxes elsewhere, Mougins is marked by its lush but careful floral displays, its manicured hedges. Christian Dior lived and worked here at the height of his fame and you can almost sense the scent of *Miss Dior* perfume along Mougins' well-tended lanes. This is the face of the Middle Ages, with its makeup intact.

Known today for its artists, its fabulous restaurants and its wonderful Automobile Museum (see below), it makes a very pleasant day out if you are visiting Cannes. Alternatively, have a quiet stay in Mougins, dipping in and out of the urbanity of Cannes, 15 minutes away.

Before it became so dainty, Mougins was the favorite haunt of some of the wild men of 20th-century art. In the 1920s, surrealist painter Francis Picabia settled there. His friends followed – Fernand Leger, Man Ray, filmmaker René Clair, Isadora Duncan, everybody's friend Jean Cocteau and Picasso. According to stories, a young Picasso painted murals and the walls of his hotel room in the 1930s. The disgruntled owner made him whitewash over them. Picasso returned, nevertheless, to spend the last 15 years of his life here.

The **Museum of Photography** *(Porte Sarrazine, Mougins Village, ☎ 33 04 93 75 85 67, fax 33 04 93 90 15 15; open Wednesday to Saturday 10 am to noon and 2 to 6 pm, Sunday 2 to 6 pm, summers until 8 pm)* is a tribute to the town's most famous artist resident, with photo portraits of Picasso by his greatest photographer contemporaries.

Picasso lived next door to **Notre Dame de Vie**, a 12th-century chapel set on a particularly striking avenue of tall, straight cypress trees at a site once sacred to the goddess Diana. In a poignant historical footnote, the chapel was once considered a "sanctuary of respite" connected with stillborn babies. Bereaved parents would bring their dead child to the church, sometimes traveling great distances. During the Mass, the baby was considered to be "alive" long enough to be baptised.

Modern Mougins is still an artists' colony with dozens of studios and galleries tucked in among the lanes and stone cottages. Le Lavoir, near the main entrance to the village, is a free showcase for young talent.

About a mile outside of the village is the **Musée de L'Automobiliste** *(Aire des Bréguières, 06250 Mougins, ☎ 33 04 93 69 27 80, fax 33 04 93 46 01 36, musauto@club-internet.fr, www.musauto.fr, open 10 am to 6 pm, October to March, and to 7 pm, April to September).* This is an absolute must for anyone who's ever fantasized taking the wheel of a classic Bugatti, a Hispano Suiza, a Rolls Royce Phantom I or Silver Wraith, a Delaunay-Belleville, or any number of classic, 20th-century racing cars. The museum, in a dramatic modern building, has an enormous collection. A few cars can be rented (with a professional driver) for weddings and other grand entrances.

Although the village is tiny, the municipality of Mougins actually covers an area larger than Cannes. Town fathers have resisted urbanization with strict limits on development. As a result, the village is surrounded by a sea of green. There are gentle walks along marked botanical trails in the **Valmasque Forest Park**. **L'Etang de Fontmerle**, on the edge of Valmasque, supports an unusual variety of giant Asian lotus, unique in Europe.

Getting Here: Mougins is about four miles north of the A8 Motorway, Cannes-Mougins exit. Both the **Sillages** *(☎ 33 04 92 38 96 38)* and **Rapides Côte d'Azur** *(☎ 33 04 93 36 08 43)* run bus services from Cannes.

More Information: Mougins Tourist Office, 15 Avenue Jean Charles Mallet, 06250 Mougins, ☎ 33 04 93 75 87 67, fax 33 04 92 92 04 03, tourisme@mougins-coteazur.org, www.mougins-coteazur.org.

La Turbie

This village of about 1,000 people, high up on the Grande Corniche, surveys the whole coast from an altitude of 480 m/1,570 feet. The view of Monte Carlo, lit up at night, is one of the great sights of the Riviera and watching the Monte Carlo fireworks competitions from here is sublime.

The views were the unexpected bonus I discovered when I came to see **La Trophée des Alpes**, the most prominent structure on the entire Grande Corniche. The Emperor Augustus, who built the monument that rises over this town, probably chose the spot for its outlook. What better way to demonstrate that Rome reigned over all it surveyed. The "trophy" was built as a kind of macho demonstration of pride and power.

After the death of Julius Caesar, the always troublesome tribes of the Maritime Alps escaped Roman domination. Although the Romans held onto most of Gaul and Spain, the Ligurians of this area continually interfered with the business of Empire on the Via Julia Augusta between those provinces and Italy. To put an end to these troubles, Augustus set out to extend Rome's authority over the Alps. It took nine years and many campaigns. Historians believe that Augustus may have led most of the campaigns personally. When the region was finally subdued, he built the

Trophée des Alpes on a pass that straddles the Via Julia Augusta as a visible sign of Imperial power. Originally 50 m/165 feet tall, the ruined white stone tower still stands an impressive 30 m/98 feet – almost as tall as a 10-story building. Inside, the names of the 44 conquered Ligurian families are carved in a surprisingly modern looking script. What I found even more surprising is that the names of these ancient tribes are so contemporary they could be on a cast list of *The Sopranos* – Bruni, Vindelici, Rugusci, Salassi, Brigiani, Brodionti and Trumpilini among them.

Understandably, this is a busy little town. In the summer, avoid the traffic jams by arriving early enough to have breakfast in one of the cafés. At other times of the year, La Turbie is a good place to take a break during a drive above the coast on the Grande Corniche.

Getting Here: The village is 18 km/11 miles from Nice on the Grande Corniche.

More Information: Mairie de la Turbie, ☎ 33 04 92 41 51 61, fax 33 04 92 41 13 99, info@ville-la-turbie.fr, www.ville-la-turbie.fr.

■ Festivals & Fêtes

Antibes-Juan Les Pins

Jazz à Juan: Having begun more than 43 years ago, this annual festival claims to be France's oldest celebration of jazz and what better place to hold it than the town where the Jazz Age was invented. The festival is usually held the third week in July, and attracts top jazz and contemporary musicians. Performances are held in the Pinède Gould, a pinewood named for an American millionaire who donated it and which gave its name to the village of Juan les Pins. Tickets and information are available from the Antibes-Juan Les Pins tourist office (page 383).

Festival Pyromélodique: Every year during August, Europe's top fireworks makers and artists gather to show off their works in a series of *son et lumières*, combining fireworks displays with music, along the beaches and bays of Antibes-Juan les Pins. Thousands line the shore and pack the restaurants to watch. Dates and beach locations are available from the Antibes-Juan les Pins tourist office (page 383).

Feu d'Artifice at the Fireworks Festival in Antibes. OT Antibes

The International Festival of Underwater Pictures: The *Festival Mondial de l'Image Sous-Marine* is a feast of all kinds of underwater artwork, a celebration, competition and trade showcase all rolled into one. Films, reportages, documentries, slide shows, paintings and photography are exhibited and judged in a variety of competitions. Commercial exhibitors offer books, travel, and all kinds of underwater photography and diving equipment. The festival takes place at the Palais des Congrès, Juan-les-Pins, in September or October and is usually organized around a theme. In 2004, for example, the theme was Polynesia. *Festival Mondial de l'Image Sous-Marine, 62 Avenue des Pins du Cap, 06160 Antibes,* ☎ *33 04 93 61 45 45, fax 33 04 93 67 34 93, spondyle@wanadoo.fr, www.underwater-festival.com.*

Nice

Carnival: As if you needed an excuse to come to Nice, the Carnival is the best one I can think of for combining some Alpine skiing in the Haut Pays Niçois with a February visit to the city. The Carnival has been going on since 1873 and is the biggest winter celebration on the Riviera. It attracts more than 1.2 million people to the city for two weeks of madness, including processions featuring hundreds of "Big Heads" (papier maché caricatures), decorated floats, flower parades, evening torchlight flower parades, flower wars, tons of confetti, rock and techno concerts, hundreds of troupes of entertainers and brilliant fireworks. Each year the name chosen for the King of the Carnival becomes the theme set to inspire the float makers and designers. Themes can be bizarre – in 2005, for example, "King of the Deranged Climate" was

Theme float at the Carnival of Nice. Office du Tourisme et des Congrès de Nice, A. Hanel

the theme! For more information, contact the Nice Tourist Office (page 385).

Nice Jazz Fest: If you are a jazz fan, you have plenty of options in July on the Riviera. Like Antibes, Nice also has a major jazz festival that has been going on for decades. Held in Cimiez Park and the Roman Amphitheater, it attracts 45,000 jazz buffs for eight days of music, 75 concerts, 500 musicians. Three stages are kept busy from 7 pm to midnight every night of the festival. Spectators wander among them – the Roman amphitheater, the Matisse Stage and the Cimiez Gardens, sampling creole food in the restaurant, or trying local specialties at various food stalls. Meanwhile, all over Nice, an alternative festival fills the city with music all day long until 6 pm. *Nice Jazz Fest, Viviane Sicnasi Promotion, 28 Avenue*

Marceau, 75008 Paris, fax 33 01 47 23 07 58, V.S.P@nicejazzfest.com, www.nicejazzfest.com.

Menton

Fête du Citron: Held in February and March, this 15-day celebration of the Menton lemon has been going on since the 1930s. Festivities include a parade with citrus-decorated floats, giant designs and sculptures made of citrus fruits and carnival-style partying all over the town. Information from the tourist office.

Fête des Bazaïs: If you are around Menton in August, ask at the tourist office about this ancient, traditional event. Said to have originated in the Middle Ages, the "feast" gathers the whole town on Henry Bennet Quay around a giant cauldron of bean soup into which all kinds of vegetables and bits of meat are stirred. According to tradition, the event originated when Barbary pirates were besieging the town and causing a famine among the population, already decimated by plague. The survivors made a giant cauldron of soup, everyone contributing all the food they had left to the pot. Seeing this, the pirates imagined that despite their long siege, the townsfolk still had abundant supplies. Discouraged, they fled.

■ Shopping

Cannes

Shop hounds won't be bored in Cannes. People say **La Croisette** is a sort of Faubourg St. Honoré south. Together with **Rue d'Antibes**, which runs parallel to it, practically all the major Paris designers, jewelers and purveyors of luxury goods are represented. Of the two streets, La Croisette tends to have more of the internationally established names – jewelers Bulgari, Cartier, Chanel, Chopard and Fred; fashion designers Christian Lacroix, Dior, Escada, Fendi, Jean-Paul Gaultier, Valentino and Celine, with leathers from Longchamp and Louis Vuitton. Shops on the Rue d'Antibes are no less elegant and expensive but may be less well known. Between the two avenues are small cross-streets and pedestrian walks lined with dozens of smart boutiques. perfumeries, florists, pâtisseries and salons de thé.

Rue Meynadier marks the border between Le Suquet and modern Cannes. It's a pedestrian district for neighborhood shopping where you can find clothing shops, delicatessens, wine merchants and shops dealing in Provencal specialities – food, scents, herbs, fabrics, arts and crafts.

Market Days

- Every morning – **Forville** holds a traditional *Marché Provençal* in a covered *halle*. This is Cannes' main daily market, held two blocks north of the Hotel de Ville on the **Rue Félix Faure**. It changes to a flea market on Mondays. At **Place Gambetta**, there is a smaller covered market in the center of the square. One block north of Rue d'Antibes, east of the train station. Closed on Mondays. On **Allées de la Liberté**, every morning there is a flower market under the trees.

- Mondays – A *marché brocante* (flea market) takes place from 8 am to 6 pm at **Forville**.
- Saturdays and the first and third Sunday of the month – A *marché brocante* (flea market), takes place from 8 am to 6 pm under the trees along the **Allées de la Liberté**.
- Saturday and Sunday – Paintings and arts and crafts along the **Allées de la Liberté** from 9 am to 6 pm.

In Antibes

Small shops in the *Vieille Ville* are good places to look for traditional Provençal products, especially the wonderfully scented olive oil-based soaps and the colorful table linens. Just for the pleasure, fill your arms with flowers at one of the many market stalls; you can't find fresher roses anywhere. Antibes has a busy covered market, the ***Marché Provençal***, that is fun and very photogenic. It's on the Cours Masséna in front of the Mairie. Look for spices and scents to take home as well as the sorts of kitchen gadgets, sauce mix packets, sweets and convenience foods that no French housewife could live without.

Market Days

- Tuesday and Sunday mornings, September through May; every morning June through August – fresh fruit, vegetables, fish, flowers and regional products at the *Marché Provençal*.
- Sunday afternoons – arts and crafts, *Marché Provençal*.
- Thursdays – clothing on **Rue Fontvieille**, behind the post office.
- Thursday and Saturdays – all day, bric a brac on **Place Jacques Audiberti**.

In Nice

Nice is one of France's largest cities and a vacation destination for well-heeled visitors for more than 200 years. As you might expect, it is paradise for shoppers. Shops are usually open from Monday to Saturday, 9 am to noon and from 2 to 7 pm. Shops in the pedestrian areas as well as the big department stores along **Rue Masséna** stay open through lunch, from 9 am to 7 pm. The shopping center, **Carrefour Nice**, on **Boulevard Delfino**, as well as hypermarkets on the outskirts, sometimes stay open to 9 or 10 pm. Sunday openings are still very uncommon in France, except for small food stores and bakeries (what would the French do without their fresh-baked bread and Sunday lunch patisserie?).

There are several good shopping areas:
- Luxury shops and designer boutiques are concentrated in the town center pedestrian zone, near **Place Masséna**.
- **L'Avenue Jean Médecin** and the roads leading off it are lively and commercial.
- **Avenue de la République**, across from the Palais des Congrès et du Tourisme, is a good area for dipping in and out of boutiques of all kinds.
- Stylish (and pricey) antique dealers can be found on **Rue Ségurane**, near the port.
- The **Cours Saleya**, the most charming and colorful shopping area of the *Vieille Ville*, is the site of one of the best daily markets on the Riviera (see *Markets*, below). Elsewhere in the *Vieille Ville*, at least 600 shops are tucked in among the lanes and "ruelles."

The Markets

The **Marché aux Fleurs** is a huge and fabulous flower market held Tuesday through Saturday, from 6 am to 5:30 pm, along the **Cours Saleya**. Just about every artist of note in the 19th and 20th centuries has painted it. If you visit Nice, don't miss it. On Mondays, when there is no flower market, the Cours Saleya is taken over by the **Marché à la Brocante**, a flea market, held from 8 am to 5 pm. Another good flea market, **Les Puces de Nice**, is open Tuesday to Saturday, from 10 am to 6 pm along the **Place Robilante**, near the port. If you like poking around in flea markets, you might also like **Le Paradise de l'Occasion** (literally second-hand paradise), a store on Boulevard Raimbaldi (☎ 33 04 93 92 29 98). And take your camera to the **Marché aux Poissons**, the fish market, **Place Saint François**, 6 am to 1 pm every morning except Monday.

Other Nice markets of interest include:
- **Antique Books** – Place du Palais de Justice, every Saturday.
- **Artists Market** – Place du Palais de Justice, every second Saturday of the month.
- **Stamps, postcards and coins** – Square Durandy, Sunday mornings. Pins and telephone cards are among the more modern collectibles.

In Menton

Most shopping is along the broad, pedestrian **Rue Saint Michel**, which is lined with shops and restaurants and busy every day. The town also has a covered market, **Halles Municipales**, between the old port and the old town.

Where to Stay

Deluxe

CANNES: Some hotels are so wreathed in legend that they are lifted above the field of competition and just entering them makes you feel like a legend yourself.

It isn't a question of price. Although the first two hotels aren't cheap, there are many far more expensive hotels (some costing upwards of €1,000 per night) along the Riviera. It isn't even a question of luxury and glamor – neither of these hotels, though well outfitted, tops their class. It's more about story and romance, about history and spirit. If you haven't got a taste for those, you need read no further.

HOTEL PRICE CHART	
Rates are per room based on double occupancy.	
	Under €55
€	€56-€96
€€	€97-€135
€€€	€136-€195
€€€€	Over €195

☆☆☆☆ **The Hotel Negresco** *(37 Promenade des Anglais, 06000 Nice,* ☎ *0 4 93 16 64 00, fax 04 93 88 35 68, reservations@hotel-negresco.com, www.hotel-negresco-nice.com/index-gb.htm, €€€€).* Built in 1912, the Negresco was classified as a National Historic Monument in 1974, and a National Historic Building in 2003. If you have seen the classic picture of Nice – the view of the Promenade des Anglais with its palm trees and flowers – then you have seen this hotel. It's one of the best-known Belle Époque hotels in the world. From the pink domes of its roof to its ruffly white façade, the hotel oozes extravagance. The current owner has filled its public rooms, several of which are extraordinary, with five centuries of French paintings and artwork – classical and historic paintings, royal portraits and 20th-century works by Salvador Dali and Nikki de Saint Phalle. In keeping with Nice's important place in the jazz scene, there's a sensational portrait of Louis Armstrong. The rooms, which have been individually decorated in styles that range from Louis XIII to Art Deco, have the usual modern conveniences, carefully concealed among the fripperies and furbelows. Across the street, the hotel's private beach includes rows of immaculate blue and white beach chairs and umbrellas. The few complaints we've heard were from people who prefered antiseptic modern perfection to regal character. This is a grand dowager of a hotel. You can save 30 to 40% off the standard room price by booking through an online travel service. But, if you can't stay, you can always visit one of the hotel's two atmospheric bars – the English Bar and the Carousel Bar.

☆☆☆☆ **Hotel Belles Rives** *(33 Boulevard Edouard Baudoin, 06160 Juan les Pins-Cap d'Antibes,* ☎ *33 04 93 61 02 79, fax 33 04 93 67 43 51, message@bellesrives.com, www.bellesrives.com/uk, €€€€, but in the off-season, a few rooms drop down to €€).*

"We are in a perfect spot," the young American wrote in 1926. "Our big house is right on the sea and has a private beach. The casino is scarcely

100 meters away and we are looking forward to a splendid summer." The young man was F. Scott Fitzgerald and he was writing to friends about the Villa Saint Louis, a house that he and Zelda had rented in Juan that summer. A few years later, a Rumanian emigré bought the house, added a few wings and, presto, the Hotel Belles Rives was created.

The hotel exterior looks strangely like a very clean, 1930s-era apartment building plonked down on a beach. The beach itself is tiny and almost completely covered with loungers and stripey blue and white beach cushions called *matelas*. This is not a place for people who like to touch the sand (but then hardly any of the private Riviera beaches are). There is a long pier (also lined with loungers) with facilities to dock speedboats. Watersports professionals are available for waterskiing, wake boarding, parascending and diving. Recently redone in an authentic Art Deco style to reflect the hotel's heyday, the rooms have a sober, masculine luxury. A couple of nice restaurants on the beach, a flower-covered terrace and a clubby bar and there you have it. If, like me, you are a sucker for literary landmarks, it's worth trying to get a room – not all that easy since the hotel is small (45 rooms) and popular. And all bets are off during the Cannes Film Festival, the Cannes Advertising Festival and the Grand Prix de Monaco.

THE PALACE HOTELS OF CANNES

Modern Cannes began in the early 19th century as an aristocrats' playground. The first hotels, built in the 1860s, were designed to offer a level of *grand luxe* of the highest order. That objective continued into the 20th century. Today Cannes has four hotels considered above the conventional star ratings of the French tourist authorities, with a total of 1,300 luxury rooms and suites. It goes without saying that all these hotels are used to catering to executives, as well as vacationers and celebrities. So, if you are totally plugged-in and can't be separated from your e-mails and Internet, don't worry – you'll find all the electronics you need at any one of them.

Tip: For numerous reasons, not least of which are the changing vacation tastes of young European glitterati, Cannes' grand palaces have been less fully booked than they would like in recent years. Bargain packages can be found, even in the high season, so it's always worth checking, or – if you have the nerve – making an offer.

The Carlton Intercontinental *(58 La Croisette, BP155, 06400 Cannes,* ☎ *33 04 93 06 40 06, fax 33 04 94 06 40 25, cannes@interconti.com, www.cannes.interconti.com; 338 rooms and suites; open year-round, €€€€+).* With its saucily inspired domes, this is virtually a symbol of La Croisette. The simplicity of its cool, marble-columned lobby gives a sense of the accommodations – fine materials and polished surfaces, tastefully rather than extravagantly arranged. If you can, peak into the ballrooms to see where the "palace" designation comes from. Built in 1912, the hotel is regularly refurbished and has recently had a multi-million-euro facelift. There are several bars and restaurants, a private beach and pier for speedboat and water-ski enthusiasts, an aerobic gym, an indoor pool and a casino.

The Majestic Barrière *(10 La Croisette, BP 163, 06407 Cannes, ☎ 33 04 92 98 77 00, fax 33 04 93 38 97 90, majestic@lucienbarriere.com, www.lucienbarriere.com; 305 rooms and suites; closed mid-November to just after Christmas, €€€€+).* This inherits the site of The Beau Rivage, Cannes' second great luxury hotel, built in 1863. Rebuilt in an Art Deco style in 1926, it is all glamour and a favorite with movie stars during the festival. Forget the silk furnishings and crystal chandeliers in the public rooms and take in the amazing black marble bathrooms instead. The hotel's huge pool is surrounded by pink umbrellas. Owners, the Lucien Barrière chain, offer some short breaks and good value packages. It's worth checking the website.

The Hotel Martinez *(73 La Croisette, 06406 Cannes, ☎ 33 04 92 98 73 00, fax 33 04 93 39 67 82, martinez@hotel-martinez.com, www.hotel-martinez.com; 397 rooms and suites; open year-round €€€€+).* Opened in 1929, at the climax of the Roaring Twenties, the Martinez has had its ups and downs but recent refurbishment has restored it to former glories. Rooms with sea views are particularly spectacular and the hotel's restaurant, the Palme d'Or, is one of the most highly rated in Cannes.

The Noga Hilton *(50 La Croisette, BP224, 06414 Cannes, ☎ 33 04 92 99 70 00, fax 33 04 92 99 70 11, sales_cannes@hilton.com, www.hiltoncannes.com; 234 rooms; open year-round, €€€€+).* This is Cannes' newest and, within its class, least expensive of the palace hotels. It's six storeys of blue glass, modern and cool, with a rooftop pool, an underground shopping mall and large, covered parking lot. The hotel's auditorium/theater seats more than 800 people. So, between festivals, the hotel is usually busy with trade shows. Room prices vary with the view.

SAINT JEAN CAP FERRAT: The Grand Hotel du Cap Ferrat is another legendary hotel and vies with the Hotel du Cap in Cap d'Antibes, as one of the most expensive in the world *(Boulevard Géneral de Gaulle au Cap Ferrat, 06230 Saint Jean Cap Ferrat, ☎ 33 04 93 76 50 50, fax 33 04 93 76 04 52, reserv@grand-hotel-cap-ferrat.com, www.grand-hotel-cap-ferrat/com, €€€€€).* Standard rooms range in price from €580 to €1,100 per night. Parking in the covered garage is €75 a night! For that price, they throw in breakfast. You also get a perch high up on the tip of a promontory, surrounded by water on three sides, acres and acres of manicured lawns with specimen trees, an infinity pool that was once avant garde but is now de rigueur at dozens of Riviera hotels, and a private cable car, in case you want to descend to mingle with the hoi polloi. The rooms are plush and grand but the place is, frankly, so regal you feel as if you have to whisper. And I've always thought the lawns look suspiciously like the grounds of the kind of posh asylum that you might see in the movies. Speaking of movies, if you manage to visit during the Cannes Film Festival (don't hold your breath) you might spot the odd mega star, a super model or Elton John.

CAP D'ANTIBES: The **Hotel du Cap Eden Roc** in Cap d'Antibes (*Boulevard Kennedy, BP29, 06601 Antibes,* ☎ *33 04 93 61 39 01, fax reservations 33 04 93, 67 13 83, edenroc-hotel@wanadoo.fr, www.edenroc-hotel.fr,* €€€€€). This was probably the model for the Hotel des Etrangers in F. Scott Fitzgerald's *Tender is the Night*. Built in 1870 in the style of a seaside château, the hotel is now composed of three buildings set right into the rocks at the end of Cap d'Antibes. The building known as the Eden Roc has suites and a well-known restaurant with huge windows overlooking the sea. The seawater pool, with its rocky back wall and overflowing infinity edge, is particularly dramatic. Like the Grand Hotel du Cap in Saint Jean Cap Ferrat, this is a place that takes itself very seriously. Although the rooms are, perhaps, breezier and less frigidly status-aware, the staff is not. Expect to tip handsomely. The hotel is far too grand to accept anything as vulgar as a credit card, so plan to pay for your room (doubles start at €550 and there are only a few "standard" doubles) with cash or wire funds ahead. Interestingly, it's not too grand to use its celebrity clientele for sales advantage. Check out the A to Z listing of celebrity guests on their website. By the way, this hotel has no "off season" – it is open from April through September.

Beware The Alphabet Soup

Finding a room in Cannes can be complicated by the tremendous number of festivals and trade meetings that take place at the Palais des Festivals and Des Congrès. One festival season flows right into another and room prices bob up and down, so that there is no real high season and low season. In addition to the Bridge and Games festivals, the Film Festival in May and the International Advertising Festival in June, you may run across MIDEM, MIPIM, MAPIC and so forth on accommodation rate cards (as in, "the price is €€€ except for MIDEM"). Here is what some of these mean:

MIDEM – International Music Market (Marché International de la Musique)

MIPIM – International Property Market (Marché International des Professionnels de l'Immobilier)

MIPTV – International Audiovisual and Digital Content Market

MIPCOM – International Marketplace for Entertainment Content

MAPIC – International Market for Retail Real Estate

GSM-Cannes – International GSM telecoms show

As you can see, a lot of industries like to wheel and deal in Cannes, driving up room rates in the process. The best way to find out what's going on when you want to go is to check with the tourist office about the schedule at the Palais. You can also look at **www.whatsonwhen.com**, a very useful site for up-to-date information.

CANNES: Le Cavendish bills itself as Cannes' only boutique hotel *(11 Boulevard Carnot, 06400 Cannes, ☎ 33 04 97 06 26 00, fax 33 04 97 06 26 01, www.cavendish-cannes.com, €€€€)*. The 34 rooms in a Belle Époque town mansion have been recently rebuilt and redecorated by a trendy designer using jewel box colors to give the whole place the ambiance of an opulent 19th-century boudoir – a boudoir with Internet access, air conditioning and sound proofing of course. Well-located near the Croisette and the Palais des Festivals, this is for those who want their luxury on a more intimate scale.

MOUGINS: Le Moulin de Mougins has about seven relatively simple rooms and suites and serves a lovely breakfast (not included) on the terrace *(Notre Dame de Vie, 06250 Mougins, ☎ 33 04 93 75 78 24, fax 33 04 93 90 18 55, reservation@moulindemougins.com, www.moulindemougins.com, restaurant 4-star Relais & Chateaux €€€€€)*. Keep an eye on the website, if you are interested, as spring and fall offers can be quite reasonably priced.

Le Mas Candille has a pretty terrace restaurant as well as its gastronomic restaurant, and the only Shiseido Spa in Europe. *(Boulevard Clément Rebuffel, 06250 Mougins, ☎ 33 04 92 28 43 43, fax 33 04 92 28 43 40, info@lemascandille.com, www.lemascandille.com, €€€€)*. Forget all that "charming Provençal decor" – these rooms reek of serious wealth with their plush, slightly masculine decor.

The **Hotel de Mougins** is spread across four lavishly decorated farmhouses arranged around a pool *(205 Avenue du Golf, 06250 Mougins, ☎ 33 04 92 92 17 07, fax 33 04 92 92 17 08, info@hotel-de-mougins.fr, www.hotel-de-mougins.com, €€-€€€€)*. Supposedly Jean Cocteau wanted to build a film studio on this site. Not surprisingly, this hotel, like a lot of Mougins, has the feeling of a film set about it. Come in the winter – until the end of April – and rooms are almost half-price.

RENT A RIVIERA APARTMENT

For the price of a single night in one of Cannes' tonier hotels on La Croisette (sometimes even less) it's possible to buy a whole week's rental of a stylish apartment or a beautiful villa, overlooking the Vieux Port, the Bay of Cannes, a garden or a swimming pool. At the cocktail hour, enjoying your Campari soda while the sun sets over the sparkling bay, it's easy to play at being a 1960s-era jetsetter, for a remarkably reasonable price.

Residential hotels and privately rented furnished apartments are readily available through the Cannes Tourist Office (Palais des Festivals et des Congrès, La Croisette, 06400 Cannes, ☎ 33 04 93 39 24 53, fax 33 04 92 99 84 23, tourisme@semec.com, www.cannes.fr.) and a number of useful websites. With rents for a studio apartment for two starting at about €460 per week (going up to €1,000 to €1,400 for the same apartment during the film festival) it's possible to have a relaxed, private vacation with plenty of spare change for the Casino, a rented car and dining out.

Rents rise and fall dramatically with the festival season. For example, at **La Loggia** *(4 Quai Saint Pierre, 06400 Cannes; contact Hélène Leao, Directrice, ☎ 33 06 84 60 58 29 or 33 04 92 18 84 50, fax 33 04 03 16 la-loggia@wanadoo.fr, www.la-loggia.com, nine apartments ranging from studio to three rooms, €€-€€€€)*. This is a really charming apartment building on the Vieux Port, a serviced studio apartment with terrace rents for €700 per week (which puts it in the €€ range, less without maid service) between January and June, bouncing up to €1,500 per week during the film festival, with another €1,500 added for the terrace (which otherwise might be strung with a film advertising banner). If you time your visit to avoid the festival, you can stay like a film star here.

Riviera Rentals is run by an English speaking couple with roots in Cannes *(contacts in the USA, ☎ 804-921-8041 or 804-921-3331, fax 804-355-2125, info@rivierarental.com, www.rivierarental.com)*. It's a good source of economically priced rental apartments that are usually excellent value – pools, sea views and so forth. Typical weekly rental at the Santa Barbara Apartments (a modern apartment block with sea views that they offer in the Croix les Gardes residential area of Cannes) ranges from €600 to about €1,000.

To rent apartments and villas at the deluxe end of the spectrum, the **John Taylor Agency** on the Croisette in Cannes is acknowledged as the expert local realtor. They claim to have been around as long as the very oldest hotel in Cannes. Prices for the properties they rent are available only on request. *(55 La*

Croisette, 06400 Cannes, ☎ 33 04 97 06 65 65, fax 33 04 93 39 13 65, infos@john-taylor.fr, www.john-taylor.fr/real-estate-cannes.htm).

Abercrombie & Kent, the British luxury travel company, offers large villas with maid service in the Cannes area. Though apparently expensive, the villas accommodate eight to 10 people, making them a relatively moderate investment for a group of friends or family (☎ 44 0845 070 0618, www.villa-rentals.com).

British vacationers are particularly enthusiastic about villa rentals in France so there are some excellent and knowledgeable British companies worth consulting on line or by telephone. Try:

- **Balfour France**, who have a 24-hour rental brochure hotline (326 Upper Richmond Road West, London SW14 7JN, UK, ☎ 44 20 8878 9955, 24-hour brochure hotline ☎ 44 020 8878 1211, fax 44 020 8878 9876; enquiries@balfourfrance.com, www.balfourfrance.com).

- **Holiday-Rentals.com** is an advertising service with a good search engine that can help you find flights and insurance as well as villas and will quote prices in whatever currency you choose (1st Floor, Westpoint, 33/34 Warple Way, London W3 0RG, UK, ☎ 44 020 8743 5577, fax 44 020 8740 3863, www.holiday-rentals.com).

- **Susan Paradise, Holidays in France** is a small, independent booking agency that can put you in touch with about 150 properties, some of which are on the Riviera. The company claims to have first-hand knowledge of the properties represented and their website offers good descriptions with plenty of pictures. (Queens House, New Street, Honiton, Devon EX14 1BJ, UK, ☎ 44 01395 597 759, fax 44 01395 597 859, susan@susanparadise.co.uk, www.susanparadise.co.uk).

Mougins is also a pleasant place to rent a furnished apartment or villa and the tourist office (page 338) publishes a constantly changing list of landlords and available properties for a range of rents. This is serious movie star territory, though, so don't even bother during film festival season. If you don't find yourself competing for a property with Sharon Stone, you'll probably be competing with her hairdresser.

Moderate

CANNES: In La Bocca, a quiet green enclave and beach on the western edge of Cannes, **Chateau de la Tour** is a reasonably priced surprise (10 Avenue Font-de-Veyre, 06150 Cannes, ☎ 33 04 93 90 52 52, fax 33 04 93 47 86 61, hotelchateaulatour@wanadoo.fr, www.hotelduchateaudelatour.com,

€€-€€€). A pink washed 19th-century mansion/faux castle, it is charmingly decorated and cosy. Located a few blocks from the beach, upper rooms have sea views. The pool, set in a garden and surrounded by lawns and classical statues, is stunning.

Bleu Rivage in Cannes is remarkably good value for La Croisette *(61 La Croisette, 06400 Cannes,* ☎ *33 04 93 94 24 25, fax 33 04 93 43 74 92, bleurivage@wanadoo.fr, www.frenchriviera-online/bleurivage,* €€-€€€). The 61 rooms are nicely decorated, some with serene garden views, and the public rooms cosy. But bear in mind that many of the smaller hotels along this stretch don't publish film festival room rates until the last moment when they have a sense of how much the traffic will bear.

At the **Hotel de France**, rooms are simple and neat, public spaces recently redone in an Art Deco theme *(85 Rue d'Antibes, 06400 Cannes,* ☎ *33 04 93 06 54 54, fax 33 04 93 68 53 43, infos@h-de-france.com, www.h-de-france.com,* €€-€€€). But if you are planning some designed shopping in Cannes, you could not be better placed – the hotel is on one of the most town's most important shopping streets.

Jacques Offenbach spent the winter of 1874 at the **Hotel Splendid**, three years after it opened *(4-6 Rue Felix Faure, 06400 Cannes,* ☎ *33 04 97 06 22 22, fax 33 04 93 99 55 02, accueil@splendid-hotel-cannes.fr, www.splendid-hotel-cannes.fr,* €€-€€€). This sugary confection of a hotel, overlooking the Vieux Port and Le Suquet, is still popular with musicians and performers. Colorfully decorated rooms, some with brass beds, have terrific views. Small, neat bathrooms are slightly Victorian.

The **Hotel Regina**, on a quiet street not far from the beaches and La Croisette, is a four-storey picture in pink, with white window shutters *(31 Rue Pasteur, 06400 Cannes,* ☎ *33 04 93 94 05 43, fax 33 04 93 43 20 54, reception@hotel-regina-cannes.com, www.hotel-regina-cannes.com, B&B,* €€-€€€). Twelve of the hotel's 19 rooms have flower-bedecked balconies. Unusually, breakfast is included in the price.

ANTIBES-JUAN-LES-PINS: **Le Mas Djoliba** *(29 Avenue de Provence, 06600 Antibes-Juan-les-Pins,* ☎ *33 04 93 34 02 48, fax 33 04 93 34 05 81, info@hotel-djoliba.com, www.hotel-djoliba.com,* €-€€) is a traditional, farmhouse not far from Antibes' *Vieille Ville*. It operates as a pension/hotel, which means you can arrange half-board but don't have to. Rooms are spacious and relatively simple, with bath or shower, TV, mini-bar, direct telephone. The hotel is close to the beach.

NICE: **Villa L'Aimée** *(5 Avenue Piatti, 06100 Nice,* ☎*/fax 33 04 93 52 34 13, bookings@villa-aimee.co.uk, www.villa-aimee.co.uk,* €€) is a splendid, Belle Époque B&B in the posh Cimiez district of Nice. It has three rooms which are excellent value – if you can bag one. The house, built in 1929, has been restored, with great attention to detail, by an English couple. Rates include continental breakfast.

MENTON: The location of the **Hôtel Riva** *(600 Promenade du Soleil, 06500 Menton,* ☎ *33 04 92 10 92 10, fax 33 04 93 28 87 87, contact@rivahotel.com, www.rivahotel.com, €€)* couldn't be better. It's right across from the beach, with sea-view rooms that have picture book views across the bay to the *Vieille Ville*. The mountain-view rooms, which are slightly cheaper, aren't bad either. Apart from those views, the modern rooms are ordinary. The public rooms, however, are furnished with overstuffed blue and white sofas and are very charming. The newish rooftop solarium, with its restaurant and Jacuzzi, provides a scenic alternative to the beach.

Budget

CANNES: Hotel de Provence has earned itself Logis de France status for good value right in the center of Cannes *(9 Rue Molière, 06400 Cannes,* ☎ *33 04 93 38 44 35, fax 33 04 93 39 63 14, contact@hotel-de-provence.com, www.hotel-de-provence.com, €-€€)*. Set about a block from La Croisette, the 30-room hotel has a quiet, hidden garden and privileges on a private beach for a small fee. Rooms are basic but pretty.

La Bocca, a beachy suburb just west of Cannes center is a good area to look for budget accommodations. Both the Mercure and Ibis hotel chains (see page 131) have establishments there, Ibis being the more basic and inexpensive of the two, but both offering excellent value. **Mercure Cannes Mandelieu** is arranged around a pool, a few blocks from the seafront *(6 Allée des Cormorans, Cannes La Bocca, 06150 Cannes,* ☎ *33 04 93 90 43 00, fax 33 04 93 90 98 98, H1190@accor.com, www.accorhotels.com, €€-€€€)*. **Ibis Cannes Plage, La Bocca** is on the beach *(23 Avenue Francis Tonner, 06150 Cannes,* ☎ *33 04 93 47 18 46, fax 33 04 93 47 46 55, www.accorhotels.com, €)*.

If you've every wondered where struggling young movie makers stay when they've spent every penny on the film they're trying to sell at Cannes, take a peek at the **Hotel Florella**, near the Cannes train station. It is clean, adequate, basic and cheap but small enough to be surprisingly friendly. *(55 Boulevard de la République, 06400 Cannes,* ☎ *33 04 93 38 48 11, fax 33 04 93 99 22 15, reservations@hotelflorella.com, www.hotelflorella.com, € or less)*.

The Hotel Florian a small and friendly, family-run hotel in Cannes *(8 Rue du Commandant André, 06400 Cannes,* ☎ *33 04 93 39 24 82, fax 33 04 92 99 18 30, info@hotel-florian-cannes.com, €)*. It's about as central as you can get for both shopping and the beach – on a street that runs between La Croisette and Rue d'Antibes (see *Shopping*, page 341). The price of its tiny but looked-after rooms will leave you change to spend in the tempting designer boutiques all around.

The **Albert Ier**, not far from Cannes' Forville market (page 341), has its fans *(Albert Ier, 68 Avenue de Grasse, 06400 Cannes,* ☎ *33 04 93 39 24 04, fax 33 04 93 38 83 75, contact@hotelalbert1ercannes.com, €)*. It's an Art

Deco-style townhouse with nicely decorated rooms and a very pretty flowered terrace. It is a bit of an uphill hike from the beach through streets you won't really want to traverse in your beach sarong and flip flops. So if the beach features large in your plans, you'll have to factor in the €20-€25 per day cost of the private beaches, with their changing facilities, on La Croisette.

ANTIBES: Le Ponteil Hotel *(11 Impasse Jean Mensier, 06600 Antibes, ☎ 33 04 93 34 67 92, fax 33 04 93 34 49 47, service-reservation@leponteil.com, www.leponteil.com, €)* looks like a big, family house, in a garden full of flowers. Inside, the rooms are almost spartan, but the beach is only about 150 yards away. Because of all the festivals and trade shows in this area, rates seem to vary by €15 this way or that every couple of weeks – but they're usually within the budget range. During the summer months, the hotel only operates on a half-board basis. It's B&B the rest of the year. Just make sure you ask for a room with private WC – at least one of the rooms has a shared bath.

Hôtel Le Village de Fabulite *(Traverse de Nielles, 06160 Cap d'Antibes, ☎ 0 4 93 61 47 45, fabulite@wanadoo.fr, www.fabulite.com, € or less)*. Divers always seem to get the best deals. This B&B-cum-bungalow colony is attached to a dive center operating out of the tiny Port Olivette. Rooms for two, three or four people are simple but have their own little shaded porches and open onto a garden. There's a popular, casual restaurant that serves pizza and menus in the € range, including coffee and wine.

The oddly named ☆☆☆ **Hotel Paris Rome** *(79 Avenue Porte de France, 06500 Menton-Garavan, ☎ 33 04 93 35 73 45, fax 33 04 93 35 29 30, paris-rome@wanadoo.fr, www.hotel-paris-rome.com, € or less)* has been owned by the same family since 1908. It has the kind of warm Mediterranean style that is, frankly, often lacking in the less expensive hotels of the Riviera. There are also a number of interesting three- and four-day packages – go fishing on a private yacht, or have guided tours of several gardens. The three-star establishment also has three *Logis de France* chimneys for the Italian and French cooking in its pretty little restaurant. It's just a few yards from the beach and about 1,000 feet from the Italian border, which you can hop over whenever you like.

Location all depends on your point of view. No doubt the very low prices at Nice's **Hôtel Floride** *(52 Boulevard de Cimiez, 06000 Nice, ☎ 33 04 93 53 11 02, fax 33 04 93 81 57 46, info@hotel-floride.fr, www.hotel-floride.fr)* are due to the fact that it's in the residential Cimiez district, a bus ride away from the popular town center, the *Vieille Ville* and the Promenade des Anglais. But if you are interested in Nice's Belle Époque heritage or want to be close to the Matisse and Chagall museums, and the Roman baths, then the location is perfect. The hotel is a bright white Belle Époque building, with small, unexciting rooms that are, nevertheless, nicely fitted out for the price. There's a covered verandah off the room for breakfast and a great neighborhood (which was once the fashionable summer retreat of most of Europe's crowned heads) to explore.

Camping

I am not a great fan of camping on the Riviera, but I would make an exception for **Camping Les Romarins** on the Grande Corniche *(06360 Èze, Grande Corniche, ☎ 33 04 93 01 81 64, fax 33 04 93 76 70 43, romarins06@aol.com, www.campingromarins.com. Open April 7 to October 15, €13.30 to €16.25).* It's a small, quiet camping area with 41 shaded spaces above Èze. This isn't one of those jolly French family campsites with noisy entertainment that are like summer camps for grownups. It's just a place to sleep under the stars at one of the highest points on the Corniche. The views are brilliant.

■ Where to Eat

CANNES: Wherever you find celebrities and businessmen with expense accounts, you are bound to find the kind of restaurants that gather galaxies of stars and toques from all the best foodie guides. Cannes is that kind of place and it doesn't disappoint. Two of the best restaurants on the Riviera are within a few blocks of each other on La Croisette. A third is in nearby La Napoule.

DINING PRICE CHART

Prices are for a typical prix fixe menu of two courses and a glass of house wine for one.

	€14-€19
€	€21-€34
€€	€35-€49
€€€	€50-€69
€€€€	€70-€140
€€€€€	The sky's the limit

La Palme d'Or at the Hotel Martinez reflects the champagne standards of the Taittinger family, who own the hotel *(73 La Croisette, 06406 Cannes, ☎ 33 04 92 98 73 00, fax 33 04 93 39 67 82, martinez@concorde-hotels.com, www.hotel-martinez.com; lunch and dinner, Tuesday to Saturday, €€€€€).* Arranged in a series of rooms and on a terrace overlooking the promenade and Mediterranean, the restaurant is decorated like a plush, Art Deco club. Imaginative and luxurious dishes include pumpkin soup with a poached egg and black truffle, gnocchi of baby carrots and lemon, wild Mediterranean sea bass, fillet of beef with a mustard sauce flavored with vanilla.

At **The Villa Des Lys** in the Hôtel Majestic Barrière, diners can choose wild rice risotto with zucchini flowers, lemon and thyme, wild sea bass with chorizo and coconut cooked with sweet peppers, crayfish quenelles and tails in shallots. The cool, sunny room is all dark wood and coral banquettes, with plenty of glass. *(10 La Croisette, BP 163, 06407 Cannes, ☎ 33 04 92 98 77 00, fax 33 04 93 38 97 90, villadeslys@lucienbarriere.com, www.lucienbarriere.com; Tuesday to Saturday, dinner only, €€€€.)*

In La Napoule the three Raimbault brothers run **L'Oasis** – Stéphane heading the team, François in charge of desserts and patisserie, and younger brother Antoine just recently joining the business. *(L'Oasis, Rue*

Jean Honoré Carle, 06210 La Napoule, ☎ 33 04 93 49 95 52, fax 33 04 93 49 64 13, oasis@relaischateaux.com, www.oasis-raimbault.com, €€€€). They offer a fusion cuisine, combining traditional Mediterranean dishes with Oriental and Asian-influenced menus. Dishes include oysters marinated in horseradish, with puffed rice petals and seawater sorbet, Mediterranean crayfish roasted with Thai herbs, sea bass in a tarragon crust. The dessert list is worth saving room for – hazelnut macaroon filled with anis, tarragon and raspberry cream, 'Spice Route' iced nougat.

Cannes has its fair share of modest restaurants as well. **Mi-Figue Mi-Raisin** is a comfortable restaurant on the hill of Le Suquet, where the dishes feature strong Provençal flavors. *(27 Rue du Suquet, 06400 Cannes, ☎ 33 04 93 39 51 25, fax 33 04 93 39 51 25, dinner only, €€.)* The brasserie-style restaurant also serves pizza. It's a good choice for a relaxed, low-key meal.

La Mère Besson has been around forever and is always reliable for traditional Provençal cooking – especially a generous aïoli and fragrant boeuf en daub. *(13 Rue des Frérés-Pradignac, 06400 Cannes, ☎ 33 04 93 39 59 24, lamerebesson@wanadoo.fr, €€-€€€).*

Try **Gaston-Gastounette** for very good seafood, apparently fresh from the sea. *(7 Quai St-Pierre, 06400 Cannes, ☎ 33 04 93 39 47 92, fax 33 04 93 99 45 34, €€-€€€.)* The restaurant has terrific views of the Vieux Port. Not everything is traditional – there are Japanese influences to some of the fish dishes. If you'd like to try bouillabaisse but are intimidated by the rigamarole connected with the dish, this is a good place to dip your spoon in. The restaurant serves a small, starter-sized portion.

La Cave is the very model of a casual bistro, crowded, buzzy and relaxed. The menu is enormous, full of comfortably familiar dishes and reasonably priced, with changing specials chalked on the blackboards around the room. Zucchini flower fritters, soupe au pistou, grilled sardines, aïoli, magret de canard are among the options. *(9 Boulevard de la République, 06400 Cannes, ☎ 33 04 93 99 79 87. www.restaurant-lacave.com, €€).*

MOUGINS: A lunch or dinner date in Mougins makes a complete change of pace from the hustle and bustle of the nearby coast. Even at the height of the summer season, when its little lanes are packed with visitors, the village seems to maintain a discreet serenity. There are about 60 restaurants tucked here and there around the town, several of them serious foodie pilgrimage sites.

Many consider Roger Vergé the man responsible for the blossoming of restaurants in Mougins. There were only a handful here when in the late 1960s he established **Le Moulin de Mougins** *(Notre Dame de Vie, 06250 Mougins, ☎ 33 04 93 75 78 24, fax 33 04 93 90 18 55, reservation@moulindemougins.com, www.moulindemougins.com, restaurant and four-star Relais & Chateaux hotel, lunch €€€€, dinner €€€€€)* and the less expensive **L'Amandier** *(Place des Patriotes, Mougins Village, ☎ 33 04 93 90 00 91, fax 33 04 92 92 89 95, www.amandier.fr, €€).*

The two restaurants are considered to have put Mougins on the map. In the 1970s it had more Michelin stars than any other town in France. Vergé's handpicked successor at Le Moulin, Alain Llorca (formerly head chef at the Hotel Negresco in Nice) has recently introduced an innovative light menu and a tapas menu – a full meal of little bites (for €160 per table). Dishes include a Nice-influenced stew with spinach ravioli and chickpea pancake and roast Aveyron lamb with citrus fruits and almonds, simmered fennel and eggplant royale. The restaurant is an old oil mill, just outside the village. The dining room is decorated in minimalist cream and burgundy and there is a smart terrace. Llorca runs a cooking school and there is also a shop. Unless you're Elizabeth Taylor (who hosts an Aids fund raiser at the restaurant during the Cannes Film Festival), book long before you leave home. You can make reservations for both the restaurant and hotel online.

Also worth a look is **Restaurant Candille** at Le Mas Candille, a hotel with two restaurants on the edge of town *(Boulevard Clément Rebuffel, 06250 Mougins,* ☎ *33 04 92 28 43 43, fax 33 04 92 28 43 40. info@lemascandille.com, www.restaurantcandille.com, lunch €€€, dinner €€€€)*. Here the chef dresses lentil soup with roast crayfish, poached quail's egg and deep-fried parsley. He wraps the omnipresent sea bass in a tobacco leaf, and punctuates cauliflower with pecans and pistachios.

For something completely different, **Le Ban Noï** *(538 Avenue de Tournamy, 06250 Mougins,* ☎ *33 04 92 28 08 88. ban-noi@wanadoo.fr, €)* serves good Thai food.

BIOT: For a tiny perched village, Biot is packed with good restaurants in every price range, from crêperies and pizzerias through good brasseries and bistros to the height of haute cuisine. At the moment, because of the chef's Michelin star, **Les Terraillers** is the hot reservation *(11 Route du Chemin Neuf, 06460 Biot,* ☎ *33 04 93 65 01 59, fax 33 04 93 65 13 78, contact@lesterraillers.com, www.lesteraillers.com; lunch €€, dinner €€€)*. Set in a 16th-century pottery on the edge of the village, it has a vaulted dining room with bare stone walls and beams. The pretty terrace has pink-washed walls. The set menu of classic dishes might include gratin or warm oysters with champagne butter, or a spring roll of Dublin Bay prawns with vegetables. Leave room for chocolate desserts worth every mile you'll have to walk to work them off. The pottery's old kiln is a private dining room for 10.

I prefer **Chez Odile** *(Chemin des Bâchettes, 06410 Biot,* ☎ *33 04 93 65 15 63, €€€)*, where the fixed price menu emphasizes regional cooking in a rustic atmosphere. The kitchen is open to view so it isn't the quietest of places, but the atmosphere is colorful and food very good. The restaurant is closed in December and January and closing days (or nights) vary throughout the year, so call ahead.

NICE: Lately, some restaurateurs in Nice have been displaying a label of *La Cuisine Nissarda* to show that they prepare the traditional dishes of

Nice in an undiluted, traditional way. I suspect that this is probably one of those marketing gimmicks that tourist boards are so fond of dreaming up. Even if it is, anything that focuses attention on Nice's unique culinary style can't be bad. Some Niçoise dishes, like stockfish (*estocaficada* in the local language) – a stew of dried cod or haddock and vegetables – can be an acquired taste. And *socca*, the chickpea flour pancake that seems like such a good idea, can be heavy and greasy if not served by an expert. But well-prepared Nissard food is distinctive and delicious.

Casalinga, which has the *Cuisine Nissarda* label, serves Provence-influenced food as well as good Niçoise stockfish and stuffed zucchini blossoms *(4 Rue de l'Abbaye, 06300 Nice, ☎ 33 04 93 80 12 40, 11:30 am to 3 pm and 3 to 7 pm, closed Sunday, €€)*.

Don Camillo, another with the *Cuisine Nissarda* quality label, is not far from the Cours Saleya, where its fresh produce probably originates *(5 Rue des Ponchettes, 06300 Nice, ☎ 33 04 93 85 67 95, vianostephane@wanadoo.fr, dinner 7 to 10 pm, Monday through Saturday, Sundays and Monday lunch, €€€-€€€€)*. The restaurant, which gets a lot of good local press, offers gourmet gastronomy alongside traditional menus. Chef Stephane Viano is something of a local celebrity.

Go to the **Grand Café de Turin** in Nice for the freshest seafood and shellfish *(5 Place Garibaldi, 06300 Nice, ☎ 33 04 93 62 29 52, fax 33 04 93 13 03 49, 8 am to 11 pm, no reservations, €-€€)*. This is an old-fashioned seafood brasserie with a great atmosphere, a lively terrace and some unusual house specialties like roast asparagus salad. It's open nonstop, all day long and if you want a plate of scampi for breakfast, no one will raise an eyebrow.

La Zucca Magica, is that genuine rarity in France, a gourmet vegetarian restaurant *(4 bis Quai Papacino, 06300 Nice, ☎ 33 04 93 56 25 27, open Tuesday to Saturday, lunch 12:30-2:30 pm, €, dinner 7:30 to 10:30, €-€€)*. Zucca means pumpkin and the place is decorated with pumpkins of every shape and size. Apparently this is one of the symbols of Nice. Owner Marco Folicardi was a successful vegetarian chef and TV personality in Rome before setting up in Nice. His restaurant, near the Old Port, is tiny, with only 18 tables. The menu is basically Italian, but original for all that. Ravioli might be served open, like an open-faced sandwich on a slice of fine pasta. The "meatballs" are made of goat cheese and eggplant. The menu changes regularly, depending upon that day's market. If I had any problem it's that I always find staff in vegetarian restaurants either cranky or bossy. Signor Folicardi's charming staff is anything but cranky. But don't be surprised if you end up eating what they think you should order.

ANTIBES: L'Oursin, which means sea urchin, is an institution *(16 Rue Republic, 06600 Antibes, ☎ 33 04 93 34 13 46, €)*. No stay in the town would be complete without a drop in at this crowded and popular seafood joint. The menu is reasonable, the terrace is noisy and friendly. There's also an inexpensive children's menu.

Oscar's, also in Antibes, is a cosy place with Italo-Provençal cuisine *(8 Rue Rostan, 06600 Antibes, ☎ 33 04 93 34 90 14, fax 33 04 93 34 90 14, €-€€)*. The dining room is small, with bare stone walls, pink napery and frilly white chairs. Menus change with the market but the restaurant's four-course menu of entrée, fish or meat course, cheese and dessert is always a good value.

MENTON: La Calanque is a rustic, waterside restaurant near the harbor *(13 Square Victoria, 06500 Menton, ☎ 33 04 93 35-83 15, noon to 2 pm and 7:15 to 9:30 pm, Tuesday to Saturday; Sunday lunch, noon to 2 pm, €€)*. It serves fat, fresh charcoal-grilled sardines (have the waiter show you how to debone them, there's a knack to it), soup de poisson and local seafood. The menu is also dotted with such Niçoise specialties as *barbajuan* – a ravioli stuffed with Swiss chard and cheese and then fried – don't knock it till you've tried it. Given the ambiance and the location in this smart little town, the set-price menus are quite reasonable.

ÈZE: Have lunch on the beach in Èze. **Anjuna Plage** is named after a popular beach in Goa but the only thing vaguely Indian about this place are the exotic plants and statues arranged around the terrace restaurant *(58 Avenue de la Liberte, RN98, 06360 Eze Bord de Mer, ☎/fax 33 04 93 01 58 21, nadia@anjunabay.com, www.anjunabay.com, €-€€)*. Food is traditional seafood with an occasional touch of exotic spice. The beach is pebble and shingle so you will need to rent one of their pale blue *matelas*. About €9 buys you a place on the beach for half a day, with a few spaces available for non-diners.

Light Meals & Snacks

NICE: The best places to sample *socca* in Nice (and you should at least try some) are the stalls and snack bars that make them fresh along most of the markets. These pancakes, made of chick pea flour fried in olive oil, are rich and can be a bit heavy. A little goes a long way. Everyone who likes *socca* has a favorite stand on a special streetcorner where they buy it. Ask at your hotel or among the market traders for a recommendation.

ÈZE BORD DE MER: The beach bar and restaurant **La Cigale** serves pizza and ice cream *(06360 Eze sur Mer, ☎ 33 04 93 01 58 87, open for lunch from spring through fall and evenings in July and August)*. Toy with a drink here while you watch the passing scene and celebrity-spot. There aren't many pizza joints that will organize a wedding on the beach for you but that's the kind of place Èze is.

Up in Èze Village, the aptly named **Le Nid d'Aigle** (The Eagle's Nest) serves afternoon snacks and traditional family-style cooking on a terrace in the sky *(1 Rue du Château, 06360 Èze, ☎/fax 33 04 93 41 19 08, closed Tuesdays and Wednesday night, €)*.

Le Cactus is another place to refresh yourself from climbing up to Èze, with crêpes, salads and ice creams. It's at the entrance to the old town *(La Placette, Èze Village, ☎ 33 04 93 41 19 02).*

BIOT has a particularly nice salon de thé, **Le Mas des Orangers** *(3 Rue des Roses, 06410 Biot, ☎/fax 33 04 93 65 18 10, sylvie.rekkas@libertysurf.fr , www.lemasdesorangers.com)* where you can take a break from all your hot shopping in the glass studios. They offer splendid patisserie, light salad lunches, fruit juices, gourmet teas, local beer, oddly enough, olive oil, gourmet treats and house wares for sale.

■ Adventures

On Foot

Hiking in the Haut Pays Niçois

Before You Go: Within 60 km/37 miles of the Riviera, the mountains here are every bit as rugged and abrupt as any in the entire Alpine region. If you are thinking of hiking in the Alpes Maritime, be honest with yourself and consider whether you are fit enough and experienced enough for the route you have in mind. Some of the peaks in the Parc du Mercantour and those nearby, close to the Italian border, rise to nearly 4,000 m/13,000 feet, with trail passes at 2,000 m/6,500 feet.

More than 4,000 km/2,500 miles of hiking trails snake through the mountains. Among them, there is bound to be something for everyone – including relatively gentle rambles close to villages and along the cross-country skiing *(ski du fond)* trails. Nevertheless, some of the most interesting hikes are steep and challenging, suitable for mountain hikers who are used to covering varied terrain while carrying overnight gear in backpacks.

The itineraries suggested in this chapter, along the GR52A and the GR510, were originally planned along existing roads, forestry paths and pastures. Since their creation, changes have regularly taken place. Landslips, land use alterations, the construction of new roads and forestry activities all contribute to new and often unpredictable difficulties.

If you are keen to try but uncertain about heading off on your own, guides are available (page 368) to help physically fit visitors with good stamina discover mountain hiking in the Alps.

When to Go: Mid-June to the beginning of July is the best time to hike the Alpes Maritime. Hotels and refuges are not busy, the days are long and wild flowers are at their peak.

During July and August, the mountains attract violent thunderstorms in the afternoons. The French Ramblers Association (FFRP) advises hikers to avoid ridges and peaks after midday at that time of year.

The GR52A and the GR510 travel through two distinctly different habitats, each with its own climatic conditions. Trails above 1,000 m/3,280 feet are usually snowbound and virtually impassable from November to May. Some of the highest passes have snow until mid-June.

Closer to the Mediterranean, the hills are dry and sunbaked. Here, trails below the 1,000-m mark can be hiked throughout the year (depending upon the risk of forest fire), but tend to be very hot in the summer, with natural sources of water rare.

What to Wear: Even in the summer, carry warm, waterproof clothing and wear good-quality, waterproof hiking boots. The experts recommend that you carry a compass to avoid becoming lost in sudden mists.

Three Days in the High Mountains

Along the western flanks of the Massif du Mercantour, this early summer hike travels between lovely perched villages and near several of the area's ski resorts. As you climb, panoramic vistas of the highest Alpine ranges begin to reveal themselves. The villages become more rough-hewn and Alpine, with houses built of local, reddish stone or wood. Instead of the typical tiles of Provence, roofs are covered with red or mauve slates, called *laures*. Along the way, watch the mountainsides for chamois, ibex, mouflon, stag, roe deer and European elk as well as some of the 60 mating pairs of eagles that nest in this region. Trails are marked with a white stripe above a red stripe.

> **Planning Your Route:** These IGN 1:25,000 maps cover the territory traversed on this hike – 3741 ET and OT; 3641 ET; 3640 OT.

- **Day One**

Saint Martin Vésubie: This medieval village likes to call itself "La petite Suisse Niçoise," boasting of the freshness of its mountain air at an altitude of 964 m/3,162 feet. The village, with a population of more than 1,000, is relatively large for this region, where hamlets of a few hundred residents are common. Its streets are laid out along a rocky ridge that separates the river valleys of the Boréon and the Madone de Fenestre. It is surrounded by dramatic peaks, including la Cime du Gélas, at 3,143 m/10,311 feet.

The 17th-century parish church has 13th-century Templar origins. Inside is a 12th-century, painted wooden Madonna, Notre Dame de Fenestre, which is carried in procession to a mountain sanctuary every September. One of the town's interesting curiosities is the pedestrian Rue du Docteur-Cagnoli, a steep, narrow cobbled lane overhung with substantial Gothic houses. The apparent "drain" down the center of the street, which you step over again and again, is actually a tiny canal, called a *gargouille*.

The village is a popular starting point for winter sports enthusiasts and a base for exploring the Parc Mercantour and the *arrière-pays Niçois*; there is a good selection of accommodations and restaurants.

Getting Here: The Nice-based bus company, **TRAM** (☎ 33 04 93 89 47 14), runs twice daily bus service, Monday through Saturday, leaving from Nice Gare Routière at 9 am and 5 pm. The 60-km/37-mile trip takes two hours and costs €10 for a one-way ticket.

For More Information: Office de Tourisme, Place Félix Faure, BP 12 06450 St Martin Vésubie, ☎ 0 4 93 03 21 28, fax 33 04 93 03 21 44. o-t-hautevésubie@wanadoo.fr, www.pays-vesubie.com.

How Long Will It Take?

The suggested times for the stages of these hikes are based on the recommendations of the FFRP, the French Ramblers Association. They are meant to indicate the average time for a fit hiker accustomed to varied terrain, in dry conditions, without snow. Depending upon the load you are carrying, you should adjust the times to suit yourself – particularly if you are carrying gear for a bivouac.

The Walk: In the center of Saint Martin Vésubie, look for signs for the **GR52A**.

- Leave the village heading north along the valley of the River Boréon. Cross the river to the district known as Saint Nicholas. Look for the path heading west and then southwest, which crosses the Vallon de Vernet. At this point, the path follows an ancient Roman road, climbing through a forest. This first leg of the hike climbs about 1,800 feet to the first mountain pass and is one of the steepest sections. When you've reached the top at Col Saint Martin la Colmiane, you can take heart in knowing the hardest climb of the day is over. After you have gained some altitude above the village, you will see a range of high mountains which cut across the horizon to the east. This is the border between Italy and France.

- Continue along the path that joins the **D2565**. As you near the pass of **Col Saint Martin La Colmiane** (one hour and 45 minutes, 1,500 m/4,921 feet), look north to **Baus de la Fréma**, a peak of 2,246 m/7,369 feet. **La Colmiane** is a ski resort and has a few restaurants and hotels.

- From the Col, the route descends. At the first fork, leave the paved road and take the path to the left. After about half an hour you will reach **Saint Dalmas Valdeblore** (1,290 m/4,232 feet). Saint Dalmas is one of three communities that make up **Valdeblore**. It is a hub of GR paths (the GR5 goes south to Nice and the GR52 goes southeast to Menton).

The village has plenty of accommodation, camping and restaurants. You can also catch a bus for Nice here.

- The trail continues along the **D2565** towards the west. Just after the bridge, you can either stay with the **GR5** (which continues along the road) or take the **GR52A**, which is the path to the left. Both join up at La Bolline with the GR5 route being about 25% shorter. If you choose the GR52A, the trail descends into the **Bramafam River Valley**. Follow the left bank, which becomes the **Route de la Goune**. To the south, you will see the **Bois Noir** (Black Forest).
- At the neck of land marked "1123 m," turn sharply to the northeast and descend to the floor of the valley. Cross the valley and rejoin the D2565 (also the GR5) at a bend in the road near the church of Saint Jacques in **La Bolline** (995 m/3,264 feet), which you should reach in about an hour and 10 minutes.

La Bolline

At this point, if you have been keeping up an average pace, you will have been walking at least three hours and 25 minutes. La Bolline is a good place to take a break. It has two, casual bistros – **Ô Délices** (☎ 33 04 93 02 89 79) and **Lou Bramafam** (☎ 33 04 93 02 83 09), as well as shops for stocking up with climbing and camping supplies. You can also catch buses here to other towns in the area.

- From the bend near the church in La Bolline, the GR5/GR52A continues along the Bramafan Valley before crossing the route of an ancient branch of a glacier, now buried under a meadow. Cross the Gros Valley on a medieval bridge and rejoin the **D2565** at **Planet**.
- The road climbs out of the valley. Continue to the next bend after Planet and take the lane from the **Collet de Raglas** to the village of **Rimplas** (1,016 m/3,333 feet), which should take another hour and 10 minutes. Like La Bolline, Rimplas has a few basic shops and restaurants, as well as some simple accommodations. If you have enough daylight left to finish the day's hike, spend some time looking around. The village is built on an ancient fortification and has a chapel dedicated to Mary Magdalen that tops a narrow rocky outcrop.
- At the base of the village, the trail heads in a northwesterly direction on a recently widened, paved road between steep cliffs. The path drops down, relatively rapidly, through a ravine and a small valley to the **Chapelle of Saint Roch**.
- At the foot of the chapel, leave the paved lane and take a sharp left turn onto a descending path.

- The path makes a sharp turn to the right. Just below this, it rejoins a paved road. Continue on this road to reach **Saint Sauveur sur Tinée** (496 m/1,627 feet), about an hour and 10 minutes beyond Rimplas.

This completes the first day after just under six hours of walking. Stop here for the night or catch a bus to Nice.

• Day Two

Saint Sauveur sur Tinée is a typically Alpine village that, nevertheless, reveals itself to be Provençal in the colorful trompe l'oeil exteriors of some of its buildings. It is a hidden jewel, clasped between the heavily forested walls of the Tinée Valley at a bend in the Tinée River, where it is joined by the Vionène. It is in the geographic center of what is called the Middle Valley of the Tinée and has a population of just over 300.

The 14th-century stone parish church stands beside a Gallo-Roman bell tower, decorated with gargoyles and a famous 14th-century marble statue of Saint Peter. Among the works of medieval and Renaissance art inside, an anonymous painting of the "Mystic Marriage of Saint Catherine" includes a view of the ancient village in the background.

Saint Sauveur has a small riverside campsite, a basic hotel-restaurant and a few simple bars and cafés. There are also a few small shops for restocking with camping necessities.

A number of local loop paths reveal stunning views of the village, the valley and the perched villages of **Roure** and **Roubion**, higher up. Saint Sauveur is also close enough to the edge of the **Parc Mercantour** (page 380) for a day excursion into the nature reserve. There is enough to do here to plan an extra night in the village before climbing up to Roure.

Regular bus service on the Nice-Isola 2000 line, makes this an easy place to start or end your hike. Nice is only about an hour and a half away, so even a day-trip is reasonable.

Getting Here: Santa Azur runs several bus trips a day between the Nice bus station and Isola 2000, stopping at Saint Sauveur sur Tinée *(Santa Azur, Gare Routière de Nice, 5 Boulevard Jean-Jaurès, 06300 Nice, ☎ 33 04 93 85 92 60, fax 33 04 93 85 48 74, www.santa-azur.com).* The number of trips varies with the season but there is usually at least one morning and one evening bus in each direction, with more on weekends. The journey takes a little over an hour and a half.

For More Information: Lacking a tourist information office, the **Syndicat d'Initiative**, a kind of French Chamber of Commerce, provides information and hiking maps from an office in the village hall (Mairie, 06420 Saint Sauveur sur Tinée, ☎ 33 04 93 02 00 22, fax 33 04 93 02 05 20, www.ville-saint-sauveursurtinee.fr). Their hours seem to be a bit random, but the **Parc Mercantour Office** is usually open and can provide local walking itineraries *(11 Avenue des Blavets,*

06420 Saint Sauveur sur Tinée, ☎ 33 04 93 02 01 63, *mercantour.moyenne.tinee@wanadoo.fr*).

The Walk: Day two of the walk is uncomplicated but very steep. After the Church in Saint Sauveur, the trail descends across the river and passes the cemetery:

- At the bottom of the cemetery, take the path that climbs to the right and stay on it, all the way up to **Roure** (1,096 m/3,596 feet). Simple directions but not a simple stroll. This is a very steep and rough climb, the steepest on this three-day itinerary. The path winds back and forth in dozens of switchbacks. It crosses the D30 and then the D130, the narrow motor roads up to Roure, several times. The climb will take you about two hours of hard walking. Roure is a genuine *village perchée*. It clings to the side of the mountain in a way that really brings home how dangerous the times must have been when these defensive settlements were established. The town has a small multi-purpose shop/café where you can usually have drink or a snack. Out of season, however, it may be open only on weekends. It also has an *auberge*, **Le Robur**, which serves meals and has a few rooms available between April and November. Before moving on, enjoy another panoramic view from the ruins of the village château.
- Leave the village heading north toward the **Chapelle St Sébastien**. Just beyond the chapel, the trails fork. The **GR5** veers off to the right and contiues north. Take the trail to the left, the **GR52A**, which heads in a northwesterly direction, past farm buildings at **La Cerise**.
- At La Cerise, after the farm buildings, leave the path and descend through a series of switchbacks to a hidden canal. Cross through the valley by following the canal and then climb back up to the path, following the edge of the valley's right flank.
- Continue in a northwesterly direction as far as the underground passage, then climb carefully, following the contour of the alluvial cone.
- Cross the **Vionène**, which is a wide stream here, rushing through a tumble of red boulders. Then climb the path on the other side of the valley going in a southerly direction, following the **Vignols path** to **Roubion** (1,314 m/4,311 feet).

This is a very dramatic walk, which should take about three hours. Roubion perches like an eagle's nest on a rocky spur above the stream. This completes the second day, after five hours walking. Stop here for the night.

- **Day Three**

Roubion is a base for winter and summer sports. It is near several ski lifts and is linked to a number of mountain biking trails suitable for families. It has several hotels, at least three restaurants, a snack bar, *gîtes* and a *gîte d'étape*.

The views from Roubion are spectacular. The village is almost suspended in the sky above the Vionène. The close horizon is filled with the mass of two Alpine giants. To the northeast, **Mont Saint Sauveur** rises 2,711 m/8,894 feet, while to the northwest **Mont Mounier**, at 2,817 m/9,242 feet, dominates the sky.

But this village is much more than a mountain resort. Founded by Celto-Ligurians in 800 BC, it was a Roman outpost, a medieval fortress and the site of long-term border conflicts between the kingdoms of France and Savoy. It didn't actually agree to join France until 1860 and traces of its many pasts are all around. Several buildings, including its ruined châteaux, 12th-century ramparts and gates, are listed historic monuments. Should you decide to take a break and stay a while, there is plenty to do here.

For More Information: Tourist information is available through the Mairie (☎ 33 04 93 02 10 30, fax 33 04 93 02 10 30, ot.roubion@smtm06.fr, www.ville-roubion.fr/index.cfm).

Getting Here: Roubion is not on a scheduled **bus** route, but it can be reached via Roure, which is served by regular service through Santa Azur (☎ 33 04 93 85 34 06). I've found the staff at the Santa Azur office at the Nice bus station helpful, usually able to speak English and knowledgeable about services throughout this area. You can hire a **taxi** in Roure to take you up to Roubion (☎ 0 800 06 01 06 – this is a local, toll free number). It is probably a good idea to check with the Tourist Information office in Roure about the status and phone numbers of local taxis, just to be on the safe side *(Office de Tourisme, Roure, Rue Centrale, 06420 Roure,* ☎ *04 93 02 00 70, fax 04 93 02 00 72)*. By **car** from Nice, take the D2205 to Saint Sauveur sur Tinée (60 km/37 miles). Leave the village going west on the D30 to Roubion (12 km/7½ miles). These are narrow, winding mountain roads with lots of switchbacks and hairpin turns, so allow plenty of time.

The Walk: Today's walk lasts about four hours and 15 minutes. It begins with a short, sharp uphill climb to the highest pass on this itinerary and then includes gentle ascents and descents for the rest of the walk. The **GR52A** leaves town next to the church, heading west toward the hamlet of Vallons:

- Climb to **Col de la Couillole** at 1,678 m/5,505 feet. Though steep, this is a relatively straightforward stretch and shouldn't take much more than an hour and a half. There is an *auberge* at the pass where you can stop for refreshments.

- Descend into the **Couillole Valley**, along its left slopes. Cross the valley to the right bank and climb to the small mountain chapel. From the chapel, follow the tarred road north. Cross the **Cians**, here a mountain stream, and climb an old mountain road to **Beuil** at (1,450 m/4,757 feet). This should take a little less than an hour.

- Beuil is a town of reasonable size with bus service to Nice and Valberg, several hotels, restaurants and shops for camping supplies. It is also a center for cross-country skiing. Go right through the village, and continue west, climbing to **Col Saint Anne**. It should take about half an hour to reach the pass at 1,550 m/5,085 feet.
- There is a chapel at the pass. Go south of it and then southwest, skirting the hamlet of **Les Launes**.
- Descend into the small **Chalandre Valley**, with its (usually) dry stream bed, and then climb a good path up the north-facing slope to **Atres Pass**, at 1,684 m/5,525 feet, the highest point on this itinerary.
- From **Atres**, continue northwest until you join a paved road near a swimming pool. Follow the road, descending into **Valberg** (1,670 m/5,479 feet). You should reach Valberg about an hour and 20 minutes after the Saint Anne Pass.

Valberg is a winter and summer resort with hotels, shops and restaurants. It's a major ski resort with 52 Alpine pistes and 22 lifts, as well as 25 km/15½ miles of cross-country ski trails. In the summer, there are miles of marked hiking trails through the larch forests, as well as river fishing and mountain bike trails. Spend the night here or catch a Santa Azur bus back to Nice.

This completes the three-day hike.

• Where to Stay & Eat on this Itinerary

In Saint Martin Vésubie: The village has a handful of small, hotels, most providing basic comfort with a few modern additions, such as satellite television and direct telephones, but don't expect a modem link for your laptop. All the village hotels fall below the lowest budget price in this guide.

Logis de France awards ☆☆ **La Bonne Auberge** two hearths for the quality and value of a room and three-course meal *(Allées de Verdun, 06450 Saint Martin Vésubie, ☎ 33 04 93 03 20 49, fax 33 04 93 03 20 69, louis.roberi@wanadoo.fr, 13 rooms, closed November 16 to February 1, breakfast extra. Dinner menus €, half-board available for between €39 to €44).*

Camping at ☆☆ **Le Champouns** offers a wider than usual choice of options – from spaces for one-person bivouac tents up to furnished apartments available by advanced reservation *(Route de Venanson, 06450 Saint Martin Vésubie, ☎ 33 04 93 03 23 72, cell 33 06 80 13 77 02, champouns@yahoo.fr, myweb.vector.ch/champouns, €).* The site is close to the village and inexpensive, with 50 spaces starting at about €3 per person per night. The camp's website has a good rundown of facilities and prices.

Look for restaurants and cafés along **Rue Docteur Cagnoli**, the street with the *gargouille* running down its center, and **Place Félix Faure**, near the Mairie. You'll notice the Alpine and Italian influence on the local cuisine.

In Saint Sauveur sur Tinée: Visitors have recommended ☆☆ **Le Relais d'Auron** to me for comfortable accommodation and simple but nicely done meals served on a terrace by the river *(18 Avenue des Blavets, 06420 Saint Sauveur sur Tinée, ☎ 33 04 93 02 00 03)*. It only has a few rooms but if it's full, you could try camping at the municipal site by the river or staying at the *gîte d'étape*, also run by the community. Both are open from June 15 to September 15 *(☎ 33 04 93 02 03 20 or phone the Mairie at ☎ 33 04 93 02 00 22)*.

L'Auberge de la Gare, near the bus station, also has its fans for simple, traditional cooking *(☎ 33 04 93 02 00 67, restaurant only, no rooms)*.

In Roubion: A rustic, mountain B&B, **Le Rupicapra**, is on the GR52A at the northern end of the village *(Ginette et Jean-Claude Rimoldi, Le Haut Village, 06420 Roubion, ☎ 33 06 85 04 13 91, accueil@rupicapra-roubion.com, http://rupicapra-roubion.com/chambres_d_hotes.html)*. Rooms are very simple and spare but the welcome is warm. The house has four rooms, two of which have a shared bathroom. Rupicapra is a Provençal word for chamois. Little chamois signs are scattered around the routes into the village, leading you to this inn, near the medieval ramparts and several restaurants.

Also worth trying are **Restaurant Les Écureuils** *(☎ 33 04 93 02 09 71)* and **La Crébasse** *(☎ 33 04 93 02 01 57)* for snacks and pizzas.

In Valberg: After roughing it in the mountains for a few days, Valberg is a good place to indulge yourself a little. It is a typical Alpine resort – skiing in winter, hiking, biking, accrobranching, tennis and so forth in the summer. Hotels are styled to look like Swiss chalets and have all the cozy comforts that skiers expect, such as fireplaces, balconies for enjoying the view, saunas, gyms and steambaths. Among the six hotels in the heart of the resort, ☆☆☆ **L'Adrech de Lagas** has 20 colorful rooms, some with galleries for extra guests *(63 Avenue de Valberg, 06470 Valberg, ☎ 33 04 93 02 51 64, fax 33 04 93 02 52 33, adrech-hotel@wanadoo.fr, www.adrech-hotel.com, 20 rooms, buffet breakfast extra, €)*. Every room has a big balcony, shaded by the deep chalet eaves. The hotel has a sunny restaurant with beamed ceilings, stone floors and big views. There is a small, modestly equipped gym.

☆☆ **Blanche Neige**, with 17 rooms in the center of town, is a small chalet hotel with a difference *(10 Avenue de Valberg, 06470 Valberg, ☎ 33 04 93 02 50 04, fax 33 04 93 02 61 90, 17 rooms, €, closed October and November)*. *Blanche Neige* is Snow White in French and the hotel is decorated as if she is still keeping house and the Seven Dwarves will be home from a hard day on the slopes any minute. Lots of hand-painted wooden furniture, floral fabrics. Very cute.

Valberg has 21 restaurants and bars, most serving casual meals and snacks with more ambitious regional cuisine available in some of the hotels.

• Mountain Guides

Local tourist offices and offices of the Parc Mercantour can suggest guides for mountain walks. In **Roubion**, try **Bureau des Guides OEROC** (☎ *33 06 12 21 01 30*) or **Arnaud Van Caneghem** (☎ *33 04 93 02 10 84*). In **Colmiane**, contact **Maison de la Montagne/Bureau des Guides Escapade** (☎ *33 04 93 02 88 30*) for all kinds of Alpine activities including via ferrata, escalade, canyoning and hikes.

A Two-Day Trek in the Mercantour to the Valley of Marvels

La Vallée des Merveilles is a magic place scattered with thousands of stone carvings, created by primitive people over a period of 4,000 years. The carvings decorate slabs of colored shale – green, orange, pink, and violet – polished by a receding glacier at the end of the last ice age. The valley is paved with these stones. There are at least 36,000 carvings, which appear to be concerned with the sacred rites and everyday preoccupations – agriculture, hunting and herding – of the Ligurian and proto-Ligurian people who made them. At least half of the carvings are horned figures. These probably represent a bull god, ruler of the lightening that often crowns **Mt. Bego**. The mountain, which rises 2,872 m/9,423 feet above the valley floor, may also have been an object of ancient veneration and pilgrimage. The most celebrated of the carvings have nicknames – *Christ, The Sorcerer, The Tribal Chief, The Ballerina*. Authorized trails with special, interpretative circuits guide visitors to the most interesting carvings.

La Vallée des Merveilles is located deep within the Parc Mercantour in the high Alps. There are several ways to visit it. If this two-day, independent trek doesn't appeal to you, you could join a hiking group with a certified guide, or take part in a Jeep tour. For information about these options, see page 371.

This hike is best undertaken between July and October. The first leg is a short (2½ hours, 710 m/2,329 feet), easy but steep climb to a mountain refuge where you spend the night. The second day takes longer (five hours) and includes the 440-m/1,444-foot climb into La Vallée des Merveilles, before descending 830 m/2,723 feet to the finish. Day One is considered to be of average difficulty while Day Two is an Alpine hike. Food is available at the refuge where you will spend the night and at another refuge along the trail but you should carry some high energy snacks and water.

Using the Balisages to Plan Your Route

Key points along the local park paths are marked with numbered signs, called *Balisages*. Throughout the directions for this trek, *Balisage* points are indicated with the letter "b" and a number – such as b-82. Within the Parc Mercantour, you should be

In the Safranier quarter *(© Bompuis, OT Antibes)*

Above: Baie des Anges, Nice, with private beach on the left
(Office du Tourisme et des Congrès de Nice)

Below: The back country of the Riviera (©MDF/J/Sierpinski, courtesy of CRT PACA)

In Menton Old Town, narrow streets break into flights of steps to climb the Colla Rogna hill (OT Menton)

Basilique St. Michel, Menton's Baroque masterpiece (© Komenda, OT Menton)

able to find wooden signs or trail markers with corresponding numbers carved into them.

To be on the safe side, also carry IGN 1:25, 000 Topo 25 Map, 3841OT, "Vallée de la Roya," which covers the whole of this trek.

- **Day One - Climb to the Refuge des Merveilles**
- Start from the parking area at **Lac des Meches** (1,380 m/4,528 feet) and take the wide lane that climbs into the larch forests (**b-82**).
- Just past the National Park Information Office (**b-86**), continue to the left, climbing a gentle slope on a road suitable for Jeeps and 4X4 vehicles. This route takes you along the **Vallon de la Minière** (**b-87**, **b-88**, **b-89**) above a small lake.
- At **b-89**, you can leave the Jeep road and take the path. This is a steeper route but will shorten the way considerably, since the Jeep road goes back and forth through several switchbacks. If you choose to do this, you can rejoin the Jeep road at **b-90**.
- From **b-90**, the road climbs for a short distance, passing between **Lac Saorgine** on the left and the lower part of **Lac Long** on the right.
- As you reach **Lac Long Supérieur des Merveilles**, the upper section of the lake (2,111 m/6,926 feet), look for the **Refuge CAF des Merveilles** (**b-92**) on the south bank. This is the *gîte d'étape* where you will spend the night. Food is available here.

The Club Alpin Français de Nice

The Club Alpin Français (CAF) is a good source for information, insurance, mountaineering events, guides, climbing lessons and all kinds of Alpine activities including: canyoning, cliff and mountain climbing, lessons, paragliding, hiking and snow shoe hiking, downhill and cross-country skiing, spelunking, mountain biking and Via Ferratta. Joining also gets you big reductions at all the club's mountain refuges. **For Information:** *CAF des Alpes-Maritimes, 14 Avenue Mirabeau, 06000 Nice,* ☎ *33 04, 93 62 59 99, fax 33 04 93 92 09 55, cafnice@cafnice.org, www.cafnice.org/cafbase/accueil.php.*

Staying at a CAF Refuge

The CAF refuges encountered along this walk are inexpensive to stay in. You can make half-board arrangements, including continental breakfast and a four-course evening meal (soup, main course, cheese and dessert) for about €32 per person, less for CAF members. Places in the refuges are limited, so whether you want to stay the night, or simply stop for refreshments, you must book in advance. In the **Refuge CAF des Merveilles**, there are 20 places in winter and 75 in the summer. The **Refuge de Valmasque** (where you can stop for food on this itinerary) has 54 places in the summer, 12 in winter.

To make a reservation, contact the refuge guardian at least three weeks before your visit. To stay at the Refuge CAF des Merveilles between June 15 and September 26, write to: Alex Ferrier Refuge des Merveilles, 06430 Tende, France, indicating dates, number of people and whether you want to have a meal or stay with half-board. Enclose a self-addressed envelope and a money order for €8 per person. If you are writing from outside of France, add a few extra euros for postage and indicate this in your letter. The deposit will be returned if no places are available. Between October 2 and the beginning of June, you can visit the Refuge by reservation through Jochen Boggero, ☎ 33 04 93 04 88 90 or 0 6 22 46 01 16.

To enquire about the Refuge de Valmasque, contact Michel Duranti, ☎ 33 04 92 31 91 20, June 15 to September 26, or ☎ 33 04 93 04 62 74 at other times of the year. Current price information is available on the CAF Refuge at www.cafnice.org/cafbase/refuges.php.

- **Day Two - Through the Baisse de Valmasque**
- Before you leave the Refuge CAF des Merveilles, stock up on chocolates and energy snack foods. Then follow the **GR52**, which becomes a cliff path, above the south side of the lake.
- At **b-93** take the right fork (still the GR52), which will take you deeper into the Vallée des Merveilles.
- You enter the valley across a gigantic amphitheater of smooth slices of rock (called *chiappes* in the local dialect) and tumbled boulders. Inside, a marked *circuit d'interprétation*, with commentary and information on plaques, will lead you to some of the most famous carvings. Stay on the marked path and the sign-posted itinerary.
- Continue along the small Lac des Merveilles and climb through several switchbacks to the **Baisse de Valmasque (b-94)** at 2,549 m/8,362 feet.
- Staying on the GR52, descend, heading north toward **Lac du Basto (b-95)**, the largest of the lakes encountered on this itinerary.
- At **b-96**, leave the GR52, and take the path on the right toward the **Refuge de Valmasque**.
- Stay close to the shores of **Lac Noir** and **Lac Vert de Valmasque** (**b-97, b-98**).
- From b-98, you can take the path on the left for the short walk to the Refuge if you need water or supplies and have made an advance reservation for this stop (see above).

- From **b-98**, begin the long but easy descent to the entrance of the National Park (**b-374**, **b-393**, **b-394**).
- From the gates, continue downhill on the **D91** to **Castérino** (1,550 m/5,085 feet). From Castérino you can catch a taxi (**Taxis Rossi**, ☎ 0 6 70 70 70 19, or **Taxis Souchon**, 0 6 80 27 41 82) back to the parking lot or to Tende train station.

Accompanied Visits to La Vallée des Merveilles

Guides certified by the Parc Mercantour can lead you into the Valley. A list of certified guides is available from the **Tende Tourist Office** *(Office de Tourisme, Avenue du 16 Septembre 1947, 06430 Tende-Val des Merveilles,* ☎ *0 4 93 04 73 71, fax 33 04 93 04 35 09, info@tendemerveilles.com, www.tendemerveilles.com)* or from **Maisons du Parc National du Mercantour** *(Parc National du Mercantour, 23 Rue d'Italie, BP 1316, 06006 Nice,* ☎ *33 04 93 16 78 88, fax 33 04 93 88 79 05, mercantour@wanadoo.fr, www.parc-mercantour.fr or Secteur Roya-Bévéra, Bureau du Parc National, 103 Avenue du 16 Septembre 1947, 06430 Tende,* ☎ *33 04 93 04 67 00).* During the summer, information is also available from the **Castérino Park Information Point** in Chalet de Castérino *(*☎ *33 04 93 04 89 79).*

Guided group tours are regularly organized by various companies and clubs. For information, contact **L'Association Merveilles Gravures et Découverte** *(18 Rue Antoine Operto, 06430 Tende,* ☎ *33 06 86 03 90 13, fax 33 04 93 04 20 75, gravureinfo@yahoo.fr).* They run regularly scheduled group tours of the valley, leaving from either Tende or Fontanalbe.

Jeep and 4x4 tours are run by members of the the **Association des Accompagnateurs des Merveilles**. They cost between about €50 and €100, depending upon what is included. Information is available from the **Haute-Roya Tourist Office** *(Office de Tourisme, La Haute-Roya,* ☎ *33 04 93 04 73 71),* the **Tourist Information Portal of the Roya and Bévéra Valleys** *(*☎ *33 04 93 04 92 05, fax 04 93 04 99 91, royabevera@wanadoo.fr, www.royabevera.com)* and from the **Tende Tourist Office** (see above).

Resorts in the Provence Alps have a genuine alpine spirit. © Manu Molle, OT Pra Loup

Getting Here: The easiest gateway to this region is by **SNCF train** from Nice to Tende or Saint Dalmas de Tende. Direct trains from Gare de

Nice take two hours. *(Contact SNCF, ☎ 33 08 36 35 35 35).* By **car**, take the A8 Autoroute from Nice to Vintimille, just across the Italian border from the French town of Ventimiglia. Then take the N204 to Col de Tende, which is 40 km/25 miles.

In the Snow

Ski resorts in the Alpes Maritime and the Alpes de Haute Provence are focused sports rather than après ski and shopping. For that reason they're attractive to anyone who likes to spend as much time as possible on the slopes.

That doesn't mean there is nothing else to do. Most offer a range of other sports and nighttime entertainments, ski boarding, ice skating, heli-skiing and snowshoeing *(raquettes)*.

Within 90 minutes of Nice by car (even less by train), the Alpes Maritime have more than 300 ski slopes, between 1,150 and 2,610 m/3,773 to 8,563 feet and a total of 147 ski lifts. Of the 561 km/348 miles of skiable slopes, there are 239 km/150 miles of cross-country trails. From the highest resorts, such as Isola 2000, you can see sailboats on the Mediterranean. Pra Loup, which is farther west in the Alpes de Haute Provence, is a bit harder to get to but is a beautiful resort with lovely 17th- and 18th-century farm and *auberge* accommodations. It is also a much bigger resort than the three others covered below, with more pistes and a greater variety of activities.

Ski Resorts

Each of the major ski resorts offers something extra for nature lovers and thrill seekers. Progressive downhill, acrobatic and artistic skiing, slalom, jumps, cross-country, ski touring, skidoo, snowshoeing and so forth. Here's a rundown:

Auron

The Ski Slopes: Forty slopes covering 132 km/82 miles. A total of 20 ski lifts capable of moving 20,000 skiers per hour. Slopes for all abilities – eight black, 17 red, 13 blue, two green.

Other Winter Sports: Surfing and mono skiing at the Auron Snow Park. Preformed structures, including half pipe, and modules (table, gap, spine, quarter) are ready with the first snows. Cross-country and snowshoeing at Saint Dalmas le Selvage, 15 minutes away. Ski touring, cross-country and snowshoe hiking over a 50-km/31-mile area. Ice skating in a small, natural rink. Paraskiing.

Getting Here: 90 km/55 miles from Nice. By **bus** with **Santa Azur**, ☎ 33 04 93 85 92 60 or 33 04 93 85 37 06, fax 33 04 93 13 42 28, www.santa-azur.fr. By **train** from Nice SNCF Station, ☎ 33 08 36 35 35 35 or 33 08 36 67 68 69.

For More Information: Auron Office de Tourisme, Grange Cossa, 06660 Auron, ☎ 33 04 93 23 02 66, fax 33 04 93 23 07 39, auron@wanadoo.fr, www.auron.com. Also **Saint Étienne de Tinée Office de Tourisme**, 06660 Saint Étienne de Tinée, ☎ 33 04 93 02 41 96, fax 33 04 93 02 48 50.

Isola 2000

The Ski Slopes: 15 summits between 2,450 m and 2,974 m/8,038 and 9,757 feet. The actual ski runs are between 1,810 and 2,610 m/5,938 and 8,563 feet. There are 45 pistes, covering 120 km/75 miles of skiable slopes from 24 lifts. Slopes for all abilities – four black, 14 red, 20 blue, seven green.

Other Winter Sports: Ice track for car, kart and quad racing, lake diving under the ice, surfing and mono skiing. Isola has no cross-country but there are four km/2.4 miles of snowshoe trails.

Getting Here: 90 km/55 miles from Nice Airport. By **bus** from Nice Airport Bus/Railway Station, ☎ 33 04 93 85 92 60, the cost is about €17.50 for a two-hour trip. By **train** from Nice SNCF station, ☎ 33 08 36 35 35 35 or 33 08 36 67 68 69. By **taxi**, up to five people can go to the resort from Nice Airport for a total of about €155 each way (☎ 33 04 93 23 13 67).

For More Information: Office du Tourisme, ISOLA 2000, 06420 Isola 2000, ☎ 33 04 93 23 15 15, fax 33 04 93 23 14 25, info@isola2000.com, www.isola2000.com and www.skifrance.fr.

Valberg

The Ski Slopes: 52 pistes, with 90 km/55 miles of skiable slopes. Runs for all abilities – six black, 22 red, 13 blue and 11 green. The 22 ski lifts include six chairlifts. There are also 25 km/15½ miles of cross-country trails.

Other Winter Sports: Ice karting, paraskiing, heli-skiing and, for the really fearless, climbing frozen Alpine waterfalls.

Getting Here: 86 km/53 miles from Nice Airport. By **bus**, daily service from Société Broch starting at Nice bus station, Promenade du Paillon, and stopping at the SNCF station and Nice Airport, ☎ 33 04 93 85 61 81, 33 04 93 31 10 52 or 33 04 93 07 63 28. By **train** from Nice SNCF station, as above.

For More Information: Office du Tourisme, 4 Place du Quartier, 06470 Valberg, ☎ 33 04 93 23 24 25, fax 33 04 93 02 52 27, ot@valberg.com, www.valberg.com.

Pra Loup

The Ski Slopes: 170 km/106 miles of skiable slopes on 73 pistes at between 1,500 and 2,600 m/4,921 and 8,530 feet. Skiing for all levels – five black, 30 red, 19 green and 19 blue, plus one "mauve" baby slope. 53 ski lifts, including 11 chairlifts.

Other Winter Sports: Ice circuit for go karts, skimobiles, ski scooters, 4x4 snow treks. 30 km/18.6 miles of cross-country/ski touring trails in the Mercantour (about 45 minutes away at **Ski de Fond à Larche**, 04400 Larche, ☎ 33 04 92 84 32 97). Winter skydiving and hang-gliding. Paragliding at Ubaye (**Ubaye Parapente**, ☎ 33 04 92 81 34 93, www.haute-ubaye.com).

Getting Here: The resort is most easily reached from the TGV station in Aix en Provence. During Pra Loup's opening season, a snow shuttle **bus** leaves at 2:20 pm every Saturday from the Aix-Arbois TGV station, arriving at Pra Loup at 6:15 pm. Reservations for round-trips must be made at least 72 hours in advance. Tickets cost €20 (☎ 33 08 20 20 62 10).

For More Information: Office de Tourisme, 04400 Pra Loup, ☎ 33 04 92 84 10 04, fax 33 04 92 84 02 93, info@praloup.com, www.praloup.com. For lift information, **Pra Loup Developpement**, Immeuble le Génépi, 04400 Pra Loup, ☎ 33 04 92 84 11 54, fax 33 04 92 84 18 94, transmontagne@skipass-praloup.com, www.skipass-praloup.com.

Adventures on Water

Le Ski Nautique & Water-Tow Sports

Antibes-Juan les Pins claims to be the birthplace of that quintessential Riviera sport, waterskiing. According to the local story, Léo Roman and two brothers named Le Bihan experimented with the new-fangled activity off Juan les Pins, invented and named it in 1931. As usual with such claims, there are counter-claims and there's a school of thought that says waterskiing was invented on a Minnesota lake in the 1920s.

Regardless, they have been doing it here for a long time. Certainly it is where the sport was introduced to the Riviera; the first international waterskiing federation was founded here and the first world championships were held here in 1949.

Naturally, it is something of a mecca for enthusiasts and good-quality lessons are available at half a dozen beaches. Nowadays, other boat-tow sports, like wake boarding and parascending, are available at the same beaches, clubs and hotels. Try these:

- **Belles Rives Ski Club**, ☎ 33 04 93 74 45 54.
- **Azur Water Sport**, Plage du Méridien Garden Beach, ☎ 33 04 92 93 57 57.
- **Hélios Ski Club**, Plage le Colombier, ☎ 33 04 93 61 51 10.
- **Star Ski Club**, Plage Neptune, ☎ 33 04 93 61 92 29.
- **Le Ski Club de la Grande Bleue**, Plage Petit Navire, ☎ 33 04 93 61 38 56.

- **Cap d'Antibes Ski Nautique**, Plage de la Baie Dorée, ☎ 33 04 93 67 30 67.
- **Plage de la Siesta**, ☎ 33 04 93 33 31 31.
- **Plage Royale**, ☎ 33 04 93 73 64 60.

Deep-Sea Fishing

If you like the idea of 12 hours on the high seas and can get a group together, you can go deep-sea fishing for tuna and dolphin from a number of Riviera ports. Typically, a day-trip from 6 am to 6 pm, on a radar- and safety-equipped powerboat, costs about €200 per person, including all food, drinks and fishing gear. **Guigo Marine** (☎ 33 04 93 34 17 17, *contact@guigomarine.com*), based in Cannes, takes groups of six people or more after tuna, swordfish or dolphin on its 14-m/46-foot boat. If you can fill the boat, the captain will pick up your group in Antibes or another nearby port.

Diving

Antibes-Juan les Pins hosts an annual underwater photography festival (page 339). Divers from a number of its diving centers are either participants or enthusiasts and will take divers to particularly photogenic areas.

We've heard good reports about **Côté Plongée**, which operates from a small center on Graillon Beach, Cap d'Antibes (☎ 33 06 72 74 34 94, *coteplongee@wanadoo.fr, www.reverbmedia.com/coteplongee/content/accueil/accueileng.html*). Their center gives access to both a private beach – with sun loungers, umbrellas, showers, a seafood restaurant and taxi-boat pickup – and a small, untouched public beach with natural calanques and clear waters that is off-limits to boats. They offer a range of dive packages, starting with a three-dive, open-water package at €145.

École de Plongée d'Antibes-Juan les Pins (EPAJ, ☎ 33 04 93 67 52 59, fax 33 04 93 33 60 16, *francis.brunner@free.fr, www.multimania.com/epaj*) has also been highly recommended. Francis Brunner, a "Guide de la Mer" and founder of EPAJ, is particularly interested in underwater photography and dives that focus on flora, fauna and local archaeology. Brunner and his team lead groups of up to 25 people – from eight years and up – to 60 different sites. Lessons up to various qualification levels are available in the ocean or a pool. EPAJ also has its own sandy beach.

Nice also has plenty of good diving sites in the **Baie des Anges** and Villefranche Bay. Every year, thousands of divers explore the underwater cliffs that begin at the foot of the Cap de Nice. The cliffs are covered with brilliantly colored marine life, including the frequently photographed spectacle of hundreds of magnificent gorgones waving their fans to strain the current for plankton. **Villefranche Bay**, on the other side of Cap Ferrat, is only a 15-minute boat ride from the Port of Nice and its shape and sheltered configuration makes almost all-weather diving a reality.

Closer to the beaches, the waters are very good for snorkling, with hundreds of fish, shellfish and plant life thriving among the rocky outcrops just a few feet underwater.

Le Poseidon Ecole de Plongée *(Quai Lunel, Port de Nice, 06300 Nice, ☎/fax 33 04 92 00 43 86, cell 33 06 11 80 81 81, tlo@poseidon-nice.com, www.poseidon-nice.com/en/index.html)* is a full-service PADI diving center offering discovery dives and courses as well as a range of dive packages for qualified divers, starting at about €26 for a single dive. Poseidon visits 20 different sites, most located in Villefranche Bay.

Activities at the **Centre International de Plongée de Nice**, another PADI center based in the Port of Nice, include dives themed around biology and underwater video *(Raymond Lefevre, 2 Ruelle des Moulins, Rue du Lazaret, BP 4022, 06301 Nice, ☎/fax 33 04 93 55 59 50, ray.lefevre-cip@wanadoo.fr, www.cip-nice.com)*.

MEDUSA ALERT

If you head out early, before swimmers, windsurfers and speedboats have disturbed the water, you have a good chance of spotting a Medusa, or one of several other fantastically colored jellyfish off the beaches of Nice. Don't approach these strange creatures – their sting can be very painful – but don't worry; if you keep your distance they won't approach you either. If you do get stung, the city of Nice offers this advice:

- Wash the area well with sea water to remove filaments and barbs. Do not use fresh water.
- Rub the irritated area gently with fine sand.
- Head for a pharmacy for disinfectant and balm.

Adventures on Wheels

Mountain Biking

The Alpine forests of the Alpes Maritime have a good selection of well-maintained mountain bike *(VTT)* trails connecting the small perched villages and ski resorts. Ranging from challenging itineraries for mountain bike athletes to paths for gentle family outings, the routes in the outer section of the **Parc du Mercantour** are among the best and most scenic.

> **Tip:** The **Conseil General des Alpes Maritime** has created a series of maps and itineraries for hikes and VTT tours called **Les Guides Randoxygène**. The guides are available from their French-language website (www.cg06.fr/w_rando/pageaccueil/index.html).

A Mountain Bike Circuit in the Black Forest

This 11-km/6.8-mile circuit is easy and suitable for families and groups of mixed abilities. It is a good route to try in hot weather because it is shaded by tall fir and spruce trees.

> **Tip:** This forest is maintained for timber so woodcutting operators are often active. Pay attention and obey safety signs in marked woodcutting *(coupe de bois)* zones.

Getting to the Start: The circuit starts in St. Dalmas Valdeblore, which is on both the Nice-Auron (**Route 740**) and Nice-Isola 2000 (**Route 750**) regular bus routes from Nice bus station. Services are frequent throughout the day and take about an hour and a half along either route.

For More Information: Santa-Azur, Gare Routière de Nice, 5 Boulevard Jean Jaurès, 06300 Nice, ☎ 33 04 93 85 92 60, www.santa-azur.com.

The circuit will take about an hour and a half. It is posted with the same kind of numbered "balisage" signs described in the Vallée des Merveilles hiking itinerary above.

- From **Dalmas Valdeblore** (**b79**) at 1,289 m/4,232 feet, take the **GR52A** (red and white trail markers). Descend on a small, blacktopped road, which quickly changes into a dirt road and then a trail along the Vallon de Bramafan.
- At **b136**, (1,082 m/3,550 feet), go straight ahead on the **La Gourre forestry road** – **b137** and **b138** – which circumnavigates the peak of La Séréna on a relatively level track.
- At the intersection with the trail leading to the village of Marie, take the left fork and climb to the **Col de la Séréna** (**b128**) at 1,307 m/4,288 feet. Turn left here for a quick trip up to the viewpoint at the top and a view over Valdeblore.
- Return to **b128** and continue along the **Bois Noir forestry road** to the **Collet du Puei** – **b126**. Here, at 1,334 m/4,376 feet, there are some picnic tables.
- Descend on a gently rolling path to the village of **Saint-Dalmas Valdeblore** – **b76**.

Driving the Corniches de la Riviera

Drive between Nice and Menton on one or two of the three Corniches de la Riviera to enjoy dramatic views, fascinating hilltop villages and some of the best scenery this coast has to offer.

A *corniche* is a path or road along a rocky ledge. These three famous roads twist and wind along the contours of a landscape that becomes ever steeper and wilder as France and Italy crumple into each other at their Alpine border.

The distance between Nice and Menton is only about 20 miles, but if you are in a hurry, take the A8 Motorway instead. The Corniches are the slow roads, made for frequent stops to enjoy the views.

The **Basse Corniche**, also referred to as the Corniche Inférieure (or, more boringly, the N98), hugs the coast along the bottom of the hills and cliffs. It connects all the beach resorts and seaside villages, giving access to the Mediterranean and to some exceptional views. Of the three Corniches, this is the only one that actually goes through the tiny principality of Monaco.

It's 33 km/20½ miles between Nice and Menton on this route, but there's more than enough to fill a day-trip (then return on the A8 in less than half an hour). Among the highlights of the route:

- **Views from Mount Boron** – East of Nice, stop to enjoy the view over Villefranche Bay to Cap Ferrat (home to movie stars, princes and probably a few deposed dictators), reputed to have some of the most expensive real estate on the planet.
- **Presqu'ile du Cap Ferrat** – Follow signs to the D25 and then the D125 to make a circuit of Cap Ferrat. An 11-km/6.8-mile footpath starts at Plage de Passable and goes all around the peninsula, giving fascinating glimpses of some of the homes.
- **Beaulieu Sur Mer** – A pricey little resort that is concentrated on the hills above the route. Below the railroad, there are shops and a market square and, looking up from the main street, a terrific view of the railway viaduct and the Moyenne Corniche. Beaulieu has an usually wide, sandy and quiet beach, below the Corniche.
- **Èze Bord de Mer** – Pine-shaded beaches and private estates surrounded by paths and flights of steps. Above it all, the 14th-century heart of Èze, perched on a needle of rock about 1,500 feet above the beach. There are footpaths between the beach and Èze village, but they are not for the faint-hearted or the casual walker.

The Moyenne Corniche (N7): Of the three, this mid-level Corniche has the potential to be the most hair-raising to drive as it is cut into the side of the cliffs and includes a few tight curves and switchbacks. But it is a well-marked, wide road, with a few tunnels to take you through the steepest ridges. A parapet often blocks the view so take advantage of the parking areas to stop and have a look. There are usually marked parking areas near the best views. Allow about two hours to enjoy the 31 km/19 miles of this road:

- The birds'-eye views of the beaches and coastal villages make it feel like you are flying. I especially enjoy the view over the railroad tracks to the tiny beach and intensely blue waters of **Villefrance sur Mer**.
- The Moyenne Corniche provides access to **Èze village**. Just past the village, there's a link to the Grande Corniche, over the steep and narrow D45.

- Farther along, the French town of **Beausoleil** hangs over Monaco like a balcony. From the village, narrow lanes and staircases climb to the summit of **Mont des Mules**, where there is an orientation table to describe the indescribable panorama.
- Near Beausoleil, the road intersects with the **D53** which descends, via switchbacks from the Grande Corniche all the way down to the beach at Monaco.

The Grande Corniche (D2564): The highest of the Corniches, reaching an altitude of 550 m/1,804 feet above Èze village, this road was built by Napoleon. For most of the way, it follows the ancient Roman road, the Via Julia Augusta. Plan on about three hours for this 31-km/19-mile drive:

- The Grande Corniche starts after **Cap Martin**, west of Menton. As you enter the town of **Roquebrune Cap Martin**, look for a sign for a little road (a right turn if you are heading west) that will take you up to the town's medieval *village perchée* – worth a visit.
- Farther west, near the fabulous **Hotel le Vistaero** (on a cliff, 333 m/1,093 feet high, with rooms starting at about €1,500 per night), stop to enjoy a view that takes in the whole of Monte Carlo and the Italian Coast, as well as a good prospect of the **Trophée des Alpes**.
- The road goes through **La Turbie**, which was a high pass on the Via Julia Augusta. Stop here to see the Trophée des Alpes and to enjoy looking down on Monaco.
- There are very good views from the highest lookouts on the route at Col d' Èze and Belvédère Èze. A bit farther along, at the **Col des 4 Chemins**, look north along the deep Paillon Valley for a glimpse of the snow-covered Alps.
- A steep descent takes you into Nice, with lovely views of the city, its château, Mont Boron and the Baie des Anges.

In the Air

Paragliding

Mountains overlooking broad stretches of beach, or winter meadows covered in snow. The Riviera and the high country behind it are prime territory for what the French call *parapente*. To find out where to launch or where to learn, or to talk with fellow enthusiasts about local conditions, get in touch with one of the many clubs in the area. They will usually put you in touch with teachers or guides:

- **Mont Bastide**, over Èze, is a registered launch site for experienced sail flyers. The site is open throughout the winter, from October 1 to March 1, with landing on Èze beach. Contact **Fédération Française**

de Vol Libre, ☎ *33 04 93 88 62 89,* or **Monaco Voltige,** ☎ *377 93 30 59 29.*
- From sites in **Tende** and **Col de Tende**, in the Alpes Maritimes, it is possible to soar over the military forts of the Maginot Line and the summits of the Italian Alps. Contact **Club de Parapente de Tende,** *Maurice Baldi, Bar des Sports, 06430 Tende,* ☎ *33 04 93 04 61 17,* or **Royaparapente,** *http://royaparapente.free.fr.*
- Not far from Grasse, you can learn parasailing at a launch site in **Gourdon**, then soar over hilltop villages and the Pre-Alps of Grasse. Contact **Ascendance**, *Ecole Professionnelle de Parapente, Label F.F.V.L., Gourdon,* ☎ *33 04 93 09 44 09, contact@ascendance06.com, http://membres.lycos.fr/cdvl06.*
- From a free-flying site at Mont Gros above **Roquebrune Cap Martin**, sail over the coastal beaches. The site is near an airport and the town has strict regulations about when and where you can launch. The site is managed by **Le Club Roquebrun'ailes,** *Alex Dordor,* ☎ *33 04 93 41 06 64* or *33 06 75 70 87 14, club@roquebrunailes.com.*

Eco-Travel

Mercantour National Park

The Parc National du Mercantour in the Alpes Maritimes, together with its cross-border partner, the Parco Naturale Alpi Marittime, protect an extraordinary Alpine habitat. On the French side alone, 830 square miles of wild, mountainous landscapes are maintained primarily for the benefit of the natural environment – educational and recreational uses being secondary.

That's not to say the park is off-limits. Unlike parts of the wetlands reserve of the Camargue, where thousands of acres are closed to the public, most of the Mercantour can be sensitively explored. The reward, to the careful walker, is the opportunity to see species of flora and fauna that, until recently, were nearly extinct in this region.

Two Parks in One: A core area, covering about 265 square miles, is maintained for the protection of nature. Within this area, all vehicles are banned (including mountain bikes), as are fires, noise, weapons, dogs and camping. Bivouacs (without tents) are allowed between 7 pm and 9 am but only in areas more than an hour's walk from park boundaries or access roads. You can't even paraglide over this area lower than 1,000 m/3,280 feet above ground.

The peripheral area, covering about 565 square miles, includes 28 mountain resorts and a handful of ski resorts. It is managed to insure a balance between environmental protection, visitors, local development and traditional activities.

The Mercantour includes seven river valleys in France, all of which offer access to the park through different natural environments: Ubaye, Verdon, Var-Cians, Tinée, Vésubie, Bévéra and Roya. The park also includes the Vallée des Merveilles.

Wildlife Walks: As a meeting place of Alpine and Mediterranean climates, the Mercantour's variety of wildlife and of changing landscapes is unmatched. On the upper slopes of the core area, quiet walkers may see ibex and chamois as well as large birds of prey – golden eagles and bearded vultures. In the lower slopes, look for stags, roe deer and wild boar, along with black grouse, rock ptarmigan and nutcrackers. Small mammals include marmots and stoats.

A mark of the success of this conservation area is the return of wolves, crossing into the region from Italy after an absence from France of 70 years. Contrary to their fairy-tale image, they are shy of humans and very hard to spot.

Of the more than 2,000 plant species identified in the Mercantour, 220 are extremely rare and 40 are found nowhere else. These include the florulenta saxifrage and the bright orange martagon lily. The feathery larch cover allows the Mediterranean sun to penetrate to the forest floor, encouraging wild rhododendrons and blueberries.

Getting Here: The following villages are convenient gateways to the park: Tende, La Brigue, Breil sur Roya, Saint Martin Vésubie, Isola, Saint Etienne de Tinée. Gateway villages can be reached via SNCF trains from Gare de Nice or by Santa Azur bus from Nice bus station.

For More Information: Information about the Parc Mercantour is available from several Visitors Centers (*Maisons du Parc*), from tourist offices and from information points scattered throughout the region. *Parc du Mercantour, 23 Rue d'Italie, BP 1316, 06006 Nice, ☎ 33 04 93 16 78 88, fax 33 04 93 88 79 05, mercantour@ wanadoo.fr, www.parc-mercantour.com and www.parks.it/parco.alpi. marittime.*

Appendix

■ Tourist Information Offices

Les Adrets de l'Estérel – Office du Tourisme des Adrets de l'Estérel, Place de la Mairie, 83600 les Adrets de l'Estérel, ☎ 33 04 94 40 93 57, fax 33 04 94 19 36 69, otsi@mairie-adrets-esterel.fr, www.mairie-adrets-esterel.fr/NewSite.

Agay – Office du Tourisme d'Agay, Boulevard de la Plage next to the Gendarmerie, ☎ 33 04 94 82 01 85, info@agay.fr or agay.tourisme@wanadoo.fr, www.agay.fr.

Aix en Provence – Office de Tourisme d'Aix en Provence, 2 Place du Général de Gaulle BP 160, 13605 Aix en Provence, ☎ 33 04 42 16 11 61, 33 04 42 16 11 62, infos@aixenprovencetourism.com, www.aixenprovencetourism.com.

Antibes – Office de Tourisme et des Congrès, 11 Place de Gaulle, BP 37, 06601 Antibes, ☎ 33 04 92 90 53 00/05, fax 33 04 92 90 53 01, accueil@antibes-juanlespins.com, www.antibesjuanlespins.com.

Apt – Office de Tourisme, 20 Avenue Philippe de Girard, 84400 Apt, ☎ 0 4 90 74 03 18, fax 33 04 90 04 64 30, ot@apt.fr, www.ot-apt.fr .

Arles – Office de Tourisme d'Arles, Boulevard des Lices,13200 Arles, ☎ 33 04 90 18 41 20, fax 33 04 90 18 41 29, ot-arles@visitprovence.com, www.tourisme.ville-arles.fr.

Auron – Office de Tourisme, Grange Cossa, 06660 Auron, ☎ 33 04 93 23 02 66, fax 33 04 93 23 07 39, auron@wanadoo.fr, www.auron.com.

Avignon – Office de Tourisme, 41 Cours Jean Jaurès, ☎ 33 04 32 74 32 74, information@ot-avignon.fr, www.avignon-tourisme.com.

Les Baux de Provence – Municipal Office of Tourism des Baux de Provence, Maison du Roy, Rue Porte Mage, 13520 Les Baux de Provence, ☎ 33 04 90 54 34 39, fax 33 04 90 54 51 15, tourisme@lesbauxdeprovence.com, www.lesbauxdeprovence.com.

Beaucaire – Office de Tourisme, 24 Cours Gambetta, BP 61, 30301 Beaucaire, ☎ 33 04 66 59 26 57, fax 33 04 66 59 68 51, info@ot-beaucaire.fr, www.ot-beaucaire.fr.

Cannes – Palais des Festivals et des Congrès, La Croisette, 06400 Cannes, ☎ 33 04 93 39 24 53, fax 33 04 92 99 84 23, tourisme@semec.com, www.cannes.fr.

Carpentras – Office de Tourisme, Hotel-Dieu, Place Aristide-Briand, Carpentras, 33 04 90 63 00 78, fax 33 04 90 60 41 02, tourist.carpentras@axit.fr, www.ville-carpentras.fr/english/index.html or www.tourisme.fr/carpentras/e-index.htm.

Cassis – Office Municipal du Tourisme de Cassis, Quai des Moulins, Oustau Calendal, 13260 Cassis, ☎ 33 04 42 01 71 17, fax 33 04 42 01 28 31, omt@cassis.fr, http://www.cassis.fr.

Châteauneuf du Pape – Tourist Office, Place du Portail, 84230 Châteauneuf du Pape, ☎ 33 04 90 83 71 08, fax 33 04 90 83 50 34, tourisme-chato9-pape@wanadoo.fr, http://perso.wanadoo.fr/ot-chato9-pape.

La Ciotat – Office de Tourisme, Boulevard Anatole France, 13600 La Ciotat, ☎ 33 04 42 08 61 32, fax 33 04 42 08 17 88, tourismeciotat@wanadoo.fr, www.laciotatourisme.com.

Collobrières – Office de Tourisme de Collobrières, ☎ 33 04 94 48 08 00, fax 33 04 94 48 04 10, ot@collotour.com, www.collotour.com.

L'Etang de Berre – Office de Tourisme Berre L'Etang, Avenue Roger Salengro, 13130 Berre l'Etang, ☎ 33 04 42 85 01 70, fax 33 04 42 85 07 15, tourisme.berreletang@free.fr.

Èze – Office de Tourisme, Place du Général de Gaulle, 06360 Èze Village, ☎ 33 04 93 41 26 00, fax 33 04 93 41 04 80, www.eze-riviera.com.

Fontaine de Vaucluse – Maison de Tourisme, Avenue Robert Garcin, ☎ 33 04 90 20 31 44, officetourisme.vaucluse@wanadoo.fr, or fontainedevaucluse@oti-delasorgue.fr, www.oti-delasorgue.fr/fontaine.php.

Fréjus – Office de Tourisme de la Culture et de l'Animation de Fréjus, 325 Rue Jean Jaurès, 83600 Fréjus, ☎ 33 04 94 51 83 83, fax 33 04 94 51 00 26, tourisme@frejus.fr, www.frejus.fr.

La Garde Freinet – Maison du Tourisme, Chapelle St. Jean, Place de la Mairie, 83680 La Garde Freinet, ☎ 33 04 94 43 67 41, fax 33 04 94 43 08 69, ot_lgf@club-internet.fr, www.lagardefreinet-tourisme.com.

Gordes – Office de Tourisme, Le Château, 84220 Gordes, ☎ 0 4 90 72 02 75, fax 33 04 90 72 02 26, office.gordes@wanadoo.fr, www.gordes-village.com.

Grasse – Office de Tourisme, Place du Cours Honoré Cresp, 06130 Grasse, ☎ 33 04 93 36 03 56, info@grasse-riviera.com, www.grasse-riviera.com/en.

Haute Roya – Office de Tourisme, La Haute-Roya, ☎ 33 04 93 04 73 71.

L'Isle sur la Sorgue – Office de Tourisme, Place de la Liberté, 84800 Isle sur la Sorgue, ☎ 33 04 90 38 04 78, fax 33 04 90 38 35 43, contact@ot-islesurlasorgue.fr, http://www.ot-islesurlasorgue.fr.

ISOLA 2000 – Office du tourisme, ISOLA 2000, 06420 Isola 2000, ☎ 33 04 93 23 15 15, fax 33 04 93 23 14 25, info@isola2000.com, www.isola2000.com and www.skifrance.fr.

Marseille – Office de Tourisme et des Congrès de Marseille, 4 La Canebière, 13001 Marseille, ☎ 33 04 91 13 89 00, fax 33 04 91 13 89 20, accueil@marseille-tourisme.com, www.marseille-tourisme.com.

Martigues – Office de Tourisme, Rond-point de l'Hôtel de Ville, 13500 Martigues, ☎ 33 04 42 42 31 10, fax 33 04 42 42 31 11, info@martigues-tourisme.com, www.martigues-tourisme.com.

Maussane – Office de Tourisme, Place Laugier de Monblan, 13520 Maussane les Alpilles, ☎ 33 04 90 54 52 04, contact@maussane.com. www.maussane.com.

Menton – Office de Tourisme, 8 Avenue Boyer, BP239, 06506 Menton, ☎ 33 04 92 41 76 76, fax 33 04 92 41 76 78, tourisme@menton.fr, www.villedementon.com.

Mouriès – Tourist Office, 2 Rue du Temple, BP 37, 13890 Mouriès, ☎ 33 04 90 47 56 58, office@mouries.com, www.mouries.com.

Nice – Office du Tourisme et des Congres, 5 Promenade des Anglais, BP 4079, 06302 Nice, ☎ 33 08 92 70 74 07, fax 33 04 92 14 48 03, info@nicetourism.com, www.nicetourism.com.

Nîmes – Office de Tourisme, 6 Rue August, ☎ 33 04 66 67 29 11, info@ot-nimes.fr, www.ot-nimes.fr.

Orange – Office de Tourisme, 5 Cours Aristide Briand, 84100 Orange, ☎ 33 04 90 34 70 88, fax 33 04 90 34 99 62, officetourismeorange@wannadoo.fr, www.provence-orange.com/indexuk.htm.

Pays de Fayence region – www.paysdefayence.com. Villages of the Pays de Fayence:

- **Callian** – 3 Place Bourguignon, 83440 Callian, ☎/fax 33 04 94 47 75 77, tourisme-callian@wanadoo.fr, www.callian.fr.
- **Fayence** – Office de Tourisme de Fayence, Place Léon Roux, 83440 Fayence, ☎ 33 04 94 76 20 08, fax 33 04 94 39 15 96, ot.fayence@wanadoo.fr, www.mairiedefayence.com.
- **Montauroux** – Office de Tourisme de Montauroux, Place du Clos, Village Center, ☎ 33 04 94 47 75 90, fax 33 04 94 47 61 97, montauroux.tourisme@wanadoo.fr, http://tourisme.montauroux.com.
- **Mons** – Office de Tourisme, Place St. Sébastien, 83440 Mons ☎/fax 33 04 94 76 39 54, o.t.mons@wanadoo.fr.
- **Saint Paul en Forêt** – Office de Tourisme, Rue de la Mairie, 83440 Saint Paul en Forêt, ☎ 33 04 94 39 08 80, fax 33 04 94 39 08 89.
- **Seillans** – Office de Tourisme, Le Valat, 83440 Seillans, ☎ 33 04 94 76 85 91, fax 33 04 94 39 13 53, ot.seillans@wanadoo.fr.
- **Tanneron** – Office de Tourisme, Place de la Mairie, 83440 Tanneron, ☎/fax 33 04 93 60 71 73, officetourismetanneron@wanadoo.fr.
- **Tourrettes** – Office de Tourisme, Place de la Mairie, 83440 Tourrettes, ☎ 33 04 94 39 07 20, fax 33 04 94 39 07 25.

Pierrefeu du Var – Office de Tourisme, 20 Boulevard Henri Guérin, 83 390 Pierrefeu du Var, ☎ 33 04 94 28 27 30, fax 33 04 94 28 21 78, contact@ot-pierrefeu.com, www.ot-pierrefeu.com.

Pont du Gard – Tourist Office of the Pont du Gard, Place des Grands Jours, 30210 Remoulins, ☎ 33 04 66 37 22 34, ot.remoulins@free.fr, www.ot-pontdugard.com/ang/index.htm.

Pra Loup – Office de Tourisme, 04400 Pra Loup, ☎ 33 04 92 84 10 04, fax 33 04 92 84 02 93, info@praloup.com, www.praloup.com. For lift information: Pra Loup Developpement, Immeuble le Génépi, 04400 Pra Loup, ☎ 33 04 92 84 11 54, fax 33 04 92 84 18 94, transmontagne@skipass-praloup.com, www.skipass-praloup.com.

Roubion – Mairie, ☎ 33 04 93 02 10 30, fax 33 04 93 02 10 30, ot.roubion@smtm06.fr, www.ville-roubion.fr/index.cfm.

Roure – Office de Tourisme, Roure, Rue Centrale, 06420 Roure, ☎ 04 93 02 00 70, fax 04 93 02 00 72, www.ville-roure.fr/index.cfm.

Roussillon – Office de Tourisme, Place de la Poste, 84220 Roussillon, ☎ 33 04 90 05 60 25, ☎/fax 33 04 90 05 63 31, ot-roussillon@axit.fr, www.roussillon-provence.com.

Saint Étienne de Tinée – Office de Tourisme, 06660 Saint Étienne de Tinée, ☎ 33 04 93 02 41 96, fax 33 04 93 02 48 50.

Saint Martin Vésubie – Office de Tourisme, Place Félix Faure, BP 12, 06450 St-Martin-Vésubie, ☎ 33 04 93 03 21 28, fax 33 04 93 03 21 44, o-t-hautevésubie@wanadoo.fr, www.pays-vesubie.com.

Saint Raphaël – Office Municipal de Tourisme et des Congrès, Rue Waldeck Rousseau, BP 210, 83702 Saint Raphaël, ☎ 33 04 94 19 52 52, fax 33 04 94 83 85 40, information@saint-raphael.com, www.saint-raphael.com.

Saint Rémy de Provence – Office du Tourisme, Place Jean Jaurès, 13210 Saint Rémy de Provence, ☎ 33 04 90 92 05, www.saintremy-de-provence.com. Also, Place du Général de Gaulle, Z.A.C. de la Gare, 13210 Saint Rémy de Provence, ☎ 33 04 90 92 05 22, fax 33 04 90 92 38 52.

Saint Saveur sur Tinée – Syndicat d'Initiative, Mairie, 06420 Saint Sauveur sur Tinée, ☎ 33 04 93 02 00 22, fax 33 04 93 02 05 20 or Parc National du Mercantour, 11 Avenue des Blavets, 06420 Saint Sauveur sur Tinée, ☎ 33 04 93 02 01 63, mercantour.moyenne.tinee@wanadoo.fr.

Saintes Maries de la Mer – Office de Tourisme, 5 Avenue Van Gogh, BP 73, 13732 Saintes Maries de la Mer, ☎ 33 04 90 97 82 55, fax 33 04 90 97 71 15, info@saintesmaries.com, www.saintesmaries.com.

Salon de Provence – Office de Tourisme, 56 Cours Gimon, 133 00 Salon de Provence, ☎ 33 04 90 56 27 60, fax 33 04 90 56 77 09, ot.salon@wanadoo.fr.

Tarascon – Office de Tourisme, 59 Rue des Halles, 13150 Tarascon, ☎ 33 04 90 91 03 52, fax 33 04 90 91 22 96, tourisme@tarascon.org, www.tarascon.org.

Tende – Office de Tourisme, Avenue du 16 Septembre 1947, 06430 Tende-Val des Merveilles, ☎ 0 4 93 04 73 71, fax 33 04 93 04 35 09, info@tendemerveilles.com, www.tendemerveilles.com.

La Turbie – Mairie de la Turbie, ☎ 33 04 92 41 51 61, fax 33 04 92 41 13 99, info@ville-la-turbie.fr, www.ville-la-turbie.fr.

Vaison La Romaine – Office de Tourisme, BP 53 Place du Chanoine Sautel, ☎ 33 04 90 36 02 11, fax 33 04 90 28 76 04, tourisme@Vaison la Romaine.com or ot-vaison@axit.fr, www.vaison-la-romaine.com.

Valberg – Office du Tourisme, 4 Place du Quartier, 06470 Valberg, ☎ 33 04 93 23 24 25, fax 33 04 93 02 52 27, ot@valberg.com, www.valberg.com.

Uzès – Office de Tourisme d'Uzès et de l'Uzège, Chapelle des Capuçins, Place Albert 1er, BP 129, 30703 Uzès, ☎ 33 04 66 22 68 88, otuzes@wanadoo.fr.

■ Regional Tourist Boards

Alpes de Haute Provence, Comité Départemental du Tourisme des Alpes de Haute Provence, Maison des Alpes de Haute Provence, 19 Rue du Docteur Honnorat, BP 170, 04005 Digne les Bains, ☎ 33 04 92 31 57 29, fax 33 04 92 32 24 94, info@alpes-haute-provence.com, www.alpes-haute-provence.com.

Alpes Maritime, Conseil General des Alpes Martime, Tourisme, www.cg06.fr/tourisme/tourisme-liens.html.

Bouches du Rhône, Comité Départemental du Tourisme des Bouches du Rhône, 13 Rue Roux de Brignoles, 13006 Marseille, ☎ 33 04 91 13 84 13, fax 33 04 91 33 01 82, dt13@visitprovence.com, www.visitprovence.com/servlet/esolution?langue=2&dist=2GP.

La Drome, Comité Départemental du Tourisme de la Drôme, 8 Rue Baudin, BP 531, 26005 Valence, ☎ 33 04 75 82 19 26, fax 33 04 75 56 01 65, info@drometourisme.com, http://www.drometourisme.com.

Gard, Comité Départemental du Tourisme du Gard, 3 Place des Arènes, BP 122, 30010 Nimes, ☎ 33 04 66 36 96 30, fax 33 04 66 36 13 14, contact@tourismegard.com, www.cdt-gard.fr.

Provence Alps-Côte d'Azur (PACA), Comité Régional du Tourisme PACA, Les Docks, Atrium 10.5, 10 Place de la Joliette, BP 46214, 13267 Marseille, ☎ 33 04 91 56 47 00, fax 33 04 91 56 47 01, information@crt-paca.fr, www.crt-paca.fr.

Roya and Bevera Valley, Roya-Bévéra, Pôle Touristique, ☎ 33 04 93 04 92 05, fax 04 93 04 99 91, royabevera@wanadoo.fr, www.royabevera.com.

Var, Comité Départemental du Tourisme du Var, 1 Boulevard Foch, 83003 Draguignan, ☎ 33 04 94 50 55 50, fax 33 04 94 50 55, info@cdtvar.com, www.tourismevar.com.

Vaucluse, Comité Départemental du Tourisme de Vaucluse, 12 Rue Collège de la Croix, BP 147, 84008 Avignon Cedex, ☎ 33 04 90 86 43 42.

■ Useful Contacts

Information

Universal Currency Converter – www.xe.com/ucc.

Relais Routiers – www.relais-routiers.com. An online directory of inexpensive restaurants near major routes. The site is in French but not too difficult to work out. Clicking on *Choissisez Votre Relais Routiers* in the middle of the page redirects you to an interactive page where you can choose the area you're interested in.

Accommodations

Gîtes de France – La Maison des Gîtes de France et du Tourisme Vert, 59 Rue Saint-Lazare, 75 439 PARIS Cedex 09, ☎ 33 01 49 70 75 75, fax 33 01 42 81.28 53, info@gites-de-france.fr, www.gites-de-france.fr/eng.

Gîte de France Alpes de Haute Provence – Rond Point du 11 Novembre, 04000 Digne-le-Bains, ☎ 33 04 92 31 52 39, fax 33 04 92 32 32 63.

Gîte de France Vaucluse Place Campana – BP 164, 84008 Avignon, ☎ 33 04 90 85 45 00, fax 33 04 90 85 88 49.

Fédération Française de Camping et de Caravaning – 78 Rue de Rivoli, 75004 Paris, ☎ 33 01 42 72 84 08, fax 33 01 42 72 70 21, info@ffcc.fr, www.ffcc.fr (click on *Campings* at this French-language site for links to English-language campsites).

L'Annuaire Hébergement Rural en France (HRFrance) – www.hrfrance.com/index.php. Online source for rural and village accommodation. French-language site.

Ibis Hotels – Basic, modern budget hotels all over France. Not much character but good value for money. Book online. The website has a good interactive map. www.ibishotel.com/ibis.

Logis de France – Fédération Nationale des Logis de France, 83 Avenue d'Italie, 75013 Paris, ☎ 33 01 45 84 83 84, fax 33 01 45 83 59 66, www.logis-de-france.fr. A ratings and listing service for a huge number of independently owned restaurant-hotels which must meet strict standards of quality and service. A very reliable indicator of comfortable accommodation.

Mercure Hotels – 1 Rue Jean Vilar, 84000 Avignon, ☎ 33 04 90 80 93 00, fax 33 04 90 80 93 01, H1952@accor-hotels.com, www.mercure.com. Comfortable independent hotels, often in town centers or interesting locations.

Activities

Cycling

Fédération Française de Cyclisme – Bat. Jean Monnet, 5, Rue de Rome, 93561 Rosny sous Bois, ☎ 33 01 49 35 69 00, www.ffc.fr. French-language cycling site full of easy-to-understand cycling information and contacts.

Fishing

Gard Fishing and Environment Association – 34 Rue Gustave Eiffel, 3000 Nîmes, ☎ 33 04 66 02 91 61.

Riding

Association Departmentale de Tourisme Equestre en Vaucluse – ADTEV, Comité Departmental D'Equitation, President René Francois, Chemin de Saint-Julien. 30133 Les Angles, ☎/fax 33 04 90 25 38 91. List of riding centers, classes, accompanied rides, lodgings for riders and horses.

Walking & Hiking

Fédération Française de la Randonée Pédestre and Centre d'Information de la Randonnée Pédestre – FFRP, 14 Rue Riquet, 75019 Paris, ☎ 33 01 44 89 93 93, fax 33 01 40 35 85 67, info@ffrp.asso.fr, www.ffrp.asso.fr. The French Rambler's Association, with information on GR trails, Topo-Guides, maps.

Club Alpin Français CAF des Alpes-Maritimes – 14 Avenue Mirabeau, 06000 Nice, ☎ 33 04, 93 62 59 99, fax 33 04 93 92 09 55, cafnice@cafnice.org, www.cafnice.org/cafbase/accueil.php.

Parc National du Mercantour – 11 Avenue des Blavets, 06420 Saint Sauveur sur Tinée, ☎ 33 04 93 02 01 63, mercantour.moyenne.tinee@wanadoo.fr, or Parc du Mercantour, 23 Rue d'Italie, BP 1316, 06006 Nice, ☎ 33 04 93 16 78 88, fax 33 04 93 88 79 05, mercantour@wanadoo.fr, www.parc-mercantour.com and www.parks.it/parco.alpi.marittime.

Paragliding

Fédération Française de Vol Libre (FFVL) – 4 Rue de Suisse, 06000 Nice, ☎ 33 04 97 03 82 82, fax 33 04 97 03 82 83, ffvl@ffvl.fr, www.ffvl.fr.

Transportation

Air

Marseille-Provence Airport – contact@marseille-provence.aeroport.fr, 24-hour information desk, ☎ 33 04 42 14 21 14.

Nice Côte d'Azur Airport – www.nice.aeroport.fr, ☎ (from within France only) 08 36 69 55 55.

Rail

TGV Méditerranée – www.tgv.com, tgv@voyages-sncf.com. High-speed, long-distance rail schedules and information.

Rail Pass – www.railpass.com, from the US, ☎ 877-RAILPASS. US-only access to European Rail network.

Rail Europe – www.raileurope.com, from the US, ☎ 877-257-2887; from Canada, ☎ 800-361-RAIL. From the UK contact www.raileurope.co.uk, reservations@raileurope.co.uk, ☎ 08705-848-848.

Car

Rail Europe – ☎ 877-EUROVAC from the US and Canada. Offers below-advertised rates for popular brand rental cars.

France Car Rental – from the US ☎ 786-866-2865, info@francecarrental.net.

Local Bus Services

Santa Azur – Gare Routière de Nice, 5 Boulevard Jean-Jaurès, 06300 Nice, ☎ 33 04 93 85 92 60, fax 33 04 93 85 48 74, www.santa-azur.com.

Emergencies

To report a lost or stolen credit card in France:

American Express – ☎ 01 47 77-72 00.

Diners Club – ☎ 08 10 31 41 59.

MasterCard – ☎ 08 00 90 13 87.

VISA – Global customer assistance, ☎ 08 00 90 11 79 or call US collect 001-410-581-9994 or 001-410-581-3836.

Consular Services

USA – US Consul General Marseille, Place Varian Fry, 13286 Marseille Cedex 6, ☎ 04 91 54 92 00, amcongenmars@fr.inter.net.

Canada – For 24/7 emergency assistance for Canadian citizens in distress, dial the Canadian Embassy switchboard at ☎ 01 44 43 29 00 or paris-consulaire@dfait-maeci.gc.ca.

United Kingdom – British Consular Services, 24 Avenue du Prado, 13006 Marseille, ☎ 04 91 15 72 10, consulare-mailpavis.consulare-mailpavis2@fco.gov.uk.

Maps & Guidebooks

IGN Maps

Institut Géographique National (IGN) – Purchase online at the French-language site, www.ign.fr.

Map Link Inc, Map Distributors, 30 S. La Patera Lane, Unit 5, Santa Barbara, CA 93117, ☎ 805-692-6777, billhunt@maplinkinc.com.

Navigator Maps Ltd, 4 Devonshire Street, Ambergate PO Box 6242, DE56 2GJ, Derby, ☎ 01773 857 996, www.navimaps.co.uk.

Stanfords, 12-14 Long Acre, London, WC2E 9LP, ☎ 020 7836 1321, fax 020 7836 0189, customer.services@stanfords.co.uk, www.stanfords.co.uk.

Glossary

À la ferme (aa lah FAIRM) – Describes open-air and tent camping. Literally "on the farm."

À la mode (aa lah mod) – In the style of. Used with food and usually combined with the name of a town or region, as in *boeuf à la mode de Beaucaire* to describe a way of cooking beef.

Abrivados (ah-bree-VAH-do) – Running of small numbers of bulls through the streets, accompanied by *gardians de taureaux* (see below). Popular in Alpilles and Camargue areas of Provence.

Aïoli (eye-OH-lee) – A garlicky mayonnaise sauce eaten with vegetables and fish. A *Grande Aïoli* is a banquette of many dishes served with this sauce. It is often served at public celebrations and includes raw and cooked vegetables, steamed fish, shellfish and crustaceans.

Appellation d'Origine Contrôlée (ap-LAH-ssion dory-ZHEEN cahn-tro-LAY) – A certification of wine and some key heritage products (olives, olive oil) guaranteeing their area of origin. Usually abbreviated as *AOC*.

Arrière pays (aa-ree-AIR pay-YEE) – Back country.

Attributs (AAH-tree-bu) – Tokens removed from the bull's horns in the *Course Camarguaise* (see below)

Auberge (oh-BAIRZH) – A country inn, usually with a restaurant.

Bac (Bahck) – A river ferry.

Balisage (baa-lee-SAZH) – A signposted trail for hiking or cycling.

Bar tabac (bar taBAHK) – More like a pub than a bar, this is a local place where you can have an alcoholic beverage, a coffee or a soft drink, buy a lottery ticket or cigarettes. Sometimes sandwiches are available. All towns have tabacs. In the smaller towns, they may be open for coffee and croissants at breakfast time.

Basilic (BAA-zil-eek) – Basil.

Bastide (ba-STEED) – A substantial farmhouse or rural house.

Berlingots (burl-ing-GOAT) – Hard candies, a specialty of Carpentras.

Billets (BEE-yay) – Transportation tickets or notes of currency.

Biòu (Byou) – Bull in Provençal language.

Bis (BEE-ss) – Usually indicates an alternative or secondary road, or a smaller branch of a larger store. The word actually means "again."

Bories (BOHR-eez) – Beehive-shaped, dry stone buildings used for different purposes, erected from ancient times until about the 18th century, common on the Lubéron.

Boulangerie (boo-LAHNZH-er-ee) – Bakery that sells bread and yeast-risen baked goods.

Brandade de Morue (brahn-DAHD duh maw-ROO) – A spread or dip made of salt cod, garlic and olive oil.

Brocantes (broke-AUNTS) – Bric-a-brac.

Cabanes (ka-BAHN) – Traditional, thatch-roofed dwelling in the Camargue.

Calades (ka-LAHD) – Steep village streets where the paving includes cobbled steps.

Calanques (ka-LAHNK) – Rocky Mediterranean inlet, often lined with limestone needles or cliffs. Mini-fiords.

Calissons d'Aix (KAH-lee-sone DAYKS) – Traditional almond and melon sweet. Specialty of Aix en Provence.

Camelles, les (ka-MEL) – Pyramids of sea salt.

Caves du vin (KAHV doo VAAN) – Wine cellars. Usually used to indicate a place where wines are not only kept but also sold.

Chambre d'hôte (SHAHM-bruh DOHT) – Bed and breakfast accommodation. Other meals may also be served.

Champêtre (SHAHM-peh-truh) – An adjective describing something pertaining to rural or country life.

Chemin de fer (shuh-MAA duh FAIR) – Railroad, or a gambling game played in Riviera casinos.

Col (KOAL) – Mountain pass.

Colline (ka-LEEN) – Hillside.

Compté (kon-TAY) – Old French spelling for county. Today it is usually spelled Comté but the old spelling is sometimes found in traditional Provence place names.

Confiserie (cahn-FEESS-ree) – A shop where candy and sweets are sold. Traditionally, this is also a place where they are made.

Corniche (kor-NEESH) – Particularly scenic coastal road. The corniches of the Côte d'Azur overlook the sea from ledges on the massifs and the Alps.

Course Camarguaise (koorss kaa-mar-GAZE) – A game with bulls in which participants try to grab tokens or *attributs* (see above) from the animals' horns. Popular in the arenas and stadiums of the Alpilles and the Camargue, where both the players and the bulls can become celebrities. The game is a traditional part of festivals and celebrations as well as a weekend pastime from spring through late fall.

Cuisine du terroir (kwee-ZEEN doo teh-WAHR) – Regional cooking using local ingredients. The word terroir comes from terre, the French word for earth.

Cyste (seasste) – Rock roses or eglantine, a common plant in the garrigue and on the massifs.

Déjeuner (DAY-jun-ay) – Lunch.

Département (DAY-part-mont) – An administrative division and government, similar to a US state.

Distributeurs automatiques de billets (dis-trib-eu-TURRS auto-mah-TEEK duh bee-YAY) – ATMs, often abbreviated as DAB.

École (ay-KOAL) – School.

En vrac (on VRAK) – In bulk. Wine that is poured into your own containers from barrels is sold *en vrac*.

Escalade (ehs-cuh-LAHD) – Cliff climbing.

Étang (ay-TONG) – Coastal lake lagoon, usually large and shallow.

Évasion verte (ay-VAH-zyon vairt) – Vacation in the country. Literally "green getaway."

Feu d'artifice (fuh dart'FEESS) – Fireworks.

Feu de bois (fuh duh BWAH) – Wood fire. Describes a method of cooking, as in pizza *feu de bois* – pizza cooked in a wood-burning oven.

Fougasse (foo-GAHSS) – Soft, flat bread made with olive oil and often flavored with olives or herbs.

Fruits de mer (frou-EE d'MAIR) – Shellfish and crustaceans.

Galoubet (GAL-oo-bay) – A flute or pipe used in traditional Provençal music, similar to an Irish tin whistle or an American fife.

Gardianne de taureau (Gard-YAAN duh tor-ROW) – A stew of bull or beef in red wine, traditional in the Camargue and often served at *manades* (see below).

Gardians (gard-YAHN) – Traditional Camargue cowboy and herder of bulls.

Gardonnades (gar-doe-NADE) – Sudden sharp storm that sends a torrent down the River Gardon. A weather danger for canyoners.

Gare (Gar) – Train station. A bus station is a Gare Routière.

Garrigue (gaa-REEG) – Dry scrubby plants as well as the arid limestone landscape in which they are found.

Gitan (zhee-TAHN) – A kind of gypsy.

Gîte (zheet) – A cabin or house with kitchen, usually rented by the week. They range from basic comfort to luxury.

Gîte d'étape (zheet day-TAP) – A basic shelter for hikers or cyclists. Like a hostel. Accommodation may be dormitory-style with shared cooking and sanitary facilities.

Glacières (GLAS-yaire) – Antique ice houses.

Hébergement (ay-BAIRZH-uh-mon) – Accommodation. General term taking in all categories.

Horloge (oar-LOGHE) – Clock tower.

Immeuble (em-MUHB-luh) – Apartment or flat.

Journée (zhoor-NAY) – One form of the word for day (jour), which suggests the passage of a whole day rather than simply a date on a calendar. *Toute la journée* means all day long.

Joutes – Jousting, particularly boat jousting, popular at festivals in Provence.

La farniente (la far-NYEN-tay) – Loafing around, idling. From the Italian phrase *la dolce farniente*, meaning the sweetness of doing nothing. A popular way to describe the main pastime on the Riviera.

Lac (lack) – Lake.

Lavoire (Laav-WAHR) – A public washhouse, found in ancient villages and among Roman or medieval ruins. Also a public well for washing clothes.

Les Halles (Lay AHL) – Covered market.

Loisirs (lwah-ZEER) – Leisure activities and pastimes.

Grand magasin (Grahn mag-uh-ZAAN) – Department store.

Mairie (mair-REE) – Town hall.

Maison forestière (may-ZONE faw-rest-YAIR) – Forest ranger station.

Manade (mahn-AHD) – A herd of semi-wild Camargue bulls or the ranch that tends them.

Manadier (mahn-ahd-YEAH) – A Camargue rancher, particularly a herder of bulls and ponies.

Mas (Mahss) – A traditional Provencal farmhouse with vaulted rooms on the lower floors that were once stables and barns. Houses have no windows on the northern side to protect from the Mistral.

Massif (mass-EEF) – A compact group of mountains.

Médecin (maid-SAA) – Doctor.

Micocoulier (mick-koh-cool-YEAH) – Deciduous shade tree, common in the dryer regions of Provence, particularly in the Alpilles.

Monstre-sacré (MOHN-struh s'CRAY) – An idiomatic expression for someone or something esteemed and above criticism. It means sacred monster. Think "sacred cow" and you've got it.

Navette (nah-VET) – Shuttle bus.

Neroli (ne-roll-EE) – Orange blossom oil.

Patisserie (Pah-TEESS-ree) – A bakery specializing in fancy cakes and pastries or the pastries sold there. Often operating in connection with a *salon de thé* (see below) or a *confiserie* (see above).

Pan bagnat (Pan ban-YAH) – Traditional sandwich in Nice – basically a salade niçoise on bread.

Patrimoine (pat-ri-MWAHNE) – Heritage and tradition.

Pétanque (pay-TAHNK) – Southern version of the game of boules. Played, almost always by men, in town squares all over Provence.

Phare (fahr) – Lighthouse.

Pichet (pee-SHAY) – A small jug or pitcher for serving portions of water or wine.

Pierres et poutres (p'YAIR ay POO-truh) – Stone walls and exposed beams.

Plage (PLAZH) – Beach.

Planche à voile (plahnsh aa VWAHL) – Windsurfing.

Pression (press-YAWN) – Draft beer.

Randonnée (RAN-dun-AY) – A ramble. The word is used to describe either a purposeful hike along a trail or a similar cycle ride.

Repas (ruh-PAH) – A meal, usually lunch and dinner, not breakfast.

Romarin (ROW-muh-RAA) – Rosemary.

Rond-point (RAHN-PWAH) – Roundabout, traffic circle.

Rouille (roo-EEE) – A pungent mayonnaise, colored with saffron and flavored with liberal quantities of chilis and garlic. Traditionally served with bouillabaisse and fish dishes.

Rouille de poulpes (roo-EEE duh POOL-puh) – Octopus in a *rouille* (see above) sauce.

Ruelles (roo-ELLE) – Tiny lanes found in the old centers of medieval villages. Usually pedestrian-only.

Salon de thé (SAL-ohn duh TAY) – Tea shop. This is a place where *patisseries* (rich pastries) are consumed with tea, hot chocolate and sometimes coffee. Savory pastries may be served at lunch time. Generally these are operated in connection with a *patisserie* or *confiserie*.

Sansouire (saahn-SWEER) – A salt plain on the edge of marshes in the Camargue and other littoral wetlands.

Santons (saahn-TONE) – Small, handpainted terra cotta figures of saints, typical Provençal characters and ordinary people. The figures originated for use in Christmas crêches and major festivals selling them are still held around Christmas. A classic and very popular craft of Provence.

Saucisson sec (saucy-SONE seck) – Salami.

Service compris (sair-VEESS come-PREE) – Indicates that a gratuity is included in the price. Also *compris* or *non compris* to indicate that something (usually wine or coffee and dessert) is or is not included in the price.

Site classé (SEAT klass-AY) – A site classified because of its historic or ecological importance, or because it is an area of outstanding natural beauty.

Socca (SAW-ka) – A large pancake made with chickpea flour, cut in squares, and peppered. A traditional midmorning snack with a glass of wine in Nice.

Soupe de poisson (SOUP duh pwah-SONE) – Very spicy, garlicy fish soup which combines many different kinds of Mediterranean fish.

Tambourin (tam-boo-RAAHN) – A traditional drum, tall in shape, played with one stick and carried by the player in marches.

Tapenade (TOP-n-ODD) – A paste made of crushed olives, spread on bread and used in regional dishes.

Télécarte (tele-CART) – A card needed for public pay telephones. Sold in Bar-Tabacs and sometimes at newstands.

Tellines (tell-EEN) – Small, highly prized clams.

TER (TAY AY AR or sometimes TAIR) – Regional rail service, connecting larger towns. Short for *Trains Express Regionaux*.

TGV (TAY ZHAY VAY) – National high-speed, long-distance rail service. Short for *Trains à Grand Vitesse*.

Thermes (TAIRM) – Spas or hot springs – usually referring to ancient Roman baths.

Vélo (VAY-low) – Bicycle.

VTT (VAY TAY TAY) – Mountain bike; it stands for *vélo tout terrain,* bike for all terrain.

Véloroutes (VAY-low-ROOT) – Cycle paths.

Vieille (VYAY) – A feminine version of the word for old, as in *Vieille Ville*, meaning old town.

Vieux (Vyuh) – A masculine version of old, as in *Vieux Port*, or old port.

Village perchée (vee-LAHZH pair-SHAY) – Fortified, hilltop village.

Voie (Vwah) – Way or route, usually used in the names of ancient Roman roads.

Voile (Vwahl) – Sail. *A planche à voile* is a windsurfer.

Index

Abbaye Saint Victor: *Marseille,* 160
Abseiling: *Castellane,* 197
Accrobranching: *Vaucluse,* 138
Agay, 266-67, 286
Aigues Mortes, 49; camping, 92; festivals, 88-89; gîtes, 94; history, 81-82; restaurants, 94; shopping, 89-90; sightseeing, 83; travel to, 83
Airports, 26-27, 38
Aix en Provence, 6, 147-48, 147-49; art and architecture, 172-73; camping, 180-81; festivals, 171-72; gîtes, 181; hotels, 177-80; markets, 176; restaurants, 182-84; shopping, 173-75; sightseeing, 151-53; transportation, 151; travel to, 149
Alpilles, 37; boating, 67-68; cycling, 65-66; driving tours, 64; hiking/walking paths, 62-63; hot air ballooning, 68; hotels, 66-67; rock climbing, 63-64; transportation, 39; travel to, 38-39
Anatole Jakovsky International Museum of Naive Art: *Nice,* 323
Anthéor, 267-68
Antibes-Juan Les Pins, 5, 308-10, 311-12; beaches, 314; festivals, 339-40; hotels, 351, 353; jazz, 310-11; markets, 342; restaurants, 357-58; shopping, 342; sightseeing, 315-16; travel to, 312-13; watersports, 374-75
Apt, 109-11; eco-tourism, 144-45; markets, 127; sightseeing, 111; travel to, 110
Arbaud Museum: *Aix en Provence,* 170
Archaeology Museum: *Antibes-Juan Les Pins,* 315
Archaeology Museum of Nice-Cimiez: *Nice,* 323, 325
Arles, 37; camping, 92; festivals, 87-88; gîtes, 93-94; history, 74-77; hotels, 90, 91-92; map, 75; restaurants, 94-96; shopping, 89; sightseeing, 76-77, 77-79; travel to, 77
Arrière, 321-22
Art and architecture, 16-17, 17-18
ATM machines, 32
Auberges, 29

Avignon, 8, 39-42; airport, 38; camping, 59; festivals, 18, 41, 54; hotels, 56, 58; markets, 54; shopping, 54, 55; sightseeing, 42

Bakeries, 19
Banks. *See* Currency exchange
Bar tabac, 20
Basilica of Notre Dame de la Garde: *Marseille,* 160
Basilique Saint Michel Archange: *Menton,* 326, 330
Beaches: *Antibes-Juan Les Pins,* 314; *Camargue,* 85-87; *Les Saintes Maries de la Mer,* 81; map, 84; *Marseille,* 192; *St. Tropez,* 236-37
Beaucaire, 50-51; festivals, 54; hotels, 57-58, 59; restaurants, 61-62
Biot, 333-34, 356
Bistros, 20. *See also* Restaurants
Blot, 333-34
Boating: *Alpilles,* 67-68; *Camargue,* 101-2; *Massif de l'Estérel,* 276-77, 277-78; *Saint Raphaël,* 276-78
Boulangeries, 19
Boulouris, 263-64
Bureaux de Change, 32

Cabanes, 81
Cabs. *See* Taxi services
Cafés, 20. *See also* Restaurants
Calanques of Marseille, 162-65, 184-85
Camargue, 22, 71-74; beaches, 85-87; birdwatching, 103-4; canoeing, 101; climate, 96; cycling, 97-99; fishing, 102-3; habitats, 72-74; hiking/walking, 97; horseback riding, 99-100; jeep safaris, 99; kayaking, 101; map, 84; restaurants, 94-96; sailing, 100-101; transportation, 72; windsurfing and sailing, 100-101
Camping, 30; *Aigues Mortes,* 92; *Aix,* 180-81; *Arles,* 92; *Avignon,* 59; *Camargue,* 92; *Eygalières,* 59; *French Riviera,* 354; *Les Adrets de l'Estérel,* 286; *Les Saintes Maries de la Mer,* 92; *Marseille,* 180-81; *Massif des Maures,* 228; *Mauresque Coast,* 248; *Saint*

Raphaël, 286; *St. Rémy de Provence,* 59; *Vaucluse,* 128-32
Cannes: cinema, 303-4; history, 302-3; hotels, 344-46, 347-48, 349-51, 352-53; map, 301; markets, 341-42; restaurants, 354-55; shopping, 341; sightseeing, 304-7; travel to, 307-8
Canoeing: *Camargue,* 101; *Massif de l'Estérel,* 274-75
Cap d'Antibes, 347
Carpentras, 111-13, 127
Carré d'Art: *Nîmes,* 46
Car rentals, 28
Cassis, 165-66, 170, 177
Castellane: abseiling, 197; driving tour, 204, 205-6; hiking, 198-200; hotels, 207-8, 210, 211; restaurants, 211; tourist information, 211
Cathedral de la Madeleine: *Martigues,* 168
Cathedrale Sainte Réparate: *Nice,* 324
Cathedral of Notre Dame and Cloister: *Vaison la Romaine,* 121
Cathedral of Saint Sauveur: *Aix en Provence,* 152-53
Cathedral of St. Trophime: *Arles,* 76, 78
Cathedral of Ste. Anne: *Apt,* 11, 110
Cathedral of St Siffrein: *Carpentras,* 112
Cathedral Saint Sauveur: *Aix en Provence,* 152
Cézanne, Paul, 148, 152, 173, 176, 177
Chambre d'hôtes, 30, 284-85
Chapelle Cocteau: *Fréjus,* 258
Chapelle de la Miséricorde: *Nice,* 324
Chapelle des Pénitents Blancs: *Menton,* 326
Chapelle de St. Sixte: *Eygalières,* 51
Châteauneuf-du-Pape, 37, 106, 121, 125, 134; markets, 127; shopping, 126, 127
Churches and cathedrals: *Aigues Mortes,* 81; *Aix en Provence,* 152, 168; *Apt,* 11, 110; *Arles,* 76, 78, 79; *Carpentras,* 112; *Fréjus,* 257-58; *Marseille,* 160; *Menton,* 326, 330; *Mougins,* 337; *Nice,* 319, 324-25; *Nîmes,* 48-49; *Saint Raphaël,* 263; *St Rémy de Provence,* 48-49, 50; *Vaison la Romaine,* 121; *Vers Pont du Gard,* 67

Church of Notre Dame de la Mer: *Aigues Mortes,* 81
Climate, 12
Climbing. See Rock climbing
Collobrières, 218-20; map, 219
Comtat Venaissin, 108
Consular services, 35, 390
Corniche des Crêtes, 190
Cost of Living, 33
Crau, 74
Credit cards, 32
Cristallerie des Papes: *Fontaine de Vaucluse,* 122
Currency exchange, 31-32, 32, 388
Customs regulations, 30-31
Cycling, 23-25, 29, 389; *Camargue,* 97-99; *Garrigues,* 65-66; itineraries, 140-42, 187-90; *La Sainte Baume,* 186-90; *Marseille,* 186-90; *Massif du Tanneron,* 289-90; *Pierrefeu du Var,* 223-26; tours, 142-43; *Vaucluse,* 139-43

Deep-sea fishing: *French Riviera,* 375
Digne les Bains, 212-13
Dining. See Restaurants
Discount passes, 33, 42, 158
Diving: *Antibes-Juan Les Pins,* 375; *Marseille,* 190-91; *Nice,* 375-76; *Saint Raphaël,* 278-79
Driving tours: *Alpilles,* 64; *Castellane,* 204, 205-6; *French Riviera,* 377-79; *Les Gorges du Verdon,* 204-6; *Marseille,* 190

Economy, 13-14
Eco-travel/tourism: *Alpilles,* 68-69; *Apt,* 144-45; *Camargue,* 70; *Fréjus,* 273-74; *French Riviera,* 380-81; *Gorges du Gardon,* 68-69; *Lubéron,* 144-45; *Mercantour,* 380-81; *Sault en Provence,* 144-45; *Vaucluse,* 144-45
Eglise Saint Raphaël: *Saint Raphaël,* 263
Emergencies, 35, 390
Entry requirements, 30-31
Escalade: *Les Gorges du Verdon,* 197; *Marseille,* 185
Eygalières, 51; camping, 59; gîtes, 60; hiking, 62-63; hotels, 57; markets, 55; restaurants, 60-61
Èze, 335-36, 358-59

Index ■ 401

Fauna, 15
Ferme, 30
Festivals & Fêtes, 7, 87; *Aix*, 171-72; *Antibes-Juan Les Pins*, 339-40; *Arles*, 88; *Avignon*, 41, 54; *Beaucaire*, 54; *Châteauneuf du Pape*, 125; *Les Saintes Maries de la Mer*, 79, 88; *L'Isle Sur La Sorgue*, 125; *Marseille*, 170-71; *Massif de l'Estérel*, 295-96; *Menton*, 341; *Nice*, 340-41; *Nîmes*, 54; *Vaison la Romaine*, 125
Fine Arts Museum: *Nice*, 323, 325
Fine dining, 20
Fishing, 14, 389; *Camargue*, 102-3; *Les Gorges du Verdon*, 207
Flora, 14-15
Fontaine de Vaucluse, 121-23
Food and drink, 18-19. *See also* Restaurants
Fougasse, 10, 19
Fragonard Museum: *Grasse*, 334
Fréjus, 253-58; map, 254; shopping, 293-94; sightseeing, 255-58
French Riviera/Maritime Alps, 299-300; camping, 354; deep-sea fishing, 375; diving, 375-76; driving tours, 377-79; eco-tourism, 380-81; hotels, 344-53; map, 296; mountain biking, 376-77; paragliding, 379-80; restaurants, 354-59

Garrigues, 37-39
Gîtes, 22; *Aigues Mortes*, 94; *Aix*, 181; *Arles*, 93-94; *Camargue*, 93-94; *Eygalières*, 60; *Fréjus*, 285-86; *Marseille*, 181; *Mouriès*, 60; *Saint Raphaël*, 285; *St. Rémy de Provence*, 60; *Vaucluse*, 132-33
Glossary of Terms, 393-98
Gorges du Gardon, 38, 68-69, 113-16, 128
Granet Museum: *Aix en Provence*, 153
Grasse, 334-35
Grimaud, 238
Groupe Épiscopal: *Fréjus*, 257-58
Guidebooks, 198, 390-91

Haute Provence, 22; *Gorges du Verdon*, 196-207; hotels, 207-10; map, 194; restaurants, 210-11; taxi services, 212-13; tourist information, 211; travel to, 193-96

Haut Pays Niçois, 321-22; hiking itineraries, 359-72
Haut Vaucluse, 106
Hiking, 22, 23, 389; *Calanques*, 184-85; *Camargue*, 97; *Eygalières*, 62-63; *Haut Pays Niçois*, 359-60; itineraries, 197-204, 360-72; *Marseille*, 184-85; *Mont Sainte Victoire*, 185-86; *Pierrefeu du Var*, 221-23; *Pont du Gard*, 63; tours, 185-86, 197-204; *Vaucluse*, 136-37
History, 4-12
Holidays, 33-34
Horseback riding: *Camargue*, 99-100; *Saint Raphaël*, 272-73; *Vaucluse*, 144
Hostels, 210
Hot air ballooning: *Alpilles*, 68; *Pont du Gard*, 68; *Vaucluse*, 143-44
Hotels: *Aix*, 177-80; *Alpilles*, 66-67; *Antibes-Juan Les Pins*, 351, 353; *Arles*, 90, 91-92; Auberges, 29; *Avignon*, 56, 58; *Beaucaire*, 57-58, 59; *Camargue*, 90-92; *Cannes*, 344-46, 347-48, 349-51, 352-53; *Castellance*, 207-8; chambre d'hôtes, 30, 284-85; *Eygalières*, 57; ferme, 30; *La Maline*, 209; *Les Saintes Maries de la Mer*, 90-91, 92; *Marseille*, 177-80; *Massif de l'Estérel*, 280-84; *Massif des Maures*, 226-28; *Mauresque Coast*, 239-48; *Menton*, 352; *Mougins*, 348; *Moustiers Saint Marie*, 209-10; *Nice*, 351; *Nîmes*, 58; *Rougon*, 208-9; *Saint Jean Cap Ferrat*, 346-47; *St. Rémy de Provence*, 56-57, 58-59; star ratings, 29-30; *Uzès*, 67; villas, 30. *See also* camping; gîtes

Industry, 14
Information sources, 25-26
Isle sur la Sorgue, 21

Jeep tours, 368, 369, 371; *Camargue*, 99; *Massif de l'Estérel*, 271-72
Jet skiing: *Camargue*, 101-2
Kayaking: *Camargue*, 101; *Saint Raphaël*, 274-75

La Begude Saint Pierre: *Vers Pont du Gard*, 67
La Cathédral des Images: *St Rémy de Provence*, 50
La Ciotat, 167

La Garde Freinet, 6, 220-21
La Grande Camargue, 72-73
La Maline, 209
La Musée de Castre: *Cannes,* 305
La Napoule, 336-37
Language, 16
La Petite Camargue, 73
La Sainte Baume, cycling, 186-90
La Turbie, 338-39
Le Cap Dramont, 264-65
Le Cathédral des Images, 50
Le Lavandou, 237-38
Le Moulin de Bouillons: *Gordes,* 116
Le Pays de Fayence, 290-93
Les Adrets de L'Estérel, 268-69
Les Baux de Provence, 49-50; *restaurants,* 61
Les bories, 114
Les Calanques of Cassis, 165
Les Gorges du Verdon, 196-97, 196-207; abseiling, 197; climbing, 197; driving tour, 204-6; escalade, 197; fly fishing, 207; hiking tour, 197-204; transportation, 196; trekking, 197; watersports, 207; whitewater rafting, 206-7
Les Saintes Maries de la Mer, 79-81; beaches, 81; camping, 92; festivals, 79, 88; hotels, 90-91, 92; shopping, 89; sightseeing, 81; travel to, 81
Les Salins, 74
Le Trayas, 267-68
L'Isle Sur La Sorgue, 123, 125, 126-27, 128
Lodging. *See* Hotels
Logis de France, 30
Lubéron, 22; eco-tourism, 144-45. *See also specific cities*

Mail service. *See* Post offices
Maison Carré: *Nîmes,* 17, 44, 46
Mandelieu, 336-37
Maps: *Aix-en-Provence,* 150; *Aix to Marseille,* 146; *Antibes Peninsula,* 309; *Arles,* 75; *Avignon,* 40; buying, 25-26, 198, 390-91; *Camargue Beaches,* 84; *Cannes,* 301; *Collobrières,* 219; cycling, 23-24; *Fréjus,* 254; *French Riviera/Maritime Alps,* 296; *Haute Provence,* 194; *Maritime Alps,* 298; *Marseille,* 150; *Massif des Maures,* 216; *Massif l'Estérel,* 252; *Menton Region,* 328;

Nice Center, 320; *Nîmes,* 43; *Pays Niçois,* 317; *Provence,* 2; *St Raphaël Center,* 261; *St Raphaël Region,* 259; *St Tropez - Western Côte d'Azur,* 231; *Vaucluse,* 107; *Vieille Antibes,* 312; *Vieux Marseille,* 155
Marc Chagall Museum: *Nice,* 325
Maritime Alps, 299-300; map, 296; mountain biking, 376-77; skiing, 372-74. *See also* specific cities
Marseille, 147-48, 153-54; art and architecture, 172-73; beaches, 192; camping, 180-81; climbing, 184-85; cycling, 186-90; diving, 190-91; driving tour, 190; escalade, 185; festivals, 170-71; gîtes, 181; hiking, 184-85, 185-86; history, 154, 156; map, 146, 155, 159; markets, 175-76; museums, 161; restaurants, 182-84; sailing, 192; shopping, 173-75; sightseeing, 157-58, 160; transportation, 157; travel to, 156-57; windsurfing, 192
Marseille-Provence Airport, 26, 38
Martigues, 167-68
Massif de l'Estérel, 251-53; boat excursions, 277-78; camping, 286; canoeing, 274-75; chambre d'hôtes, 284-85; diving, 278-79; eco-tourism, 273-74; festivals, 295-96; gîtes, 285-86; guided walks, 270-71; horseback riding, 272-73; hotels, 280-84; jeep tours, 271-72; kayaking, 274-75; map, 252; markets, 294-95; mountain biking, 272; powerboating, 276-77; restaurants, 286-88; sailing, 275-76; shopping, 293-95; transportation, 253; travel to, 253; watersports, 279-80; windsurfing, 275-76; yacht rentals, 276
Massif des Maures, 215-18; camping, 228; *Collobrières,* 218-20; hotels, 226-28; La Garde Freinet, 6, 220-21; map, 216; *Pierrefeu du Var,* 221-26, 229; restaurants, 228-29; travel to, 218
Massif du Tanneron, 288-89; cycling, 289-90; *Le Pays de Fayence,* 291-93
Matisse Museum: *Nice,* 323, 325
Mauresque Coast, 229-30; camping, 248; hotels, 239-48; restaurants, 248-51
Maussane les Alpilles, 51-52; shopping, 55

Index ■ 403

Maussane les Alpilles, 51-52; shopping, 55
Medical services, 34
Menton, 326-28; festivals, 341; history, 328-29; hotels, 352; restaurants, 358; shopping, 343; sightseeing, 330-33; travel to, 329
Mentonese Faiences: *Menton,* 330-31
Mercantour: eco-tourism, 380-81
Metric system, 29, 36
Modern art, 17-18
Monastery of St. Paul de Mausole: *St Rémy de Provence,* 48-49
Money. *See* Currency exchange
Monoprix, 55
Montagne du Lubéron, 108-9
Mont Sainte Victoire, 185-86
Monts de Vaucluse, 108
Mougins, 337-38; hotels, 348; restaurants, 355-56
Mountain biking: *Maritime Alps,* 376-77; *Massif de l'Estérel,* 272
Mouriès, 51-52; gîtes, 60; rock climbing, 63-64
Moustiers Saint Marie: hotels, 209-10; restaurants, 209-11
Mt Ventoux, 3, 39, 108
Musée Archéologique: *Fréjus,* 256
Musée Cantini: *Marseille,* 161
Musée d'Archeologie Mediterranéenne: *Marseille,* 161
Musée de la Mer: *Cannes,* 307
Musée de la Mode: *Marseille,* 161
Musée de l'Annonciade: *St. Tropez,* 232
Musée de L'Automobiliste: *Mougins,* 337, 338
Musée des Beaux Arts: *Marseille,* 161
Musée des Beaux-Arts: *Menton,* 320
Musée des Docks Romains: *Marseille,* 161
Musée d'Histoire Naturelle: *Marseille,* 161
Musée du Bonbon: *Uzès,* 53
Musée Grobet-Labadié: *Marseille,* 161
Musée Jean Cocteau: *Menton,* 330
Musée National Fernand Leger: *Biot,* 333
Musée Picasso: *Antibes-Juan Les Pins,* 315
Museum of Art and History: *Nice,* 323
Museum of Modern and Contemporary Art: *Nice,* 323
Museum of Natural History (Musée Barla): *Nice,* 323
Museum of Photography: *Mougins,* 337, 338
Museums: *Aix en Provence,* 153, 170; *Antibes-Juan Les Pins,* 315; *Avignon,* 42; *Biot,* 333; *Cannes,* 305, 307; discount passes, 42, 77, 305; *Fontaine de Vaucluse,* 122; *Fréjus,* 256; *Gordes,* 116; *Grasse,* 334; *Marseille,* 161; *Menton,* 320, 330-31; *Nice,* 4, 319, 323, 325-26; *Nîmes,* 42, 46; *Orange,* 117; *St. Tropez,* 232; *Uzès,* 53; *Vaison la Romaine,* 118-19, 118-20, 119-20

Nice: map, 5, 6, 316-18, 320; airport, 26, 27; cuisine, 320-21; festivals, 340-41; history and culture, 318-19; hotels, 351; markets, 343; museums, 325-26; restaurants, 356-57, 358; shopping, 342-43; sightseeing, 323-25; transportation, 322; travel to, 322
Nice Côte d'Azur Airport, 26, 27
Nîmes, 37, 42-45; festivals, 54; hotels, 58; map, 43; markets, 54-55; shopping, 54-55, 55; sightseeing, 44-45, 46; travel to, 45
Nostradamus, Michel de, 47
Notre Dame de Vie: *Mougins,* 337

Orange, 116-18, 126, 128

Palais des Papes: *Avignon,* 8, 9, 42
Palais Lascaris: *Nice,* 323
Paragliding, 389; *French Riviera,* 379-80; *Vaucluse,* 143-44
Passports, 30-31
Patisseries, 19
Pays de Sault, 108
Pays de Sorgues, 108
Performing arts, 18
Petit Palais: *Avignon,* 42
Petrarch Museum and Library: *Fontaine de Vaucluse,* 122
Pharmacies, 34
Pierrefeu du Var: cycling, 223-26; hiking, 221-23
Plage de Beauduc, 85-86, 95
Plage de L'Espiguette, 86-87
Plage Est, 85
Pont du Gard, 37, 44, 52-53; hiking, 63; hot air ballooning, 68

404 ■ Index

Pont St. Bénézet, 39, 41-42
Port Grimaud, 238, 251
Post offices, 32, 34
Prehistoric Museum of Terra Amata: *Nice*, 4
Prieuré du Vieux-Logis: *Nice*, 323, 326
Public Holidays, 33-34
Puget Theniers, 213

Quartier de Puymin: *Vaison la Romaine*, 119-20

Rail Europe, 27, 28
Restaurants, 85; *Aigues Mortes*, 94; *Aix*, 182-84; *Antibes-Juan Les Pins*, 357-58; *Arles*, 94-96; *Beaucaire*, 61-62; *Biot*, 356; boulangeries, 19; budgeting for, 20; *Cannes*, 354-55; *Castellane*, 211; *Eygalières*, 60-61; *Èze*, 358-59; *Les Baux de Provence*, 61; *Marseille*, 182-84; *Massif des Maures*, 228-29; *Mauresque Coast*, 248-51; *Menton*, 358; *Mougins*, 355-56; *Moustiers*, 210-11; *Nice*, 356-57, 358; patisseries, 19; tea shops, 19; tipping, 33; types of establishments, 19-20; *Western Côte d'Azur*, 286-88
Rock climbing: *Les Gorges du Verdon*, 197; *Marseille*, 184-85; *Mouriès*, 63-64; *Vaucluse*, 138
Rougon: hotels, 208-9
Roussillon, 124, 128
Route Napoléon, 214
Russian Orthodox Church: *Nice*, 319, 324-25

Saint Jean Cap Ferrat, 346-47
Saint Raphaël, 215, 258-60; boating, 276-77; *Boulouris*, 263-64; *Le Cap Dramont*, 264-65; *Santa Lucia Port*, 263; shopping, 294; sightseeing, 260-63
Salon de Provence, 169
Santa Lucia Port, 263
Sault en Provence: eco-tourism, 144-45
Shopping, 20-21; *Aigues Mortes*, 89-90; *Antibes-Juan Les Pins*, 342; *Arles*, 89; *Avignon*, 54; boutiques, 20-21; *Cannes*, 341; department stores, 55; *Eygalières*, 55; *Fréjus*, 293-94; *Les Saintes de la Mer*, 89; *Maussane des Alpilles*, 55; *Menton*, 343; *Nice*, 342-43; *Nîmes*, 54-55; specialties, 21, 55; sporting goods, 55; *St. Rémy de Provence*, 89-90; *St. Tropez*, 234; *Uzès*, 55; VAT (Value Added Tax), 31
Spelunking: *Les Calanques*, 162; *Vaucluse*, 138, 139
St. Anne's Church: *Arles*, 79
St. Rémy de Provence, 21, 46-47; camping, 59; gîtes, 60; hotels, 56-57, 58-59; markets, 54; shopping, 54; sightseeing, 48-49; travel to, 48; Van Gogh tour, 47
St. Tropez, 5, 230-37; beaches, 236-37; map, 231; shopping, 234; sightseeing, 232-34; travel to, 234-35
Stamps, 34
Ste Maxime, 239
St Maximin La Ste Baume, 169-70
Synagogue: *Carpentras*, 112
Taxi services, 212-13
Tea shops, 19
Telephones, 26, 34-35; calling cards, 34
Terra Amata Human Paleontology Museum: *Nice*, 319, 323
Terrain, 1-4
Théâtre Antique and Museum: *Orange*, 117
Tipping, 33
Tourist Information Offices, 383-87
Transportation, 26-29
Traveler's checks, 32

Uzès, 53-54, 55, 67

Vaison la Romaine, 118-21, 125, 126
Vallon de la Fontaine, 49
Van Gogh, Vincent, 12, 18, 37, 47, 48-49, 58-59, 76-77, 79, 90, 95
Vasarely Foundation, 173
VAT (Value Added Tax), 31
Vaucluse/Lubéron, 105-6; accrobranching, 138-39; camping, 128-32; cycling, 139-40, 142-43; cycling itineraries, 140-42; eco-tourism, 144-45; festivals, 125; gîtes, 132-33; horseback riding, 144; hot air ballooning, 143-44; hotels, 128-31; map, 107; markets, 127-28; music and dance, 126; regions, 106-9; restaurants, 134-36; rock climbing, 138; shopping, 126-27; spelunking, 138,

139; travel to, 106; windsailing, 143-44
Villas, 30
Villeneuve-les-Avignon, 42

Walking tours: *Massif de l'Estérel,* 270-71; *Mont Vinaigre,* 269-71

Watersports: *Antibes-Juan Les Pins,* 374-75; *Saint Raphaël,* 279-80
Whitewater rafting: *Les Gorges du Verdon,* 206-7
Wildlife, 15-16
Windsailing: *Marseille,* 192; *Saint Raphaël,* 275-76
World Heritage Site, 39, 52, 76

ADVENTURE GUIDES
from Hunter Publishing

This signature Hunter series targets travelers eager to explore the destination. Extensively researched and offering the very latest information, Adventure Guides are written by knowledgeable, experienced authors, often residents of the destination. A comprehensive introductory section provides background on history, geography, climate, culture, when to go, transportation and planning. These very readable guides then take a region-by-region approach, plunging into the very heart of each area and the adventures offered, giving a full range of accommodations, shopping, restaurants for every budget, and festivals. All books have town and regional maps; most have color photos. Fully indexed.

Below are some of the recent Adventure Guides. For a complete list of titles in this series, visit www.hunterpublishing.com or call ☎ 800-255-0343 to request a free catalog.

THE BAHAMAS
3rd Edition, Blair Howard
Fully updated reports for Grand Bahama, Freeport, Eleuthera, Bimini, Andros, the Exumas, Nassau, New Providence Island, plus new sections on San Salvador, Long Island, Cat Island, the Acklins, the Inaguas and the Berry Islands. Mailboat schedules, package vacations and snorkeling trips by Jean-Michel Cousteau.
6 x 9 pbk, 384 pp, $18.99, 1-58843-318-9

BELIZE
5th Edition, Vivien Lougheed
"Down-to-earth advice.... An excellent travel guide."
– *Library Journal*
Extensive coverage of the country's political, social and economic history, along with the plant and animal life. Encouraging you to mingle with the locals, Pariser entices you with descriptions of local dishes and festivals. Maps, color photos.
6 x 9 pbk, 400 pp, $18.95, 1-58843-289-0

COSTA RICA
5th Edition, Bruce & June Conord

"... most comprehensive... Excellent sections on national parks, flora, fauna & history."
– *CompuServe Travel Forum*

Incredible detail on culture, plants, animals, where to stay & eat, as well as practicalities of travel. E-mail and website directory.

6 x 9 pbk, 384 pp, $17.99, 1-58843-502-4

DOMINICAN REPUBLIC
4th Edition, Fe Liza Bencosme & Clark Norton

Virgin beaches, 16th-century Spanish ruins, the Caribbean's highest mountain, exotic wildlife, vast forests. Visit Santa Domingo, revel in Sosúa's European sophistication or explore the Samaná Peninsula's jungle. Color photos.

6 x 9 pbk, 360 pp, $17.99, 1-58843-402-8

DOMINICA & ST. LUCIA
Lynne Sullivan

An in-depth guide to these highly popular English-speaking Caribbean islands by the author of our top-selling Virgin Islands Adventure Guide. Dominica is unique in that it was never farmed over; it remains jungle-covered, mountainous and the only island still occupied by the original Carib Indians. St. Lucia is more developed, but is breathtaking in its beauty, with high peaks and azure-blue bays dotted with colorful boats. Town and regional maps, color photos, fully indexed.

6 x 9 pbk, 244 pp, $19.99, 1-58843-393-5

THE FLORIDA KEYS & EVERGLADES NATIONAL PARK
4th Edition, Bruce Morris

"... vastly informative, absolutely user-friendly, chock full of information..." – Dr. Susan Cropper

"... practical & easy to use." – *Wilderness Southeast*

Canoe trails, airboat rides, nature hikes, Key West, diving, sailing, fishing. Color.

6 x 9 pbk, 344 pp, $18.99, 1-558843-403-6

PUERTO RICO
4th Edition, Kurt Pitzer

"A quality book that covers all aspects... it's all here & well done." – *The San Diego Tribune*

"... well researched. They include helpful facts... filled with insightful tips." – *The Shoestring Traveler*

Crumbling watchtowers and fascinating folklore enchant visitors. Color photos.

6 x 9 pbk, 432 pp, $18.95, 1-558843-116-9

THE YUCATAN, Cancún & Cozumel

3rd Edition, Bruce & June Conord

"This in-depth travel guide opens the doors to our enchanted Yucatán" – Mexico Ministry of Tourism "A valuable resource." – *Travel & Leisure* magazine Takes you to places not covered in competing guides. Take to the mountain trails, swim in hidden cenotes, watch the sun rise on a beach near the ancient Maya port of Polé (where the authors celebrated the dawn of the new millennium). Visit Bohemian Playa del Carmen, or history-rich Cozumel, where the Spanish first set foot on the North American continent.

6 x 9 pbk, 456 pp, $19.99, 1-558843-370-6

TAMPA BAY & FLORIDA'S WEST COAST

3rd Edition, Chelle Koster Walton

Visit vibrant cities, charming hometowns, nature preserves, wilderness areas and the famous white-sand beaches of Florida's Gulf shore. Covers all of Tampa Bay/St. Petersburg and north to Withlacoochee State Forest, and south to Sanibel Island, Naples and Everglades National Park. Canoeing the Everglades, fishing on Marco Island, biking in Boca Grande, diving with manatees in Crystal River, sailing along St. Pete Beach, theater-going in Sarasota, shopping the sponge markets of Greek-flavored Tarpon Springs, exploring the history of Tampa's Latin Ybor City - it's all here! Town and regional maps. Fully indexed. Color photos.

6 x 9 pbk, 320 pp, $18.99, 1-58843-350-1

TUSCANY & UMBRIA

Emma Jones

This history-rich region offers some of Italy's classic landscapes – pole-straight cypress trees lining dusty farm roads, rolling hills that stretch as far as the eye can see, fields of vibrant sunflowers, medieval villages perched on rocky spurs above crashing surf. Visit them all with this comprehensive guide that helps you explore the very best places. A largely untouched coastline and protected wild areas only add to the appeal of this top vacation destination. Town and regional maps, color photos, fully indexed.

6 x 9 pbk, 500 pp, $19.99, 1-58843-399-4

SWITZERLAND

Kimberly Rinker

With azure-blue lakes that shine brilliantly against the greenest slopes of the surrounding Alps, its picturesque villages and chic towns are accessible via high-speed trains, though many opt to travel by longboat on some of the country's tranquil waterways. It is one of the world's most advanced industrialized nations, yet its towns and cities are incredibly clean. Part-time Swiss resident Kimberly Rinker has lived and worked here for years. She tells of little-known attractions as well as major tourist draws and everything in-between. Color photos.

6 X 9 pbk, 528 pp, $21.99, 1-58843-369-2

ST. MARTIN & ST. BARTS
Lynne Sullivan

Half-French, half-Dutch, St. Martin offers Orient Bay; duty-free shopping in Philipsburg; Marigot, with chic French boutiques and superb food; and Restaurant Row in Grand Case, with great eateries in charming Creole houses. St. Barts has few buildings higher than one story, no large hotels, memorable food and 22 beautiful beaches along turquoise seas. Lynne Sullivan, author of our best-selling Adventure Guide to the Virgin Islands and several other guides, shows you how to discover and enjoy these islands to the fullest, with island tours, shopping tips, historic sightseeing, watersports and hundreds of places to stay and eat. Color photos. Maps. 6 x 9 pbk, 240 pp, $19.99, 1-58843-348-X

SPAIN
Kelly Lipscomb

A resident of Spain, the author delves into every province and town. He tells of the history and culture, and provides innumerableuseful traveling tips. Everything is explored – the cities, the parks, the islands, the mountains, the foods. Covers the entire country, from Ibiza to Granada, Andalucia, Barcelona, Madrid and Toledo. Town and regional maps, color photos, fully indexed. 6 x 9 pbk, 730 pp, $21.99, 1-58843-398-6

SCOTLAND
Martin Li

The definitive guide to every aspect of Scotland – the legends, the clans, the castles and romantic hotels, the Highland games and, of course, the whisky. This long-time Scotland resident takes us from Edinburgh to Glasgow, Argyll and the Isles, Loch Lomond, the Highlands and to the Outer Isles. Fascinating details on the Loch Ness monster, Shakespeare's "Macbeth" castle, Mary Queen of Scots, the Viking legacy, Burns Night and the royal castles. This book covers it all, and has color photos, maps and index. 6 x 9 pbk, 750 pp, $21.99, 1-58843-406-0

PANAMA

Mother nature has bequeathed Panama with some stunning spots, rich soils and a vast bio-diversity. White- and black-sand beaches alternate with mangrove mazes along the coast. Sparkling wild rivers overflowing with trout run through jungle-clad canyons filled with colorful flowers. Mist-crowned Baru Volcano towers above them all. This book explores every region from tip to toe, including the San Blas Islands, offshore Barro Colorado, and urban Panama City, gateway for visitors. Walking tours visit historic forts, gold museums, classic city parks and bustling crafts markets. Special attention is given to the national parks. 6 x 9 pbk, 360 pp, $19.99, 1-58843-368-4

MEXICO'S GULF COAST
Joanie Sanchez

The area of Veracruz, Tabasco and north to the US border is a throwback to Mexico of old. It has volcanoes, rainforests, Maya ruins and such abundant wildlife that you will see hundreds of toucans and an island filled with monkeys. Experience the dance and music of Veracruz (birthplace of La Bamba), the fabulous local foods of Xalapa, the local festivals, the miles of pristine coastline, Mexico's tallest mountain, the sheer beauty of the jungles. Town and regional maps, color photos, fully indexed.

6 x 9 pbk, 400 pp, $19.99, 1-58843-394-3

MEXICO'S PACIFIC COAST
Vivien Lougheed

The Pacific coast of Mexico is a playground for active travelers. Warm waves and sunny skies attract the beach crowd with watersports, while volcanoes, mountains and jungles appeal to hikers, naturalists and the culturally curious. Visit a pearl farm in San Carlos, ride a train through Copper Canyon, go crocodile hunting on La Tovara River, surf the big waves at Playa Las Islitas, or visit the village of Ajejic, where DH Lawrence once got inspiration. Town and regional maps, color photos, fully indexed.

6 x 9 pbk, 500 pp, $19.99, 1-58843-395-1

JAMAICA 5th Edition
Paris Permenter & John Bigley

This travel guide walks with the adventurous traveler to the heart of Jamaica, to the miles of sand beaches, to the rugged Blue Mountains, to the country villages that provide a peek at the real Jamaica. The authors focus on the adventures this popular Caribbean island has to offer: scuba diving along coral reefs, biking mountain trails, deep sea fishing, parasailing, windsurfing, horseback riding, and other adventures that range from mild to wild. Special sections include a look at Jamaica's Meet the People program, home visits, local nightspots, festivals, and more. Maps and photos enliven the down-to-earth text.

6 x 9 pbk, 360 pp, $18.99, 1-58843-504-0

NEW ZEALAND
Bette Flagler

Written by a local, this guide covers every region and town, with in-depth information on the Maori culture, the remarkable places to stay and eat, vineyard tours, cooking schools, thermal springs, albatross and whale encounters, scenic drives, and more. Canoe the Whanganui River, ride in a hot air balloon, hike the Waikaremoana Track, explore Whirikana Forest Park, take a glacier tour. There's even a section on how to talk Kiwi English! Color photos, maps and a thorough index.

6 x 9 pbk, 650 pp, $21.99, 1-58843-405-2

GERMANY
Henk Bekker

Bavaria, the Mosel Valley, the Rhine region, the Black Forest, Dresden, Berlin, Hamburg – this highly detailed guide covers every part of the country in depth. The author, a German resident, shows you how to experience the best, through town walks, drives in the countryside and immersing yourself in the entertainment, the sights, the history and culture. Hundreds of hotel and restaurant reviews. Maps, color photos, index.

6 x 9 pbk, 550 pp, $19.99, 1-58843-503-2

IRELAND
Tina Neylon

Ireland is steeped in history, tradition and culture, making it one of the most popular vacation destinations worldwide. Its story is told in centuries-old castles (some of which now welcome overnight guests); stone circles strategically placed to shine in the winter solstice moon; and, of course, in its pubs, where local residents gladly share a pint and a tale. Its cities are a treat to explore, with winding streets packed with tiny antique stores. Trips along the coast take you to traditional fishing villages and past some of the world's best golf courses. This book, written by an Ireland native, tells it all. Color photos.

6 x 9 pbk, 624 pp, $21.99, 1-58843-367-6

PARIS & ILE DE FRANCE
Heather Stimmler-Hall

Written by a Paris resident, here is every neighborhood of the city, the forests and parks, plus recommended day-trips to majestic châteaux and authentic medieval villages. Shopping adventures, wine and food, dance and drama, language and literature, nightlife and entertainment – the author shows you how to get involved in it all, whether through cooking classes, dance lessons, language courses, luxury spas or wine festivals. Town and regional maps, color photos, fully indexed.

6 x 9 pbk, 448 pp, $19.99, 1-58843-396-X

All Hunter titles are available at bookstores nationwide or from the publisher. To order direct, send a check for the total of the book(s) ordered plus $3 shipping and handling to Hunter Publishing, 130 Campus Drive, Edison NJ 08818. Secure credit card orders may be made on the Hunter website, www.hunterpublishing.com, where you will also find in-depth descriptions of the hundreds of travel guides we offer.

---

w w w . h u n t e r p u b l i s h i n g . c o m